DATE DUE

MAY 1 2 2013

Blood and Rage

By the same author

Prussian Society and the German Order

Germany Turns Eastwards

The Racial State: Germany 1933–1945

(ed.) *Confronting the Nazi Past*

Ethics and Extermination: Reflections on Nazi Genocide

The Third Reich: A New History

*Earthly Powers: Religion and Politics from
the French Revolution to the Great War*

*Sacred Causes: The Clash of Religion and Politics from
the Great War to the War on Terror*

MICHAEL BURLEIGH

Blood and Rage

A CULTURAL HISTORY OF TERRORISM

HARPER

An Imprint of HarperCollins*Publishers*

www.harpercollins.com

HarperCollins books may be purchased for educational, business, or sales
promotional use. For information, please write: Special Markets Department,
HarperCollins Publishers, 10 East 53rd Street, New York, NY 10022.

First published in Great Britain in 2008 by HarperPress, an imprint of
HarperCollins Publishers.

FIRST U.S. EDITION

Library of Congress Cataloging-in-Publication Data is available upon request.

ISBN 978-0-06-117385-1

09 10 11 12 13   OFF/RRD   10 9 8 7 6 5 4 3 2 1

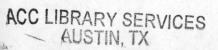

In their basic relation to themselves most people are narrators ... What they like is the orderly sequence of facts, because it has the look of a necessity, and by means of the impression that their life has a 'course' they manage to feel some- how sheltered in the midst of chaos.

Robert Musil, *The Man without Qualities*

CONTENTS

PREFACE

This book's starting point is the moment when recognisably modern terrorist organisations emerged in the mid-nineteenth century, dubious precedence being accorded here to the Irish Fenians. We could venture back to the medieval Assassins of Syria or the early modern British Gunpowder Plot, but my knowledge of both has faded with age and I do not regard either as especially helpful in understanding contemporary terrorism. The book's working assumptions are evident throughout. There are well over a hundred definitions of terrorism and it is possible to aggregate those elements that recur most frequently. Terrorism is a tactic primarily used by non-state actors, who can be an acephalous entity as well as a hierarchical organisation, to create a psychological climate of fear in order to compensate for the legitimate political power they do not possess. It can be distinguished from, say, guerrilla warfare, political assassination or economic sabotage, although organisations that practise terror have certainly resorted to these too.

That modern states, from the Jacobins in the 1790s onwards, have been responsible for the most lethal instances of terrorism, including self-styled counter-terror campaigns, is taken as a given, which does not absolve non-state actors through repetition of this historical truism. State violence is currently on the defensive, as various rabble armies run amok under the guise of Islamic or liberation or people's revolution or whatever they call themselves. Nor does the cliché that yesterday's terrorist is tomorrow's statesman really get us very far. If you imagine that Osama bin Laden is going to evolve into Nelson Mandela, you need a psychiatrist rather than an historian. The Al Qaeda leader does not want to negotiate with us since what he desires is for all infidels and apostates to submit or be killed.

This book focuses on life histories and actions rather than the theories which validate them, roughly in accord with St Matthew's precept 'By their fruits ye shall know them'. This is not because I am dismissive of ideas and ideology – quite the contrary – but because these seem a relatively neglected part of the picture. Ideology is like a detonator that enables a pre-existing chemical mix to explode. Terrorists make choices all along their journey, and it is these I am most interested in. Hence the book is about terrorism as a career, a culture and a way of life, although obviously one involving death, for the terrorists' victims and sometimes for the terrorists themselves, unless they deliberately court this through suicidal operations like Hamas, Hizbollah or the Tamil Tigers. Terrorism is violent, which is why there is much detailed discussion of violence in the book, as well as material intended to demystify and deglamorise terrorist operations. Some terrorists do indeed kill people; many others spend their time laundering money or stealing vehicles. Since much of this material is in the public domain, it is of no operational use to would-be terrorists.

As the book tries to make crystal clear, especially to anyone who might appear to harbour a sneaking admiration for those who wish to change the world by violence, the milieu of terrorists is invariably morally squalid, when it is not merely criminal. That is especially evident in the chapters below on Russian nihilists, the Baader–Meinhof gang, and both loyalist and republican terrorists in Northern Ireland. The unexpressed goal of bringing about transformative chaos becomes the element in which terrorists are most at home. Destruction and self-destruction briefly compensate for some perceived slight or more abstract grievances that cause their hysterical rage. As endless studies of terrorist psychology reveal, they are morally insane, without being clinically psychotic. If that affliction unites most terrorists, then their victims usually have one thing in common, regardless of their social class, politics or religious faith. That is a desire to live unexceptional lives settled amid their families and friends, without some resentful radical loser – who can be a millionaire loser harbouring delusions of victimhood – wishing to destroy and maim them so as to realise a world that almost nobody wants. That unites the victims of terror from Algiers, Baghdad, Cairo, via London, Madrid and New York, to Nairobi, Singapore and Jakarta. They all bleed and grieve in the same way.

If this book were to be absolutely comprehensive, it would be doubly long, losing its human focus. That is why such subjects as terrorism in Latin America from the Tupamaros to FARC, the US itself, and the Sinhalese–Tamil conflict in Sri Lanka have been omitted, although there is passing allusion to them all. Alert readers will realise that buried in the history are suggestions about which past policies worked, and which didn't, regarding, for example, how to deal with imprisoned terrorists who routinely try to convert jails into universities or how to derange terrorist financing by encouraging organised crime. In this I have learned a great deal from studies and programmes in such varied places as Italy, France, Indonesia, Saudi Arabia and Singapore, whose existence and importance are routinely ignored. Since this is not a counter-terrorism manual, any prescriptions are highly tentative, such as disaggregating terrorist movements along their inner fault lines, while emphasising the commonality of suffering that terrorism produces in all our respective civilisations. As long as people hardly react to the news that x number of people, remarkably like ourselves in longing for life, have been killed by a bomb in Egypt or Malaysia, there will be no effective global response to this current epidemic. A properly funded police, intelligence and military response is essential; but so are improved public diplomacy and efforts to deradicalise potential terrorists, for the Hot and Cold Wars are now parallel. They have to learn not only that they cannot win, with even 9/11 merely affecting the operations of Wall Street for a few days, but that they are fighting precisely those societies that can most help their own societies overcome their wounding intellectual and material dependency on the West. When the cause is discredited, Islamist terrorism, like that of anarchists or Nihilists, will significantly abate, although die-hards will never stop.

Nothing would be gained in these pages by attempting to impose uniformity on the spelling of Muslim names. Many Western Muslims have their own preferred forms; French transliterations from the Arabic, for example, differ from English; and there is even debate about the most respectful way to spell the Prophet's name. My policy is to aim for consistency with each person's name and not to worry that one is Mohammed, another Mahomed, a third Muhammad and so on. I have similarly left it to my sources to determine whether measurements are imperial or metric.

I would like to offer warm thanks to Heather Higgins of the Randolph Trust and Director John Raisian of the Hoover Institution, Stanford University for making it possible for me to research and write this book under the aegis of a leading US think-tank. Self-evidently it is not one that espouses the sanctimonious ethos of the *New York Times* and is all the better for that. Andrew Wylie, Peter James and several friends at HarperCollins have made producing this book a pleasure despite a subject matter that frequently lowers one's spirits. Among the people who have afforded insight and encouragement from within the counterterrorism milieu, I would especially like to thank Shmuel Bar, Paul Bew, Adrian Weale and Dean Godson as well as others who wish to remain anonymous.

Michael Burleigh
August 2007

Blood and Rage

CHAPTER 1

Green: The Fenian Dynamiters

I FRIENDS ACROSS THE OCEAN

Irish grievances against the British in the nineteenth century were many. The British had garrisoned Ireland with troops, and favoured the industrious Protestant Scots-Irish of the North, because they suspected that its predominantly Roman Catholic inhabitants would rebel with the aid of a foreign foe at the first opportunity. In addition to the Ulster Presbyterians, there was an established, that is privileged, Protestant Church of Ireland, even though most of the population were Catholics. There was a fine Protestant university, Trinity College, Dublin, but none for Catholics. Ireland was part of a global empire, but was often treated as an offshore agricultural colony where labourers and poorer tenant farmers lived in chronic insecurity at the whim of absentee English landlords. Millions had left for the US (and industrialising Britain) where they adopted radical views that were far in advance of those of most people in Ireland itself. Confronted by virulent strains of American Protestantism, they compensated for discrimination by becoming more aggressively Irish, caricaturing the English as latter-day Normans and sentimentalising the old country with its ancient barrows, bogs, castles and mists. That these were historically authentic was partly due to their being noted, from 1824 onwards, on detailed Ordnance Survey maps, while another British intrusion – the national census – ironically contributed to a growth of Irish cultural nationalism. Successive censuses had startling revelations. Whereas in 1845 half the population spoke Irish (or Gaelic), by 1851 this had fallen to 23 per cent, and below 15 per cent forty years later. The Gaelic League was born of a desire for an Irish-Irish patriotic literature at a time when the brightest stars in that firmament were Anglo-Irish Protestant nationalists like J. M. Synge, Sean O'Casey or W. B. Yeats.[1]

Many complexities about the real, as opposed to imaginary, Ireland were lost in the Atlantic translation as fond hearts filled with hatred. Irish volunteers for the British army, replete with their own Catholic military chaplains, won a disproportionately high number of Victoria Crosses during the Crimean War. English and Irish liberals, led by the High Anglican prime minister William Ewart Gladstone, combined with British nonconformists to disestablish the anomalous Church of Ireland in 1869. Partly due to the disruptive ingenuity of a caucus of Irish MPs in the House of Commons, notably under Charles Stewart Parnell, and endemic rural criminality, Land Acts alleviated the insecurity of the smallest class of tenants. Finally, more and more British politicians, led eventually by Gladstone himself, were persuaded that Ireland's future lay in some degree of Home Rule, with separate legislatures benefiting both England and Ireland, the two countries joined at a more exalted level for defence or foreign policy by an imperial parliament continuing to sit at Westminster. That prospect, which became real enough on the eve of the First World War, was sufficient for the Protestant majority in Ulster to seek German arms to preserve their membership of a more developed Belfast–Glasgow–Liverpool industrialised axis, if necessary detached from the benighted clerical South.[2]

Irish terrorism grew out of a venerable insurrectionary tradition that was manifestly failing by the mid-nineteenth century, only to return with a vengeance after an intervening lull in the late 1960s. The older history created many of the myths and martyrs of the more recent Troubles, as well as patterns of behaviour and thought that have survived in armed Irish republicanism within our lifetimes. There were many malign ghosts.

On 17 March 1858 an organisation was founded in Dublin by a railway engineer called James Stephens. It was St Patrick's Day. Within a few years this mutated into the Irish Republican Brotherhood, although that name was never employed as widely as 'Fenians'. This referred to a mythical band of pre-Christian Irish warriors, or the Fianna, roughly similar to romantic English legends about the Knights of King Arthur. For the English it meant a dastardly gang of murdering desperadoes. Fenianism encompassed a range of activities, with harmless conviviality and labour activism at the legal end of the spectrum, through to rural disturbances, insurrection and terrorism on the illegal margins.

Incubated in the political underworld of Paris, or the rough-and-ready slums of North America's eastern seaboard, the culture was heavily indebted to that of secret societies, with arcane rituals, masonic oaths and signs, a major reason why the Roman Catholic Church was largely unsympathetic. The general goal was the 'disenthralment' of the Irish race and the achievement of an Irish republic through violent struggle, all this within a broader context of Gaelic cultural self-assertion to which there has been some allusion.[3]

The strategy, ultimately derived from the 1798 Wolfe Tone rebellion, was to transform British imperial difficulties into Irish opportunities. The imperial difficulties included the Crimean War, the Indian Mutiny and the Zulu, Sudan and Boer Wars, as well as crises in British relations with France in the 1850s, with the US in the 1860s, and with Russia in the 1870s, for a war with any of these would enhance the prospects of an independent Irish republic. While the number of Irish heroes in the Crimea seemed to suggest that this strategy had failed, the Fenians took courage from the war's exposure of Britain's military deficiencies and the barely concealed rift with its French ally. In addition to trying to arm the Zulus, even the mahdi's 'swarthy desert warriors' became objects of Fenian interest, a trend that would continue into the late twentieth century in the form of Irish Republican Army links with the Palestine Liberation Organisation and Libya.[4]

The Fenians drew upon the wider Irish emigration, whether in mainland Britain or the United States of America. They included refugees from the conditions that had produced the mid-nineteenth-century famine, of which many Irish-Americans had raw memories. Life in the urban Irish ghettos of the US (or industrial Britain) was primitive. The Irish were also heartily disliked by the Protestant aristocracy that dominated the US, a fact which may explain their flight into a vehement Irishness which had much purchase in Boston or 'New Cork'. The American Civil War marked an important turning point since Britain was perceived to have supported the Confederate South, at a time when 150,000 Irish-Americans were fighting predominantly for the North. The Irish-Americans would inject Fenianism with money and military expertise.

The US government was culpably indulgent towards Fenian terrorism, as it would be for the next hundred years. Despite British government protests, nothing was done by the American authorities to stop the Fenians openly soliciting money in the US for anti-British outrages, notably through the so-called Dynamite Press. The Fenians were even allowed openly to use riverbank yards to develop a submarine whose sole object was to harass British shipping. US authorities rejected all British attempts to extradite Irish fugitives. All of which is to say that the Fenians had discovered an important terrorist tactic, that of using a benign foreign base for fund-raising and launching terrorist operations. British protests to Washington might have been taken more seriously had England, and especially London, not itself been a welcoming haven for every species of foreign radical. The French, who reacted with alacrity in detecting and deporting Paris-based Fenian supporters, chivalrously overlooked the fact that the bombs used by Orsini in his 1857 bid to kill Napoleon III had been manufactured in Birmingham.

Within six years, the Fenians had over fifty thousand supporters in Ireland. There, Fenianism was often little more than an assertive badge of identity and an opportunity for politicised recreation, in which young men joined a parallel society based on military drill, picnics and the adoption of non-deferential American manners towards priests, police-men and squires.[5] The movement had its own newspaper, *Irish People*, and in James Kickham at least one writer of note. Across the Atlantic it enabled demobilised veterans of the Civil War to defer their return to civilian normality and to act on behalf of an Ireland that assumed mythical proportions through greater distance from its complex realities. In February 1867 a Civil War veteran and Fenian, captain Thomas J. Kelly (he promoted himself to colonel when he entered the service of Ireland), ordered a series of risings in Ireland, to be accompanied by diversionary supporting incidents in England, and two invasions of Canada, in the name of the US, which were frustrated by a British secret agent and the US government itself.

One escapade involved the capture of Chester Castle, which contained an arsenal with thirty thousand stands of rifles. The Fenian plan was to commandeer a train to take the arms to the port of Holyhead where a steamer would ship them to Ireland. Telegraph wires would be cut and rail track ripped up in the train's wake so as to stymie pursuit. Fires in the city and interference with the water works would create even greater chaos, the first manifestations of future co-ordinated terrorist campaigns. The raid on the castle involved a hard core of American veterans, supported by several hundred ruffians who infiltrated them-selves into Chester by rail from Liverpool and other northern cities with large Irish minorities.

The raid was halted before it started. Tipped off by spies, and concerned about the convergence of large groups of young Irishmen on Chester, the British authorities poured troops and police into the city, the mere sight of whom led to the dispersal of the Fenians. They dropped their cartridges, clubs and revolvers into the River Dee or the nearest ditch. The rising in Ireland was crushed as a result of the suspension of habeas corpus and the arrest of prominent nationalists; increases in troop numbers; and deployment of ships to watch the Atlantic approaches. It coincided with the worst snowstorm in fifty years, which put paid to national deliverance by Irish-American soldiers on *Erin's Hope*. Fifty thousand British troops and police mopped up a few thousand Fenians, although not before they had issued their proclamation:

> We therefore declare that, unable to endure the curse of Monarchical government, we aim at founding a republic based on universal suffrage, which shall secure to all the intrinsic value of their labour. The soil of Ireland in the possession of an oligarchy belongs to us, the Irish people, and to us it must be restored. We declare also in favour of absolute liberty of conscience, and complete separation of Church and State.[6]

Colonel Kelly, who in the interim had created an assassination unit to deal with agents and informers, and captain Timothy Deasy were initially picked up in Manchester under the Vagrancy Act. News of their arrest spread throughout Manchester's substantial Irish minority, and eventually reached the ears of two Irish-American officers, Edward O'Meagher Condon and Michael O'Brien. Together they assembled a team of ten to rescue Kelly and Deasy as they were being transferred in a Black Maria for remand hearings at another city prison. Six policemen rode on top of the horse-drawn box, in which a sergeant Brett sat with the keys to the prisoners' locked cage. Four more officers followed in a carriage behind. None of the ten policemen was armed.

The carriage was ambushed as it passed beneath a railway bridge. Once shots were fired to kill the off-side horse, the escort ran for cover. The rescuers then fired at the lock on the prison van, contriving to hit sergeant Brett in the head as he peeped apprehensively through the ventilator grille. Kelly and Deasy seized his keys and joined their rescuers, who made a run for it across Manchester's criss-crossed railway tracks. Neither man was captured – although Deasy in his dark pea jacket, grey trousers, deerstalker and handcuffs might have been thought conspicuous. They resurfaced as heroes in America.

The authorities had more luck in apprehending the rescuers and their penumbra of supporters. Twenty-eight people appeared in the dock of Manchester magistrates' court, of whom five were then sent for trial by judge and jury for murder, felony and misdemeanour. As an indication of how seriously the government regarded the trial, the prosecution case, which was one of common cause due to uncertainty about which individual had murdered sergeant Brett, was put by the attorney-general, the Crown's leading law officer. After a five-day hearing, all of the defendants were found guilty of murder and sentenced to execution by hanging. The British press managed to have one of the convictions quashed, because the convicted man had a cast-iron alibi, an anomaly that might have affected the sentences handed down on the four found guilty. While *The Times* opined that terrorism 'must be repelled by lawful terrorism', twenty-five thousand sympathetic working-men demonstrated for royal clemency on Clerkenwell Green in London. Domestic and foreign middle-class radicals drew attention to the paradox whereby the British lionised the Italian radical Garibaldi while treating his Irish equivalents as common or garden murderers, an early manifestation of the claim that yesterday's terrorist is tomorrow's statesman. Petitions were drawn up by such progressive celebrities as Charles Bradlaugh, John Stuart Mill and Karl Marx. Two days before the executions were to be staged, the single American convicted – Condon – was reprieved so as to avoid diplomatic complications with the US.

Meanwhile, a thirty-foot section of the prison wall was dismantled, on which arose a cross-beamed gallows shrouded in black drapery. Next morning, five hundred soldiers and two thousand constables interposed themselves between the gallows and a large crowd of spectators. Other army units took up positions throughout the city. There was dense fog as the three men were led up the thirty-five to forty steps of the scaffold for their rendezvous with William Calcraft, the alcoholic white-haired executioner, whose sinister forte was to leap on the backs of men whose necks had not been instantaneously broken. All three men were hanged together. Allen died instantaneously. Calcraft descended to finish off Larkin, but was prevented by a Catholic priest from performing a similar service for O'Brien, who duly choked to death three-quarters of an hour later.

Friedrich Engels, whose wife was a Fenian, wrote that 'The only thing the Fenians lacked were martyrs. They have been provided with these.' Outrage at the executions was evident in America, Australia, Canada, South Africa and New Zealand, as well as across Europe. In Ireland itself, huge mock funeral processions were held, which suggested that the Catholic hierarchy had modified its earlier condemnations of godless Fenian 'socialists' in favour of endorsing the sentimental Irish national-ism often espoused by its priests. The death of Brett was regarded as merely collateral damage in such circles.

The Fenians at large in England resolved to redouble their violence, in anticipation of which they stepped up their arms procurements. Crucial to these endeavours was another Civil War veteran, Ricard O'Sullivan Burke, who had fought from Bull Run to Appomattox, before going on to become a Fenian arms procurer in Birmingham, where as 'Mr Barry' or 'Mr Winslow' he purchased arms allegedly on behalf of the Chilean government. Burke was identified to Scotland Yard detectives while staying in Bloomsbury in central London. After a scuffle he was arrested together with his confederate Joseph Casey in Woburn Square. Burke was remanded to the Clerkenwell House of Detention, one of two prisons in an area favoured by English artisan radicals, Welsh milk suppliers and many Irish, Italian and Swiss immigrants. The area was known for clock-making and printing, as well as demonstrations on its Green. The House of Detention, which included an exercise yard, was ringed by a wall that was three feet thick at the base and twenty-five feet high. Tenement houses ran parallel with the wall along one side of respectively Corporation Lane and Corporation Row.

Aided by sympathetic female visitors, who included his sister, the imprisoned Burke was in contact with Fenians in London with whom he exchanged messages written in invisible ink. He devised his own escape plan. In the yard he had noticed that the outer wall had been weakened by men repairing pipes buried under the road. The escape bid was led by another Civil War veteran, James Murphy, formerly of the 20th Massachusetts Infantry Regiment, who together with a Fenian from Fermanagh called Michael Barrett misused the proceeds of a collection for a new church to assemble enormous quantities of gunpowder. These purchases alerted the police to what was afoot, although they also had agents within the Fenian conspiracy.

On 12 December 1867 Murphy and two helpers wheeled a tarpaulin-covered barrow through the darkening winter streets of Clerken-well. Underneath was a thirty-six-gallon kerosene barrel filled with gunpowder. They lobbed a white ball over the wall, the signal for Burke – who was circling the yard on exercise – to halt as if to remove a stone from his boot. Outside, Murphy lit the initiatory fuse, which spluttered and went out. Undertaking one of the most dangerous things to do with gunpowder, whose main drawback as an explosive is that it easily becomes damp, he returned twice more to relight the increasingly short fuse. Eventually the three called it a day and left; inside the walls Burke was returned to his cell.

On Friday the 13th at 3.30 p.m. the barrow and barrel reappeared alongside the prison. Some of the children playing in the street were co-opted into what became a game of fireworks. One of the bombers, dressed in a brown overcoat and black hat, even lit the squib used to ignite the barrel by taking a light from a boy smoking a cigarette. Although a low rather than a high explosive, which creates what experts call a burning event, gunpowder delivers a prolonged and steady propellant push useful for quarrying rocks or expelling projectiles from cannons. When the bomb went off, most of the explosive force hit the tenements opposite rather than the prison wall, although an inverted wedge was blown out of that, sixty feet long at the top and narrower at the wall's thicker base. The breach in the wall was irrelevant since, as a precautionary measure, the suspicious prison authorities had relocated Burke and Casey to cells in a remote part of the jail. The explosion was heard in suburban Brixton south-east of the Thames, and even, according to a man who wrote to the *Standard*, some forty miles away. Fifty firemen arrived to pick their way through the rubble, while hundreds of policemen milled around. Guards units took up station in and around the prison. Gas mains were excavated to provide light for rescuers combing through the rubble. Three people were dead, a seven-year-old child called Minnie Abbott, a thirty-six-year-old housewife, Sarah Hodgkinson, and a forty-seven-year-old brass finisher, William Clutton. Terrible injuries were inflicted, many involving fractures to the facial bones, although an eight-year-old girl coming home with a jug of milk sustained terrible lacerations to her knee. An eleven-year-old boy had to have eight fingers amputated. The death toll of local residents rose to twelve over the following weeks, while hundreds more had sustained injuries. Four hundred houses had been damaged. Rumours flew about Fenian plots to blow up the Arsenal at Woolwich, the Tower of London and York Minster. Fifty thousand special constables volunteered to patrol the streets and civil servants went about armed. There was dark talk in the *Spectator* of the need for bayonets to be deployed, although the magazine had been sympathetic to the demotic nobility of the Fenian uprising in Ireland. More practically, a local clergyman organised a Clerkenwell Explosion Relief Fund that dispensed aid and pensions to the victims and their rescuers.[7]

Michael Barrett was caught test-firing a revolver while in Glasgow and brought back to London. He and five others went on trial at the Old Bailey in April 1868. The cases against Ann Justice and John O'Keefe were dismissed by the judge, and the jury went on to acquit three other defendants. Barrett alone was found guilty of murder. He spoke at great length before sentence was passed, disputing the evidence and the witnesses brought against him, one of whom he dismissed as a 'prince of perverts'. He was sentenced to hang. In another trial, Ricard O'Sullivan Burke was sentenced to fourteen years' penal servitude. Attempts to reprieve Barrett took place at a time when the authorities in Australia and Canada had hanged Fenians who had shot a renegade Fenian (he had since become a Canadian cabinet minister) and wounded the duke of Edinburgh on a tour of the Antipodes. Barrett was taken out from Newgate prison to be executed on a fine May morning, as people who had rented gallows side seats in the Magpie and Stump for up to £10 sang 'Champagne Charlie' or 'Oh My, I've Got to Die'. When Barrett appeared the crowd cheered, with boos and hisses for Calcraft. Barrett died instantly, the last man to be executed in public in England. After an interval of an hour, Calcraft appeared – to shouts of 'Come on, body snatcher!' – to cut the corpse down. The bells on St Sepulchre's rang nine times. A martyr had been born. So had the habit of calling the Irish 'Micks', because thenceforth the Fenians (and the Irish Guards) were popularly referred to as the 'Mick Barretts'.

As Barrett assumed his place in Irish martyrology, the sufferings of some eighty imprisoned Fenians became the stuff of legend and the object of complex calculations on the part of the British authorities who, regardless of party, were pursuing a moderate reform agenda in Ireland, with Disraeli's Tories emollient towards the Catholic Church, and Gladstone seeking land reform and disestablishment of the Protestant Church of Ireland. The majority of Irish nationalists responded with calls for land reform and Home Rule. At the extreme margins of Irish politics, the Fenian prisoners taxed the dispassionate ingenuity of British statesmen. The need to maintain law and order – ultimately through executions and imprisonment – had to be balanced against the spiral of violence this might unleash, and against the wider political repercussions in Ireland and further afield, especially in the US, where politicians were hungry for the Irish-American vote. Did one treat them as criminals or as political prisoners?

While the Fenian convicts were spared the full disciplinary rigours of Victorian jails, those who acted up were kept in solitary confinement or in irons for periods of time that seemed cruel. Tales of the plight of the prisoners swelled the ranks of Fenian activists and sympathisers, for they were the objects of emotive campaigns on their behalf, campaigns which routinely highlighted the sufferings of the prisoners' innocent wives and children. Everywhere as the cold-blooded facts of terrorist outrages responsible for their conviction faded from memory, the plight of the imprisoned occupied the emotional foreground. Gladstone's administration eventually opted for the sensible tactic of releasing the small fry, then expatriating the ringleaders, while keeping Fenians who had been members of the armed forces in detention, that being the issue on which queen Victoria refused to be persuaded towards leniency.[8]

Rage at the 'injustices' and 'indignities' heaped upon imprisoned Fenians also led to thoughts of retaliation and revenge among their supporters. The enraged included Jeremiah O'Donovan Rossa, who in 1871 had been amnestied by the Gladstone government from a fifteen-year jail sentence on condition he remove himself to America. A dipsomaniac over-fond of whiskey and cigars, Rossa was given to sanguinary bombast, threatening to reduce London to ashes with the aid of a dozen arsonists, who would bring 'the fires of Hell' to the imperial capital. The erratic Rossa, known to detractors as O'Dynamite, was only fitfully connected to Clan na Gael, a US-based secret society founded in June 1867 under John Devoy to oppose Irishmen lured into supporting Home Rule.

In 1876 this secret society mounted the daring escape from the Imperial prison at Fremantle in Western Australia of six imprisoned Fenians, who were spirited out to international waters on a US-registered whaler called the Catalpa. Its flag can still be seen in the national museum in Dublin. This propaganda coup fuelled the notion of a skirmishing fund to finance attacks against Britain and its global interests, the first project being an invasion of Canada, which it was hoped the US would take advantage of. This resulted in a few inconsequential border skirmishes. A great deal of Clan money was mercifully squandered on a schoolmaster and inventor called John Holland, the genius who offered to build a Fenian submarine. Ever more elaborate models led to actual boats initially propelled by steam lines from a surface ship, and then, after the successful installation of engines, unaccompanied. Mishaps included a Fenian flying through the air when, having forgotten to tighten a hatch, an air bubble propelled him skywards. Holland's habit of suing all and sundry eventually led the Clan to steal his boat, which then was left to rust – like a riveted porpoise – while others spirited away its engines. But an idea had been born. In 1900 the same inventor's USS *Holland* would become the first submarine purchased by the US Navy.

John Devoy, the Clan's most intelligent leader, decided on what he called a New Departure in 1878 which supported Charles Parnell's constitutional form of Irish nationalism, but others in the leadership simultaneously embarked on a campaign of terror, as did O'Donovan Rossa, with whom, to complicate matters, the Clan occasionally cooperated. Much of the rhetoric familiar from more contemporary terrorist movements was evident in embryonic form among these Fenians in the 1880s, although their avoidance of the term terrorism means that more emphasis has been placed on Russian nihilists as the progenitors of the tactic. In fact, what the Russians did, rather than what they said, was more akin to the targeted assassination of key imperial figures, with a view to isolating the government from society, than an attempt to create mass panic so as to influence the political process.[9]

The early Fenian notion of a people's army representing the oppressed nation's will through insurrectionary violence was gradually displaced by that of terror campaigns designed to sap the morale of the more mighty imperial enemy. This change of tactics was because there was no substantial support for the insurrection, a truth that was cleverly concealed within the Fenians' own analysis: 'We should oppose a general insurrection in Ireland as untimely and ill-advised. But we believe in action nonetheless. The Irish cause requires Skirmishers. It requires a little band of heroes who will initiate and keep up without intermission guerrilla warfare – men who will fly over land and sea like invisible beings – now striking the enemy in Ireland, now in India, now in England itself as occasion may present.' The conceit of the enlightened vanguard would become familiar to all manner of modern terrorists.

The preferred weapon was influenced by the Russian nihilist attacks that had culminated in the assassination of tsar Alexander II on 1 March 1881 by terrorists hurling small grenade-like explosives at their target.

Nitroglycerine had been invented by Ascanio Sobrero, a Piedmontese chemist, who by mixing glycerine with sulphuric and nitric acids made a yellowish, sweet-smelling liquid with curious properties. A small quantity blew up in his face. Pursuing a different tack, Sobrero tried a trace on a dog, which died in agony, but which was revealed to have hugely distended blood vessels in its heart and brain. British doctors subsequently discovered that nitroglycerine brought relief for the paralysing pain of angina pectoris. In the 1860s the Swedish inventor Alfred Nobel discovered how to stabilise nitroglycerine by absorbing it into a solid, using such things as kieselguhr, sawdust or gelatine, the end product being sticks of dynamite with names like Atlas. Nobel also invented gunpowder-based detonators to trigger the dynamite explosion.[10]

The Fenian terrorist Rossa endeavoured to bask in the remote glow of the Russian nihilist assassins by advertising in his newspaper courses in manufacturing bombs by a Professor Mezzeroff, 'England's invisible enemy'. Mezzeroff was a tall, sharp-faced man with curly hair arranged around his pate and a 'grizzly moustache'. Habitual wearing of black clothes and steely spectacles rounded off the sinister effect of a character straight out of Dostoevsky or Conrad. His origins were mysterious, although he had the accents of an Irishman. His father was Russian, but his mother was said to have been a Highlander and he enjoyed US citizenship. Students were encouraged to pay US$30 for a thirty-day course in making dynamite, although Mezzeroff's enthusiasm was greater than his knowledge of chemistry. He claimed that dynamite 'was the best way for oppressed peoples from all countries to get free from tyranny and oppression'. A pound of the stuff contained more force than 'a million speeches'.[11]

Instead of initiating a burning event, with pressures up to 6,000 atmospheres in milliseconds, dynamite causes a shock wave with pressures of up to 275,000 atmospheres. In other words, compared with gunpowder, a dynamite explosion is like the difference between being knocked off a bicycle by a car and being hit by an express train. Moreover, unlike cumbersome barrels of gunpowder, lightweight dynamite could be concealed within small containers or included in brass grenades whose fragments would cause death and injury when thrown. Different detonators became available to bombers, beyond the gunpowder-based fuses that had to be lit. They included systems based on acids burning through wads of paper pushed into holes in a series of pipes; percussive mechanisms involving timers and a revolver; or alarm-clock-based 'infernal machines' that ticked away to oblivion. These enabled terrorists to minimise personal risk by practising place and leave, although there was considerable risk to anyone who happened along. A weapon of such lethality would inevitably entail collateral civilian casualties, even when it was used to decapitate a state's leadership or against fixed strategic assets such as arsenals or dockyards. Hence the anticipatory formulation of ethical evasions before the Fenian campaign had even started. Dynamite terrorism was the tactic of the weak in an otherwise impossible conflict. There were no immutable laws of war because evolving technologies tended to make them redundant. In any case, as Ireland was not a sovereign state, Irishmen were absolved of international inter-state conventions. In obeisance to the spirit of the Victorian era, the ultimate rationalisation was that dynamite was the apogee of scientific warfare. Hence the respect accorded to Mezzeroff, later immortalised as the 'Professor' by Joseph Conrad in *The Secret Agent*.

Both Rossa and the Clan embarked on campaigns of terror, using Irish-American bombers rather than British- or Irish-based Fenian sympathisers who were thought to be too susceptible to penetration by British detectives and secret agents, some of whom like Henri le Caron operated across the Atlantic.[12]

These were not random attacks against high-profile individual human targets, but campaigns with their own rhythm of multiple successive strikes whose object was to spread fear and panic. Their opening target was chosen for its symbolic value: an army barracks in the town where three Irish martyrs had been hanged. On 14 January 1881 Rossa's bombers struck in dense fog at Regent Road Barracks in Salford, although the bomb placed in a ventilator shaft in the wall did most damage to a neighbouring butcher's shop and a rope factory where a seven-year-old boy was slain. Further attacks in February were foiled when police raided a steamer named the SS *Malta*, with a cargo of cement from New York, in whose hold they found cases containing six bombs fitted with clock-work detonators. Three months later an alert policeman extinguished the burning fuse of a blasting-powder-based bomb placed in a recess below the Egyptian Hall in London's Mansion House. In May, a crude pipe bomb caused minimal damage to Liverpool's police headquarters. A month later, two of the bombers were caught after they left a bomb built into a cast-iron gas pipe outside the town hall in the same city.

Some brave policemen dragged it down the steps of the town hall just before it exploded. The two Fenian bombers received sentences of life and twelve years' imprisonment. The sole other success the police enjoyed was to discover a Fenian arms dump in a stables which a Mr Sadgrove had rented from a Swiss watch maker in Clerkenwell. This contained four hundred rifles, with shamrocks embossed on their stocks, sixty revolvers and about seventy-five thousand rounds of ammunition. Sadgrove, or John Walsh as he was called, was sentenced to seven years' penal servitude. Although the lethal effects of Rossa's campaign were minimal, it added to the horror occasioned by the murders in Phoenix Park of lord Frederick Cavendish and Thomas Burke, senior members of the Dublin administration, who were slashed to death with twelve-inch surgical knives by a gang called the Irish Invincibles, and ensured that the general public were stricken with anxiety and terror. They had good reason because Rossa's shambolic Skirmishers were about to be augmented by killers with a more professional approach, although the irrepressible Rossa helped fund them. His newspaper the *United Irishman* openly solicited donations to terrorism, sometimes publishing donor letters: 'Dear Sir, Inclosed [sic] find $3; $2 for my yearly subscription for "the United Irishman"; and $1 for dynamite. I think it the most consistent remedy for old tyrant England. Wishing you and the "United Irishman" success, I remain, etc. Thos. O'Neill.'

More substantial funds came from the US Clan leader, a Chicago lawyer called Alexander Sullivan, who simply redirected some of the impressive sums which Irish-Americans had given to the Irish Land League's rural activities. A rock of a fellow, always armed and wearing cowboy boots, Sullivan had earlier killed a man who called his wife 'a tool of Jesuits' and had subsequently shot and wounded a political rival in New Mexico. Despite this background, Sullivan reinvented himself as a lawyer with vice-presidential ambitions in any party that would have him. Rossa and Sullivan effectively ran parallel campaigns of terror, although the sources of funding and some of the personnel overlapped.[13]

Rossa's men struck first in late January 1883 in Glasgow. Two large bombs destroyed a gasometer in the city gasworks, causing considerable damage to neighbouring industries and injuring eleven people. In the early hours of the following day, late-night revellers happened upon a bomb designed to bring down a stone aqueduct carrying the Forth and Clyde Canal over a road. An off-duty soldier poked around in an oval bonnet box made of tin which erupted in his face. The bombers moved to London.

Seven weeks later, a policeman discovered another bonnet box, this time behind the offices of *The Times* newspaper in Playhouse Yard. He managed to kick it away, causing the crude lignine bomb to malfunction. Shortly afterwards, just as Big Ben was striking nine, a massive explosion went off amid new government buildings in Parliament Street. These buildings and the headquarters of the Metropolitan Police 'A' Division looked as if they had survived a major riot. Gladstone appeared next morning to survey the scene. Policemen were stationed at all key buildings and guarded key public figures. A new Irish Special Branch, under chief inspector 'Dolly' Williamson, and dedicated to Fenian terrorism, was established in a small building at the centre of Great Scotland Yard, a warren of narrow streets and courtyards off the east side of Whitehall where the Metropolitan Police still stable horses. On 21 May *The Times* published a letter from 'a considerate dynamiter' warning that 'thousands, perhaps millions, of your innocent citizens, before another April comes around, will be no more'. Writing from Colorado, the correspondent advised the British to evacuate women and children before the Fenian bombers returned.[14]

The weakest link in Rossa's campaign was that his explosives were being smuggled into Britain on American ships bound for Cork or Liverpool, a procedure that gave the watching police their biggest breaks. The next wave of bombers, despatched by Sullivan's Clan rather than Rossa, resolved to manufacture their bombs in England, to avoid having to run the gauntlet at Irish and British ports where security had been stepped up. Their leader, Dr Thomas Gallagher, visited Britain in the guise of an American tourist in 1882. From a large family of Irish immigrants, Gallagher had worked in a foundry as a teenager, studying medicine in his spare time. He had the natural authority of a healer in his part of Brooklyn, while his studies had also involved the chemistry needed to make bombs.

Gallagher sent one Alfred George Whitehead – or Jemmy Murphy, to give him his real name – to England to establish a cover for a bomb factory. Whitehead rented a shop in the Ladywood district of Birmingham, where he set up a phoney paint and decorating business, with £10 of brushes and wallpaper on display for customers. This cover enabled him to purchase large quantities of chemicals, whose odour would be masked by that of oil and paint. Alert suppliers began to wonder about the quantities of pure glycerine Whitehead was buying, and noted his Irish accent, stained fingernails and acid-bitten clothes. Undercover police officers began to purchase brushes and wallpaper, finally breaking into the shop at night to take samples of the chemicals littered around. They noticed that acids burned holes in their socks. The most ominous clue was a coat with the label Brooks Brothers, Broadway, New York, then and now a famous US clothing firm.

Although they had the bomb master under surveillance, the police had no clue to the identity of the bombers. Gallagher had recruited them the previous year from young men who belonged to New York's many Fenian clubs, with names like Emerald Club or Napper Tandy. Gallagher himself sailed to Britain, together with his alcoholic brother Bernard, whom he left in steerage. Gallagher was carrying $2,300 and a letter of credit for £600. He and his bombers made trips from London to Birmingham to pick up Whitehead's explosives. Despite the doctor's clear instructions, the less bright members of his team imagined that one could pour nitroglycerine into a bag or trunk without the need for rubber bags inside. On one occasion, eighty pounds of nitroglycerine were poured into two fishing waders, which, tied off at the knees, were then taken to London in a portmanteau. Station and hotel porters buckled under the weight, speculating that the case contained gold sovereigns or iron bars. The police followed the bombers from Birmingham to London and then pounced to effect their arrests. Whitehead was detained in his bomb factory. The entire cell were sentenced to life imprisonment. In another triumph for the authorities, some ten Glasgow 'Ribbonmen' (violent Catholic nationalists who wore green ribbons) and two of their Irish-American recruiters were convicted in December 1883 of the Glasgow bombing campaign. A more stringent Explosive Substances Act put the onus of proof that possession of certain chemical compounds or actual explosives was entirely innocent upon the person caught with these substances.

These trials took place during the summer as a final bombing campaign, focused on London, geared up for its attacks. The team leader, William Mackey Lomasney, had been born in Ohio, and had been amnestied by the British authorities in 1871 after serving part of a sentence for arms-related offences and attempted murder. From a family with deep roots in Irish insurrectionism – his great-grandfather had died fighting for Wolfe Tone – Lomasney was a slight man with a lisping voice and a face that became instantly unrecognisable through the simple device of growing or shaving off his beard. Lomasney's team commenced their campaign by bombing the London Underground railways in November 1883. The stations and dark tunnels provided plenty of ways to evade capture, as did the ever present crowds. Bombs in bags were dropped from the front first-class carriages, detonating by the time the third-class carriages passed the spot where the bags had fallen. The first such attack occurred as a Metropolitan Line train pulled out of Praed Street station, the Underground connection with Paddington rail terminus. Seventy-two people in the cheaper carriages were injured by splinters of wood and shards of flying glass. Twenty minutes later, another bomb exploded as a District Line train left Charing Cross on a journey towards Westminster; it caused limited damage to subterranean cables and pipes and to the tunnel itself. The injured included various artisans and shopkeepers as well as two schoolboys visiting the capital for the day from Clacton. Meanwhile, a further Fenian team had brought bomb components over on the boat from France. In February 1884, four bombs with alarm-clock detonators were left in cases deposited at four main railway terminals: Charing Cross, Ludgate Hill, Paddington and Victoria. Three of them failed to detonate, although the bomb at Victoria devastated the left-luggage room when it went off at one in the morning when the station was deserted. The bombers were en route to France before the bombs had even been set to explode. Police surveillance of the ports was stepped up.[15]

With the help of an informer, the police arrested an Irish-American called John Daly with three brass-encased dynamite bombs. His intention had been to throw them from the Strangers' Gallery on to the floor of the House of Commons, an outrage that would have killed the government and opposition leaders on the front benches below. A jury took fifteen minutes to find Daly guilty. Meanwhile, Lomasney's men struck in May 1884 at the Junior Carlton Club, injuring the kitchen staff rather than members, at the home of Sir Watkin Wynn, and most audaciously at the offices of the Irish Special Branch. A bomb was left in a cast-iron urinal of the Rising Sun pub which shared a corner of Great Scotland Yard with the Irish Special Branch. It caused considerable damage to the building and destroyed many of the police records on the Fenians themselves. After a lull during summer and autumn, at six in the evening on 13 December 1884 a bomb exploded at the south-west end of London Bridge, hurling pedestrians to the ground and blowing a hole in the road. The wreckage of a rowing boat, rented earlier by

William Mackey Lomasney and two accomplices, drifted out on the ebb tide, indicating that the bombers were no more. Lomasney's store of dynamite, manufactured in San Francisco, was discovered at a house in Harrow Road a year later.

In the new year, a fresh team of Irish-American terrorists, under James Gilbert Cunningham and Henry Burton, respectively aged twenty-three and thirty-three, successfully smuggled in sixty pounds of Atlas Powder A dynamite as they entered the United Kingdom. Their first bomb exploded on 2 January 1885 on a Metropolitan Line train as it approached Goodge Street station. On Saturday 24 January Burton – with a team mate disguised as a female – tried to explode a diversionary bomb in Westminster's Crypt, so as to enable the other unmolested to drop a bomb into the chamber of the House of Commons. Virtually simultaneously Cunningham slipped away from a party of sightseers in the Tower of London and placed a bomb behind a gun carriage in the central White Tower. The carriage absorbed much of the blast, although four young sightseers were hurt. Cunningham was caught as he ran through the Tower's maze of walls and gardens; Burton was apprehended shortly afterwards. Both men were jailed for life for these attacks as well as for bombs at Gower Street and the four London mainline stations. In mid-March 1885, the French authorities rounded up and deported Fenians gathering for an alleged dynamite conference. Their number included James Stephens, the creator of the original organisation who ironically had always opposed terrorist bombings. Fears that the US government might finally be persuaded to follow suit led the Clan to abandon its plans for further campaigns. A final conspiracy by the implacable Rossa and a wing of the Clan to cause explosions during the Queen's 1887 Golden Jubilee was thwarted because of high-level penetration of the Clan by a British agent.

II HEWING THE WAY

The Fenians, or Irish Republican Brotherhood, were at the historic core of, and the mythologised model for, what became the Irish Republican Army or IRA. Ironically, the success of the (not entirely) opposed constitutional tradition in getting the British government to concede Irish Home Rule in 1914 had already engendered a blocking Unionist paramilitary response – the formation in 1913 of the Ulster Volunteer Force (UVF). Outrageous British government acquiescence in this first paramilitary army – with its links to the Conservative Party and the British armed forces – contributed to the creation in Dublin of the Irish Volunteers, elements of which would fuse with the IRB to become the IRA.[16]

In line with the established Fenian strategy of capitalising on Britain's imperial woes, elements within the IRB and Irish Volunteers – both supporters of imperial Germany in the Great War – launched the 1916 Easter Rising, taking over a handful of buildings in Dublin for five days. Involving about a thousand insurgents, this was as much intended to discredit the constitutional pragmatism of John Redmond's Irish Parliamentary Party, which had achieved the goal of Home Rule (albeit deferred for the war's duration), as it was directed against a Liberal-dominated British government mired on the Western Front in a war which the Catholic Church and most Irishmen supported. Coldly considered, the Rising was hopelessly ill conceived, commencing before a crucial consignment of German weapons had arrived, let alone an invasion of Britain by Ireland's gallant ally the Kaiser. About fifteen hundred men took part in the Rising, or about 1 per cent of the number of Irish volunteers simultaneously fighting imperial Germany in the British army. But that was not the point, because this crucifixion had been conceived and choreographed as a form of blood sacrifice witnessing the birth of the nation. It was crushed with relative ease, by Irish soldiers of the 10th Royal Dublin Fusiliers, after it had cost about 450 civilian Irish lives, as well as those of 116 soldiers and sixteen policemen. But the manner of the judicial response became, in republican eyes, the constitutive epiphany in the creation of an armed republican movement with widespread support among those Irish Catholics who had conflated religion and nationalism into one sacral tribal entity while dissimulating their own rabid Catholic sectarianism. They had even managed to assimilate such Protestant and Enlightenment precursors as Wolfe Tone or Robert Emmet into a mythologised Catholic nationalist Emerald Isle story. Coming a day after Easter Sunday, in the eyes of mystical nationalists like Padraig Pearse the Rising was the blood sacrifice necessary for Ireland's liberation. In a pamphlet entitled *Ghosts* written on the eve of the Rising, Pearse wrote: 'There is only one way to appease a ghost, you must do the thing it asks you. The ghosts of a nation sometimes ask very big things; and they must be appeased at whatever the cost.' Pearse's own ghost has been appeased ever since, notably at the animist rites of IRA funerals, but also at the expense of living people who became innocent dead too.[17]

The judicial consequences of the Rising only succeeded in engendering 'maximum resentment, minimum fear'. Sixteen of the leaders were sentenced to death, by military courts, with the executions being dragged out for an unconscionably long time, in two cases involving men physically incapable of standing before a firing squad. Whereas the Dublin Rising had hardly elicited widespread support, there was general outrage at the manner of its suppression, as well as at the internment in Britain of hundreds of its participants. Their revolutionary commitment was deepened in Frognoch and Reading jails. Just as the Rising's leading ideologue, headmaster Padraig Pearse, had traded on memories of martyrs past in his various proclamations of an Irish republic, so he and his fifteen executed comrades became mythological martyrs themselves, inspiring republicans to this day. Even the Marxists among them clutched crucifixes as they died in a hail of bullets, enhancing their posthumous appeal to the majority of their countrymen.

The Rising could well have been relegated to the status of minor might-have-been had the British government not made the mistake of extending to Ireland the principle of conscription for men under fifty-one (it had existed in the rest of the United Kingdom since 1916) to cover the huge losses caused by the March 1918 German offensive on the Western Front. Why should the Irish be exempt from fighting when they benefited from newly introduced old-age pensions and the wartime hike in agricultural prices? Taken together with the stalling of talks between constitutional nationalists, Unionists and the British government, the Military Service Bill dramatically boosted the fortunes of Sinn Féin in the December 1918 general election, in which an enlarged electorate of over two million voted for the first time. The party name meant Ourselves, or Ourselves Alone, depending on how one translates from the Gaelic, and was indicative of both solipsism and the Cosa Nostra.

Originally a non-violent, non-republican nationalist party, with an eccentric enthusiasm for the Austro-Hungarian Dual Monarchy as a model for Britain and Ireland, Sinn Féin won 48 per cent of the vote in the whole of Ireland, but a striking 65 per cent in the southern twenty-six counties that would become the Irish Free State. By that time, the party had been hijacked by surviving leaders of the Rising, with Eamon de Valera – sprung from British captivity – becoming president of the party at the October 1917 ard-fheis convention. In addition to being reconfigured as a republican party, Sinn Féin was formally linked with militant separatism when de Valera was elected president of the Irish Volunteers, who in 1919 became the IRA. They set up an alternative parliament, called the Dáil Éireann, which met on 21 January 1919, when a Declaration of Independence was proclaimed. Three months later de Valera became president of the Council of Ministers, the rebel provisional government in which also sat such luminaries as Michael Collins, W. T. Cosgrave, Arthur Griffith and Constance Markievicz. The ministers operated from flats above shops or private houses to avoid arrest by the British. Sinn Féin supporters quietly set up a parallel system of courts and local government so as to nullify the power of Dublin Castle, the symbol of imperial rule. The IRA embarked on a military campaign combining elements of guerrilla warfare with terrorism.

Although the IRA had a military command structure modelled on that of the British army, this did not efficiently curb the desire of locally based bands to kill representatives of the Crown forces. An IRA unit in Tipperary shot dead two Royal Irish Constabulary officers in January 1919, the first blow in what became an ugly vortex of violence. The IRA carried out a systematic campaign of terror, beginning with attacks on isolated police officers as well as a detective in the Dublin Metropolitan Police. This developed into larger attacks on police barracks, a strategy designed to sever any connection between the police and people, and to establish the IRA as an alternative authority. Enforcing the quarantining of the police, women who had liaisons with them, or who cooked for them, were threatened with death or had their heads shaved. A seventy-year-old woman who informed the police of a planned IRA ambush was shot dead. In an atmosphere paranoid about spies and fifth-columnists, epitomised by Church of Ireland and Methodist churches, Orange lodges and masonic temples, Ireland's Protestant minority became targets, with about a third of their number being forced out of their homes in these years. This was only partially a response to the British policy of burning down the homes of known rebels, although it did not quite amount to the ethnic cleansing in Smyrna in the 1920s or Yugoslavia in the 1990s.

These were the classic years of the romance of the gunman, a leather-jacketed or trench-coated figure armed with a pistol, rifle or Tommy gun. This last was an American submachine gun with a cylindrical magazine originally designed to be used at close quarters to clear wartime trenches, but, produced too late for the Western Front, adopted as the weapon of choice for Chicago gangsters. It was useless in shootouts across fields. Other aspects of the learning curve included the realisation that a .45 is more useful in close-quarter assassination than a .38. Most of the hundred thousand or so IRA volunteers were young, single Catholic males from urban backgrounds ranging from shop assistants to medical students. Many had served in the British armed forces or had been educated by the Christian Brothers. In addition to small hit teams, there were larger flying columns of mobile guerrillas in the countryside, consisting of full-time paid rebels, released from whatever restraints being part of a family or community may have imposed. The women's organisation Cumann na mBann provided vital intelligence, nursing, and material and spiritual support during this period.[18]

Much of the violence had a tit-for-tat character in a society where there were long hatreds. When a police constable was shot dead by the IRA, mystery assassins killed Tomas McCurtain, the lord mayor of Cork and a commandant in the IRA. His successor, Terence MacSwiney, was jailed for IRA activities, and expired on the seventy-fifth day of his hunger strike in London's Brixton prison. A shopkeeper and his friend refused to share in the general lamentations involving kneeling women praying for the Blessed MacSwiney in front of a bearded Capuchin. These men were both assassinated by the IRA. After shooting most of the Dublin Metropolitan 'G' division which dealt with political crime, IRA gunmen – who included future taoiseach Sean Lemass – struck at Britain's intelligence presence in Ireland, killing twelve army officers (who stuck out like sore thumbs) in their homes on what became known as (the original) Bloody Sunday. Most of the victims were laid out in the morgue still wearing blood-stained pyjamas. These killings were in reprisal for the execution of medical student Kevin Barry for the murder of a soldier younger than himself. Some of the victims had nothing to do with intelligence, unless their cover was veterinary officers come to Dublin to purchase mules. Enraged by this attack, the British struck back at Croke Park, the mecca of Gaelic football, when during a hunt for fleeing IRA men they fired into, or back at, the crowd (for the causes are contentious), killing twelve people including a player from Tipperary who fell dead on the pitch. This was a result of the deployment of thirteen thousand battle-hardened veterans of the recent war as auxiliaries to the Royal Irish Constabulary. These Black 'n' Tans, named after their mix-and-match combat garb, brought a certain indiscriminate vigour to the conflict that has passed into Irish folklore and that was condemned at the time by senior British statesmen.

Less well known, about a thousand IRA men were also active in mainland Britain, particularly London, Liverpool and Tyneside. Their wilder schemes included plans to kill Lloyd George, to truck-bomb the House of Commons or to poison the horses in Buckingham Palace. In practice, a hundred IRA men caused extensive damage to Liverpool's docks, destroying nineteen warehouses. Between February and July 1921 they launched co-ordinated arson attacks on farms around London and Liverpool, in response to British reprisal burnings of farms of IRA sympathisers in Ireland, as well as extensive attacks on telegraph and telephone lines and railway signal boxes. Such attacks caused an estimated £1,000,000 damage. The IRA stalked high-profile military and police targets, notably Basil Thompson, the head of the Special Branch responsible for political criminality. On 22 June 1922, two young IRA men, Reginald Dunne and Joseph O'Sullivan, shot dead field marshal Sir Henry Wilson as he reached his doorstep after spending the morning unveiling a war memorial at Liverpool Street station. O'Sullivan had a wooden leg after being wounded while serving in the British army in the same war Wilson was commemorating. Wilson had once snubbed Michael Collins at a 10 Downing Street meeting. Despite shooting two policemen and a civilian who pursued them, the two assassins were captured, and in August were tried and executed. The British responded to this campaign by giving about fifty prominent figures armed body-guards, installing barriers around government buildings and parliament, and from time to time deploying soldiers to guard railway lines and telegraph poles.[19]

By that time, the IRA had effectively run out of ammunition and weapons, while the British had succeeded in capturing about 5,500 of their estimated 7,500 active personnel. Collins estimated that within about three weeks the IRA would not be in a position to fight. Worse, IRA intelligence told the leadership that the British were thinking of trebling the number of troops in Ireland while imposing martial law. This inclined the IRA, which had long been talking with the British government through clerical back channels, to a political settlement, albeit one that many of them would regard as temporary. A truce in the summer of 1921 led to negotiations in Downing Street which de Valera was shrewd enough to leave in the hands of Collins. Three months of talks resulted in the establishment of the twenty-six-county Irish Free

State, its autonomy qualified by various residual links to the British Crown akin to those which connected the Dominions of Canada or South Africa to the motherland. Six, rather than nine, counties of Ulster would remain in the United Kingdom, although Collins hoped that when boundaries were drawn this would be reduced to an unviable, and indubitably Protestant, three. The readiness of the British government to treat with individuals it had recently dismissed as murderers was noteworthy, with the lengthy talks themselves generating all manner of human sympathies among the negotiating parties. Just in case they failed, Lloyd George threatened to wage all-out war with the entire resources of the British empire within three days.

The Treaty was adopted in the Dáil by a narrow majority of 64 to 57, indicating how far the issue served to aggravate pre-existing personal and political animosities. Those who backed the Treaty, including Michael Collins and Arthur Griffith, thought that a bird in hand was better than one in the bush, and that full independence could be achieved in due course. In these circles, the Protestants of the six northerly counties were a second-order issue – an inexplicable extension of the industrial civilisation of Glasgow or Manchester in the otherwise Irish pastoral idyll. Opponents were more exercised by the exclusion of the six counties, or by the failure to achieve a fully independent republic based on the renunciation of the symbolic features of union that the Free State still retained through Dominion status. A general election in June 1922 overwhelmingly confirmed the pro-Treaty view. Government structures were based on British exemplars, although significantly there was no Ministry of Education. That was the quid pro quo for endorsement of the Free State by the Catholic Church, which already envisaged it as the Atlantic bastion of anti-modernity that it would remain for the next fifty years. Archbishop Walsh voted Sinn Féin.

Since the purest of the republican pure derived their spiritual legitimacy from the martyrs of 1916 and back beyond to a Catholicised Wolfe Tone in 1798, rather than from democratic elections, they ventured ahead with their military quest for the establishment of an independent republic. Roughly 50 per cent of the IRA merged into the newly formed Irish army, while the remaining half comprised Irregulars or Republicans – the forerunners of the modern IRA. These were the armed temple virgins of the flames of Padraig Pearse.[20]

In March 1922 IRA men opposed to the Dáil's decision took over buildings in Dublin, in a symbolic re-run of the Easter Rising. This was hopeless because the Free State's army was deployed against them, using arms provided by the British. The British army even lent it a couple of cannon. 'What's artillery like?' asked one IRA man of a veteran of 1916. 'You get used to it, it's not bad,' replied his comrade. The Dublin insurgency was easily suppressed, as it was in other cities and towns. The IRA reverted to the sort of rural guerrilla war it and its pro-Treaty foes had recently fought against the British, with one unit happening to ambush and kill Michael Collins on 22 August 1922. Ironically, the Provisional Government resorted to measures indistinguishable from the British to win what had become a civil war – although unlike the British it had the support of the Catholic Church, which eagerly excommunicated the IRA. A special-powers resolution perpetuated the draconian military reprisals that had commenced with the British Restoration of Order in Ireland Act two years before. A spiral of violence recommenced. Some seventy-seven republican captives were executed, regardless of whatever services they had performed on behalf of Irish patriotism. When the Irish authorities shot the fifty-two-year-old republican writer Erskine Childers, the IRA announced that members of the government and its supporters were fair game.

The first victim was Seán Hales, a pro-Treaty deputy to the Dáil. The Provisional Government responded to his killing by executing four republican prisoners, thereby putting a stop to this particular cycle of publicly acknowledged violence. However, it did not stop murderous warfare between the IRA and Free State troops. Some of the latter seem to have killed IRA prisoners by tying them up and exploding mines beneath them. Perhaps as many as four to five thousand people were killed in the civil war, the majority of them IRA personnel, as recorded Free State military losses were about eight hundred. In May 1923 the IRA declared a ceasefire and hid its arms, prompting president William T. Cosgrave to remark that the organisation's members might need them 'any time they took it into their heads to interview a bank manager'. Be that as it may, in republican circles the Rising became a foundational myth that one criticised at one's peril. In 1926 the working-class Protestant playwright Sean O'Casey did just that, in *The Plough and the Stars*, performed in the national Abbey Theatre a decade after the Rising. The wives and widows of republican martyrs, including the mother of Pearse, created pandemonium on stage as the Irish tricolour was paraded in a pub to the ghostly tones of Pearse proclaiming his republic. O'Casey left Ireland and never returned.[21]

One inadvertent consequence of the civil war that convulsed the South was that it enabled Ulster Unionists – the secession within the secession – to consolidate partition by forming the state of Northern Ireland. This was accelerated by the quiet decampment of a third of southern Protestants after an IRA campaign of sectarian murder less well known than ugly Unionist riots against Catholics in Belfast. The ambiguities and unsuppressed hopes emitted by the southern Treatyites had unfortunate repercussions in the North. Catholic nationalists abstained from political involvement in the crucial formative years of Northern Ireland, a stance that enabled the Unionist majority to abolish proportional representation and to gerrymander its local government arrangements. This fed a sense of Catholic nationalist grievance that the victims themselves were partly responsible for because of their wish to maintain the provisional character of the new northern polity. This still exists as part of the United Kingdom in the early twenty-first century, with Belfast, but not Dublin, on British television weather maps.[22]

CHAPTER 2

Red: Russian Nihilists and Revolutionaries

Alexis de Tocqueville thought that the most critical time for the pre-revolutionary French monarchy had been when it conceded limited reforms. That assertion held good for late-nineteenth-century tsarist Russia too. Tsar Alexander II, who succeeded to the throne in 1855, embarked on liberalisation measures after the Crimean War had brutally exposed Russian backwardness. His principal reforming measures were the abolition of serfdom in 1861, and the modernisation of provincial government, the law courts and the army. Even the universities, which under his forbidding predecessor Nicholas I resembled socially exclusive reformatories, were opened to students from modest backgrounds who enjoyed a heady period of self-government. A gentler hand was initially evident too in the Russian regime in partitioned Poland, while disabilities imposed on religious sectarians and Jews were relaxed. The latter were allowed to live outside the Pale of Settlement, and Jewish converts to Orthodox Christianity could be, and were, appointed to high office.

Discontent developed because Alexander was torn between the liberal spirit of these reforms and the dying exhortation of his father Nicholas: 'Hold on to everything.' The tsar would not consider any constitutional concessions, thereby antagonising many Western-orientated liberals who sought some form of parliamentary government. Expanding higher education was all very well, but there was no corresponding increase in the positions open to graduates; many humanities graduates faced a life in penurious limbo that failed to match their ambitions. Similarly, there were no official steps taken to satisfy the desire of many educated young women to do something socially useful, or to attain parity of esteem with their male contemporaries. Most crucially, once the excitement was over, the emancipation of the serfs fell far below their heightened expectations, since they had to compensate their former masters for relinquishing a valuable commodity. Having forfeited their feudal authority through governmental edict, the landowners faced an ugly mood from peasants who felt they had been defrauded. In a village called Bezdna, a holy fool cum village idiot enjoined the peasants to resist soldiers who had come to enforce the rights of the landlords. He claimed to have the 'real' edict 'written in golden letters'. Forty-one villagers were shot dead and seventy injured by the army. Despite evidence that the soldiers' captain was insane, he was court-martialled and shot. Hopes rose in radical circles that such incidents of peasant unrest would lead to a general explosion of rural violence. Although Alexander had wanted to increase Polish self-government, this seemed only to fuel nationalist demonstrations – which were violently suppressed by Russian soldiers – and the romantic insurrectionism rife in Polish circles. As with the British and Ireland, so Russia's troubles in Poland – and in the Baltic, Caucasus and Finland – were always regarded as an opportunity by Russia's own domestic radicals.

Russian policy in Poland oscillated between concessions and repression: these equivocations resulted in the bizarre spectacle of the viceroy and the general commanding Warsaw fighting a so-called American duel, in which, after drawing the short straw, the general duly shot himself in the head and the viceroy resigned. In early 1863 the Russian authorities, sensing that an insurrection was imminent, decided to round up Warsaw's radical young, sending them as conscripts to the depths of the Russian interior, a measure that duly triggered the insurrection. Polish partisans were easily crushed by Russian regulars. Twenty thousand insurgents were killed, and in the subsequent crackdown four hundred rebels went to the gallows and a further eighteen thousand to Siberia. The real beneficiaries of the Rising were Prussia and the USA. Alexander II looked on benevolently as Bismarck defeated Austria and France in the name of a united Germany, while to spite the British and French who supported both the Confederacy and the Polish rebels Alexander sold to the Union the wastes of Alaska for US$7 million. The final area in which Alexander took fright and pulled back from his earlier concessions was in the febrile universities. Confronted by evidence that the students were running an informal dictatorship over the professors, student assemblies were banned and limits were placed on the numbers receiving subsidised tuition. Two elderly generals were placed in charge of higher education. This led to student demonstrations which were suppressed with erratic brutality, for it was Alexander's tragedy that, having failed to institute thoroughgoing liberal reforms, he proved incapable of re-establishing his father's austere police regime too.[1]

Severally, these events led to the multiplication of revolutionary conspiracies among people whose general emotional and philosophical outlook needs to be briefly elaborated, for this was the milieu from which more select numbers of terrorists emerged. Although the ranks of terrorists included a few notorious psychopaths, the more typical pathology was a misdirected or frustrated altruism, experienced by people – from a variety of family and socioeconomic backgrounds – whose political goals ranged from the impeccably liberal to the most sanguinary Jacobin totalitarianism.[2]

The common idealistic fantasy was called Populism – that is, the belief that, once the crushing weight of the autocracy and aristocracy had been lifted off by revolution, the structures and habits of socialism allegedly inherent in the traditional peasant commune would be revealed. This was nonsense, albeit inspired by a moralising concern with social equality and justice, on the part of predominantly decent-minded people who wished to overcome the boredom and purposelessness of their own lives by doing good to others.

One can see this impulse at work in the young Vera Figner, the pretty daughter of a well-to-do justice of the peace of noble lineage, who attended one of Russia's elite boarding schools. There she received a very limited education, chiefly in the art of deportment, essential training for society balls and ensnaring an acceptable husband. In her memoirs, Figner gave a presentiment of the lady she was not destined to be: dressed in a cloud-like gauzy white dress with white slippers and her dark hair in ringlets, about to make her lonely debut in a brilliantly lit ballroom filled with elegantly smart people. Nothing in her childhood explains her subsequent career – which she embarked on aged twenty-four – of lifelong revolutionary. There were no signs of psychological disorder; indeed, although rather frail, she was happy and not given to excessive introspection. As a teenager she was virtually unaware of the squalor in the surrounding villages of which her father was lord and master. It was her very happiness, however, that put her on her chosen path in life. Her 'superabundance of joy' awoke diffuse feelings of altruistic gratitude which, given the aimlessness of her privileged life, resulted in a vocation to do good. Late one night she was stung when, overhearing an aunt and cousin indulging in family gossip, they said that she, Vera, 'is a beautiful doll'.

Liberal-minded relatives in her tight family circle introduced her to the heady ideas common among prosperous liberal Russians at the time. A chance reading of an article about the first, Swiss-trained, female physician led to her choice of a medical career. In an early display of feminine resolve, Figner persuaded her young lawyer husband to abandon his career so that she could study medicine in Zurich. There, she became rapidly alienated from her more conservative husband – notwithstanding his having given up his career for her – and so sceptical about her new-found vocation that she failed to qualify. Under the impact of radical student groups, she 'came to see in the practice of medicine only a palliative for an evil which could be cured only by social and political means'. Vera had fallen for the myth of deep causes. She wrote to her husband renouncing any further relations with him and his future financial support. She consciously disavowed her own narrow ambitions, and the 'egotism' of the family that had encouraged them, in favour of the life of denial and sacrifice practised by revolutionaries in Russia. She returned to the – disillusioning – chaos of the revolutionary underground in Moscow. This seemed squalid, for nothing in Figner's genteel background had prepared her for bribing policemen or consorting with gnarled criminals. Deeply depressed, she left to continue the work of propaganda in the countryside, after qualifying as a midwife. She would return to the city as a terrorist.[3]

Figner was an example of the many young upper-class women who engaged in terrorism. Why did they get involved? Apart from the keen sense of altruism many of them felt, terrorism was one of the few areas where women could play an active role, with their views being accorded equal respect to those of men and their lives exposed to the same hazards. Vera Zasulich, who became a revolutionary at the age of seventeen when her elder sister inducted her into radical student circles, regarded this as a way to escape the dismal fate of being a governess in a gentry household, the only future open to poor relations of rich people such as herself: 'Of course it would have been much easier if I had been a boy; then I could have done what I wanted . . . And then, the distant specter of revolution appeared, making me the equal of any boy; I too could dream of "action", of "exploits", and of "the great struggle" . . . I too could join those "who perished for the great cause".'[4]

Much of the inspiration behind Populism was a form of guilt on the part of the leisured educated and upper classes – for, instead of ruthlessly espousing their own selfish interests as Marxism avers, many members of Russia's elites were only too eager to repudiate themselves. As Figner discovered in the villages, 'only there could one have a clean soul and a quiet conscience'. Despite its outward espousal of atheism, Populism was an essentially Christian vision, in which redemptive virtue was ascribed to the lowest of the low, and paradise would dawn after their consciousness had been raised to revolutionary levels. Towards the end of her twenty-two years in prison, Figner told her family of a dream she had had:

> I dreamed we four sisters were riding in a sleigh, over a perfectly black road, bare of snow, and that we were driving through a village, now uphill, now downhill. We passed rows of fine peasants' houses, with sloping stone steps for pedestrians built everywhere, squares with leafless trees, and arbors with golden-yellow roofs. In the centre, on a hillock, rose a white church, a mass of stone, with many graceful, golden cupolas. And when I looked up, suspended from the sky, I saw over the church and the whole hill a crystal canopy which amazed me by its beauty, and for some reason reminded me of the Northern Lights. When we had left the village there spread before us a limitless field, covered with tender green, and above it shone a hot sun in a blue sky. For some reason it reminded me of a picture I saw some time ago: tired pilgrims are walking; and ahead of them in the distance, as though hanging in the clouds a fine outline of a city is visible, with an inscription: 'hail, ye who seek the city of the Lord!'[5]

Where did the bit about the glass canopy come from? And were all terrorists as benign as Vera Figner? It is necessary to review briefly some of the ideas which tantalised the Russian intelligentsia, a species of being that requires comment in itself.

They are not to be confused with the great nineteenth-century Russian novelists, for as a count and a Christian living in seclusion on his estates Tolstoy was not some hack Moscow or Petersburg journalist possessed of a single big idea but otherwise lacking in humanity. Dostoevsky wrote his best novel about this self-selecting group, or rather, about the destruction they had wrought on society and themselves. He committed the heresy of submitting the intelligentsia to the sociological and psychological investigation from which they regarded themselves as exempt, cloaked as they were in the fashionable uniformed ideas of the age – a bit of Comte, Darwin, Feuerbach and so on.

Nor did the intelligentsia coincide with those who might have known a lot about a little, such as professors of ancient history, law, medicine or physics, dispassionately pursuing their subject to the bemusement of radicalised students who worshipped newer foreign gods like Marx and Nietzsche. Rather, the intelligentsia were a sub-set of the educated classes, encompassing those who talked about books they had never read, distinguished both by a disavowal of a class or occupation, such as bureaucrat or soldier, and by their conformist subscription to such supposedly progressive ideas as atheism, socialism and revolution. They were kept afloat like some speculative fraud, on a bubble of liberal good taste, for among an older generation corrupted by liberalism it was not done to challenge youth or its progressive causes until the example of the renegade Dostoevsky gave birth to a right-wing intelligentsia late in the day. The intelligentsia also exercised their own informal censorship, more insidious and pernicious than some minor government bureaucrat blundering around with the prose of Dostoevsky. As Chekhov wrote: 'I do not believe in our intelligentsia, which is hypocritical, false, hysterical, ill-bred, and lazy. I do not believe in it even when it suffers and complains, for its oppressors come from the same womb.' There was another hazard there, brought forth in a hellish light by Dostoevsky, namely that self-styled victims could become the worst oppressors if given the chance. As Shigalev says in *The Possessed*: 'I am perplexed by my own data and my conclusion is a direct contradiction of the idea from which I start. Starting from unlimited freedom, I arrive at absolute despotism. I will add, however, that there can be no solution of the social problem but mine.' He foresees the death of 'a hundred million' to realise a utopia that involves total spying designed to eliminate the private realm. In order to achieve human equality, 'Cicero will have his tongue cut out, Copernicus will have his eyes put out, Shakespeare will be stoned.'[6]

Nihilism was the philosophy of choice for the younger generation of Russian radicals benignly caricatured in Turgenev's *Fathers and Sons* and rendered demonic in Dostoevsky's *The Possessed*. Strictly speaking, nihilism is the rejection of all religious and moral principles, often in the belief that life is meaningless. In that form it is usually the philosophy of choice for adolescents who have read a bit of Camus, but the appeal seems to have seeped across cultures and religions too.[7]

In nineteenth-century Russia, nihilism meant an inordinate credulity towards any number of 'isms', notably positivism, materialism, ethical utilitarianism and, inevitably, terrorism. Generational conflicts were involved. A liberal older generation of well-to-do gentry, with their love of art for art's sake and peregrinations between their Russian estates and German casinos and spas, faced rude competition from earnest plebian intellectuals, many the sons of humble clerics, who thought that the only point of a seascape was to inform those who had never seen the sea, while a novel was merely a didactic means of reforging moral personality in the service of political goals. Any complex social institution could be taken apart and examined for evidence of its utilitarian reasonableness, with the same clinical detachment that a biologist brought to cutting up a frog. In addition to ill-digested ideas, there was a mode of conduct for those who could not be bothered to think. A contrived boorishness was obligatory as well as a conforming nonconformity in long hair, spectacles and slovenly dress. Like the Fenians, who adopted American manners to betoken cultural independence from the British, the nihilists dismissed social graces out of 'the same impulses which make Americans put their feet on the table and spit tobacco on the floor of a luxury hotel'. The nihilist who deliberately collided with a uniformed general in a park, rather than deferentially moving out of his way, probably took things too far as the general turned out to be the tsar.

The living inspiration for the nihilist 'new man' was the literary critic and social theorist Nikolai Chernyshevsky, author of an execrable utopian novel called *What is to be Done?*[8] The book was written in prison, which does not redeem it unless one is sentimental. Its characters were like ideograms, the new moral personalities, for whom the personal was always the political, and who would inhabit the light-filled Crystal Palaces of glass and steel he envisaged as the human race's future. Others, above all Dostoevsky, who had visited the real Crystal Palace on a short trip to London, thought that such futuristic visions suggested the creative finality of an ant-heap, his implication being that the human ants would not improve either through architectural innovation alone. As has been pointed out, Chernyshevsky's 'vision of a terrestrial paradise was a kind of oleograph of the kind of writings he must have read in his seminary days'. Although few of his admirers noticed, his crass scientific reductionism went hand in hand with airy ethical idealism. A great religious philosopher expressed the contradiction through a striking pseudo-syllogism: 'Man is descended from the ape, and *therefore* we must sacrifice ourselves for one another.'[9]

Along with the exiled, and temporarily unfastidious, liberal Alexander Herzen, and the gross and slovenly fugitive anarchist Nikolai Bakunin, Chernyshevsky was one of the architects of a revolutionary conspiracy called Land and Freedom. This revolutionary organisation briefly flourished between 1861 and 1864, in which period it became prototypical for the many conspiracies that followed. It was a predominantly student response to the government's partial rescinding of its university reforms, although the name suggested nobler outrage at the way in which the liberated serfs had had to put themselves in hock for land grudgingly relinquished by their erstwhile masters. There were unsuccessful attempts too to subvert the armed forces, on the part of officers already corrupted by a liberalism they had acquired in partitioned Poland. Mysterious fires in the poorer parts of St Petersburg conduced to a febrile atmosphere and suspicions of plots. Already under open surveillance by his janitor and cook, Chernyshevsky was arrested in 1862 and held in custody for two years while the government manufactured evidence to frame him. This invidious treatment led to his going on one of the first hunger strikes in penal history. Evidence was forged to prove his authorship of inflammatory tracts, which he had in fact written, and he was given six years' hard labour, with exile to Siberia upon his release. The experience killed him. A revolutionary martyr had been born; forty years later an admirer called Lenin would pay explicit homage to Chernyshevsky with a new tract called *What is to be Done?*

Even the most radical members of Land and Freedom, not to speak of Chernyshevsky himself, doubted whether killing the tsar would have any long-term effect, for another Romanov would simply succeed and the masses, whether in town or country, by way of vengeance would probably wipe out the long-haired intelligentsia, with their blue-tinted spectacles. Such thoughts did not deter the dispersed remnants of Land and Freedom, largely consisting of social misfits drawn from demi-educated plebeians and impoverished clerical or gentry families. Contemptuous of the older generation of liberals like Herzen, these men and women were mightily taken with Chernyshevsky's literary embodiment of revolutionary implacability – the character of Rakhmetov – upon whom they modelled themselves.

The first nihilist terrorist group, the Organisation, was founded with the prime intention of liberating Chernyshevsky himself. Its leading lights were Ivan Khudyakov and Nikolai Ishutin, the latter a fantasist who used political causes to dominate other people, the former an unhappy young man plagued by a sexually voracious wife. An air of fanatical intent was propagated through claims that one recruit had offered to poison his rich father so as to donate his inheritance to the Organisation's cause. Early in 1866, Ishutin formed a tighter group within the Organisation with the appropriate title Hell. While the members of the wider Organisation would continue with their mixture of agitprop and social work, members of Hell would devote themselves to assassination, blackmail and robbery. At night the youthful members of Hell discussed the minutiae of such subjects as using planted servants to blackmail their employers, or carrying out assassinations after using acids to disfigure one's face. Phials of strychnine would prevent capture after the event.

These psychopathic fantasies might have remained the stuff of the time between midnight and dawn, but for Ishutin's depressed first cousin Dmitry Karakozov. On 4 April 1866 tsar Alexander II entered a St Petersburg public park for his afternoon stroll with his setter Milord. He left his carriage and escorts at the gate. The forty-seven-year-old ruler of Russia had a brief talk with some aristocratic relatives, and then made his way back to the gate, hardly noticing the gathering crowd of admirers, some of whom were already bowing as a gesture of respect. As Alexander reached his carriage a shot rang out, the bullet narrowly missing his head. This good fortune was due to an alcoholic hatter's apprentice, who inadvertently jogged the assassin Karakozov's arm. Karakozov was quickly apprehended, with phials of acid and strychnine unused about his person. The tsar strode up to him for the following cryptic exchange:

'Who are you?'

'A Russian.'

'What do you want?'

'Nothing, nothing.'

The hatter's apprentice was ennobled and given the wherewithal to drink himself to death. A terrified regime handed the investigation of this minuscule conspiracy of juvenile fantasists to count Michael Muraviev, known dramatically as the hangman, but whose wider investigations were clumsily repressive rather than brutal. Some radical journals were closed down and apartments raided. Instead of publishing the investigation's findings to expose the psychopathic fantasies of the conspirators, or using a local jury which would have executed the lot, the government opted for a special trial by elderly members of the Supreme Criminal Court, with capable lawyers for the defence, in itself testimony to Alexander's reforms. Karakozov and Ishutin were sentenced to death and hanged, while Khudyakov was sent to Siberia, turning down the offer to accompany him from his loyally importunate spouse. Other members of Hell received lesser sentences.[10]

In the years that followed, Alexander turned to more conservative advisers, without effectively clamping down on subversive ideas and those who expressed them. He forfeited much of his dignity when, in late middle age, he became besotted with a teenage girl. It was in this atmosphere of indecision that nihilist terrorism was born. In 1865, a peasant boy who had hauled himself up to become a rather louche schoolmaster had arrived in Moscow. His name was Serge Nechaev. He was introduced to radical intelligentsia circles by the Jacobin lawyer Peter Tkachev, whose odder ideas included the view that Russia could be reformed by killing everyone over the age of twenty-five. The two men collaborated in producing revolutionary tracts. Nechaev, meanwhile, was tantalising radical-chic upper-class ladies with claims that, despite being illiterate until sixteen, he had nevertheless mastered the philosophy of Kant. Such liberal ladies were almost impossible to parody, although Dostoevsky managed it, as they recalled Nechaev fondly: 'He loved to joke and had such a good-natured laugh.' One can meet such people any night of the week in London, New York or Sydney. Nechaev looked like the US outlaw Jesse James, which was appropriate since he admired the ferocious bandits of Russian history, but the inexplicability of his malicious deeds, and the fine plots he wove, are more suggestive of the evil of Shakespeare's Iago.[11] His practical jokes included sending subversive materials to his enemies, knowing that it would be intercepted by the police. Resentment would be a great recruiting agent. In early 1869, Nechaev decided to embroider his revolutionary mystique by faking his own arrest. He sent a cryptic note to eighteen-year-old Vera Zasulich, towards whom he had clumsily professed his love, which sensationally claimed that he had been taken to the government's most intimidating penal fortress. In fact, he was en route to Moscow, where sympathisers procured him a passport to go abroad. He left Odessa bound for Switzerland. There he quickly insinuated himself into illustrious exiled circles. The shambolic Bakunin, who, compensating for lifelong impotence with rhetorical violence, was an early fan: 'They are magnificent these young fanatics. Believers without God, and heroes without phrases.' Nechaev painted a colourful tale of flight from the Peter and Paul fortress, and of the imminent revolution his Committee was about to unleash. Bakunin mobilised the alcoholic Nikolai Ogarev and Herzen to transfer ten thousand francs to help Nechaev's cause.

Nechaev also flattered Bakunin's vanity by encouraging him to co-author a *Revolutionary's Catechism*. This advocated a lethal Spartanic asceticism: 'The revolutionary is a doomed man. He has no personal interests, no business affairs, no emotions, no attachments, no property, and no name. Everything in him is wholly absorbed in the single thought and the single passion for revolution.' All bonds with the civilised world 'of laws, moralities, and customs, and with its generally accepted conventions', were severed. Only two things were worth studying: the sciences of destruction, and the psychology of those whom the revolutionary would abuse and exploit. How the words flowed from Bakunin's pen: 'Moved by the sober passion for revolution, he [the revolutionary] should stifle in himself all considerations of kinship, love, friendship, and even honour.' Tyrannical towards himself, he would be tyrannical over others. Some revolutionaries were more equal than others, for only the first grade would possess gnosis, and could freely exploit grades two and three. They were 'capital' to be disposed of at will. In a novel departure, revolutionaries were to collaborate with the ultimate primitive rebels, the lumpen criminal underclass. Turning to a theme that animates many revolutionaries, Bakunin and Nechaev eagerly established who was to be first for the chop. Humanity was divided into those 'to be liquidated immediately', while various categories of usefully idiot liberals were to be exploited and discarded, including 'empty-headed women' whose salons Nechaev had adorned. A further pamphlet, *The People's Justice*, began to fill the ranks of those to be liquidated with real names drawn from what Nechaev charmingly called 'the scum of contemporary Russian learning and literature ... the mass of publicists, hacks, and pseudo-scientists'. Reams of these tracts were malevolently mailed to Russian radicals, knowing that it would result in their arrest. The whole of this programme, whose goal was 'terrible, total, universal, and merciless destruction', was notionally designed to benefit 'the people'. In fact, things had to get worse before they got better because 'the Society will use all its resources and energy toward increasing and intensifying the evils and miseries of the people until at last their patience is exhausted and they are driven to a general uprising'.

Equipped with a certificate endorsed by Bakunin announcing 'The carrier of this is one of the World Revolutionary Alliance No. 2771', Nechaev returned to Moscow in September 1868. There he established an eight-man revolutionary cell, grandiloquently called People's Justice, consisting of young men like Ivan Ivanov and Peter Uspensky, and an older man called Ivan Pryzhov, an alcoholic down-at-heel writer, who earned a few kopecks explaining the meaning of life to fellow barflies. Even suicide eluded Pryzhov: when he threw himself and his dog into a lake, the dog dragged him out. The original eight each received a number – Ivanov was 2 – which then became the first digit used to identify each man's recruits from an allocated sector of society. Nechaev went after army officers, Ivanov after students, while Pryzhov's mission was to the underworld. True to the terms of the *Catechism*, Nechaev's recruitment and fund-raising strategies were not subject to moral concerns. One student joined the conspiracy when Nechaev threatened him with a knife. Another man was invited to tea, given subversive tracts, and then arrested when he left by bogus policemen wearing false beards and wigs. This persuaded him to part with six thousand rubles on the spot.

These escapades took a more serious turn when on 16 November Nechaev informed his confederates that it was necessary to kill Ivan Ivanov, whom he suspected of being a police spy. In fact, Ivanov had merely demurred when Nechaev had ordered him to distribute in-criminating literature among the innocent students of the Petrovsky Agricultural Academy. On the afternoon of 21 November, Ivanov was lured to the grounds of the Academy with claims that the conspirators had found some useful printing equipment concealed in a grotto a few yards from a frozen pond. At five in the afternoon, the five assassins bushwhacked the unsuspecting Ivanov, pinning him down while Nechaev strangled him. Although Ivanov was dead already, Nechaev shot him in the head. The five weighed the body down with bricks, broke a hole in the ice and dropped it into the pond. But this was ineptly done, and the corpse bobbed up shortly afterwards. As they had forgotten to take a library card which Ivanov had borrowed from one of his future murderers, the police were soon on the trail of the right men. All except Nechaev were quickly rounded up, but the instigator and chief murderer managed to flee abroad. He re-established contact with Bakunin, chillingly offering to kill a publisher who was harassing the anarchist for delivery of his translation of Marx's *Kapital*. Nechaev then focused his sinister attentions on Natalia Herzen, the wealthy daughter of the deceased liberal exile. Luckily for her, she had a vigilant stepmother who knew what Nechaev was about. Moreover, his attempts to 'blackmail and frighten' 'Tata' were beginning to worry Bakunin, who began to compare the protégé he called 'the boy' with Savonarola and Machiavelli. In early 1872 Nechaev moved from Geneva to Zurich, where he began plotting bank robberies. Although most of the European socialist press swallowed Nechaev's lies about his reasons for killing Ivanov, the Swiss authorities determined to extradite him to Russia for his criminal enterprises rather than his 'political' crime. He found himself confined to the Peter and Paul fortress of his fantasies.

What followed these events was, arguably, as disturbing as the deeds of Nechaev and his friends, which became the starting point for Dostoevsky's great reckoning with his own revolutionary demons in *The Possessed*. With breathtaking stupidity, the authorities elected to dissolve the squalid essence of the charge relating to Ivanov's murder by tacking on loosely related cases when the murderers came to trial. This meant that instead of five accused, there were eighty-seven, many with walk-on parts in the original conspiracy, or ironically, people whom Nechaev had himself framed when he sent them his incriminatory pamphlets. Not for the first or last time, elite alienation from what they regarded as a reactionary government meant that well-to-do liberal folk made the most grotesque apologists for murderers, blissfully unaware that when half a century later the Nechaevs came to power, their property would be looted while they disappeared into exile or Arctic concentration camps. Middle-aged and elderly dupes saw in Nechaev the wayward idealism of youth, rather than a psychopathic conman. The public gallery was filled with students, impressionable young ladies and artillery officers who lapped up the theatre unfolding before them, vicariously thrilled by the frisson of animal violence that Nechaev brought with him. The prosecutor was predictably inept, while the defence lawyers acted like activist demagogues, a recurrent pattern in the history of terrorism. The liberal-minded chief judge indulged the accused, allowing them to read newspapers and wave to their admiring audience. A squalid little gang of murderers were emboldened by whispers of 'brave boys and girls, they do not lose heart'. In these circumstances, four of the accused received mild sentences of between seven and fifteen years' hard labour. Twenty-nine others were given prison terms. The rest were acquitted.

The chief demon was given twenty years. The authorities even botched this. Instead of sending Nechaev to a remote mine in Siberia, the tsar personally intervened to consign him to solitary confinement in the Peter and Paul fortress, thereby seeming to betray the terms of Nechaev's extradition as a common felon. The murderer became a myth. Inevitably, a man of Nechaev's indomitable will was able to suborn long-serving guards who identified more with their charges than with the world beyond. This enabled Nechaev to establish contacts with each new generation of revolutionaries, who, as his crimes faded into rosy memory, more keenly admired his ferocious energy and will. This endured long after Nechaev had expired in jail from dropsy, on the thirteenth anniversary of his murder of Ivanov.

Although the spirit of Nechaev lingered, the main thrust of Russian radicalism in the 1870s took the form of a redemptive Populist crusade, in which members of the liberal and radical intelligentsia descended among the people to serve and guide. There was something distastefully anthropological about this venture, as if the Populists were going among remote tribes, which in a profound sense they were. A rift quickly opened between the people as abstraction and the multifarious people themselves.

The service part of the agenda was entirely acceptable to the peasantry. From 1873 until the end of the decade, countless numbers of young idealists went on a 'Pilgrimage to the People'. Vera Figner and her sister went to dwell in remote villages, where Vera worked as a peripatetic physician. This was challenging since 'I had no idea how to approach a common person.' Given that her knowledge of the common people was entirely derived from books, Figner coped pretty well at overcoming her distaste for the squalor and rampant syphilis, and such novelties as dossing down on a bed of louse-riddled straw. The muzhiks or peasants seem to have regarded the miracle-working 'she-healer' with affection and gratitude, even if they confused medicine with magic charms. They eagerly took up her offer of teaching their children how to read in her spare time. Only one thing spoiled this idyll, the malign counter-moves of landlords and priests which prevented the further revolutionary message from getting through.

Much of this crusade was harmless in a utopian well-meaning way: teaching illiterates to read, providing medical services or acting as midwives. Young radicalised Jews threw themselves into working among the Orthodox people, some of them going as far as converting to

Christianity, in the hope that here at least they would find acceptance by sloughing off historic deformations that widespread anti-Semitism had forced upon them. Some educated professionals abandoned their own skills to practise carpentry or joinery, a lifestyle choice that struck the peasants as eccentric at best. The political part of the Populist crusade led to mutual animosities and resentments, or at best a dialogue of the deaf. Deeply religious peasants who were in awe of the tsar were profoundly offended by the Populists' disdain for Orthodoxy, or worse, by their crude attempts to amalgamate Christianity with socialism by clothing the latter in the idioms of the former. In 1873, two folksily attired Populist artillery officers tried to engage a peasant on his sled: 'We started to tell him that one should not pay taxes, that officials are robbers, and that the Bible preaches the need for a revolution. The peasant urged on his horse, we hastened our step. He put it into a trot, but we kept running, shouting about taxes and revolution . . . until we could not breathe.' In peasant eyes, the remote tsar was a force for good. Only deceitful nobles and officials were preventing the realisation of his will.

While many peasants proved immune to Populist attempts to subvert their faith or reverence for authority, others were all too keen to affect the accoutrements of modern society that the primitivist Populists despised. These mutual incomprehensions bred frustration and resentment, especially as carefully crafted tracts and pamphlets were torn up and used as cigarette paper or to wipe an arse. Those who tried to shed their elitism came to loathe the obdurate mass to whom they preached, like some recalcitrant beast that would not move. Had the authorities left the Populists alone, disillusionment with the objects of their enthusiasms would have caused the movement to peter out. With characteristic ineptness, however, some of the more militant Populists were tried for sedition and given harsh sentences. Wider society thought their rights had been infringed when they were subsequently held imprisoned in limbo rather than despatched to the relative liberty of Siberia where remoteness was the only prison wall. This was a largely false perception. In fact, the authorities simply equivocated. They did not want to turn these agitators loose on the villagers of Siberia, and were also reluctant to inflict on young Russian idealists the sort of fate that had befallen Poles and ordinary criminals. Hence convicted Populists languished in tsarist jails, in circumstances that were far from onerous. The food was so good they could not get enough of it, while interrogations were more like avuncular admonitions to mend one's juvenile errors than sessions with a chair leg or iron bar in the basement of Stalin's Lubyanka.

Despite these realities of the age, the minds of some Populists turned to terrorist violence, as a way of circumventing the bovine immobility of the peasants and of striking back at an allegedly repressive regime whose jails were actually breeding grounds for terrorism. Vera Figner was disingenuous about this mutation. The balance of forces between the authorities and the landowners was so loaded against the peasants that she thought a campaign of rural terrorism was inevitable. But this relied upon a constant flow of Populist idealists going into the countryside. The failure of their crusade meant that the flow had all but dried up. So she became sympathetic to the idea of one cataclysmic strike – against the person of the tsar. As she admitted, 'we saw clearly that our work among the people was of no avail', although the Populist ideal remained morally good. This was an early example of how a refusal to acknowledge the failure of one revolutionary delusion was superseded by the adoption of another of a more radical kind.

In 1876 a northern revolutionary group which borrowed the name Land and Freedom managed to deliver prince Peter Kropotkin from a military hospital; in the south, a more radical branch based in Kiev purchased weapons with a view to assassinating the government's more stridently reactionary supporters. Although both groups continued to pay lip-service to the idea that slow agitation would raise peasant consciousness to the boiling point of revolution, terrorism – understood as disorganising and annihilating the existing regime – gradually acquired its own momentum as an end in itself. In 1876, Land and Freedom tried to convert a mass being celebrated in the church of Our Lady of Kazan into 'the first workers' demonstration in Russian history' by mingling fifty factory workers with the congregation exiting the cathedral. In fact, many of the workers who did participate had been bribed by Land and Freedom to attend, for most factory workers were more interested in Western-style trades unionism than in being pawns for middle-class revolutionaries. The government's inept insistence on arresting and trying anyone remotely connected with this sort of agitation led to a series of political trials, in which the accused declined defence lawyers so as to make ringing declarations of revolutionary intent from the witness box.

Meanwhile, the more venturesome Kievan group hit upon the idea of forging tsarist rescripts so as to stimulate defiance on the part of peasants who were unhappy with the land they had received after 1861. One rescript ordered the peasants to form 'secret bands' to fall upon the necks of noblemen and officialdom. While this absurd plot was unfurling, the leading members of the Kievan group decided to murder the twenty-year-old Nikolai Gorinovich, who, recently released from jail, they imagined was a police informer. In echoes of Nechaev's murder of Ivanov, they beat him senseless with an iron ball attached to a chain, and then poured acid over his face to frustrate identification. Unfortunately for them, the blind and scarred Gorinovich survived this murderous attack – photographs of his injuries are almost unbearable to look at – and went to the police. They may have apprehended the culprits, but they did little to publicise the psychopathic nature of the attack, the paranoia that triggered it, and the way in which the group had set up a kangaroo court to convict someone on the basis of entirely circumstantial evidence.

The authorities' oscillation between indulgent slackness and repression culminated in an incident in St Petersburg's preliminary-arrest jail, where a few hundred political prisoners freely consorted with one another in a sort of university behind bars. On 13 July 1877, general Fydor Trepov, the governor of the capital, visited the jail and encountered scenes of fraternisation that appalled him. Out in the yard, Arkhip Bogoliubov, a founder member of Land and Freedom, enraged him by arguing the rights of political prisoners as if he were addressing an equal. Trepov knocked the man's cap off, and ordered that he should be flogged twenty-five times. In addition to being technically illegal, this treatment also violated the unspoken assumption that the government would not treat political criminals drawn from the intelligentsia with the customary brutality meted out to ordinary felons. These were gentlemen whom the prison guards called 'sir'. They could tell the guards to make tea.

On 24 January 1877, Vera Zasulich called at general Trepov's offices to obtain a licence to teach. After two years' imprisonment and four years of exile because of her association with Nechaev, Zasulich had become a gaunt, chain-smoking, professional revolutionary. While Trepov scribbled something down, Zasulich produced a gun from her muff and shot him in the side. She claimed to have been motivated by moral outrage at the treatment of Bogoliubov. Her trial for attempted murder was a great setpiece occasion, with both the foreign minister and Dostoevsky present. The government did its best to remind the judge of his 'duty', but it was a credit to Alexander's reforms that the judge remained scrupulously impartial. It quickly became Trepov's rather than

Zasulich's trial. Dressed in her customary grey linen smock, and instructed by her lawyer not to bite her nails – a sign of evil thoughts in Russian folklore – Zasulich turned in a tear-jerking performance, with no one questioning why, if her response to the brutality of Trepov had been 'spontaneous', she had waited six months before seeking revenge, returning to the capital from a revolutionary commune where she rode about with a gun in her belt. The defence lawyer went into rhetorical overdrive when he compared this political assassin with women 'who had imbrued their hands in the blood of lovers who jilted them or that of their successful rivals', crimes of passion for which they had been acquitted. This had the public gallery in tears, while Zasulich herself sobbed demurely. Few paid much attention to the prosecution's cogent argument that 'every public figure, whoever he may be, has the right to a legal trial and not trial by Zasulich'. After deliberating for seven minutes, the jury duly acquitted Zasulich to cries of 'Bravo! Our little Vera!' from the gallery. Smart society (and the jury) had effectively endorsed political violence. The government promptly undid any credit it was due for the fairness of its courts by seeking to rearrest Zasulich, who fled abroad, where already the London *Times* was celebrating her as a latterday Charlotte Corday, who, it failed to recall, had actually killed the Jacobin terrorist Marat. She did not return to Russia until 1905.[12]

Most Russian terrorists sought to limit terrorism to killing suspected informers and the most egregiously harsh officials like Trepov. In the south, however, a more Machiavellian strategy was adopted, of killing the most liberal members of the regime so as to foster repression as a recruiting mechanism, a tactic employed by many later terrorists the world over, especially if their sect was manifestly bereft of a wider follow-ing. In February 1878, Verian Osinsky unsuccessfully shot the chief prosecutor in Kiev, whose life was saved by a thick fur coat, and then in May stabbed to death the rather ineffectual chief of the city's police. A few days later he successfully sprang the assailants of Gorinovich from jail. Since, ironically, the liberal elite objected to his killing of ineffectual policemen, Osinsky concentrated on trying to co-opt them into joint advocacy of constitutional and legal reforms that he anticipated would fail, the covert aim being to radicalise these hapless confederates to the point of supporting his tactic of terror.

A rather different sort of policeman was on Osinsky's trail. This was Georgy Sudeykin. Born in 1850 into an impoverished and landless gentry family, Sudeykin graduated top of his class from the Infantry Cadet

School. He was a tall, well-built man, with piercing eyes and a persuasive manner. A lack of money, and a fascination with crime and its detection, led him to join the Corps of Gendarmes rather than the elite and flashy Guards. Sudeykin adopted the chameleon life of his terrorist prey, never sleeping in one apartment too long and carrying multiple identity papers. Lacking the mentality of the stereotypical tsarist martinet, he used his ostensibly flexible political opinions to insinuate himself into revolutionary circles and to win over those he captured by treating them as potential collaborators in the cause of reform. Being inordinately ambitious himself, he knew how to play on the ambitions of terrorists, who after all were part of career structures themselves.

In January 1879 Osinsky and his older lover, Sophia Leshern von Hertzfeldt, were detained despite their attempts to shoot Sudeykin and the other arresting officers – the revolutionaries earlier having resorted to revolvers against policemen armed only with sabres. Osinsky's death and Sophia's exile to Siberia left a legacy of revolutionary romanticism that proved contagious. Meanwhile, the organisers of Land and Freedom issued a revised programme that effectively downgraded traditional Populist belief in the revolutionary potentialities of the people in favour of full-blown terrorism. Other innovations were the creation of discrete cells with no cognisance of one another, and the licensing of freelance acts of terrorism under Land and Freedom's ideological franchise, a tactic that in our time would serve Al Qaeda rather well. Throughout late 1878–9 the terrorist nucleus within Land and Freedom under Alexander Mikhailov carried out a series of high-profile assassinations. Victims included Mezentsov, chief of the ineffectual Third Department, and prince Dmitry Kropotkin, governor of Kharkov and cousin of the anarchist aristocrat – as well as comrades suspected of being agents or informers. Early that year, a disillusioned Populist named Alexander Soloviev contacted Land and Freedom offering to assassinate the tsar. He explained: 'The death of the emperor will effect a change in public life. The dissatisfaction that is expressed in quiet mumbling will explode in regions where it is most deeply felt. And then it will spread everywhere. It just needs an impetus for everything to rise up.' Mikhailov purchased for Soloviev a large-calibre American pistol known as a Bear Hunter. Soloviev had competition, because a young Jew called Goldenberg was also volunteering as suicide–assassin. Since Goldenberg's ethnicity would have prompted a pogrom had he been successful, Mikhailov stuck with Soloviev.

Given the enormity of the undertaking, the scheme had to be vetted by the full membership of Land and Freedom, rather than that hidden part of it that had few qualms about terrorism. This meeting degenerated into angry exchanges between Mikhailov and the leading Populist theorist Georgy Plekhanov. The outcome was that, although Land and Freedom would not formally endorse the assassination, it would not prevent individual members from aiding and abetting Soloviev. At 8 a.m. on 2 April 1879, Soloviev approached the tsar on his morning walk as he returned to the square in front of his palace. Something about Soloviev – in his long black coat and official's cockaded hat – caught Alexander's attention. He turned and saw a gun pointed at his head. When the first shot missed, the tsar took flight and ran zigzagging into the palace as four more shots passed by. His bodyguard felled Soloviev, and managed to stop the would-be assassin from swallowing a nugget impregnated with cyanide. 'God saved me,' wrote the tsar in his diary. Although the church bells rang and the Guards shouted 'Hurrah!', others joked on hearing the bells, 'Missed again?' Meanwhile, Soloviev reclined on a sofa, with a basin of his stomach contents beside him. He told his ineffably polite interrogators, men with epaulettes betokening high rank who hung on this rascal's every word, that he had seen the 'ghosts' of political martyrs. He had been impelled by a sense of social justice to bring 'closer the radiant future', although he was rather vague about what this might be save that no one would harm anyone else. Soloviev was tried by a Special Court and executed in Semenovsky Square.

The advocates of 'terrorism first' within Land and Freedom met at a seaside resort in June 1879 to conspire not only against the regime, but also against those comrades who favoured the mainstream Populist agenda of patient agitation among the peasantry, as they all gathered for a further plenary meeting in Voronezh. There, sentiments flowed this way and that, as the terrorists argued that their campaign would force the government to grant a constitution, while the older Populists around Plekhanov, who rejected constitutionalism as an obstacle to socialism, argued for radical land redistribution instead. The tensions became unsustainable. Plekhanov stormed out and founded a movement called Black Repartition. Interestingly, Vera Zasulich had tried to slip back into Russia for this meeting but she arrived too late. Prone to bouts of depression and morbid self-reflection, she had become convinced that she had started the spiral of terrorist violence in Russia. She had developed major reservations about the tactic, except when, as in her own case, terrorists acted for purely selfless reasons. Terrorism was divisive and exhausting, and it provided the government with too easy a pretext for massive repression. More importantly it led to pathological behaviour: 'in order to carry out terrorist acts all one's energies must be expended, and a particular frame of mind almost always results: either one of great vanity or one in which life has lost all its attractiveness'. The advocates of terrorism dissolved Land and Freedom – whose name both factions agreed to renounce – for a new conspiracy called People's Will in conscious rejection of rule by the will of a single man.

On being invited to join People's Will, Vera Figner initially exclaimed, 'But this is pure Nechaev!' In fact, the terrorist nucleus of Land and Freedom had already adopted many of Nechaev's dubious practices, including bank robberies and murdering informers. People's Will also borrowed his tactic of suggesting to the credulous that it was the tip of a much larger revolutionary organisation – the Russian Social Revolutionary Party – which in reality was non-existent. There was an imposing-sounding Executive Committee all right, but this was co-terminous with the entire membership of People's Will . Further deceptions included claims that members of this Executive were themselves merely 'third-degree agents', the insinuation being that there were limitless levels of revolutionary talent above them. In fact, People's Will never had more than thirty or forty members, who would then recruit 'agents' for specific tasks or to establish affiliate cells within sections of society deemed to have revolutionary potential. Efforts were made to co-opt the leading lights of the arts and intelligentsia with a liberal-sounding public platform. After all, which reasonable person could quibble with the Party's explicit goals? Its programme espoused liberal and democratic-socialist aims: a parliament, universal male suffrage, the classic liberal freedoms of speech and the press, together with peasant and worker control of land and the factories. Much was unsaid about how these aims were related to the tactical goal of a revolutionary coup by an elite Jacobin minority. No wonder Lenin would recommend that his associates study the structure and modus operandi of this precursor organisation to the Bolsheviks.

Like the contemporary Irish Fenians, People's Will discovered the unique killing properties of dynamite. Having sentenced Alexander II to death, in one of its pseudo-popular conclaves of three individuals who were judge, jury and executioner, People's Will made seven attempts to kill him before they succeeded on 1 March 1881. Their first efforts focused on Odessa, near which the tsar would pass on his return to the north from his annual vacation in the southerly Crimea. After being rebuffed as an assassin, Vera Figner was allowed to move dynamite there. She rented an apartment with a man posing as her husband, where the explosives expert Kibalchich set about his work with dynamite, guncotton and fulminates. Since the plan was to put a mine under the railway track some distance from Odessa, Figner – temporarily reverting to her old posh self – boldly secured a post as a railway section master for one of her fellow conspirators by interceding on his behalf with baron Ungern-Shternberg, an acquaintance of the governor-general. In the event, the plan was aborted since Goldenberg requested most of their dynamite for a northerly plot that had much greater chance of success, while they learned anyway that the tsar was taking another route home. Goldenberg was arrested at a railway station after an alert policeman became suspicious about his trunk, which he discovered contained fifty pounds of dynamite. Of a weak disposition, Goldenberg became progressively deranged in the loneliness of his cell. His concerned jailers offered him a deal that calmed his distress: he would betray People's Will in order to end senseless violence and to speed the reforms the jailers admitted were necessary.

Meanwhile, People's Will had set two further railway attacks in motion just in case the tsar changed his route. At Alexandrovsk, a second group of conspirators, whose cover was a tannery business, had crawled through a gully so as to dig holes under the railway line into which they placed two canisters of explosives, linked with wires which in turn led to a command detonator. However, when the tsar's train passed overhead, no explosion resulted owing to a failure in the electric circuit. A third team of railway bombers, this time nearer Moscow, had also buried bombs under railway track, reached by tunnelling from a nearby house they had rented. Bad timing on 19 November 1880 meant that they missed the train conveying the tsar, but they did manage to derail eight carriages of a second train, carrying his entourage and baggage.

Although the police had raided an apartment and discovered both dynamite and a plan of the Winter Palace with an 'X' marking the dining room, with typical sloth the Palace's commandant did nothing about it. He was a wounded general who had fought at Sebastopol, operating in a palace where there were too many doddery chiefs while most of the Indians were thieves. Below stairs, a carpenter called Stephen Khalturin who belonged to People's Will had got himself on the Palace payroll, after performing well while repairing the tsar's yacht. Khalturin shared a basement room with a police guard, who began to entertain the conceit that this respectable tradesman might make a worthy son-in-law. Khalturin was a strapping, cheery fellow, adept at affecting peasant stupidity by scratching his ear when anyone asked a question. He had the run of the palace, which he quickly realised was not a tight ship. Theft was so normative that even officers practised it, as Tolstoy amusingly described in the story of the officer with stolen food hidden under his helmet. On one occasion Khalturin found himself working in the tsar's study. Surveying the back of the emperor's bald head, Khalturin thought of smashing it with his hammer, but decided that this would be too mundane a fate for the purposes of People's Will.

Instead, Khalturin collected dynamite, smuggled in by the Executive Committee, which he stored under his pillow. Since sleeping on nitroglycerine made his eyes stream and his skin turn the colour of clay, he bought a trunk, ostensibly to house the dowry of a future bride. Instead of petticoats and the like, this filled with dynamite, although Khalturin never got the 360 pounds he thought necessary to penetrate two floors. On the evening of 5 February 1880, Khalturin hosted an engagement party in a restaurant, coolly returning to the palace on some spurious pretext, so as to light the Rumford fuse to his bomb. Then he returned to the restaurant. It was snowing. The explosion tore through the floor above, killing or maiming fifty members of the Finland Regiment, but only shaking the floor of the Yellow Dining Room which the tsar and prince Alexander of Battenberg were about to enter. The room was a vision of dust and fallen plaster that lay upon the dishes and decorative table palms. The gas lights had been blown out, the chandeliers destroyed, and the cold howled in through the shattered windows. The tsar and his guests were unhurt.

In response to this attack so close to home, the tsar appointed a Supreme Commission under prince Michael Loris-Melikov with a remit to fight sedition. The choice bewildered conservatives. A subtle, liberal-minded and wily Armenian, who had fought 180 battles against Caucasian tribesmen and the Turks, Loris-Melikov abolished the hated Third Department, by transferring its secret police functions to the Interior Ministry, a move designed to appeal to liberal opinion. He had the unpopular education minister Tolstoy sacked. He pandered to the power of the press by asking editors for their opinions and advice. It was Loris-Melikov's apparent reasonableness that made him a high-priority target for People's Will terrorists. They tried to shoot him in February. The prospect that Loris-Melikov might succeed in introducing sufficiently meaningful reforms to appease the intelligentsia made it all the more urgent to press ahead with the tsar's assassination. One plan involved sinking 250 pounds of dynamite within sealed rubber bags under the waters beneath the Kammeny Bridge. But when the royal carriage swept over the bridge in mid-August, no bomb went off, for the bomber had overslept. The method finally employed to kill Alexander was first essayed in Odessa where Vera Figner and her associates rented a shop and then tunnelled their way under the street with a view to laying a mine to blow up the tsar when he visited the city. A version of this was replayed in St Petersburg. A couple called Kobozev – this was not their name and they were not married – rented basement premises in Little Garden Street where they opened a cheese shop. He had a sun-burnished face and a jolly spade-shaped beard; she spoke in reassuringly provincial accents. The shop was along the route the tsar took each Sunday from the Winter Palace to the Hippodrome where he inspected his guardsmen. There was enough cheese displayed on the counter to satisfy any customer – Vera Figner tested this by purchasing some Roquefort – but close inspection of the cheese barrels to the rear would have revealed excavated earth rather than Camembert. For, each night, a team of terrorists visited the shop to burrow a tunnel beneath the road. In the event that the mine which was to be laid under the road missed the tsar, there were two back-up teams of assassins. Four men would ambush him with dynamite bombs in kerosene cans at the end of another street, while a lone assassin would lurk with a knife should he survive the second-wave attacks. In fact, this last assassin was arrested before he could be put in position.

Vera Figner was one of those who sat up all night with Kibalchich, the benign master bomber, in an apartment where they nervously assembled the bombs, while a large mine was hastily placed in the tunnel leading from the cheese shop. In the morning the bombers collected their weapons from a safe house. These men were chosen for their representational symbolic effect, an aristocrat, a scion of the middle class, a worker and a peasant. One was virtually a moron; another was very conspicuously tall.

In the event, after lunch with his morganatic wife, whom he rapidly 'took' on a table to deflect her pleas that he should stay at home, the tsar did not go to the Hippodrome via Little Garden Street. But at three that afternoon he ordered a return route that brought him very close to where his killers loitered. As his carriage and Cossack escort passed the assassin Rysakov, the latter hurled what appeared to be a chocolate box beneath the carriage. When it exploded it threw one of the Cossacks to the ground, while various passersby were injured. The tsar, who was unharmed, got out of the carriage, saying to an officer who inquired after him: 'No, thank God, but—' as he gestured to the injured. As appeared to be his habit, Alexander strode up to the captured bomber and said, 'You're a fine one!' By now ringed by soldiers, the tsar returned to the carriage, hardly noticing a young Pole holding a newspaper-wrapped parcel. It exploded, killing the Pole and mortally wounding the tsar in his legs and lower body. His left leg was so mangled that it was impossible to staunch the bleeding by squeezing an artery. Whispering that he felt cold, the tsar said he wanted to go home to the Winter Palace. He died there about fifty minutes later. Perhaps his final thoughts were on how his day had started, when he and Loris-Melikov had agreed that elected representatives should be appointed to the State Council to advise on reforms.

Six members of the conspiracy to kill the tsar were put on trial in late March. All six were sentenced to death, although when it was discovered that Gesia Helfman was pregnant, she was reprieved. The remaining five were publicly hanged, with placards reading 'Regicide' around their necks. Kibalchich, the bomb maker, tried to interest the authorities in a propellant rocket as a way of securing a reprieve, but they were not to be diverted. The fact that Helfman was from an Orthodox Jewish background was one of the reasons for violent anti-Semitic pogroms that erupted in the rural Ukraine. While the new tsar Alexander III endeavoured to suppress the pogroms, the remnants of People's Will actively welcomed them as evidence of forces that might one day be directed against the state. They issued pamphlets in Ukrainian, which Vera Figner distributed in Odessa, claiming: 'It is from the Jews that the Ukrainian folk suffer most of all. Who has gobbled up all the lands and forests? Who runs every tavern? Jews! . . . Whatever you do, wherever you turn, you run into the Jew. It is he who bosses and cheats you, he who drinks the peasant's blood.' It is common knowledge that the tsarist secret police would exploit anti-Semitism to canalise popular anger; it should be equally well known that, some time before, the revolutionaries had rather welcomed anti-Semitism too. The authorities had much success in rounding up many of those involved in earlier conspiracies to assassinate

Alexander II, including the pair who ran the phoney cheese shop on Little Garden Street. Soon Vera Figner was the sole surviving member of the Executive Committee, although its associated Military Organisation – consisting of dissident army officers – was in better shape, having been kept aloof from terrorism.

A fatal new development, the Degaev affair, unfolded in a bizarre period during which the People's Will offered the new tsar Alexander III a truce, provided he permit an elected assembly and release political prisoners. Although this offer was rejected, some members of the government, and a rather ineffective clandestine counter-terror grouping called the Sacred Band, thought that negotiations with People's Will might at least defer the latter's assassination attempts until after the new tsar's coronation. Nothing came of these talks – which took place in Geneva – because the regime had discovered that People's Will was a shambles. The coronation went ahead in May 1883 without incident.

The reason why the authorities were so accurately apprised of the state of the revolutionary underground can be traced back to Vera Figner's decision to appoint a capable former artillery officer, Serge Degaev, to run the military wing of People's Will on behalf of the decimated Executive Committee. Degaev had impeccable revolutionary credentials, having helped dig the tunnel from the cheese shop in Little Garden Street. His mother and siblings were all involved in the wider movement. This proved Figner's undoing because, when Degaev's young brother Vladimir was arrested for sedition, he began to receive visits in his cell from major Sudeykin, the most capable of the tsar's policemen. Appearing to be sympathetic to the cause, Sudeykin offered Vladimir his freedom if he would merely keep him abreast of general trends within the underground. He required no names. Vladimir agreed to these arrangements, confidently boasting to his associates that he was the one really in charge. In December 1882, Serge Degaev himself was arrested in Odessa with the apparatus of the clandestine press of the People's Will. He recalled his brother Vladimir's dealings with Sudeykin as he grimly contemplated fifteen years' hard labour. Upon receiving a letter from Degaev, Sudeykin hastened south to see him. Some sort of murky deal developed in which, in return for ratting on the remnants of People's Will, Sudeykin would recommend to the tsar that Degaev be allowed to lead a radical party committed to non-violent reform. Sudeykin offered Degaev a chance to meet the tsar in person, although that was impossible since Sudeykin himself was too lowly in rank to have such access himself.

What Sudeykin actually wanted was to control the revolutionary movement through Degaev.

A few weeks later, Degaev miraculously escaped from a carriage escorting him to the railway station, kicking one guard out of the door, and throwing snuff into the eyes of his colleague, before vanishing into the snow. He re-established his contacts with People's Will. Meeting him, Vera Figner forgot that Degaev was no snuff-user and that prisoners were usually manacled in transit. He appeared more concerned with her safety, inquiring whether her apartment had a rear exit. Two days later she left the front door of the apartment and was arrested. The tsar rejoiced, writing in his diary: 'Thank God they finally got that horrid woman.' He asked for a photograph of her, just to remind himself how horrid she was. Her death sentence was commuted to life imprisonment. The genteel conditions within the Peter and Paul fortress where she was held for two years, dining on partridge and pears and wearing a splendid blue gown, gave way to the isolation and soiled grey garb of the Schlüsselburg where she spent the following twenty years.

Meanwhile, Sudeykin was on a slippery slope, steeper even than that being descended by the traitor Degaev. To cover his agent, with whom he had become close, Sudeykin offered up a rather ineffectual informer for Degaev to identify to People's Will, who duly murdered him. As the number of those betrayed by Degaev mounted, the traitor worried that he would run out of victims. He suggested to Sudeykin a trip to Switzerland where he could extend his treachery to Russian exiles. In Geneva, Degaev reflected on the squalid nature of his relationship with the major with whom he had shared drinks and dishes of pirogi. He had thought he could control how Sudeykin used the information he supplied; in fact, Sudeykin made indiscriminate arrests. Degaev was the major's slave, and, he realised, not an especially indispensable one either since Sudeykin had allowed him to repair to Switzerland. In this state of self-disgust, Degaev confessed his role to the leading revolutionary Tikhomirov. Although the latter dearly wanted Sudeykin dead, the swathe the latter had cut through the revolutionaries meant that assassins were in short supply. But then there was the major's friend himself. Degaev was given the unenviable choice of either killing Sudeykin or being murdered himself. Although a more steely revolutionary had to be posted to stiffen the double-agent's resolve, after a series of false starts Degaev did indeed murder the major. On the afternoon of 16 December, he lured Sudeykin to his apartment on the pretext of meeting an Italian revolutionary. The major brought his nephew, which complicated things. Degaev knew Sudeykin was always armed and wore a bullet-proof vest. Inviting him into his study, he shot him low in the back (the bullet went through his liver), while an accomplice pummelled the terrified nephew to the floor with a crowbar in the hallway. Mortally wounded, Sudeykin tried to lock himself in the water closet. Degaev's accomplice forced his way in and used the crowbar to finish the major off with four blows to the back of his head. The scene was like an abattoir, with the major sprawled half in and half out of the closet. Sudeykin received a lavish funeral, with the tsarina sending a wreath of white lilies and a note, 'To him who has fulfilled his sacred duty'. After fleeing to western Europe, Degaev resurfaced in the 1890s as one Professor Alexander Pell of the University of South Dakota where he taught mathematics.[13]

People's Will never recovered from the Degaev affair. Fear of police informers hidden in their ranks was almost as acute as the government's paranoia that nihilists were behind every untoward event. Disillusion-ment with the response of the peasants during the 1870s, and relentless repression throughout the 1880s, led many in the Russian revolutionary movement to rethink their goals and the means of attaining them. Terrorism was not the crucial issue, since all were more or less agreed that it was a legitimate tactic, although there were disagreements over how central it should be and against whom it should be directed. Rather, the disputes were about the processes and social groups that would drive revolutionary change.

For an important minority, the idyll of communal peasant socialism seemed outmoded in a rapidly industrialising country. Plekhanov was the leading exponent of social democracy and a Russian Marxism (his sect was called the Emancipation of Labour Group) in which capitalism, rather than the rural commune, would give birth to socialism, as described in the laws of history. The fact that the authorities were relatively indulgent towards working-class Social Democrats – the police tended to sympathise more with striking workers than with grasping factory owners – further inclined many revolutionaries to favour allow-ing the iron laws of history to do their work rather than jump-starting a revolution with bombs and guns. In their view, and one should note the uncontroversial acceptance of mass murder, terror was something that should succeed, rather than precede, the revolution. As Plekhanov himself wrote: 'Each Social Democrat must be a terrorist à la

Robespierre. We will not shoot at the tsar and his servants now as the Socialist-Revolutionaries do, but after the victory we will erect a guillotine in Kazansky Square for them and many others.'

Some revolutionaries, however, were not prepared to abandon the idea of the 'big bang' approach to revolution, believing in the enormous propaganda value of terrorism directed against the state's principal actors as the essential precondition to seizing power.[14] One such group was formed at St Petersburg University, where students chafed against the regime's introduction of higher fees designed to reduce the number of lower-class radical students, as well as against the reimposition of other petty restrictions in the 1884 university Charter. Students began talking about regicide and about the killing of the tsar's key conservative supporters.

Peter Shevyrev created the Terrorist Fraction of the People's Will in early 1886, one of its recruits being a brilliant zoology student hitherto expert in the biology of annular worms. He had two things in his favour. He was a literate scientist, who could give the group's tracts a spurious air of 'inevitability', and he knew chemistry, essential to the manufacture of explosives. His name was Alexander Ulyanov; his younger sibling was Vladimir Ulyanov, better know to posterity as Lenin. Alexander argued that the Terrorist Fraction had been driven to act because of the regime's frustration of non-violent reform. A campaign of constant terror would also serve to raise the people's revolutionary spirit. The Fraction incorporated further revolutionaries into the conspiracy, including Józef Piłsudski, the future head of state in independent Poland, and a number of radicalised Jews, an ever growing presence in revolutionary and terrorist circles. By 1900 they constituted 50 per cent of the membership of revolutionary parties, even though there were only 7 million Jews in a population of 136 million.

Alexander Ulyanov was responsible for the group's bomb factory. One bomb was concealed within a large tome called *Digest of the Laws*, while others were within cylindrical tubes. On 26 and 28 February and 1 March, the bombers stalked the Nevsky Prospect, hoping to waylay the tsar as he crossed it towards St Isaac's Cathedral. Acting suspiciously, the bombers were snatched by the police, who probably had information about them already since the ramification of the conspiracy had been too casual. Sloppiness led to the arrest of the other principal conspirators including Ulyanov. Although he was not the main architect of the conspiracy, Ulyanov bravely became its spokesman during the trial. They were all sentenced to hang. Despite the urging of his mother, Ulyanov refused to make a plea for pardon. He and five others were hanged on 8 May 1887; fifty students were exiled to Siberia including Piłsudski.

At the time this may have seemed like the death rattle of terrorist groups that between the 1860s and 1900 had 'only' caused about one hundred casualties, even if one of them happened to be the tsar of Russia. However, in the first decade of the twentieth century there was a massive escalation of terrorist atrocities in imperial Russia, with perhaps as many as seventeen thousand people succumbing to terrorist activities between 1901 and 1916, before even these shocking statistics were dwarfed by the onset of Bolshevik state violence, much of it the handiwork of the terrorists turned Chekist secret policemen described in the following pages.

There were various reasons for this recrudescence of terrorism on a huge scale. A major famine in 1891, followed by cholera and typhus epidemics in European Russia a year later, saw renewed attempts by radicals to mobilise the starving peasantry, efforts which were as doomed as trying to ignite sodden sticks. Minds turned to an alternative means of combustion: acts of exemplary violence that would jolt the rural masses out of their somnolence. The disaster of the Russo-Japanese War of 1904–5, and Bloody Sunday in January 1905 when protests in St Petersburg were brutally suppressed, contributed to the climate of crisis, as did the darker side of Silver Age literary culture with its emphasis on the pathologically morbid. Less luridly, and more culpably, many people with liberal views – including many members of the legal profession – irresponsibly sympathised with the terrorists up to the point of aiding and abetting them, rather than supporting the regime's efforts to reform itself. This especially applied to the liberal Kadet Party, which adopted the dubious doctrine that there were no enemies to the left, and whose members became the leading apologists for terror within respectable opinion. A ghastly moral relativism infected smart circles as when a leading Kadet politician made the following analogy: 'Remember that Christ, too, was declared to be a criminal and was subjected to a shameful execution on the cross. The years passed, and this criminal – Christ – has conquered the whole world and become a model of virtue. The attitude towards political criminals is a similar act of violence on the part of the authorities.' Liberals deliberately eschewed the term terrorist, preferring to view the aggressors as 'minors' who were really the victims of repressive authority. While no Kadet newspaper ever condemned a single act of leftist terrorism, pages were devoted to the almost insignificant instances of extreme right-wing violence, which assumed mythic proportions in the left-liberal imagination. This poison affected many liberals and leftists in foreign countries, with the British Labour Party and the German Social Democrats acting as ignorant cheerleaders for terrorist murderers in Russia. Indeed, fear of foreign liberal opinion inhibited a tsarist regime sensitive to the charge of being Asiatic from adopting effective measures to repress terrorism.

The tentative attempts at reform of the new tsar Nicholas II, specifically the Imperial Manifesto of 17 October 1905 guaranteeing basic rights and granting legislative powers to the State Duma, incentivised violent revolutionaries who took such concessions as signs of weakness. Some also thought that acts of terrorism would provoke the regime to lash out, with its lack of discrimination serving to radicalise greater numbers of people. Terrorist attacks on government officials, both high and humble, as well as what were called expropriations (actually robberies) and murders of private individuals, reached epidemic proportions. This did not apply just to Russia itself but to the Baltic provinces, the Caucasus, Finland and Poland, where the Russians (and German landowners in the Baltic) were regarded as alien occupiers by nationalist terrorists for whom any atrocity was legitimate. An improved technology, enabling the miniaturisation of explosives, meant that people feared there were bombs planted everywhere:

> People have started getting wary,
> They consider fruit quite scary.
> A friend of mine as tough as granite
> Is frightened of the pomegranate.
> Policemen, ready to bark and grumble,
> At the sight of an orange now tremble.[15]

Like the Fenians, the new generation of Russian terrorists preferred to manufacture their own explosives rather than risk capture by importing them ready-made from abroad. It was risky work, in which a trembling alcoholic hand or less than perfect concentration could cost a man his life. In 1904–5 two terrorists inadvertently blew themselves up in hotel rooms; one was identified only by his tiny hands, while bits of another were found in a neighbouring park. As with the Fenians, there was an eagerness to explore new technologies with which to kill – in the Russian case, involving aircraft designed to bomb the tsar at his residences at Tsarskoe Selo and Peterhof.

In these years, terrorism became both indiscriminate and inextricably entwined with banditry and other forms of criminality, such as kidnapping, armed robbery and extortion. These exploits were lauded in the left-liberal press, as if they were the actions of a Robin Hood or William Tell. In fact, these robberies were used to boost the profile of particular political factions – notably the Bolsheviks – or, more usually, simply to enable the terrorists to enjoy the good things of life on the run. There was a perceptible moral slippage, as human life lost any kind of value in the eyes of terrorists who were often from rougher social milieux than their genteel predecessors in the 1870s and early 1880s. These were truly Nechaev's children, in a literal sense, for many terrorists were minors, some as young as fourteen or fifteen. A deadly game could be camouflaged with idealistic rhetoric. Some 30 per cent of those arrested for political crimes were Jewish, as were 50 per cent of those involved in revolutionary organisations, even though Jews were a mere 5 per cent of the overall population. Pogroms and discrimination when combined with a moralising and secularised messianic streak led many of these young people on to the path of terrorism, regardless of the impact this would have on the rest of the Jewish population, for the sins of the sons and daughters were very quickly visited on the fathers and mothers. The feebleness of the regime's sanctions also encouraged people to embrace terrorism, for liberal lawyers invariably succeeded in commuting death sentences, while the courts passed remarkably lenient sentences, thereby indirectly demoralising the police who had to investigate such offences. Tsarist prisons and hard-labour camps became a cross between clubs and universities for radicals, where supervision of the inmates was so notoriously slack that conservatives pressed for the adoption of 'English' conditions – that is, all bread and water, chains and floggings.

Barely literate, the new wave of terrorists possessed no sophisticated theoretical reasons for their actions, which were more likely to be the product of frustration, anger and resentment, or because the perpetrators were amoral, hysterical or mad. A surprising number acted out of existential boredom with the quotidian frustrations of their lives: 'I cannot live peacefully. I like danger, so as to feel the thrill.' The young terrorist who eventually succeeded in killing prime minister Stolypin in 1911 claimed to be in despair at the future prospect of 'nothing but an endless number of cutlets'. This accidie easily translated into a megalomaniac and sadistic desire to dominate and humiliate others, not least those terrorists suspected of being informers or merely weak, who were routinely tortured by colleagues whose view of an interrogation was to hold a gun to the victim's temple. Killing people became addictive. A Polish terrorist with the alias 'Gypsy' murdered nineteen policemen. He explained why he experienced an uncontrollable urge to go to the funerals of his victims where he could check to see the accuracy of his marksmanship on the person displayed in an open coffin: 'In the beginning it was difficult for him to kill, but by the third or fourth time the act of taking a life was already making an unusually pleasant impression on him. Seeing the blood of his victim gave him a special feeling, and therefore he felt an increasing urge to experience this sweet sensation again. This is why he has committed so many murders of which he does not repent in the least.' Still others were acting in accordance with a death-wish, undertaking attacks from which they knew there was no prospect of escaping either being shot or executed if captured. Many lost what small moral compass they originally possessed: 'Tell me, why can one not lie? Why can one not steal? What does "dishonest" mean? Why is it dishonest to lie? What is morality? What is moral filth? These are but conventions.' Dmitry Bogrov, the young lawyer's clerk from an assimilated Jewish background who in 1911 assassinated Stolypin in a Kievan opera house, 'always laughed at "good" and "bad". Despising conventional morals, he developed his own, whimsical and not always comprehensible.' A bad gambling habit meant that he was always short of money, which probably explained why he became a police informer.

II BOLSHEVIKS AND BANDITS

Whereas in the 1870s and 1880s the People's Will had endeavoured to confine its murderous activities to specific highly placed individuals, its successors indiscriminately attacked anyone connected with the state, or indeed private citizens and their families. Humble constables patrolling the streets were either gunned down or had sulphuric acid thrown in their faces. Innocent civilians who got in the way were killed, regardless of age or gender. As government officials took increased security measures, from installing triple locks and peepholes on doors to hiring thuggish bodyguards or wearing undergarments of chain mail, so terrorists sought them out in such public places as church services or while in transit. Anarchist terrorists, who were especially vicious, targeted entire classes of people, hurling bombs into churches, restaurants, synagogues and theatres, or simply shot anyone whose white gloves signified the bourgeoisie's mark of Cain. The Bolsheviks similarly used the generic libel that any alleged opponent belonged to the Black Hundreds – that is, what the left claimed was Russia's proto-fascist movement – as when they threw three bombs into a shipyard workers' tavern, on the grounds that some of the workers supported the monarchist Union of the Russian People. Those who survived these explosions were shot as they sought to flee outside.

In a further shocking development, the new-wave terrorists resorted to suicide bombings, in addition to attacks that were already a subliminal form of killing oneself. In 1904 terrorists connected to anarchist groups walked into gendarme or secret police buildings and blew themselves up. On 12 August 1906, three terrorists dressed as gendarmes tried to enter prime minister Stolypin's villa on an island near St Petersburg. The minister's guards held them in an antechamber, where, shouting 'Long live freedom, long live anarchy!', they blew themselves up with sixteen-pound bombs. The explosion was so powerful that it tore the façade off the villa, burying the minister's horse and carriage. There were human body parts and blood everywhere. Twenty-seven people were killed and thirty-three injured, including many elderly people, women and Stolypin's four-year-old son and fourteen-year-old daughter. The minister himself suffered no greater indignity than having the inkwell fly from his desk, splashing ink all over his face and shirt front. In 1908 nine members of a terrorist group were arrested for plotting a suicide attack on the justice minister. One of their number was kitted out as a human bomb, the idea being that he would hurl himself beneath the minister's carriage, simultaneously detonating the bomb. When the police tried to arrest this Conradian figure, he warned: 'Be careful. I am wrapped around with dynamite. If I blow up, the entire street will be destroyed.' Seven of this group were sentenced to death and hanged.

In addition to acts of murder, the new terrorists of the 1900s carried out acts of extortion, hostage-seizures and armed robbery, the latter leading to gunfights on city streets that resembled scenes from a Western set amid snow. A man of means would receive a note scrawled: 'The Worker's Organisation of the Party of Socialist-Revolutionaries in

Belostok requires you to contribute immediately ... seventy-five rubles ... The Organisation warns you that if you fail to give the above-stated sum, it will resort to severe measures against you, transferring your case to the Combat Detachment.' In the Caucasus where Armenian and Georgian terrorists were notoriously violent (one group was called Horror, another Terror of the City of Tiflis) and hardly distinguishable from criminal gangs, they intimidated people into not paying the state's taxes while imposing regular levies of their own. This was sometimes done under the self-delusion that the gangs were like latterday Robin Hoods.

Who were the groups responsible for this new wave of terror? The group most identified with the tactic was the Party of Socialist-Revolutionaries (SRs) which had coalesced out of various neo-Populist groups shortly after 1900. It established a special Combat Organisation solely dedicated to acts of terrorism under a former pharmacist Grigory Gershuni, a cunning figure who recruited many of the Organisation's assassins. He led the Combat Organisation until his capture in 1903, when Boris Savinkov, the son of a Warsaw judge, replaced him. The person who acted as the link between the SR's Central Committee and the Combat Organisation was Evno Filipovich Azef, the son of a Jewish tailor who had studied electrical engineering at Darmstadt university in Germany. For fifteen years Azef was at the heart of SR terrorist activities – a remarkable run of luck, for since the early 1890s he had been working for the Okhrana, the tsarist secret police, in return for a monthly salary.

The SRs acknowledged the People's Will as their immediate inspiration, but tried to reconcile acts of terror with Marxist concerns with history's larger motions in which neither the individual pulling the trigger nor the individual on the receiving end of a bullet was of much import. Marxified terror had several purposes. It could be a defensive response to repressive acts by the state. It would serve to disorganise the regime. Above all, in the SRs' view, terrorism had propaganda value, 'inciting a revolutionary mood among the masses'. In practice, things were never so clear cut as this theoretical exposition implies. There was a strong esprit de corps among the terrorists themselves, independent of the ideological niceties that served to differentiate each group. Besides, many of the terrorists had such limited education that they could scarcely articulate the ideological justifications for their actions at all. Many of the lower-level cadres who committed acts of terror were motivated by hatred and revenge, or simply became habituated to violence.

Such people tended to be contemptuous of the Party's deskbound theoreticians, who did not practise the violence their theories licensed. In addition to the centrally controlled Combat Organisation, the SR leadership also encouraged local terrorist groups, whose attacks were less discriminating than those of the central terrorist organisation. When the SRs decided in October 1905 to halt their terrorist attacks in the wake of the tsar's reforming platform, locally based terrorist groups broke away to form the Union of SR-Maximalists, which, as the name suggests, ploughed ahead with terrorism against all and sundry. As the Maximalists put it: 'Where it is not enough to remove one person, it is necessary to eliminate them by the dozen; where dozens are not enough, they must be got rid of in hundreds.'

In 1907 one of the leading Maximalist theoreticians, Ivan Pavlov, published a pamphlet entitled *The Purification of Mankind*. Anyone still harbouring the illusion that the class killings of the left were somehow morally superior to the race-based killings of the far right might wish to reconsider in the light of this tract. Pavlov argued that mankind was divided into ethical as well as ethnic races. Those in any kind of economic or state authority were so heinous that they literally constituted another race, 'morally inferior to our animal predecessors: the vile characteristics of the gorilla and the orangutan progressed and developed in it to proportions unprecedented in the animal kingdom. There is no beast in comparison with which these types do not appear to be monsters.' Since this group villainy was heritable, it followed, by this weird logic, that the children of these beasts in human form had to be exterminated. Other Maximalists sought to put a number on the exploiters who had to be killed, with one coming up with a round twelve million. Oddly enough, these pathological zoomorphic fantasies – which would be turned into Soviet reality by the rival Bolsheviks – have received far less scholarly attention than every minor Austrian or German *völkisch* racist who passed the days and nights wondering how to castrate or kill Jews.

While the Socialist-Revolutionaries did not conceal their campaign of terror, the rival factions of the Social Democratic Labour Party ostentatiously disavowed terrorism as incompatible with Marxism's emphasis on forming revolutionary consciousness through agitation, while practising it on a massive scale. This distinctive theoretical stance enabled them to identify a separate niche from the SRs; acts of individual terrorism, Lenin averred, were a minor distraction from the serious business of mobilising and organising the revolutionary masses. Both the impact of terrorist campaigns in the early 1900s and the social provenance of many new-wave terrorists meant that the exiled Lenin had to revise his opinions to keep step with events on the ground in Russia. By 1905 he had come to realise the complementary value of terrorism, openly exhorting his followers to form armed units and to attack Cossacks, gendarmes, policemen and informers, with bombs, guns, acid or boiling water. Local Bolshevik terrorist groups extended this campaign from servants of the state to the captains of industry. Moreover, they also used violence to disrupt the elections to the first State Duma, attacking polling stations and destroying the records of the results, since elections might undermine the prospects for revolution in Russia.

Lenin had few scruples about political finance. On one occasion he ordered his subordinates to seduce the unremarkable daughters of a rich industrialist so as to grab their inheritance. He also helped establish a clandestine Bolshevik Centre specifically tasked to carry out armed robberies. The Bolshevik robbers were especially active in the wildly exotic Caucasus, where Lenin's Georgian associate Josef Stalin had graduated from leading street gangs to political violence on an epic scale. His right-hand man was the Armenian psychopath Semen Ter-Petrosian, or 'Kamo the Caucasus brigand' as Lenin affectionately knew him. Stalin's Outfit was responsible for extortion against businessmen and armed robberies, the most spectacular being a June 1907 bomb and gun raid on carriages taking money to the State Bank in Tiflis which netted at least a quarter of a million rubles.[16] Many leading Bolsheviks who benefited from the proceeds of this crime were arrested abroad as they tried to exchange high-value 500-ruble notes for smaller denominations in Western banks.[17] Kamo was betrayed in Berlin, but managed to feign insanity sufficiently well to be confined in a mental institution when he was extradited to Russia. He was released after the Revolution; a statue of him replaced that of Pushkin in Tiflis's Yerevan Square, scene of his most notorious exploit.

Although the Bolsheviks' rivals, the Mensheviks, included among their leaders men like Iuly Martov and Pavel Aksel'rod who opposed terrorism, things were not so straightforward either in theory or in practice. Again, many Menshevik activists simply ignored the leadership's strictures against terrorism, which were rarely accompanied in any case by condemnations of terrorist attacks committed by rival groupings. In entire regions, such as the Caucasus, revolutionaries were unaware of any rift between Bolsheviks and Mensheviks in the first place, and hence continued to commit acts of terrorist violence under a common Social Democrat banner. The vast majority of terrorist killings, however, should be ascribed to anarchists, drawn from craftsmen, students and the underworld, all conjoined by belief that theoretical niceties were irrelevant and that reformism merely served to perpetuate an evil system. They practised what they called 'motiveless terror', in other words violence that was utterly disconnected from any alleged wrongdoing on the part of the victim. So instead of killing a member of the regime known for persecuting revolutionaries, anarchist terrorists regarded all the regime's servants as legitimate targets. Moreover, since the anarchists regarded private property as an evil on a par with the evil of the state, all estate and factory owners and their managers became targets too. The ideological enemy was included, whether clerics or reactionary writers and intellectuals. These generous guidelines meant that anarchist groups were responsible for the majority of terrorist attacks in Russia, although the anarchists' disavowal of central organisation and emphasis on the spontaneous violence of dispersed local groups meant that their responsibility was not reflected in any sort of accounting of atrocities.

The new wave of terrorism decelerated for various reasons. Following the assassination attempt at his villa in August 1906, prime minister Stolypin resorted to emergency decrees which bypassed the Duma, a step he took with regret since he respected the rule of law. In areas where disturbances were endemic, governors were licensed to use field court martials, where military judges passed summary justice on anyone indicted for terrorist attacks, assassinations, possession of explosives or robberies. Death sentences were frequent and, in a new departure, they were invariably carried out – a thousand within the first eight months of these new courts being established. The noose was known at 'Stolypin's necktie'. The regular civil and military courts were also encouraged to be less indulgent towards political criminals. Measures were introduced to improve the calibre and training of the police who investigated terrorist offences, while efforts were made to render imprisonment more stringent, by denying political offenders the privileged status that distinguished them from common criminals. In a few cases, government forces exceeded their authority, as when the commandant of Yalta in 1907 shocked civilised Europe by burning down the house from which a terrorist had tried to shoot him before killing himself. These measures were successful for they demonstrated the regime's resolve, while the costs to the terrorists became real. Parallel agrarian and economic reforms diminished the wider grievances upon which terrorism fed. Then there was the demoralising effect of what came to be known as the Azef affair, after the spy hidden within the SR Combat Organisation. Azef was so dedicated and senior a revolutionary that those comrades who suspected that he was a police spy were ignored. One man, Vladimir Burtsev, the editor of an SR journal, persisted with these accusations, supporting them with evidence that the Party leadership could not dismiss. A Judicial Commission confirmed Burtsev's allegations in a way that cast a poor light on the entire SR leadership group.

The exposure of further highly placed police agents led many revolutionaries to question the value of terrorism as a tactic, a feeling that spread to other leftist parties which otherwise enjoyed the SRs' discomfort. Terrorism directed from the centre went into abeyance, although it continued to be practised by locally based groups of diehard radicals. Dmitry Bogrov, the Okhrana agent and terrorist, belonged to such a group in Kiev. In August 1911 he received a visit from a fellow revolutionary who presented him with the unenviable choice of being killed as a traitor or assassinating the head of the Kievan Okhrana for whom Bogrov acted as an agent. Deciding that he had bigger fish to fry, Bogrov managed to persuade the same Okhrana chief that there was a plot abroad to kill Stolypin on a visit to the Ukrainian capital; in return for this information, which he failed to pass on since the only threat that concerned him would have been against the tsar, the police chief presented Bogrov with a ticket for that night's performance of Rimsky-Korsakov's *Tale of Tsar Saltan*, allegedly to provide Bogrov with an alibi to use with his suspecting terrorist friends. During the opera's second interval, Stolypin stood chatting in front of the orchestra pit, while Nicholas II and his daughters remained in their nearby box. Stolypin was hit by two shots fired from close range, one of which went through his hand, injuring one of the musicians on its further trajectory, while the second ricocheted off one of his medals and burrowed its way into his liver. The prime minister placed his hat and gloves on the edge of the balcony and unbuttoned his tunic, revealing a spreading red patch on his white shirt. The tsar came to the box, where his dying prime minister blessed his monarch with a final move of his hand. Bogrov was sentenced to death four days later and hanged the following week.

Although the tsarist regime succeeded in temporarily containing the epidemic of terrorism, it had fatally weakened the capacity and willingness of the government's bureaucratic servants to resist further assaults in future, especially when these occurred in the context of Russia's catastrophic conduct of the First World War. The repression represented by the field courts martial was a temporary success, but the tactic itself did nothing to foster a liberal camp that might have combined an insistence on legality with an unambiguous condemnation of terrorism. Instead, 'liberalism' was represented by the revolutionary Kadets with their soft tolerance of appalling terrorist violence. As for the terrorists, many of them slipped effortlessly into the apparatus of state terror that Lenin and his comrades established, beginning with the Cheka and from 1922 onwards the dread GPU. Kamo the Caucasian bandit re-emerged as a Chekist state terrorist, whose method of ascertaining the political loyalty of his Bolshevik subordinates was to torture them, to sort out the weaklings whom he then summarily executed. But even he was dispensable. In 1922, as the black joke went, the only bicycle in Tiflis, the one he was riding, was hit by the city's sole truck. The Bolsheviks' leading terrorist Leonid Krasin became their first ambassador to the Court of St James; Maxim Litvinov, their chief arms procurer, was a Soviet foreign minister under Stalin, the former terrorist who erected a tactic into a system of government.

CHAPTER 3

Black: Anarchists and Terrorism

I 'SHOOT, STAB, BURN, POISON AND BOMB':
THEORISTS OF TERROR

Anarchists, including some who never touched a stick of dynamite, theorised a violence that Fenians and nihilists practised, although there were more obscure precursors. In organisation and spirit nineteenth-century terrorist groups owed something to organised banditry and the conspiratorial societies of late-eighteenth- and early-nineteenth-century Europe, notably 'Gracchus' Babeuf's 'Conspiracy of the Equals' against the bourgeois Directory that ruled France after 9th Thermidor and the execution of Robespierre. This failed attempt to restore the dictatorship of the purest of the pure had some of the salient characteristics of modern terrorism, not least the infatuation with the most sanguinary phase of the French Revolution. The conspirators had faith in the redemptive powers of chaos: 'May everything return to chaos, and out of chaos may there emerge a new and regenerated world.' Babeuf and his co-conspirator and biographer Buonarroti pioneered the view that 'no means are criminal which are employed to obtain a sacred end'. This became a founding commandment of future terrorists, even when they practised something resembling an operational morality.

The Italian anarchists Carlo Pisacane, Carlo Cafiero and Errico Malatesta, and more especially the French doctor Paul Brousse, would convert this into the slogan 'propaganda by the deed', meaning the mobilising and symbolic power of acts of revolutionary violence. After an abortive rising in Bologna, Malatesta claimed that 'the revolution consists more in deeds than words ... each time a spontaneous movement of the people erupts ... it is the duty of every revolutionary socialist to declare his solidarity with the movement in the making'. The obvious inspiration for this was the 1871 Paris Commune, in which twenty-five thousand people were killed, an event with huge symbolic value since it epitomised the most polarised form of class struggle. Malatesta may have been an advocate of insurrectional violence, believing that 'a river of blood separated them from the future', but he condemned acts of terrorism and regarded revolutionary syndicalism as utopian.

A further crucial anarchist contribution to the matrix that comprised terrorism was prince Peter Kropotkin, the leading anarchist ideologue. Although Kropotkin was widely regarded as a figure of almost saintly virtue, who condemned the 'mindless terror' of chucking bombs into restaurants and theatres, he was nevertheless keen on the multiplier effects of force, in which one evil deed was repaid by another, setting in motion a spiral of violence that would duly undermine the most repressive of governments. Kropotkin was also a leading apologist for terrorism, justifying anything motivated by the structural violence bearing down on desperate people. 'Individuals are not to blame,' he wrote to a Danish anarchist friend, 'they are driven mad by horrible conditions.' What Kropotkin's own apologists seem to be saying is that the prince was a more decent, honourable fellow than Bakunin, who as we saw in the previous chapter swam in the deceitful depths of the maniacal Nechaev.[1]

Kropotkin was a leading theoretician of anarchism, rather than of terrorism, which has a less involuted theoretical history of its own. The dubious honour of originator belonged to a German radical democrat who revised classical notions of tyrannicide so as to legitimise terrorism. Karl Heinzen was born near Düsseldorf in 1809, the son of a Prussian forestry official with radical political sympathies. He studied medicine at the University of Bonn, before being rusticated for idleness. Another legacy of that time were the nine duelling scars on his face; one, shaped like an inverted L, ran down beside his chin, and was still clearly visible in later life. Heinzen served briefly with the Dutch foreign legion in Java and Sumatra, before returning to the Prussian army. He fell in love with the widow of an officer, who died before Heinzen could marry her, although he would go on to wed the widow's eldest daughter. Released to civilian life, he slogged his way up the hierarchy of the Prussian customs and excise service. This involved eight years of sheer drudgery, and his mounting alienation from the Prussian state. He was a petulant subordinate, frequently passed over for promotion, who resigned from the civil service in a sour mood.

Heinzen wrote a coruscating attack on the Prussian bureaucracy, so intemperate that he had to flee over the border to Holland to evade arrest. His radical republicanism deepened in exile in Belgium and Switzerland. In 1847 he made his first trip to America, where his various articles advocating republican revolution led to his being fêted as 'an authority on revolution' in the German-language press. He became editor of New York's *Deutsche Schnellpost* on the eve of the 1848 Revolutions which convulsed most of Europe, but he raced back to Germany to take part in the rising in Baden before standing, unsuccessfully, for election to the Frankfurt parliament. Inevitably an exponent of the most radical measures, he fell out with his more liberal-minded colleagues, and was obliged to flee as the forces of reaction regrouped.

During this turbulent period, Heinzen wrote 'Murder', an essay in which he claimed that 'murder is the principal agent of historical progress'. The reasoning was simple enough. The state had introduced murder as a political practice, so revolutionaries were regretfully entitled to resort to the same tactic. Murder, Heinzen argued, would generate fear. There was something psychotic in the repetitive details:

> The revolutionaries must try to bring about a situation where the barbarians are afraid for their lives every hour of the day and night. They must think that every drink of water, every mouthful of food, every bed, every bush, every paving stone, every path and footpath, every hole in the wall, every slate, every bundle of straw, every pipe bowl, every stick, and every pin may be a killer. For them, as for us, may fear be the herald and murder the executor. Murder is their motto, so let murder be their answer, murder is their need, so let murder be their payment, murder is their argument, so let murder be their refutation.

In a later rehashing of the essay, now entitled 'Murder and Liberty', Heinzen elaborated his thoughts on murder into a philosophy of tyrannicide that ineluctably slid into a justification of terrorism. Being German, he had to flourish analytical categories to give his obsessions the simulacrum of scientific respectability. There was 'the mere passion of annihilation' as when the Conquistadors wiped out the Amerindians, followed by 'the murder of pitched battle' such as the Carthaginian slaughter of the Romans at Cannae. Next came 'the murder of stupidity', by which Heinzen, the Catholic turned atheist, meant religious wars that might have led a resurrected Jesus to proclaim 'my kingdom is the cemetery'. Employing the accounting skills he had acquired in the Prussian tax offices, he claimed that there had been 2,000,000,000 murders in four thousand years of human history. The vast majority of these were the crimes not of ordinary individuals, but of princes and priests; by contrast, the number of murders committed by 'the champions of justice and truth' was insignificant, perhaps as few as one victim for every fifty thousand slain by the powerful. Heinzen next displayed his knowledge of classical tyrannicide to highlight the contrast between posterity's knowledge of the killing of a single man, say Julius Caesar, with the innumerable anonymous people that tyrants slaughtered. The despot was like a rabid dog or rogue tiger on the loose, an outlaw against whom any counter-measures were justified. However, Heinzen was not content to rehearse classical teachings on tyrannicide.

Arguing that the 1848 revolutionaries had been too weak-willed, he insisted on the need to kill 'all the representatives of the system of violence and murder which rules the world and lays it waste'. By these grim lights, 'the most warm-hearted of man of the French Revolution was – Robespierre'. The spirits of Babeuf and Buonarroti inspired his hope that 'History will judge us in accordance with this, and our fate will only be determined by the use we make of our victory, not the manner of gaining it over enemies, who have banished every humane consideration from the world.' It was now a matter of 'rooting out' the tyrant's 'helpers', who, like the disarmed bandit or the captured tiger, are 'incurable'. The entire people were to help identify and kill these aides of tyrants. Heinzen added aphoristically, 'the road to humanity lies over the summit of cruelty'.

In the writings of Heinzen, the ancient doctrine of tyrannicide was amplified into one of modern, indiscriminate terrorism. Although he never terrorised anyone, he had a fertile imagination as a writer. Putting himself in the shoes of a future reporter, he imagined a series of terrorist killings. A royal train snaking around an Alpine precipice would be hurled over the edge by a massive explosion caused by a revolutionary laying a thimbleful of 'fulminating silver' on the track. Another fictional report had revolutionary guerrillas armed with heavy guns which would emit showers of poisoned shot. A third had Prussian soldiers fleeing from iron tubes that fired showers of molten lead; but as they retreated they stepped on pressure mines set beneath the pavements. Other psychopathic reveries included the use of poisons delivered in every conceivable manner from pinpricks to glass bullets. Copper explosive balls would blast every palace, and all those, from cleaners to kings, dwelling within them. One day ballistic missiles and mines might be powerful enough 'to destroy whole cities with 100,000 inhabitants'.

These were the violent fantasies of a life that settled into agreeable domesticity after the initial difficulties of exile, for in October 1850 Heinzen and his family returned to New York. He reverted to editing and lecturing, settling in Louisville, Cincinnati, and finally back in New York, where the family's chronic money troubles were partially alleviated by Mrs Heinzen's millinery and needlework trade. In early 1860 they moved to Boston, where they lodged for the next twenty years in the home of a fellow radical, a Polish woman doctor who founded the New England Hospital for Women and Children. There Heinzen enjoyed something like peace of mind, tending his garden and growing vines to remind him of his native Rhineland. Having enjoyed robust health all his life, in late 1879 he suffered an apoplectic stroke and slowly died.[2]

Heinzen's younger German contemporary Johann Most was more a man of action than a theoretician. For anarchists of his persuasion, violence was attractive because it was unencumbered with theories that seemed designed to frustrate action. It hardly needs to be said that many anarchists – notably the Russian novelist Leo Tolstoy – were opposed to violence, thinking there were other routes to the federalism and mutualism their creed desired.

Born in 1846 in Bavaria, Most experienced terrible facial disfigurement at a young age when a disease resulting from parental neglect was treated by incompetent surgeons. He became a bookbinder as well as a committed Social Democrat, being sentenced in Austria in 1870 to five years' imprisonment for high treason. He had played a leading role in a rowdy demonstration before Vienna's parliament building. This was the first of many spells in jail that Most underwent on two continents; like Kropotkin, he became something of an authority on comparative penology. After his early release, he caused further provocation by going about with a group of 'Jacobins' threatening the extermination of 'mankind's' enemies.

Deported to Germany, Most quickly became one of the leading figures in the Social Democratic Party. In 1874 he was elected a member of the Reichstag, which he attended by day, while editing socialist newspapers at night. His rhetorical intemperance meant that the sergeant at arms frequently had to eject him from the chamber where even his own comrades dreaded his interjections. In 1874 he was sentenced to eighteen months in Plötzensee prison for inciting violence during a speech commemorating the Paris Commune. In 1878, Bismarck's introduction of anti-socialist laws, following two failed attempts on the life of the Kaiser, meant that Most had to flee abroad. He chose England; as the Berlin Political Police claimed, 'The whole of European revolutionary agitation is directed from London,' in ominous anticipation of the delusional laxities of contemporary 'Londonistan'. Most founded a paper, called *Freiheit*, whose revolutionary stridency embarrassed German Social Democrats trying to negotiate the twilight of legality and illegality that Bismarck had consigned them to by allowing them a presence in the Reichstag while suppressing their larger organisation and its propaganda organs. The German Social Democrat leadership began to mock Most as 'General Boom Boom', slinking about London with his red scarf and wide-brimmed black hat, a dagger in one hand and a pistol in the other. The Party leadership duly expelled their erstwhile comrade, who reacted by moving from being a socialist revolutionary to an anarchist–Communist under the influence of people he met in London, though his grasp of anarchist theory was shaky as he did not have French. He became a convinced advocate of 'propaganda by the deed' or as he vividly put it: 'Shoot, burn, stab, poison and bomb'. In England, his intemperance was ignored – much to the annoyance of foreign authorities – until he responded to the assassination of Alexander II ('Triumph, Triumph') by calling for the death of 'a monarch a month'.

At the instigation of a German teacher shocked by his paper, Most was arrested and charged with seditious libel. Convicted by an English jury, he was sentenced to sixteen months' hard labour, which he served at Coldbath Fields in Clerkenwell on the site of what is nowadays the Mount Pleasant Royal Mail sorting office. Despite being in solitary confinement, he managed to write articles for *Freiheit* with the aid of needles and lavatory paper which were smuggled out of the prison. The paper contrived to celebrate the Phoenix Park murders in Dublin – 'We side with the brave Irish rebels and tender them hearty brotherly compliments' – a stance that led to police raids on the temporary editors and the impounding of their typesetting equipment. Upon his release from prison, Most resolved to take himself and *Freiheit* to America. He sailed for New York in December 1882, quickly setting himself up among the foreign radicals huddled together in the slums of the East Side. Schwab's saloon was where Most held court, with a bust of Marat glowering from amid the bar's rows of bottles glinting in the gaslight and the fug of cigar smoke. In this milieu, with its cacophonous revolutionary talk in German, Russian and Yiddish, the bushy-haired and bearded Most would meet 'Red' Emma Goldman, an uneducated seamstress of Russian Jewish origin who fell in love with the short and grim veteran revolutionary.[3]

The violence of American labour disputes in the 1870s and 1880s was visceral in the smudge-like cities where vast impoverished immigrant populations speaking a Babel of tongues seemed like a threatening alien race to comfortable native elites. Wage cuts, layoffs and mechanisation were every employer's solution to downturns in profits. Strikes were met with extreme violence, reminiscent of a modern banana republic. In Pennsylvania, militant miners of Irish extraction nicknamed the Molly Maguires shot it out with the strike-breaking Pinkerton Detective Agency and ten of the former were hanged. During major emergencies when club-wielding or pistol-firing police or militias proved inadequate to quell violent disorders that arose during strikes, sun-burnished regular infantrymen were given a break from annihilating the Sioux. For weren't alien anarchists the white equivalent of anarchistic Apaches or ravening packs of wolves?

The press contributed to an atmosphere of hysteria. In Chicago, newspaper editors openly called for the throwing of grenades into the ranks of striking sailors or advocated lacing the food dispensed to the city's army of tramps with arsenic. By the same token, anarchists equally openly called for a 'war of extermination' against the rich: 'Let us devastate the avenues where the wealthy live as [the Civil War general] Sheridan devastated the beautiful valley of the Shenandoah'. Many anarchists were inspired by a murderous, exterminatory resentment towards the rich, and especially those gathered at fancy dinner parties, where their own bombs lurked 'like Banquo's ghost'. Anarchist papers like the *Alarm* advocated the assassination of heads of government and the use of dynamite against those 'social fiends' the police. Such papers contained detailed descriptions, many translated from Most's *Freiheit*, of how to manufacture bombs and handle explosives. 'The dear stuff', as anarchists called it, 'beats a bushel of ballots all hollow, and don't you forget it.'[4] If this anticipated the ease with which contemporary terrorists can access information about explosives on the internet, future co-operation between far-flung terrorist groups was evident in how in the 1880s the US based Clan na Gael extended a thuggish hand to striking Bohemian or German factory workers in North American cities, while apparently taking instruction in explosives from immigrant Russian nihilists.

Most was in his element here. He was a great crowd-puller on speaking tours organised by American radicals, his punch-line in either German or broken English being 'I shall stamp on ruling heads!' According to the Berlin Political Police, whose agents monitored some of the two hundred speeches he delivered in his first six months in the United States, 'he promises to kill people of property and position and that's why he's popular'. In 1883 at Pittsburgh, he proclaimed an American Federation of the International Working People's Association, or Black International for short, his solution to the problem of how to avoid organising loose federations of anarchist groups, whose cardinal tenet, after all, was to resist the authoritarian impulse reflected in the word organisation itself. He also systematised his long-standing interest in political violence. He published a series of articles in *Freiheit* which were subsequently published as *The Science of Revolutionary Warfare*. This was a terrorist primer, replete with details of codes, invisible inks, guns, poisons and manufacturing explosives, including his own favourite device, the letter bomb. He did much original research for this publication, poring over military manuals freely available in public libraries, and finding temporary employ in a munitions factory. He claimed that dynamite would redress the asymmetric inequalities which anarchist insurgents faced against regular forces.

In Chicago, Most's faith in dynamite was echoed in anarchist circles. The leading anarchist August Spies provocatively showed a newspaper reporter the empty spherical casing of a bomb. 'Take it to your boss and tell him we have 9,000 more like it – only loaded,' he added with much bravado. Lucy Parsons, the African-American wife of the charismatic anarchist war veteran Albert Parsons, proclaimed: 'The voice of dynamite is the voice of force, the only voice that tyranny has ever been able to understand.' Beyond the 'bomb talk' of these prominent figures, a handful of dedicated anarchists drew lessons from the contemporaneous terror campaigns of the Irish Fenians and the 'tsar bombs' of the Russian Nihilists, a fateful turn as America underwent the Great Upheaval of co-ordinated labour unrest in the winter of 1886.

Commencing in the spring, the Upheaval saw the country hit by fourteen hundred strikes involving over six hundred thousand employees. The strikers wanted an eight-hour working day, paid at the going rate for ten. In Chicago, where some forty thousand men went on strike, the epicentre was at the McCormick Reaper Works, a combine-harvester plant, which its intransigent boss turned into a fortress with the aid of four hundred policemen stationed to protect strike-breaking 'scabs'. These strikes became very ugly. In nearby Illinois, sheriff's deputies shot dead seven striking railwaymen and wounded many more. Inevitably, violence reached what was known as Fort McCormick when a gathering of striking railwaymen whom August Spies was addressing near the plant turned on strike-breakers as they were escorted from work. The police opened fire and shot dead several of the assailants. Spies hastened to his newspaper office to produce an incendiary 'revenge' circular which urged: 'To arms, we call you. To arms!' Although a colleague thought better of this and had the circular reprinted with this exhortation deleted, a few hundred copies of the original were nonetheless distributed.

A group of militant anarchists meeting in a saloon cellar resolved that night to bomb police stations and to shoot policemen if the latter persisted with violence against the strikers. They began putting explosives into pipes or into metal hemispheres which when screwed together formed grapefruit-sized bombs with ten inches of protruding fuse. In the meantime, there was to be a big protest rally in Market Square the following day. In his *Arbeiter-Zeitung* Spies argued that the striking McCormick workers would not have been slain so promiscuously had they possessed guns and a dynamite bomb. Unknown to him, two young anarchist carpenters, Louis Lingg and William Seliger, were concurrently manufacturing thirty or forty small bombs in Seliger's home. Large numbers of policemen under the conspicuously implacable inspector Bonfield were gathering at Desplaines Street police station near where the rally was held. The rather liberal governor decided against the deployment of militiamen in the city, arguing that the police could cope. This combination of factors proved fatal.

That evening Spies was the first speaker to mount a wagon in the Haymarket before a crowd of about three thousand strikers. Because of his poor English, he quickly turned the podium over to Albert Parsons, who had returned that day exhausted from agitating among striking workers in Cincinnati. Since Parsons had brought his wife and two young children to the rally, it seems unlikely that he anticipated bombs. In their speeches, both Spies and Parsons were mainly concerned to disclaim any personal responsibility for the recent violence at the McCormick plant. The mayor of Chicago, a genial Kentucky gentleman who frequently showed his presence by lighting cigars to illumine his face, was so sure that nothing untoward was being said that he mounted his horse to return home, after telling the police that the event was pretty tame.

By this time, Lingg and Seliger had moved their bombs in a trunk to the vicinity of the Haymarket, where they were distributed to persons unknown. The final speaker at the rally, an anarchist workman called Samuel Fielden, was inveighing against the police and the law in general, crying, 'Throttle it. Kill it. Stop it. Do everything you can to wound it – to impede its progress.' A plainclothes detective relayed a version of these incendiary remarks to Bonfield. The inspector set nearly two hundred blue-coated policemen on a rapid march along Desplaines Street, using their drawn revolvers to force a passage through the crowd. When he reached the rally, a police captain called out, 'I command you in the name of the people of the state of Illinois to immediately and peaceably disperse.' After a pause, Fielden got down from his podium, grudgingly remarking, 'All right, we will go.' At that moment, people were distracted as a round hissing object arced overhead, falling as a bright light at the feet of the policemen. There was a vivid orange flash and a loud detonation. One officer was killed instantly although a further seven would die of appalling wounds and many more had to have limbs amputated. Terrified out of their wits, the police started firing so indiscriminately that many of their victims were from among their own ranks. Someone tried to shoot the fleeing Spies with a revolver shoved into his back, although the anarchist leader managed to grapple with the gun so that when it went off the bullet penetrated his thigh. Sam Fielden was shot in the leg as he fled the scene. Albert Parsons, convinced he was a marked man, fled Chicago for Geneva, Illinois and then, heavily disguised, to Waukesha, Wisconsin.[5]

Over the following days, the press filled with murderous exhortations: 'Let us whip these Slavic wolves back to the European dens from which they issue, or in some way exterminate them.' In the financial district, brokers and traders offered personally to lynch anarchists and hang them from the city's lampposts, while businessmen financed the police investigation. The prosecuting attorney Julius Grinnell urged the police not to bother with such niceties as warrants: 'make the raids first, and look up the law afterwards'. The police descended on the offices of the

Arbeiter-Zeitung, dragging August Spies and Michael Schwab to Central Police Station where the leading officer fell upon Schwab screaming, 'You dirty Dutch sons of bitches, you dirty hounds, you rascals, we will choke you, we will kill you.' The paper's assistant manager, Oscar Neebe, was picked up the following day. The police then came for Fielden, who was nursing his leg wound at home. The chief officer pointed his finger at Fielden's head and said: 'Damn your soul, it should have gone here.' Next the police pulled in Seliger and Lingg. Lingg put up a desperate fight in his hidey-hole; a policeman had to bite the anarchist's thumb to stop him cocking his revolver. The police managed to detain and then release the person most widely suspected of throwing the bomb, who of course was never seen again. A middle-aged anarchist toy-shop owner, George Engel, was arrested and thrown in a police sweat-box to encourage him to talk. Eventually, eight anarchists were indicted for conspiracy to commit murder. Sensationally, on the opening day of the trial, a relaxed Albert Parsons walked into the courtroom, his previously dyed hair restored to its black sheen. His defence counsel had persuaded him to surrender himself as his continued flight seemed like an admission of guilt. Although the accused had decently courageous defence lawyers, both the judge and the jury were openly biased against them. The jury selection dragged on over twenty-one days in order to weed out any working-class men who might view the anarchists with sympathy. Once the defence had exhausted its right to query some 160 candidates, the court bailiff was allowed to go out into the streets to select jurors who had already condemned the defendants.

The charge of murder was outrageous, because how could one have a trial of accessories without the bomb-throwing principal? The star prosecution witness, a Swiss anarchist cabinet-maker, had been given money and immunity from prosecution for his testimony that two of the accused had conspired to use bombs at the fateful meeting in the saloon cellar. The prosecution was allowed to lay before the court lavish displays of bomb-making paraphernalia with obscure connections to the matter in hand. Inevitably, Most's bomb-making manual became People's Exhibit 16. As the prosecution and defence witnesses testified to the events of that night, it seemed that they were recalling two entirely unrelated scenarios. On 19 August the jury retired, rapidly reclining in armchairs to smoke cigars, after apparently reaching an instant verdict. The following morning they announced that seven of the defendants were guilty of murder and would hang, while Oscar Neebe should serve fifteen years' hard labour. Parsons was allowed an incredible eight hours to address the court, further adding to the theatrical nature of the proceedings. After the appeals process had been exhausted, the four men, who refused to seek clemency, on the grounds of their belief in their innocence, were hanged wearing white shrouds. There should have been five executions, but Louis Lingg – a search of whose cell had earlier revealed four sticks of dynamite – cheated the hangman by exploding a small detonator cap in his mouth which blew away half of his face, a scene that became an illustrators' favourite. It was an agonising death.

II THE BLACK INTERNATIONAL

These dramatic events in Chicago were symptomatic of the near-global panic that the anarchist Black International inspired in the late nineteenth and early twentieth centuries. Such an entity did exist, for in July 1881, a few months after the assassination of Alexander II, forty-five radicals gathered in London to form an International Anarchist Congress, although it failed to reconvene until 1907. While use of violence was controversial in these circles, it was nonetheless resolved by the participants to pay greater attention to explosives chemistry and technology so as to match the evolving forces of repression. This gathering, replete with loose talk about dynamite, 'the proletariat's artillery', gave substance to the widespread fear that there was a single controlling intelligence behind each and every manifestation of political violence that could not be attributed to Fenians or nihilists.

It has long been almost axiomatic to regard a ramified anarchist conspiracy as the product of fevered bourgeois imaginations. Certainly, people in authority thought there was a single conspiracy animating anarchist deeds just as today Al Qaeda is blamed for, and opportunistically takes credit for, a welter of terrorist atrocities. The Spanish ambassador to Rome wrote of an 'international anarchist impulse' which informed the spirit if not the letter of anarchist deeds. The Italian press was convinced that the killing of king Umberto was part of 'the vastness of the plan of the anarchists and of the aims they propose, the assassination of all of Europe's monarchs'.

Although in reality there was no single directing conspiracy, and no single anarchist party, there were good reasons for contemporaries to believe that individual anarchists were acting in response to generalised injunctions to destroy bourgeois civilisation. That anarchists were often foreigners, with unpronounceable names like Bresci or Czolgosz, automatically fostered the impression of a very cosmopolitan conspiracy, as did the international circulation of the multilingual anarchist press, copies of which were invariably found in the homes of dynamiters and their sympathisers. That press also sedulously propagated the idea of a worldwide army of anarchists willing to avenge suffering humanity. In other words, the anarchists themselves propagated the notion of a worldwide conspiracy. Improved telegraphy and successive daily newspaper editions updating the cycle of atrocity, arrest, trial, speeches from the dock, imprisonment or execution meant that readers could quite justifiably conclude that the activities of bomb-throwing maniacs were being co-ordinated on behalf of sinister objectives across Europe or North and South America, for Argentina too was not spared propaganda by the deed. Detailed and extensive press coverage had its drawbacks, since even the most hostile newspapers invariably printed the courtroom justifications of convicted anarchists virtually verbatim, fuelling the lethal ardour of anarchists everywhere. The reporting of the killing of king Umberto of Italy directly inspired the assassin of US president William McKinley. As Sir Howard Vincent, one of the founders of Scotland Yard's Criminal Investigation Department (CID), put it: 'The "advertisement" of anarchism, as of many other crimes, infallibly leads to imitation.' That was why the French Chamber of Deputies made serious legislative efforts to prohibit reporting of trials of anarchists.

The sheer repetition of high-level assassinations also inclined people to think a vast conspiracy was abroad, even though the politics of the assassins – assuming they were not madmen – were hardly uniform. In 1878 Hödel and Nobiling made successive attempts on the life of the German emperor, the second of which resulted in his being badly wounded. That year a republican cook stabbed king Umberto of Italy, twenty-two years before his eventual assassination, while there was a bomb attack on a monarchist parade the following day. In 1881 a young French anarchist and unemployed weaver, Emile Florion, shot a total stranger having failed to find the republican politician Léon Gambetta. Florion then unsuccessfully tried to shoot himself. In the autumn of 1883 an anarchist plot was uncovered to blow up the German Kaiser, the crown prince and several leading military and political figures as they gathered to open the monument to Germania on the Niederwald above Rüdesheim. Sixteen pounds of dynamite were concealed in a drainage pipe beneath the road so as to blow up the imperial entourage as it passed overhead. Luckily, one of the terrorist assassins had decided to save a few pfennigs by purchasing cheap fuse cable that was not water-proof; the cheap fuse was so damp it could not be lit. The chief anarchist plotter, August Reinsdorf, and an accomplice were beheaded two years later. In January 1885 the chief of police in Frankfurt, who had played a major role in capturing Reinsdorf, was stabbed to death by an unknown assailant; circumstantial evidence was used to convict the anarchist Julius Lieske of the crime. Instead of an unending chain reaction of terror and counter-terror, these events resulted in the virtual demise of the German anarchist movement. Foreign policemen hastened to Berlin to discover the secrets of Prussian policing.

In France, meanwhile, anarchists were responsible for a series of random attacks, some of them indicative of the perpetrators' mental derangement. Too inept to make a bomb, the young cobbler Léon Léauthier simply sat down in an expensive restaurant and knifed a neighbouring customer who turned out to be the Serbian ambassador. Charles Gallo threw a bottle of prussic acid on to the floor of the Stock Exchange, crying 'Vive l'Anarchie!' at the startled traders, as he fired a revolver into their midst. The lethal suppression of labour disputes served as a pretext for anarchist attacks. On 1 May 1891 police used a newly invented machine gun to break up a demonstration for the eight-hour day at Fourmies in the Nord department. Nine people were killed, including four women and three children. Simultaneously at Clichy the police employed excessive violence to break up an anarchist procession following a woman bearing a red flag. Despite being unlawfully beaten by the police, two men received considerable sentences of hard labour. By way of revenge for these incidents, the anarchist former dyer François-Claudius Ravachol placed bombs in the homes of Benoit, the advocate-general, who lived on the smart Boulevard Saint-Germain, and Bulot, the judge who had presided in the Clichy affair. In the second incident, a smartly dressed Ravachol walked up to the second floor of the building with a bomb in a briefcase, set the fuse and left, bringing the entire four floors crashing down, although the judge survived unscathed. A little too exultant about his recent accomplishments, the thirty-two-year-old Ravachol was betrayed by a waiter in the Restaurant Véry. A brave police detective was summoned, who after scrutinising his fellow diner apprehended Ravachol before he could draw his revolver or deploy his sword cane.

The restaurant was bombed the day before Ravachol stood trial. The proprietor died a slow death after losing most of a leg, while an equally innocent customer, rather than the waiter, was killed. Ravachol – whose name became the verb *ravacholiser* (to blow up) – was sentenced to life imprisonment for these offences. He blamed unemployment for his criminal turn: 'I worked to live and to make a living of my own; as long as neither myself nor my own suffered too much, I remained that which you call honest. Then work got scarce and with unemployment came hunger. It was then that great law of nature, that imperious voice that allows no retort – the instinct for survival – pushed me to commit some of the crimes and offences that you accuse me of and that I recognise being the author of.' He was subsequently tried in Montbrison for offences committed long before he became a bomber for murdering and robbing 'the Hermit of Chambles', an elderly miser called Brunel with much gold and silver hidden in his cupboard, and for profaning the grave of baroness de Rochetaillée where he hoped to find the jewels she had reportedly been buried with, but which instead contained a wooden crucifix and a single medal. When he recommenced his lofty claims to being the arm of justice for the oppressed, the judge snapped back: 'Do not pretend to speak for the working men, but only for murderers.' Ravachol was guillotined before he had time to make further speeches. One of his admirers, the novelist Octave Mirbeau, described him as 'the peal of thunder to which succeeds the joy of sunlight and of peaceful skies', one of a number of instances when idiot liberal artists and men of letters glorified common criminals, such career felons increasingly describing themselves as anarchists so as to bask in refracted acclaim.[6]

The anarchist response to Ravachol's execution came from Auguste Vaillant, who on 9 December 1893 threw a bomb hidden in an oval tin box on to the floor of the Chamber of Deputies, although the accidental jogging of his arm meant that the bomb exploded over the deputies' heads, causing cuts and fractures rather than fatalities. In addition to installing iron grilles in the public gallery, and prohibiting the wearing of coats or cloaks inside the building, the Chamber promulgated the 'scroundrelly laws' proscribing publications that incited acts of terrorism. One of the first to be convicted as a 'professor of Anarchy' was Jean Grave, who received two years' imprisonment for passages in a book that appeared to incite anarchist violence. Vaillant had his admirers in an artistic milieu where, among others, Courbet, Pissarro and Signac were anarchist supporters. The poet Laurent Tailharde shocked a literary supper when he exclaimed: 'What do the victims matter, as long as the gesture is beautiful?' – a view he probably revised when a random anarchist bomb took out one of his eyes in a restaurant. The execution of Vaillant allegedly provoked the young anarchist Emile Henry to detonate a bomb in the Café Terminus in the Gare Saint-Lazare, killing one person and wounding twenty. He chose this target after failing to get in to a theatre that was sold out, and after inspecting a restaurant with only a scattering of diners. The station café was full of commuting workers, a fact that did not disturb the workers' advocate unduly. Henry was a cold-blooded killer whose avowed intent was to murder as many people as possible. At his trial he confessed to a murderous moralism with his infamous remark 'there are no innocent bourgeois': 'I wanted to show the bourgeoisie that henceforth their pleasures would not be untouched, that their insolent triumphs would be disturbed, that their golden calf would rock violently on its pedestal until the final shock that would cast it down among filth and blood.'

That resentful desire to inflict chaos on ordinary people going about unremarkable lives would become a recurrent terrorist motive; what the victims of terrorists usually have in common is often overlooked. Henry warned the jury that 'It [anarchism] is everywhere, which makes it impossible to contain. It will end by killing you.' He was guillotined early on the morning of 21 May 1894. In retaliation for his refusal to grant Henry and Vaillant pardons, president Marie François Sadi Carnot was stabbed in the heart by an Italian anarchist Santo Jeronimo Caserio as he rode through Lyons in his carriage.

This was the first in a spate of assassinations of heads of state that made the years 1894–1901 more lethal for rulers than any other in modern history, forcing them to use bodyguards for the first time. Following the killing of Carnot, the prime minister of Spain was assassin-ated by Italian anarchists in 1897, in retaliation for confirming the death sentences passed on anarchists who had been rounded up and tortured after a bomb flew into a Corpus Christi procession in Barcelona. He was followed by Elizabeth empress of Austria, stabbed by an Italian anarchist drifter in 1898; king Umberto of Italy, shot dead in Monza by an Italian-American anarchist Gaetano Bresci in 1900; and president McKinley, assassinated in 1901. McKinley's assassin was an Ohio farmboy turned factory worker called Leon Czolgosz, although he sometimes used the aliases John Doe and Fred Nobody. He was inspired by Emma Goldman's passionate espousal of anarchism, although the direct inspiration to shoot McKinley at the Pan-American Expositon in Buffalo came from his reading of a newspaper report of Bresci's shooting of king Umberto that July. Czolgosz approached McKinley outside the Temple of Music, where he shot him at close range; one bullet was deflected by the president's breast bone, but the second went so deep into his abdomen that surgeons could not recover it. The president slowly bled to death. A search revealed that Czolgosz not only had a folded newspaper clipping in his pocket of Umberto's murder, but that he had used the same .32-calibre Iver Johnson revolver as Bresci. Narrowly surviving the beating he received from McKinley's security officers as they pummelled him to the floor, Czolgosz went to the electric chair after a trial that lasted eight-and-a-half hours from jury selection to verdict.

In 1892 Alexander Berkman had been inspired by Emma Goldman to stab Henry Clay Frick, the managing director of Carnegie Steel, in Frick's Pittsburgh offices. Henry's attack on commuters nursing a beer or glass of wine had already been preceded by the bombing of Barcelona's Liceo Opera House during a performance of Rossini's *William Tell* that killed more than thirty people, one of several bomb attacks in major European cities. The assassin chose the opera house as a target because it seemed to epitomise bourgeois conspicuous consumption. Six anarchists were subsequently shot by firing squad at the Montjuich fortress for this outrage. In the same year, 1893, Paulino Pallás threw two bombs at the military governor of Catalonia, to avenge the torture of hundreds of anarchists detained in the wake of the Corpus Christi attack and the garrotting of their five colleagues. The would-be assassin warned at his trial that 'Vengeance will be terrible!' In Italy, government repression of demonstrations in Sicily and of a rising by Tuscan quarry workers resulted in a bomb attack outside the parliament building and an attempt on the life of the prime minister. Anarchists also stabbed to death a journalist who had condemned the Italian anarchists responsible for killing president Carnot. When a Portuguese psychiatrist certified an anarchist insane, after the latter had hurled a rock at the king, a bomb tore apart the asylum building in which the doctor dwelt.

Even the tranquillity of London's Greenwich Park was not immune from anarchist activity. On a wintry February evening in 1894 park keepers heard the muffled thud of an explosion from the winding path leading up to Wren's Royal Observatory. They raced to the scene where they saw a young man kneeling on the ground with agonising wounds to his abdomen and thighs and a missing hand. This was Martial Bourdin, a young anarchist, who had accidentally set off the 'infernal machine' he was carrying towards the Observatory, embedding iron shards in his own body. His brother-in-law probably gave him the bomb, in his sinister dual capacity of anarchist cum police agent, the basis for 'Verloc' in Conrad's *Secret Agent*. Bourdin expired in the delightful Seamen's Hospital down on the river front fifty minutes after the explosion. A search of his clothing revealed a membership card for the Autonomie Club, a notorious haunt of 'cosmopolitan desperadoes' on Tottenham Court Road. Emile Henry had allegedly been seen there a few weeks before the Terminus bombing. *The Times* took the commonsense view that perhaps the theory of 'liberty for everybody on British soil' had been taken 'a little too far', although no British government was disposed to address this, then or now.[7]

These multifarious acts of anarchist violence achieved nothing beyond the individual tragedies of those people killed and maimed. They had no significant impact on the domestic or international politics of any of the countries concerned, and certainly did not collapse the social order in favour of whatever infantile arrangements the Henrys, Ravachols and Vaillants of the time desired.

The burghers of Chicago probably took things too far when they built a huge fortified Armoury in the city and insisted on basing a regular army division only thirty miles away from the seething alien helots of the South Side. President Theodore Roosevelt fulminated against anarchism, this 'daughter of degenerate lunacy, a vicious pest', and in 1903 introduced laws prohibiting anarchists from entering the United States, along with paupers, prostitutes and the insane. Immigrants who 'converted' to anarchism during their first three years in the country could be deported, an interesting example of conditional citizenship. Similar expulsions of dangerous foreigners were adopted in France and Italy, and in France two thousand anarchists were simultaneously raided by the police in twenty-two departments, resulting in a host of prosecutions for petty offences that kept some of them in jail. Refusing to take lessons in good governance from concerned friendly governments, the British persisted in maintaining liberal asylum laws that anarchists were manifestly abusing. One minor concession was that the Metropolitan Police hauled in anyone looking like an anarchist (and there was indeed an almost obligatory sartorial code in such circles) in order to photograph them – thereby making them less elusive in future – while drawing up a list of anarchist suspects, whom they encouraged to talk freely in East End pubs. They gave these lists to employers in the expectation that, impoverished by chronic unemployment, these men might be forced to leave Britain's welcoming shores. There were a few fitful attempts to organise international police co-operation – notably the 1898 International Anti-Anarchist Conference of police chiefs and interior ministers – but Britain and Belgium insisted that anarchist violence could be adequately contained by existing domestic laws. Inevitably, in their dealings with the subterranean world of anarchist conspiracy, the police forces of Europe recruited agents or involved themselves too deeply in financing anarchist journals, lending some substance to Chesterton's surreal vision in *The Man Who Was Thursday* of the police chasing anarchists who were themselves.

Anarchist terrorism did manage to generate widespread fear of a single conspiracy, with fake threatening letters from 'Ravachol' or suspicious boxes and packages contributing to urban psychosis. Fanciful journalists and novelists imagined weapons of greater destructive power rather than the modest explosive devices that anarchist plotters disposed of, although that may not be how the patrons of the Café Terminus or the Liceo Opera House would have seen things. Politicians and monarchs could no longer go among their citizens and subjects with relative ease, and government buildings took on some of the forbidding, fortified character they often possess today. Above all, perhaps, anarchist violence served to discredit political philosophies whose libertarian impulses might otherwise strike some as praiseworthy, by associating them, however unfairly, with the murderous vanity of sad little men labouring over their bombs in dingy rooms. A philosophy which regards the state as nothing more than the organisation of violence on behalf of vested interests came to be universally identified with murderous violence, obliterating the more harmless aspects of the underlying philosophy. One observer of these anarchists felt that 'All these people are not revolutionaries – they are shams.' This was the Anglo-Polish novelist Joseph Conrad, a man too admiringly grateful to England to breach its unspoken etiquette by publicly criticising how it had afforded asylum to 'the infernal doctrines born in continental back-slums'. Edward Garnett paid him an immense (backhanded) compliment when he reviewed *The Secret Agent*: 'It is good for us English to have Mr Conrad in our midst visualising for us aspects of life we are constitutionally unable to perceive.'[8]

Partly inspired by Bourdin's death in Greenwich Park, in 1907 Conrad devoted *The Secret Agent* to the theme of 'pests in the streets of men', notably the pain and suffering they inflicted on everyone they touched in their immediate private circle. Although in the wake of 9/11 many commentators rightly discovered precursors of the Saudi hijackers in Conrad's depiction of squalid anarchists blindly following a plot elaborated by a tsarist diplomat in 1900s London, this was not where the author's primary interests lay. The chief focus is Winnie Verloc, who commits suicide after murdering Adolf Verloc, her anarchist, agent-provocateur and pornographer husband who acts on behalf of a sinister Russian diplomat seeking to make London inhospitable to terrorists by inciting them to blow up Greenwich Observatory as a symbol of bourgeois belief in scientific progress. Winnie inadvertently discovers that her husband was responsible for the death, while carrying a bomb destined for the Observatory, of her simpleton half-brother Stevie, the other innocent victim in a tale that Conrad invested with little political significance. The anarchists depicted in the book are composite characters drawn from several real people we have encountered already. The character of Verloc was indebted to the fact that Bourdin's brother-in-law was a police agent as well as editor of an anarchist paper. Karl Yundt is based on Mikhail Bakunin and Johann Most. Michaelis is a fusion of the Fenians Edward O'Meagher Condon, who attacked the prison van in Manchester in 1867, and Michael Davitt, like Michaelis author of a book about his experiences in prison. The 'Professor' is probably none other than the eponymous 'Russian' bomb-making genius who figured in O'Donovan Rossa's newspapers.[9]

The private moral squalor, shabbiness and smallness of the men who terrorise a major city are among the novel's most striking features beneath their grandiose apocalyptic talk: 'no pity for anything on earth, including themselves, and death enlisted for good and all in the service of humanity – that's what I would like to see', says Yundt. 'They depend on life, which, in this connection, is a historical fact surrounded by all sorts of restraints and considerations, a complex, organised fact open to attack at every point; whereas I depend on death, which knows no restraint and cannot be attacked. My superiority is evident,' opines the Professor. In reality he was not a 'Professor' at all, but the meanly countenanced son of a preacher in an obscure Christian sect who had discovered in science a faith to replace that of 'conventicles' so as to realise his limitless ambitions without effort or talent. Conrad continues: 'By exercising his agency with ruthless defiance he procured for himself the appearance of power and personal prestige. That was undeniable to his bitter vengeance.' He believed in nothing: ' "Prophecy! What's the good of thinking what will be!" He raised his glass. "To the destruction of what is," he said, calmly.'[10]

CHAPTER 4

Death in the Sun: Terror and Decolonisation

I HOLY LAND, HOLY WAR

At the time of the 1917 Balfour Declaration, favouring 'the establishment in Palestine of a National Home for the Jewish People', land designated by the Roman name of Palestine was part of the Ottoman Empire, with which Britain was at war. The Ottoman Empire, and Kemal Atatürk's regime that superseded it, had sought to draw closer to European civilisation. One measure of this was how religious minorities were treated within an Islamic tradition that traditionally accorded non-Muslims dhimmitude or submissive status. This was not quite what it sounds. Throughout urban centres, Jews could become members of parliament, hold government posts and, after 1909, be recruited into the military. Following on from this late and poignant flourishing of Islamic modernism, Atatürk abolished sharia law in 1924, while in Egypt this applied only in the private realm. All of which is to say that Islam was contained by the nation state rather than the other way around.

The Jewish community in Palestine was known as the settlement or Yishuv, and consisted of about eighty-five thousand people; some had been there for half a century or more, others were recent emigrants. There were three-quarters of a million Arabs. The League of Nations accorded Britain mandatory authority over Palestine in 1919. In welcoming Zionist settlers, the British were in step with educated Arab opinion in the Middle East. The editor of Egypt's *Al-Ahram* wrote: 'The Zionists are necessary for this region. The money they bring in, their intelligence and the diligence which is one of their characteristics will, without doubt, bring new life to the country.'[1] The Zionists colonised desolate lands where absentee Arab landlordism was rife, although tenant graziers did not regard this as creating entitlement.[2] Zionists felt that development would register a moral claim, irrespective of conflicting Arab and Jewish versions of the venerability of their respective presences in the region. Israel Zangwill's 1901 dictum, 'a land without a people for a people without a land', indicated that some Zionists apparently did not notice the Arab inhabitants. Theoretically, in the minds of both the British and some Zionists, Jewish settlement could be achieved without prejudice to the indigenous Arab inhabitants, for everyone would benefit from improved irrigation, medicine and sanitation.

Zionist immigrants regarded themselves not as colonial subjects, but as fellow colonists alongside the British. Their intention was to create a durable Jewish state under the temporary aegis of the imperial Mandate. They were diligent and purposeful state-builders pursuing a secularised messianic ideal. Long before the European Holocaust, Zionists argued that, as the Arab nation disposed of a million square miles of territory, the Jews were morally entitled to a tiny polity roughly the size of Scotland and with much the same sporadic population density. By contrast, the Palestinians were more reactive, divided by allegiances to clan or tribe, and dependent upon the British for a state infrastructure. Only their religious leaders were more politically engaged than those of the Jews.[3]

Among some contemporary Israelis the British Mandate has come to be viewed nostalgically. Although Palestine did not have the elephants, maharajahs and tigers of the Indian Raj, the same culture of Highland reels, polo and pink gins in the King David hotel flourished. So did an incorruptible civil service, possibly a novelty in the region.[4] Under this aegis, the Jews of the Yishuv determinedly elaborated proto-national institutions, including a Jewish Agency, while immigrants – many of them idealistic Zionist socialist kibbutzim – set about bringing life to stony ground rich in associations among people who had never seen it except in their mind's eye. An ancillary Zionist objective was to confound the anti-Semitic claim that Jews had no 'racial' aptitude for farming or manual labour, a notion hard to square with the orderly citrus trees, vegetables and vines that appeared in the new Jewish settlements. Entirely new cities, like Tel Aviv, arose beside Arab Jaffa, essential elements in the Zionist equivalent of the Whig view of history, but based on exchanging the dark and cold of eastern Europe for a light-filled modernist seaside setting.[5] It is salutary to recall that, below the antagon-isms of Arab and Jewish notables, on a local level ordinary Jews and Arabs co-operated with one another. They shopped in each other's stores, worked alongside one another in bakeries, petroleum and salt plants, transport, post and telegraphy, and from time to time went on strike together to protest against some arbitrary decision of their Mandatory employer. Moreover, as late as 1933, the Egyptian govern-ment gladly allowed a thousand Jewish emigrants to disembark at Port Said en route to Palestine.[6]

Jewish immigration, and the eviction of Arab tenants from land the Jews bought from absentee landlords based in Beirut or Damascus, triggered Arab unrest in 1920-1 and 1929, which acquired focus in Haj-Amin al-Husseini. A gangling teacher with a ginger beard and a red fez, Husseini was the scion of a notable Palestinian family. Despite having been sentenced to ten years' imprisonment in absentia for orchestrating mob violence in 1920, the British pardoned him a year later and rigged his election as grand mufti of Jerusalem, to balance the appointment to the city's mayoralty of a man from the rival Nashashibi clan. As a pupil of the Wahhabist Rashid Rida, the mufti's primary objection to the Jews was that they were symptomatic of a threatening Western modernity: 'They have also spread here their customs and usages that are opposed to our religion and to our whole way of life. Above all, our youth is being morally shattered. The Jewish girls who run around in shorts demoralise our youth by their mere presence.' Careful to wipe his fingerprints from Arab urban violence, the mufti was mainly responsible for inciting it.[7]

Anti-Jewish violence led to the creation in 1921 of an underground Jewish defence force, the Haganah, designed to protect remote Jewish settlements when the British authorities wouldn't or couldn't. Weapons were smuggled in from Europe hidden in beehives and steamrollers. Such self-consciously tough Jews would confound common anti-Semitic stereotypes about the Jews being averse to a fight. In 1924 the Haganah assassinated the Orthodox Jewish leader Israel de Haan who was endeav-ouring to have the British exclude his co-religionists from rule by secular Zionists. Not for the last time, the British sought to appease Arab sentiment – at least as expressed by notables like the mufti – by limiting Jewish immigration to what the country's economy could satisfactorily absorb, a policy that took little notice of the evil currents abroad in Europe which were pushing Jews in Poland or the Ukraine to emigrate.

With the exception of those like Winston Churchill who had keen

Zionist sympathies, British officials imbued with nostalgic memories of colonel T. E. Lawrence were keen not to do anything to unsettle the sixty million Muslims in India on behalf of Jews in Palestine or Britain itself, towards whom some members of the British Establishment (and opposition Labour movement) harboured old-fashioned prejudices. In one of its slippery retreats from the airy grandiosity of the Balfour Declaration, in 1928 the British cabinet rejected Chaim Weizmann's request for a substantial loan designed to buy further Arab land to build more Jewish settlements and thenceforth tried to restrain immigration.[8]

The following year, the mufti incited attacks on Jewish worshippers at Jerusalem's Wailing Wall, claiming that they planned to demolish the Al-Aqsa mosque, events that led to the deaths of sixty Jews in the Old City. Even as he pretended to calm the mobs, the mufti was actually egging them on. These casualties were some of the 133 Jews killed that year by Arab violence throughout Palestine. Such murderous riots had an international dimension, as Arabs in Syria, Transjordan and Iraq threatened military involvement if Jewish immigration to Palestine was not halted. One consequence of the riots was that a number of Haganah's military commanders led by Avraham Tahomi, its chief in Jerusalem, seceded from the parent body, forming a National Military Organisation (Irgun Zvai Leumi or Etzel for short after its Hebrew acronym), arguing that Haganah itself was too close to one political party, a notion they felt did not apply to themselves.

Arab unrest at the prospect of Jewish hegemony led the British to carry out two investigations, in 1929–30, which concluded that Jewish immigration had allegedly exceeded the absorptive capacity of the economy in Palestine, although the country would sustain a much larger population in future. They were shocked by the extent of pauperisation among the Arab population, which either eked out a miserable existence on the land or tried its luck as a proletariat in the cities, but they did little to alleviate it through aid or investment. In and around the shanty districts of the port of Haifa, ironically one of the towns where Arabs and Jews lived in conspicuous amity, some of these people joined the guerrilla army formed by a charismatic Syrian Wahhabist preacher, Izz al-Din al-Qassam, who for two years from 1933 launched attacks on the Jews and British policemen until the latter killed him and three associates in 1935. He is commemorated in the name of present-day teams of Palestinian suicide bombers, since his was the first armed Palestinian nationalist grouping.

Broadly speaking, the Zionist Establishment was either socialist or Marxist, a characteristic evidenced by the fact that it was not until 1977 that the state of Israel elected a right-wing government. While the majority of Zionists in the Yishuv supported its left-leaning and pro-British leadership, a right-wing minority were adherents of a Polish-based Revisionist Zionism that followed the charismatic Zeev Jabotinsky. Although Jabotinsky subscribed to an expansive version of otherwise thoroughly Zionist objectives, namely to return all Jews to a pre-dominantly Jewish 'Eretz Israel' on both sides of the Jordan, which would act as a 'laboratory' for a 'model Jewish citizen', the means were heavily permeated with the political culture of inter-war Poland. This is almost impossible for anyone brought up in a stable liberal Western democracy to comprehend, but it would probably resonate with historically minded Italians. Jabotinsky was much taken with the nineteenth-century revolutionary Garibaldi's legion, which had played such a major role in the creation of Italian statehood. This had served as a model for the Polish Legion of Marshal Józef Piłsudski, which had made itself sufficiently indispensable to the Allies in the Great War for them to favour the restoration of Polish independence after an interval of more than a century of partition.[9] Other features typical of the 1920s and 1930s included the creation of a youth movement, called Betar, with its red-brown uniforms and anti-Marxist middle-class intellectual membership. The model for this was the Ballila youth movement of Italian Fascism. Unsurprisingly, the Marxist–Zionist leadership of the Yishuv referred to these Betarim as Fascists, although only the most implacable of them had active flirtations with Mussolini and Hitler. In 1929 the British banned Jabotinsky from Palestine while his Arab antipode, the grand mufti, fled abroad; two years later Jabotinsky withdrew from the World Zionist Organisation.

In Palestine, frustration among Jabotinsky's followers with the cautious land reclamation and settlement policy of the Yishuv's socialist-Zionist leadership led to the formation of a virulently anti-Marxist nationalist movement called the Bironyim, which roughly translates as 'Zealots'. They hoped that a Jewish state could be created quickly through terrorist violence against the British Mandatory authorities. The extent to which they were swimming in dangerous waters can be gauged from the fact that the journalist Aba Achimeir, who had been seared by experience of the Bolshevik Revolution, wrote a Hebrew column called 'From a Fascist Notebook'. 'We need a Mussolini,' he argued, although he would also have settled for something like Sinn Féin/IRA, the model for how to achieve independence from the British through armed insurrection. These ideologues inspired what became the main radical-right Zionist terrorist cum guerrilla organisation, called Irgun here for short.

On 16 June 1933 one of Achimeir's protégés, Avraham Stavsky, shot dead Chaim Arlosoroff, head of the Jewish Agency's Political Department, as he walked with his wife along the beachfront at Tel Aviv. The pretext for this assassination was that Arlosoroff was negotiating with Hitler's Germany to transfer the assets of persecuted Jews to Palestine. This assassination poisoned relations between the socialist Zionists and the Revisionists, which descended into mutual slurs. The parents of the boy Ariel Sharon, the prime minister of Israel seventy years later, who favoured Arlosoroff's killers, were reminded of the culture of public denunciation they had experienced in Bolshevik Russia as they were ostracised by the leftist community of their neighbours. Charges of anti-Semitism were hurled back and forth with the usual tedious abandon. Jabotinsky himself weighed in with an article entitled 'Blood Libel' arguing that his opponents were using the tactics of medieval Christian anti-Semites to smear not only Stavsky but the Revisionist movement as a whole. Stavsky was acquitted of murder, but Achimeir was arrested and jailed.

Although in 1933 Avraham Tahomi abandoned Irgun to return to the bosom of Haganah, some of its supporters, notably Avraham Stern, decided to colonise the youthful Betarim – much like aggressive African bees taking over a relatively placid hive – with a view to fighting the perfidious British Mandatory authority. Stern may have been romanticised subsequently by his Israeli admirers, but there is no doubt that he was a terrorist.

The right-wing and anti-Semitic colonels who ruled Poland actively connived at Irgun establishment of training facilities in Poland, while weapons were shipped to Palestine from Gdansk. The worsening climate for Jews in Europe led to an acceleration of emigration and corresponding Arab fears of inundation, as the Jewish population of Palestine surged from 20 to 30 per cent in the three years 1933–6 alone. Because unemployed Jewish immigrants would confirm British beliefs that the country had reached the population density it could absorb, the Zionists consciously adopted the policy of 'Hebrew labour' which discriminated against Christian or Muslim Arabs. Both the death of Izz al-Din al-Qassam and the discovery of ammunition in barrels of 'cement' landed at Jaffa and intended for the Haganah prompted Arab leaders into more radical action, as they abandoned urban rioting for guerrilla activity in the countryside.

In 1936 the mufti's Higher Committee declared a general strike, with follow-up mass demonstrations, that were forcibly suppressed by the British. The strike meant that Arab peasants lost the urban seasonal work on which many depended, one of the main reasons why some were available for guerrilla fighting. Arabs attacked Jewish-owned stores and cut down or uprooted orchards. Twenty-one Jews were killed, the British shot dead 140 Arabs, and thirty-three British soldiers were killed in clashes with Arab gunmen. The British despatched the Peel Commission, which recommended the absorption of most of Palestine into Transjordan, continued British control of such strategic points as Haifa and Lydda, and a small Jewish state. While David Ben-Gurion, Labour Party leader, accepted partition as the basis for future negotiations, radical Arab leaders including the exiled mufti's nephew decided upon violence, telling the British to choose 'between our friendship and the Jews'. At this point the Nazis became interested in resisting the creation of a Jewish state, using their short-wave radio transmitter at Zeesen outside Berlin to beam a mixture of Arabic music, Koranic quotations and their own brand of racial anti-Semitism to the Arab world. The Nazi contribution, as mediated by the mufti in his various writings, was to transform Muslim disdain for Jews – whom the Muslims had ruled for centuries – into Muslim fear of Jews as powerful global conspirators with a money-smoothed line to the ears of the world's most powerful rulers.

In the remoter countryside the British were confronted by armed bands, often fifty to seventy strong, which ambushed trucks, cut telegraph wires and blew up railway track with discarded First World War artillery shells wired up as improvised explosive devices. One four-man team blew up the railway from Lydda to Haifa. Its leader was Hassan Salameh, a barefoot peasant boy from Kulleh who by early adulthood had a reputation as a tough guy, as symbolised by his nickname 'the Cut-throat'. Although his three cousins were killed in the gunfight that ensued after the railway attack, Salameh lived to fight another day, forming his own guerrilla band under the patronage of Aref Abd-el-Razek. The legend of his escape led to his being dubbed 'Sheikh'. Sheikh Hassan's army was a motley crew, clad in white robes with criss-crossed ammunition belts and colourful keffiyeh headdresses, bearing an assortment of British, German, Italian and Turkish rifles. These bands menaced isolated Jewish settlements, while practising robbery and extortion against fellow Arabs. Their ranks were made up of villagers, some of them part-time fighters who returned home each day, others full-timers armed and paid by the Higher Arab Committee, with the occasional contribution from Mussolini who was keen to cause trouble for the British to distract from his war in Abyssinia. This composition gave the fighting a seasonal character as it waxed and waned according to whether the fighters were needed to bring in the harvest. Wider Arab nationalism was evident as two hundred Iraqis, Jordanians and Syrians arrived to aid the armed uprising under a former Ottoman Iraqi officer Fawzi al-Qawuqji. These were effective fighters since they were capable of waging a six-hour battle with British troops who eventually called in RAF support. They even managed to shoot down one of the British aircraft. By the autumn of 1937 most of the uplands of Palestine were in rebel hands. In September Arab terrorists killed the district commissioner for Galilee who had shepherded the Peel commissioners around Palestine.[10]

The British response to this Arab Revolt was brutal and based on techniques imported from the Indian North West Frontier and Sudan.[11] Between 1937 and 1939 British military courts executed a hundred Arabs and imposed many life sentences, while captured rebels were detained in special camps. An identity-card system was introduced to impede rebel movement on the country's roads. When Arab guerrillas briefly occupied Jerusalem's Old City, the British used Arab human shields to wrest back control. They constructed roads to penetrate remote mountainous regions. They used aircraft to bomb and strafe concentrations of guerrillas, although the RAF unaccountably broke off a raid on a guerrilla general assembly at Dir Assana. British troops routinely demolished houses and orange groves wherever they were fired upon, applying the doctrine of collective reprisals that was commonplace in other colonies. To prevent attacks on trains, male relatives of local guerrilla commanders were placed on inspection trolleys attached to the front of each train, a tactic that proved an effective deterrent. Suspected terrorists were so roughly handled that the local Anglican clergy was moved to protest at practices that were christened 'duffing up' after an especially robust police officer called Douglas Duff. In addition to giving the British its intelligence on these Arab bands, the Haganah undertook its own patrols, based on the maxim that the best defence was attack. The chiliastic Christian soldier captain Orde Wingate advised and led Special

Night Squads of Haganah troops in Lower Galilee, whose ranks included such future military eminences as Moshe Dayan and Yigal Allon.

There was much about the Arab rebels that was brutal too, a fact often overlooked in literatures that excoriate the Irgun and the Stern Gang on the other side, perhaps as a reaction to the air of Jewish moralism which claims that Zionist forces always fought the good fight. The Arab insurgents set up a Court of the Revolt to hand out summary justice to those who did not get the message, including informers, Arabs who sold land to Jews, political moderates and policemen. The punishments were floggings and execution. Capture sometimes involved being dropped into pits filled with scorpions and snakes, or one's corpse left lying in the road with a shoe in the mouth as a symbol of disgrace. Financial levies on ordinary villagers by these bands gave way to outright extortion. As moderate Arab leaders learned to go about with bodyguards, village sheikhs formed their own defensive groups to ward off these Arab nationalist bands, a few of which were covertly operated by the British to discredit the wider enemy in the eyes of the local population. The guerrillas also made use of the British by informing on opponents in order to have the British liquidate them. Sometimes the sheikhs even asked their Jewish neighbours for advice and support as fellow victims of these depredations. With British help, moderate Arab leaders paid one of the rebel leaders to defect and to lead so-called 'peace bands' which fought the nationalist guerrillas in a war that began to assume an intra-Arab character. Out of six thousand Arab casualties of the Revolt, only fifteen hundred were slain by the British or the Haganah; the rest were done in by fellow Arabs. The Revolt petered out amid endless blood feuds and vendettas.[12]

The Peel Commission and the Arab Revolt also divided the Zionists. While the Jewish Agency and the socialist Zionists wanted to work with the British and condemned Jewish terrorism against Arabs, the Revisionists rejected attempts to renege on promises to the Jewish people. Their extreme supporters in Palestine decided to meet Arab terror with terror, meaning the indiscriminate killing of innocent civilians. Parallel with the Arab Revolt against the British, Arab and Jewish terrorists targeted each other's civilian populations. Throughout the summer of 1938 there were vicious killings by Arab and Jewish extremists, including the murder of Arabs who worked for Jews. On 29 June an Arab terrorist threw a bomb into a Jewish wedding in Tiberias; on 25 July thirty-nine Arabs were killed when a Jewish terrorist bomb exploded in Haifa's

melon market. It should be carefully noted that both the Jewish Agency
and the Hisradut trades union were explicit in their condemnation of the
'miserable (Jewish) cowards' who executed these attacks.

At a time when the major and minor powers, led by the United States,
were doing their best to impede the flight of European Jews from
Nazism at the 1938 Evian Conference, the 1939 British 'Black Paper' (the
sinister name for a class of policy documents that were routinely white in
colour) proposed drastic cuts to the number of legal Jewish emigrants to
Palestine – effectively to twenty-five thousand a year – while promising
to institute Arab majority rule. There were also to be restrictions
on Jewish purchases of land beyond existing settlements. The British
calculation was that with war looming in Europe, the Jews would have no
alternative other than to back the Western Allies, while Arab loyalties
might be biddable to the Rome–Berlin Axis, into whose camp the
exiled mufti (as a dedicated anti-Semite) steadily drifted. He fled French-
controlled Syria for Iraqi Baghdad, where he was joined by Hassan
Salameh, whose wife gave birth there to a son named Ali Hassan
Salameh, the future leader of Black September. Since Jewish illegal
immigration continued unabated – with the added urgency of the
extension of Hitler's sway – the British retaliated by halting all legal
immigration to Palestine. Illegal immigrants who did reach its shores
were interned, with a view to repatriating them after the duration, while
mean minded efforts were made by the Foreign Office to prevent Jews
seeking access to Greek or Turkish merchant shipping if they reached
the mouth of the Danube. The Haganah established an intelligence arm
called Mossad le-Aliyah Bet to facilitate transport of illegal immigrants
by sea.

The outbreak of war between Britain and Nazi Germany saw some
curious reversals of allegiance. The mufti was forced to flee first Iraq and
then Persia, as British forces invaded. After a spell hiding in the Japanese
embassy in Teheran, Italian agents spirited him to Rome, where the Duce
installed him in the Villa Colonna and promised to liberate Palestine.
A written plea for aid submitted to the Nazi Führer led to his translation
to Berlin and a new home in the splendid Bellevue Palace. In November
1940 he had an agreeable meeting with Hitler, who promised to make
him a German Lawrence of Arabia. The Nazi leader evidently admired
his guest in the red fez: 'He looks like a peaceful angel, but under his robe
hides a real bull!' Not forgetting his friends, the mufti had the Germans
fly Hassan Salameh from Aleppo to Berlin, where he and others received

military training. In the absence of volunteers, however, no large Arab
Legion materialised, although the mufti helped recruit a Bosnian Muslim
SS division to fight in the Balkans. Only when in 1944 the British formed
the Jewish Brigade did Hitler decide to facilitate the mufti's scaled-down
schemes. In November that year Hassan Salameh and Abdul Latif were
dropped with three German agents from a Heinkel-111 in the vicinity of
Jericho. Along with bags of banknotes and gold coins, their equipment
included ten cylinders of poison, the intention being to contaminate the
water supplying Tel Aviv, thereby killing or forcing out its inhabitants.
Latif and the Germans were captured; Salameh limped off injured to
fight another day.

By contrast, the mainstream Yishuv rallied to the Allied cause. The
Haganah was quietly refashioned from a local defence force into a model
army, with crop-dusting light aircraft standing in for an air force. Elite
Palmach commandos took part in Allied operations against the Vichy
French in Lebanon and Syria. It was on one such operation that the
young soldier Moshe Dayan lost an eye. In total, some twenty-seven
thousand Jews served with the British armed forces, some in the famous
Jewish Brigade, while the corresponding figure for Arab Palestinians
was twelve thousand. This disparity in military experience would prove
decisive in future. While supporting the British war effort, the Haganah
simultaneously tried to circumvent British restrictions on Jewish
immigration. This resulted in the tragedy of the *Patria*.

This was a French liner which the British intended to use to ship to
Mauritius illegal migrants who had arrived off Haifa in the *Milos*
and *Pacific* in November 1940. The Haganah determined to disable the
Patria in Haifa harbour, but used too large a consignment of explosives.
The ship sank in fifteen minutes, drowning two hundred and fifty
refugees. While the British decided on compassionate grounds to allow
the nineteen hundred survivors of the *Patria* to remain in Palestine –
against, it has to be noted, the vehement protests of general Wavell – they
resolved to deport a further seventeen hundred refugees newly arrived
on a ship called the *Atlantic*. Only Churchill's personal intervention
saved the day for those on the *Patria*.

Although the leaders of the Yishuv and Haganah – and indeed
Jabotinsky until his sudden death in New York in 1940 – supported
the British war effort, this was not true of the outright terrorist
groups. The poet–gunman and romantic elitist Avraham Stern – who
adopted the name Yair in honour of the leader of the ancient uprising

against the Romans at Masada – believed that 'alliances will be formed with anyone who is interested in helping Eretz Israel'. Strategic realities and romantic fervour inclined him to strange alliances. With Italian and then German forces advancing through Egypt, an Axis victory seemed certain. To this end, Stern tried to contact Mussolini, in the hope that Italian conquest of the Middle East might expedite the formation of a Jewish state in Palestine. This was to have corporatist features, with Jerusalem placed under the authority of a Vatican which was not consulted about these schemes. Failing that, Stern put out feelers to Nazi Germany via Vichy authorities in Syria, with a view to securing a pact that would allow a 'national totalitarian' Jewish state once the Führer had defeated the British. Underlying these bizarre gambits was a specious distinction between the evanescent 'enemy' (Britain) and the historical 'persecutor' (Nazi Germany), and the delusion that the Jews could use the latter to see off the former. This was too clever by half. Efforts to reconstrue these contacts with the Germans as part of some 'rescue' endeavour on behalf of Europe's Jews are unconvincing.[13]

Having already countenanced a modern Israeli postage stamp, Stern is also commemorated in the name of a small town populated by many of the current Israeli ruling elite. Admirers of the Stern Gang like to situate it within the deep stream of Jewish history, which made its violence seem both historically determined and divinely ordained: 'Because there is a religion of redemption – a religion of the war of liberation/Whoever accepts it – be blessed; whoever denies it – be cursed' ran one of Stern's poems. The British were Nazis and the leadership of the Zionist Yishuv a latterday *Judenrat* (the councils that administered Jewish existence in the wartime ghettos).[14]

Deceitful mythologies apart, Stern was responsible for a handful of fanatics, perhaps three hundred at most, their identity oscillating between gangsters, guerrillas and terrorists depending on the nature of specific activities. Their favoured tactics were bank robbery and assassination; half of their victims were fellow Jews whom they regarded as collaborators with the British, a proportion reflected in the 'disciplinary' killings conducted by many subsequent terrorist groups such as the FLN in Algeria. Both the British CID and the Haganah endeavoured to track down Stern himself. Eventually he was surrounded in a house, where a CID officer called Geoffrey Morton found him hiding in a closet. Despite being unarmed, the handcuffed Stern was shot dead, although Morton claimed he was shot trying to jump out of a window.

Many people think he was assassinated. Sternist death threats would haunt Morton's future postings in the Caribbean and East Africa. The remnants of the Stern Gang, including the future (seventh) prime minister of Israel, Yitzhak Shamir, who adopted the nom de guerre 'Michael' in honour of Sinn Féin's Michael Collins, took the name Lehi, shorthand for Lohamei Herut Israel or 'Fighters for the Freedom of Israel', and pronounced like 'Lechi' in Hebrew, although 'Stern Gang' tended to stick in the minds of their British and Jewish opponents.

Meanwhile Menachem Begin, Irgun's new leader, was nearing the end of a modern odyssey. Having moved from Poland to Vilnius in Lithuania to escape the Nazis, he was arrested by Stalin's secret police and shipped to a gulag; on his release he joined the Anders army, the Polish force which Stalin licensed after the German invasion of the USSR. Begin, the future sixth prime minister of Israel and Nobel laureate, was a young Polish-Jewish lawyer and Revisionist activist, who as a deskbound corporal in the Anders army finally reached Palestine via Iran and Iraq. Although he was a leading Betari ideologue, it was his lack of military experience and Polish origins that paradoxically inclined the military leaders of Irgun in Palestine to appoint him chief. There was another reason to choose this colourless and humourless little man, 'that bespectacled petty Polish solicitor' as Ben-Gurion described him in one of his politer formulations. Having never been to Palestine, Begin was invisible to the British CID who had no record of him. Like Stern, always dressed in a suit and tie, regardless of the heat, Begin lived with his wife an unexceptional middle-class life, where in between meetings with Irgun commanders he read the newspapers, learned English by listening to the BBC and issued his florid, hate-filled communiqués.

Begin's hatred of the British was implacable and his rhetoric intemperate. His Polish background inclined him to the view that they were unreliable allies, while their restrictions on Jewish immigration to Palestine even as the Nazis and their confederates annihilated Jewish communities across Europe confirmed his view that they tacitly sought the Jews' destruction. This charge, based on the conceit that Christians secretly wanted the Jews to disappear, was as unfair as it was outrageous, although one hears it repeated from time to time. Whereas his men were 'soldiers', the British were 'terrorists', or 'tsarists', 'Hitlerites' and 'Nazis': 'The [British] terrorist government in Eretz Israel conducts an unheard-of terror campaign. This terror is hidden behind laws, statutes, regulations and "books" [the White Paper, a policy document on Jewish immigration to Palestine]. Great Britain conquered the land with the help of the Jews [the Yishuv]. With their help it has received legitimacy ... They are worse than the Tsars. The Tsars oppressed their nation, but the British help to annihilate the nation.' As for the Arabs, Begin was so contemptuous of them that he thought that with the British defeated they would simply run away.

Under his leadership Irgun carried out probing attacks on the sinews of British power in Palestine, where the British had a hundred thousand soldiers as well as a substantial MI5 (Defence Security Office) and CID presence. Begin could not destroy this imposing apparatus, but he could damage its morale, and tarnish its international image, by provoking the British into actions they would come to regret. Unlike Lehi, which carried out forty-two assassinations, the Irgun was keen to avoid killing British soldiers or assassinating senior Mandate figures; instead it hit land and tax offices. Begin's band grew from about 250 to 800 fighters between 1944 and 1948. It also became more mainstream in the sense that as, in the wake of Alamein and Stalingrad, the British reverted to more inflexible policies towards the Jews, even elements of the Haganah and Palmach began to share Begin's desire for an anti-Mandatory revolt. This was exactly what Begin had anticipated. His forces would act as the catalyst for a wider revolt involving the more mainstream Zionists in the Yishuv, not least by provoking the British into indiscriminate repression against myriad Zionist groups whose precise coloration and contours they barely understood.

Initially, Irgun and Lehi terrorist activities triggered a diametrically opposite response from the leadership of the Yishuv. In 1944 two Lehi gunmen assassinated lord Moyne (and his driver) in Cairo. Moyne was a very wealthy member of the Guinness dynasty, and a close personal friend of Churchill. He and Churchill had founded an exclusive dining club called the Other Club, while Churchill's wife was an honoured guest on a converted ferry that Moyne used to cruise the Pacific in search of rare lizards. Killing such a figure brought down on the heads of Lehi the condemnation of Irgun – 'irresponsible, despicable, a deed soiled in treachery' – while the socialist Zionists of the Yishuv decided to help the British eliminate the 'Fascists' and 'Nazis' of Lehi and Irgun.

To that end, Ben-Gurion and his colleagues declared a 'hunting season' (the Sezon) on 'the gangsters and gangs of Irgun and Lehi', although the sneaking admiration they had for the authentically Hebrew Lehi meant that most of their efforts were directed against the less lunatic

Revisionists of Irgun who constituted the greater political threat. Ben-Gurion and the Jewish Agency did not mince their words: 'The Jewish community is called upon to spew forth all the members of this harmful, destructive gang, to deny them any shelter or haven, not to give in to their threats, and to extend to the authorities all the necessary assistance to prevent terror acts and to wipe out [the terror] organisations, for this is a matter of life and death.'[15]

A 250-strong squad of Palmach commandos was let loose to track down key terrorist figures, while buffer mechanisms were created to hand information on five hundred Irgun and Lehi members to the British CID. Apparently the future mayor of Jerusalem, Teddy Kollek, identified a number of Irgun members, including the father of a current Israeli cabinet minister, to his handlers in MI5. None of this effort managed to snare Begin. Never having been directed at those who had ordered the killing of Moyne, notably Yitshak Shamir, the open season was called off. It should be emphasised that fellow Jews had sought to crush what are all too casually described as 'Jewish terrorists'; such opposition by fellow Arabs was a rarer phenomenon in the concurrent history of Arab terrorism.

While Begin continued to set the overall direction of Irgun strategy, operational control was in the hands of Amichai 'Gidi' Paglin, a former socialist Zionist who had crossed over to the dark side. Even as the war in Europe ended, Irgun stepped up attacks on oil pipelines and police stations in Palestine. The Cairo–Haifa railway was blown up and banks were robbed in Tel Aviv. Paradoxically, the landslide victory of the Labour Party in Britain, which continued to implement the 1939 White Paper strategy, had the effect of temporarily bringing Irgun and the mainstream left-wing Zionists closer together in an ad-hoc military alliance.

In October 1945, the Haganah, Irgun and Lehi established a joint Hebrew Resistance Movement, the first attempt to co-ordinate the Zionist underground in Palestine. This was subject to poor political control – the X-Committee under the chairmanship of a rabbi Fishman. While Irgun wanted to pursue a broad assault on the Mandatory power, the Haganah wished to concentrate on those assets – such as coastal radar stations – which directly impeded illegal immigration. In other words, the Haganah was combating a policy while Begin's group was at war with the Mandatory regime as a whole, a strategy that included seeking support from the Soviet Union in the developing Cold War. That chimed with those kibbutzim who had gleefully followed the progress of Stalin's legions on maps pinned to the wall.[16] All that held them together was a desire not to be left out at the birth of Jewish statehood. Between October 1946 and April 1947, some eighty British personnel were killed, as were forty-two Jews and an unknown number of Arabs. The British commander in chief, field marshal Bernard Montgomery, advocated the most brutal response, including the assassination of the top fifty Yishuv leaders, a recommendation that the British cabinet vetoed. Since the Haganah bore the brunt of British reprisals for Irgun operations, it decided to scale down the latter's more spectacular operations. Specifically, in June the Haganah discovered that Irgun had dug a tunnel leading to the Citrus House in Tel Aviv, a British security zone, where it planned to detonate an enormous quantity of explosives after giving the British due warning to evacuate. Haganah succeeded in removing most of the charges, although some of its members were killed when the remainder detonated accidentally. By way of tribute, British personnel attended their funerals.

Irgun and Lehi terrorism inevitably provoked a tough British response, which included the beating and torture of terrorist suspects. On the night of 29 June 1946 – known as Black Sabbath because it was a Friday – seventeen thousand British paratroops imposed a curfew on the Yishuv and made strenuous efforts to arrest its leaders, who were then held in Jerusalem's Latrun prison. Teams of soldiers trawled for arms in thirty kibbutzes and settlements. Confiscated papers of the Yishuv found their way to the British military headquarters in the King David hotel. In the eyes of the wider world, and especially the United States, these actions were part of a continuum that also consisted of a British Labour government detaining concentration-camp survivors in Displaced Persons' Camps to thwart their desire to go to Eretz Israel.[17]

These actions, and the rebarbative tone of foreign minister Ernest Bevin when speaking on Jewish questions, set the scene for Operation Chick – Begin and Paglin's plan to blow up Jerusalem's King David hotel, one floor of which housed British military headquarters. This was the country's most luxurious hotel, at whose bar British officers could relax over their pink gins. Although some Israelis seek to qualify this operation by pointing to telephoned warnings, in fact it was an act of indiscriminate terror, qualitatively different from the assassination of key figures like Moyne.

At 12.10 p.m. on 22 July 1946, a truck pulled up near the hotel's basement. Several men dressed as Arabs unloaded milk churns and placed them below the floor containing the offices of the Palestine Government Secretariat. A Royal Signals officer who came upon the group was shot twice in the stomach. The fourteen or fifteen terrorists fled in a truck and several cars. Shortly afterwards, a colossal explosion demolished a wing of the hotel, killing ninety-one people, many of them buried under falling masonry. The victims included the postmaster-general of Palestine, several Arab and Jewish administrative staff, and twenty British soldiers. Many others sustained horrific injuries, as one clerk had his face cut almost in half by shards of flying glass. The terrorist bosses claimed that they had given the British adequate warning. A young Irgun courier, Adina Hay-Nissan, had made three calls to the British Command, the French consulate and the *Palestine Post*, warning the British to evacuate the hotel immediately. However, her bosses knew full well that there had been so many bomb warnings that the British had become blasé; in this instance the terrorists had also shortened the time between warning and explosion to thirty minutes, to stop the British salvaging confiscated Irgun papers. In fact, the explosion occurred within fifteen or twenty minutes of the warning, leaving little time for the building to be evacuated. The Jewish Agency called the bombing a 'dastardly crime' committed by 'a gang of desperadoes'. It served to end the intra-Zionist co-operation symbolised by the Hebrew Resistance Movement. At the 22nd Zionist Congress in December 1946, veteran leader Chaim Weizmann bravely castigated American Zionists for advocating resistance in Tel Aviv from the comfort and safety of New York and called the murder of Moyne 'the greatest disaster to overtake us in the last few years'.

Regardless of widespread abhorrence among Jews for these atrocities, Irgun pressed on with its anti-British terror campaign. The British introduced the practice of corporal punishment, which may have been acceptable in Africa or Asia but was an outrage against people who had vivid memories of such practices in Nazi concentration camps. When the British army flogged persons caught in possession of arms, Irgun retaliated in December 1946 by seizing a major and three sergeants and giving them eighteen strokes of the cane. The practice stopped. On 1 March 1947 Irgun blew up the British Officers' Club in Jerusalem, killing fourteen officers. In April, it smuggled hand grenades into a prison where two of its members were awaiting execution, the intention being that they would throw these at the British CID. When a rabbi appeared to read them the last rites, the two condemned men simply blew themselves up. A major raid was also launched on Acre prison to free Irgun and Lehi fighters. Disguised as British soldiers, Irgun men blocked the road to the prison and then bluffed their way inside, where their imprisoned comrades had already used smuggled explosives to blow the locks off their cell doors. In a fire-fight with British squaddies returning from a swim, nine of the thirty-nine escaped prisoners were shot and six of their rescuers captured. The American screenwriter Ben Hecht outraged the British by taking out a full-page advertisement addressed to 'my brave friends' in which he wrote: 'Every time you blow up a British arsenal, or wreck a British jail, or send a British railroad train sky high, or rob a British bank, or let go with your guns and bombs at British betrayers and invaders of your homeland, the Jews of America make a little holiday in their hearts.'[18]

Three of the attacking force, Avshalom Habib, Yaacov Weis and Meir Necker, were condemned to death and executed. Irgun kidnapped two British policemen as hostages to stop the executions, although the presence of an Anglo-American Commission in Palestine, which took testimony from Begin himself, led to their reluctant release. Begin then ordered the kidnapping of two British army sergeants, Clifford Martin and Marvin Paice, who following the execution of the condemned Irgun men were hanged in a factory basement near Natanya. One of their corpses was booby-trapped and both were left hanging in nearby woods, where a British officer was injured trying to retrieve them. According to Begin, the two sergeants were 'criminals that belong to the British–Nazi criminal army of occupation'. Such acts led some British officials to extend their animosity towards Zionist terrorists to Jews in general, just as many Israelis would come to hate all Arabs. 'It's quite time I left Palestine,' wrote Ivan Lloyd Phillips. 'I never had any sympathy with Zionist aspirations, but now I'm fast becoming anti-Jewish in my whole approach to this difficult problem, & it is very difficult to keep a balance & view matters objectively with a growing (a very real feeling) of personal antipathy.'[19] Under these circumstances discipline collapsed, giving further impetus to conflict. On 31 July British soldiers shot dead five innocent Jewish people and wounded twenty-four others, in an act of retaliatory indiscipline that would typify other colonial terrorist conflicts. British personnel had to fortify their living quarters, which resembled fortresses ringed with barbed wire and guarded by Bren gunners. Unremitting terrorist attacks wore down the will of the British people to remain in Palestine, a subject remote from their hearts during a harsh winter when they were experiencing a fuel crisis – although pictures of the two hanged sergeants published in every newspaper gave them the temporary warmth of outrage.

Although anti-Semitic reprisals were negligible in Britain, any international sympathy the British might have expected was cancelled out by the callous and unfeeling attitude of the Labour government to illegal migrants, a major error of public diplomacy given the intense United States interest in these events under a new president, Harry Truman, who was less capable of double-dealing both Arabs and Jews than his illustrious predecessor and all too aware that most Jews voted Democrat.

The manipulation of international public opinion was a crucial part of the struggle between Zionists and British and the former won. In July 1947 a ship called the *President Warfield* (subsequently renamed *Exodus 47*) arrived off Haifa overflowing with five thousand German and Polish camp survivors. This voyage was set up to attract the maximum publicity. The clever move would have been to allow them to disembark on humanitarian grounds. Instead, the short-fused Bevin decided to 'teach the Jews a lesson' and had the ship intercepted by the Royal Navy, which managed to kill three of the passengers. At that point, Bevin instructed that the Jews should be put on three ships to take them, not to internment in Cyprus, as was normal, but back to Sète near Marseilles, where the British encouraged them to leave their ships while Haganah activists told them to stay on board. Newsreel footage was an essential part of a propaganda war in which the passengers were encouraged to hang Union Jacks daubed with swastikas from the portholes. In the end a ship called *Empire Rival* took them to Hamburg where, despite having been well treated on the voyage, they were herded off by British soldiers using rifle butts, hoses and tear gas. As the book and the film readily indicated, the saga of *Exodus 47* was a major propaganda victory for Zionism.[20]

Revisionist Zionist terrorism alone did not cause the British to relinquish their Palestinian Mandate. Britain's resources were overstretched and exhausted by global war against Germans, Italians and Japanese, not to speak of the concurrent reconquest of South-east Asia to stop Communists and nationalists stepping into the vacuum left by the Japanese. Indeed, five hundred sergeants from the Palestinian police were rapidly redeployed to Malaya. The conflict between Arabs and Jews seemed not only intractable, but damaging to Britain's international image since the violence took place beneath the spotlight of world opinion and involved a people whose victimhood had recently been revealed through shocking newsreels and the Nuremberg trials. As Begin himself put it: 'Arms were our weapons of attack; transparency was the shield of our defence.'[21]

In November 1947 the UN voted to partition Palestine, with British withdrawal scheduled for mid-May 1948. Neither the British nor the UN helped the situation by failing to make adequate arrangements for the transition. It therefore became exceptionally bloody even before it had started, as neither Arab nor Jewish extreme nationalists accepted this solution. In the fortnight following the UN decision, Arab terrorists killed eighty Jews. The first victims were passengers on a bus heading from Natanya to Jerusalem. As it turned a sharp bend the bus driver saw a tall Arab man standing in the road who signalled him to stop. As the bus halted the Arab man pulled out a submachine gun and raked the bus with gunfire, while comrades opened up from both sides of the road. Five of the passengers were killed, including a young woman on her way to her wedding. The leader of the attack was Hassan Salameh, whom the Beirut-based mufti had appointed commander of guerrilla forces in central Palestine. Vowing during his intermittent public appearances that 'Palestine will become a bloodbath,' Salameh launched several deadly attacks on lone buses and taxis plying the roads that were the Yishuv's most vulnerable point. In January 1948 Salameh ambushed a food convoy in the village of Yazoor, using a dead dog packed with explosives to stop the Jewish police escort, seven of whom were then bludgeoned and knifed to death.

Reasonably enough the Haganah decided to deter Arab terrorists, warning 'Expel those among you who want blood to be shed, and accept the hand which is outstretched to you in brotherhood and peace.' This was usually done by killing individuals, including a night-time assault on Hassan Salameh's Yazoor headquarters, led by future prime minister Rabin, which resulted in the building being demolished with explosive charges. Salameh was elsewhere. The Haganah was also not above attacks with wanton consequences for civilian bystanders, notably the attack on the Najada headquarters in Jerusalem's Semiramis hotel, which killed the Spanish consul and eleven Arab Christians.

In dealing with Palestinian Arabs, Irgun refused to confine its response to the targeting of bona-fide Arab killers; instead, it tossed a grenade into an Arab vegetable market near the Damascus gate, killing twelve Arab civilians. On 5 January 1948, two Stern Gang members parked a truck loaded with oranges in an Arab quarter of Jaffa, pausing to have a coffee before leaving on foot for Tel Aviv. The resulting explosion killed more than twenty Arabs. On 14 January, British deserters and former German POWs working for the Arab cause exploded a postal van in the Jewish quarter of Haifa, killing fifty Jewish civilians. British army deserters also demolished the offices of the *Palestine Post*. Towards the end of February, further British deserters exploded three vehicle bombs in a night-time attack on a Jerusalem residential street, killing fifty-two Jews as they slept. On 11 March, ten days after the establishment of a Jewish Provisional Council, an Arab terrorist used a car bomb which killed thirteen people in the courtyard of the Jewish Agency.

Aided and abetted by fanatical supporters in the US and Europe who were seeking to downgrade Irgun from a politico-military movement into their own paramilitary arm, the right-wing Zionist underground resisted attempts to absorb it into the new Israeli Defence Force or IDF that was preparing to fight a war with the Arabs the moment the British relinquished control. It also attempted to make the shift from terrorist attacks to regular military activity in the immediate context of the battle for control of roads and strategic villages being waged between Haganah and Arab fighters. Deir Yassin was a medium-sized Arab village west of Jerusalem. Its inhabitants were described by the Haganah intelligence service as 'loyal to the peace arrangements' they had already initiated with the Jews. With tacit Haganah approval, Irgun and Lehi forces numbering 120 men attacked Deir Yassin at dawn on 9 April 1948. They met with some fire from Iraqi volunteers in the schoolhouse; five of their number were killed and thirty-one wounded. Having failed to take the village cleanly and expeditiously, the Irgun–Lehi forces – already vengeful because of earlier defeats at the hands of the Arab Legion elsewhere – ran amok in Deir Yassin, firing and throwing hand grenades into houses. Depending on whom you believe, between 120 and 254 Arabs, mainly women and children, were killed in this armed riot by Jewish terrorists masquerading as professional soldiers. Both Irgun (which wanted to spread fear) and the Palestinians (who wished to bolster Arab resistance) exaggerated the number of casualties. What is not in doubt, for there is contemporary evidence from a Red Cross official and the Haganah officer Meir Pa'il, is that there was some sort of massacre.

Prime minister Ben-Gurion immediately apologised to the king of

Jordan for this massacre. Attempts by American and European supporters of the Irgun to arm the latter so as to give it a military capacity
independent of the Haganah and emerging IDF resulted in the *Altalena*
affair (the ship was named after Jabotinsky's old nom de plume). This
involved the government of Ben-Gurion asserting its legitimacy by using
artillery to sink the *Altalena* before its arms consignment could be used
for the madcap adventures of Irgun. Firing at a range of 350 yards, a
cannon hit the ship's hold and killed fourteen members of the Irgun.
Begin inveighed hysterically against Ben-Gurion from the underground
radio, while the latter could never bring himself even to say his opponent's name. Ben-Gurion and Begin anathematised and cursed each other
well into the 1950s about the sinking of the ship. These curses endured,
several decades later costing prime minister Yitzhak Rabin his life, for he
had also been involved in firing on the *Altalena*.

As Arabs and Jews went to war in the interval heedlessly caused by
the end of the Mandate and the UN's failure to implement adequate
transitional arrangements, some seventy thousand leading Palestinians
fled, including virtually all of their leaders. The Zionists enjoyed several
advantages over the Arabs. They had coherent and tight command
structures, more recent military experience, interior lines of communication, and good intelligence, including the ability to tap phones used by
their opponents. By contrast, the Palestinian leadership was tainted
by cowardice and rife with internecine feuding, even as control of the
Arab campaign passed to neighbouring Arab states, each with ulterior
objectives.

The Palestinians did not flock to fight for their own cause, as only
twelve thousand volunteered to fight alongside regular Arab forces. As
Deir Yassin already indicates, these were the months when the dragon's
teeth of 'ancient' hatreds were sown. In April 1948 the Haganah had
another go at Hassan Salameh, attacking a four-storey concrete building
in an orange grove where he and his men were sheltering. After a fierce
gun battle, the building was blown up with eight hundred pounds of
dynamite. Salameh was not among the casualties. Nonetheless, Haganah
activity was taking its toll on the Palestinian leadership, with the
commander in chief, Abd el-Kader el-Husseini, shot dead after a chance
encounter with an alert Haganah sentry. Hassan Salameh seems to have
had intimations of mortality, for on his appointment as Kader's successor he told his wife: 'If I am killed I want my son to carry on my
battle.' As invading Arab armies began to dominate the struggle with the

Zionists, Salameh calculated that he needed to reassert the Palestinian contribution through dramatic military action. In May 1948 Irgun fighters had taken an Arab village called Ras el-Ein, a former crusader fortress whose wells supplied Jerusalem and Tel Aviv below. Salameh led three hundred fighters to retake the village, which they did to shouts of 'Allahu Akhbar!' As the Irgun men fled, leaving eleven dead behind, their mortar fire hit a small group of the attackers, killing Salameh's cousin and wounding his nephew. The sheikh himself received mortal injuries as pieces of shrapnel penetrated his lungs. He died in a Ramleh hospital a few hours later, leaving the battle for his son to fight.

Although it is far from clear whether the leaderless Palestinians fled or were driven out in accordance with the Haganah's master-plan, some 650,000 Palestinians left in a very short space of time that seems inexplicable unless they were terrified. Whether they had reason to be terrified is a contentious matter. The Zionists acted swiftly and ruthlessly wherever they encountered anything less than unconditional surrender. Some 370 villages were deliberately erased and their inhabitants expelled, although some of the claims regarding outright massacres have become the subject of libel suits by old soldiers directed at the Israeli 'New Historians' who are making them.[22] It is also important to note that even future Palestinian terrorist leaders, such as Abu Iyad, who at the age of fifteen fled Haifa by boat, partly blame overblown propaganda – about rape and disembowelling – put about by the Palestinians themselves, and the false expectation that after a brief interval Arab armies would enter the fray to restore the Palestinians to their homes.[23] Only 160,000 Palestinians remained in situ, while nearly a million found themselves in refugee camps, notably in the Gaza Strip and the West Bank, a problem for the UN and neighbouring Arab governments down to the present. Jewish immigrants were settled in places whose names were deliberately 'Hebraised', particularly along the borders with Arab states with which Israel concluded an uneasy ceasefire. Although it is often forgotten in a discussion where sympathies tend to be unilateral, in the next few years some 850,000 Jews fled Egypt, Iraq, Morocco, Tunisia and Yemen, often under duress as rulers made wholly unwarranted connections between Jews and Zionists and mobs perpetuated atrocities. In the case of Iraq, the Jewish Agency may have helped chaos along by covertly exploding bombs in the vicinity of Baghdad synagogues to encourage a general atmosphere of paranoia. Many of these Mizrahi Jews faced an uncongenial future in Israel.[24] Beyond questions of who did what to whom, the

fact is that two peoples with an acute sense of dispossession and persecution would covet the same small territory. In the case of the Palestinians,
some talismanic item – a rusty key or yellowing land deeds – would
give credence to the legends that the older generations would inculcate in
young people, a process of 'retraumatisation' that was all too evident
among their Israeli opponents, as the European Holocaust went from
being something the heroic sabras (a term derived from the prickly pear
with a sweet centre to describe native-born Israeli Jews) viewed as a
source of embarrassment to becoming a central feature of Israeli national
identity.[25]

II THE BATTLE OF THE CASBAH

While this conflict was developing by the Levantine shores of the
Mediterranean, its North African littoral witnessed a vicious eight-
year colonial struggle which had a major influence on future national
liberation movements that resorted to terrorism, while offering many
negative instances of how not to combat these which are being studied by
the US military in Iraq today. This struggle was played out in Algeria –
with Tunisia and Morocco one of the countries of the Maghreb, that
immense coastal plain stretching from the Mediterranean to the interior
mountain ranges.

France had conquered Algeria between 1830 and 1870 in a series of
murderous campaigns led by marshal Bugeaud, which one of his main
supporters, Alexis de Tocqueville, thought might toughen up the degenerate French of his time. Although there was the usual rhetoric
of France's *mission civilisatrice*, Algeria was run in the interests of the
tough-minded European colonial minority, including many Corsican,
Italian, Maltese and Spanish settlers as well as Frenchmen, rather than
the majority Muslim population of Arabs and Berbers who were in a
condition of tutelage. Within this European minority a tiny wealthy elite
took over most of the fertile lands, which were converted from cereal
production to viticulture, with Algeria becoming the third-largest wine
producer in the world. The urban centres may have gleamed with white
stone and sparkling fountains, but the non-European rural population
derived little benefit from this. Poverty and a high birth rate forced many
to seek work in the cities or in metropolitan France. There some of the

more thoughtful Muslim emigrants imbibed democratic and egalitarian principles not evident in the French colonial regime in Algeria, and began to organise among the migrant proletariat in their favourite cafés. They contrasted an abstract France of universal principles with the real France of their experience, and found the latter wanting.

In 1926 Messali Hadj founded a pan-Maghrebi movement called the Etoile Nord-Africaine. Constantly harassed by the French authorities, this was relaunched in 1937 with a narrower focus as the Parti du Peuple Algérien. Simultaneously, those in favour of a puritanical form of Islam organised as the Association of Algerian Ulamas under sheikh Ben Badis. There were also Algerian Communists, organised as a separate party from 1935 onwards, as well as liberal leaders who sought the assimilation of all Algerians into France.

As in other parts of the world, the humiliation of the colonial power by the wartime Axis gave renewed impetus to Algerian nationalists, just as they would later take heart from France's defeat in Indo-China and its ignominious role in the Suez conspiracy against Nasser. The *baraka* or magic aura of European invincibility was broken. Since most of the European *colons* or *pieds noirs* (a term referring to their shiny black shoes) supported Pétain's Vichy, Algerian nationalists offered conditional support to the Free French. When the latter sought to conscript Arabs and Berbers in 1942, nationalist leaders replied with a Manifesto of the Algerian People, which reminded the French of American commitments to the liberation of colonial peoples. Refusing to countenance future Algerian autonomy, the French abolished some of the more discriminatory aspects of their rule, notably by according Arabs and Berbers judicial equality with Europeans, giving sixty-five thousand of them French citizenship, and allowing all adult males the right to vote for a separate Muslim parliament. This was too little, too late.

Tensions boiled just beneath the surface. In May 1945 Arab nationalists tried to attach pro-independence demonstrations to European celebrations of Victory Day. At Sétif in the Constantois district the police forcibly stopped demonstrators unfurling political banners and the green-and-white national flag. Arabs turned on Europeans, killing 103 and wounding another hundred in a week of murderous rioting resembling a medieval peasant jacquerie. An eighty-year-old woman was among those raped. In the course of the official and unofficial response, *pied-noir* vigilantes and Senegalese regulars – supported by air and naval bombardments – killed between one thousand and forty-five thousand

Muslims, although more reliable estimates range between six and twelve thousand. Over five thousand Muslims were arrested, with nearly a hundred condemned to death and hundreds sentenced to life imprisonment. Ironically, those arrested included the most moderate Arab leader, Ferhat Abbas, who was detained in the anteroom to the governor-general's office where he had gone to congratulate the Frenchman on the Allied victory over Nazism.

At a time when France was determining the constitution of the Fourth Republic, attempts at limited reform in the governance of Algeria disappointed Arab and Berber nationalists while increasing the insecurity of the ruling European minority. The September 1947 Organic Statute on Algeria established a dual electoral college system, in which half a million voters with French civil status enjoyed equal representation with one and a half million Muslim voters of local civil status, despite there being nine million Muslims. The *colons* engineered the recall to Paris of the governor-general they blamed for these limited concessions and his replacement by one more sympathetic to their intransigent views. To ensure the electoral defeat of the Mouvement pour le Triomphe des Libertés Démocratiques (MTLD), the most radical nationalist party, police and troops were used to scare voters away, and Muslim nationalist candidates were arrested both before and after their election. Some ballot boxes were either stuffed with fraudulent votes or vanished in transit. Let us be entirely clear that the French were deliberately frustrating the extension of democracy to the Arab and Berber populations.[76]

There was particular shock at these corrupt arrangements among Arabs and Berbers who had loyally served in the French armed forces, only to revert to being treated as second-class citizens awaiting France's decision as to when they had become sufficiently civilised to be admitted to a political process that was rigged in favour of the European minority. The future FLN commander, Belkacem Krim, remarked: 'My brother returned from Europe with medals and frost-bitten feet! There everyone was equal. Why not here?' Facing imprisonment for civil disobedience, Krim fled into the mountains of his native Kabilya, where one of his first acts in a career of violence was to shoot dead a Muslim village constable. Together with another war veteran, Omar Ouamrane, Krim formed a guerrilla band that had five hundred active members. Among those appalled by the violence at Sétif was a young former warrant officer, Ahmed Ben Bella, holder of the Croix de Guerre and Médaille Militaire awarded for bravery during his service in France and Italy. A municipal councillor, Ben Bella was forced to flee the law after shooting a fellow Muslim who may have been set up to take over Ben Bella's father's farm. While underground Ben Bella formed an Organisation Spéciale (OS) as the armed wing of the MTLD. Although it carried out a few bank robberies, and had an estimated 4,500 men, the OS was rapidly penetrated by French agents and its leaders imprisoned or forced to flee. Ben Bella himself managed to escape his eight-year jail sentence by sawing his way out with a blade concealed in a loaf of bread. He fled to Cairo where he received sympathy rather than weapons.

The exiled Ben Bella, along with Belkacem Krim, became one of the nine founder leaders of a revolutionary action committee. In November 1954 this adopted the nom de guerre of FLN with an armed wing called the ALN. Just as France's defeat in 1940 had contributed to the first stirrings of Muslim Algerian nationalism, so the loss of fifteen thousand French (and Muslim Algerian) troops at Dien Bien Phu in Indo-China directly influenced the decision in favour of armed revolt, especially since the victorious Viet Minh were not slow to ask Muslim Arab captives why on earth they were fighting fellow victims of French colonialism halfway around the world.[27]

The FLN distributed its limited and poorly armed forces in five Wilayas or major military districts which were subdivided in turn down to individual cells. A separate organisation would be built up in Algiers. Consciously restricting themselves to targeting the police, military and communications infrastructure, for the experience of Sétif made an anti-European pogrom inadvisable, the FLN commenced its revolt on All Saints Day, 1 November 1954, with a series of low-level attacks on barracks and police stations, as well as the destruction of telegraph poles, or cork and tobacco stores. An attack on oil tankers failed when the bomb did not explode. Despite the desire to avoid civilian casualties, two young liberal French teachers were dragged off a bus, shot and left to die on the road, an act which the FLN did not disavow. The FLN's opening 'Toussaint' campaign seemed patchy and ineffectual, with the fighting in the remote countryside making little or no impression on the urban European civilian minority who continued their sun-filled life by the sea.

Heavy-handed deployment of police or soldiers against entire civilian populations has invariably been one of the best recruiting mechanisms for terrorist organisations. No one appreciates armed men kicking the door down, manhandling women and rifling through possessions, let alone blowing up one's home. That the FLN survived its first dismal winter was due to indiscriminate French responses, including the destruction of entire villages as reprisal for nearby attacks; this propelled yet more resentful Algerians into the movement's ranks. A guerrilla war acquired terrorist characteristics as some FLN commanders decided to get the Europeans' attention, for hitherto the fighting had seemed abstract and remote from them.

The commander of Wilaya 2, Youssef Zighout, consciously decided to treat all Europeans, regardless of age or gender, as legitimate targets. Terrorism would provoke intensified and indiscriminate repression which would boost FLN support, for much of the FLN's efforts were directed to mobilising a nationalist movement. Terror would psychologically force Arabs and Europeans into mutually antagonistic camps. There was no room either for ambiguous identities or dual loyalties, as can be seen from the fact that in its first two-and-a-half years of existence, the FLN killed six times as many Muslims as it did Europeans. Anyone who served the French administration or worked for Europeans became a target, as did those who consumed alcohol or tobacco. The former had their lips cut off, the latter their noses, by way of warning; repeat offences resulted in the 'Kabyle smile', the dark term for having their throat cut, a deliberate indignity otherwise inflicted upon sheep.

Anti-European terrorism was first demonstrated in several coastal towns in the Constantois in August 1955. On the 20th of that month the town of Philippeville was attacked by a large FLN force that had infiltrated the city, emerging to throw grenades into cafés patronised by *colons* and to drag Europeans out of their cars in order to hack and slash them to death with knives. The French military intelligence officer Paul Aussaresses, a former wartime secret agent, who had accurately read the signs that this attack was imminent, joined four hundred French troops who emerged to engage the FLN in a ferocious gun battle. When the FLN attackers retreated, they left 130 of their own dead and over a hundred wounded.[28]

Elsewhere, the FLN struck with truly shocking effect. At a pyrites mining settlement located in a Philippeville suburb called El-Halia, groups of FLN-supporting miners burst into the homes of European workers where they and their families were settling down to lunch out of the intense midday sun. Men, women and children had their throats cut, to the encouraging sounds of ululating Arab women. Miners who had not made it home were found stabbed in their cars. Children kicked in the head of an old woman already dying in the street. The ages of the victims ranged from five days to seventy-two years. This was not some frenzied occurrence but the result of deliberate planning, with phone communications cut and the local policeman abducted before he could fire a flare to alert nearby troops. The arrival of French para-troopers led to an extended bloodbath. After failing to restore order with warning shots, they opened fire on every Arab, mowing down batches of prisoners afterwards. There were so many corpses, and the ground was so solid, that bulldozers were used to bury them. In a further in-dication that the government was losing control not only of its own soldiers, but of the French colonial population, armed *pieds noirs* tracked down any Muslims who survived the paratroopers' lethal ire. Anywhere between twelve hundred and twelve thousand Arabs perished, the obvious disparity representing French government and FLN statistics. Perhaps more importantly what had been too lightly described as the *drôle de rebellion* would now be fought across what the reforming governor-general Jacques Soustelle called a ravine of spilled blood.

During this period, the FLN surreptitiously elaborated a network of institutions, courts, taxes, pensions and welfare provision, to refocus the loyalties of the Arab and Berber population away from the colonial power, at the same time killing those foolhardy enough to continue to work for the French administration in any capacity. People with complex identities, like the Kabyle educator Mouloud Feraoun who kept a remarkable journal of these years until he was murdered by settler terrorists in 1962, felt themselves torn apart by this insistence upon people conforming to crude political labels. Never blind to the atrocities committed by the French, Feraoun also acknowledged and condemned the tyrannical pathologies beneath the rhetoric of liberation used by the FLN:

> Has the time for unbridled furor arrived? Can people who kill innocents in cold blood be called liberators? If so, have they considered for a moment that their 'violence' will en-gender more 'violence', will legitimize it, and will hasten its terrible manifestation? They know that the people are unarmed, bunched together in their villages, immensely vulnerable. Are they knowingly prepared for the massacre of 'their brothers'? Even by admitting that they are bloodthirsty brutes – which in

any case does not excuse them but, on the contrary, goes against them, against us, against the ideal that they claim to defend – they have to consider sparing us so as not to provoke repression. Unless liberation means something different to them than it does for us. We thought that they wanted to liberate the country along with its inhabitants. But maybe they feel that this generation of cowards that is proliferating in Algeria must first disappear, and that a truly free Algeria must be repopulated with new men who have not known the yoke of the secular invader. One can logically defend this point of view. Too logically, unfortunately. And gradually, from suspicions to compromises and from compromises to betrayals, we will all be declared guilty and summarily executed in the end.[29]

At its clandestine Soummam Valley Congress in the autumn of 1956, the FLN established the primacy of the political over the military, and of the internal leadership over those exiled abroad. This was achieved by preventing the external leaders from attending the Congress by holding them in Tripoli until it was over. The French themselves delayed this politics of the underhand developing into murderous internecine rifts. For in October a plane carrying Ben Bella and four colleagues from Rabat to Tunis was forced down at Oran, and the external leaders landed in a French prison. This act of air piracy hugely antagonised the newly independent governments of Morocco and Tunisia, which became safe havens for FLN regular forces. The FLN skilfully exploited international opportunities by forcing their grievances into the limelight of the United Nations. This undermined French efforts to treat Algeria as a domestic issue involving FLN 'criminals' leading astray otherwise placid Muslims, through terror or such devices as giving them hashish, a claim that sat ill with the FLN's grim vestiges of Islamic puritanism.

The French increased their forces in Algeria from eighty thousand in 1954 to nearly five hundred thousand two years later, the level of commitment maintained until the end of the war. Indo-China had taught some commanders hard lessons in counter-revolutionary warfare. The Foreign Legion, nearly half of whose ranks were Germans, had lost ten thousand men in Indo-China alone. Counter-insurgency techniques learned in Indo-China were reapplied against the FLN, whom French officers often referred to as 'les Viets'. A special counter-insurgency warfare school was established at a barracks in Arzew near Oran, whose two- to five-week courses were compulsory for arriving officers and NCOs. The French copied counter-terror tactics which the British had recently employed in Malaya, namely the internal deportation of some half a million Chinese squatters into 'protected villages' designed to cut off the predominantly Chinese 'Communist terrorists' from local sources of supply. The historical model was hardly the most edifying that might have been chosen as one British district officer had his moment of illumination: 'The Japs put barbed wire around Titi and Pertang, garrisoned these with troops and made all the Chinese of the locality live within the defended areas . . . Could we not try the same idea?'[30]

To drain the sea in which the FLN swam, the French army corralled villagers into bleak *centres de regroupement*, whose only effect was to create anti-French solidarities among embittered people who had been arbitrarily lifted out of their traditional communities. They ensured 'the concentrated hatred and frustration of thousands' among the two millions so affected. The French tried redistributing government-owned land, only for the FLN to cut the throats of any farmer rash enough to take it. A high density of French troops was maintained in fertile and populous areas, while sparsely inhabited districts were declared free-fire zones where anyone going about was presumed to be an FLN fighter, even if this involved dressing the corpse of some elderly herdsman in an FLN uniform to bump up the body count. Banana-shaped Vertol H-21 helicopters enabled up to twenty-one thousand French troops to be inserted per month to intercept FLN bands while T-6 Texas trainer aircraft were used to bomb and strafe FLN formations. There was extensive aerial reconnaissance designed to track FLN movements. Beyond France and Algeria shadowy operatives from the SDECE – the French secret service – went into business to adulterate weapons and munitions destined for the FLN and hired assassins of mysterious provenance to murder the mainly ex-Nazi or Swiss arms dealers involved with devices ranging from car bombs to darts poisoned with curare.[31]

In Algeria itself machismo was the dominant tone among both the elite soldiers and the *colon* males, an ideology exemplified in the novels of Jean Larteguy with his philosopher heroes resplendent in leopard-striped camouflage gear clutching their distinctive MAT 49 submachine guns with the long under-slung magazines. Some of this spirit is evident in the composite anti-hero para colonel 'Mathieu' in Gillo Pontecorvo's 1966 cinematic masterpiece *La battaglia di Algeri*. His lean face never smiles and the eyes are perpetually occluded by sunglasses. Many of the civilian *colons* had fond memories of Charles Maurras and Pierre Poujade, espousing a bar-room brand of Fascism and inter-communal hatred. Limited and localised hearts-and-minds initiatives, one of which we will look at in detail, were regarded grudgingly by senior French commanders, and were invariably undone if a new dawn brought paratroopers crashing through an Arab home.[32] The occasional commander who advocated more subtle strategies or who opposed torture, such as Jacques Pâris de Bollardière, was encouraged to resign his commission.

The first person of note to publicise torture was the Catholic novelist François Mauriac in an article that appeared in January 1955. Various administrators in Algeria itself also voiced their disquiet. Starting in February 1957, the Catholic weekly *Témoignage Chrétien* published a 'Jean Muller dossier' by a recalled reservist in Algeria, in which he said, 'we are desperate to see how low human nature can stoop, and to see the French use procedures stemming from Nazi barbarism'. The Catholic journal *Esprit* also published an account by Robert Bonnaud in which he declared: 'If France's honour can go along with these acts of torture, then France is a country without honour.' In September 1957 Paul Teitgen resigned as secretary-general of police in Algiers, because he recognised on the bodies of detainees 'the deep marks of abuse or torture that I personally endured fourteen years ago in the basement of the Gestapo in Nancy'. Communist militants and Catholic priests were especially active in making torture known to the wider public.[33]

As well as assassinating international arms dealers, for whom hearts may not bleed, the counter-terrorist war in Algeria acquired very dark accents at the explicit behest of the French socialist government, whose ranks included the justice minister François Mitterrand. Few prisoners were taken, and those that were, were systematically tortured along with anyone suspected of FLN sympathies. This was sometimes a case of those who had experienced or who feared abuse becoming abusers themselves, although the word abuse does not begin to convey the reality, and not every victim of torture became a torturer.

As the case of the then major Paul Aussaresses suggests (he had feared Gestapo or Milice torture every time he was parachuted into occupied France by Britain's SOE), French officers and men, including those who had fought in the wartime resistance, had few apparent scruples about torturing captives and suspects to glean information about FLN personnel and operations. Suspects were beaten or kicked and then subjected to such techniques as electric shocks or simulated drowning, sometimes to the accompaniment of gramophones or radios to drown out the screaming that victims of torture resort to by way of delaying the breaking point. After such sessions, which sometimes involved activities best described as refocused sexual sadism, such as jamming broken bottles into a person's anus, the victims were then routinely killed. Degrading and psychologically damaging as this was not only for the victims but for the torturers too, how did the French army seek to justify this?

Senior commanders, such as general Jacques Massu of the elite 10th Paratroop Regiment, argued (as a matter of faith perhaps) that torture was scrupulously focused on those guilty of aiding and abetting or committing acts of terrorism: 'There were few errors affecting the innocent; in very few cases did we arrest, interrogate, and beat up individuals who had nothing to do with torture.' Torturers routinely used the 'ticking time-bomb' argument that torture was resorted to in order to save people from imminent terrorist attacks. Actually, except in the minds of torturers or academic philosophy seminars, such attacks never figured in the information desired or extracted. Since the FLN were trained to survive interrogation, the information given was usually out of date, or was deliberately rendered to incriminate members of the rival National Algerian Movement, who were then picked up and tortured too.

Even more slippery was Massu's claim to Aussaresses that the army would have to adopt 'implacable' measures – the euphemism for torture – to forestall some morally insane act by the *pieds noirs* – in other words a variant on the claim that torture was the lesser of two evils. Specifically Massu indicated that the *colon* ultras were plotting to park several petrol tankers on an incline at the top of the Casbah, the old Turkish quarter of Algiers. Petrol would be streamed down the sloping alleys and streets which, when ignited, would incinerate '70,000' Muslim residents. Here Massu's memory may have been playing tricks for he was back-projecting to the start of the conflict a plot that the OAS undertook in the final days of French Algeria. If Massu had any religious qualms about what he ordered, these were presumably allayed by the army chaplain who explained:

> Faced with a choice between two evils, either to cause temporary
> suffering to a bandit taken in the act who in any case may

deserve to die, or to leave large numbers of innocent people to be massacred by this criminal's gang, when it could be destroyed as a result of his information, there can be no hesitation in choosing the lesser of the two evils, in an effective but not sadistic interrogation.[34]

Torture led smoothly to the murder of suspects, like the lawyer Ali Boumendjel, who, arrested for organising terrorist killings, was thrown off a sixth-floor walkway connecting police buildings. The justification for murder was that there were so many FLN suspects awaiting trial that the courts were clogged to the point of immobility while liberal lawyers were ever ready to get the accused off. Rather than risk acquittal, it was better to throw a man off a high building, a clear illustration of how torture tends to be a slippery slope. Much, much later, Massu – who with his wife adopted two Algerian children – would concede that torture had been militarily superfluous.[35]

Massu had arrived in Algiers with his 4,600 paratroops, just as the more extreme *colons* in the capital were hurling tomatoes at the new socialist premier Guy Mollet at a wreath-laying ceremony, forcing him to rescind the appointment of a seventy-nine-year-old former general as governor-general to replace the popular Soustelle. Instead Algeria got Robert Lacoste, another hero of the wartime resistance. In addition to being defeated by an angry urban mob, Mollet decided to increase the military presence to half a million men by calling up reservists and extending the service of conscripts. This resulted almost immediately not only in the FLN ambushing a platoon of inexperienced soldiers at Palestro, but in the grim discovery that the FLN had taken prisoners, some of whom were later found disembowelled with their genitals cut off, and with stones stuffed in their body cavities. Although Massu's paratroops wiped out most of the band responsible, governor-general Lacoste ordered the execution of two FLN prisoners and a massive armed raid on the Casbah that resulted in the detention of five thousand people. The battle of the Casbah was on.

Fatefully, the FLN simultaneously took the decision to focus its terrorist efforts on the capital, for as Ramdane Abane argued: 'one corpse in a jacket is always worth more than twenty in uniform'. He instructed the head of the FLN in Algiers, Saadi Yacef, to 'kill any European between the ages of eighteen and fifty-four. But no women, no children, no old people.' The objective of this urban terror campaign was to get the maximum international visibility for the FLN: 'Is it preferable for our cause to kill ten enemies in an oued [a dry riverbed] when no one will, talk of it, or a single man in Algiers which will be noted the next day in the American press?'[36]

Yacef was a twenty-nine-year-old baker, who in a short period of time assembled fourteen hundred fighters, while constructing an elaborate network of bomb manufactories, arms dumps and hiding places in the courtyard houses of the Casbah, home to eighty thousand Muslims. One of his most implacable fighters was the former pimp Ali La Pointe, the hero of Pontecorvo's film, in which Yacef played himself. A classic in the revolutionary-insurgency genre, the film is required viewing for soldiers deployed in Iraq, for whom the message of how to win a battle while losing a war is pertinent. In the summer of 1956, almost fifty Europeans were shot dead by the FLN in a series of random killings in the European quarters of the city. Probably in response to this, settler extremists (perhaps including members of the local police) detonated a bomb in the Casbah's Rue de Thèbes, allegedly to destroy an FLN bomb factory; it demolished four houses, killing seventy Muslim men, women and children.

In September 1956, Yacef despatched three young middle-class women, including two law students, into the European quarter of Algiers. One of them subsequently married Jacques Vergès, the half-Vietnamese lawyer who defended the Lyons Gestapo chief Klaus Barbie, although the couple have since divorced. Yacef reminded them of the atrocity in the Rue de Thèbes – whose effect was heightened, according to twenty-two-year-old Zohra Drif, by the knowledge that carefree and indifferent Europeans were at the beach or swimming in the city below when Arab children were being picked out of the rubble. Dressed as if going to the beach, and with their hair dyed to pass as Europeans, the girls flirted their way past French military checkpoints. One terrorist went to the Milk-Bar where families liked to go after a day at the beach; another, accompanied by her mother, to a café patronised by students dancing the mambo; and a third to the Air France terminus. The bombs were slipped under tables and the women left. When they exploded, a total of three people were killed and fifty injured, many by shards of flying glass. When the doctor who was hiding Ramdane Abane protested, the FLN chief replied: 'I see hardly any difference between the girl who places a bomb in the Milk-Bar and the French aviator who bombards a *mechta* or who drops napalm in a *zone interdite*'.[37] To worsen relations between Europeans and Muslims further, Ali La Pointe was instructed to assassinate the seventy-four-year-old president of the Federation of Algerian Mayors, Amédée Froger, a veteran of the Great War and a popular *pied noir* leader.

The governor-general of Algeria handed overall responsibility for public order to the newly arrived commander in chief, general Raoul Salan, and his subordinate Massu. Massu was an extremely distinguished soldier; his chief of staff Yves Godard was a former *maquisard* and veteran of the war in Indo-China.

These men used brutal force to break an FLN-inspired general strike intended to impress the United Nations as it opened in New York, dragooning strikers back to work or ripping off the grilles of closed shop fronts. By these actions the French authorities were prohibiting the right to strike, having already corrupted Algeria's limited democracy. Yacef responded by despatching more young female bombers, who killed five people and wounded sixty in a brasserie, a bar and a café. A fortnight later, bombers struck at two popular stadiums, killing ten and injuring forty-five people. Godard used diagrams, called organograms, based on information from informers and tortured suspects, to give firm organisational outlines to a shadowy opponent camouflaged by the civilian population of the Casbah. Each house was daubed with a number and Nazi-style block wardens were appointed to monitor the comings and goings of the inhabitants. Hooded informers stood ready to identify FLN suspects at the choke points through which Arabs entered and left the Casbah. The French concentrated on finding the bomb makers and weapons stores, sometimes using helicopters to land troops on flat roofs at night. Some bomb makers elected to blow themselves up rather than surrender to the French, in further illustration of the deleterious effects of torture in stiffening resistance. These methods led to the arrest of Larbi Ben M'Hidi, who allegedly hanged himself in French custody shortly afterwards, but was in fact hanged by Aussaresses in a remote barn. This left Yacef in total charge of the campaign of terror. The latter moved from hideout to hideout, sometimes dressed as a woman, with a submachine gun hidden under 'her' capacious robes.

The battle degenerated into the tit-for-tat killings which in 1956 the leading *pied noir* writer Albert Camus vainly tried to halt through a civil truce committee designed to stop the indiscriminate murder of innocents. When two paratroopers were shot leaving a cinema, their comrades burst into a Turkish bath and raked the place with gunfire, leaving as many as eighty people dead, the majority beggars using it as a cheap shelter. By way of revenge, the FLN placed bombs inside heavy cast-iron lampposts, which caused grievous head injuries to passing Muslims and Europeans as they exploded, sending out heavy shrapnel. On 9 June the FLN managed to put a bomb under the bandstand at the Casino, which was packed with regular Sunday dancers. The band leader, Lucky Starway, proved highly unlucky as he was disembowelled, while his singer had her feet blown off. Nine people were killed and eighty-five wounded, many of them losing feet or legs because the bomb was positioned on the floor and the bandstand focused its blast. Men from the working-class European quarters went berserk, rounding on local Arab shopkeepers. Five people were killed and fifty injured while the army and police turned a blind eye or quickly released anyone they arrested. Meanwhile, a French patrol managed to detain Djamila Bouhired, one of Yacef's closest collaborators, as they passed the pair in the Casbah. Yacef tried to shoot her before fleeing. Although she did not betray Yacef, further chance arrests, and the deployment of agents inside the Casbah, meant that his hiding place in the Rue Caton was nearing discovery.

Before that, Yacef took part in the celebrated dialogue with the ethnologist and former Gaullist resister Germaine Tillion, who had been incarcerated in Ravensbruck by the Nazis. She smuggled herself into the Casbah in an attempt to persuade a senior FLN commander (who she did not know was Yacef) in a four-hour meeting to halt the terror bombing of civilians. Their encounters were revealing:

> 'We are neither criminals, nor assassins' [said Yacef]. Very sadly and very firmly, I replied: 'You are assassins.' He was so disconcerted that for a moment he remained without speaking, as if suffocated. Then, his eyes filled with tears and he said to me, in so many words: 'Yes, Madame Tillion, we are assassins ... It's the only way in which we can express ourselves.'

Yacef claimed that a former *pied noir* friend had died in the Casino bombing and that the man's fiancée had lost both her legs. He agreed to call off attacks on civilians, and he proved as good as his word until his capture.

Yacef's whereabouts were revealed after Godard captured his main courier to the outside world. The man also told Godard about the secret contacts between Tillion and Yacef which his captors were outraged to learn had occurred with the complicity of the French government. Godard's paratroopers found Yacef in a concealed hideaway in the Rue Caton, from which he lobbed grenades or dropped *plastique* to buy time to burn crucial documents. He and his companion Zohra Drif eventually surrendered to avoid choking from smoke inhalation. Across the street, Ali La Pointe slipped away. He was eventually tracked down to another hideout, where he crouched resignedly with Hassiba Ben Bouali and the twelve-year-old Petit Omar. Refusing to surrender, the three of them were killed when bombs designed to expose their hideaway detonated a store of explosives which destroyed several houses. Seventeen Muslim neighbours, including four children, died in the blast. The battle of Algiers was over and the French army had won it, although their disgraceful methods would lose them the wider war.

The FLN's internal leadership in Algeria fled to Tunis, where the 'externals' blamed them for a failed general strike, for a failed urban terrorist campaign, and for handing the French a major propaganda coup which they were calling the FLN's Dien Bien Phu. Worse, the French were now decimating the FLN out in the countryside, while installing high-voltage fencing and minefields, with troops stationed at one-mile intervals, to prevent the FLN from raiding from Morocco or Tunisia.

The 584th Infantry Battalion was stationed in the southern Sahara around Tizi-Ouzou, Oued Chair and Ain Rich. Until major Jean Pouget took command, it was an indisciplined rabble whose soldiers had vandalised the train taking them to Marseilles for transhipment to Algeria. Pouget, a wartime resister who had narrowly avoided execution by the Nazis, and had then spent five years in a Viet Minh prison camp after Dien Bien Phu, resolved to clean them up. Thefts and vandalism were punished by making the entire battalion sleep outside in night-time temperatures of −5 degrees Centigrade. Having been tortured himself, Pouget forbade abusive treatment of FLN captives. When he encountered a captive whom a conscript had assaulted, the major punched the conscript twice in the face: 'That is on behalf of the prisoner … do not forget that a prisoner is a disarmed soldier. He is no longer an enemy and could be a friend of tomorrow. So long as I am in command of this battalion the prisoners will be treated as if they are already our comrades. Now untie him! Medic, check out his wounds.' Routinely, FLN prisoners were so overcome by such treatment that they gushed out information that was not even solicited. Nor would Pouget tolerate any abuse of the local civilians, imprisoning a lieutenant who had put his arm round the waist of a dignitary's daughter and then ordering him to sweep the base courtyard. He also whole-heartedly believed in Specialist Administrative Sections. These were hearts-and-minds outposts staffed by young Arabic-speaking officers, who gleaned intelligence while improving local animal husbandry, education, irrigation and medical provision. They went from village to village, listening rather than talking to the inhabitants. If they had problems with their sheep, then the SAS officer would open a disinfection station with no questions asked. They also used mobile medical clinics and cinemas to win over the locals. They sent out doctors under the protection of the village elders, a way of breaking the vice-like grip of the FLN on the population. A twenty-one-year-old philosophy student conscript volunteered to run a village school in a remote location. He was popular. When the FLN killed him, Pouget took no retaliatory action, waiting for the village elders to ask for French protection. Through such calculations, counter-insurgency wars are sometimes won.[38]

The FLN were also faced with the prospective nightmare of an ethnic split between Arabs and Berbers when an Arab FLN commander shot dead his Berber political commissar who he imagined was abusing local Arab women. He then took his men over as Harkis or Muslim irregulars, who quickly outnumbered the Algerian Muslims fighting for the FLN. French intelligence also successfully inserted high-level agents into the FLN, sowing fear and murderous paranoia in its ranks. In view of these setbacks it is not surprising that there were bitter recriminations and power struggles within the FLN leadership, notoriously involving the luring to Morocco in December 1957 of its most charismatic leader, Ramdane Abane, where he was strangled on the orders of the five Wilaya colonels who increasingly dominated the FLN. A communiqué announced that he had been killed by the French while on a secret mission in Algeria. As the external FLN forces became more professionalised and played an increasingly important part in the fighting, leadership passed to such figures as Colonel Houari Boumedienne, the grimly taciturn figure who would become Algeria's second president.

That the FLN recovered from apparent defeat was paradoxically due to tensions among the French victors. Success in the battle of Algiers went to the heads of many regular army officers who, already explicitly sympathetic to the *colon* minority, grew impatient with the succession of indecisive politicians who determined their destinies from Paris. On

8 February 1958 they caused a major international incident when, responding to FLN anti-aircraft fire from within neighbouring Tunisia, they despatched bombers which levelled the town of Sakiet, killing eighty people. This attack was never authorised by the French government and provoked international outrage. Moreover, since the disaster at Palestro, the French public was beginning to question the cost, human, moral and material, of underwriting the *pied noir* presence in Algeria. It was one thing for regular troops, Foreign Legionnaires and Harkis to die in a war in Algeria's scrubland, but they felt differently when conscription meant that it involved sons of metropolitan families. Discontent spread to the army as conscript soldiers were used to control areas of scrub and sand while the paras got the glamour, girls and glory in the cities. The conduct of the war, and in particular the systematic use of torture, also discredited France in the eyes of the world, even though the FLN's own terror tactics included disembowelling people and braining small children against walls. Clumsy attempts by the French government to censor accounts of torture were counter-productive since they could not control the international press, and the use of torture against European supporters of the FLN was a public relations catastrophe.

In May 1958, the *colons* launched a direct challenge to the French government when they forced Lacoste to leave his post – over government failure to stop the FLN from carrying out reprisal executions – and proclaimed a reluctant general Massu president of a Committee of Public Safety. In the background Salan threatened to extend this coup to France, bringing paratroopers as close as Corsica during Operation Resurrection designed to lever general Charles de Gaulle into power. As Parisians scanned the skies for massed mushrooming parachutes, the aged president René Coty summoned de Gaulle, granting him the right to rule for six months by decree and to draw up a constitution for a Fifth Republic. Playing his cards very close to his chest, de Gaulle had a vision of France that ranged high above the squalid little war in Algeria, to a world in which economic might and nuclear bombs were a surer index of global great-power status than a string of colonies undergoing rancid disputes between colonial dinosaurs and national liberation movements.

De Gaulle flew to Algeria in early June 1958, where he praised the army, claimed he 'had understood' the mutinous *colons*, and slightly opened a door to those 'Muslim Frenchmen' whom the FLN had temporarily led astray through the offer of a settlement that would acknowledge the honour of France's opponents. His Constantine Plan that autumn promised universal suffrage, a single electoral college, and two-thirds Algerian Muslim representation in the metropolitan parliament. Integration was to be accelerated through crash economic and educational reforms. The new constitution became a trial of strength with the FLN. It lost in the sense that nearly 80 per cent of Muslims turned out to vote, and 96.6 per cent voted to approve the constitution of the Fifth Republic. The FLN responded by announcing a provisional government to be based at Tunis, with the erstwhile moderate Ferhat Abbas as president and the imprisoned Ben Bella as his deputy. This entity rejected the Constantine Plan and de Gaulle's offer of an honourable *paix des braves*. Worse, in November, the FLN succeeded in deterring anyone of note from standing for election to the electoral college, thereby underlining the fact that the French would have to talk to its representatives. Paradoxically, de Gaulle had more success in reining in the army – general Salan was replaced by Maurice Challe – which then virtually crushed the FLN in three of the Wilayas. That displaced the centre of FLN military activity to Morocco and Tunisia, where quasi-regular forces could be carefully trained and equipped with the increasing flow of Chinese and Soviet-bloc weaponry.

In September 1959 de Gaulle gave radio and television addresses which made the first calculated play with the term 'auto-determination'. A referendum on this would come about if peace could be established and maintained for four years. The FLN rejected these proposals, which were designed to reach over its head, even as the first crack in the French façade boosted nationalist morale. By contrast the more militant settlers, sensing betrayal, launched a week-long uprising in January 1960 which was viewed sympathetically by likeminded spirits in the regular army as the *colons* clashed violently with French gendarmes and riot police. Although de Gaulle was able to use radio and television appearances to hold the inconstant soldiery onside, for the next two years both *colon* intransigence and the uncertain loyalty of the army proved the major obstacle to a swift resolution of the nightmare in Algeria.

Disunity within the FLN was a further obstacle, for it too was divided between accommodationists and maximalists, the latter chiefly represented within its armed formations. That summer de Gaulle endeavoured to split the FLN by holding clandestine talks at Melun with dissident leaders from Wilaya Four in southern Algiers who were disenchanted with the external leadership. Although these talks came to nothing, and these dissidents were subsequently killed by the FLN and the French, it put enormous pressure on the FLN leadership to commence their own negotiations. In November, de Gaulle opened the door a little wider when he said in a public address that he could envisage an Algerian republic, a vision preparatory to a referendum in Algeria and France on Algerian self-determination.

In February 1956 Ferhat Abbas had heard a *pied noir* demonstrator remark: 'The FLN has taught us that violence is profitable for the Muslims. We are going to organise violence by the Europeans and prove that that too is profitable.' During 1960 extremists among the *colons* organised as the Front de l'Algérie Française or FAF. Its supporters among metropolitan notables included Jacques Soustelle, the centre-right politician Georges Bidault and generals Jouhaud and Salan. When de Gaulle visited Algeria, but not Algiers itself, in December, the most implacable elements in the FAF tried to assassinate him. Booed by *colons* everywhere, the president was greeted respectfully by Algerian Muslims. On 11 December the FLN organised a huge demonstration of nationalist sentiment in the capital, which was awash with white-and-green FLN flags and banners. In early 1961, around 75 per cent of the metropolitan electorate voted in favour of Algerian self-determination, a figure that sank to 55 per cent in the colony where the FLN urged a Muslim boycott. That month de Gaulle banned the FAF, whose more virile adherents formed an Organisation Armée Secrète or OAS, under a triarchy led by the exiled Salan. Shockingly, the retired general Maurice Challe flew to Algeria to take charge of the military putsch the OAS was planning.

On the night of 21 April 1961, the 1st Foreign Legion Parachute Regiment seized government and security facilities in Algiers and took the military commander and government-delegate captive. The following morning Challe broadcast that he and his colleagues had assumed power in Algeria and the Sahara. However, the putsch was not supported by the commander of the Oranie, while the commander of the Constantois havered. The army in metropolitan France remained loyal to de Gaulle's government. Stalled at the outset, the putsch collapsed, with Challe surrendering himself to the authorities and the other leaders fleeing abroad. De Gaulle took the opportunity to rearrange the high command of the army. Thus the main means by which France sought to contain the FLN had disabled itself. As the putsch gave way to the nihilistic violence of the OAS, de Gaulle used Georges Pompidou to establish clandestine contacts with the external leadership of the FLN.

Talks commenced at Evian, with Belkacem Krim and the FLN delegates commuting from neutral Switzerland. The OAS assassinated the mayor of the host city in a gesture that was as barbarous as it was irrelevant. The French called a unilateral ceasefire and released thousands of prisoners as a goodwill gesture. After a series of meetings the talks broke down over the FLN's refusal to accord European settlers dual citizenship or recognise France's claim that the (oil- and gas-rich) Sahara had never been an integral part of Algeria.

As this future was being arranged in a remote part of the Jura, the OAS developed an organisational structure to support its five hundred or so Delta terrorists. These were drawn from the *colon* ultras, soldiers enraged by what they saw as de Gaulle's sell-out, and from the criminal underworld, which, on the Muslim side, was not entirely unrepresented in the ranks of the FLN either. Insofar as they had any coherent long-term ideas – and such an absence had been no obstacle to the FLN either – these consisted of admiration for the toughness of the Zionist Haganah and of apartheid in South Africa. To urgent chants and hooting of 'Al-gé-rie fran-çais', which became a sort of counterpoint to the FLN's ululations, the Delta men used plastic explosives or guns and daggers to kill liberal-minded Europeans or senior members of the police. This escalated into indiscriminate drive-by shootings of any group of innocent Muslims after each FLN attack. The war spread to France when, in response to orders to the army to suppress the OAS, its operatives blew up the Parisian apartment of the chief of staff, narrowly missing the general's wife. Ironically, French detectives in Algiers were soon resorting to organograms to pinpoint the organisational structures of the OAS, many of whose members had helped construct these diagrams in the war against the FLN.

Unsure of the loyalties of the local Algerian police, the heads of counter-terrorism in Algiers resorted to the slightly fantastical *barbouzes* or false beards, a motley crew of bar-room toughs, Vietnamese and local Jews, who collectively might have strayed out of a Humphrey Bogart movie. Since the Vietnamese were hardly inconspicuous, the OAS Delta teams were able to track down their whereabouts with relative ease. One 'secret' villa was shot to pieces with a devastating display of fire-power; its replacement was demolished when the Deltas smuggled in a massive bomb inside a crate bearing a printing press, which blew many of the *barbouzes* to pieces. The remnants tried to flee the country, but were cornered inside a hotel; the four men who managed to get out as the OAS shot up the place were trapped in a car and burned alive.

Unfortunately for the OAS the colourful *barbouzes* had distracted them from the activities of a team of expert metropolitan detectives, two hundred men strong, who brought their skill to bear on unravelling the OAS, rotating out of Algeria every two months so as to avoid going native with the European community. In order to publicise their cause in the metropolis, the OAS extended their campaign of terror to the mainland. There was a series of increasingly daring attempts to assassinate de Gaulle, the closest being thwarted by the skill of the president's driver, as well as crazed schemes to bring down the Eiffel Tower. Most OAS machine-gunnings and *plastiquages* were directed at prominent opponents of the war in Algeria, including the headquarters of the Communist Party and Jean-Paul Sartre, that loathsome academic enthusiast for the purifying effects of political violence. In February 1962, an OAS attempt to kill the minister of culture went badly awry when the bomb intended for him sent three hundred glass splinters into the face and body of four-year-old Delphine Renard as she played in a ground-floor apartment. She was blinded in one eye and badly disfigured. Shocking newspaper coverage of this atrocity led to a small demonstration by left-wing and Roman Catholic trades unionists the following day, which ended in scenes of police violence at the Charonne Métro station where the police threw people downstairs, leading to the deaths of eight people. Half a million protesters took to the streets the following day.

Talks resumed at Yéti high in the Jura in early 1962 when the FLN had become as concerned as the French government about the indiscriminate terror campaign launched by the OAS. In February alone this resulted in the deaths of 553 people. Stringent night-time curfews meant that only killers moved around in the darkened streets of Algiers and Oran. In these talks, France dropped its claim to the Sahara, although it was granted exploration and production rights on a leased basis, and the FLN allowed France to maintain air and naval facilities, while keeping Algeria within the franc zone. Algerians would still be welcome to work in France, with which preferential trading arrangements were established. France would grant Algeria a generous aid package to ease the transition to independence. This deal was overwhelmingly endorsed through referenda held in mainland France and Algeria.

As news of this settlement reached the OAS leadership, Salan ordered an indiscriminate assault on every manifestation of governmental authority, which apparently took in postmen, foreign correspondents and flower-sellers on street corners. Many of these were drive-by shootings. OAS killers also came for Mouloud Feraoun, who was killed along with five other French and Muslim educators in a Chicago-style hit as they discussed vocational education for homeless Algerian children. Although the ensuing Evian Agreements seemed to protect the rights of the *pieds noirs*, the OAS ignored the stipulated ceasefire, beginning with a mortar attack on a square where Muslims were celebrating the proclamation of Algerian independence. Murderous OAS attacks on French police and conscript soldiers followed. In response to this, the French army launched an all-out assault on the OAS heartland in the suburb of Bab el-Oued, using tanks and aircraft to reduce sniper positions in the blocks of flats. When the *pieds noirs* held a mass demonstration to protest this siege, the OAS provoked a massacre by firing from a rooftop on the Algerian Tirailleurs brought in to police the demonstration. Totally unsuited for this role, and newly returned from hunting FLN fighters in the countryside, these troops opened fire and left forty-six demonstrators dead as well as two hundred wounded. Even as it unleashed this orgy of violence, intrepid policemen and soldiers were on the tracks of the OAS leadership.

Among those picked up were Salan himself and Roger Degueldre, the organisation's most feared gunman, both of whom were flown to captivity in France. The OAS top brass including Challe, Jouhaud and Salan escaped with their lives, while their murderous myrmidons like Degueldre went to the firing squads. By way of response to these arrests, the OAS used a powerful car bomb to kill sixty-two Muslim dockers seeking work; and an attempt to roll a petrol tanker down into the Casbah was narrowly averted. In a uniquely mean-minded attack, the OAS murdered seven aged cleaners on their way to work, bringing one week's death toll to 230 people. As the FLN responded with attacks on bars and cafés that were known OAS haunts, one hundred thousand Europeans slipped out of Algeria, which the OAS now decided to destroy as it was abandoned. As everything from libraries to oil refineries went up in flames, some 350,000 Europeans left in June 1962 alone. In total, some 1,380,000 Europeans departed, as well as one hundred thousand, mainly FLN-supporting, Algerian Jews, leaving a mere thirty thousand *pieds noirs* behind. When in Oran a few diehards rashly opened fire on the incoming FLN, a Muslim crowd went berserk and cut the throats of any men, women and children they encountered in the almost deserted European quarter of the city. On Tuesday 3 July 1962 a plane carrying the Provisional Government landed in Algeria from Tunisia. The president, Ben Youssef Ben Khedda, drove into Algiers where hundreds of thousands of people waving white-and-green flags awaited him. There were chants and whistles of 'Ya-ya, Dje-za-ir!' or 'Long live Algeria!'. Peace meant the onset of faction-fighting in the FLN which cost the lives of fifteen thousand former comrades. It also brought a bloody reckoning with those Muslim Algerians who had fought for France, as the FLN murdered an unknown number of former Harkis, the most conservative estimate being thirty thousand, the most sensational one hundred and fifty thousand. The much smaller number who escaped to the metropolis experienced the full ingratitude of the French and the neighbourly hostility of the Muslim Algerians who migrated in subsequent years as remittance men to France.

There was one further important aspect to the celebrations of Algeria's liberation from France. Among the invited guests was Yasser Arafat, whose elder brother Gamal had befriended the exiled FLN leader Mohammed Khider in Cairo. Arafat was a former student militant with connections to the Egyptian Muslim Brotherhood and with a family relationship to the chief adviser of the grand mufti. He was one of the five young Palestinian exiles, by 1958 all working in Kuwait, who founded a movement called Fatah for the liberation of Palestine. The name was based on the initials of the Palestine Liberation Movement – Harakat Tahrir Filastin – spelled backwards. Forwards they gave 'Hataf' or 'Death', backwards they spelled 'Conquest'. Initially there were twenty members who swore an oath before being admitted to its cell-based structure:

> I swear by God the Almighty,
> I swear by my honour and my conviction,
> I swear that I will be truly devoted to Palestine,
> That I will work actively for the liberation of Palestine,
> That I will do everything that lies within my capabilities,
> That I will not give away Fatah's secrets,
> That this is a voluntary oath, and God is my witness.

Arafat had initially gone to Kuwait to work as an engineer building roads. From this starting point he developed business interests in the construction industry, which enabled him to travel and to recruit from among professionals in the wider Palestinian diaspora in the Gulf and western Europe. Arafat's friend Khalil al-Wazir, also known as Abu Jihad, became full-time head of a Palestinian Bureau in Algeria, which along with Baathist Syria was the Palestinians' most valuable patron. Cordial relations with the chilly Boumedienne enabled al-Wazir to open a guerrilla training camp at Blida while sending a select few to the Cherchel Military Academy. It must have been a heady atmosphere as Palestinians met such living legends as Ernesto Che Guevara or established contacts with foreign diplomats, which in early 1964 resulted in Arafat's first visit to China.[39]

At this time Fatah was merely one of a host of organisations claiming to represent the Palestinians. In January 1964 an Arab summit in Cairo had created a Palestine Liberation Organisation under a diplomat and lawyer named Ahmad al-Shuqairi with the highly undiplomatic habit of calling for the Jews to be hurled into the sea. Worse, al-Shuqairi talked about establishing an armed wing of the PLO, thereby siphoning off Fatah's potential pool of recruits. Using Wazir as an intermediary, Arafat proposed that the Palestinians should copy the Zionists' example, with Fatah acting as the terrorist equivalent of Irgun or Lehi to the PLO's version of the underground Haganah army of the Jewish Agency. Fatah's extremely limited resources led to a series of strategic debates between the so-called 'sane ones' advocating caution and the 'mad ones', including Arafat, who argued that even apparently futile attacks on Israel would provoke a massive reaction that would bolster Fatah's cause. A compromise was agreed between the two factions, in the sense that Fatah would create a pseudonymous armed formation called Al-Asifa, or the Storm, whose failures could be denied by Fatah itself, dissimulation repeated in the 1970s with the more deadly Black September organisation.

The first fedayeen consisted of twenty-six men armed with three weapons and financed by a modest bank overdraft. Their initial campaign was not impressive as one raiding party was arrested by the Lebanese while the Jordanian army was responsible for the first casualty when it shot a Palestinian guerrilla returning across the border from Israel. Despite the huge disparity between Fatah's rhetoric and its piffling attacks on Israeli water-pumping stations from its bases in Jordan, money started to flow from rich Kuwaitis and such new benefactors as Saudi's sheikh Ahmed Zaki Yamani. A Saudi diplomat in Ankara was deputed to drive weapons to Fatah from Turkey via Syria into Lebanon. Paradoxically, Israel's swift and comprehensive defeat of the Arab nations in the Six-Day War in June 1967 benefited Fatah, while more radical rival actors such as Dr George Habash's Marxist-Leninist Popular Front for the Liberation of Palestine entered the scene bent on revolutionising the entire Arab world and defeating US imperialism.[40] Rather than rely on feeble Arab patrons, Arafat persuaded his Fatah colleagues to organise guerrilla activity inside the territories newly occupied by Israel. Although the response inside the West Bank was poor, and the Israelis quickly killed or captured most of the guerrilla fighters, four hundred more Palestinian volunteers flew to Algeria from Germany for military training. Fatah also established bases for cross-border raids on the Israeli–Jordanian river frontier, which it could ford at night using primitive rafts. To the increasing alarm of its Hashemite ruler, Jordan became for Fatah what Hanoi was for the Viet Cong. The Israelis responded with artillery fire and the occasional air strike.

On 18 March 1968 an Israeli school bus drove over a Fatah mine, killing a doctor and a schoolboy and injuring twenty-nine children. Well informed, thanks to a CIA tip to his Jordanian hosts, about massive Israeli reprisals, Arafat made the maverick decision to stand and fight the Israelis at a border base camp at Karameh, one of the few successful rural resettlements of Palestinians by the United Nations Relief and Works Agency (UNRWA) that administered Palestinian refugee camps. Appropriately the name meant 'Dignity' in Arabic. Israel's operation went awry when paratroops despatched to cut off the guerrillas' escape route into the hills found themselves ambushed by Habash's PFLP, while the main force ran into a regular Jordanian division commanded by a general sympathetic to the Palestinians, which after an intense fight forced the Israelis to withdraw at a loss of twenty-eight dead and nearly seventy wounded. Fatah lost around 150. The Fatah guerrillas distinguished themselves in the fight, including the seventeen men who died firing rocket-propelled grenades (RPGs) at point-blank range into tanks, a feat commemorated in the name of Arafat's elite bodyguards, Force 17. Relations between Israel and Jordan conspired to make this a Fatah, as opposed to a Jordanian, 'victory'. The movement was inundated with volunteers, while for the first time the name of the mystery commander allegedly responsible for Israel's 'defeat' was bruited abroad: Abu Ammar, the nom de guerre of Yasser Arafat. The Palestinian cause acquired a stubbly face, with the trademark chequered *keffiyeh* and wraparound sunglasses, his Egyptian-accented Arabic switching into broken English for the increasing number of Western interviewers.

Once again emulating the Zionists, Arafat used the increased resources flowing to Fatah from oil-rich Libya and Saudi Arabia to ramify a series of non-military institutions as a sort of state in waiting, which also gradually marginalised the authority of UNRWA in the camps. Although Egypt's president Nasser was suspicious of Arafat's connections with the Muslim Brotherhood, after a key meeting in April 1968 he offered the Fatah leader his protection. This enabled Palestinians to train at Egyptian military bases and to begin broadcasting from their own Voice of Fatah station in Cairo. With considerable shrewdness, Arafat managed to get financial support from the ultra-conservative Saudis to purchase arms from the Communist Chinese, who also supplied the PFLP. France's president de Gaulle allowed Fatah to open its first official European mission in Paris, from which the Palestinians were able to forge contacts with the new left, whose sympathies migrated from the FLN to the Palestinians as the chic international cause of the day. In a further adroit move, Fatah finally took over the moribund Palestinian Liberation Organisation, thereby benefiting from its connections with the leaders of the Arab world and the erratic mandate of the Palestinian so-called parliament. In February 1969 Fatah leaders installed in the Palestinian National Council elected Arafat chairman of the ruling Executive Committee of the PLO. Although there was a parliament the modus operandi owed more to Marxist-Leninist democratic centralism than to Westminster. There was also an explicit and unequivocal commitment to armed struggle as the only means of liberating Palestine. That December Arafat sat as the leader of the Palestinians among other Arab leaders at a summit in Rabat, unaware that it was from some of the friends around the table, rather than the Israelis, that he had most to fear.

III RELUCTANT TERRORISTS

The newly installed FLN regime in Algeria also gave hope to another liberation struggle at the other end of the African continent. In early 1962 a tall, graceful, middle-aged African stood on the edge of a dusty little Moroccan town called Oujda, borrowing field glasses from an FLN commander to take a look at French troops operating across the nearby border in Algeria. Their uniforms reminded him of the South African Defence Force. The FLN's campaign against the colonial regime in

Algeria seemed the closest contemporary counterpart to the African National Congress's struggle against white minority rule in South Africa. The following day, Nelson Mandela attended a military parade honouring the recently released Ahmed Ben Bella, watching a march-past by tough FLN fighters equipped with modern weapons as well as axes and spears. In the rear a huge African marked time with a ceremonial mace for an FLN military band. There was a warm flash of ethnic fellow feeling.

There was little of the soldier about Mandela, yet he was in North Africa as the newly appointed founder leader of Umkhonto we Sizwe (MK), or the Spear of the Nation. This was to become the armed wing of the ANC. The son of a Xhosa clan closely connected with the royal house of the Transkei, Mandela had received a decent British education at Methodist schools before qualifying as a lawyer, with his own thriving (Black) practice in Johannesburg with his friend Oliver Tambo. The pose of being a simple country bumpkin made good masked a man of great political intelligence who was radicalised by the thousand quotidian systemic slights that *baaskap* or White mastery entailed:

> To be an African in South Africa means that one is politicised from the moment of one's birth, whether one acknowledges it or not. An African child is born in an Africans Only hospital, taken home in an Africans Only bus, lives in an Africans Only area and attends Africans Only schools, if he attends school at all. When he grows up, he can hold Africans Only jobs, rent a house in Africans Only townships, ride Africans Only trains and be stopped at any time of the day or night and be ordered to produce a pass, without which he can be arrested and thrown in jail. His life is circumscribed by racist laws and regulations that cripple his growth, dim his potential and stunt his life. This was the reality, and one could deal with it in a myriad of ways.[41]

As he had done earlier in his life – for example, when he wanted to understand Roman law or Communism – Mandela began by resorting to study, this time brushing up on military matters. Living clandestinely on a farm, he borrowed Clausewitz's *On War* from a friend who had fought in North Africa and Italy. He went on to read Castro, Guevara and Mao on guerrilla warfare, as well as *The Revolt* by Menachem Begin. Fortuitously, Arthur Goldreich, who provided cover for Mandela by renting the farm on which the MK leader was ostensibly the hired hand, had fought in the Zionist Palmach against the British. Even more experience came from Jack Hodgson, another war veteran, who showed Mandela how to blow things up with nitroglycerine. The path to violence, largely against inanimate objects rather than people it must be stressed, was paved with the obstacles that apartheid had placed in the way to the aspirations of the majority.

Black Africans were subject to pass laws in the nineteenth century by the British so as to restrict their movements into and within White and Coloured areas. Blacks were not allowed on to the streets of towns in Cape Province or Natal and had to carry a pass at all times. British liberals had also reserved the three protectorates of Basutoland, Bechuanaland and Swaziland from the Union of South Africa allegedly to protect Black African interests within a White-dominated Union. These pass laws were the object of a campaign by the South African Native National Convention, founded in 1912 to co-ordinate the expression of Black opinion after it was ignored by the Union's White founders. The campaign's model was the passive resistance espoused by Gandhi, the Indian lawyer who spent twenty years living in Natal until he returned home in 1914. Protests by Indians (and Coloureds) forced the government to drop discriminatory measures affecting these communities. Passive resistance also reflected the fact that the majority of members of what in 1923 became the ANC had a Christian background – preventing some of them such as chief Albert Luthuli from ever endorsing political violence – which also made them suspicious of the machinations of the tiny South African Communist Party. Moreover, the Communists had sought to promote white working-class interests, as typified by the slogan 'Workers of the World Unite for a White South Africa' during the 1922 Rand revolt in which troops were used to shoot down white miners striking in protest against being deskilled through the employment of Blacks. It was only when as a result of Comintern pressure the Communists advocated an 'independent native republic' that the Party was able to expand its influence within the ANC, although it would continue to be viewed with suspicion by pan-Africanists who resented any leading role being assumed by Coloureds, Indians or White liberals and leftists.

It is important to remember that Afrikaner nationalism was also long in the making.[42] The semi-secret Broederbund was established to encourage Afrikaner culture and language and to practise a sort of Trotskyite entryism into all major institutions, while the Dutch Reformed Church gave transcendental purpose to the Afrikaner version of the toils and travails of this southerly Chosen People. The poet cum theologian J. D. du Toit claimed that racial differences were part of God's ordinances of creation. The National Party was the political vehicle for the expression of Afrikaner interests.[43]

The outbreak of the Second World War meant that, regardless of the Anglo-South Africans who volunteered for the RAF, and the third of Afrikaner males who joined them, many Afrikaners sympathised with a Nazi camp whose propagandists were not slow to emphasise the historical sufferings of the Boers and Irish. Radio Zeesen was active here too, with the former headteacher Eric Holm acting as an Afrikaner 'Lord Haw Haw'. There were nasty mass brawls between the Red Lice, that is men in uniform with Dominion insignia, and members of the para-military Ossewabrandwag. Extremist elements in that movement formed terrorist *Stormjaers*, who tried to sabotage communications and ended up killing a bystander when they blew up a post office.[44] A society at war discombobulated many of the racial verities of farmers in the Transvaal. Increased wartime production also meant heavy demand for Black labour, which drained away from the interior's Afrikaner farms, thereby nullifying the efforts of the National Party in the previous decade. Prime minister Smuts seemed to be going along with the de-facto abrogation of segregation until the National Party under Daniel François Malan stiffened his resistance. Idealistic Anglo-American talk about a better post-war world gave a fillip to the ANC, whose new Youth League became a training ground for a remarkable and more resilient generation of future leaders including Nelson Mandela, Walter Sisulu and Robert Sobuke. Instead of dividing and ruling, the government also picked concurrent fights with the Coloured and Indian communities, who instituted tentative contacts with the ANC. Finally, the Communists, their prestige enhanced by the westward march of Stalin's legions, succeeded in penetrating and radicalising Black African trades unions, leading to such events as the Rand goldmine strike that resulted in the police forcing Black miners back to work at gunpoint.

The National Party's victory in the May 1948 elections brought the first all-Afrikaner cabinet in South Africa's history, all but two ministers being members of the Broederbund. The Afrikaners believed in and practised affirmative action. Men serving sentences for treasonable collusion with Nazi Germany were released from jail, while the English deputy chief of the Defence Staff was transferred to Germany and his post abolished. Official bilingualism meant that many linguistically challenged English-speaking South Africans lost their jobs while bilingual Afrikaners replaced them. To augment his slim parliamentary majority, Malan invented six new seats for South West Africa, still under a UN mandate. New rules made it hard for Cape Coloureds to register to vote; after a protracted legal battle that ran over five years they emerged entitled to vote only for four White representatives.

Unanimity of outlook in successive Afrikaner administrations enabled them to implement the racist principles inherent within the ideology of apartheid, which was presented as a form of separate development for each of South Africa's various 'tribes'. That this was enshrined in law made it more enforceable than the informal segregation of the US South of the day; that the rule of law still largely functioned made it less murderous than Nazi Germany with its vast supra-legal SS state. Comparisons between either apartheid or Nazism and the modern state of Israel are both inaccurate and offensively absurd, quite apart from the generous representation of South African Jews in the South African Communist Party and the ANC.

Apartheid was imposed incrementally over several years by legislation, its intellectual afflatus supplied by social psychologists and the like at the university of Stellenbosch. It began with racial classification according to crude physiognomic criteria, and regardless of the absurdly hurtful consequences in a society where Creolisation was at an advanced stage. Under legislation introduced in 1949–50 race determined who a person could marry or have sexual relations with. The 1950 Group Areas Act and the 1952 Native Laws Amendment Act made race the determinant of where a person was allowed to live. The former licensed the wholesale eviction and resettlement of Coloureds and Indians away from White districts, while trying to freeze the existing Black African urban population through stringent criteria and restrictions on intra-urban mobility.

These Black Africans were thenceforth treated as foreign guest-workers in the 87 per cent of land reserved for Whites, Coloureds and Indians, and the vast majority of the Black population was allocated some 13 per cent of the remaining land, despite the fact that they were 80 per cent of the total population. These territories were divided into ten 'homelands', the idea being that once they had achieved independence the Blacks living there would forfeit their South African citizenship. The 1953 Bantu Authorities Act confirmed the impression that these were analogous to the reservations of Native Americans in the US when they accorded power to government-selected tribal chiefs. In the coming decades, vast numbers of people, including six hundred thousand Coloured, Indian and Chinese as well as forty thousand Whites and millions of Black Africans, were moved around in this bizarre experiment in racial engineering, with bulldozers erasing each anomalous 'black spot'. A ban on the South African Communist Party was loosely framed to cover not only past Party members but also others deemed to have similar sympathies.

Laws also reserved the enjoyment of quotidian 'amenities' along racial lines. Non-whites needed special permits to run businesses or to practise professions within White areas. No Black was permitted to employ a White, and no White could be arrested by a Black African police officer. The transport system was segregated, with Blacks consigned to the third class on trains. Whites enjoyed significantly better educational and medical facilities than Blacks. Perhaps most perniciously, the limited avenues for intellectual and social advancement that Christian schools and colleges had provided were choked off by the restriction of Black education only to those skills – such as taking orders – that were deemed necessary by the Afrikaner economy. A Black man wishing to study astrophysics could go abroad, if the funding was there, but it would take an age to get a passport and his citizenship would be cancelled the moment he left. On a less exalted scale, there were no Black vets until 1980, simply because many cattle-dip inspectors were White and Whites could not take orders from Black vets. Black Africans were made to feel on edge in their own country by myriad petty restrictions that facilitated harassment. Car parks, drive-in cinemas, hotels, restaurants, theatres, beaches, public parks and swimming pools were all segregated, requiring a plethora of trilingual warning signs and zealous jobsworths. Black African mobility was further restricted by the issuance of passes which recorded a person's employment history and without which he or she was liable to arrest.

Although in 1955 a broad front of opponents of apartheid promulgated a Freedom Charter at a historic meeting at Klipstown, the role of White Communists in its drafting led to the formation in 1959 of a separate Pan-African Congress, and hence an unfortunate radicalising rivalry among both groups of militants in their respective campaigns against the pass laws. The PAC was under the spell of the Ghanaian leader Kwame Nkrumah and wanted a totally Africanised state to be called Azania. In March 1960 a PAC-organised demonstration converged on a police station at Sharpeville in the Afrikaners' Transvaal heartland, with the intention of having themselves arrested for not carrying the necessary identity passes which the demonstrators had left at home. Apparently the fact that a stone hit the car of the local police chief was sufficient justification for his men to open fire, which resulted in sixty-nine unarmed Africans being shot in the back and a further 186 wounded. Press photographs caught the police reloading their weapons to fire another salvo which undermined the idea that they had responded impulsively to some imminent threat. Separate violent confrontations occurred in the townships around Cape Town. A state of emergency was declared in many areas. Shocking photographs of White policemen with snarling dogs bludgeoning Black Africans were relayed around the world.

Nelson Mandela recalled that 'We in the ANC had to make rapid adjustments to this new situation, and we did so.' By then Mandela was a defendant in the longest treason trial in history. In late March chief Luthuli led the way in symbolically burning his pass, a gesture followed by thousands of ANC supporters. In early April both the ANC and PAC were banned under the Suppression of Communism Act. It was at this time that the ANC elaborated underground structures, with key personnel, including Mandela, living clandestinely. After his acquittal in the treason trial, for the court could find no evidence that the ANC advocated violence, Mandela went underground. This coincided with a huge 'stay away' campaign, in which Black withdrawal of labour by simply remaining at home rather than going to work was designed to make lethal confrontation less possible. The government responded by having armoured vehicles and helicopters patrol the townships in order to intimidate with a display of military might. The PAC unhelpfully exhorted people to go to work as part of its rivalry with the ANC, and the campaign quickly collapsed in a couple of days.

This was the immediate background to discussions within the ANC in 1961 regarding the abandonment of non-violent protest, ironically just at the time chief Luthuli won the Nobel Peace Prize. Mandela argued that 'the attacks of the wild beast cannot be averted with only bare hands'. Moreover, there was the risk that spasmodic grassroots violence would result in further massacres while encouraging the view that Africans were barbaric savages. By directing violence, the ANC stood a chance of limiting its effects. Persuasively Mandela reasoned that non-violence was a tactic rather than an inviolable principle, which could be abandoned as political circumstances dictated. After interminable discussions, in which

Indian ANC supporters clung to the strategy of non-violence, Mandela won the day, and was authorised to establish a military capability, Umkhonto we Sizwe, semi-detached from the ANC.[45]

Umkhonto recruited volunteers through still-legal trades unions, many of whose branch leaders were Umkhonto commanders. The Communist Party secured nearly US$3 million in aid for arms purchases from the Soviet Union and Czechoslovakia, the majority surplus AK-47s, or Skorpion, Makarov and Tokarev machine pistols and hand grenades. Because neighbouring states had their own colonial regimes, training camps for would-be saboteurs were opened in Dar es Salaam in Tanganyika (or Tanzania as it became after 1964). The journey there by train, foot and only later aeroplane via British protectorates in Basutoland, Bechuanaland and Swaziland and then via the two Rhodesias was arduous and dangerous. Although sabotage was regarded as preparatory for full-scale guerrilla war, by being directed at things rather than people it would not harm the ANC's considerable moral authority in the eyes of world opinion. Little thought was given to the logistics of such a campaign or how to attract and maintain international attention.

The campaign opened on 16 December 1961, the day Afrikaners celebrated a victory over a Zulu host at Blood River in 1838. The intention was to cause widespread economic disruption and a cessation of foreign investment. Bombs went off in electric power stations and government offices in Johannesburg and Port Elizabeth. Leaflets left at the scenes explained: 'The time comes in the life of any nation when there remain two choices: submit or fight . . . we shall not submit and we have no choice but to hit back by all means within our power.' There were some 194 attacks on further targets until July 1963, the average causing a mere US$125 damage. There were also disciplinary attacks on suspected collaborators, informers and state witnesses in terrorism trials. The South African state did not idly watch these developments. A Sabotage Act enabled it to ban individuals suspected of terrorism, proscribing even the reproduction of their words, while a year later the police were allowed to detain suspects for ninety days, the thin end of the wedge for widespread detainee abuse. For reasons that seem obscure, the Umkhonto leadership purchased a farm called Lilliesleaf in the White Johannesburg suburb of Rivonia to house a radio transmitter and duplicating equipment. Police penetration of the organisation led to a raid on the farm in July 1963 and the detention of almost the entire Umkhonto leadership.

Several of these men, including Mandela, who was already in jail, received life sentences. Leadership of the ANC passed to the London-based Oliver Tambo, Mandela's former law partner, who became acting president of the ANC. Parallel attempts by the PAC to organise an armed campaign from Masera in Basutoland were undone when the British colonial police raided its headquarters and handed the entire membership lists of the guerrilla organisation to their South African colleagues. The South African police also successfully smashed a break-away PAC faction called Poqo which was active in the Cape and Transkei. This had murdered pro-government chiefs and seven Whites. Surveying the ANC in the early 1960s it seems a miracle that it survived at all.

Although the internal military organisation had been decimated, in Tanzania the exiled Umkhonto leadership under the peripatetic Oliver Tambo rebuilt its military cadres. Men who managed to make the two-thousand-kilometre journey into exile were relayed to Algeria, Egypt, Ethiopia and Morocco for military training, although some five hundred went for year-long courses to Odessa in the southern Soviet Union where the climate was relatively familiar. In 1965 Tanzanian president Julius Nyerere allowed the ANC to open its own training camp at a disused railway station at Dodoma. Zambian achievement of independence that year enabled the ANC to move one country closer to South Africa and to set up operations in Lusaka. There it co-operated with the exiled leadership of the Zimbabwe African People's Union (ZAPU) fighting the newly independent Ian Smith regime in Rhodesia. The first joint operation by ZAPU and the MK Luthuli Detachment crossed into Rhodesia in 1967, the idea being for the main body of this force to venture into South Africa to set up further guerrilla bands. It fought a number of engagements with Rhodesian Selous Scouts in the bush of the Wankie Game Reserve, before being confronted by reinforcements from the South African Defence Force. Short of water and supplies, the MK survivors, including their commander Chris Hani, limped into Botswana without having fired a shot on South African soil.[46]

This disaster, whatever its symbolic significance, and the success of the government of John Vorster in persuading the heads of fourteen African states to back a non-violent solution to southern Africa's multiple conflicts, led the ANC to consider its long-term strategies at the Morogoro Conference. The view of the Côte d'Ivoire president that 'Apartheid falls within the domestic jurisdiction of South Africa and will not be eliminated by force' was especially ominous. Emerging from nearly two years in a Botswana jail, Hani was angrily exercised by the corruption and brutality abroad in the ANC training camps where recruits dressed in rags went on marches while their leaders rode behind in Land Rovers sipping Scotch. There was widespread resentment at the globe-trotting lifestyle of some of the senior leadership, who appeared to be swanning around on a sort of international anti-apartheid circuit. The Conference served to clear the air while both opening the ANC to all races and streamlining its operations. It established a sense of direction, namely an 'indivisible theatre of war' with 'interlocking and inter-weaving of international, African and southern African developments which play on our situation'.

This was just as well since the ANC was in danger of being left behind by the tide of events. Portuguese colonial rule collapsed dramatically in Angola and Mozambique, giving a morale boost to the anti-apartheid movement within South Africa. Or so it seemed. For in addition to deploying its economic weight to bring those countries' new governments to heel, South Africa also backed guerrilla armies such as UNITA in Angola, RENAMO in Mozambique and ZAPU in what after 1980 became Zimbabwe, while deposing the government of Lesotho in a coup. Car and letter bombs, one of which killed Ruth First in 1982, or armed incursions and bombing raids kept up pressure on exiled ANC headquarters in each of the five frontline states, until all but three thought better of it. Cuban, East German and Soviet aides evened up these conflicts while forcing the West to construe them in Cold War terms, softening its moral outrage towards apartheid which had been declared a crime by the United Nations.

Within South Africa, where the ANC was hardly present as an organised force, a younger generation of radicals had discovered Black Consciousness, partly in emulation of the US Black Power movement of the time, with an emphasis upon Black (including Coloured and Indian) pride and values. The charismatic medical student Steve Biko emerged as its most representative figure, at a time when the ANC within the Republic was led by a seventy-seven-year-old. Based in Black universities and schools in the homelands, the movement's rejection of violence and its interest in raising consciousness meant that the White government initially welcomed it as an alternative to the semi-Stalinist leadership of the ANC. By way of respectful osmosis, the regime began to substitute the term 'Black' for the fussily suburban 'Non-White' in its descriptions of the majority population. Student protests led to expulsions while Biko himself was placed under a banning order. The expelled students became teachers in township schools, spreading their radicalism down through the age groups.

In 1976 children at a Soweto school protested against hitherto un-enforced rules that half the instruction should be in Afrikaans. With their unerring ability to misjudge the impact on international opinion, the South African police shot into a march by protesting schoolchildren, killing a twelve-year-old boy. The trouble spread to a hundred urban areas, leaving a total of six hundred people dead by 1977. For the first time in South Africa's history, young people took control of the protest movement, and effectively assumed control of the townships. Violence was employed to eliminate collaborators and the drinking dens that undermined township discipline. Biko himself passed into legend when, after being arrested in August 1977, he was beaten in police custody, taken on a long ride in a police van, and left to die in a cell. That autumn all Black Consciousness organisations were banned and many of its supporters fled abroad, providing fresh blood for the ANC. Even before then, South Africa was losing 450 dissidents a month, many going to ANC bases in Angola, Mozambique and Zambia. The average age of Umkhonto fighters fell from thirty-five to twenty-eight as a result of this infusion of energy and commitment, even if much of it was dissipated in the ANC's sinister military encampments.[47]

Between 1977 and 1982 Umkhonto stepped up guerrilla attacks within South Africa, striking communications links, industrial installations – including both of South Africa's oil-synthesising plants and its nuclear power station – and the administrative offices of the townships. Police stations had to be heavily sandbagged against possible RPG attacks. During the 1980s these armed attacks included some which involved the bombing of innocent civilians, despite the ANC in 1980 being the first national liberation movement to sign the Geneva Convention as modified three years earlier to include guerrilla wars. Nineteen people were killed in downtown Pretoria in 1983 by an ANC bomb, prompting Nelson Mandela to criticise the attack for its lack of concern for civilians. The ANC defended the use of landmines in the context of its Operation Kletswayo on the ground that the government treated border areas as conflict zones. Most victims were innocent civilians, like thirty-four-year-old Kobie van Eck and her daughters Nasie, aged two, and Nelmari, aged eight, together with Kobus, aged three, Carla, aged eight, and their grandmother Marie de Nyschen, all slaughtered on holiday in a game reserve by a mine laid by three MK personnel acting on the orders of several members of the current South African cabinet.[48]

In that year the ANC launched a United Democratic Front, an umbrella organisation for all those who were opposed to apartheid, and which functioned as a surrogate within the Republic for the exiled or imprisoned ANC leadership. Enthusiastic White liberal involvement with ANC cadres occasionally brought the disillusioning realisation that they included steely Stalinists, although that message rarely filtered back to the ANC's more credulous supporters in the West, notably in its Churches, ever receptive to the secularised messianisms of their time. In 1985 the UDF decreed a campaign to make South Africa ungovernable, while also qualifying Umkhonto's earlier concentration on hard targets. This decision was taken partly because the hard targets had become harder to attack because of beefed-up defences, but also because in the eyes of the ANC it was time to remind Whites that the victims of their security forces were not just Blacks but civilians too. Among some Blacks there was the feeling that Whites had evaded the sort of carnage they had undergone, sipping drinks and frying sausages and steaks by their swimming pools. Car bombs, copied from events in Lebanon, exploded outside a bar in Durban while in Johannesburg a small bomb outside a court lured policemen who were killed by a much larger second explosion. Two days before Christmas 1985, ANC guerrilla Andrew Zondo left a bomb in a waste bin in a crowded shopping centre at Amanzimtoti, which exploded killing five Whites and injuring forty-eight others. He said he couldn't find an unvandalised phone to call in a warning. In 1986 Umkhonto began planting limpet mines on White farms, regardless of whether those killed or maimed were the farmers or their Black labourers; some twenty-five people died and seventy-six were injured.[49]

This broadly focused campaign, which included boycotts, the campaign to free Mandela, withholding rent and strikes, led to a steady exodus of Whites, reducing their proportion of the population from 20 to 11 per cent. Their experience of South Africa passed into the great hole of forgetting that awaits unpopular lost causes, especially since charm was not the average Afrikaner's strong suit. The South African state became progressively militarised, symbolised by the armoured high-axel Hippos careening through townships in clouds of dust and firing bursts of birdshot, while assuming state terrorist features, ranging from torture to murdering people at home and abroad. The security service BOSS was sometimes caught red handed practising any number of dirty tricks including burglary and blackmail as well as murder. In addition to the growing number of detainees who hanged themselves in cells or fell off police-station roofs, balaclava-clad security personnel were responsible for the disappearance and killing of ANC suspects.[50] Of course, violence was not simply White on Black. Kangaroo courts in the townships meted out some seven hundred necklacings (death by blazing tyres), and a further four hundred other forms of burning, while inter-tribal violence erupted between the predominantly Xhosa supporters of the ANC and the Zulus of chief Mangosuthu Buthelezi's Inkatha Freedom Party. Although one cannot overlook the asymmetry between state and sub-statal violence, White South Africans have a point when they argue that attempts to bring apartheid-era officials before the courts should be matched by trials of ANC figures responsible for these actions, if the principle of equality before the law is a reality in their country.[51] The ANC's armed campaign made little or no impact on the massive military might of the South African state, which was ultimately undermined by chronic disorder, economic failure and the seismic reverberations of the collapse of Communism which gave momentum to several peace initiatives in the 1990s. In P. W. de Klerk the Afrikaners found a leader of the calibre of Mikhail Gorbachev, a realist who rose to the occasion. The precise relationship between the ANC's armed struggle and the chronic crime and violence that afflicts post-apartheid South Africa remains to be established.

Methods of fighting which had been peripheral to the vast indus-trialised clashes of the Second World War became commonplace in the wars of decolonisation that succeeded it. Guerrilla movements became the norm, with many resorting to terrorism partly to magnetise inter-national opinion, but also because clever men like the psychiatrist–revolutionary Frantz Fanon (or his modish spokesperson Sartre) told them that violence was both bonding and liberating – a new man would emerge upright from the deformed personality created by colonialism. They had less to say about how violence could develop its own psycho-pathic momentum, a habit that it was impossible to shake off, or how in some left-wing circles it would be invested with a spurious glamour.

In none of the cases discussed here was terrorism the crucial factor in forcing the colonial powers, or the minority elites, to abandon Palestine and Algeria, or to agree to surrender power in South Africa. The former reflected the wider strategic picture during the Cold War, which led the British or French metropolis to regard Palestine and Algeria as super-fluous liabilities which cost too much blood and treasure. The British did a quick flit; the French fought an eight-year war. International isolation, chronic economic problems, a deleterious demographic imbalance, and the end of the Cold War as a covering excuse for combating alleged Communists did for the regime in South Africa. The terrorism of Irgun and the Stern Gang never amounted to more than an irritant to the British in Palestine and an embarrassment to the leaders of Labour Zionism, for whom the moral heights were always paramount. Despite the constant Afrikaner talk of terrorists, terrorism was marginal to the ANC's broadly based strategies, which for most of its existence revolved around non-violence. When this was abandoned it was in favour of guerrilla warfare and sabotage, both unsuccessful in any military sense, with terrorist attacks on civilians adopted at a late stage of their oper-ations. That is not to excuse it. Arguably, the passive–aggressive war of children against policemen and soldiers in the townships had far greater impact. Even the US ambassador came to the funeral of Steve Biko. By contrast, terrorism became endemic in Algeria, initially to grab the headlines, but then increasingly as part of a cycle of vengeful attacks, which in due course was emulated by ultras among the *colons* and their regular army supporters in a terrorist onslaught that became mindless, discrediting their already lost cause. Finally, Arafat's Fatah drew entirely inappropriate lessons from the FLN campaign against the French, regardless of the ways in which military activity boosted its support at a time when the Arab nations were reluctant to undertake it. The Israelis were a majority rather than a colonial minority in Israel. Unlike the *colons* of Algeria they were not dependent upon mood swings in the metropolitan public or on the strategic capriciousness of its statesmen. Given the background of the Holocaust, the Israelis had nowhere to retreat to – certainly not Europe, which they regarded as a vast Jewish graveyard. They were where they were and that is where they remain.

Armed national liberation struggles also led to the adoption of counter-terrorist methods which could be terroristic in themselves, in the sense of being designed to create widespread fear among civilian populations or involving such counter-productive methods as torture. Only in a few specific contexts where the insurgents, as in Malaya, were from an ethnic minority could they be isolated through political conces-sions to the majority. Even then, the Malayan Emergency took the British twelve years to suppress, by careful police work as much as by Dayak head-hunters or the Special Air Service Regiment (SAS). In Algeria, similar tactics, with more force and less concern for hearts and minds, failed to work, for the cause of national independence was widely shared by the Arab and Berber majority. Worse, the hearts and minds of most metropolitan French people ceased to be with 'Algérie française', associated as it was with hapless conscripts and mutinous regulars and the lethal nihilism of the OAS, whose final contribution was to blind four-year-old Parisians and to blow the country they loved apart as it slid from their control. State brutality was matched by the horrors perpetrated by the FLN. Similarly in South Africa, the Afrikaner state readily resorted to assassination and torture to perpetuate racist domination of the Black African majority, whose leaders' espousal of non-violence for so long is remarkable. Sharpeville came to symbolise that struggle, along with the carefully honed image of the imprisoned Nelson Mandela, with any less attractive features of the ANC – or the grassroots township leaderships – suppressed in the liberal imagination. Afrikanerdom came to be synonymous with a brutal security state that undercut all the rhetoric about civilisation.

The ways in which the experiences of national liberation struggle, and the brutalities which that involved, may have become encoded in the DNA of the newly independent states, as Mouloud Feraoun predicted in the case of Algeria, has never received the sort of attention that colonialist state violence has incurred, although present-day Algeria indicates that this is a major oversight. The historian of South Africa, R. W. Johnson, claims that the exiled ANC began to assume some of the unattractive characteristics of the regime it was fighting. The PLO under Arafat became a byword for corruption, with huge sums of money destined for Palestinian causes ending up in obscure bank accounts which were inherited by the leader's widow rather than by those in refugee camps. Despite this, the era of national liberation struggles powerfully conveyed the message that terrorism worked, and that the pariah's mark of 'terrorist' – which made it impossible to negotiate with those imprinted with it – could be expunged. Ben Bella, Boumedienne, Begin, Shamir, Mandela and Tambo all became leaders of their respective countries, while Arafat became 'Mr Palestine' for his corrupt lifetime. That beguiling message was received in many parts of the world, as well as by terrorists in impeccably democratic states who represented causes with virtually no popular backing. The idea that it is 'always good to talk' has become folkloric in some circles, with the credulous imagining that dialogue is possible with Al Qaeda. There was a further lesson. The colonial struggles all involved playing to international public opinion via the mass media. Terrorists learned that too. That takes us to how a series of events in Jordan played out in and beyond Munich: grim harbingers of transnational terrorism that has become spectacular in our lifetimes.

CHAPTER 5

Attention-Seeking: Black September and International Terrorism

I 'A GRAVEYARD FOR PLOTTERS'

By 1951, when king Abdullah annexed the teeming West Bank, and was promptly assassinated by a Palestinian, the Hashemite kingdom of Jordan had become home to the largest number of Palestinian refugees, constituting two-thirds of its two million people. The CIA referred to the capital, Amman, as a 'Palestinian city'. Jordan was an important Western ally, to which the United States contributed aid worth US$47 million per annum. It was also where the main Fatah bases were situated, from which cross-border raids were launched into Israel. This raised grave problems, not all of them connected with Israeli reprisals, which because of their scale and focused firepower attracted more attention than the spasmodic lethal raids that provoked them.

Very few Westerners have any experience of armed paramilitaries in their midst, unless they have memories of the occupying Wehrmacht or the Provos in Dundalk, a town in Eire nicknamed 'El Paso'. The posturing arrogance of armed Palestinian fighters compounded older animosities between the refugees and the indigenous Transjordanian population. The Jordanians, like many Arabs, regarded the Palestinians as akin to Jews: better educated, go-getting, more cosmopolitan and more urbanised than they were. In their eyes the Palestinians were cowards who had failed to fight for their own country in 1948. Many Palestinians were correspondingly contemptuous of the 'barefoot' Jordanian Bedouin, the fiercely proud nomads who were heavily represented in the Jordanian armed forces. By the late 1960s there were some fifty-two separate armed Palestinian groups active in Jordan. Sometimes Yasser Arafat appeared to be in control of these multifarious groups; mostly he preferred to indulge his lifelong affinity with drama and chaos, for as events unfolded there seemed little method behind his actions as he flitted from one attention-seeking drama to another.

Some of these armed groups were tools of neighbouring states, such as Iraq or Syria, others – notably the Popular Front for the Liberation of Palestine led by the former medical practitioner George Habash – sought to overthrow reactionary Arab governments, including that of his host king Hussein. As we shall see, the former Fatah member Sabri el-Banna, known as Abu Nidal, would constitute a further layer of complication when as a self-proclaimed rejectionist he declared war on the PLO as well as the Jews and Israelis, while acting as a hired assassin for various Arab governments. His role was emulated with gusto by the freelance Venezuelan Marxist-Leninist murderer Illich Ramírez Sánchez, nicknamed 'Carlos the Jackal'. The Japanese Red Army would contribute a peculiarly sadistic note to these years. Its internal practices, evident from the tortured corpses of comrades buried around the scene of the winter 1972 siege of its snowy hideaway north of Tokyo, were more redolent of the cultic American mass murderer Charles Manson than of a typical terrorist movement. In addition to the dramatis personae, the tactics employed went international too.

Most of these radical Palestinian factions believed in internationalising their cause through the tactic of air piracy, a crime hitherto mostly confined to political refugees or, in the US where it was most frequent, to extortionists, the deranged and admirers of Fidel Castro, for virtually every hijacked aircraft in the 1960s was diverted from the US to Cuba. Uniquely horrifying because of the vulnerabilities of people held at gunpoint at thirty thousand feet, hijackings occurred so often – for there were no armed sky marshals, passenger screening or reinforced cabins – that pilots took plans of Havana's José Martí runways on flights south to Florida, the routes where most hijackings occurred. There was even a routine form for the US to complete and lodge with the neutral Swiss embassy in Washington, to extricate stranded aircraft, passengers and crew from Cuba. In the summer of 1968 the tactic was globalised when PFLP terrorists commandeered an El Al flight and diverted it to Algeria, releasing non-Israelis while keeping the Israelis captive, in a clear act of ethno-religious malice. After two months, a threat by the International Airline Pilots Association to boycott Algeria resulted in the release of the hijacked passengers. When in August 1969 two Palestinians hijacked a TWA flight to Syria, the US quietly put pressure on the Israelis to release Palestinian prisoners to secure the freedom of the hijackers' Israeli hostages. This would not be repeated, *pour décourager les autres*.[1]

Israeli armed intervention in Jordan to suppress guerrilla bands at source, and the strutting, extortionate behaviour of Palestinian fighters on the streets of Amman and elsewhere, forced king Hussein to crack down on the state within a state developing in his kingdom. For that is how one Palestinian fedayeen leader recalled it: 'We were mini-states and institutions. Every sector commander considered himself God ... everyone set up a state for himself and did what he pleased.' Weapons were openly brandished and Palestinian fighters went around in vehicles without Jordanian licence plates. Local policemen were treated with contempt whenever they tried to do their job.

After armed clashes between the Jordanian army and Palestinian fighters, in which the latter allegedly celebrated one victory by playing football with the head of a Jordanian soldier, Hussein instituted a crackdown. He banned Palestinians from roaming around brandishing weapons, while Arafat agreed not to venture cross-border raids without the kingdom's express agreement. This undertaking, and the many similar agreements between Arafat and Hussein afterwards, were systematically flouted by the Fatah leader whose word invariably failed to bond. In February 1970 Hussein instituted yet another attempt to curb fedayeen activity, in an atmosphere in which Palestinian militants thought Jordan (and Egypt) might betray them in the interests of a US-brokered deal with Israel. At a graduation ceremony for Fatah recruits in August 1970, Arafat warned Hussein: 'We shall turn Jordan into a graveyard for plotters.' This tough Palestinian rhetoric was invariably followed by Jordanian appeasement as the king reversed his own earlier measures to constrain the fedayeen.

Armed clashes between Jordanian troops and Palestinian fedayeen grew more serious, including two attempts on the life of the king, in one of which his motorcade was sprayed with machine-gun fire. Both sides sought external support. Arafat thought he had secured promises of military help from Syria as well as from the seventeen thousand Iraqi expeditionary troops permanently stationed in Jordan. However, he also managed to alienate Nasser by criticising his acceptance of a US-brokered peace with Israel. With US assistance, Hussein desperately turned to Israel to see whether it would deter Syria from intervening in the civil war threatening to break out in his kingdom. He also quietly squared the Iraqis, securing an agreement with the army commander, general Hardan al-Takriti, that Iraq's Eastern Command would not intervene. The deal was even secretly taped by Hussein, and played back to demoralise captured Palestinian leaders. Some time later Iraq's president Ahmad Hassan al-Bakr explained to the PLO leaders why he had cut a deal with Hussein: 'you in the Palestinian resistance have nine lives, like a cat. If they kill you, you can rise again. But we are a regime!'[2]

Hussein's fear that he was losing control of Jordan was confirmed when in early September 1970 Habash's PFLP hijacked three aircraft, landing two of them – a Swissair DC-8 and a TWA Boeing 707 – at Dawsons Field, a remote airfield at Zarka in Jordan's deserts. The hijackers demanded the release of Palestinians held by Israel and various European governments; the US held no Palestinians prisoner, with the exception of the lunatic who had shot Robert Kennedy. A week later a BOAC VC-10 joined the other aircraft, so around four hundred people were trapped in what felt like metal cigar containers left out in the relentless desert sun. The British government of Edward Heath immediately capitulated to PFLP demands by releasing the svelte guerrilla Leila Khaled whom El Al security personnel had delivered to the British authorities after she was overpowered in an earlier hijacking. More concerned with the Soviet Union, China and Vietnam than a second-tier problem like the Middle East, president Richard Nixon persuaded the Israelis to release some Palestinian prisoners, while also insisting on improved security measures on US airlines. The hijacking opened up rifts between the PLO and PFLP, since Arafat did not want all of this international attention focused on Jordan as he prepared to overthrow its government. Fifty hostages remained, not on the three aircraft, which were blown up in a fit of maniacal pique, but in Amman, even as king Hussein and Arafat went to war.

On 17 September loyal Jordanian forces converged on the PLO headquarters in Amman, while Arafat, who had taken no preparatory steps to fight a hot war, impertinently told the king to leave his own country, a demand he repeated later on Radio Baghdad. A 'Republic of Palestine' was proclaimed in the northern city of Irbid. Heavily armed Jordanian troops used artillery and tanks to crush the PLO within the refugee camps, in eleven days of fighting that left some three thousand people dead. Seventy Palestinian guerrillas elected to wade across the Jordan to surrender to the Israelis rather than put themselves at the tender mercies of the Jordanians, a telling comment on the fragilities of intra-Arab solidarities. The US reinforced its Sixth Fleet and despatched elements of the 82nd Airborne Division from North Carolina, although they were recalled in mid-air. Israeli armoured convoys rumbled towards the small Syrian tank force that intervened, sending the latter scuttling homewards. After bold intervention by the Sudanese leader, acting as a proxy for the Arab League in Cairo, Arafat was smuggled out of Jordan dressed as a Kuwaiti dignitary. In Cairo, he and Hussein made their respective cases to the Arab leaders, with each accusing the other of betrayal. While they glowered at each other outside the conference room, the Arab leaders on 27 September patched together a deal regularising Palestinian guerrilla activity within Jordan that both men were obliged to accept. Of course, neither did, and fighting erupted again. The new Jordanian prime minister, Wasfi Tal, pushed the guerrillas out of the capital while confining the remainder to ever diminishing pockets around Ajlun and Jerash. After arranging a meeting with the king in Amman, Arafat thought better of it while en route to Amman, and ordered the car to cross over into Syria, while many of his fighters withdrew to Lebanon in what amounted to a second flight. The so-called Nakbah (catastrophe) of 1948 had been joined by the 1970 'Black September' in the Palestinian mythology of noble fighters and dark betrayals. Shortly afterwards, Abu Nidal in Baghdad began broadcasting attacks on his former Fatah colleagues, accusing them of cowardice and condemning them for concluding a ceasefire with king Hussein.

In 1971 Arafat joined his men in Lebanon, who eventually numbered about 2,400, making Beirut the headquarters for future Palestinian operations. Southern Lebanon was soon dubbed 'Fatahland'. President Nixon was less polite, asking, 'Why is Lebanon harbouring those sons of bitches?' Although Lebanon did not have the large Palestinian presence Arafat had left behind in Jordan, it had other advantages. Beirut was a major cosmopolitan city, for guerrillas were not immune to the high life, with easy access to the international media, some of whom were susceptible to the lure of revolutionary chic. More importantly the Lebanese government was weak and based on delicate ethno-religious compromises that could be undone with the slightest tip in the demographic balance. In 1948 there were already 180,000 Palestinian refugees in camps dotted along Lebanon's southern coast and in Beirut's western suburbs. By the 1960s they constituted 10 per cent of Lebanon's population. Fedayeen fighters in the south attacked Israel's northern settlements, disregarding the ineffectual Lebanese army and the mounting concerns of Lebanon's Maronite Christians. Armed clashes between Lebanese troops and Fatah guerrillas led Nasser to broker a deal in November 1969, whereby the Palestinians would co-ordinate their activities with the Lebanese armed forces while refraining from interference in the internal politics of the host country. In reality, this Cairo Agreement included no mechanisms to ensure such co-ordination or to police infractions of it. Moreover, Arafat was increasingly partial to the ambitious Druze leftist Kamal Jumblatt (the Druze were a minority religious sect) and was help-ing to train the Lebanese Shia Amal militia, evidence of his persistent meddling in the politics of the host country. When Syria's president Hafaz al-Assad imposed tighter controls on the three to four thousand Fatah fedayeen he had allowed in from Jordan, they decamped and joined their fellow militants in the Arqoub region of southern Lebanon, swelling the number of available fighters.[3]

With some organisational skill, Arafat and his colleagues set about constructing a state within a state in Lebanon, resembling the one they had been forced to abandon in Jordan. For it is surely noteworthy that just as the Palestinians had baulked at UN partition in 1947, a better deal than they would ever achieve in the ensuing decades, they also repeated in Lebanon the behaviour that had led them to being thrown out of Jordan. Donations from Arab states, above all Saudi Arabia, and the tithe levied on expatriate Palestinians working in Europe, the Middle East and the US were used to construct a parallel polity, with courts, hospitals, schools and training camps for the Palestinian refugee com-munity. The PLO opened some thirty-five industrial concerns, manu-facturing a variety of consumer goods, in and around Beirut, with Arafat as chief executive officer of this PLO Inc. In addition to these legitimate activities, PLO militants carried out bank robberies and kidnappings, making their own contribution to the destabilisation of one of the few parliamentary democracies ever to have existed in the Middle East.

II MUNICH

Revenge for those blamed for Black September came fast, as Arabs practised the old way of an eye for an eye. At lunchtime on 28 November 1971, the Jordanian prime minister Wasfi Tal went up the steps of the

Sheraton hotel in Cairo to meet his wife after a morning of Arab League negotiations. As he crossed the crowded lobby looking for her, a young man, later identified as Essat Rabah, fired five shots into him, scattering his bodyguards. Tal's dying words were 'They've killed me. Murderers, they believe only in fire and destruction.' Another assassin, Manzur Khalifa, knelt down to lap up blood from the pool spreading beneath Tal's body. His lower face smeared red, Khalifa shouted: 'I am proud! Finally I have done it. We have taken our revenge on a traitor.' Stumbling towards the commotion, Tal's wife screamed: 'Palestine is finished!' As the assassins were captured and driven away by Egyptian security officials, they shouted triumphantly: 'We are Black September!' Two weeks later an Algerian gunman loitering on a quiet Kensington street emptied a submachine gun into the car carrying Zeid al-Rifai, the Jordanian ambassador to London and a key adviser to king Hussein. The ambassador was wounded in the hand. Egypt quietly released on the PLO's recognisance the four men sent for trial for murdering Tal. They vanished. Similarly, although the French authorities captured Frazeh Khelfa, the man who had shot at the Jordanian ambassador in London, they quickly put him on a plane to Algeria where he was allegedly wanted for earlier offences. Meanwhile, Black September struck at various targets in Europe. Five Jordanians said to have collaborated with Israel were murdered in a St Valentine's Day-style massacre in a basement in Brühl in Germany. Gulf Oil storage tanks were blown up in Holland, while an Esso pipeline was attacked near Hamburg.

Black September was the terrorist organisation which Arafat founded in Damascus in August and September 1971, initially to wage a terrorist war against the Jordanian monarchy. He admitted as much when, referring to Tal's murder on PLO Radio, he described the assassins as 'four of our revolutionaries'. The point of Black September was that it was deniable. In the words of one of its commanders: '[Black September] was separate from Fatah so that Fatah and the PLO would not have to carry opprobrium for our operations. The group, as individuals and as a leadership, was responsible for its own successes and failures without compromising the legitimate leadership of the Palestinian people [the PLO].'[4]

It had a collective leadership, with the officers able to draw upon Fatah and the PFLP's existing pool of men for each operation. The leaders included the former school teacher Salah Khalef (or Abu Iyad), Abu Youssef (Mohammed Youssef al-Najjar), Ghazi el-Husseini (a relative of the mufti), Fakhri al-Umari, Abu Daoud and Abu Hassan (Ali Hassan Salameh), all senior Fatah figures working under this new flag of convenience. Abu Iyad was head of Fatah's secretive Reconnaissance Department, Jihaz el-Razd, into which he had recruited the young Ali Hassan Salameh, the son of the renowned Hassan Salameh, with a brief to uncover and kill Israeli double-agents. Arafat sent all of these future Black September leaders on specialised training courses organised by the Egyptian Mukhabarat, the generic name for Arab intelligence agencies.[5]

At the age of twenty-five, Salameh had walked into the PLO's Amman offices during the 1967 Six-Day Arab war with Israel. This was a victory of family sentiment. Salameh's father had been killed when he was six. His mother, and a sister named Jihad, never allowed him to forget the heroic life of his father, or the ancestral home in Kulleh which the victorious Israelis had flattened. For women, and especially mothers and grand-mothers, were crucial in fanning the fires of hatred across the family generations, constantly reminding young males of the great deeds of their fathers, or jolting their emotions with idealised details of a way of life the family and an entire people had lost. It is worth quoting the sort of emotional pressures this super-terrorist was subjected to:

> The influence of my father posed a personal problem to me. I grew up in a family which considered struggle a matter of heri-tage which should be carried on by generation after generation. My upbringing was politicised. I lived the Palestinian cause.
>
> When my father fell as a martyr, Palestine was passed to me, so to speak. My mother wanted me to be another Hassan Salameh at a time when the most any Palestinian could hope for was to live a normal life.

Clearly that included him, for it was not automatic that he wished to become a terrorist:

> I wanted to be myself. The fact that I was required to live up to the image of my father created a problem for me. Even as a child, I had to follow a certain pattern of behaviour. I could not afford to live my childhood. I was made constantly conscious of the fact that I was the son of Hassan Salameh and had to live up to that, even without being told how the son of Hassan Salameh should live.

It was not a deprived childhood, in material respects, for the father had bequeathed the large sums he had accrued before and during the Arab Revolt. The family lived in Damascus and then Beirut, with Ali Hassan Salameh sent to the famous Maqassed College and then Bir-Zeit university in the West Bank. He spent time at various German universities, studying engineering, but mainly indulging his taste for fancy sports cars and attractive women. Salameh cultivated a macho image, always dressing in black – with gold medallions – and spending a lot of time body-building and learning karate. In 1963 his mother persuaded him to marry a member of the Husseini clan, a union to which the aged mufti gave his blessing, although the groom would quickly embark on extramarital liaisons. The Six-Day War was the first intimation that he was responsive to family obligation, his illustrious name guaranteeing that the new recruit would soon come to the notice of Arafat. That is a key way ahead in many terrorist organisations.[6]

Black September's first attempt to outdo Habash's PFLP in the arena of spectacular hijackings was a disaster. In early May 1972, four terrorists – two men and two women – commandeered a Sabena flight from Brussels to Tel Aviv shortly after it left Vienna on the second leg of its journey. The British pilot relayed to Tel Aviv the hijackers' demand for two hundred Palestinian prisoners to be released in exchange for the eighty-seven passengers. When the aircraft landed at Tel Aviv, Israeli special forces, disguised in white ground-crew overalls, sabotaged it – draining the hydraulics and deflating its tyres – while negotiators sought to wear down the hijackers. Meanwhile, special forces personnel practised storming a Boeing 707 at another airport, honing their assault to ninety seconds' duration. It took less than that time to carry out the mission when it happened. One hijacker was shot between the eyes by a soldier who appeared through an emergency hatch; another was killed with a couple of pistol shots. The two females were overpowered and captured. Any rejoicing at this operation proved premature. For Abu Iyad and other members of Black September had been to an international terrorist convention hosted by Habash at the Baddawi refugee camp in Lebanon, where it was decided to thwart attempts to profile terrorists by making use of a sort of double-indemnity method like the murders which two strangers plot while on a train in the 1951 Hitchcock thriller. Here the participating Japanese Red Army became relevant, its very strangeness in a Middle East context almost guaranteeing world interest. Its members were warriors who went to war with Rimbaud poems and small origami dolls in their pockets.

On 30 May 1972 an Air France jet landed at Israel's Lod airport after a final stopover at Rome on its long flight from Puerto Rico. It was 10 p.m. before the passengers, many of them Baptist and Pentecostal pilgrims visiting the Holy Land, entered the hall to retrieve their baggage. No one paid much attention to three young Japanese men, Takeshi Okidoro, Yasuiki Yashuda and Kozo Okamoto, none of these names being the ones on their passports, which by now had no photographs either, as they lifted three fibreglass cases from the conveyor belt.

Instead of exiting through customs, they laid the cases on the floor and withdrew grenades and Czech VZI-58 submachine guns. They raked the baggage hall with gunfire, pausing to toss grenades amid their fellow passengers. The hall filled with smoke, noise, screams and the pungent reek of cordite. The pilgrims' leader, Reverend Manuel Vega, saw his wife shot dead before a sharp pain hit him in the chest. Fortunately for him, what would have been a fatal bullet lost propulsion as it passed through his pocket Bible. Twenty-four people were killed, and a further seventy wounded, before Yashuda was accidentally shot by one of his comrades and Okidoro blew his own head off with a hand grenade that exploded prematurely as he tried to throw it through the luggage aperture to the parking bays. Only Okamoto attempted to escape via the airport runways, throwing grenades at stationary planes as he weaved past, before a brave El Al employee managed to floor him. During interrogations – which yielded a response from the silent Japanese only when the Israelis (falsely) promised to supply him with a revolver and a bullet to commit suicide – Okamoto shed some light on how he and his Rengo Sekigun (Japanese Red Army) comrades had decided to turn an airport into a charnel house, with spidery channels or long splashes of blood between corpses and abandoned luggage.

The son of a primary school head and a teacher, Okamoto had studied agriculture at a minor college, quickly becoming disillusioned with the 'mere masturbation' of student politics with silly posters of Che Guevara on the college dorm walls. He followed his elder brother Takeshi into the Red Army, his first task being to screen to students a movie entitled *Declaration of World War by the Red Army and PFLP*. In September 1971 he went to Beirut for military training. In early summer 1972 the PFLP put him through a more rigorous programme including handling explosives, the last three days being devoted to the layout of Lod airport. He then embarked on a sightseeing trip to Europe with his two comrades, the cover needed for them to board the Air France jet as it made its final stop at Rome from Puerto Rico. In keeping with the bizarre, cultic character of the Red Army, whose chief casualties hitherto had been members sexually abused, tortured and done to death by their comrades, Okamoto made several Delphic utterances about desiring to become a star within Orion, the fate he wished to share with his victims. Sentenced to life imprisonment, Okamoto eventually converted to Judaism, using nail clippers to perform a botched circumcision that nearly killed him. He currently lives somewhere in Lebanon after his release from prison in 1985 as part of a hostage exchange involving three captured Israeli soldiers who were swapped for 1,150 Palestinians.

Responses to this attack varied. In Japan, where the father of another terrorist had been so ashamed that he hung himself, Okamoto's own father wrote the following to the Israeli authorities: 'For forty years I thought I had devoted myself faithfully to the education of our young people. Please punish my son with the death sentence without delay.' The Japanese government also paid substantial compensation to the families of the victims. In Puerto Rico, Japanese engineers at the Panasonic factory were advised to leave the country because of the intensity of popular outrage provoked by the events at Lod airport. Libya's eccentric leader colonel Ghaddafi typically held the Japanese up as a model for the Palestinians: 'Why should a Palestinian not carry out such an operation? You will see them writing books and magazines full of theories, but otherwise unable to carry out one daring operation like that carried out by the Japanese.'[7]

As if this enormity were not enough, Black September was plotting its most spectacular attack. The pretext was that the International Olympic Committee had brusquely ignored a request from the Palestinians to be represented in September 1972 at the Munich Games. More relevant was possibly the presence of some six thousand print, radio and television journalists, with the first live satellite broadcasts – the US media pioneered this in 1968 – capable of reaching audiences of billions. A huge television tower would ensure that the world watched as sports commentators found themselves spectators at a massacre, with both commentators and terrorists having a vested interest in the telling detail and the longevity of the unfolding drama. The modern dialectic of commentators, studio-based experts and terrorists had come of age.

The projected attack, on a small Israeli team consisting mainly of fencers, weightlifters and wrestlers, was plotted by leading figures in

Fatah and Black September, namely Abu Iyad, Abu Daoud, Fuad al-Shamali, and Ali Hassan Salameh. 'We have to kill their most import-ant and most famous people. Since we cannot come close to their statesmen, we have to kill artists and sportsmen,' in the words of Fuad al-Shamali, the Lebanese Christian who plotted the Munich attack before his death in August 1972 from cancer. These men selected the two leaders of the attacking terrorist team, while the latter in turn selected six accomplices from a pool of men put through specialist training some-where in Lebanon. These six then received intensified training, especially in jumping from high walls, at an Egyptian secret police facility near Cairo. Insofar as these men had any common profile it was that they had grown up in the Chatila refugee camp in Beirut and four, including the team leader Luttif Afif, code-named 'Issa', had studied or worked in Germany. One had worked on the construction of the Olympic Village; another had been a cook or waiter in one of the canteens; a third had a German wife.

Their weapons arrived in Germany in late August 1972. Abu Iyad shepherded a well-dressed middle-aged Arab couple through Frankfurt airport. A customs officer stopped them and asked to inspect their suitcases, much to the annoyance of the supposed businessman, who protested loudly. The first and only case he opened revealed piles of women's underwear which in turn triggered voluble protests from the man's wife. The customs officer waved them through. The other two cases contained grenades, pistols and eight AK-47 Kalashnikovs. Abu Daoud met the group and helped store the weapons in lockers at Munich's railway station; he then waited for the attacks in his hotel room. Ali Hassan Salameh flew to East Berlin to watch the discomfort of the Federal Republic unfold from the safe haven of its Marxist-Leninist rival.

The full terrorist team met for the first time at a restaurant in Munich station on the eve of the attack. It was code-named 'Ikrit and Birim' in honour of two Maronite villages that the Israelis had destroyed in 1948. It commenced at 4.30 a.m. on 5 September when eight Palestinians, wearing tracksuits and carrying heavy sports bags, sauntered towards the fence surrounding the Olympic Village. A group of drunken Americans returning from a party obligingly helped them climb the fence. They made for Connollystrasse 31, one of a series of low-rise flats where athletes and their trainers were housed. There they donned ski masks and took out weapons from the sports bags. Using a key they had purloined,

the group quietly tried the lock of the door to apartment 1. This scratching sound awoke a wrestling referee called Yossef Gutfreund who,
half asleep, went to the door. On seeing armed men through the crack,
he used his capacious bulk to keep them outside. Gutfreund's desperate
shouts led a weightlifting trainer to smash a window and flee outside.
The terrorists forced their way past Gutfreund and burst into the
apartment. The wrestling coach Moshe Weinberg grabbed a fruit knife
and slashed at Luttif. Another terrorist shot Weinberg in the face. Taking
Weinberg with them, the terrorists went past apartment 2, which contained more Israeli athletes, and headed along the street to apartment
3 where the weightlifters and wrestlers lodged. They were captured and
taken back out into the street towards apartment 1. In that moment
a wrestler managed to break loose and flee into an underground car
park. The wounded Weinberg smashed one of the terrorists in the face,
breaking his jaw, before he was scythed down by submachine-gun fire
and left dying in the street. As lights flashed on as a result of the commotion, the terrorists herded their captives back into apartment 1 and up
its internal stairs. At that point, a weightlifter called Yossef Romano, who
was on crutches because of a ligament injury, hurled himself at his
guards. He was shot dead and left in the middle of the floor of the room
where the Israeli hostages were held. At around 5 a.m. the first calls
alerting the head of the Munich police and, forty-five minutes later,
Golda Meir's government began to make this a major diplomatic, as well
as a human, crisis.

Hostage-taking is the simple preliminary to the more complex process
of demands and negotiation. The attack had been facilitated by major
security lapses. The Israelis themselves had not made enough of
where their team was housed, in a building with direct access from the
street, nor had they insisted on having armed security guards. Keen to
dispel memories of the 1936 Berlin Games, the Bavarian authorities had
decided to convert policemen into friendly stewards, equipped with
walkie-talkies and a smile rather than pistols and submachine guns, to
underline the 'Peace and Joy' theme of their Games. Access to the
Olympic Village seemed incredibly easy to effect.[8]

The Black September team had been given two sets of written terms;
the first demanded the release by 9 a.m. of two hundred Palestinian and
foreign terrorist prisoners, including the two female Sabena hijackers
and Okamoto; the second offered an extended period for negotiations,
but demanded a plane to fly the terrorists and their captives out of

Germany, preferably to Egypt or Morocco. These conditions were backed up by threats to execute their hostages by specific deadlines. In practice the first demand was otiose since the deadline had almost expired before the first senior German officials in Bonn had been notified of these events. Initial negotiations with Issa were conducted by the Munich police chief, Manfred Schreiber, first on the telephone and then face to face. During these meetings Schreiber wondered whether he could seize the grenade clasped in Issa's hand as the two men talked across a low balcony. Since the Israeli government ruled out any hostages-for-prisoners exchange, the ball was firmly in the Germans' court, their only option being to spin out the negotiations – postponing the looming deadlines – while they considered what to do. One delaying tactic was to introduce a senior political figure into the talks who could guarantee whatever bargains were struck, this being the lot of Hans-Dietrich Genscher, the federal government interior minister. At one point he courageously offered to enter the apartment to see the Israeli captives; he was horrified by the sight of them tied to chairs, with Romano's corpse on the floor, and bloodstains and bullet holes up and down the walls. This visit reinforced the feeling among the Germans that they were dealing with fanatics.

While German negotiators tried to wear down their terrorist interlocutors, the Bavarian police took up positions for a rescue attempt. This collapsed at the initial hurdle as thousands of spectators sitting on neighbouring high ground cheered the police on as they crawled over rooftops, while the Palestinian terrorists in Connollystrasse 31 watched their approach on television. Recognising that storming a building in which terrorists had had time to entrench themselves was a bad idea, the Germans decided to effect the hostages' release somewhere along their transfer from Connollystrasse to a neighbouring airport. Gradually a plan evolved to fly the terrorists and their hostages in two helicopters to a military airfield at Fürstenfeldbruck, where the terrorists would become vulnerable to police snipers as they crossed to a waiting Lufthansa jet primed to fly them to a destination yet to be determined. This plan went awry when the police suddenly flew the snipers back to the Olympic Village, having thought they could bushwhack the terrorists as they went through an underground car park to the helicopters. On an inspection, Issa noticed figures flitting about in the car-park shadows and demanded a door-to-door bus to the helicopters instead. The five police snipers were hastily returned to the airport. At around ten, eight terrorists emerged, guns at the ready, and shepherded their nine hostages – all bound together – on to the bus. Two helicopters lifted them into the night sky towards Fürstenfeldbruck airfield. Already there was a major flaw in the police plan because until then they had assumed there were only five terrorists. Now there seemed to be eight, with only five snipers to shoot them. Soon there would be four more hostages; the four crew of the police helicopters flying the terrorists to Fürstenfeldbruck.

The original police plan had assumed that at least two terrorists, including Issa their leader, would seek to inspect the waiting Lufthansa Boeing jet on the tarmac. They could be shot or captured by police masquerading as flight crew in and around the aircraft, while the snipers simultaneously shot their 'three' comrades guarding the hostages in the two helicopters. On inspecting the Boeing the police commandos realised their own potential vulnerability once bullets started flying around its flimsy interior. Taking German democracy too far they held a vote and refused to take on the mission. That left the snipers on their own. The helicopters bearing the terrorists and their captives landed, their stationary rotor blades casting confusing shadows because a handful of badly positioned floodlights had been switched on. Not only did the police snipers, who were amateur competition marksmen rather than uniformed assassins, not have a clear line of fire, but they had not been equipped with radios to communicate with each other or their controllers. They had no helmets or protective vests either, which meant that they lacked confidence to shoot from exposed positions. Their rifles lacked both long barrels and telescopic or night sights, meaning that when they fired it was not very discriminating. Issa and his deputy inspected the Lufthansa jet, quickly realising that something was amiss. As they ran back towards the helicopters, the police snipers opened fire, bringing down Issa's deputy with a shot in his leg. So did the terrorists, who, lying beneath the two helicopters, raked the surrounding buildings with automatic gunfire. As police bullets whacked into the two helicopters, the terrorists inside machine-gunned their Israeli hostages, blowing up one of the helicopters with hand grenades. This turned into an inferno, carbonising the bodies of the hostages inside. After two and a half hours of gunfire, it emerged that five of the terrorists had been shot dead, and all nine hostages had been killed. The remaining three terrorists survived and were captured by the police. As the world mourned the dead athletes, the bodies of the dead terrorists were flown to Libya where they were welcomed as martyrs. Ali Hassan Salameh quietly slipped out of East Germany to Lebanon where he was accorded a hero's welcome. Arafat himself embraced him saying: 'I love you as my son.'

III WAR OF THE SPOOKS

Munich was a tactical failure for the Palestinians but a strategic success. They had not succeeded in having a single Palestinian terrorist released, and two-thirds of their men had died along with the Israeli hostages. However, an indifferent world could no longer plead ignorance of the Palestinian cause, since nearly a billion people had watched these events on television and many more had probably read about them in their newspapers. The PLO was inundated with recruits in the Arab world. Moreover, they had forced their way into an international event from which they had been excluded, albeit in a way that was the antithesis of the Olympic spirit. The fiasco on the airport tarmac had other repercussions, notably in the field of counter-terrorism. President Nixon instituted the first Inter-Departmental Working Group on Terrorism, under national security advisor Henry Kissinger. US airport security was considerably tightened, through screening of passengers and their baggage, and the close scrutiny of Arabs seeking visas. European governments took the more radical step of forming specialised anti-terrorist units to effect the rescue of hostages. These included Germany's Grenzschutzgruppe Neun, or GSG-9, France's Groupe d'Intervention de la Gendarmerie Nationale (GIGN) and the counter-revolutionary warfare detachment of Britain's SAS. It was not until 1977 that the US formed something called Blue Light, the precursor of its Delta Force, the model being the German border police's GSG-9.

Israel's response to this international outrage against its sportsmen was immediate, once the nation had recovered from the initial shock of Jews being murdered on German soil three decades after the Holocaust. Warplanes bombed ten Palestinian guerrilla encampments in Syria and Lebanon, causing two hundred civilian casualties. Three armoured columns clanked and rumbled into southern Lebanon, destroying over a hundred houses of suspected PLO guerrillas. Such attacks may have expressed Israel's rage and fury, but they did not touch the leaders of Black September in their Beirut apartments. More focused operations were launched, albeit with the risk of killing or maiming postmen and zealous secretaries. Israel had done this before. In the mid-1950s Israel had assassinated two Egyptian colonels whom they blamed for orchestrating horrifying fedayeen attacks on civilians within Israel. Both men were killed by bombs hidden in books. In the early 1960s Israel waged a campaign of intimidation, kidnapping and assassination against German engineers and scientists helping Nasser develop long-range rockets. A number of innocent people were also maimed or killed as the targets did not always oblige by opening their own mail.

Immediately after Munich, several Fatah leaders in Algeria, Egypt and Libya were seriously injured by mysterious letter bombs. By way of retaliation a Mossad agent in the Israeli embassy in Brussels was lured to a café where a putative Arab double-agent suddenly shot him in the body and head. A short while later, Black September members assassinated a Syrian radio reporter in Paris who had allegedly collaborated with Mossad. A total of sixty-four letter bombs arrived at Israeli embassies; one exploded in London killing an agricultural attaché eagerly expecting a package of seeds from Holland. It worked on the same principle as a mousetrap. As soon as the package was opened, it released a spring detonator which set off a strip of plastic explosive. Israeli letter bombs severely injured Palestinian student activists in Bonn and Stockholm.

This tit-for-tat climate influenced the Mossad chief, Zvi Zamir, who after returning from Munich – where he had watched the shambolic performance of the Germans, who ignored his sage advice – urged prime minister Golda Meir to focus on bringing terror to the terrorists by assassinating the leaders of Black September and anyone who had helped facilitate its Munich operation. General Aharon Yariv was brought in to force discrete Israeli intelligence agencies to pull together in the common cause, while computers were introduced to speed up the collation of intelligence data on people with complex Arabic patronymics and operational pseudonyms.

The modus operandi was clothed in pseudo-legality. Israeli overseas intelligence would gather information on a terrorist suspect, building up a dossier that became the basis of an indictment. Acting as 'prosecutor' the head of Mossad would then present this to the prime minister and members of her (or his) cabinet, constituting the judge and jury. There was no 'defence' attorney. A special Mossad unit, code-named 'Caesarea', led by a veteran agent, who may have been named Mike Hariri, forty-six years old, would then set in motion operational planning. Over time Caesarea developed three specialised sub-services. Logistics experts arranged lodgings and transport, and usually spoke the local language of the target theatre. Surveillance teams, including a large number of women, kept the target under observation, sometimes for months at a time. The killers, who worked in pairs – and were known as number 1 and number 2 – were drawn from Israeli special forces. Usually they were covered by two others to expedite their getaway. There were also experts in bomb making and burglary whom we have still to encounter. Once an assassination was imminent, the plans would be referred back to the prime minister's Committee X for a final verdict. So much for the theory.

In fact, the targets for these assassinations were chosen as much for their operational feasibility as for the subject's links with the Munich slayings, as Mossad figures have subsequently conceded. This is an important point which needs to be heard from the horse's mouth, a senior intelligence officer involved:

> You didn't need blood on your hands for us to assassinate you. If there was intelligence information, the target was reachable, and if there was an opportunity, we took it. As far as we were concerned we were creating deterrence, forcing them to crawl into a defensive shell and not plan offensive attacks against us. But in this field there is also a slippery slope. Sometimes decisions are made based on operational ease. It's not that the assassinated were innocent, but if a plan existed, and those were often easiest for the soft targets, you were condemned to death.

In other words, the preliminary analytical intelligence on a given person could be bent or sensationalised by the operatives who carried out these assassinations because of that target's relative accessibility.

The first 'soft target' was Wael Zu'aytir, a thirty-six-year-old translator at the Libyan embassy in Rome, whose chief claim to fame was an Italian translation of *One Thousand and One Nights*. He mixed in sophisticated Italian literary circles and had an Australian girlfriend. He had had nothing to do with the Munich attack, although he stupidly claimed that the Israelis themselves had plotted it, but he had been interviewed by the Italian police in connection with Palestinian terrorist attacks on oil installations in Italy. This probably sealed his fate. Entering his Rome apartment building one autumn night, carrying a bag of groceries, he was shot twelve times by Mossad agents using .22 revolvers muffled with silencers. The agents, as well as Hariri and Zamir, who oversaw the operation, were out of Italy within four hours of Zu'aytir's demise. Any residual scruples Israel may have had about such operations disappeared when Black September hijacked a Lufthansa flight on 29 October 1972 as it neared Cyprus en route from Damascus to Frankfurt. The lead hijacker explained to the terrified pilot that this was Operation Munich, the aim being to secure the release of the three terrorists held in the wake of Fürstenfeldbruck. If they were not released by the German authorities, he and his colleagues would blow the plane up in mid-air. The German government immediately obliged, taking the three men to Riem airport. Suddenly their hijacker rescuers diverted the Lufthansa jet to Zagreb, where they circled the aircraft which was already running low on aviation spirit. The Germans hastened to fly the three prisoners to Zagreb, where the hijacked plane also landed. Instead of releasing the thirteen passengers and crew, the hijackers took the three Palestinian prisoners on board and ordered the pilot to fly to Libya. The suspiciously sparse complement of passengers has suggested to some that this entire saga had been arranged by the German government and the PFLP, which carried out the hijacking, in order to be free of their three terrorist prisoners before Germany became the victim of more terror. Be that as it may, a physically sickened Golda Meir immediately sanctioned the next Caesarea operation.

Mahamoud Hamshari was a thirty-eight-year-old Palestinian with a PhD in history. He acted as the PLO's mouthpiece in Paris. As an un-official diplomat he lived in some style on the Rue d'Alésia, with his French wife Marie-Claude and his daughter Amina. He saw nothing untoward when an Italian journalist asked for a meeting, although the man was a Mossad agent seeking Hamshari's address and phone number. The same man lured Hamshari out of his apartment long enough to allow burglars from Mossad's Keshet unit to case the premises, photographing the interior from every angle. A second visit by the burglars enabled them to affix a thin slab of plastic explosive under the telephone on the desk where Hamshari worked during the day. A small detonator was wired to an antenna capable of picking up coded radio signals. Late the next morning, Hamshari took a phone call. 'Hello?' he asked. A voice said: 'Can I please speak with Dr Hamshari?' 'He is speaking,' Hamshari replied. At that point the apartment erupted as an explosion showered glass on to the street below. Hamshari died three weeks later in hospital, still muttering about the mystery Italian journalist. The method of his murder, since he could just as easily have been shot on a dark street, was indicative of how Mossad was readily learning from terrorists. A bomb attack in Paris would attract press and public notice in a way that shooting would not, arousing fear among Palestinian terrorists. As a former Caesarea operative elaborated: 'If I could take them down with a missile from twenty miles away, I would.' That came in the future too. The third target was a thirty-six-year-old PLO representative, Hussain Abu-Kair, who operated from the Olympic hotel on Nicosia's President Makarios Avenue. As far as anyone knows, he was the PLO's clandestine contact with the Soviet KGB, which provided arms and training for Fatah militants. He does not appear to have had any direct involvement with the Munich killings. Keshet burglars got into his hotel room and placed a remote-activated bomb under his bed. On 25 January 1972, Abu-Kair returned to his room late at night, briefly switched the light on and off and went to bed. Outside, someone flicked a switch which blew him apart. In April 1973 the Caesarea team shot dead Dr Basil al-Kubaissi, a law professor at Beirut University, as he left an expensive restaurant in Paris.

Israeli counter-terror operations in Europe forced Black September to mount its attacks in remoter places considered to be softer targets. On 28 December 1972, Black September terrorists invaded the Israeli embassy in Bangkok, taking advantage of the festive atmosphere surrounding the investiture of the Thai crown prince. Six Israeli diplomats were taken hostage. Only the intervention of the Egyptian ambassador prevented a bloodbath; the weary terrorists (and the ambassador) were flown from Bangkok to Cairo.

This very public setback so infuriated Ali Hassan Salameh that he insisted on a further operation that appalled even his Fatah colleagues because of its political ramifications. Urgency was added when an alert Jordanian army patrol managed to detain Abu Daoud, masquerading as a Saudi sheikh, but carrying out reconnaissance for a Black September attempt to hold Jordanian ministers hostage so as to effect the release of a thousand Fatah members from the kingdom's prisons. In order to free Daoud, Black September launched an attack on the Saudi embassy in Khartoum just as the ambassador was hosting a party for the outgoing deputy chief of mission at the US embassy to Sudan. Local PLO figures made all the preparations for the attack, with a Fatah official driving the terrorists to the embassy, where they burst into a diplomatic reception. Extraordinarily, a secret US navy listening post in Cyprus had already

recorded Arafat and Abu Iyad in Beirut discussing the arrival of operatives for something codenamed 'Cold River' (Nahr al-Bared) with the
PLO's representative in Khartoum. The National Security Agency passed
this information on to the State Department, but there were then delays
as the two agencies tried to decide the importance of the information.
Urgent messages now arrived at the State Department from the embassy
in Khartoum, about events at the Saudi reception. There, the terrorists
separated out the US ambassador, Cleo Noel, and his deputy, George
Moore, as well as the Belgian chargé d'affaires, Guy Eid, whom they
mistakenly and maliciously imagined was Jewish. It soon became clear
that Egyptian mediation was pointless since the Palestinians were bent
on killing someone. The orders to 'carry out Cold River' came from
Arafat in Beirut, unaware that his conversations with the terrorists in
Khartoum were being monitored by the US and Israel. A gentleman to
the last, Noel apologised to his Saudi host for ruining the party. The
terrorists took the three diplomats down to the basement where they
were shot several times, starting from the feet and working upwards until
they were dead. Arafat called half an hour afterwards saying: 'Have you
carried out Cold River yet? Why didn't I hear about this? Why wasn't it
on the news?'[9]

Salameh also set in motion a plot to assassinate Golda Meir when
Black September learned of her plans to visit the Holy Father in Rome.
Having personally scouted her likely route from Rome's Fiumicino
airport into Vatican City, Salameh determined that his best shot would
be with a Russian shoulder-launched missile as her plane landed. Cases
of such rockets were moved by yacht from Dubrovnik to Bari in Apulia
and then transported to Rome. Fortuitously, Mossad intercepts on the
phone of a high-end Brussels call-girl used by PLO clients revealed calls
from Salameh to a flat in Rome. He spoke in code about moving fourteen 'cakes'. The Rome address was traced and searched, and the Israelis
found scraps of paper relating to Russian missiles, including instructions
on their use. They and the Italian police then scoured Fiumicino airport
a few hours before the prime minister was scheduled to land. The Israelis
soon intercepted one of two terrorist teams and managed to capture one
of its members. With little time to lose, they beat him up, and extracted
the information that another team lay in waiting, one of the few
occasions when excessive force has directly proved of any use. By chance,
another Mossad agent patrolling the airport in his car noticed a café-van
with three strange tubes protruding from its roof. Not taking any

chances, he rammed the van, which turned over, trapping the terrorists inside with their missiles akimbo even as Meir's plane prepared to land. The plot had failed.

In April 1973 the Israelis struck at three Palestinian leaders living in neighbouring seaside apartment blocks in the a-Sir district of Beirut. They were Abu Youssef, the second in command of Fatah, Kamal Adwan, the young commander of Fatah operations inside Israel, and Kamal Nasser, the PLO's Christian chief spokesman. Although the first two were heavily engaged in acts of terrorism, they had no discernible links with the killings in Munich, while Kamal Nasser was a propagandist rather than a fighter, a distinction some might regard as too precious. While Mossad provided the intelligence picture for this raid, it was conducted by Israeli special forces, Sayaret Matkal, under the command of lieutenant-colonel Ehud Barak, Israel's future prime minister. His deputy was Yoni Netanyahu, the elder brother of another future Israeli politician. The planning for the attack, in the heart of a city with a population of a million and home to dozens of international terrorists, was meticulous. Agents landed from a submarine carried out reconnaissance, establishing that a private beach on a spring night was most likely to be clear of fishermen or young couples, while the night-time cold would keep hotel guests away from their balconies. The entire operation was rehearsed at the construction site of two apartment blocks in northern Tel Aviv, much to the consternation of neighbours who began to wonder about armed men moving in and out of buildings.

On the night of 9 April, sixteen commandos were ferried from Haifa to Beirut in torpedo boats and then transferred to inflatables, which they paddled on the final voyage inshore. The parting words of the IDF chief of staff were 'Kill the bastards' which left no room for any ambiguity about attempting to capture the PLO leaders. In Beirut they were met by Caesarea agents masquerading as tourists who used wide American sedans to drive these bulky and heavily armed figures to their target. There was one further act of deception. Barak and Amiram Levine were dressed as women, with Barak in a brunette wig and Levine done up as a blonde. They brazenly walked, arm in arm with their respective 'boyfriends', past two Lebanese policemen who did not give these couples a second glance. At the apartment blocks, things suddenly speeded up. Three commandos raced up to the sixth floor and inserted strips of explosive into the door frame of an apartment. After receiving a signal from Barak, they burst into the apartment and shot dead Abu

Youssef, killing his wife too. Other commandos hit Kamal Nasser, as he worked on a speech at his desk, having rejected Abu Iyad's request to sleep over, which saved the latter's life. Kamal Adwan was shot in front of his wife and children before he had managed even to aim the AK-47 by his bedside. Ziad Helou, one of the assassins of Wasfi Tal, was badly wounded in the attack, having narrowly missed being killed by the Jordanians the previous week.[10] An elderly Italian lady who was roused by the commotion was shot dead by the Israelis as she opened her door. By this time a gun battle was raging in the street below, as the brunette and blonde sprayed bullets from their Uzis at Palestinian security guards and Lebanese policemen. A police jeep was blown up with a grenade, killing all its occupants. Elsewhere in Beirut, Israeli paratroopers carried out further attacks, blowing up an apartment block housing militants from the Democratic Front for the Liberation of Palestine. All these commandos and paratroopers left Beirut the way they had come before dawn broke. The Mossad logistics team left their rental cars neatly parked in line with the ignition keys on the dashboards. As angry Palestinians attended their three leaders' funerals, Israelis basked in the expert ferocity of their armed forces as displayed in this operation 'Spring of Youth'. There were also furious anti-government demonstrations in Beirut, for many Palestinians and Lebanese leftists suspected that the Lebanese authorities had turned a blind eye to this audacious Israeli strike. Increasingly open clashes between the Palestinians and government forces led president Franjieh to authorise the Lebanese air force to dive-bomb the Sabra and Chatila refugee camps, which were hotbeds of Palestinian militancy.

Flushed with this success, the Israelis continued their 'Wrath of God' campaign against Palestinian targets. Although he had no apparent links to Munich, in April 1973 the PLO's replacement representative in Cyprus was killed by a bomb in his hotel room. A few months later, a key Black September associate of Ali Hassan Salameh momentarily let down his guard by leaving his hotel in Athens to buy a newspaper, giving Mossad enough time to burgle his room and leave a bomb under the bed. Just before dawn the next day he woke to answer the telephone to a strange caller, and was blown to smithereens when the line went dead. In June, two Palestinians who had been reconnoitring El Al's offices in Rome were blown up in their Mercedes. Before the month was over, Mossad struck at Muhammed Boudia, an Algerian working as a theatre director in Paris, who while having no connection to Munich had been responsible for the attacks on the oil-storage facility at Trieste in August 1972. His fatal mistake was to make his security checks a habit. Living in Paris he drove a grey Renault 16 whose underside he carefully inspected each morning. Burglars broke into the car at night, while he visited a girl-friend, fixing a landmine packed with nuts and bolts under the seat. When Boudia got into the vehicle and switched the ignition key he was blown to pieces and engulfed in flames. Black September immediately took its revenge when a Palestinian gunman shot dead colonel Yosef Alon, the Israeli deputy defence attaché to the embassy in Washington, on his suburban lawn as he went to garage his car after returning from a party.

Mention of the US raises another reason why Mossad was so keen to kill Ali Hassan Salameh, beyond his responsibility for Munich. Since 1969 he had been in contact with Robert Ames, the head of the CIA Beirut station and a key Agency analyst of the Middle East. The CIA was interested in recruiting senior Fatah figures, probably to forestall attacks on Americans around the world. Mistaking his man, Ames twice offered Salameh huge sums of money (on one occasion US$3,000,000) only to be rebuffed by the playboy terrorist, who had money enough. These contacts, which doubtless came to the notice of Mossad, increased the urgency of killing Salameh.

In 1973 Mossad began to assemble plausible evidence that he was in Scandinavia, searching for a soft Israeli target on Europe's northern periphery. When agents in Switzerland monitored the movements of a twenty-eight-year-old Algerian, Kemal Benaman, who flew from Geneva to Copenhagen and then on to Oslo, they thought they had a firm lead. A dozen Mossad agents were flown to the Norwegian capital to trail Benaman. When Benaman drove north to Lillehammer, they followed him. They thought that one of the men he met in a café was Ali Hassan Salameh. This person was tracked in turn, even into the municipal swimming pool where he was watched by an innocent-seeming female bather as he chatted in French with another Arab or North African swimmer in the middle of the pool. Agents followed 'Salameh' to an apartment in the Nivo district where he appeared to be living with a pregnant Norwegian woman. That he went about on a bicycle or by bus and appeared to know the small town well did not seem to raise any questions. When Mike Hariri's agents contacted Zvi Zamir for authorisation to kill this personage, any queries were perfunctory. Late one night 'Salameh' and his girlfriend left a cinema showing *Where*

Eagles Dare and took the bus homewards. Holding hands they walked up the hill to their flat. A car pulled up on the opposite side of the street, two men jumped out, and shot 'Salameh' ten times with silenced Berettas. He was in fact a young Moroccan waiter, with an extra job as a pool attendant, called Achmed Bouchiki, out for a night with Toril Larsen Bouchiki, his expectant wife. Any meetings with Arabs or North Africans he had had were chance encounters in which, far from home, he had merely desired to speak languages that came easier to him than Norwegian.

This time, the Mossad agents were not allowed to go quietly into the night. They had stuck out like sore thumbs in a small provincial town where their Mediterranean appearance and clumsy surveillance operations had aroused suspicions. As they headed back to Oslo in their rental cars, the Norwegian police were not idle, having noted the licence plate of a car that sped out of Lillehammer on the night of the attack. They detained a foreign couple who tried to return the car to the airport rental firm, and quickly broke their badly rehearsed cover story. The man was an Israeli citizen of Danish origin who, suffering from claustro-phobia, cracked the moment he was shown a police cell. This led to the arrest of two further foreigners, a 'British' teacher from Leeds and a 'Canadian' freelance journalist who had spontaneously decided to visit Norway after a chance meeting at Zurich airport. When the police searched the belongings of the first couple, they uncovered addresses and phone numbers that led to two further names of persons who turned out to be lodging at the home of the security officer at the Israeli embassy in Oslo. Although Hariri managed to get out of Norway along with the two trigger-men who had shot Bouchiki, six of his agents were now in Norwegian custody. Five of them received sentences of up to five and half years' imprisonment as accessories to premeditated murder. Their testimony included the Tel Aviv phone number of Mossad – which was rapidly disconnected – but Israel denied all responsibility for their actions.

While this fiasco convulsed Mossad, forcing it to suspend the series of assassinations, Black September launched a vicious attack at Athens airport. In August 1973 two young Palestinians produced guns in the departure lounge and began blasting their fellow travellers. They killed three American tourists and an Indian passenger, wounding a further fifty-five. The two men then surrendered. The Greek government let them go when Palestinian terrorists hijacked a Greek ship in Karachi.

Despite these killings of Americans, in early November 1973 Ali Hassan Salameh had a meeting in Morocco with general Vernon Walters, the deputy director of the CIA. He agreed to suspend attacks on US citizens. One unexpected result of their accord was that Salameh warned the CIA of an imminent plot to kill national security advisor Henry Kissinger with a missile attack as he landed in Beirut for talks. The pay-off came the following year when, as Arafat flourished an olive branch at the UN in New York, revealing a shoulder holster under his upraised jacket, the CIA entertained Salameh at the Waldorf Astoria. In 1975 Salameh provided Force 17 guards for Americans evacuated in a convoy from Beirut as civil war erupted, a gesture for which he was received in person at the CIA's Langley headquarters. Two years later, after Salameh had married Georgina Rizak, a one-time Miss Lebanon cum Miss Universe, the CIA paid for the couple's honeymoon in Hawaii and threw in a no-expenses-spared visit to Florida's Disney World. Despite these amicable relations, technically the CIA denied that Salameh was its agent when the Israelis inquired some time in 1978. That sealed his fate.

Mossad teams arrived in Beirut to keep a close watch on Salameh's movements. He spent his afternoons with his second wife Georgina in an apartment on Beka Street. A female Mossad agent rented an apartment there, posing as a batty English artist, who worked for a Palestinian orphans' charity and fed feral cats. Another Mossad agent pretended to be a Canadian selling kitchenware to local Beirut shopkeepers. In mid-January 1979, Israeli frogmen swam ashore at Beirut and handed over a package to Mossad agents. The agents returned to a safe house and built thirty kilograms of hexagene explosives (a very potent bomb material) into a rented VW car. They parked this in Beka Street where Salameh was wont to visit Georgina. On the afternoon of 22 January, Salameh left her apartment, intending to visit his mother's flat to celebrate the third birthday of his niece. He and his two bodyguards got into his Chevrolet, while three other guards followed in a jeep. As this convoy passed the parked VW it exploded, killing eight people including all of Salameh's guards. He died an hour later in hospital from a shrapnel wound to his brain. A hundred thousand people came to his funeral. Photographs show Yasser Arafat with his arm consolingly draped around Salameh's thirteen-year-old son.

By that time, the PLO leadership had itself decided to turn off Black September, because its depredations were becoming counter-productive. Abu Iyad and a trusted colleague devised a novel solution that did not involve killing them. They travelled to PLO offices in Middle Eastern countries with large Palestinian populations. They identified about one hundred of the most attractive girls they could find, urging them to go to Beirut on a mission of great national importance. There they were introduced to members of Black September. The latter were told that if they agreed to marry these women, they would receive US$3,000, a fridge, a gas stove and a television, as well as a regular job in a non-violent PLO-affiliated organisation. If they had a child within a year, they would receive a further US$5,000. Many of these men did marry, settled down and started families. To test their resolve, the PLO handed them legitimate passports and asked them to go to Geneva or Paris on PLO business. They mostly refused, not wishing to jeopardise their settled existence. Modified versions of this decontamination strategy have been tried from Northern Ireland to Saudi Arabia, but it seems to have been the PLO that pioneered it.[11]

Although it is invariably overlooked, the PLO were also victims of another campaign of assassinations running parallel with the activities of Mossad. Several PLO breakaway factions advertised themselves as 'rejectionists', opposed to Arafat's ceasefire with king Hussein and, from his 1974 UN address onwards, to his readiness to negotiate a political settlement with the Israelis. From 1974 onwards there were clandestine contacts between the Israelis and Palestinian moderates, which were informally institutionalised through the Israel–Palestine Friendship League. The Austrian socialist chancellor Bruno Kreisky and the former French premier Pierre Mendès-France were important facilitators of these dialogues.[12] Although Fatah continued to hit Israel through guerrilla activities, it scaled back its involvement in international terrorism. The rejectionists included George Habash's PFLP, Ahmad Jibril's PFLP-General Command and, last but not least, Abu Nidal, whom the Iraqis cultivated as their Palestinian client at a time when the PLO in Lebanon seemed to be slipping under the suasion of their Syrian rival for dominance within the pan-Arab national socialist Baath movement. Abu Nidal was the first terrorist to turn murder into an international business, although he has had many rivals since. He was not the first, nor the last, terrorist to enjoy violence for its own sake, an Arab Nechaev for our times.

Born in 1937 in Jaffa, Sabri Khalil al-Banna, or Abu Nidal, was one of the many sons, by a maid turned wife, of a wealthy citrus-grower, for whom the exchange of luxurious homes with servants for refugee tents

Irish-American Civil War veterans were prominent among the Fenians who terrorised Britain from the 1860s onwards. Ricard O'Sullivan Burke, seen here in Union officer's uniform, was the leader of the Irish Republican Brotherhood in England.

The Irish-American terrorist John Holland in the turret of his 'Fenian Ram', a submarine designed to sink British shipping. Modern terrorists resort to the less sophisticated tactic of ramming ships with explosives-laden boats, as the USS *Cole* experienced off Aden a few years ago.

After several botched attempts, Russian Nihilists finally succeeded in killing the reforming Tsar Alexander II in March 1881.

Across Europe anarchists directed terror not simply against heads of state but at the rich and powerful in general, including the opera-goers who were bombed in Barcelona in 1893. Envy and resentment, whether against individuals or entire ways of life, remain powerful motives for many contemporary terrorists.

Much of the edginess of Gillo Pontecorvo's *The Battle of Algiers* derives from its being shot during the 1965 coup which removed the first elected president of independent Algeria, Ahmed Ben Bella. French paratroopers, seen here in the film entering the city, won the localised battle of the Casbah, but went on to lose the wider war.

Some of the FLN figures in the film were played by their real life equivalents. Saadi Yacef (*second from left*) is seen here with the film's anti-hero, Ali la Pointe (*far right*), who was played by actor Brahim Hadjadj.

Anarchistische Gewalttäter
– Baader/Meinhof-Bande –

Wegen Beteiligung an Morden, Sprengstoffverbrechen, Banküberfällen und anderen Straftaten werden steckbrieflich gesucht:

Für Hinweise, die zur Ergreifung der Gesuchten führen, sind insgesamt 100 000 DM Belohnung ausgesetzt, die nicht für Beamte bestimmt sind, zu deren Berufspflichten die Verfolgung strafbarer Handlungen gehört. Die Zuerkennung und die Verteilung erfolgen unter Ausschluß des Rechtsweges.

Mitteilungen, die auf Wunsch vertraulich behandelt werden, nehmen entgegen:

Bundeskriminalamt – Abteilung Sicherungsgruppe –
53 Bonn-Bad Godesberg, Friedrich-Ebert-Straße 1 – Telefon: 02229 / 53001
oder jede Polizeidienststelle

Vorsicht! Diese Gewalttäter machen von der Schußwaffe rücksichtslos Gebrauch!

A 1972 'wanted' poster for members of the West German Baader–Meinhof gang. Many of them exhibited an unappetising combination of middle-class Leftist guilt about the German past and the self-righteous amoralism of the 1960s.

The former Red Brigade killer, Mario Moretti, who turned state's witness and went on to write revealing accounts of life inside the organisation

Moretti's sophistication was notably absent from the pronouncements of the German 'wild child' Andreas Baader, who went on a brief terroristic rampage in the 1970s before committing suicide in Stammheim prison.

The basic intention of projecting shards of metal into human flesh has not changed from the lead-cased projectiles hurled by US anarchists in Chicago's Haymarket atrocity in 1886 (*right*) to the hydrogen peroxide-based bomb designed to spray nuts and bolts that was abandoned after the 21 July 2005 London bombing by an Islamist terrorist who had masqueraded as an asylum seeker.

BATF Explosive Standards

ATF	Vehicle Description	Maximum Explosive Capacity	Lethal Air Blast Range	Minimum Evacuation Distance	Falling Glass Hazard
	Compact Sedan	500 pounds 227 kilos (in trunk)	100 feet 30 meters	1,500 feet 457 meters	1,250 feet 381 meters
	Full Size Sedan	1,000 pounds 455 kilos (in trunk)	125 feet 38 meters	1,750 feet 534 meters	1,750 feet 534 meters
	Passenger Van or Cargo Van	4,000 pounds 1,818 kilos	200 feet 61 meters	2,750 feet 838 meters	2,750 feet 838 meters
	Small Box Van (14 ft. box)	10,000 pounds 4,545 kilos	300 feet 91 meters	3,750 feet 1,143 meters	3,750 feet 1,143 meters
	Box Van or Water/Fuel Truck	30,000 pounds 13,636 kilos	450 feet 137 meters	6,500 feet 1,982 meters	6,500 feet 1,982 meters
	Semi-Trailer	60,000 pounds 27,273 kilos	600 feet 183 meters	7,000 feet 2,134 meters	7,000 feet 2,134 meters

This Bureau of Alcohol, Tobacco, Firearms and Explosives chart soberly calculates the blast radius of different types of vehicular bomb used in park-and-leave or suicide attacks by modern terrorists.

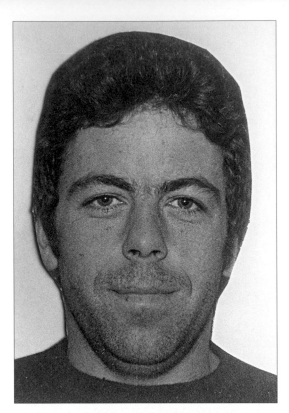

Not all terrorists are psychopaths, but Lenny Murphy of the Shankill Butchers undoubtedly was.

'Mad Dog' Johnny Adair (*second from right*) of the Ulster Freedom Fighters with colleagues outside the Maze prison on his premature release from a sixteen-year sentence for directing acts of terrorism.

This triumphalist road sign appeared after the IRA equipped themselves with high-powered sniper rifles to menace troops operating in South Armagh.

Brian Gillen was a prominent IRA 'face' who sought less publicity than his Loyalist equivalents.

The IRA's Padraic Wilson (*front left*) with colleagues in the IRA wing of the Maze.

Senior IRA figure Brian Keenan at a republican funeral. Politicised funerals are a favoured means used by terrorists of many persuasions to re-stimulate rage and hatred in their respective communities.

The transition from political violence to democratic politics has been made by, among others, Martin Ferris (*left*), a member of the Irish Dail, and Gerry Adams (*front*), a member of Northern Ireland's Stormont Assembly.

may have been too much to bear. After periods as an odd-job man in Saudi Arabia, Nidal returned to Nablus in the West Bank working as an electrician, and then moved to the Jordanian capital where he founded a trading company named Impex that provided a cover for his increasingly murky political activities. Abu Iyad sent him to run the PLO office in Iraq, about two months before king Hussein obliterated the PLO in Jordan. In Iraq, Abu Nidal vented his fury at the direction in which Arafat was taking the Palestinian movement. His first independent operation, code-named 'The Punishment', was to take hostage eleven Saudi diplomats in the Paris embassy so as to secure the release of Abu Daoud from the Jordanians, and to distract attention from the Non-Aligned Conference which, to the annoyance of Iraq's leaders, Algeria was hosting. This maverick operation, which did secure the release of Abu Daoud after Kuwait paid Jordan US$12,000,000, was condemned by Abu Iyad, who sent the current Palestinian leader, Mahmoud Abbas, to Baghdad to reason with Abu Nidal. He failed and stormed out of the meeting. Abu Nidal was expelled from Fatah in March 1974.

In late 1974 Nidal announced the formation of 'Fatah: The Revolutionary Council'. The Iraqis paid Nidal a monthly retainer of US$150,000 plus a one-off golden-hello of between US$3,000,000 and US$5,000,000. They also handed over various training facilities and US$15,000,000 worth of Chinese weapons originally earmarked for the PLO. War was declared between these Palestinian factions when the PLO's Fatah killed Abu Nidal's friend and former Black September member Ahmad Abd al-Ghafur in Beirut, where he was putting in place the logistics for major terrorist strikes against Western interests that would have been blamed on the PLO itself.

At this stage, Abu Nidal was a minor figure, temporarily eclipsed by the more exotic and publicity-hungry celebrity terrorist Carlos the Jackal (Illich Ramírez Sánchez). Sánchez was born in Caracas in October 1949, the spoilt son of a millionaire Stalinist who would bask in the son's exploits. Never straying far from the paternal tree, Sánchez attended a guerrilla training camp run by the Cuban secret service – the Dirección General de Inteligencia – and then the Lumumba university in Moscow, where the KGB identified future guerrillas, saboteurs and terrorists from among its twenty-thousand-strong corps of foreign students. Always the ladies' man, despite the corpulence that since childhood had earned him the nickname 'El Gordo' or 'the Fat One', Carlos was expelled for ostentatious skirt-chasing among the earnest comrades. He seems to have gone to the Middle East to fight against the Jordanians, gradually being accepted as an associate of Habash's PFLP. By the early 1970s he was living near his mother in London, ostensibly studying at the London School of Economics – even then notorious for welcoming any foreigner with an open chequebook – but in one reality living the life of a Latin American playboy, whose fashionable revolutionary chat-up lines appealed to the credulous young women he gathered around him, using their homes as arms stores and safe houses. The other reality surfaced when on 30 December 1973 Carlos forced his way into the St John's Wood home of the president of Marks and Spencer, and shot Joseph Sieff in the face. A month later, the same elusive figure opened the door of the Israeli Hapoalim bank in Cheapside and threw a bomb into the lobby injuring a typist. El Gordo had mutated into 'the Jackal', a name given to him by journalists familiar with Frederick Forsyth's 1970 best-seller. Carlos resurfaced in Paris. In August 1974 bombs exploded at the offices of papers deemed sympathetic to Israel. The next month a hand grenade was thrown into the Drugstore nightclub, this being an attempt to add extra pressure on the French government to release a Japanese Red Army operative, at a time when JRA terrorists had taken the French ambassador to the Netherlands hostage with the aid of guns and grenades supplied by Carlos. In January 1975 there were two successive attacks, using Russian-made rockets, against El Al flights leaving Orly airport. All of these attacks were the handiwork of Carlos.

His luck temporarily ran out when Lebanese security police detained Michel Moukharbel in Beirut, for he was responsible for administering the logistics of Carlos's outrages in Paris. They kept him for five days before allowing him to leave for France, where the Direction de la Surveillance du Territoire (or DST) kept an eye on him and eventually arrested him. Moukharbel eventually volunteered the address of the fat youth the DST had photographed him with, although he insisted that the man was of no importance. Three DST agents took Moukharbel to the address, a flat on the Left Bank's Rue Toullier, although as their shift was about to end they checked in their weapons before leaving, a time-saving gesture that proved mistaken. The sound of guitar music and the Mexican song 'Give Thanks for Life' drew them to a small flat where the lead DST officer entered, leaving Moukharbel with his two colleagues along the hall. The DST agent chatted amiably with the fat young man in sunglasses who was the life and soul of a small party for his fellow Latin Americans. Then the inspector decided to go up a gear by calling in Moukharbel to see what would happen when the two men were confronted with one another. That was a mistake. As the three agents and Moukharbel entered the apartment, Carlos pulled out a .38 Czech automatic and in seconds had shot Moukharbel and two of the agents dead. The lead DST agent was wounded in the neck. While British and French police put together the various links between the spate of assassinations and bombings both countries had recently experienced, Carlos slipped out of Marseilles on a fruit-boat bound for Algeria.

Carlos re-entered the spotlight when with remarkable audacity he and various Arab and German colleagues shot their way into the head-quarters of OPEC (the Organisation of Petroleum-Exporting Countries) in Vienna shortly before Christmas 1975. An Austrian policeman and an Iraqi security guard were clinically assassinated by a German woman terrorist. A Libyan economist who tried to wrestle Carlos's submachine gun away from him was killed when the Jackal used his free hand to whip out a 9 mm automatic. These people meant business, and now they had eleven oil ministers cowering under their guns, including Iran's Jamshid Amousagar and Saudi Arabia's Ahmed Zaki Yamani, both of whom they intended to kill as representative of the most reactionary Gulf-region monarchies. For, in addition to a diffuse desire to strike at multinational capitalism, the raid was probably a warning from the progressive supporters of the Palestinians, that is Algeria, Libya and Iraq, to the con-servative Arab states and the shah of Iran. The Austrian chancellor Kreisky rapidly caved in to terrorist demands which were backed up by threats to shoot a minister on the hour. One lighter moment came when an Iraqi mediator asked to know who they were dealing with. 'We are revolutionaries, not criminals,' replied Carlos, 'we are the Arm of the Arab Revolution.' 'But you are not Arab,' exclaimed a perplexed Riyadh al-Azzawi. Within hours, the Austrian interior minister was hugging Carlos farewell on the tarmac as the group and their hostages took off in a DC-9. Although the Nigerian minister felt sufficiently relaxed to ask the Jackal for his autograph – 'Flight Vienna–Algiers 22/xii/75 – Carlos' – Yamani and the Iranian spent the flight under the cloud of his threats to shoot them. The plane landed at Algiers and then took off for Tripoli. Carlos boasted that the Libyan prime minister would be there to greet them and to provide them with a fresh jet with the range to reach Baghdad. True to form, the Libyan prime minister slept soundly in his bed, while the jet failed to materialise. Back they returned to Algiers where, probably in exchange for a king's ransom, they eventually released the eminent hostages and disappeared. A swelling folder of press cuttings about his crimes was as important to Carlos as his burgeoning bank accounts.[13]

In April 1975 unknown gunmen had tried to assassinate the leading Maronite in Lebanon, Pierre Gemayel, at a ceremony to consecrate a church. Before the morning was over, Maronite gunmen had massacred twenty-eight Palestinians as they journeyed by bus to Ain Rummaneh. Inter-communal fighting escalated, becoming all-out war when, not without reason, Gemayel accused the PLO of abusing Lebanese hospitality and called for a referendum regarding the Palestinians' continued presence in his country. This prompted Kamal Jumblatt, the leader of a so-called Lebanese National Movement, to demand the removal of the right-wing authoritarian Maronite Phalangists from the coalition government. When the Maronites besieged three Palestinian refugee camps, massacring the inhabitants of Dbayeh, Palestinian guerrillas shelled and overran the small town of Damour, killing most of its inhabitants.

The responses of the wider Arab world to this conflict were disappointing when viewed from Arafat's perspective. The Egyptian president Sadat's preoccupation with a unilateral peace deal with Israel meant that Arafat could not bank on the support of the largest and most powerful Arab country. To his suspicious mind, it seemed that Egypt was doing a deal at the expense of the Palestinians. Worse, although Syria's wily president Assad had begun by supporting the Lebanese radicals and Palestinians, he switched to the Maronites when the former seemed like winning and Jumblatt had bluntly warned him to keep out of Lebanese politics. When Arafat presumptuously upbraided Assad, the Syrian leader shouted: 'You do not represent the Palestinians more than we do. Don't you forget . . . There is no Palestinian people and there is no Palestinian entity. There is only Syria.' There was some truth in much of that.

With Israeli and US approval, in June 1976 twelve thousand Syrian troops moved into Lebanon. Under their protective cover, the Maronites attacked the vast Palestinian refugee camp at Tal al-Zaatar. After a siege of fifty-two days the thirty thousand inhabitants were forced to surrender, some of them being killed as they departed. Following some eighteen months of fighting, Saudi mediation resulted in Lebanon being carved into spheres of influence, all supposedly guaranteed by a Syrian Arab Deterrent Force. The PLO alone had lost an estimated five thousand casualties. They soon included their local protector, Kamal Jumblatt, who felt Assad's vengeance when he was shot dead at a Syrian roadblock in March 1977. Iraq also unleashed Abu Nidal against the Syrians, who had committed the major sin of turning their guns against the Palestinians in Lebanon. He dubbed his campaign of bomb and gun attacks against such Syrian interests as airline offices and embassies around Europe and the Middle East 'Black June' after the date of the Syrian invasion of Lebanon. This culminated in an attempt to assassinate the Syrian foreign minister at Abu Dhabi airport, an attack that resulted in the death of the United Arab Emirates minister of state for foreign affairs. After Saddam Hussein came to power and went to war with Iran, Abu Nidal was used to assassinate exiled Iraqi dissidents, in between his endeavours to kill such senior PLO leaders as Abu Iyad, whose men came to Baghdad attempting to kill Nidal in turn.

They had good reason, for, commencing in January 1978, Abu Nidal had launched a campaign of assassination against PLO moderates, especially those in contact with Israeli peaceniks or who advocated a two-state solution to the Israeli–Palestinian problem. In that month the PLO's representative in London, Sa'id Hammani, was shot dead by Kayid Hussein, one of Abu Nidal's Tunisian gunmen. That summer Abu Nidal's organisation struck at Ali Yassin, Fatah's spokesman in Kuwait, Izz al-Din Qalaq, its man in France, and narrowly missed Yusif Abu Hantash, in the PLO's Islamabad offices. In 1981 they killed Heinz Nittal, a Vienna city councillor and close friend of chancellor Kreisky, in a clear warning that the latter should halt his attempts to develop Israeli–Palestinian dialogue. The PLO knew exactly who was to blame, firing rockets into the Iraqi embassy in Beirut and attacking Nidal's offices in Tripoli. Although some claim that Nidal's 'strategy' was being 'manipulated' by Israeli agents secreted within his organisation, this seems unlikely, given that his terrorists simultaneously carried out attacks against soft Israeli and Jewish targets across Europe, that being a euphemism for shooting up worshippers in a Viennese synagogue and throwing grenades into a party of schoolchildren in Antwerp. In April 1983 Nidal's men murdered the prominent PLO dove Isam Sartawi at a socialist conference in Portugal. These killings were carried out by gunmen who had survived the rigours of Abu Nidal's various training camps. Since Abu Nidal at one point thought that his own wife was a CIA agent, one can only imagine the levels of paranoia that prevailed in these hellholes, recreations of camps he had himself received training at in China and North Korea. He insisted on the old Communist practice of making recruits constantly rewrite their autobiographies, with the slightest inconsistency resulting in bouts of monstrous torture in Section 16, the interrogation and punishment block. Those who failed this test ended up buried in the desert.

Although the PLO had suffered a major defeat in the first Israeli invasion of the Lebanon, it was not a calamity. For, among the fiefdoms into which Lebanon was divided, there was one for the loser too. Arafat was able to have his state within a state, based in the Farqhani district of west Beirut and stretching southwards to the Litani river on Israel's northern border. This emboldened Arafat to transform his guerrilla fighters into a pastiche regular army, including sixty defunct Soviet T-34 tanks and an arsenal of anti-aircraft guns and rocket launchers. Apparently oblivious to the geostrategic changes ushered in by Sadat's visit to Jerusalem, which effectively freed the newly elected Likud government of Menachem Begin to concentrate on its northern border, Arafat sanctioned a pointless Fatah seaborne terror raid north of Haifa, which resulted in the hijacking of a bus and the deaths of thirty-four Israelis and all but two of the raiders. Israeli public pressure for retaliation was massive. On 14 March 1978 some twenty-eight thousand Israeli troops in huge armoured columns rumbled across the border, flattening Lebanese villages and killing two hundred PLO fighters. Sadat condemned the guerrilla raid and Israel's retaliation; Syrian troops prudently kept out of the way until this juggernaut had turned home-wards. Before they left, the Israelis installed a friendly Maronite Christian militia to provide an added line of defence in addition to the UN interim force in the buffer zone along their northern border. A pattern of violence that continues over thirty years later involved relatively under-reported Palestinian cross-border attacks, to which the Israelis regularly responded with either air strikes or expeditions using their prodigious armour, a spectacle that enabled the Palestinians to posture as David versus Goliath to an international media that always found the response more newsworthy than whatever had provoked it, not being interested either, it seems, in who ordered the guerrilla fighters on the border to attack Israel.

Violence flared up again in the summer of 1981 when, following Israeli air strikes in southern Lebanon, the PLO embarked on a sustained two-week campaign of launching Katyusha rockets into northern Israel, causing thousands of Israelis to flee southwards, increasing demands on the government to do something to stop it. The Israeli air force was despatched to bomb west Beirut, where it killed three hundred and injured a further seven hundred, in yet another display of raw firepower that was starting to alienate much uninvolved opinion, for the Israelis were neither parsimonious in their use of expensive ordnance nor too scrupulous about where they used it. Arafat derived some consolation from an American-brokered ceasefire which implicitly meant that the Israelis had recognised the PLO terrorists. Although Arafat was by this time involved in back-channel negotiations designed to win US recognition of the PLO, the new Israeli defence minister, Ariel Sharon, was effectively conducting Israel's foreign policy, and held discussions with a US interlocutor, Alexander Haig, whose mind seems to have been distracted by the prospect of higher office. Sharon came away from meetings with Haig in May 1982 convinced he had the green light for major operations in Lebanon, although Haig had in fact given him a vaguely qualified red. Sharon discreetly flew into Lebanon to establish a Christian–Jewish partnership designed to recast the Lebanon after a successful Israeli invasion. Israel stepped up pressure by annexing the Golan Heights, to test Syria's non-existent resolve, and by ousting pro-PLO mayors in the occupied territories. On 3 June 1982 Sharon got his pretext for war when Abu Nidal's men shot the Israeli ambassador to Britain as he left a function at London's Dorchester Hotel. When told that this renegade Palestinian terrorist was responsible, the Israeli army commander Raphael Eitan remarked: 'Abu Nidal, Abu Schmidal.'

The Israeli air force returned to bomb west Beirut, killing sixty people, and prompting the PLO to fire rockets over the southern border. On the morning of 6 June Israeli armoured formations, with forty thousand troops, crossed into Lebanon, while navy units landed near the PLO stronghold of Sidon. Although the Israeli cabinet had earlier vetoed Sharon's most expansive war plans, the headstrong commander immediately set about implementing them, escalating the war from a limited campaign to secure Israel's northern border from Fatah attacks to a radical attempt to reorganise the politics of Israel's northerly neighbour. Any prospect of Syrian intervention disappeared when the Israeli air force destroyed a quarter of Syria's air force in a brief series of engagements. Israel did not entirely have things its way, however, since the Maronite leader Bashir Gemayel, son of Pierre, proved highly resistant to being used as Sharon's cat's-paw, thus removing one of the lynchpins of the general's battle plans. That left Sharon and Arafat to slog it out personally. Arafat was also subjected to mounting pressure from a newly formed Lebanese Council of National Salvation, consisting of his Sunni Muslim allies, to get out of Lebanon before the Israelis blew it apart. Although Arafat felt pricks of conscience about the disaster he had brought upon his friendly hosts, he also spoke darkly of Beirut becoming a Palestinian Stalingrad. Libya's madcap ruler Ghaddafi helpfully suggested that the PLO commit collective suicide in Beirut rather than leave. Arafat sourly remarked that he would have fought to the last if Ghaddafi had not failed to provide weapons. This was possibly overly melodramatic because as they negotiated their evacuation with Ronald Reagan's envoy, Philip Habib, the PLO team were insistent on the shipment of their fleets of BMWs and Mercedes, and other manifestations of the good life in their Beirut strongholds.

Although Israel was under considerable pressure to conclude a cease-fire, Begin and Sharon unleashed a final eight-day assault on west Beirut itself, hoping to kill Arafat as a tangible sign of victory. He switched from bunker to bunker as the Israelis attempted assassination by F-15. They failed to notice the shocking effect of sustained aerial bombing and shelling on wider international opinion, one of the major flaws in their future responses to cross-border terrorism. This prompted a tense telephone exchange between Reagan and Begin. 'Menachem, this is a holocaust,' the president remarked. 'Mr President, I'm aware of what a holocaust is,' the Israeli leader replied. The bombing ceased and the PLO prepared to embark on its third exodus, having brought nothing but chaos and violence to Lebanon. Nearly eleven thousand Palestinian fighters were shipped out on vessels chartered by the US. Arafat himself left for Greece on the *Atlantis*, his final destination being Tunis, as remote from Palestine as it is possible to be in the Arab world. He left a city in ruins with nineteen thousand dead and another thirty thousand wounded. Four hundred Israelis had also died.

The killing was not quite over. On 14 September the long hand of Syria's Assad reached out to Bashir Gemayel, the president elect of Lebanon, who was killed by a bomb that destroyed his east Beirut headquarters. Israeli troops took the opportunity to comb west Beirut to hunt down any remaining Palestinian fighters. They also enabled Phalangist militiamen to enter Palestinian refugee camps at Sabra and Chatila on the same pretext, where they butchered anywhere between seven hundred and fifteen hundred people, depending on whose figures are deemed most reliable. This massacre appalled international opinion and many Israelis including such patriots as Abba Eban, the former foreign minister, while the monomaniacal former terrorist Menachem Begin merely commented: 'Goyim are killing goyim, and the world is trying to hang the Jews for the crime.' Israel was starting to pay in hard-won moral capital, along with the IDF its most precious asset.

Beyond the wars that destroyed the Lebanon, some of the more extreme Palestinian factions were joining Carlos the Jackal as freelance murderers working for the highest bidder, activities they combined with extortion. While Carlos, having broken with the PFLP, hired himself out to the Romanian secret service or the East German Ministry of State Security (the Stasi) to kill dissidents or to attack Radio Free Europe in Munich, Abu Nidal had switched his allegiances from the Iraqis to the Syrians. They saw him as a useful weapon against Jordan whose king was encouraging the Muslim Brothers against the Syrian Baathists while claiming that he could do the best deal with Israel on behalf of the Palestinians.

Commencing in the autumn of 1983, Nidal's carefully constructed international terror network, which he directed while posing as a businessman based in Communist Warsaw, killed the Jordanian ambassador to India and wounded Jordanian officials in separate attacks in Athens, Madrid and Rome. Jordanian diplomats were also murdered in Ankara and Bucharest. Jordan responded with a series of hits against Syrian diplomatic and commercial interests until the two countries concluded a ceasefire of sorts. Abu Nidal also increased his formidable financial resources, having embezzled US$11,000,000 from the Iraqis in the course of an arms deal before they encouraged him to leave the country. Much of his activity was indistinguishable from criminality. He personally taped 'requests' to the rulers of the Gulf states for donations to the 'true' Palestinian revolutionary movement, giving them six months to comply. If they did not, then they received a shorter communication: 'I will kill you! I will kidnap your children and your princes! I will blow you up!' Shortly after that a Gulf Air jet was blown up in mid-air by a bomb as it landed at Abu Dhabi airport. When two UAE diplomats were attacked in Paris and Rome, the UAE ruler reluctantly transferred US$17,000,000 to Abu Nidal's accounts. Similar extortion was focused upon Kuwait which agreed to pay Nidal a large monthly retainer. When the Kuwaitis showed signs of reneging on this deal, nine people were murdered and nearly ninety injured in simultaneous bomb attacks on cafés in Kuwait City. In 1985 Nidal used three of his assassins to kill his brother-in-law and five-year-old nephew when the former refused to acknowledge Nidal's co-ownership of a substantial house in Amman. Meanwhile, Nidal quietly put out feelers to Libya's colonel Ghaddafi, who had decided to employ him to kill exiled Libyan opponents of his regime and for strikes against his 'imperialist' Western enemies. Ghaddafi provided generous facilities for Nidal's organisation in and around Tripoli, including free telephone calls and the transport of weapons through diplomatic bags. Like Carlos, the most feared international terrorist had become a hired gunman for a rogue state, the international revolutionary rhetoric starkly revealed as hollow words signifying nothing.

CHAPTER 6

Guilty White Kids: The Red Brigades and the Red Army Faction

I IDEOLOGY ADDICTS

On the afternoon of Friday 12 December 1969 an unremarkable man entered the circular hall of the Banca Nazionale dell'Agricoltura on Milan's Piazza Fontana. He slid two briefcases under a table where farmers and merchants from the rural hinterland were completing bank slips. A few minutes after the man left, eighteen pounds of explosives tore the hall apart, in a hail of glass, marble and metal office equipment. A twenty-seven-year-old clerk, Michelle Carlotto, said: 'In the smoke I saw a body fly from the public section above the counter and fall one yard away from me. I was shocked, I couldn't move.' Other survivors noted stray shoes with severed feet still in them. Sixteen people were killed and another ninety wounded by the bomb, which was accompanied by simultaneous attacks on two banks in Rome.

Within hours the police had unearthed two anarchists, one a ballet dancer, the other Giuseppe Pinelli, a railway worker. Pinelli died after a mysterious midnight fall from a fourth-floor window in Milan's police headquarters, three days after the bombing, which was considerably longer than the police were legally entitled to detain him. Some maintain that he was killed by the police, although an official inquest cleared the investigating officer and held that Pinelli had brought about his own end by accidentally falling after he had suffered a mysterious funny turn (*malore attivo*). The ballet dancer was held on remand for three years, and then jailed for a further fifteen years, for a crime he probably did not commit. Attempts to prosecute members of the neo-Fascist Ordine

Nuovo for the bombing routinely floundered, as have repeated efforts to reveal the role of Sifar, or Italian military intelligence, and maybe the CIA, in an atrocity which when blamed on 'anarchists' was intended to refashion Italian democracy in a more authoritarian direction.

The hardline *ordonovisti* regarded themselves as keepers of the Fascist flame and the revolutionary conscience of the extreme right at a time when Arturo Michelini and his successor Giorgio Almirante, leaders of the neo-Fascist Movimento Sociale Italiano (MSI), were taking the party into mainstream Italian politics so as better to realise their anti-democratic objectives. This strategy, which had its analogue on the extreme left, resulted in the creation of several neo-Fascist splinter groups, committed to the destabilisation of Italy through the kind of political violence practised and theorised by the revolutionary left around the world. They pursued a 'strategy of tension', mainly through indiscriminate terrorist bombings, such as the attack on the Milanese bank, which they hoped would provoke a response from the extreme left, thereby necessitating the formation of an authoritarian state. Insofar as these groups, which sailed under a bewildering and shifting range of flags of convenience, had any intellectually coherent objectives, these were derived from the ideologue Julius Evola, until his death in 1974 a living link with Mussolini's tawdry Salo Republic and Hitler's Third Reich, and author of *The Cult of Blood* and *Revolt against the Modern World*.

These mutations in the neo-Fascist camp had their counterparts on the anti-democratic far left, their historical memory haunted by the collapse of their political forebears under the assault of Fascism earlier in the twentieth century. The occasional bombing aside, the threat of 'neo-Fascism' was a serviceable left-wing moral panic analogous to how the right had historically sought to exploit middle-class fears of Bolshevism. The putative revival of Fascism was the necessary lifeblood of an 'anti-Fascism' whose most heroic memory was the belated spasm of armed resistance after 1943 when Allied armies coursed northwards through the peninsula. Since the wartime resistance was dominated by the left, its admirers could further claim that a far-reaching social revolution had allegedly been betrayed by the forces of Catholic conservatism that the Allies helped impose on the post-war democratic Italian Republic. Covert CIA funding and the vast parish network combined to keep the Christian Democrats in power for over forty years.

Neo-Fascist violence became a pretext for the first rather eccentric left-wing terrorist assault on Italian democracy. On 26 March 1972

Giangiacomo Feltrinelli, the multi-millionaire friend of Fidel Castro and publisher of Boris Pasternak, blew himself up while planting a bomb beneath a high-voltage electric pylon, having earlier gone underground with his Partisan Action Groups, the name echoing the wartime movement and so reflecting the elderly composition of its membership.[1] Feltrinelli's idiosyncratic trajectory, from ownership of the publishing house Mondadori to terrorist bomber, signified much wider disenchantment on the undemocratic left with the reformist course pursued by Enrico Berlinguer, the Sardinian aristocrat who led the Partito Comunista Italiano or PCI. This resulted in the 1973 'historic compromise', an attempt to reconcile Communist collectivism with the left Christian Democrats' Catholic 'solidarism', a course pursued by Berlinguer in order to avert a CIA-backed Chilean-style military coup, which was no idle fantasy in the Italy of the early 1970s. In a further notable departure from Communist subservience to the Chosen Nation, the Italian Communists definitively abandoned their already attenuated admiration for a Soviet Union that had invaded Hungary and Czechoslovakia, while hoping to find a common moral cause with the nation's Catholic majority in rejecting US-influenced individualism and materialism.[2]

The historic compromise was a betrayal too far for many of those who in the late 1960s had sought to convert widespread, but far from universal, discontent into an Italian Marxist revolution. The failure of that endeavour was the principal cause of left-wing terrorism, which failed in its turn in its attempt to destroy Italian democracy. The terrorist vanguard would be the midwives of the revolution that had so far refused to be born. While Italy did not undergo anything comparable to the effervescent moment of May 1968 in France, it experienced more than a decade of social ferment in its schools, factories and universities that directly and indirectly contributed to waves of left- and right-wing terrorism. Between 1969 and 1987 there were some 14,591 terrorist attacks; 1,182 people were wounded and 419 killed, the worst year being 1979 when there were 125 fatalities. One hundred and ninety-three of these deaths were caused by neo-Fascist terrorists, mostly in a few major bomb attacks; 143 were attributable to the extreme left, and 63 to Middle Eastern terrorist groups operating in Italy.[3]

The universities were one well-pool of a fanaticism that would fuel almost two decades of Red terrorism. This was a new development, since from the end of the war down to the late 1950s Italian students were more likely to be fervent supporters of the right, demonstrating against the transfer of Istria to Yugoslavia and the proclamation of the free status of Trieste in 1949. The mindless and supposedly economically driven over-expansion of higher education (no one thought to consider prosperous Switzerland, where the number of students was and remains small at 12 per cent of the relevant age cohorts) was largely responsible for unrest among the nation's swarms of students. In 1965 entrance to university by competitive examination was abolished. By 1968 there were 450,000 students as opposed to 268,000 three years earlier, with respectively sixty thousand, fifty thousand and thirty thousand students enrolled at Rome, Naples and Bari universities, institutions that had been designed for optimum numbers of around five thousand. By the 1970s there were one million students, or three times the number then studying at universities in Britain. Academics refused to adjust from elite to mass institutions, while liberal-minded administrators cowered in fear of faculty or student radicals. Facilities such as canteens, classrooms and lecture halls were stretched to breaking point.

The life of an Italian tenured professor was a good one, with formal commitments of fifty-two hours lecturing a year, no local residence requirement, and many opportunities to earn real money in architecture, law, medicine or politics. There were no seminars, tutorials or written examinations, a student's progress being measured by oral examinations in the mastery of basic textbooks reflecting an outmoded curriculum. Jaded academics, many of them not much older than their students, discovered an antidote for accidie and boredom through laicised left-wing messianisms and the espousal of violence for other people, an especially despicable trait among left-wing intellectuals. Especially in social sciences, notably at the first Italian sociology faculty at Trento, and the humanities in general, they indoctrinated their students in Marxist theories almost guaranteed to disable these students in the job market. This was not an immediate handicap, for students could simply hang around after failing exams, in these glorified 'social parking lots', until the attrition of penury forced them on to a job market in which their talents rarely matched their pretensions and where clientelism, corruption and nepotism were rife.

Beginning in the autumn of 1967, at the Catholic universities of Trento and Milan, students held occupations in protest against attempts to increase fees or to restrict access, protests that mushroomed into discussions about what universities were for and what should be taught by whom. There was much conformist experimentation, whether involving sex, drugs and rock 'n' roll, or collectivised housing and squatting. Remote conflicts, in Latin America and South-east Asia, or in the race-torn cities of the USA, added visceral moralising passions while inclining young people to admire guerrilla-type violence. They were especially impressed by the Brazilian revolutionary Carlos Marighella, whose *Minimanual of the Urban Guerrilla* was published by Feltrinelli. Marighella pioneered political kidnapping when he abducted the US ambassador to Brazil, releasing him only after fifteen of his own comrades were freed by way of exchange. Since most of these youthful radicals no longer subscribed to the simple-minded Communist myth of the Soviet Union, their hatred of the existing liberal capitalist democracy was devoid of any reference to an existing ideal society. As in other European countries and the US, the transmission of knowledge and culture for their own sake was despised, while the high culture of the West was repudiated in favour of popular music and the cults of the bandit and outlaw as celebrated by such figures as the British Marxist Eric Hobsbawm. Worryingly, at Turin University a student 'scientific' commission cut books into five pieces to overcome the problem of 'book fetishism'. As the mother of a student radical who became a terrorist only to be shot dead in 1976 put it, the university her son attended 'had become a shambles, not a school'.[4]

While not every rock-throwing student became a terrorist, this was the general leftish milieu from which Red terrorists often came. It was part of a wider counter-cultural scene. As a German terrorist described it: 'the new ways of life, communes, Stones music, long hair – that exerted an enormous pull on me. In addition to that, socialism and other revolutionary theories, and the sense of justice born during the revolt.'[5] A low level of militarisation was evident in the increasingly ugly confrontations between Italian students and a police force not known for its gentle approach. After the police had used considerable force to eject students occupying Rome's La Sapienza university, future demonstrators came wearing crash helmets and prepared to fight back. Some manufactured and threw Molotov cocktails or fired ball-bearings with catapults and slings, the first stage in getting used to handling weapons.

The 'autonomous' left-wing groups which sprang up everywhere developed strong-arm security squads, which would eventually detach themselves from political control, becoming terrorist groups in their own right. For a minority, this often involved first storing guns, then getting used to handling, stripping down, reassembling and loading them, and on to the life-changing decision, for the terrorist and for his or her victim, to fire weapons at a living, breathing person. This was the point of no return, where the fact of having killed someone would cast an eternal shadow. Guns also had aesthetic and sexual appeal: 'arms have a fascination of their own, it is a fascination that makes you feel in some way more ... more virile ... this sensation of feeling stronger, more manly ... I found myself ... showing them to women to try to impress them ... and then it seemed somehow more noble to use arms instead of, I don't know, fighting with one's fists let's say,' recalled a former terrorist of the Italian Red Brigades.[6]

The denigration of what universities traditionally represented did not mean an absence of ideas. The most modish thought emanated from dissidents within the two dominant religions of Italy, that is Roman Catholicism and Marxism, with left-wing priests preaching social justice and Latin American-style liberation theology and various charismatic academic charlatans espousing heterodox forms of Marxism. The latter were a clerisy in disguise, albeit preaching the autonomous organisation of workers (and students) so as to supplant the leading role of the vanguard Party hitherto occupied by grey-suited Communist bureaucrats. The radical messianic type became ubiquitous throughout the universities and colleges of the Western world, a megaphone or microphone never far from their mouths, Danny 'the Red' Cohn-Bendit in France, Rudi Dutschke in West Germany, Tariq Ali in Britain and, in Italy, Antonio Negri. All of these men became celebrities of a sort in cultures of stunning credulity.

Negri initially exchanged his youthful Catholic fervency for the International Socialist Party, an allegiance that helped him become a full professor in politics at Padua University at the age of thirty-four, as some suspect, through the intercession of such patrons as Norberto Bobbio and Raniero Panzieri. Negri was an energetic blur of long black hair, horn-rimmed glasses, trite slogans and clenched fists. Learned investigations into the writings of the young Marx went together with crackbrained belief that the Italian government was merely the local branch of SIM – the Italian acronym for 'the imperialist state of the multinationals'. Negri joined the editorial board of *Quaderni Rossi* before founding his own paper *Potere Operaio*, both key vehicles for the non-Communist revolutionary Marxist left. These journals became manifestos for the autonomous grouplets formed by students as they went adrift from their traditional party political moorings, for the journey from left Catholicism to Red was paralleled by disillusionment with the leadership of the major political parties and their established youth movements.

Negri was contemptuous of the immobilised paralysis of the Communist Party, which he called a red bourgeoisie with its 'Marxist Disneyland' in the municipal administration of Red Bologna. The Communists were the most insidious element in a gigantic system of repression, canalising and controlling the 'violent insubordination' that was inherent in the working class and those cunningly marginalised as criminals. In a revealing analogy, Negri claimed that the difference between PCI chief Enrico Berlinguer and a real revolutionary was like that between 'a water pistol and a P.38'. There was no difference, Negri and his admirers argued, between liberal democracy and authoritarian or Fascist states, although he, and the terrorists he inspired, would be assiduous in claiming the rights that liberal democracy afforded, just as they made extensive use of the existing media to publicise their cause while simultaneously deriding it as a capitalistic opiate. Apart from using the term Fascism in an irresponsibly inflationary way, Negri and his like legitimised political violence. In order to legitimise it, Negri spouted a lot of claptrap, worthy of his French friends Louis Althusser, Jacques Derrida and Michel Foucault, about the structural or systemic violence inherent in capitalism, while warning such people as judges, executives, managers and policemen that they performed their duties at their own risk. The Viet Cong showed 'how it was not at all adventurism to shoot high-level state functionaries, that it was not adventurism to assault police stations in order to procure arms and . . . to execute those high state authorities hated by the urban and rural proletariat'. While approving of 'proletarian justice', that is kangaroo courts in which self-appointed judges sentenced industrialists and politicians to death, Negri and his kind availed themselves of every stunt that his defence lawyers could dream of. But that is to anticipate. By his mid-forties Negri had become an international intellectual celebrity, invited to the Ecole Normale Supérieure by Louis Althusser, married to a successful architect, and with beautiful homes in both Milan and Padua, no disqualification of course for the resentful views he held.[7] Radical students were merely one constituent element of the Red Brigades and, arguably, not the most important. While they paralysed the universities, the vast motor-vehicle factories of the northern industrial quadrangle were convulsed by strikes. If an average of 100 million man hours were lost through strikes each year between 1959 and 1969, the figure for that last year leaped to 294 million man hours alone.[8]

Several factors contributed to these years of industrial militancy. The flood of eight million migrants from the backward south was imperfectly assimilated into insalubrious northern slums, doing mindless unskilled tasks for low pay in factories where skilled workers received much higher rewards. They were also not assimilated into trades unions which were dominated by pragmatic-minded skilled workers and attached to the major political parties. The consumer boom that screamed from every advertising hoarding made a mockery of life in overcrowded, sub-standard housing within sprawling working-class suburbs. While the Italians can make almost anything look beautiful, they failed with their slums. Then came the radical students, turning up at the factory gates in political sects such as Workers' Power, Workers' Vanguard and Unceasing Struggle and encouraging workers to organise themselves on an autonomous basis outside existing trades unions which were disparaged as 'firemen' putting out industrial conflagrations on behalf of the bosses, a slur that served to drag the socialist unions further leftwards. Independently of the students, radical workers had begun to organise cell-like structures within the factories. One of the future leaders of the Red Brigades, a telecommunications engineer called Mario Moretti, worked in a large Siemens factory in Milan. Born into a Communist-supporting family in a seaside town in Marche, Moretti hated the cold, grey anonymity of Milan, and rapidly grasped the realities of class struggle in the factories, especially since his technological education had only made him a better class of factory hand in an era of automation. From the student movement he and his comrades copied the confusion of grassroots democracy with interminable mass meetings. He was fascinated by the students' command of language, their slogans and their 'fantasy'. So much so that he and other workers began to dabble in communal housing, partly to save money, but also to share childcare – he and his wife had a boy called Marcello – in order to devote more time to activism.[9]

What commenced with demands for the equalisation of wage differentials between skilled and unskilled or between men and women escalated into calls to decouple wages from productivity, profitability and the well-being of the economy as a whole. The lexicon of industrial conflict expanded to include the 'hiccup' strike, or the abrupt alternation of work and stoppages, or the 'chessboard' strike in which an individual workshop would down tools so as to paralyse an entire factory. Strikers marched around occupied factories wearing red scarves and balaclavas, singing the golden oldies of the wartime partisan movement. A further escalation came with sabotage, including cutting off power to machinery or blocking access roads and railways. The responses of employers invariably made things worse rather than better. They transferred militants to work in the noxious paint shops, hired scabs, summoned the riot police or, finally, closed entire factories to relocate production abroad. The habit of occupying a factory rather than leaving it, so as to discuss and vote interminably, revealed the influence of students. Their counter-cultural influence was also evident in the expansion of worker demands to include housing, rents and pensions.

As with the student left's domination of the universities, bullying and coercion were evident, even though former Red Brigadists do not like to recall this climate of oppression. While few cared if the occasional local drug dealer was beaten up, righteous violence was also used to intimidate foremen and managers, and at a major Fiat plant to force female office workers to join a strike, these women being jeered at and kicked or spat upon by four thousand blue-collar colleagues. Strikes spread from large industrial plants to public and tertiary sector workers in the 1969 'hot autumn', while autonomous radical organisation leached from prisoners to their judges: only the Italians could dream up 'the assault group of stipendiary magistrates'. Even lunatics were not spared the experimentations of a leftist anti-psychiatry that regarded mental illness as a construct of repressive social structures and Enlightened ideas rather than a chemical disorder. This carnival of militancy, still evocative with nostalgic memories for many of the academics writing about it forty years later, took place without regard to the inflationary pressure of higher wages and shorter working hours or the marked tendency of capital to leave the country or to relocate production to cheap labour sources such as Spain.

The Red Brigades were the most notorious terrorists on the anti-democratic left, the most dedicated and enduring of a wide range of armed sectarian grouplets. They were ruthlessly effective, with the worker members bringing a certain craftsmanly pride in performance to their new job. They emerged from the Metropolitan Political Collective founded in Milan on 8 September 1969, gradually establishing a presence in such Milanese factories as Fiat and Pirelli, and in the surrounding working-class districts of Lambrate, Quarto Oggiaro and Giambellino.

The leading lights were the husband-and-wife team Renato Curcio and Margherita Cagol, who as recently as 1965 had exchanged the left-tinged Catholicism of Jacques Maritain for admiration of Chairman Mao's Red Guards and the Viet Cong. Once a devout Catholic and a talented classical guitar player, Cagol fell under Curcio's spell after meeting him in Trento's new sociology department. They participated in various occupations before marrying, in a church wedding, in August 1969. Moving to Milan Cagol hated the 'barbarity' of the big city, 'the true face of the society we live in'. Instead of finding a less stressful domicile – which would be the reaction of most people – Cagol said, 'we must do anything possible to change this system, because this is the profound meaning of our existence'. This was written in a series of letters to her mother, in which there was incongruous stuff about buying new curtains, which Cagol signed off, 'bye mum, lots of kisses from your revolutionary'.[10] The third founder was Alberto Franceschini, from a Communist clan in Reggio Emilia, whose grandfather was a former partisan and whose resistor father had been an inmate of Auschwitz. After attempting to study at a technical institute in Milan, Franceschini fell in with Curzio and Cagol. In a symbolic link with the wartime past, an elderly former partisan instructed them in using two Second World War-vintage machine guns. The wartime historical dimension also cleared up many moral dilemmas. As Mario Moretti has put it, 'If a partisan pumped half a kilo of lead into the belly of a German soldier, do you think you could ask him: "Didn't you think that perhaps Fritz has a wife and five children, raises cows, and doesn't want anything else?" "Yes, but I am defending my country" he would have replied.' This conveniently overlooked the fact that the partisan had no lawful way of expressing dissent, while the Red Brigades terrorists chose to ignore a mature democratic system.[11]

At a key meeting of seventy activists in Chiavari in November 1969, Curcio, Cagol and Franceschini argued that the hour of the Italian revolution was at hand and that it was time for a violent vanguard to bring it into being. On the cover of their review, *Sinistra Proletaria*, a rifle joined the ubiquitous hammer and sickle. In October 1970 the review announced the formation of the Red Brigades, 'the first moments of the proletariat's self-organisation in order to fight the bosses and their henchmen'. In other words, the initial strategy was to pose as the armed defenders of striking workers. There was something else, which an older and wiser Franceschini would concede: 'All of us in the Red Brigades were drug addicts of a particular type, of ideology. A murderous drug, worse than heroin.'[12]

Rhetorical violence in the group's review, notably 'for every eye, two eyes; for every tooth, an entire face', was initially accompanied by planting red flags on factory roofs and expelling the management and foremen, followed by burning cars belonging to managers and industrialists. There was something goliardic about these activities. Kidnapping came next. On 3 March 1972 they abducted for all of twenty minutes Idalgo Macchiarini of Sit-Siemens, caricatured as 'a neo-Fascist in a white shirt', releasing him with a sign around his neck which read 'Strike one to educate a hundred'. At that point, the ranks of the Red Brigades were augmented by the leaderless remnants of Feltrinelli's Partisan Action Groups. They carried out a few robberies, while burning the cars of nine Fiat executives at a time when they were negotiating with striking metal workers. In February 1972 they kidnapped Bruno Labiate, the provincial secretary of a right-wing union, leaving him four hours later shaven-headed and bound to the gates of Fiat Montefiori. In the spring Cagol and her husband unexpectedly joined her parents who were on vacation in an almost deserted Rimini. Curcio and her father discussed the irrevocable choice the couple had made to engage in armed activities. That summer a separate Red Brigades column was established in Turin. In December they abducted and detained Fiat executive Ettore Amerio for eight days.

If these actions could be interpreted as strategic interventions on behalf of militant workers, the kidnapping of a Genoese judge, Mario Sossi, who was held captive for over a month in the spring of 1974, was a direct challenge to the state at a time when passions were already high over a referendum on divorce. Inadvertently giving the lie to the notion that the Italian Establishment was capable of a coherent conspiracy to do anything, the Red Brigades immediately and successfully opened a rift between the police, four thousand of whom searched for Sossi, and the magistracy who wanted to call off the hunt so as to do a discreet deal regarding the prisoners whose release the Red Brigades had demanded.

Not for the last time, the Red Brigades exploited the psychological distress of the victim to sow dissension in government. Between bouts of blubbering like a baby, Sossi issued angry denunciations of a state that had failed to protect him, warning that he would take the attorney-general Coco down with him as co-responsible for the crimes the Red

Brigades accused him of. The attorney-general then flouted agreed government policy by offering to exchange eight prisoners for Sossi, and broke his own word when he then failed to keep his side of the bargain after Sossi had been released. Sossi himself was put out by the attorney-general's insinuation that he had gone insane during his captivity. There was some truth in the Red Brigades' limpid observation that 'during these thirty-five days the contradictions of the various state organs have been manifested'. Italy being what it is, many leftists either sympathised with what the Red Brigades were doing or imagined that they were some artful mirage acting on behalf of more sinister right-wing forces.

While the Red Brigades were keen to claim credit for their actions, terrorists of the extreme right preferred to envelop their carnage in an air of mystery since they acknowledged responsibility for only a few of the terrorist attacks attributed to them. Unlike the left, they preferred indiscriminate bombing, eschewing kidnapping entirely, in their bid to create maximum public insecurity. It is very likely that they received assistance from elements in the Italian security services; moreover, the judiciary did not hasten to investigate their crimes. On 28 May 1974 a powerful bomb exploded in a refuse bin amid a crowd of 2,500 people attending an anti-Fascist rally in Brescia. Eight people were killed, including two who were decapitated, and 102 injured. Two months later, on 4 August, a bomb exploded on the Rome–Brenner express as it entered a tunnel near Bologna. Twelve people were killed and forty-eight injured, the majority holidaymakers.

In September 1974, police succeeded in arresting Curcio and Franceschini, who had been too trusting of an ex-priest called Silvano Girotto, a former Bolivian revolutionary they had enthusiastically admitted to their ranks. Nicknamed 'Father Machine Gun', Girotto was in fact the police spy who identified the whereabouts of Curcio and others. Curcio was imprisoned in a low-security establishment at Casale Monferato, where he 'resembled a terrorist on sabbatical', allowed to use the telephone at will and without supervision and to receive as many visitors as he cared to in cells that were not locked. Cagol continued the struggle alone, writing to her mother: 'I am doing the right thing and History will show that I am right as it did for the Resistance in 1945 ... there are no other means. This police state is based on the use of force and it can only be fought on the same level ... I can manage in any situation and nothing scares me.' In February 1975 Cagol arrived at the prison pretending to be an engineer from SIP, the state telephone company. Three male comrades with machine guns under their coats rushed in behind her. Another member of the team used a ladder to cut the telephone wire running along the perimeter wall. They called out, 'Renato, where are you?' and made off with the Red Brigades leader.

Lying low until May in flats bought with hard cash, the Brigades introduced a new tactical method when they burst into the offices of a prominent Christian Democrat lawyer, tied him up and then shot him in the leg, the first of many *gambizzazioni* or kneecappings. In June, after they had kidnapped Vallarino Gancia, a drinks-industry magnate, the police cornered the band on a remote farm near Acqui Terme. Cagol had bought it in March 1972 claiming she was a maths teacher from Padua married to an academic. They had recently lost a baby and she needed peace and quiet to recuperate. She had indeed suffered a miscarriage, but the rest of the cover story seems like the life she had left. Neighbours did not realise that when she asked them to cut the tall grass surrounding the farm, she was clearing a field of vision. Gunshots and a grenade flew around the farm as the Brigadists tried to flee, with a policeman losing an eye and an arm, and Mara Cagol her life when she was shot twice at close range. Curcio escaped. He was recaptured in Milan after a gun battle with the police in January 1976, although this proved a mixed blessing for the Italian authorities since his release became the object of future terrorist outrages. Cagol received a Church funeral, returning to the ways of the family she had not left.

II YEARS OF LEAD

These undoubted triumphs for the forces of law and order encouraged many premature obituaries of the Red Brigades. In fact, they had set in place organisational structures that enabled them to wage a sustained terror campaign against the imminent threat, in their febrile imaginations, of *gollista* (an authoritarian reconstruction of the constitution as had occurred in France under de Gaulle) and *golpista* (a full-blown military coup). There was a central Direzione Strategica, consisting of ten to fifteen people, which met biannually or whenever requested by one of the five major regional columns in Rome, Genoa, Milan, the Veneto and Turin. These were co-ordinated by a Comitato Esecutivo. Each column consisted of several brigades which could co-operate laterally as fronts such as the 'prison front' or the 'counter-revolutionary front'. Each single brigade consisted of a cellular nucleus of regulars, who lived underground and drew a modest salary of about two hundred thousand lire a month, surrounded by a larger penumbra of irregulars who operated above in the sunlight pursuing conventional careers. For example, in Turin, there were ten underground guerrillas and about thirty people who operated in the open. New recruits, mostly from the wider left-wing subculture, underwent a training programme – it is striking that there were far more applicants than the Red Brigades either wanted or had places for. Training involved finding a remote clearing or quarry and having a go with a revolver or machine gun. The weapons were usually of Second World War vintage, or guns purchased from regular gun shops. While there may have only been three hundred or so dedicated Red Brigades terrorists, there were far larger numbers of active sympathisers, and hundreds of thousands who were sentimentally enamoured of the cause. A group of eager students tried to donate hunting rifles to the Red Brigades, blissfully ignorant that a weapon a metre and a half long is not best suited to fighting in narrow urban streets. The terrorists' favourite weapon was the short – and totally unreliable – British Sten-gun, for which it was easier to get ammunition than it was for the more exotic Soviet AK-47. Mario Moretti has pointed out that he and his colleagues were not great shots; most of what they did was achieved by surprise. Funds were raised through armed robberies, the techniques being learned from watching cops-and-robbers films.

In April 1976 the Brigades firebombed the Fiat Montefiori factory, causing a billion lire's worth of damage, and two billion more when they returned to the Fiat factory at Turin ten days later. They were no longer the only game in town. A new group, called Potere Proletario Armato, kneecapped a Milan businessman, while an oil executive, Giovanni Theodoli, was shot eight times by terrorists from Nuclei Armati Proletari on a Rome street. This southern terrorist band had been founded in 1970 by middle-class students from Naples; the father of one member was an oil executive, another member was the son of the owner of a brick-making firm, the rest the offspring of lawyers and teachers. This founding group then recruited convicted criminals in the highly politicised jails of Lecce and Perugia where imprisoned student radicals simultaneously glorified and politicised fellow inmates.

Fear of terrorism began to work its way into the judicial system. When the trial of captured Red Brigadists commenced in Turin in May 1976, the defendants warned the judges and prosecutors that they themselves would be liable to attack. It proved so difficult to find willing jurors that the trial had to be postponed. Then the Red Brigades reckoned with the duplicitous attorney-general Francesco Coco. On a sunny June afternoon his new driver, Antioco Dejana, took the judge to his home for lunch, with a bodyguard called Giovanni Saponara sitting in the front seat. On reaching their destination, Coco and Saponara walked up to the house while Dejana parked the car. Five terrorists appeared, killing Saponara before his hand had even reached his shoulder holster, and blowing most of the attorney-general's head away. Dejana was shot dead while still in the car. In the Turin courtroom, Curcio announced: 'Yesterday we put to death Coco, enemy of the proletariat.' He had probably dialled up the murder squad from a prison telephone. Before the end of July, neo-Fascist terrorists machine-gunned Judge Vittorio Occorsio in Rome.

Most Italian left-wing terrorists joined these underground armed groups after graduating from student demonstrations, or from the security sections spawned by the various autonomous political organisations. Judging from smaller groups like Prima Linea, they tended to join as small groups of close friends, where bonds of personal trust reinforced political solidarities. About 10 per cent of left-wing terrorists were women, with violence against others acting as a liberating impulse in a society where until 1975 husbands were legally entitled to beat their wives. Other girls were roped in at the insistence of, or to hold on to, their boyfriends. By contrast, Moretti's wife left him once he embarked on a career as a terrorist; he never saw her or his son again until they visited him in prison. He has described life on the run rather well. He was a temporary guest of other people, a sort of phantom, watching their everyday lives without really being a part of them. He had to judge people and situations in a split second, because the slightest mistake could have catastrophic consequences.[13] Acclimatisation to violence was incremental. It began with hurling cobblestones or Molotov cocktails at the police. Next came some proof of higher reliability, such as hiding a fugitive or storing guns and explosives, perhaps followed by reconnaissance of a potential target. This was followed by using guns in robberies and then firing them at someone, always for reasons of political necessity. They internalised Mao's dictum: 'All men must die, but death can vary in its significance.' There were weighty deaths, on behalf of the revolution, and deaths of 'Fascists' which were 'light as a feather'. As

Adriana Faranda conceded, extreme violence was inherent in the social revolutionary project: 'You convince yourself that to reach this utopia of idealized relationships it is necessary to pass through the destruction of the society which prevents your ideas from being realized. Violence is a necessary component of this destruction. The concept of the purifying bloodbath is axiomatic to the model of the socialist revolution.'[14] Sam Peckinpah's existential splatter movie *The Wild Bunch* was also a firm favourite in these circles; one Red Brigades terrorist had seen it twenty times.[15]

Kneecappings and murder represented a higher order of violence than burning cars and kidnappings. This was premeditated violence, where someone was identified as a symbol of larger political processes, and meticulous plans were laid to harm or kill them. As one former terrorist said, 'you make a person correspond to a political need', while concealing the brute facts of bloodshed within an obfuscatory, leaden language derived from sociology seminars. Having identified the target, the terrorist decides he is guilty and determines the penalty: 'so in actual fact he is not a person any more, he has been emptied and you load him up with other crimes, other responsibilities ... At this point you can't afford to be totally involved ... you are someone who is meting out justice, who is stating values, and so there is no place for ... strong emotions even if you have them inside, even if the situation is charged with feelings ... but not in that role, not at that time.' In fact, most terrorists were constantly anxious to distinguish their actions from those of mere criminals, even when they were robbing banks in order to pay for foreign holidays, for those went with the job too.

These terrorist attacks in Italy in the late 1970s took place against a backdrop of crisis, natural disaster and political scandal. Droughts were succeeded by torrential rain, and an earthquake devastated Friuli. Aid for the victims was systematically misappropriated. An accident at a Hoffmann-La Roche subsidiary manufacturing herbicides near Seveso released large quantities of dioxin gas similar to Agent Orange, which threatened an epidemiological disaster that the government badly mismanaged even as it handed out over a hundred billion lire to deal with it. At the same time it emerged that both the CIA and Exxon Corporation had been feeding tens of millions of dollars into corrupting the Italian political process, while Christian Democrat and Social Democrat politicians had taken bribes from Lockheed to rig a major aircraft contract. There were rumours that Mossad was trying to destabilise

Italy to make Israel the US's sole strategic ally in the Mediterranean. Fatally dependent on the inflated prices OPEC demanded for oil, the government of Giulio Andreotti had to go cap in hand to the IMF, the EEC, the US and West Germany. The lire was devalued by 30 per cent, while unemployment rose by 8 per cent, the same figure for the drop in industrial production.

Meanwhile, Rome's La Sapienza university was the scene of days of rioting, which turned murderous. After a police officer had been shot dead, one of his colleagues opened fire and killed two student demonstrators. Urban radicals stormed and set fire to offices of the Christian Democrats and the MSI headquarters. When a Communist trades union leader attempted to speak to students at the university, he had to flee from a mob armed with clubs, crowbars, tyre irons and wrenches. On 5 March 1977 ten thousand students fought a four-hour pitched battle with police, two of whom were shot by gunmen operating within the crowd. Later that month, fifty thousand students battled the police into the night after a demonstration to commemorate Pier Francesco Lorusso, a Lotta Continua activist killed by police in Bologna. There, only reinforcements from across the whole of Italy enabled the police to keep a grip on the model Communist city that students almost took control of after days of rioting.

The trial of Curcio and others led to the adoption of a dual strategy. The defendants would refuse to recognise the court, while outside their comrades would strike at the judiciary. They assassinated the seventy-six-year-old president of the Turin bar association responsible for selecting Curcio's defence team, together with two policemen. The trial judge had to report that, out of a pool of three hundred potential jurors, only four were willing to serve. Simultaneously, the Red Brigades extended their campaign to their foes in the mass media. Three prominent newspaper and television figures were kneecapped, including TG1 news director Emilio Rossi who was shot twenty-two times in the legs, crippling him for life. When Curcio's trial was moved from Turin to Milan, the Brigades attempted to kill the president of the Court of Appeals, but managed only to wound two of his police bodyguards. The authorities scored a minor triumph when on 1 July 1977 carabinieri ambushed Antonio Lo Muscio, the former convict who by then led the Nuclei Armata Proletaria, on the steps of Rome's San Petro in Vinculi where he and his colleagues were waiting to gun down the rector of La Sapienza. Lo Muscio was shot dead as he tried to flee.

That autumn saw interminable riots and gun battles. In November, Red Brigades terrorists shot the vice-director of *La Stampa* four times in the face, somehow construing this former resistance fighter as 'an active agent of the counter-guerrilla campaign'. During the fortnight that it took for him to die, Red Brigades terrorists shot the reform Communist Carlo Castellano a total of nine times, eight shots in his legs and one in the stomach. While recovering from the fourteen bouts of surgery, Castellano recalled his attackers: 'Eyes filled with so much hatred as if I were a wild animal to be killed, not deserving the slightest pity.' After killing the head of security at Fiat, the Red Brigades machine-gunned the elderly judge in charge of reforming Italy's parlous prisons. In Turin, where Curcio and fifteen other defendants went on trial in a court guarded by eight thousand policemen, the defendants howled abuse at the judges, lay and professional, warning: 'To the lay judges we say, with great clarity, that in this voluntary capacity as special tribunal we consider them responsible for their actions, and consequently we will hold them accountable.' Turin's head of urban security was shot dead; a Red Brigades communiqué announced, 'the trial must not go ahead'. It did, despite the antics of the accused. Curcio received a seven-year jail sentence.

As the quicker-minded policemen worked out, bank robberies or kidnappings were invariably the prelude to some major terrorist incident. A kidnapping was duly undertaken in connection with the abduction of Aldo Moro. In 1977, the Red Brigades replenished their war chest by seizing Pietro Costa, a younger son of a Genoese shipping tycoon. There were rare light moments. A man of six foot six, Costa quipped as he was compressed into a tight box that they might have gone for one of his shorter siblings. His kidnappers liked the fact that he was wearing shoes with holes in them, which he had worn all day inspecting the damp decks of ships. When they asked about his dietary requirements, he replied, 'I eat everything, the main thing is a lot of it.' After the kidnappers had told him they wanted a ransom of ten billion lire, he pleaded his father's business difficulties. They settled for one and a half billion and he was freed. When they handed back his wallet, he found one bus ticket missing which he insisted on having returned to him. That's how tycoons are made.[16]

*　　*　　*

III THE MORO AFFAIR

In the eyes of the terrorists, whose analysis of complex modern government was simple, there was a single entity called 'the state', which like
a crouched beast of prey had a single 'heart'. As early as 1974 the
Red Brigades had considered inducing a total governmental crisis by
kidnapping Giulio Andreotti, the leader of the Atlanticist right wing
of the Christian Democrats. Perhaps sensing that this fixer and friend of
the Mafia might not be missed, Mario Moretti and others resolved
to kidnap Aldo Moro, as the embodiment of the Christian Democrats –
or the 'demiurge of bourgeois power' as Moretti put it. It is difficult
to convey what a body-blow this action was, the worst crisis in post-
war Italy.

Moro had been prime minister between 1964 and 1968 and again
between 1974 and 1976 of various Christian Democrat and Socialist
coalitions, with a controversial spell as foreign minister in between.
He was the progressive Catholic responsible for the historic opening to
the reformed Communists. With their 34 per cent of the vote, the
Communists could not simply be ignored. Moro seems to have envisaged
a 'solidarity government' after which the Communists would alternate in
power with his own Christian Democrats, who might also have benefited
indirectly – morally speaking – from a break in their forty-year spell
in office. Although Christian Democrats had made the single greatest
contribution to the stabilisation of post-war democracy in Italy, they
were also heavily engaged in corruption, including that of the Mafia,
as subsequent revelations about Andreotti made plain. A British prime
minister has been interviewed about the alleged sale of honours; in Italy a
former premier was accused of consorting with murderers.

Increasingly warming to the role of wise elder statesman, Moro was
the purely ceremonial president of the Christian Democrats, combining
this with a university professorship in law. He was an impressively subtle
figure, a native southerner but with the austere phlegmatic formality
of Italian northerners. Rather endearingly, he was also a hopeless
bumbler and hypochondriac, dragging around endless pill boxes in his
briefcase. He also seems to have had presentiments of doom. Moro's
widow Eleanore remembered him punctuating their conversations with
testamentary remarks along the lines of 'If you have need of counsel . . .
of someone to whom you can open your heart, you can turn to this

person, who is a friend' or 'I would like my books to remain together as a collection.'

The Red Brigades spent five months planning their attack, which devolved on the Rome column which Moretti had established. Its key players were Adriana Faranda, a divorcee with a small daughter whom she handed over to her own mother, so as to engage fully in politics with her lover Valerio Morucci, an addict of American gangster films. These two were the commanders. Moretti also recruited Anna Laura Braghetti and Barbara Balzerani, both prominent in autonomist groups, as well as Prospero Gallinari, an escapee from Treviso prison. Using the proceeds from the Costa kidnapping, they purchased three apartments in Rome and a house at neighbouring Velletri where the Direzione Strategica could meet. They lived as three couples, keeping a polite distance from their neighbours and using assumed names. They closely monitored the movements of three potential victims. Andreotti had ten guards and moved about the city with armed escorts and motorbike outriders. Since Senate president Amintore Fanfani's movements were too erratic to be predicted, that left only Moro as a target. Months were spent watching his movements, whether at home or at Rome university's Political Science faculty where he had his professorship.

On 16 March 1978 Moro set off for parliament to celebrate the installation of Andreotti's new government, a coalition positively supported, rather than merely tolerated, by the PCI. Fortunately, his two-year-old grandson Luca had opted for a rival firemen's display rather than his usual morning outing with his grandfather. Moro sat in the rear of a dark-blue Fiat 130, driven by his long-time driver, Domenico Ricci, with Oreste 'Judo' Leonardi, his fifty-two-year-old chief bodyguard, alongside. Three further guards, all southerners aged between twenty-five and thirty, followed in a cream Alfa Romeo. There was a regrettably predictable stop en route, the church of Santa Chiara, where Moro stopped to pray for half an hour before the start of each working day. The Red Brigades first planned to attack on this square, but the prospect of shooting the two bodyguards who accompanied Moro into the church, and the likelihood that a crocodile of schoolchildren might get in the way, induced them to find another spot more suited to their task.

The point of any terrorist attack is to concentrate firepower so as temporarily to get the edge over the much vaster forces of law and order, represented in Rome that day by about ten thousand policemen.

At a bend in the Via Fani the Red Brigades team found a section of road where the vacant Bar Olivetti was separated from the road by shrubs, with a blank wall beneath a block of flats on the opposite side. This was perfect for a broadside attack. The only snag was a street flower-vendor called Antonio Spiriticchio, who set up his stall just there; the night before the attack the Red Brigades sent someone to slash the tyres of his truck. He wouldn't be selling flowers the next day. Mario Moretti drove a stolen blue Fiat 126 in front of Moro's convoy, keeping it in his rear mirror. He braked suddenly in the Via Fani, causing a three-way collision with the Fiat 130 and the Alfa Romeo. His companion, Barbara Balzerani, got out and ran up the road to halt oncoming traffic, with a lightweight submachine gun. Alvaro Loiacono and Alession Casimirri used a white Fiat 128 to block in the car containing Moro's bodyguards from the rear. Valerio Morucci, Raffaele Fiore, Franco Bonsoli and Prospero Gallinari emerged from the bushes that shielded the bar. They were wearing Alitalia uniforms and caps, which had made it seem as if they were waiting for the airline minibus with their light luggage ready for a flight. They wore bullet-proof vests. Although two of the guns jammed for a moment or two, they poured automatic fire into the front of the Fiat 130, killing Moro's driver and bodyguard, and the Alfa Romeo, where they killed two of the bodyguards instantaneously. The third guard managed to crawl out but was executed with a shot in the head. Only one of the five guards managed to get his service pistol out of its shoulder holster. Moretti dragged Moro, who was unhurt apart from scratches from flying glass, out of the Fiat, driving him a short distance before the attackers switched to a waiting van. He was put in a wooden box and removed, after another change of vehicle, to an apartment at Via Montalcini 8. Any attempts to summon help to the scene of this bloodbath were frustrated since the terrorists had disabled the local telephone junctions. For over fifty days, Moro was held in a cell created by an architect who had built a concealed partition in a bedroom. A mirror was used to recreate the illusion of lost space. Moro lay on a narrow camp bed, and was denied sanitary facilities except for a metal bowl and a cloth. Elsewhere, throughout progressive Italy, Prosecco corks popped in many apartments in celebration of this coup. In parliament there was a cross-party statement rejecting terrorism. Knee-jerk demands for the introduction of the death penalty for terrorists were refused.

The Red Brigades claimed responsibility for Moro's abduction in a series of telephone calls, one of which directed the authorities to a subway tunnel where they found a recent picture of the politician awkwardly posed before the group's five-star banner. A communiqué explained that he was being held in 'a people's prison' pending trial as the leading theorist of the Christian Democrat regime and the key agent of the nefarious multinationals, although some of his captors would subsequently report that the former prime minister had genially confounded the rubbish they spouted regarding how power in Italy 'really' functioned. From his cage in the Turin courtroom, Curcio announced that Moro was 'in the hands of the proletariat' and on trial. Using the tactic they had pioneered with the kidnapped judge Sossi, Moro's captors encouraged him to communicate with his family and political colleagues thereby using the former to put psychological pressure on the latter. Eventually, in despair the family would pursue an independent strategy to release their paterfamilias. The kidnappers engaged him in prolonged discussions, in order to influence what he wrote, assuming, of course, that they didn't simply hold a gun to his head. Moro complied, and wrote several letters, no doubt partly in the hope that the police would eventually trail one of the couriers. His letters were then edited by the kidnappers. His letters to interior minister, and future president, Francesco Cossiga warned that he was not solely responsible for decisions that had been collective, and urged the Party to involve the Vatican in negotiations to free thirteen Red Brigades prisoners.

Egged on by the US, and going against the wishes of pope Paul VI, Andreotti's government refused to negotiate with the kidnapper–murderers, while the police engaged in a massive hunt for the victim's whereabouts. The physical evidence was mishandled, while the police invited ridicule by bringing in mediums and spiritualists, although ironically a raid on a remote village called Gradoli near Lake Bolsena, recommended during a séance, might have turned up trumps at Rome's Via Gradoli, where indeed there was a Red Brigades hideout. Christian Democrat politicians put out feelers to their Mafia friends, who contacted imprisoned Red Brigades terrorists to spare Moro's life. Moro's wife and daughter, encouraged by Moro himself, endeavoured to make the government change its inflexible line. This was made infinitely harder by the fact that the Red Brigades stepped up their campaign of shootings of industrialists and prison guards, in addition to the five bodyguards they had already cold-bloodedly murdered in the Via Fani, whose own relatives were implacably opposed to negotiations. They released a communiqué giving the government forty-eight hours to commence negotiating prisoner releases. A list of thirteen names, including Curcio's, followed. These people had been convicted of eight murders, and included men serving three life sentences, and others doing a total of 172 years.[17] Meanwhile, Moro wrote his increasingly desperate letters, twenty-nine in all, claiming that he was being offered up as a sacrificial figure, and insisting that he did not want any politicians at what he imagined would soon be his funeral. While the pope and UN secretary-general Kurt Waldheim made impassioned interventions to secure Moro's release, the government divided into hawks and doves, just as the Red Brigades hoped it would, and just as they themselves were also divided between the militarist Moretti and Faranda who wanted Moro released alive. In reality, these positions were always susceptible to agonies and doubt, no matter how resolved anyone may have been in advance.

The government hawks claimed that Moro was either drugged or had gone out of his mind, and that there should be no negotiations. To give in would invite further abductions. This line was picked up by many newspapers, which proclaimed that 'Moro isn't Moro.' Newspaper editors also pondered whether they would publish any shocking revelations Moro might have made about Italian politics. Half said they would. The victim found himself in the grotesque position of having to prove that he was compos mentis when he wrote his subsequent prison letters. The opposition Communists, and Berlinguer in particular, took the hardest line against negotiations. Doves, led by Socialist Bettino Craxi, urged covert talks, a view urgently endorsed by the extra-parliamentary left who belatedly realised where their rhetorical flirtations with the Red Brigades had led them. The sinister professor Negri held seminars where he and his comrades pontificated about whether the distinguished statesman should be released or killed. Craxi opened up a back channel to the Red Brigades through Giannino Guiso, a Socialist acting as defence lawyer to Curcio and other Red Brigades defendants. From him Craxi learned that, unlike the case of Sossi, Moro would be killed if the government failed to release terrorist prisoners. The Social Democrat president of the Italian Republic, Giuseppe Saragat, weighed in by reminding his colleagues that 'no democratic form of power could exist outside the sense of humanity and pity'.

That hawks and doves were not neatly distributed along party lines only increased the pressure on the government. The former resistance fighter and leading socialist Sandro Pertini was a hardliner, as was the widow of one of Moro's bodyguards, who threatened to incinerate herself if Andreotti negotiated with terrorists. Even as it kneecapped an industrialist and a union leader, the Red Brigades issued communiqués claiming that 'The state of the multinationals has revealed its true face, without the grotesque mask of formal democracy; it is that of the armed imperialist counter-revolution, of the terrorism of mercenaries in uniform, of the political genocide of communist forces.' That sentence alone indicates how much they inhabited a world of dangerous delusions. Acting under the suasion of higher historic logic, the Red Brigades were now 'compelled' to conclude this chapter in their 'valiant struggle' by putting an end to their hostage's life.

Moro, who had stopped shaving and was refusing solid foods, was allowed to write a final letter, and was then repeatedly shot by Moretti and Gallinari on the morning of 9 May after being told to ready himself for a journey in the trunk of the car. In a bold gesture, the Red Brigades left his corpse in the car symbolically parked midway between the Christian Democrat and Communist headquarters. At noon the following day a telephone call revealed his whereabouts; Christian Democrat notables arrived to ponder the last fifty-four days and the body awkwardly slumped in the car. Renato Curcio triumphantly shouted from the dock: 'the act of revolutionary justice administered to Aldo Moro was the highest act of humanity possible in this class society' before he was led away. In line with her late husband's wishes, Eleanore Moro insisted that he be buried in a small parish church at Torrita Tiburina, with no music and little fuss, and no politicians present. No family members attended the memorial service conducted by the ailing pope, who himself died that August.

While the government contemplated its next steps, the Red Brigades sent a team to shoot Antonio Esposito, a thirty-six-year-old anti-terrorist officer, as he journeyed on a bus to work. In October, they killed Italy's director of penal affairs, followed by the country's leading expert on academic penal anthropology. In January 1979 they killed Guido Rossa, a charismatic Communist union official, for allegedly denouncing a workmate who had handed out Red Brigades literature in his plant. Shortly afterwards, sixteen thousand workers at the Italsider steel works demonstrated against 'Fascist/Brigadists', and half a million people attended Rossa's funeral in Genoa. Oblivious to such scenes, Prima Linea gunmen murdered a leading left-wing lawyer who had investigated right- as well as left-wing terrorism. When a heroic jeweller shot two Brigadists as they held up a pizza restaurant he was patronising, gunmen from the Proletari Armati per il Comunismo turned up at his shop a few days later and shot him dead.

Meanwhile, at Padua, leftists had achieved the university of their wildest dreams. 'Anti-proletarian professors', many of them Communists or Socialists, were physically attacked, including three who were beaten up for refusing to issue automatic examination passes. Even professors of impeccably working-class origins were accused of 'bourgeois tendencies', and received telephone death threats or had to walk along university corridors with 'To shoot at professors is our duty' sprayed on the walls. A bomb destroyed the entrance to the Political Science Faculty, while the homes of two 'reactionary' professors were set ablaze. Two academic psychologists were almost beaten to death by a mob of twenty students. In September 1979 Angelo Ventura, a middle-aged professor of history and director of a regional centre for the study of the wartime resistance, who had repeatedly clashed with Negri, had a narrow escape when two terrorists on a Vespa scooter attempted to shoot him. It was revealing of the depths Italian universities had reached that Ventura drove them off with five shots from his licensed handgun. In early December a team of Prima Linea terrorists took over Turin university's business school, kneecapping five professors and five students, and shooting a student who, politely in the circumstances, inquired whether he should address the lead female terrorist using the formal pronoun.

In view of these continued atrocities, the government massively augmented the resources at the disposal of the new counter-terrorism chief, general Alberto Dalla Chiesa, giving him command of twenty-five thousand carabineri in the north, while making another paramilitary police general prefect of Genoa, the first time a non-civilian had held such a post. Powers of preventative detention were extended to forty-eight hours, and the interrogation of suspects without lawyers present was introduced, a necessary step since some radical lawyers were aiding and abetting their clients by passing messages back and forth with the underground organisations.

Further measures were designed to disaggregate the terrorists, notably the penitence law of May 1982 and the dissociation law of March 1987. While anyone who killed a public official was to receive an automatic life sentence, those terrorists who actively co-operated with the police by confessing their crimes and identifying other terrorists would have their sentences reduced. This unfairly tended to favour the big players, who had more to confess than the small fry in the Red Brigades' highly atomised cells. Those who dissociated themselves from terrorism had to confess fully, abjure violence and demonstrate their reformed characters in prison, in return for which they would receive reduced sentences. Social psychologists were brought in to profile terrorist suspects so as to identify who would or would not co-operate, a procedure which isolated the implacable hard core, who were then kept in the worst circumstances in a generally poor penal system.

This procedure opened the way to the phenomenon of the *pentiti* – that is, terrorists who cut deals, rather than repented as the Italian name wrongly suggests. The first of these was Carlo Fiorino – *il professorino* – who incriminated Toni Negri, already indicted in April 1979 for his involvement, actual and by way of incitement, with left-wing terrorism. The most damaging charge was that in 1975 Negri had used criminals of his acquaintance in a faked kidnapping of fellow radical Carlo Saronio to extort 470 million lire from Saronio's wealthy parents. The kidnappers contrived to hold a chloroform-saturated cloth over Saronio's face for so long that it killed him.

The number of terrorist incidents in 1979 would reach 2,513, worse even than the 2,379 of the previous year. In January the Red Brigades shot dead Piersanti Mattarella, the Sicilian Christian Democrat leader who had most strongly taken up Moro's desire to achieve reconciliation with the Communists. They machine-gunned three Milanese policemen and injured eighteen carabinieri when they bombed a barracks in Rome. In Genoa, Prima Linea shot dead a carabiniere colonel and his driver, while blinding an army colonel. In February they struck at professor Vittorio Bachelet, a prominent liberal Catholic and vice-president of the magistracy, as he left a classroom at La Sapienza. A woman walked up to him in the crowded corridor and shot him four times in the stomach. Her male companion shot Bachelet a further three times before reaching down to put a fourth bullet in his head. In March they killed three prominent judges, shooting one of them in the back as he walked into a hall where he was due to give a lecture.

Although many Italians were thoroughly demoralised by these killings, crucial arrests and the incentives available to terrorists who turned state's evidence began to grind the Red Brigades down, while increasing the paranoia of people already living in a permanent state of alert watchfulness. The 1980 arrest of Patrizio Peci was especially significant as he had led the Turin Red Brigades column and belonged to its Direzione Strategica. According to his autobiography, dramatically entitled *I, the Vile One,* Peci was born in 1953, the son of a builder in Ripatransone, a small town in the Marche that claims the narrowest street in the world. They moved to the larger town of San Benedetto del Tronto when Peci was nine. He had an uneventful childhood, although he preferred playing cards on the beach to going to school. As a young adult, he worked as a waiter in seaside hotels, although he had joined Lotta Continua while still at school, prompted by a dispute between fishermen and the owners of their boats. Soon he was beating up his teachers, the action which attracted the Red Brigades' notice. In 1974 they recruited him and sent him to work in a factory in Milan. Whereas he had received 180,000 lire per month as a waiter, he now got 200,000 monthly expenses as a Red Brigades logistician, on top of free accommodation, utility bills, clothing and equipment. There was also an annual holiday in a property owned by the organisation. No wonder his girlfriend, Maria Rosaria Roppolo, threatened to kill herself if she could not join too.[18]

Peci reflected a lot on a job in which 'like any job' people acquired proficiency. His first task, as part of the Turin column, was to wash and dry two thousand million-lire banknotes, the proceeds of the Costa kidnapping. After the column leader, Fiore, was captured, Peci took his place. He killed his first victim on 22 April 1977, a foreman at Fiat in Turin. He thought of this in terms of doling out justice to exploiters of the proletariat: 'In technical terms, to kill someone is a lot easier than wounding them – but from the human point of view it is the exact opposite.' Actually, things were more complicated than that. Peci liked guns, reaching out for his .38 Special on the bedside table first thing each morning: 'It gave me a feeling of power and security. It was my good friend. I was more jealous towards it than towards a woman.'[19] But there was also the vomiting of his caffelatte and rolls on the morning of his first kill, with adrenaline contributing to a night of intermittent sleep. It was like the night before an exam. Deep sleep came after the job was done. This was how he regarded Antonio Munari, his first victim:

> This is a man who's doing well, he goes home for lunch while the
> workers remain at the canteen. He has a nice car given to him by
> Fiat, lives in a beautiful place, in a residential suburb, possibly
> also given to him by Fiat, while the workers, on the other

hand ... What struck me most of all was the fact that he would
go home to eat, while the workers probably ate disgusting food
in the canteen, then he'd come back, happy and well fed, and
make them work like dogs ... I was there for an act of justice.
Hit one to educate one hundred. I had no hesitation.[20]

In 1978 Peci tried to wound a man, who promptly died of a heart
attack. Violence became more difficult when he and his victim
exchanged words, breaking down the 'target's' anonymity. After killing
someone, Peci felt tense with an internal unease, which he later thought
was 'sorrow for the end of a life'. By 1979 he was exhausted and disillusioned with an organisation that had failed to increase its support
in the factories. He collapsed almost immediately after he fell into
the hands of the state; the police did not treat him as the big shot he
imagined himself to be, a strategy which may have led him to confess
so as to reassert his own importance. Kept in isolation he was free to
contemplate the prospect of a lifetime behind bars, where the main
obsessions, apart from cooking – Italian prisons had no communal mess
– were acquiring cosmetics and hair dye to disguise the ageing process
and trying to avoid getting knifed in a Mafia gang fight. The future
consisted of watching oneself grow pallid, thin, bald, grey-haired, sick
and old. He trusted general Dalla Chiesa, and began to like the policemen and judges he dealt with more than his erstwhile comrades. Pressure
to turn was intense. The sentence for illegal possession of a firearm alone
was three years and four months in jail; he had committed eight
murders. Then he heard that Alberto Franceschini had rejoiced at Peci's
arrest as it would spur others to release him. He was already a derisory
'object' to the police; now apparently he was just a functional object for
a senior comrade.

Having deromanticised himself, Peci took a long hard look at the
organisation he belonged to. The Red Brigades had no popular support.
Their actions were diminishing the space available to legitimate protest
by filling the public sphere with paranoia. And finally what they called
the armed struggle was harming working-class interests: 'All in all, we
were beaten, militarily and politically.' Further rationalisations followed.
Like the medieval crusaders who regarded killing in this light, he claimed
that his betrayals were acts of love, for former comrades whose errant
ways he had prematurely halted. Betrayal was also a form of recompense
towards his own victims and a form of personal redemption.[21] One of

Peci's first revelations was the location of a hideout in Genoa. When the carabinieri stormed this in force, five Red Brigades terrorists decided to make a stand; all five were killed by withering police fire. Two policemen were indicted (and acquitted) for summarily shooting two of them. In his two hundred hours of taped confessions, Peci – quickly dubbed 'the infamous one' or 'that bastard' by his former comrades – revealed the whereabouts of major arms dumps and who was who in the Red Brigades operation. In total, he was responsible for the arrest of over seventy 'ferocious beasts' as he called his former colleagues. Another *pentito*, Antonio Savasta, was more eloquent on why he had betrayed his comrades:

> The necessity and the inevitability of armed struggle represented our bet with history. Well, we lost that bet, and our isolation and defeat are the price we paid for having defined reality by abstract theories which oversimplified it, for having concentrated the social reasons for change in an instrument unable to express it, for having diminished our own force and capacity for change and isolated them in an absurd and futile project.[22]

The arrest of Sergio Zedda and Roberto Sandalo gave the police similar insights into the workings of the *piellini* – that is, the terrorist group Primea Linea – thirteen of whom were immediately arrested. Quite independently of the *pentiti* the Moro affair had triggered ructions within the Red Brigades between those who wished to embed the organisation in the wider revolutionary movement and those of a hard-line militaristic frame of mind for whom killing people had become a career. When the Red Brigades sought help from Prima Linea it caused a fatal split between those prepared to go along and those who thought the armed struggle had had its day. Virtually all of Prima Linea's leaders were arrested, including Marco Donat Cattin, the son of one of the Christian Democrats' most anti-Communist politicians. Clearly buckling under the hostility of the 'prostitutes' of the 'Establishment' press, terrorists from a new XXVIII March Brigade murdered Walter Tobagi, an energetic *Corriera della Sera* correspondent and historian at Milan university who had repeatedly attacked the intellectual godfathers of terrorism ensconced at leading universities.

While immense reserves of manpower, and the lire equivalent of £13,000 per day, were put into combating Red Brigades terrorism, the extreme-right species were not idle. They killed a thirty-seven-year-old detective famous for arresting drug dealers as he sat in his car monitoring pushers operating outside a school. On 23 June 1980 they killed judge Mario Amato, who had specialised in investigating neo-Fascist violence. Then on 2 August 1980, at the start of the Italian summer holiday season, a huge bomb tore through Bologna railway station, collapsing an entire wing and its roof. Eighty-five people were killed in the blast, and a further two hundred injured. The mortuary was lined with small corpses wearing shorts, T-shirts and sandals for the beach.

Patient police work, facilitated by the mounting number of terrorist turncoats, led to the arrest of the leadership of Prima Linea and the liquidation of the group XXVIII March. Although the Red Brigades were capable of further assassinations, the police mounted simultaneous raids on several cities that saw the arrest of twenty-six key figures. They also found a haul of weapons and incriminating documents, the most significant to date. The Red Brigades struck back by kidnapping judge Giovanni D'Urso, the head of Italy's prison system. They demanded the closure of a maximum-security facility at Asinara, an island off Sardinia, which the government had already decided to shut down. That conjuncture enabled the government to deny that it made concessions when the Red Brigades released the judge, who after thirty-three days was found in a car left outside the Ministry of Justice. On New Year's Eve two loitering youths shot dead Dalla Chiesa's chief associate, general Enrico Galviagi, as he and his wife returned from mass. In the new year, the police captured Maurice Bignami, the final founder of Prima Linea still at liberty, who was useful in incriminating Negri, dismissed contemptuously by Dalla Chiesa as the only instigator of terrorist attacks to be in receipt of grants from the National Research Council. This was not entirely accurate since among further arrests there was professor Enrico Fenzi, a distinguished scholar of Dante, who had become a Red Brigadist.

The Red Brigades carried out a number of kidnappings, lifting a Montedison petrochemical director while he was having lunch with his wife at home. After three weeks his corpse was found in a car parked outside his plant. Contrary to the illusion that such actions would trigger a proletarian revolution, sixty thousand workers marched through Mestre to denounce the 'Nazi Red Brigadists'. The Brigades also hoped to make the *pentiti* think again when they abducted Roberto Peci, the electrician brother of Patrizio, the state's star supergrass. After fifty-five days Roberto's body was found on a rubbish tip; his face had been badly battered and he had been shot eleven times. The Red Brigades filmed his execution. In a novel departure on 17 December 1980 four Brigadists masquerading as plumbers kidnapped US general James Lee Dozier from his home in Verona, where he was in charge of logistics for NATO's Southern European Command. They had to purchase a box of lead US toy soldiers in order to work out the ranks in the US army from the painting instructions that came with them. In this case an informer led the police to an apartment in Padua. They stormed the place and found Dozier tied up inside a small tent erected in the middle of the floor. Five terrorists, including the daughter of a prominent doctor, were detained without a fight. This in itself was a blow to the morale of the wider left-wing subculture that sustained the Red Brigades. By this time the police had also arrested forty-two-year-old Giovanni Senzani, a professor of criminology at Florence university until he went underground in 1981 as the leader of the Red Brigades. Among his past sins, Senzani had used his ability to attend international academic conferences to 'finger' three prominent opponents of the extreme left who had then been killed by the Red Brigades. In his hideout police found a weapons store which included four ground-to-air missiles which were to be used in an onslaught against the upcoming national conference of the Christian Democrats. There were also plans for attacks on the Trani maximum-security prison and the Rome police headquarters, as well as detailed profiles of six trades union leaders who were slated to be shot. Planning was also at an advanced stage for the kidnapping of the number two at Fiat, as a mini-prison to store him had already been built.

This coup was followed by the moral squalor displayed at the first trial of sixty-three people indicted in connection with the abduction and murder of Aldo Moro. Fifteen hundred policemen guarded a special court in Rome's Foro Italico with helicopters patrolling overhead. The light was icy like that of a mortuary. Journalists engaged in their usual indifferent frenzy. The relatives of victims and the relatives of terrorists tried to comprehend events none of them had sought. Lawyers scrambled for truth and money. The defendants were in cages, the informers heavily guarded. The testimony of the *pentiti* impressed the judges more than the comedic antics of the implacable defendants, thirty-two of whom were jailed for life. Curcio himself declared that he and the other leaders had misread the runes regarding the imminence of Marxist revolution, an admission of theoretical incompetence he could no longer share with the people the Red Brigades had killed or injured. Bereft of centralised leadership, the isolated Red Brigades cells could still mount sporadic shootings, of US diplomats, policemen and professors, between 1983 and 1987, but these were the dying spasms of a defunct episode in modern Italian life. Slowly the judicial system tried to comprehend the events of the past fifteen years, a process complicated by sensational revelations allegedly implicating the Propaganda Due (P2) masonic lodge and the security services of Italy and beyond in the kidnapping of Moro and subsequent events. These stories, eagerly consumed by the international left, said more about the degenerated state of the left-wing imagination than about the Red Brigades, who scoffed at the idea that they could have been anyone's unwitting tools. Painstaking judicial inquiries have established that neither the Italian secret services nor the CIA, P2, the Mafia or anyone else other than the Red Brigades were responsible for Moro's death.

There was also a reckoning, of sorts, with one intellectual godfather of terrorism, although not with the wider problem of how the self-repudiating left had insinuated itself into influential positions in the universities, one of the major systemic defects of modern Western civilisation as a whole. Although at his trial Negri disclaimed his own evil influence, while hiding behind the rhetoric of freedom of expression, only his election as a Radical deputy of parliament temporarily enabled him to evade justice. Disgusted deputies held a special vote, which they won by a majority of seven, to have him rearrested. He fled to France before the police arrived, but was sentenced to thirty years in absentia. This was reduced on appeal. In 1997 he returned to Italy and spent six more years in jail. A 'liberal' faculty at a major US university saw no ironies when Negri had to decline their job offer because he was in prison. Nowadays in his seventies, Negri has resumed his prophetic role, as a celebrity guru to the anti-globalisation movement, dividing his time, as the book flaps say, between university posts in Paris, Rome and Venice. Most surviving Red Brigades members were not so lucky, emerging broken from decades in jail, searching the mirrors for signs of their younger selves, the fortunate becoming professional experts about terrorism on television.[23]

*   *   *

IV BERLINER LUFT

On 10 June 1967 eight young people discovered a new way of circumventing a recent ban on demonstrations imposed by West Berlin's mayor
Heinrich Albertz. They stood in the middle of the Kurfürstendamm
shopping canyon, near the semi-ruined Kaiser Gedächtniskirche,
donning white T-shirts each daubed with a single letter. When the eight
alphabet protesters formed a line, including a willowy blonde pastor's
daughter called Gudrun Ensslin who wore the exclamation mark, they
spelled 'ALBERTZ!' Turning round, the group had 'ABTRETEN' on
their backs, the eight German letters for 'resign'.

Berlin had a uniquely febrile atmosphere, for it was a barometer of the
totalitarian past and present across the Wall; eruptions of international
tension rendered the city palpably close and oppressive as I recall when
the Soviets invaded Afghanistan in 1979. The louring architectural
detritus of Hitler's Reich stood amid the remnants of the Prussian–
German capital; a forbidding concrete wall demarcated garish Western
consumerism from 'real existing socialism' where, along with freedom,
the advertisements and neon lights vanished. Although it was completely
untrue that the Third Reich was a closed book until the liberal 1960s
dawned, what books there were dealt with morals and spirit and did
not directly confront the generous representation of former Nazis in
industry, medicine, the law, the police and politics. Many people openly
applauded when the Paris-based left-wing activist Beate Klarsfeld
smuggled herself into a Christian Democrat conference and slapped
the former Nazi propagandist and current federal chancellor Kurt
Georg Kiesinger in the face. The writer Heinrich Böll, once a greedy
Wehrmacht soldier in occupied France, sent her flowers. The 1960s
brought deep inter-generational problems to young people with Nazi-
era first names like Gudrun, Sieglinde and Thorwald, who sought
deliverance from themselves by hopelessly romanticising the Third
World. Older people prided themselves on having raised Germany from
dust and rubble, achieving a conspicuously high standard of living
through their focused industriousness. The consumer society was their
reward, although large numbers combined shopping with going to
church. For younger people, ashamed of being German, and taking high
living standards for granted, this economic vocation no longer sufficed.
They were encouraged in their radical snobbery towards cars, fridges and

garden gnomes (but not towards jeans, records and stereos) by the, often Jewish, gurus of the New Left, notably Herbert Marcuse, Max Horkheimer, Theodor Adorno and the younger Jürgen Habermas, although only Marcuse wholeheartedly endorsed the attempt to convert theory into action from Berlin to Berkeley.

New Left ideology was a fusion of Freud and Marx, leavened with a bit of Gramsci. It was, and remains, so stunningly tedious, except for a generation of academics, that we do not need to deal with it in any detail. As a former German terrorist quipped: 'theory was something that we half read but fully understood'. In many universities of the time this arcane secularised theology was served up as degree courses in subjects like economics, history or political science which almost disabled graduates in the marketplace. Consumerism created, but never satisfied, bogus needs – hence the phrase 'consumption terror' – with 'repressive tolerance' masking the 'structural violence' of an imperfectly dismantled Fascist regime. At any time the 'Brown' crowd could return. Especially when in 1967–8 the government attempted to amend the Basic Law by assuming some of the emergency powers hitherto exclusively vested in the Allied occupation authorities. In addition to times of invasion or civil war, the Christian Democrats sought to include periods of civil disturbance in the list of circumstances when the government could pass laws, draft citizens, override the federal states, and deploy the police without parliamentary approval. The Social Democrats successfully resisted this extension of what constituted an emergency, but the amendments passed through the Bundestag with a hefty majority.[24] On the left there was dark talk of new Enabling Laws with the term *Notstandsgesetze* (Emergency Laws) sinisterly abbreviated to 'NS'. Like their French contemporaries, with their crass identification of the riot police with the Nazi Schutzstaffel in the slogan 'CRS = SS', morally self-righteous middle-class young Germans indiscriminately threw around charges of 'Fascism' – or 'Auschwitz', 'Gestapo' and 'Nazis' – thereby damaging democratic discourse and ensuring that only their increasingly totalitarian voice was heard. Their colossal intolerance reminded many of their professors of scenes they had witnessed in 1933–4 when most students had been fervent Nazis.[25]

German student radicalism was centred upon Frankfurt am Main, Hamburg, Munich and West Berlin. Berlin magnetised young leftist radicals from the German provinces because those who studied there were exempt from military service, while bars and pubs with no official licensing hours encouraged a heavy Teutonic sociability. Many wealthy people had fled the city, leaving an abundance of cheap and spacious apartments, laboratories for alternative lifestyles. Communal apartments and squats had the usual atmosphere of overflowing ashtrays – even hub caps were never big enough – soiled sheets, blankets used as curtains, and the lingering odours of dope and unwashed clothes. The Cold War ensured that the place was subsidised up to the hilt as a beacon of Western democracy in the surrounding Red sea. Free of the constraints of parental homes and small towns and villages, young people bobbed about in the city's anomic hugeness, for, unlike New York, Berlin had been built on an extensive basis, the reason why Allied bombers found it hard to obliterate. A giant overhead railway network, called the S-Bahn, connected the city through its infamous Wall.

Books on German left-wing terrorism never include chapters on the working class, a revealing omission that distinguishes Germany from Italy. There was no significant working-class radicalism in West Germany, unless you count young neo-Nazis, chiefly because workers were generally represented, as of right, on the managing boards of most companies. Among German workers, Communism was associated with the Stalinist dictatorship of the German Democratic Republic, although they sometimes also idealised its alleged egalitarianism, just as they had done with Hitler's fictive 'economic miracle' in the 1930s. Hence, for many student leftists it was essential to demythologise *Western* workers – with talk of the metropolitan 'labour aristocracy' – while projecting heroic characteristics on to the real downtrodden helots of the Third World, who were above any form of criticism, and about whose reality the students knew as little as the Christ cum Che they had on the wall.

As in Italy, the West German higher-education system had been massified, with the number of students climbing from 384,000 in 1965 to 510,000 five years later. The transition from elite to mass higher education made reform urgent, with the complication that education policy was in the hands of federal governments of different political complexions. In some places, the absolutist regime of senior professors gave way to three-way power-sharing arrangements, between professors, untenured faculty and the so-called representatives of the students, arrangements that would not be tolerated among cobblers or watch makers who pass on skills. The most revolutionary students were organised in the Sozialistischer Deutscher Studentenbund, founded in 1949 as the student wing of the Sozialdemokratischen Partei Deutschlands.

Future chancellor Helmut Schmidt was its first chairman. However, by 1961 the SPD had disowned the SDS because of its campaigns against rearmament and conscription. In turn, the SDS was part of a broader 'Extra-parliamentary opposition' (APO), which was partly a response to the formation of a Christian Democrat and Social Democrat 'Grand Coalition' cabinet that, in their eyes, seemed to negate a pluralist democracy. Its leading light was Rudi Dutschke, whose fascination with violence, a common trait among intellectuals, was not merely rhetorical. He would advocate and experience it.

The left were anti-imperialist too, hysterically claiming that the US was exterminating the Vietnamese. The lawyer Horst Mahler collected money for the Viet Cong which he schlepped into East Berlin's North Vietnamese embassy. In a further twist, many leftists construed Israel as a Fascist power, camouflaging their anti-Semitism as anti-Zionism so that the erstwhile victims of their parents and grandparents could be viewed as oppressors. SDS students prevented the Israeli ambassador, and visiting Israeli academics, from speaking when they visited universities to make Israel's case. On 9 November 1969 a bomb placed by a grouplet calling themselves the West Berlin Tupamaros went off in the Berlin Jewish community building, a singularly inappropriate date to warn the Jewish 'Fascists' off 'their' colonialist oppression of the Palestinians, it being revealing that Berlin's tiny Jewish community was unreflectively conflated with Israel.[26]

Violent confrontations with the Berlin police had begun in February 1966 when SDS-supporting students blocked traffic and then stormed the Amerika-Haus cultural centre, where they lowered the Stars 'n' Stripes. Shouts of 'Amis raus aus Vietnam' (Yanks out of Vietnam) were their response to the terrible news footage and magazine photographs they had seen of orange petrochemical explosions in lush green jungle, and teenage girls with black, brown and red napalm scorches on their flesh. Shortly afterwards demonstrations were banned both on campus and in the city centre as a whole. Mayor Albertz publicly boasted that he had ordered the police to make heavy use of their rubber batons should any further protests occur. After a student tract mocked professors at the Free university as 'skilled idiots' cloning mini 'skilled idiots' the police raided the SDS headquarters and confiscated the membership records.

Vice-president Hubert Humphrey's visit to Berlin in April 1967 resulted in eggs, flour, flans and stones raining down on the cars of his entourage as they arrived at the Axel-Springer building near the Wall.

Several students were heavily beaten by the police. Although Humphrey had been assaulted with little more than the ingredients for a pudding, eleven members of a squat called Commune 1 were arrested, according to the Springer press, for plotting against the life of the US vice-president. The evening of 2 June 1967 would pass into terrorist legend, becoming both the name of a German terrorist group and of particular actions. The Iranian emperor Reza Pahlavi and his consort were in Germany on a state visit. That afternoon the imperial couple visited the town hall where both the German police and the shah's contingent of Savak agents shouting 'Long live the shah' kept Iranian and German demonstrators away. Some of the Savak men evidently lost their cool amid the rival cries of 'Shah, shah, charlatan!', crashing through the barriers to beat the demonstrators up with wooden clubs and blackjacks that could fell a person unconscious with one blow. These scenes repeated themselves that evening when the shah and his wife attended a gala performance of Mozart's *Magic Flute*. While the shah enjoyed the opera, police charged into the demonstrators, slicing the mass up like salami, and dispersing them down side streets. A tactic called 'fox hunting' ensued to detain suspected ringleaders, usually by dint of their beard or long hair in those unsophisticated times.

Three policemen chased a young man, Benno Ohnesorg, into a dark courtyard off a side street where they pummelled him with truncheons as he curled into a ball on the ground. A member of the Political Police arrived, brandishing a Walther PPK 7.65 in his hand. The officer's gun went off, fatally shooting Ohnesorg in the head. Ohnesorg was a twenty-six-year-old student of Romance languages, an otherwise pious Protestant attending the first and last demonstration of his life. Albertz blamed the demonstrators for the death, while an investigation treated the shooting as an accident rather than negligent homicide. As he bade the shah farewell the following day, Albertz asked whether his imperial majesty had heard of Ohnesorg's demise. 'Yes,' the emperor replied, 'it doesn't perturb me. That happens in Iran every day.' One of those who carried Ohnesorg's coffin was Michael 'Bommi' Baumann, who would later join the 2 June Movement.[27] Horst Mahler, whose ex-Wehrmacht soldier father had gone out into the garden and shot himself in 1949 after the family had relocated to Dessau from Silesia, represented Ohnesorg's widow. This marked a change from his commercial practice, although he had already become the first German lawyer to avail himself of the European Convention on Human Rights, on behalf of a former SS guard at Mauthausen remanded for an inhuman five years. The SDS was flooded with membership applications as Germany's students passed from shock to rage. Much of the reaction to Ohnesorg's death was hysterical and paranoid:

> I remember exactly, when I began to study, that the SDS was rampant with fantasies of fear. One man [Franz Josef Strauss] was intent on making himself into the dictator of West Germany, possibly even with the help of the Bundeswehr! Not least because of that, we had to fight desperately hard against passage of the emergency laws: he wanted to have a legal basis for his seizure of power, we were dealing with his 'Enabling Acts' and nothing less! And now, exactly as was true then [in 1933] most people had no idea, or closed their eyes willingly to the catastrophe.

At a packed SDS meeting in Berlin a young woman shouted: 'This Fascist state intends to kill all of us. We must organise resistance. Violence can only be answered with violence. This is the generation of Auschwitz – with them one can't argue! They have weapons and we haven't any. We must arm ourselves too.' The speaker was Gudrun Ensslin.

Born in 1940, Ensslin was the fourth of seven children of a Swabian village Lutheran parson and his wife. They were vaguely left-wing, in a damp clerical sort of way, being especially exercised by the question of West German rearmament. Since 68 per cent of German terrorists came from Protestant backgrounds, some have wondered whether their intense enthusiasm for Marxism or Maoism was some form of surrogate faith. Ensslin was a model pupil at her local Gymnasium, and a leading member of the Protestant organisation for girls. In 1958–9 she spent an exchange year with Methodists in Pennsylvania, before going up to Tübingen to study English, German and pedagogy. There she fell in love with Bernward Vesper, the son of a prominent Nazi poet who had turned against his father. The two became engaged and established a small publishing house producing tracts against atomic weapons. Moving to Berlin, the two campaigned for the Social Democrats, only to be appalled when its leaders went into coalition with the conservatives in 1965. That was the beginning of Ensslin's slide into radical left politics. Meanwhile, having used her fiancé to sire a son called Felix – Rudi Dutschke was godfather – Ensslin promptly left Vesper, who eventually put the child out for adoption. In common with many of her future associates, Ensslin's concern for orphans did not include those they created themselves.

V 'THIS JOB THAT WE'RE DOING IS SERIOUS. THERE MUST BE NO FUN'

Ensslin spent the night following the 1967 alphabet protest with a small crowd smoking dope and talking politics in a Berlin apartment. One of those present was Andreas Baader. Born in 1943 in Munich, Baader was the son of a gifted young historian and archivist who as a reluctant soldier had gone missing in 1945 on the disintegrating Eastern Front. Idle but aggressively strong willed, Baader grew up in an atmosphere dominated by struggling women, which probably encouraged his narcissistic traits, a mise en scène he would recreate with Ensslin and Ulrike Meinhof. He admired his uncle, Michael Kroecher, a gay ballet dancer who went on to have a modest career in art films. After being expelled from successive schools, Baader essayed various careers in advertising and journalism, none of which came to anything. His real vocation was stealing cars (he perfected the break-in time to ten seconds) and driving them recklessly fast, albeit never having acquired a (legal) licence to drive. Being good-looking in a brooding sub-Marlon Brando or Alain Delon sort of way, in the trousers he himself sewed especially tight, he was like fresh meat for the barflies in Munich's gay pubs, even though he was strenuously heterosexual. Poncing off older gay men gave him a few minor breaks; the fashion photographer who discovered Christa Paeffgen (subsequently the gaunt Nico with the nicotine-tarred voice in The Velvet Underground) photographed Baader for a gay porn magazine. Baader was never averse to violence, deliberately starting fights in pubs in order to trigger mass brawls, or mugging other customers in the men's lavatories.

Avoiding the ever closer attentions of the Munich police, in 1963 Baader moved to West Berlin, and lodged with Elly-Leonore 'Ello' Henkel-Michel and her husband Manfred Henkel, two painters of indifferent talent, with a young son called Robert. What started as a sexless ménage à trois graduated to Andreas Baader and Ello having a daughter, Suse, successfully conceived despite the mother's prodigious ingestion of whisky, Captogen and LSD. Manfred and Ello divorced, but Manfred continued to share an apartment with Ello, Baader and the two young children. Eventually, Manfred gained custody of both children from his drink- and drug-saturated former wife. Apart from the time spent brawling in pubs or taking drugs while pretending to write a book, Baader moved into the orbit of Commune 1, the radical squat that took the 1871 Paris Commune as its model. Sexual liberation was a major pre-occupation. 'The Vietnam War is not what interests me, but difficulties with my orgasm do,' as one communard put it. In the summer of 1967 Baader joined members of Commune 1 in a mock funeral intended to offend mourners at the burial of former Reichstag president Paul Löbe. Holding up a fake coffin along with Baader was Peter Urbach, a former worker on the city's S-Bahn, known as 'S-Bahn Peter', who had become the Commune's handyman, and eager supplier of drugs and weapons. He was also an agent for the West German secret service, the Bundes Verfassungsschutz (Office for the Protection of the Constitution), insinuated into the city's left-wing underground to provoke mayhem.

Baader missed the 2 June 1967 demonstrations as he was serving a brief sentence in young-adult detention for motoring offences. Returned to Berlin as an authenticated item of rough trade, he exercised inordinate suasion over left-wing middle-class students who laboured under the false consciousness that their own druggy discussions had anything to do with revolution. He had a credibility they lacked as the spoilt offspring of the bourgeoisie. Men were intimidated by his ready resort to violence and by a temper that brought foam to his lips. Women, whom feminism had taught only how to intimidate men, seem to have especially appre-ciated Baader calling them 'Fotzen' (cunts). He deftly transferred his attentions from Ello to Gudrun Ensslin, with whom he shared a common desire for deeds rather than talk. Dope cemented their affections and they became lovers. In the meantime, Ensslin had fully sloughed off being the vicar's daughter, having starred in a short Dadaist sex movie, involving her slowly stripping off and writhing around with a man beneath some sheets while letters and papers dropped unread through the front door. Their first deed was to unfurl an 'Expropriate Springer' banner from the steeple of the Kaiser Gedächtnis Kirche while letting off smoke bombs that they had made. Next they took composer Pierre Boulez at his word, when in an interview he said he'd like to see Maoist Red Guards make short work of an opera performance. Baader, Ensslin and Thorwald Proll, the son of an architect whose mother had run off to San Francisco, stormed the stage of the Deutsches Oper before being dragged out by stewards. Maestro Boulez smiled indulgently.

A catastrophic fire in a Brussels department store, which had killed over 250 shoppers, provided the inspiration for their next attacks. For the first time revealing his capacity for leadership, Baader dominated the lengthy discussions in Commune 1. In Munich he, Ensslin and Proll were joined by a radical actor called Horst Söhnlein, who had also just parted from his wife, with whom he ran an alternative theatre with the future film director Rainer Werner Fassbinder. Before the attacks, Baader tried to borrow a 16 mm camera from a Munich acquaintance, suggesting that he was partly directing his own film. For the cinematic qualities of what he was orchestrating are its most striking features. Since we know exactly what movies he saw, it is possible to recreate his own highly cinematic fantasy world. Baader was the star, a Brando, Belmondo or Delon figure from any contemporary gangster movie. The endless, mindless speeding up and down Germany's extensive Autobahn network – an abiding impression of their activities – was an attempt to replicate the rebel motorbike odyssey in *Easy Rider*, with the odd lapse into drugged surreality as Ensslin and the others had physically to stop Baader from drowning a feral cat on the Starnberger See. Finally, Baader seems to have taken what terror tactics he knew from Pontecorvo's *La battaglia di Algeri* – notably the use of simultaneous attacks – while identifying himself with the boxer, pimp, and FLN terrorist Ali La Pointe. The problem was, this was comfortable West Germany rather than the crowded slums of colonial Algiers.[28]

On the evening of 2 April 1968, shortly before closing, Baader and Ensslin took the elevator to the first floor of the Kaufhaus Schneider, where they left a firebomb in women's coats, and another in a wardrobe in household furnishings. Others deposited similar bombs in the Kaufhof store near by. At midnight an alert taxi driver noticed that both buildings were ablaze, even as a woman telephoned a news agency with the intelligence that this was 'an act of political revenge'. Both fires caused about 800,000 DM worth of damage before they were brought under control. It took the police less than two days to arrest the perpetrators. A reward of 50,000 DM was sufficient to induce the boyfriend of the person whose flat they had stayed in the night before to identify the culprits. Ensslin claimed to be visiting a cousin; Baader to be talent scouting actors for a film. The Frankfurt police discovered a screw in Ensslin's handbag that matched one used in one of the firebombs, while a search of the car used by the foursome revealed watch parts, a battery-operated detonator, rolls of tape like those employed in binding the materials together, and miniature film rolls showing the entrances to department stores around the country. Meanwhile the Berlin police discovered combustible materials identical with those used in the Frankfurt stores when they searched Ensslin's flat.

The firebombings were temporarily overshadowed in the radical imagination when on 11 April a young right-wing house painter, Josef Bachmann, walked up to Rudi Dutschke as he set off from his Berlin apartment and shot him three times, once in the head. Bachmann later killed himself in jail; in 1979 the brain-damaged victim drowned after having an epileptic fit in his bath. Dutschke was not simply a theorist of violence. That February 1968 he and Bahman Nirumand had taken a plane from Berlin to Frankfurt. They had a bomb in their luggage intended for the American Forces Radio mast in Saarbrücken. Stopped by police at Frankfurt airport, Dutschke had the nerve to put the case in a left-luggage locker before the officers took him away. He explained it was too heavy to carry, and they concurred. His widow also recalled that in the same month Giangiacomo Feltrinelli appeared at their flat, with a car trunk full of dynamite. She and Dutschke used their baby Hosea-Che's pushchair to spirit the explosives away to a left-wing lawyer who hid them.[29]

This assassination attempt against Dutschke triggered massive demonstrations against the Axel Springer Press headquarters, for radicals held conservative newspapers such as *Bild Zeitung* responsible for inciting the attack. These demonstrations took a violent turn, partly because secret agent Peter Urbach appeared with a basket of Molotov cocktails, which were used to destroy Springer delivery vans. During parallel disturbances in Munich, a student and a press photographer were inadvertently killed in a hail of stones. One of the Berlin demonstrators, who received a ten-month suspended sentence for taking part in public disorder, was Horst Mahler, the radical SDS-supporting lawyer currently acting on Baader's behalf. While the brother of the publisher of *Der Spiegel* – the left-wing glossy weekly originally founded by the British – endeavoured to defend Mahler, outside the streets were rocked by the most violent demonstrations Berlin had seen. One hundred and thirty policemen and twenty-two demonstrators were seriously injured. One of the reasons for this disparity in casualty rates was that the demonstrators included the West Berlin Tupamaros who were fully prepared to use physical violence. For men like Michael 'Bommi' Baumann or Dieter Kunzelmann, the communard bothered about his orgasms, this was their route towards terrorism. They did not need fancy ideological justifications. Baumann himself could never understand Dutschke's learnedly abstract talks about revolution. Men like him enjoyed fighting, whether at a Rolling Stones concert or a political demonstration. It was a matter of power, seeing the police scuttle away, and getting the coppery scent of blood. He was surprisingly eloquent about how carrying a gun physically altered the central point of one's being to where hand and gun joined, creating an almost foolhardy sense of security through the element of surprise. A third of the members of the 2 June Movement, to which Baumann belonged, had criminal convictions for violent behaviour at demonstrations. As he put it: 'For me violence is a perfectly satisfactory means. I have never had inhibitions about it.'[30] Reverting to her severe Protestant roots, Ensslin once reminded Baumann: 'What are you doing, running around apartments, fucking little girls, smoking dope. Having fun. That mustn't be. This job that we're doing is serious. There must be no fun.'[31]

The trial of the Frankfurt arsonists commenced on 14 October 1968; immediately the accused tried to theatricalise the proceedings, when Proll claimed to be Baader, giving 1789 as his date of birth. Matters turned to farce when Ello, invited by Baader as a character witness to 'paint a picture' of him, turned up with a selection of her naive canvases spilling from her arms. The judges felt they could dispense with her testimony. Despite the efforts of their radical defence lawyers, including Otto Schily and Horst Mahler (the latter had formed his own Collective of Socialist Lawyers), the four accused each received three years' imprisonment. After fourteen months, they were released in June 1969, pending the outcome of their lawyers' appeals to have the initial sentences reduced.

Baader and Ensslin moved into a large flat provided rent free by the Frankfurt university branch of the SDS. To celebrate their freedom, the two injected themselves with liquefied opium, managing to contract hepatitis. At the time their SDS admirers were animated by a campaign they had been running to politicise and radicalise the problem juveniles these students encountered during visits to children's homes as the practical part of their studies. There were about half a million such young people in the Federal Republic, and the conditions they lived in were miserable, exploited as cheap labour and sometimes abused.

Baader and Ensslin took part in SDS efforts to liberate these children, disrupting the homes and providing inmates with casual refuges when they managed to escape. The pair drove between juvenile homes in a Mercedes, stoned out of their minds, occasionally exchanging the driver and passenger seats while speeding along. Baader sometimes drove while patting his face with powder in the mirror. Incredibly, for Baader and Ensslin were only free pending appeal, the regional Hesse authorities allocated them housing for thirty-three youths, while granting them funds to disburse each day. Among those who came into their orbit in this fashion was Peter Jürgen Boock, an impressionable seventeen-year-old from a disturbed background whom Ensslin invited to share a bath on his first night at their place. He and his fellows were formally educated by Baader, standing on a stool reading the thoughts of Chairman Mao, and Baader also catered for their recreational needs by taking his charges on nightly escapades to smash up discotheques and pubs. Among the juveniles Baader and Ensslin collected there was much experimental sex and drugs; useful training since many of them (excepting the few who, like Boock, became leading terrorists or those who got back on the straight and narrow) became heroin addicts and rent boys when the revolutionaries moved on.

In November 1969 the Federal Court of Appeal rejected the four arsonists' appeals. They were going back inside. Baader and Ensslin decided to flee over the French border; there a contact gave them money and the keys to the vacant Latin Quarter apartment of Régis Debray, who having fought alongside Che Guevara was into the second year of a thirty-year sentence in a Bolivian prison, from which his powerful politician father would get him released the following year. They were joined by Thorwald Proll and his sister Astrid. Despite their disguises, cutting their hair shorter or dyeing blonde Ensslin brunette, the group evidently felt sufficiently at ease in Paris to photograph themselves larking around in a café. From Amsterdam they acquired fresh identity papers; their photos were inserted into the reportedly lost passports of sympathetic comrades. The two main protagonists became 'Hans' and 'Gretel'. Baader and Ensslin drove south, dropping off Thorwald Proll in Strasbourg. Considering himself unfit for life in the underground, Proll surrendered to the German authorities, one of several people who resisted Baader's siren calls to terrorism.

From Zurich the two fugitives went to Milan, visiting Giangiacomo Feltrinelli, who received them at his office dressed in camouflage gear, with guns and grenades laid out for inspection on the desk. At a glance they ascertained his seriousness. In Rome they were fêted by the left-wing writer Louise Rinser, author of a book about Hitler's prisons, and the composer Hans Werner Henze. They tried, and failed, to recruit the lawyer and novelist Peter Chotjewitz for the armed struggle. Slipping into Denglish, Baader kept asking 'Are you ready *zu fighten*?' They had intensive discussions with Ulrich Enzensberger, the brother of the writer Hans Magnus Enzensberger, with whom Baader had taken part in the mock funeral in Berlin. Baader talked incessantly (he had acquired a liking for amphetamine) about the Russian nihilist terrorist Nechaev, Lenin and the Brazilian urban guerrilla theorist Carlos Marighella. On the basis of his experiences with the juvenile delinquents he had abandoned, Baader thought that such marginal elements could bring about a German revolution if they were incentivised by an armed vanguard minority. There was vague talk of military training with Fatah in the Middle East. Hans and Gretel also found time for vacations, visiting Positano where they lounged on a beach, chatting amiably with Tennessee Williams. Their Mercedes was broken into in Palermo, causing a furious outburst from the expert car thief Baader. Back in Rome they were visited by Horst Mahler bearing money from rich sympathisers and suggesting they convert themselves into an armed radical group. The group had no name. On 12 February 1970 they returned to Berlin, looking up a celebrity journalist acquaintance with a view to hiding in her flat. This was Ulrike Meinhof.[32]

Meinhof had interviewed Ensslin fourteen months previously for the magazine *konkret* of which she was the star columnist; she was also the ex-wife of its editor and owner Klaus Rainer Röhl. Born in 1934, Meinhof was the daughter of an art historian and museum director in Jena who died of cancer when Ulrike was four. Her widowed mother struggled through the war while training to be a teacher. The young Ulrike was an exceptionally pious Protestant as a little girl. In 1946 the mother moved to Oldenburg to flee the Russians, with her children and a younger colleague and friend called Renate Riemeck. Riemeck became Ulrike's guardian when her mother died of cancer at the age of forty. A committed pacifist and socialist she also became her role model. At her Gymnasium Ulrike stood up to the more authoritarian teachers.[33]

At the university of Münster she became engaged in protests against atomic weapons and German rearmament; a relationship with a student of nuclear physics did not work out. On a demonstration in May 1958 she met the six years older Röhl, editor of a left-wing monthly covertly subsidised by the underground Communist Party to which he belonged. She joined too. Known to friends as 'K2R' Röhl wore smart suits and drove a Porsche to work. Soon Meinhof was working as a columnist for her lover, who called her 'Riki-baby', moving up to editor in chief when he accorded himself the grander title of publisher. She was not an easy person to work for. They married and in 1962 had twin girls, Regina and Bettina. Following discovery of a suspected brain tumour, which turned out to be a benign cyst, surgeons inserted silver clamps into her head, causing her to suffer migraine for the rest of her life.

As a prominent radical media couple, Meinhof and Röhl were regular social fixtures among the so-called Schickeria living in spacious urban villas dotted along the banks of the Elbe. They could be found at every party, she wearing the white gloves still obligatory at the time, chatting amiably with Rudolf Augstein of *Spiegel* and Gert Bucerius of *Die Zeit*, or dancing frenetically to 'Dizzy Miss Lizzy' and the like. But there were worms in paradise. Röhl had other women, while his plans to fill *konkret* with tits and scandal to boost circulation did not amuse the puritanical Meinhof. She did not regard her membership of Hamburg's left Establishment as her life's destiny, and nor did she care to have her increasingly politically engaged journalism ringed with naked breasts.

In March 1968 the couple divorced and the thirty-four-year-old Meinhof moved to Berlin with the twins. They were enrolled at an anti-authoritarian kindergarten where they learned why police were called 'Bullen' ('Pigs') and about Chairman Mao and the Vietnam War. Meinhof worked remorselessly at her typewriter, clattering away sustained by coffee and incessant cigarettes. Earning a substantial 3,000 DM a month from her column in *konkret*, she diversified into radio, where her direct, socially critical tones were a novelty. Ever more radical, she claimed that Germany was undergoing the beginnings of a police state, proof of her increasing substitution of agitprop for objective journalism. She wrote her first television script for a docudrama about conditions in Germany's homes for problem children – in other words, the area in which Baader and Ensslin were simultaneously operating as saviours of the oppressed. Unsurprisingly her days as a columnist on her former husband's paper were numbered. She resigned, in a blaze of self-generated publicity, although she also threatened to occupy the magazine's offices with her radical friends. In anticipation, her ex-husband – who knew his Mao too – took the magazine underground to frustrate his ex-wife. She and thirty of her radical friends descended on the former family home. They trashed the place, the finale being to defecate and urinate on the former marital bed.

Living in Berlin proved a lonely experience for Meinhof, as it probably was too for her twins since their mother was frequently on assignment elsewhere. To solve these problems in one fell swoop, she moved into a shared apartment, with the student Jan-Carl Raspe and the radio reporter Marianne Herzog. When she conceived of the idea of moving to a bigger house so that her co-occupants could take over her childcare, there was a small mutiny and the idea was dropped. Exhausted, and perpetually on the verge of tears, she moved with the twins into an apartment on Kufsteinerstrasse. That was where Baader and Ensslin turned up. Mutual admiration was instant, because in an unpublished column Meinhof had already declared that firebombing department stores was 'a progressive moment', a leap of logic typical of those times. The drifting delinquent Baader and his eternal student comrade Ensslin were in awe of a big-time professional journalist, with her spacious apartment and flights to this or that crucial assignment. She and Ensslin, the two formerly pious little schoolgirls, were tantalised in turn by the crude, leather-jacketed thug in their midst. LSD trips cemented the relationships, accelerating the wild revolutionary scenarios bruited each night in the flat. While under the influence of this 'Sunshine' pill, Ensslin rewrote the Ten Commandments, including 'Thou must kill'.[34]

One night they invited between ten and fourteen guests, including Baader's lawyer Horst Mahler. Baader spoke of 'the project'. There was to be no more 'playacting as guerrillas', but rather, for this was still Germany, 'perfect organisation', bank robberies and blowing up the Springer headquarters. They had to move fast as already the incipient Baader–Meinhof group had competition. During the winter of 1969 a series of arson and bomb attacks had occurred in Berlin, mainly against lawyers, judges and prison officials. Mahler had taken part in one such attack, although the Molotov cocktail he threw inevitably missed. A journalist had written a rather sensational article about these attacks, which were largely carried out by the Blues Movement, a sort of organisational way-station, roughly between a crowd of pot-smokers and the terrorist 2 June Movement, led by Michael 'Bommi' Baumann. Four of these men burst into the journalist's apartment, trashed it, beat the fellow unconscious and hung a placard reading 'I am a journalist and I write shit' around his neck. The police arrived to the sounds of the

Rolling Stones 'Sympathy for the Devil' booming from the wrecked flat.

On 2 April 1970, Horst Mahler used his offices for a meeting between Baader and 'S-Bahn Peter', the purpose being to acquire guns, the collusive involvement of left-liberal lawyers with terrorists being an important part of this story. Back at Meinhof's apartment – Baader was suspicious about electronic bugs – Peter Urbach volunteered that wartime guns were buried in a cemetery. Baader, Mahler and he set off for their moonlit dig. To their disappointment there were no weapons. Urbach claimed he had got the cemetery wrong, giving him leeway for the secret service to plant deactivated pistols in the right place. The following night at a quarter to three the group set off in two cars, with Mahler wearing a large hat and sunglasses as a disguise. The Mercedes with Baader at the wheel was stopped by uniformed policemen, as an unmarked car pulled up behind. Mahler and Urbach drove off in the second car. The police asked Baader for his papers. He produced an identity card which said he was Peter Chotjewitz, born on 16 April 1934. Baader got that right. Problems began when the policeman asked for the names and dates of birth of his two children which were also recorded on the card. He was arrested. Ulrike Meinhof displayed her talent for the conspiratorial life when she shortly appeared at the police station, claiming that the Mercedes belonged to her friend Astrid Proll who had lent it to her, this being her attempt to limit the incident to a motoring violation. She could not explain how she knew that the men had been arrested. Growing angry at police questions she blurted out that neither Astrid Proll nor 'the lawyer Horst Mahler' could be reached by telephone to clear things up. Had they known it, the police would have identified the key membership of the band before it had commenced operations. They did not know they had Andreas Baader either until the following morning when Horst Mahler called a friend in the Political Police, asking to speak with Baader. The leftist lawyer was not much of a conspirator either.

Baader was sent to complete the remaining twenty-two months of his sentence for arson. Meanwhile, Ensslin and Meinhof laid plans for his escape. The publisher Klaus Wagenbach was prevailed upon to write to the authorities, claiming that Baader and Meinhof had a contract to write a book on juvenile delinquents. She needed to consult regularly with him about their co-production. The authorities decided that it would be a pity to spoil Baader's future career as a writer by refusing. Mahler provided Ensslin, who was also on the run, with false identity papers so that she could inform the imprisoned Baader of what she and Meinhof were hatching. Meinhof visited Baader in prison too, insisting to the authorities that she needed him to be escorted to the Institute for Social Questions to examine key sources for their book, for which contracts were hastily drawn up as proof. Mahler insisted that Baader was not a flight risk.

Meanwhile, Astrid Proll and Irene Goergens made their way into the unaccustomed setting of a pub frequented by neo-Nazis called the Wolfschanze after Hitler's bunker, where in return for 1,000 DM a man known as Teddy sold them a 6.35 mm Beretta with accompanying silencer. An Alfa Romeo was stolen from a car-showroom forecourt and equipped with false plates. Ulkrike Meinhof despatched the twins, by now aged eight, to a writer friend in Bremen, the last time they would see their mother at home or free in Berlin.

Shortly before 10 a.m. on Thursday 14 May 1970, Baader appeared in handcuffs escorted by two prison officers. They removed the cuffs and sat down while the two authors got down to business. The atmosphere gradually relaxed, as the room filled with cigarette smoke, and Meinhof chatted to the two guards about their wives and children. Elsewhere in the building, the bewigged Goergens and Proll appeared, insisting on seeing books they needed as students of forensic medicine, which they had selected the day before as they scouted the crime scene. After being reluctantly admitted to the reading room, just before eleven o'clock they rushed to the entrance, flinging open the doors to admit two masked figures, one of whom brandished a gun. They were most likely Gudrun Ensslin and a professional criminal brought in for this job because as yet the women were unused to shooting people. There was a brief struggle with an elderly doorman who was shot through the arm and liver from close range. The two masked gunmen were joined by Goergens and Proll, by now flourishing a Reck P8 and a machine pistol. The two prison guards were overpowered after a brief struggle. Their assailants, followed closely by Baader and Meinhof, leaped from a window and raced to the stolen Alfa Romeo. By the evening, Meinhof's surly pudding face was on twenty thousand wanted posters pasted up across Berlin, with a 10,000 DM reward offered for her capture.

*   *   *

VI DESERT DAYS

In June 1970 two groups of Germans, totalling twenty people, arrived in Beirut from East Berlin's Schönefeld airport, en route to a Fatah training camp outside Amman in Jordan. They included Baader, Ensslin, Mahler and Meinhof. Originally their PLO hosts envisaged nothing more than showing the guests the revolutionary sights, including refugee camps, field hospitals, and schools. The Germans insisted on receiving military training. All were kitted out in green uniforms and caps. Horst Mahler grew a beard and wore a Fidel Castro-style forage cap to show he was in earnest. There was a minor moment of feminist assertion when, to the incredulity of the Algerian camp commander, Baader and Ensslin insisted on men and women sharing sleeping quarters. Rations were primitive: tinned meat, rice and flat bread. One of the German women asked whether a Coca-Cola machine could be made available, a request met with more disbelief by the Arab hosts.

Each day began at 6 a.m., with a long run and then practice with rifles, submachine guns and Kalashnikov AK-47s. A fatal accident was narrowly averted as Ulrike Meinhof tried a Russian hand grenade; she unscrewed the cap and then pulled the ring, without grasping the point that she was supposed to throw the already fizzing object. Catastrophe was narrowly averted. There was also tactical training in bank robbery, of which the Algerian had considerable past experience. Inevitably there was trouble between the German amateur terrorists and the Fatah professionals. The Germans fired ammunition so profligately that they had to be restricted to ten rounds a day. The Germans went on a protest strike. Fatah fighters were shocked to see that this involved young German women sunbathing naked on the roof of their quarters, an uncommon sight in their milieu. When the Germans persistently inter-rupted a lecture by the visiting PLO commander Abu Hassan – in reality Ali Hassan Salameh – he had them disarmed and put under armed guard. There were also ructions between Baader and Peter Homann, who was being mistakenly sought for his alleged role in freeing Baader, especially after Homann overheard Baader and the others sitting as a kangaroo court, discussing the possibility of his having a shooting accident. Ensslin subsequently tried to convince Ali Hassan Salameh that Homann was an Israeli agent and that he should shoot him. She also inquired whether the PLO had an orphanage where Meinhof could deposit her twins, who were currently staying with German hippies in Sicily so as to keep them from the custody of their father. The current editor of *Der Spiegel* eventually rescued them. Aided by the East German Stasi, the group slipped back into Germany. Having fled on a false pretext, Homann promptly surrendered himself to the West German police.

In Berlin, the group made preparations for their forthcoming terror campaign. They contacted a motor-repair mechanic who helped them change the identities of a number of vehicles. These were used in the 'three blows' bank robberies which the group carried out in September 1970. In three simultaneous raids, they stole over 200,000 DM. Lawyer Mahler (code-name 'James' as in 007) accompanied Baader in a raid on a branch of the Dresdner Bank, shouting 'Robbery! Hands up and stay calm. Nothing will happen to you. It's not your money.' Typically, Meinhof came up short on her excursion, having scooped up 8,115 DM, while missing a box containing 97,000 DM. The group made jokes at her expense, saying that she could have earned the eight thousand with a couple of articles in *konkret*.

By lunchtime, the police had received an anonymous tip that Baader, Ensslin and Meinhof were at a particular Berlin address. The police put the apartment under observation, eventually searching it when no one appeared. Inside, they discovered Ingrid Schubert, as well as guns, chemicals, instructions for making bombs, and several car licence plates. The police decided to stake out the apartment. In the evening, a bewigged Horst Mahler rang at the door. He was pulled inside and arrested. They found a Llama pistol in his pocket and two magazines loaded with a total of thirty-six bullets. In the flat they also found instructions in his handwriting on how to make bombs. Later in the evening, the police dragged in a young woman who had been loitering outside the door, and who had a Reck pistol in her handbag. Two further women were detained when they rang the flat's bell. In the flat, the police also found the entire group's itemised expenses, totalling nearly 60,000 DM, much of it spent on clothing. In February 1973 Mahler was jailed for fourteen years. Thanks to the efforts of his own lawyer, future chancellor Gerhard Schröder, he was released on parole in 1978.

Meanwhile, Meinhof criss-crossed West Germany, cloning cars – so that, if stopped, the group could give the details of an entirely legitimate double of the car they were driving. The group's preference was for powerful BMWs, so much so that colloquially these were known as

Baader-Meinhof Wagen. They also burgled a provincial town hall to steal blank identity documents and the seals and stamps needed to authenticate them, necessary in a country where 'if it isn't stamped it isn't Prussian'. This burglary had to be executed twice because Meinhof managed to get the postcode wrong when she posted a packet of such documents to Baader and Ensslin. She had more success in purchasing twenty-three Firebird 9 mm pistols on the black market in Frankfurt. These were intended for the new recruits to the group, who included Holger Meins, a film student with pronounced depressive tendencies, his nineteen-year-old girlfriend Beate Sturm, and Ulrich Scholze, a twenty-three-year-old physics student. It did not take Baader long to recruit them. In addition to being of a similar political frame of mind, some of the new recruits were attracted by the romantic-rebel, criminal aspect of the terrorist enterprise. The youngest recruit was a sixteen-year-old girl, whom they nicknamed 'Teeny', the human mascot of the group. Scholze had more sophisticated reasons for becoming a terrorist, speaking of a 'particular psychological disposition'. One had to be emotionally convinced that reforms merely stabilised the existing system. Reason and emotion thereby became one. 'Persecution' by the authorities confirmed one's new worldview, while sensational press reports about 'Public Enemy Number 1' and the like could be construed as marks of success. Induction was gradual, beginning with arranging secure apartments, followed by stealing cars and robbing banks.[35]

While a hugely expanded federal criminal police service – whose manpower grew from 934 in 1970 to 1,779 in 1972 with corresponding budget increases – slowly picked off individual members of the group as they drove around the country, the leadership held gloomy discussions about names and strategy. Ulrike Meinhof coined the name Red Army Faction in a pamphlet she was invited to write called *The Urban Guerrilla Concept*. A graphic artist in the group devised the logo of a Kalashnikov AK-47, with 'RAF' emblazoned beneath. The name was unfortunate since it reminded people of the depredations of the Red Army, while the acronym conjured up Lancasters destroying German cities. Adoption of the grandiose name of 'army' also reflected the rapid militarisation of life in the group. Although opposition to the supposed militarisation of West German society was one of their key platforms, they did not seem to be aware that the armed struggle had ceased to liberate the new man, along the lines imagined by Frantz Fanon, but rather was reducing his humanity in the way that a boot camp or barracks does to recruits. They began to use deprecatory phrases like 'cowardice in the face of the enemy' that would have been worthy of the Wehrmacht or Waffen-SS.

With their numbers by now reduced to about a dozen people, the group was desperate for new recruits. Salvation came from an unlikely quarter. The mad. A radical psychiatrist at Heidelberg university, influenced by the anti-psychiatry of R. D. Laing and the anti-institutionalisation theories of Franco Basaglia, had formed a socialist collective among the mainly student clientele he was treating for various mental disturbances common to that age cohort, including depression, paranoia and mild schizophrenia. In early 1971 Baader and Ensslin visited Heidelberg where they met some of the radicalised patients. In the following years about twelve of the latter, including Gerhard Müller, Siegfried Hausner, Sieglinde Hofmann, Lutz Taufer and others became the second generation of RAF terrorists, initially under the slogan 'Crazies to Arms'.

The first death came in July 1971 when police chased a car that had gone through a random checkpoint in Hamburg. After the BMW was forced to stop, a couple alighted, firing Belgian handguns at their pursuers. The police returned fire, killing twenty-year-old Petra Schelm, a former hairdresser who had followed her boyfriend, Manfred Hoppe, arrested that day, into terrorism. In October, the police sustained their first fatality when a thirty-two-year-old officer called Norbert Schmid was shot while chasing RAF members in Hamburg. The federal criminal police acquired a new chief called Horst Herold, who introduced an information revolution while creating anti-terrorist departments in each of the federal *Länder*. The number of employees at his Wiesbaden headquarters rose from 1,113 when he took up his post in 1971 to 3,536 when he left it ten years later. The scale of the information the criminal police collected was so prodigious that people began to fear that Orwell's imaginings had been realised. There were thirty-seven different data-bases, containing information on nearly five million people and over three thousand organisations. Specialist databanks registered the names of, for example, everyone who had visited a terrorist suspect in prison. Another system identified homes in a given town where the occupants had not registered themselves or their vehicle with the authorities, who paid for utilities in cash, and who were not in receipt of child support. With considerable reason the police began to take a close interest in the left-liberal lawyers who routinely defended terrorist suspects, notably

Klaus Croissant and Otto Schily, some of whom were already on public record talking about how they would hide such a suspect if invited to do so. These lawyers' phones began to be tapped.

In these desperate encounters neither the terrorists nor their pursuers were slow to squeeze the trigger. Both sides developed a form of psychosis, believing that it was necessary to shoot first to survive. Georg von Rauch, the son of a professor at Kiel, was shot dead as he tried to pull a gun after being arrested. The son of another Kiel professor, Thomas Weisbecker, was shot dead by police in Augsburg. In the course of a police surveillance operation on a flat used as an RAF forgery centre, a detective was fatally shot and terrorist Manfred Grasshof was hit in the head and the chest. In this atmosphere, accidents were bound to happen, as a seventeen-year-old boy racer discovered when a police chase finished with an officer emptying the magazine of a machine gun into him and the car. A *Spiegel* journalist who happened to resemble Baader twice found himself staring down police gun barrels, while a Hamburg journalist who looked like Meinhof had to equip herself with an official document declaring that she was not the wanted terrorist.

Meanwhile, the nine members of the group still at large had commissioned a metal worker to manufacture several steel tubes measuring 80 cm by 20 cm, with a view to turning them into bombs. They were to be packed with ball-bearings or nails to maximise their destructive effect. The extreme amateurishness of this operation was evident when Baader wore out the motors of the coffee grinders he used to reduce lumps of ammonium nitrate and charcoal into serviceable quantities. Attempts to mix explosives with kitchen mixers were not a success, as the motors packed up, although attaching snow brushes to a drill eventually did the trick. In May 1972 the RAF bombed the US officers' club in Frankfurt am Main. Three bombs caused carnage. A thirty-nine-year-old lieutenant-colonel died when a glass shard went through his neck. Thirteen others were injured. According to a communiqué from the commemoratively named Commando Petra Schelm this was payback for the strategy of 'extermination' pursued by the US in Vietnam. On 12 May five policemen were injured when two pipe bombs went off in Augsburg's police headquarters. Two hours later a car blew up in the car park of the criminal police in Frankfurt. On 15 May the wife of a federal judge was badly injured when the car she was using to collect her husband exploded as she turned the ignition key. On 19 May three bombs went off among proofreaders in the Springer building in Hamburg, injuring seventeen of them. Three further bombs were successfully defused. On 28 May two car bombs were detonated outside barracks 28 and the mess at the US army's European headquarters in Heidelberg. Three American soldiers were killed and five injured.

These serial atrocities prompted the criminal police to launch Operation Punch in the Water, a nationwide series of raids designed to set the terrorist fish in motion. Every helicopter in government service was used to land teams of policemen suddenly next to motorways so as to erect temporary control points. The entire motoring public signalled their sympathy for the police. Independently of this operation, the police had received a tip about a garage in Frankfurt being used to store explosives. They substituted harmless materials and staked out the area. On the evening of 1 June 1972 an aubergine-coloured Porsche appeared, into which three men were crammed. It patrolled the street before two of the men went into the garage. The third man, Jan-Carl Raspe, opened fire as officers approached him. He was captured as he tried to flee. Inside the garage, the shots alerted Andreas Baader and Holger Meins that they were trapped. One hundred and fifty police reinforcements arrived together with an armoured car. The police fired tear-gas canisters into the garage, which Baader successfully hurled back, until the armoured car was used to close the garage doors. Eventually a detective took a lucky shot through a windowpane with a rifle equipped with a telescopic sight and hit Baader in the thigh. Meins was prevailed upon to come out, where he stripped off at gunpoint. The police apparently got a little carried away when they pulled him inside a van since he had to be hospitalised shortly afterwards.

A week later, the owner of a Hamburg clothes store watched as a nervous and tired-seeming young woman tried on various sweaters. As she went to tidy up the dozens of other pairs of trousers another customer had strewn around, she picked up the first customer's jacket. It felt heavy, as if there was a gun inside. She called the police. A passing patrol car was called in, and two officers quickly arrested Gudrun Ensslin. She had a silver revolver in her jacket, and a large-calibre automatic with a reserve magazine in her handbag. Taking a key from her bag, the police raided a hideout in Stuttgart, only to discover Baader's favourite reading materials – twenty Mickey Mouse comics. Two days after Ensslin's arrest, police arrested Brigitte Mohnhaupt in Berlin. After serving a prison sentence she would become the leader of the second generation of RAF terrorists.

On 16 June a teacher with a conscience informed the police in Hanover that a young woman he claimed not to know had asked him to house two strangers the following night. Three policemen were despatched to watch the building. A couple suddenly appeared asking the janitor where the teacher's apartment was. The police called in reinforcements. When the young man reappeared to use a telephone kiosk, the police disarmed him and locked him inside. Four officers then went up to the flat and rang the doorbell. As the woman answered the door the police seized her. Inside the flat guns, grenades and ammunition were strewn around. The thin, sickly-looking woman with short dark hair was Ulrike Meinhof. In her bag she had a copy of *Stern* magazine, whose cover consisted of the x-ray photograph of her skull showing the silver clamps over her cyst. In her jacket they found a note from Gudrun Ensslin, which her defence lawyer Otto Schily had smuggled to Meinhof. In early July, the arrest of Hans-Peter Konieczny enabled the police to set a trap on the streets of Offenbach. Thirty undercover officers watched as Konieczny met Klaus Jünschke as he got off a bus and promptly felt a gun pressed against his neck; later that afternoon a similar trap caught Irmgard Möller, who was kicked to the ground as she attempted to flee.

VII THE MYTHS OF STAMMHEIM

Initially these terrorist suspects were kept isolated in separate prisons, with the exception of Astrid Proll and Ulrike Meinhof who were housed in different wings of the same Cologne jail. Meinhof spent eight months in an empty hospital wing which she characterised as the 'dead tract' because of the unnatural silence. An organisation called Red Aid endeavoured to dramatise the prisoners' plight, co-opting such celebrity useful idiots as the Nobel laureate Heinrich Böll into the campaign to have their conditions alleviated. Several members of Red Aid became terrorists, as the alleged plight of the prisoners became the main recruiting mechanism for the second generation of RAF members.

Leftist lawyers ensured that their terrorist defendants were able to communicate with each other, using code-names taken from Melville's *Moby Dick*. Naturally, Baader was 'Ahab'. The lawyers photocopied the group's letters and smuggled them in amid their legal documents.

The detainees claimed they were being held in conditions resembling Auschwitz, with Meinhof writing that 'the political concept behind the "dead tract" – silent corridors – in Cologne's prison is: gas. My inner fantasies that this was Auschwitz were realistic.' In fact, she received regular visits from her ex-husband and ten-year-old twins, who in Auschwitz would have been handed over to Josef Mengele. Gudrun Ensslin was allowed to have a violin. The remand prisoners were per-mitted radios and record players, so that Baader was soon rocking to the sounds of Santana and Ten Years After. They received any reading matter they wished, which enabled Baader to study the theories he had spouted as slogans for years. In this fashion they built up extensive libraries (Baader some 974 books, Raspe a further 550) with materials on bomb making, alarm systems and police investigation techniques, as well as works entitled *German Weapons Journal, Amateur Radio, What We Can Learn from the Tupamaros, Urban Guerrilla Warfare, The Special Forces Handbook, The Master Bomber: Contemporary Explosives Technology* and the like. Insofar as the RAF prisoners had a strategy, it was to dramatise and publicise their predicament, making it seem as if the democratic German state had finally let slip its mask to reveal its Fascist inner heart. There were attempts to co-ordinate hunger strikes among the forty or so terrorist detainees. Two were called off after a short time, without achieving any improvement in the conditions of their custody. Visiting lawyers enabled Baader to gobble the occasional sandwich covertly.

In April 1974 Ensslin and Meinhof were moved to a new high-security wing at Stuttgart's Stammheim prison. They were allowed considerable periods of association with one another, but were kept apart from other inmates. Meinhof was then taken to Berlin as one of the defendants in the trial of those who in 1970 had freed Andreas Baader. She would receive an eight-year jail sentence in this trial. Her fellow accused, Horst Mahler, indicated that he had unilaterally left the RAF, part of his long journey to becoming a neo-Nazi.

In October 1974 Baader, Ensslin, Meinhof, Meins and Raspe were indicted on five counts of murder, with the trial scheduled to take place in Stammheim the following year. Baader and Raspe were also moved to Stammheim prison. They enjoyed single occupation of cells in which six prisoners were usually held. Almost immediately, Baader complained that his cell was too small. The wall to the next cell was knocked through to create a suite. When this did not suffice, the next wall into Raspe's cell was given a connecting door. After three weeks of being treated as a manservant by Baader, Raspe had the door bricked up again. All were already on hunger strike, with Holger Meins too ill to be moved. Forced feeding of the prisoners commenced. This did not avail Holger Meins, who by the time he died weighed little over six stone despite being six feet tall. Long before he had even embarked on the hunger strike, Meins wrote: 'In the event that I die in prison, it will have been murder. Regardless of what the swine maintain ... don't believe the lies of these murderers.' That would eventually become the group strategy. In reality, the only people being murdered were victims of the RAF chosen as symbolic targets. On 10 November 1974 a delivery man rang the bell of a Berlin house holding a bouquet of flowers. Thinking the blooms were a belated gift for his sixty-fourth birthday, the city's most senior judge, Günther von Drenkmann, cautiously slipped off the security chain and opened the door. Three young men burst through the door and shot him twice. He died later in hospital. The judge had no connection with terrorist cases. He was a liberal lawyer specialising in civil cases and a member of the SPD. A football crowd cried, 'Meins–Drenkmann. One all'.

Two thousand demonstrators bayed for 'revenge' at Meins's funeral. Rudi Dutschke put in a celebrity appearance to bid farewell to his comrade and friend, raising his fist and shouting 'Holger, the struggle continues!' He also took his son to visit Jan-Carl Raspe in prison. These actions, together with his involvement with bombs, were apparently compatible with his refusal to join the RAF, not on grounds of morality, but because the revolutionary constellations were inopportune.

In political terms, the imprisoned RAF terrorists managed to acquire more sympathisers than they had had while on the loose. Inflated rhetoric about the tortures they were supposed to be undergoing led to the formation of protest groups called torture committees, many of whose members – including Ralf Baptist Friedrich and Stefan Wisniewski, and the three 'Hamburg aunts', Susanne Albrecht, Silke Maier-Witt and Sigrid Sternebeck – became second-generation RAF terrorists after basking on the moral high ground as human rights activists. The police estimated that the three hundred people they were currently hunting enjoyed the active protective support of ten thousand sympathisers. Jean-Paul Sartre, the veteran armchair revolutionary, hastened from afar, with one of the later OPEC hostage-takers, Hansjoachim Klein, at the wheel and Daniel Cohn-Bendit, a fellow traveller. He spent half an hour with Baader, who gave his visitor a lecture on his cod philosophy. Afterwards Sartre's only private comment was 'What an arsehole, this Baader.'

At a televised press conference attended by a hundred reporters later that evening, he struck other tones: 'Baader had the face of a tortured man. It is not like the torture of the Nazis. It is another kind of torture. A torture designed to induce psychiatric disturbance. Baader and the others are living in white cells. In these cells they hear nothing except the steps of guards three times a day as they bring food. The lights burn for twenty-four hours a day.' The lies of this aged useful idiot were broadcast on prime-time German television. He had met Baader in the visitors' room, whose minimalist furnishings bore no relation to the cells in which the prisoners lived. The cell lights actually always went out at 10 p.m. when the power was shut off. Baader complained to the prison doctor that he had a bad back. So did his comrades. The doctor insisted they needed electric blankets, even in summer; the power stayed on through the night, enabling them to read in bed. Nor was Baader isolated; he received five or six visitors a day.

Left-liberal defence lawyers, whose cynical occupation of the moral high ground spared them from press scrutiny, played a major role in facilitating communications between their imprisoned clients and the next generation of RAF terrorists. Volker Speitel, for example, graduated from working in Klaus Croissant's law firm to a terrorist group. Croissant himself would serve a two-year jail sentence. The usual relationship between lawyers and their clients was reversed, as Baader graded them for their radicality. He received some fifty-eight visits from eight different lawyers in a single month, and over five hundred in the course of three years. He even wrote down the rules of the game, beginning by insisting that the prisoners themselves would collectively establish the overall defence strategy. Terrorists struck on 27 February 1975 when fifty-two-year-old Peter Lorenz, the Christian Democratic Union's candidate for mayor of Berlin, was abducted as he drove to work. He had been kidnapped by the 2 June Movement. A communiqué demanded the release of six prisoners, including Horst Mahler, the only (former) member of the RAF mentioned because there was not much love lost between the rival groups. Since none of the prisoners had been charged with murder, the government's crisis team capitulated to these demands, especially as Mahler declined to be freed. Five prisoners were flown to Aden, with former mayor Heinrich Albertz bravely accompanying them as a guarantee. Peter Lorenz was found the same night wandering confused in a Berlin park.

On the eve of the Baader–Meinhof trial in Stammheim, six terrorists calling themselves Commando Holger Meins took over the German embassy in Stockholm, armed with guns and bombs. They included three former members of the Heidelberg psychiatric collective, and Ulrich Wessel, the son of a prominent Hamburg millionaire. They took eleven hostages, including ambassador Dietrich Stoecker, Heinz Hillegaart, responsible for economic affairs, and baron von Mirbach, the military attaché, and locked themselves into offices on the third floor, wiring the room with explosives. They demanded the release of twenty-six prisoners, including Baader, Ensslin, Meinhof and Raspe. After urgent meetings, chancellor Helmut Schmidt informed the Swedish minister of justice that his government rejected these demands. When this message was conveyed to the terrorists, they took Hillegaart to a window and shot him three times. Shortly before midnight, the embassy was rocked by a series of explosions. Both Mirbach and the terrorist Wessel died. A second terrorist was gravely injured, which did not prevent him being flown to Germany where he died in intensive care at Stammheim a few days later. Three terrorists were arrested as they escaped the burning embassy. Two weeks later defence lawyer Siegfried Haag went underground after police searched his offices for proof that he had supplied the Stockholm embassy attackers with their weapons.

The trial of Baader, Ensslin, Meinhof and Raspe commenced in a purpose-built courtroom at Stuttgart-Stammheim on 21 May 1975. Security was intense, but, as it transpired, not tight enough. From the start, the four defendants resolved to disrupt the proceedings, beginning by rejecting the defence lawyers appointed by the court after three of their previous team were disbarred under new legislation designed to frustrate the collusive machinations of radical lawyers, the least of whose sins were calling their clients 'comrade'. In their concerted efforts to convert a criminal trial into a political spectacle, the defendants subjected the judge and prosecutor to prolonged verbal abuse, calling the former a 'Fascist arsehole' and the latter a 'terrorist', while their defence lawyer, Otto Schily, pleaded that they were unfit to stand trial. He and the other defence lawyers then walked out. Other farcical tricks included wishing to call Richard Nixon, Melvin Laird, Willy Brandt and Helmut Schmidt as witnesses. On another occasion they called five former US servicemen in order to defame the NATO alliance. When the hearings resumed,

Baader claimed that his conditions of detention were worse than those in the Third Reich. In fact, the four defendants, by now joined in Stammheim by Brigitte Mohnhaupt and Ingrid Schubert, enjoyed daily baths, extensive periods of communal association, radios and record players, and various exercise machines. Baader kept hashish in a tea tin to supplement the prodigious quantities of aspirins and anti-depressants the guards handed out each night. They also intimidated their guards, with Baader warning: 'I'll send a couple of people over. For a couple of thousand Marks I can find a killer to bump off your wife as well.' Eventually the courtroom disruptions reached such levels that Prinzing the judge availed himself of new legislation enabling hearings to proceed without the defendants. In a concession to the accused, the judge subsequently allowed them to participate in their own trial at will, so that they seemed constantly to be going in and out when they were not declaiming hundreds of pages of propaganda from prepared screeds.

As the court sessions dragged on into the new year of 1976, relations between the accused deteriorated. Baader and Ensslin sharply criticised Meinhof's maundering revolutionary writings in her capacity as 'Voice of the RAF'. There was something sado-masochistic about the delight they (and she) took in ripping her writings to shreds. They suspected that her resolve was weakening. It was, largely under the pressure of their incessant bullying, and her depressive tendencies. Early on Sunday morning, 8 May, guards opened the door of Cell 719 and found Meinhof hanging from a rope made of torn hand towels tied round the bars of the window. Extensive investigations found no sign of foul play. On the 109th day of the trial, her name was neatly crossed off the list of defendants. Four thousand people, some masked, hooded or wearing white face paint, attended her Berlin funeral. In Frankfurt a policeman was badly burned when someone threw a Molotov cocktail into his van; decades later, Meinhof's journalist daughter, whose hatred of the entire '68 generation had become strenuous, accused a minister in Schröder's government of having thrown that bomb.

Meanwhile, the former lawyer Siegfried Haag and the former psychiatric collective member Elizabeth van Dyck were in the Middle East seeking external partners for the second-generation RAF terrorists. Yasser Arafat turned them down, on the ground that the PLO currently favoured negotiation. Haag was referred to George Habash, leader of the Popular Front for the Liberation of Palestine. Rebuffed there too he made contact with Wadi Haddad, leader of a PFLP breakaway faction

called PFLP-Special Commando. Two German terrorists later participated in PFLP-SC's January 1976 hijacking of the Air France jet, during
which, Nazi style, they 'selected' out the Jewish passengers, an episode
that ended in the famous Israeli special forces raid on Entebbe in which
'Bibi' Netanyahu's brother was killed. Haddad also ran a secret training
camp for foreign terrorists at Yaal, a village in southern Yemen. Haag,
by now disguised with a toupee and a pirate beard, was on hand when
several RAF terrorists, including Peter Jürgen Boock, Verena Becker,
Rolf Clemens Wagner, Sieglinde Hofmann and Stefan Wisniewski, flew
to Aden for advanced training. They were welcomed like VIPs by the
Yemeni authorities, behind whom were men with Saxon accents from the
East German Stasi which trained the Yemeni secret service. After a hard
day's close-quarter combat, running and shooting, the group settled
down to ponder strategy, in particular two operations called Big Money
and Big Breakout.

In Stuttgart the defendants' lawyers had in the interim taken collusion
with terrorists to an unprecedented level. They all came from practices
increasingly specialising in human rights; not only did they sympathise
with the terrorists, in some cases they actively assisted or joined them.
Security at Stammheim was so stringent that even lawyers had to open
their trousers for closer inspection, although guards refrained from
poking around in their underpants. Gudrun Ensslin's lawyer, Arndt
Müller, was the first to be prevailed on to smuggle things into his client,
using the simple technique of hollowing out one of the many files of legal
documents. These were searched too, but provided the lawyer gripped
the edge of the file tight with one hand while flicking the outer pages with
the other, the guards did not bother to open the file fully. Beginning with
a Minox camera, thanks to which we have photos of the group in prison,
the lawyer graduated to smuggling in earphones, cables, an electric iron
and a cooking ring, followed by three pistols – a chrome-plated .38, a
Heckler & Koch 9 mm and a Hungarian FEK 7.65 mm – and five strips of
plastic explosive which probably arrived in his underpants. The weapons
were incorporated into the structure of empty cells when the high-
security block at Stammheim underwent modification. The prisoners
chose the wall colours.

A few other things were modified too. The prisoners used their
considerable electrical expertise to change a loud-speaker system (which
they insisted be switched off) into a radio-communication network
within the cell block. Amplifiers and stereo speakers enabled them to

communicate, especially after they demanded that the electricity should remain on at night to power their electric blankets. Meanwhile in the courtroom, Otto Schily, a future German interior minister, who clearly favoured the long march through the institutions, revealed the shocking news that some of his conversations with his clients had been bugged by the secret service. In a further effort to convert the radical lawyers into victims, the new RAF commander Brigitte Mohnhaupt, by now released after Baader had spent eight months training her for her commanding role while in prison, organised a bomb attack on Klaus Croissant's offices, which was deliberately attributed to neo-Nazis so as to stir up the 'anti-Fascist' cause. In March 1977 the defendants made their last appearance in court, refusing to participate any further until the question of whether or not their cells were bugged was cleared up.

On 7 April 1977 the federal prosecutor-general, Siegfried Buback, set off for work in his chauffeur-driven blue Mercedes. He was next to the driver while a thirty-three-year-old bodyguard sat in a rear seat. As the car waited at traffic lights, a Suzuki motorbike appeared alongside. The pillion passenger produced a submachine gun and riddled Buback's car with bullets. All three occupants died. The attack was the handiwork of the Commando Ulrike Meinhof. The organisers of the attack, Boock and Mohnhaupt, were at the time ensconced with Wadi Haddad in Baghdad, finalising plans to spring the Stammheim inmates whose trial was coming to an end. The intelligence behind the attack was Baader; Siegfried Buback had signed off his indictment.

After more than 190 days in and out of court, on 28 April Baader, Ensslin and Raspe were found guilty on several counts of murder or attempted murder and sentenced to life imprisonment. They were not in court to hear the verdict. They were confined in what was supposed to be one of the most secure facilities in the Western world, so secure that a further five terrorist prisoners were moved to Stammheim's seventh-floor maximum-security set. Outside their comrades continued their killing spree. In July 1977, Susanne Albrecht, the daughter of a Hamburg lawyer, repeatedly visited the Oberursel home of Jürgen Ponto, who was godfather to one of Albrecht's sisters. Although the Pontos did not suspect it, Albrecht was scouting the security arrangements. They invited her to tea on the afternoon of 30 July. Strangely she arrived accompanied by two men and two women, well dressed and carrying a bunch of flowers. When Ponto went to fetch a vase, one man followed him into the dining room and pulled out a gun. There was a brief struggle until a woman, Brigitte Mohnhaupt, appeared and killed Ponto with five shots. They had been attempting to kidnap him and it had gone murderously wrong. After the failure of a plot to fire multiple homemade rockets into the federal prosecutor's offices, in the late summer of 1977 Boock and Mohnhaupt finalised their next project at a meeting which they dubbed 'our Wannsee conference'. Their target was the prominent industrialist Hanns Martin Schleyer, president of the West German employers association and a board member of Daimler-Benz. He looked the part of plutocrat, well upholstered and richly besuited in that German way. The group knew much about him after an intern at Klaus Croissant's law practice pretended to be researching a PhD on business leaders at the Hamburg Institute for Global Economy and supplied a wealth of personal details.

On Monday 5 September 1977, Schleyer spent the afternoon in meetings in Cologne. After 5 p.m. he set off home in his chauffeur-driven Mercedes with three bodyguards following behind. As his car neared home, it was forced to brake hard when a woman pushed a blue pram into the road. The car with the bodyguards crashed into the back of Schleyer's car. Both vehicles were raked by submachine-gun fire. Peter Jürgen Boock recalled how his Heckler & Koch seemed to zip through the thirty shells in its magazine in a couple of seconds. Willy Peter Stoll jumped on the bonnet of the second car and emptied his gun into the men inside. All of them died. One of the killers, Stefan Wisniewski, the juvenile-delinquent son of a wartime forced labourer, who had developed a social conscience as a merchant seaman on voyages around the Third World, explained why the chauffeur had been shot too. Although not armed, this son of the proletariat had once done an evasive-driving course, which cost him his life.[36]

Schleyer, who miraculously survived this ferocious assault, was dragged out and rushed away in a VW camper van. Using an underground garage for cover, the terrorists moved him to the modified trunk of a big Mercedes and took him to the underground car park of an apartment block. Apartment number 104 at Zum Renngraben 8 had been rented, by a woman paying in cash, a few months before. Schleyer was kept in one of the bedrooms, although the 108 strands of his hair subsequently found in a wardrobe suggest that he may have been subjected to conditions far worse than anything the Stammheim prisoners could imagine. Tape machines recorded his interrogation. The former wartime SS officer and economic adviser in occupied Bohemia-Moravia turned out to be bravely jovial under the circumstances, shaking his head in a bemused fashion at the incredible ignorance his captors demonstrated about the higher workings of the German economy. Although the RAF knew about his wartime past, they never used this as a justification for his abduction.

As the police concentrated on identifying high-rise buildings with underground parking, and anyone who rented them, or purchased furniture, for cash, the kidnappers made their demands known through letters sent to clergymen and calls from random telephone booths. They wanted the release of all the major RAF prisoners, who were to be flown to destinations they selected, with 100,000 DM allocated to each prisoner, and two independent guarantors that there would be no attempts to recapture them. In Bonn, chancellor Helmut Schmidt, opposition leader Helmut Kohl and other members of Schmidt's crisis-management team resolved to free Schleyer, while not giving in to the kidnappers' demands. Tragically for Schleyer this was never going to be the case, despite the fact that the day after his kidnapping an alert policeman had visited Zum Renngraben 8, quickly ascertaining from a landlord that a single woman had rented apartment 104, revealing a 10 cm thick bundle of banknotes as she paid the deposit and rent. This information was passed around various police departments, where nobody troubled to check the woman's name, which was false, or her previous address in Wüppertal, which did not exist. By mid-September the kidnappers had moved Schleyer – hidden in a laundry basket – to an apartment they had rented in the Hague. Another potential hideaway was found in Brussels, for the RAF was realising that, if you kidnap someone, all police information systems effectively stopped at national borders.

While the kidnappers and the authorities conducted complex negotiations, which the latter obviously sought to delay, the majority of the RAF kidnap team flew to Baghdad, leaving Stefan Wisniewski in charge of the smaller team guarding Schleyer. In Baghdad, Wadi Haddad was most concerned to persuade Brigitte Mohnhaupt that the Bonn government should give each freed RAF prisoner one million DM, ten times the original sum requested. A surprise German fellow guest, Johannes Weinrich – a close associate of Carlos the Jackal – thought of putting further pressure on the German government either by storming the German embassy in Kuwait or by hijacking a Lufthansa tourist flight from Palma to Frankfurt. Wadi Haddad told Mohnhaupt that both operations were at an advanced planning stage and that she could choose one or the other. Recent experience in Stockholm inclined her and Boock to the hijacking, although they had reservations about taking holidaying Germans hostage as their connection with Schleyer was far from obvious. Haddad was responsible for the idea of using Russian hand grenades cased in glass or plastic to frustrate airport security x-ray devices. The final details of how the spoils were to be divided between the RAF and PFLP were decided in Algiers. The Algerian secret services provided a scrambled telephone apparatus so that Mohnhaupt could communicate with Schleyer's kidnappers in Europe. Another secret service was also helping the RAF terrorists since Haddad had reams of copied confidential material concerning them from the West German criminal police, on which the name 'Ministry of State Security' – that is, the Stasi – had only partially been obliterated by whoever photocopied them. The opportunity for the East Germans to make mischief was simply too tempting.

The hijack operation began by equipping four young Palestinian refugees with forged Iranian passports. They flew separately to Mallorca. They were followed by a Dutch woman, in reality Monika Haas, and her pretend husband Kamal Sarvati, together with their baby daughter. The weapons for the hijacking were concealed in the baby's things, with the ammunition in tins of sweets. Sarvati was Said Slim, a nephew of Wadi Haddad. On 13 October 1977 the four Palestinians commandeered Lufthansa flight 181 'Landshut' shortly after it left Palma. Two men rushed the cockpit and dragged out the co-pilot, while two women stood in the aisle brandishing hand grenades. The plane altered course for Rome where it landed two hours later. There the new captain Mahmoud used a loud-hailer to demand the release of the RAF prisoners. Ignoring the request of the German interior minister to shoot out the tyres, interior minister Cossiga and Communist leader Berlinguer decided to have the plane refuelled to get rid of the problem as soon as possible. The Boeing took off for Larnaka in Cyprus, from where, having again refuelled, it left for Bahrain in the Persian Gulf. Following behind was another Lufthansa jet, filled with tough-looking young men in jeans and trainers from GSG-9. No sooner had the hijacked plane arrived in Bahrain than captain Jürgen Schumann was forced to fly to Dubai. The airport runway, however, was blocked with fire engines, which were removed only when the pilot pleaded that he was running out of fuel. The ninety-one passengers and crew were trapped in the intense desert heat. Bizarrely, when he learned that it was the birthday of a Norwegian stewardess, Mahmoud ordered a cake to be brought on board and cracked open champagne. His mood changed when he realised that one of the women passengers was Jewish; hitting and kicking her, he shouted that the next day he would shoot her through the aircraft's door. Mahmoud was a Palestinian called Zohair Youssef Akache. He had studied aeronautical engineering in London. During two separate pro-Palestinian demonstrations he had hit policemen and was eventually deported. Using a different name he returned to Britain in early 1977 where he shot dead the former premier of Yemen, his wife and a Yemeni diplomat as they left the Royal Lancaster hotel. Scotland Yard had known he was in London, but failed to stop him flying out of Heathrow the same evening.

While ninety-one people sweltered on board 'Landshut', the GSG-9 commanders discussed how to storm the plane with two SAS personnel, a major and sergeant, who were training Dubai's own special forces. Before a rescue could be effected, Mahmoud had the plane in the air again, headed for Aden. The atmosphere on board was ugly as the terrorists wired up the cabin with plastic explosives. Despite being refused landing permission, Schumann managed to put the aircraft down on flat sand next to the runway which was blocked with armoured vehicles. The plane was surrounded by Yemeni soldiers. Before he took off again, Schumann insisted on inspecting the wheels and undercarriage. He took too long doing it. As soon as he re-entered the plane, Mahmoud made him kneel in the aisle and shot him. With Schumann's corpse locked in a closet, and his stray brain mass thrown out of the cockpit window, the co-pilot took the refuelled plane back up into the sky. Two-and-a-half hours later it landed at Mogadishu in Somalia, a bad choice as the Somali authorities were far less sympathetic than the Yemenis.

The hijackers informed the Somali authorities that they would blow the plane up if the RAF prisoners had not been released by 5 p.m. their time. They bound the passengers and crew, dousing them with all the alcohol on board the plane. With minutes to go before they killed the hostages, the chief German negotiators who had flown in earlier that day managed to have the deadline put back to 3.30 the following morning, claiming that the RAF prisoners were on their way. They would arrive in Somalia at 4 a.m. When darkness fell, the hijackers failed to notice the arrival of another plane with its windows darkened. Nor did they see the shadowy figures who crept about beneath the cabin, placing listening devices. German negotiators indulged Mahmoud, in order to keep him in the cockpit. At 10 p.m. local time he was blinded by stun grenades which detonated outside the windows. Within seconds the plane's doors were opened and black-clad figures worked their way through the aircraft, shouting 'Where are the bastards?' They shot three of the hijackers dead, including Mahmoud, and critically wounded the fourth. The passengers were then thrown down the escape chutes. The entire rescue mission was over in a couple of minutes. On hearing the success of Operation Magic Fire the normally reserved Hamburger Helmut Schmidt cried tears of relief.

News of this triumph was broadcast by the German media later that night. Listening to Suddeutschen Rundfunk was Jan-Carl Raspe in his cell at Stammheim. Using their cell-to-cell communication system, Baader, Raspe, Ensslin and Irmgard Möller resolved to kill themselves, while endeavouring to make this seem like an act of murder by the German government. Baader retrieved the pistol he had hidden in an empty cell from the compartment he had built in his record player. The last music he heard was Eric Clapton's 'There's One in Every Crowd'. He fired a few shots into the wall and his mattress before shooting himself through the neck. He had already put the empty cartridges near his own body to make it seem as if he had been executed. Raspe used a Heckler & Koch 9 mm to shoot himself in the temple. In Cell 720 Gudrun Ensslin took a length of cable from her stereo, fashioned a noose and threaded it through the fly mesh separating her from the cell's bars. She then hung herself by kicking away the stool she was standing on. In Cell 725 Irmgard Möller stabbed herself repeatedly in the left breast, failing to puncture her heart. She would later claim that this was the work of the German secret service acting in consort with the CIA. All of them were discovered when the cells were opened for breakfast at about eight o'clock the following morning.

In faraway Baghdad, the leaders of the RAF went into shock, with the exception of Brigitte Mohnhaupt. Long before these deaths had occurred, she had explained to Susanne Albrecht that if the hijacking was unsuccessful the Stammheim prisoners had resolved to kill themselves, in order to blame their deaths on the German government. There was one more death in this cycle of violence. On 19 October 1977, a caller informed the French newspaper *Libération* that Schleyer's body could be found in a green Audi 100 parked in Mulhouse. After forty-three days the RAF had decided to 'put an end to his lamentable and corrupt existence' by shooting him three times in the head. As Schleyer had grass in his mouth and pine needles stuck to his crumpled suit, it was presumed he had been murdered in a wood, probably in Alsace. At his funeral the German president apologised to his son and widow that they had not done enough to save him.

VIII THE SECOND AND THIRD GENERATIONS

After the deaths at Stammheim, definitive command of the RAF passed to Brigitte Mohnhaupt – who shared Baader's capacity to rave uncontrollably – together with Sieglinde Hofmann, Adelheid Schulz and Christian Klar. They had begun their terrorist campaign in 1973, and it would continue until 1982. They were initially based in Baghdad before relocating to Paris, a sort of 'Parishof' before 'Londonistan' was born. Thenceforth France was always their haven, which is why they undertook no active operations on French soil. Their depression and sense of failure in the wake of Mogadishu and Stammheim were compounded when a drug-addicted Peter Jürgen Boock despatched several RAF members to purchase drugs (and his favourite oat flakes) which he could not obtain in Baghdad. He imagined he was suffering from cancer; in fact he was a junkie. As a direct result of this mission, eight RAF terrorists were arrested in France, Holland and Yugoslavia, notably Stefan 'the Fury' Wisniewski who was detained at Orly airport using a false passport after French police compared his signature with terrorist handwriting specimens they had received from their German colleagues. He was intimately connected with the murder of Schleyer, and would spend the years 1978–99 in prison. Plans were laid, and aborted, to spring Wisniewski from jail using a chartered helicopter. Instead, as they brushed up their use of bazookas and bombs at a Palestinian camp in Aden, where several of the women terrorists had flings with their Arab hosts, the new RAF leaders resolved to kill US general Alexander Haig, who was now the commander in chief of NATO.

Several bank robberies were carried out to fund Operation Stallion. Following one such raid Elizabeth van Dyck was shot dead by the police when she revisited a safe house. The attack on Haig occurred a week before his retirement as he and five bodyguards drove from his house to NATO headquarters at Maisières in Belgium. Susanne Albrecht had conveyed explosives supplied by the Palestinians from San Remo to

Belgium to dispel the widespread impression that she was not up to the job. These were buried in a hole dug under a road. As Haig's three-car convoy sped over this spot, the road erupted, the explosion narrowly missing both Haig and his bodyguards. None of them was seriously injured. In the following months the RAF lost two members in a fatal car crash, while a third, Henning Beer, dropped out after suffering a nervous breakdown. Attempts to co-operate with the Red Brigades were not a success. In 1978 a member of the Red Brigades was sent to meet a representative of the RAF in a crowded Milan subway. The unknown contact would be carrying a crime novel. The Italian returned disconsolate as he had spotted no one looking like a German, and only young girls were reading crime novels. That observation did not amuse his feminist comrades. When the two groups did finally meet, the Italians' insistence on knowing about the RAF's 'party structures' were met with embarrassment. There were none. More successfully, a merger with the 2 June Movement restored the RAF's depleted numbers, and made it less necessary to undertake bank robberies since their new partners had extorted 4 million DM from the family of a kidnapped German industrialist. A series of RAF robberies of Swiss banks had resulted in scenes worthy of the Wild West and the death of a shopper killed in the crossfire. When the RAF robbers made off on bicycles, with their loot in plastic bags, a pursuing Swiss motorist lost them as he dutifully insisted on stopping at the traffic lights.

As the attack on Haig indicated, by the early 1980s the second generation of RAF terrorists had decided to focus their attacks on the US military presence in Europe. On 31 August 1981 a huge car bomb exploded directly outside the headquarters of the US Air Force on Ramstein airbase, causing over 7 million DM worth of damage. On 15 September they attempted to kill general Frederick Kroesen, the commander in chief of US land forces in Europe. As his armoured Mercedes – on the first day he had used it – stopped at traffic lights in Heidelberg, Christian Klar, who for several weeks had been camping in a wood above the road, fired two missiles from a Soviet RPG-7, one of which, launched from 126 metres away, exploded against the trunk of the general's car. Kroesen had a lucky escape, which he jokingly attributed to the fact that his assailants were not using American-made weapons.

The German police were in luck too. A year later two mushroom pickers combing a wood near Frankfurt came upon a dip containing two large plastic boxes. In addition to the Heckler & Koch used to shoot

Schleyer's bodyguards, there were ninety-one identity cards, fifteen passports, 55,000 DM in cash and Polaroid photos of Schleyer. Among the thousand or so items the boxes contained, there were coded documents and maps showing the location of eleven similar depots. Despite the freezing temperatures, some two thousand police officers were used to stake out these depots. The first terrorists to appear with their plastic shovels were Brigitte Mohnhaupt and Adelheid Schulz, who were seized by GSG-9 men. The women had a plastic bag with them in which was the Polish-manufactured submachine gun used to kill two Dutch customs officers two years earlier. Five days later, undercover policemen disguised as people out for a walk in the woods followed Christian Klar as he made for the depot code-named 'Daphne'. He was surrounded by three hundred and fifty waiting policemen and arrested. This effectively meant the end of 'the old RAF' as it was known in police circles, or, to be more accurate, of the 'second generation'.

Unknown to the West German police, the ranks of the RAF had already been depleted by several 'drop-outs', or *Aussteiger* in German. In 1979, a total of eight RAF members had indicated that they were no longer prepared to engage in terrorism, symbolically handing their weapons over to Klar or Mohnhaupt. Some of them were nervous wrecks, others felt guilty about their victims, especially if they were bystanders killed in the crossfire. Sigrid Sternebeck was one of those who had the realism to see that 'we live in central Europe, not under a Fascist dictatorship with a population living at subsistence levels that is ripe for revolution'. Her colleague, the former nurse Monika Helbing, was plagued by thoughts of their dead comrades. Helbing's husband, Ekkehard Freiherr von Seckendorff-Gudent, since 1977 the RAF's group doctor, also wanted to get out.

What to do about these failures presented the RAF leadership with a serious problem. If they were caught by the police, they would very likely break as they had already demonstrated their scruples and lack of fortitude. There was talk of despatching the group to Angola or Mozambique, a forlorn prospect, although they did begin to study Portuguese. The terrorist Inge Veitt came to the rescue. After the second of her two spectacular breakouts from Berlin's Lehrte Strasse women's prison – in one she sawed through the bars, in the second she used knotted blankets as a rope – she had been commissioned to spring two male 2 June Movement terrorists from Berlin-Moabit prison. En route through East Berlin's Schönefeld airport she was stopped by frontier guards who, after disarming her, handed her over to the genial, purple-nosed major 'Dirty' Harry Dahl of the Ministry of State Security. 'Good day, comrade!' he announced at their first encounter. Shortly afterwards a rearmed Veitt was on her way to West Berlin on the S-Bahn. Harry and his superiors, Erich Mielke and ultimately president Erich Honecker, solved the problem of the eight RAF drop-outs, all of whom were equipped with new identities for their fresh start in the German Democratic Republic. There were several reasons why the GDR's leaders decided to harbour terrorists.

They feared that some terrorist group might spoil a big state occasion just as Black September had done in Munich, and so were keen to know the inner workings of such groups. They liked having some of the fiercest opponents of the Federal Republic sheltering under their wings. Above all, Mielke, who as a young Communist militant had murdered two Berlin policemen in 1931, forcing him to flee to Moscow, and Honecker, who had been in a Nazi concentration camp, felt a certain fellow feeling for comrades on the run. The official line (among the dozen people who knew) was that while the strategy was wrong, the RAF terrorists had demonstrated courage, a line which overlooked the reason why the eight were in the GDR. This was how the Terrorism Department of the Stasi happened to become the protector of eight West German terrorists, despite the fact that all eight were on a list of 620 radicals whom their colleagues in the frontier police were to forbid entry to the country as it celebrated its thirty-fifth anniversary. Speaking of anniversaries, every year the Stasi organised a reunion for the former RAF members they were sheltering. This being the GDR, there were a few Orwellian touches. The homes of all eight were bugged and their telephones tapped. Three of the new GDR citizens entered into the spirit of the place by becoming active Stasi informers, spying on their friends or colleagues. It was impossible to keep their identities secret. Neighbours noticed that they easily got a Trabant car, and did not have to wait for plumbers; workmates watching West German TV realised they knew the wanted terrorists whose faces were shown on the news bulletins. All eight were rapidly detained by the newly consolidated German police force shortly after the 1989 fall of the Berlin Wall, receiving far milder sentences related to crimes for which their predecessors had been jailed for life.

Unknown to the drop-outs the Stasi were also running training courses for very active second-generation RAF terrorists. Beginning in

1980, Christian Klar, Adelheid Schulz, Helmut Pohl, Inge Veitt and others made biannual trips to the GDR where, disguised as National People's Army soldiers, they received weapons training and instruction in military-level bomb making. The high point came when the Stasi let them loose with Russian RPG-7 rocket launchers. An old Mercedes was used as a target, with four dummies – in overalls filled with sawdust – and a distressed Alsatian placed inside to gauge the effects. The rocket streaked into the car, hurling the dummies around and singeing the dog, which was given the coup de grâce by a Stasi officer. Co-operation between the Stasi (anti-)terrorism branch and the RAF terrorists continued until 1984, although the Stasi also facilitated Libyan and Syrian state terrorism in West Germany thereafter. Some of this Stasi expertise would be put to ill effect, by a third generation of RAF terrorists trained by their predecessors.

The depletion through arrests and drop-outs of the second generation of RAF terrorists did not lessen Germany's problem with RAF terrorism. In late 1982, the bank robberies recommenced, suggesting that a third generation was stirring. This was confirmed when in July 1984 an elderly electrician, resting on his sofa watching TV, heard a loud bang from the flat above. Half an hour later a blonde girl appeared at his door claiming to be tending cats for an absent friend, in whose flat she had knocked over a pail. Had any water come through his ceiling, she inquired? No, but, as it happened, later he glanced down and noticed that a spent round had. When two policemen called at the flat concerned, they found six people hiding in a rear room. They did not have enough handcuffs to restrain them. To their amazement the police discovered six revolvers, 250 rounds of ammunition, a grenade and large amounts of money. They had caught forty-year-old Helmut Pohl and five of the latest recruits to the RAF. They also discovered over eight thousand pages of documents, some with details of potential targets. Despite these arrests, in November 1984 two men raided a gun shop in Ludwigshafen, making off with twenty-two pistols, a couple of rifles and 2,800 rounds of ammunition. The RAF third generation was rearming. Its campaign would continue until 1998, although an epochal moment came in 1992 when the group formally renounced political murder.

The third generation's first attempt at atrocity was a failure. A twenty-five-pound bomb was found in a car parked within the NATO academy at Oberammergau. An alert German instructor noticed a slovenly US soldier hurriedly leaving the site, and quickly asked guards whether the man had parked a car there. The site was evacuated. A technical failure prevented the bomb from going off. The explosives had come from a quarry in Belgium, stolen by the French terror group Action Directe six months earlier. Shortly afterwards a bilingual communiqué announced that the two groups were acting in concert. As if to demonstrate this, on 25 January 1985 Action Directe terrorists shot dead general René Audran, head of weapons exports in the French Defence Ministry. Responsibility was claimed by a Commando Elisabeth van Dyck, its name commemorating the RAF terrorist shot by police earlier. A week later, a young messenger girl rang the doorbell of the Starnberger See home of Ernst Zimmermann, head of MTU, manufacturers of engines for Tornado fighters and Leopard tanks. The messenger, with a letter Zimmermann had to sign for, was followed by a young man with a gun, who after tying Zimmermann to a chair shot him dead. This was the handiwork of Commando Patsy O'Hara, named after an Irish National Liberation Army terrorist who had starved himself to death in the Maze prison. Two things were significant about these attacks. The victims were not symbolic targets like Ponto or Schleyer. They were what the RAF called 'bearers of functions', that is men who were key players in their respective defence sectors. Secondly, the international martyr nomenclature was intended to forge alliances with other European terrorist groups so that a 'West European Guerrilla' would confront an increasingly integrated EEC and NATO. How successfully this was done can be gauged from the fact that an attack was named after Vincenzo Spano (an Action Directe terrorist who was alive in a French jail) when in fact it was intended to commemorate Ciro Rizatto, a Red Brigades terrorist killed in a bank robbery. The RAF corrected the mistake in a further communiqué.[37]

In August 1985 the third generation detonated a 126-kilogram car bomb inside the US Rhein-Main airbase in Frankfurt, killing two Americans and injuring twenty-three others. The night before an attractive German woman lured a twenty-year-old US soldier from the Western Saloon on his base in Wiesbaden. He body was found the following morning, shot in the back of his head. He had been killed so that the RAF could use his ID to get the bomb on to the Frankfurt base. A roadside bomb was used to murder Karl Heinz Beckurts, the leading German industrialist and advocate of nuclear power, together with his chauffeur, both of whom resembled charred puppets flecked with blood by the time the police found them. RAF Fighting Units simultaneously attacked material targets, including the Cologne offices of the German secret service. On 10 October 1986 RAF terrorists executed Gerold von Braunmühl, deputy to foreign minister Hans-Dietrich Genscher, as he arrived home late from work in a taxi. Responsibility was claimed by the Commando Ingrid Schubert, this one commemorating the RAF terrorist who had hung herself in Munich's Stadelheim prison three weeks after the group suicide in Stammheim. When the RAF claimed that Braunmühl had been chosen because of his representative status – the RAF was now going for the state itself and especially those connected to the 'pan-German EEC' – the dead man's brothers published a moving letter, in Germany's main left-wing newspaper, asking who had appointed them to murder people. Shortly afterwards, Action Directe murdered Georges Besse, the head of Renault, in what turned out to be the group's denouement. In February 1987 French police arrested the four Action Directe leaders at a farmhouse near Orleans. Co-operation with the RAF ceased.

On 20 September 1988, RAF gunmen disguised as road surveyors narrowly missed state secretary for finance Hans Tietmeyer as he was driven to work. A year later they were all too successful when they used a seven-kilogram bomb attached to a parked bicycle to kill the Deutsche Bank chief Alfred Herrhausen as he was driven in a convoy of three armoured vehicles to work. One of the most charismatic and powerful businessmen in Germany, Herrhausen had been affectionately known as 'Don Alfredo' by his friend chancellor Kohl. The attack had been meticulously planned, with terrorists posing as a road-working gang laying a long command wire to an infra-red system which triggered the explosion as Herrhausen's car crossed the beam made by a light and a reflector. The terrorists had also found a way of focusing the explosion precisely on the rear seats of the car. Police remarked that Herrhausen would have died even if he had been in a tank. His killers have never been caught. One may wonder where the expertise evident in this attack was learned other than in the GDR. On 27 July 1990, Hans Neusel, the state secretary in the Interior Ministry responsible for internal security, narrowly escaped death when a bomb exploded as he drove by. The fact that he was driving saved his life, as the bombers had assumed he would be travelling in the rear of a chauffeur-driven car. Following the outbreak of the first Gulf War, in January 1991, RAF terrorists stationed on the

Königswinter bank of the Rhine opened fire on the US embassy in Bonn, smashing a number of windows and sending the cleaners scurrying, before disappearing in a VW Passat.

Nineteen ninety-two finally brought significant developments which signalled that the end of terrorist violence was at hand. In the teeth of bitter opposition, but in line with advice from the secret service, justice minister Klaus Kinkel announced that the state must be ready for 'reconciliation' in appropriate cases, releasing terrorist prisoners in return for the RAF abandoning violence. This was less of a concession than conservatives feared, for all prisoners were entitled to parole having served two-thirds of their sentences, which meant after fifteen years for those serving life. Kinkel and his advisers were trying to sever the Gordian knot whereby the real or imagined plight of RAF prisoners served as the main recruiting sergeant for future terrorists. The secret service also agreed with the prisoners' desire to be held in one jail, although for different reasons. Given how easily even small groups of terrorist inmates could dominate a prison, this was a calculated risk. They hoped that this policy would divide and disaggregate the terrorist prisoners, opening rifts between hardliners and moderates and weakening the organisation. This gesture elicited a response from the RAF in April 1992. Cheekily suggesting that Kinkel had revealed divisions within the ruling apparat, the RAF ruefully acknowledged that the world had changed since the collapse of socialism and the end of the Cold War. It also admitted that it had little or no public support for its campaign of terror. The group promised to 'de-escalate' its campaign and to cease killing prominent business or government figures. A longer follow-up paper published in August more explicitly renounced political murder. Between early 1992 and September 1993, the authorities released nine RAF prisoners.

That this did not mean the end of RAF attacks was dramatically evidenced when on the night of 26–27 March 1993 a masked RAF team broke into a newly built prison, scheduled to be opened five days later. Apart from three security guards who were eating chips and drinking beer, and seven prison guards who, to save money, were sleeping in otherwise empty cells, the building was unoccupied. Although the prison had six-metre perimeter walls, the RAF team had used aluminium and rope ladders to scale them. As the security men and guards were bound and loaded on to a VW truck, the reasons for this bizarre raid on an empty prison became evident. The terrorists drove a green truck into the prison. Shortly after 5 a.m. five separate bombs, totalling at least 200 kilo-grams of explosives, virtually demolished the entire building, causing 123 million DM of damage and requiring four years of restoration work. The same year also saw a police success in capturing RAF third-generation terrorists turn into disaster. The secret service had managed to infiltrate an agent into the RAF scene, who succeeded in winning the confidence of Birgit Hogefeld, another graduate of the committees against torture, who together with her partner, Wolfgang Grams, was among the key third-generation RAF leaders.

After further brief encounters, the agent and Hogefeld agreed to meet in a small town in Mecklenburg-Hither Pomerania, where Hogefeld planned a short vacation. In June 1993 the agent and Hogefeld spent a weekend in a damp seaside bungalow, watched by large numbers of undercover policemen who also overheard their conversations through bugs in the walls. A plan to snatch Hogefeld as she took a bus to the station was aborted at the last minute in order to see who she had arranged to meet. At a small town called Bad Kleinen, Hogefeld and the agent were joined by Wolfgang Grams. The police decided to spring the trap, code-named Operation Wine Harvest. As the three left the café, seven men in jeans and blousons surrounded Hogefeld, while a 'passen-ger' put a gun to her neck shouting 'Hands up!' Wolfgang Grams reacted faster, sprinting up nearby steps to the platforms, and pulling out a 9 mm pistol. He put four shots into twenty-five-year-old Michael Newrzella, one of his GSG-9 pursuers, who later died. There was a furious gun battle between Grams and the other GSG-9 men during which some forty-four shots were fired. A female train driver was shot in the arm. Badly wounded, Grams tried to flee along the tracks until he collapsed. There was some controversy over claims that GSG-9 men put a couple of extra bullets into his head, although after an inquiry they were exonerated. In fact, the wounded Grams had shot himself dead.

The dramatic events in Bad Kleinen effectively signalled the end of the RAF. With Hogefeld arrested and Grams dead, there may have been as few as three further RAF terrorists on the run in Germany, although no one could be sure. There were bitter divisions among the RAF prisoners, with some opting to make their peace with the authorities, leaving a tiny implacable group led by Brigitte Mohnhaupt. In the mid-1990s the once feared terrorist organisation only appeared in the form of readers' letters to left-wing newspapers and magazines as they sought to set this or that historical issue straight. In 1997 former RAF members held a reunion in

Zurich. Surveying their middle-aged faces, whose younger selves had adorned so many 'wanted' posters, journalists were reminded of a conference of school teachers, or rather of polytechnic lecturers, which at least semi-identified where this delusive Red plague had begun, namely in the left universities of the Western world. On 20 April 1998 Reuters received a brief communiqué: 'Almost twenty-eight years ago on 14 May 1970 the RAF emerged in the course of an act of liberation. Today we conclude the project. The urban guerrilla, in the form of the RAF, is now history.' Five sides of single-spaced type reviewed the RAF's history. There was an honour roll of the twenty-six who had 'died in the armed struggle'. In his retirement, Horst Herold, who had done more than anyone else to combat RAF criminality, remarked that this paper was 'the tombstone erected by the RAF itself'.

Not quite, however, because on 30 July 1999 a jeep and a VW Passat were used to block in an armoured security vehicle as it delivered money to Duisberg-Rheinhausen banks. The guards found themselves staring into a bazooka shouldered by one of the masked assailants. The robbers made off with one million Marks. Perhaps the third generation were arranging their pensions as there have been no further signs of life from the Red Army Faction since. By contrast, much has been heard from Horst Mahler. Following the intervention of Gerhard Schröder, Mahler was allowed to resume his commercial practice in 1988. After a decade, he became politically active again. He went back to his roots. In 2000 he joined the far-right NPD. This finally bestirred his colleagues to chuck him out of the lawyers' association, in that curious dual response to Communist and Nazi criminality that characterises the left in general. Mahler became an active Holocaust-denier, combining radical anti-Semitism with hatred of the USA which he conflated with Israel. As a lawyer he subsequently specialised in defending other Holocaust-deniers. In 2004 he was disbarred, making several court appearances for virulent anti-Semitic agitation. He wrote a book with the former SS soldier Franz Schönhuber, the leader of the Republican Party, entitled *An End to German Self-Hatred*, a title more apt for the story of the RAF itself.[38]

Now, in an ultimate victory for consumer capitalism, the RAF has become just another marketing brand. There are several coffee-table books of photos from the group's heyday, including Astrid Proll's *Hans und Grete*, or in its English version *Pictures on the Run 67–77*. When London's Institute of Contemporary Arts held an exhibition entitled

Crash, which included a section on 'Radical Chic', one smart designer house was quick off the mark with a new collection that included the slogan 'Prada Meinhof' and the outline of an AK-47, printed on the scarf worn by a fashion model.[39]

CHAPTER 7

Small-Nation Terror

The Basques have inhabited a 22,000-square-kilometre region straddling the Franco-Spanish border which they call Euskal Herria for a very long time. Exactly how long is contentious. Many Basque nationalists claim their presence is aboriginal. There are Basque anthropologists who believe that the Basques are descended from cave-dwelling bipeds that achieved human form without evolutionary contact with anyone else. That the Basque language, Euskera, is autochthonous, meaning that it has no relationship to the Indo-European tongues of the Basques' European neighbours, further fuels feelings of uniqueness. So does a conviction that they have been victims of Spanish colonialism, a hurt that the Basques compulsively explore like a person using his tongue to probe a disintegrating tooth.[1]

The Basques believe in a political version of the fall from original grace, of the loss of historic liberties. The only time the Basque country was a single political entity was when it was encompassed within the kingdom of Navarre. In medieval times Castilian monarchs annexed their territory, granting the Basques unique rights (*fueros*). So as to neutralise feuding Basque warlords, the Castilian kings granted noble rights to the inhabitants of two of the Basque provinces, Guipúzcoa and Vizcaya. This meant that the Basques were 'gentlemen' entitled to serve in the administration of the incipient Hispanic empire. They were exempt from military conscription, and enjoyed important regional fiscal privileges. There were no import duties on foreign goods entering the region, while the Basques retained the ability to tax agricultural goods arriving from the rest of Spain.

By the nineteenth century these protectionist arrangements did not suit Basque manufacturers in thriving industrial towns but they saved the livelihoods of many modest Basque farmers. Another line of division, this time political, opened with the two Carlist Wars of 1833–40 and 1873–6. The Spanish succession was contested by a Liberal camp, which supported the female line represented by the child Isabella, and the reactionary Navarese gathered around her uncle don Carlos. The countryside fought for God and king – for, as the jumping off point for the medieval Reconquista and the home of the Jesuit founder St Ignatius Loyola, the Basque country was militantly Catholic – while the city dwellers of Bilbao and elsewhere supported the Liberals. The Liberals abolished the *fueros*, except in Navarre which managed to retain them, leading to a marked aloofness between Navarre and other Basque provinces. For while the Basques claim that Navarre is their historic heartland, the majority of Navarese, including those who speak Euskera, do not regard themselves as Basques first. The general breakdown of public order in Spain after these wars led a Navarese aristocrat to found the mobile police Guardia Civil, with their distinctive *tricornio* hats, ironically to nationalist eyes the most visible symbol of Spain's colonial rule in these northerly provinces.

Migration to the cities – Bilbao had trebled in size by 1900 – meant that Spanish became the lingua franca of the streets. Unlike Catalan, which is easy for a Spanish person to acquire casually, Basque is so sui generis that it requires major effort, on a par with learning Finnish or Hungarian. Although Euskera survived in the countryside, the language was dying a death where society was most dynamic, to the horror of the Basque middle class. They felt marginalised in their own country by socialist Spanish-speaking proletarians, whose profanities also outraged their faith, and by an avaricious local oligarchy with more time for their British business partners than for their fellow countrymen.

Enter Sabino Arana (1865–1903), the son of a shipbuilder who founded the Basque Nationalist Party or PNV in 1895. Arana believed that the Basques were a distinct race, with big noses and a higher proportion of RB negative than found in the Spanish population. He was on what, to us at any rate, seems less sticky ground when he argued that the Basques had unique laws and their own language, although this overlooked those urban liberal Basques who had campaigned to abolish the *fueros* as an impediment to industry. Arana used the British Union Jack as a model for the 'ancient' Basque flag or *ikurriña* except that it is red, green and white.

Sport was integral to the distinctive local culture. There were communal games, resembling those of the Scottish Highlanders. Games included lifting and rolling around one's shoulders huge round rocks, mountaineering, and the Basque version of pelota, known as *jai alai*, in which a ball is flung around a walled court at high velocity with a curved wicker-basket extension to the hand. Other fun activities include ocean-rowing, tug-of-war and headbutting one another (a national pastime in Glasgow too) or hauling and pushing a vast rectangular rock attached to two oxen. The Basques also go in for rap-like poetic extemporisation, and have a peculiar musical instrument called a *txalaparta*, the double consonants being typical of Euskera. There is a distinctive cuisine, often involving ox and seafood, which may explain why ETA bombers have twice struck at a restaurant complex set up near Biarritz in the French Basque country by award-winning chef Alain Ducasse, forcing him out of business in the area. He had allegedly been guilty of reducing Basque culture to the folklore industry.[2]

Basque Catholicism was also of the dogmatic northern Counter-Reformation variety, eschewing the superstitious semi-pagan Andalusian south, in ways that would be familiar to a northern Frenchman or Italian. In contrast to Ireland, where Catholic priests have been IRA cheerleaders, with only a tiny contingent offering logistic support to terrorists, ETA has included a substantial number of lapsed seminarians who brought moralising single-mindedness to killing people. Seminaries and retreats were also used to hold covert ETA meetings. Finally, economic facts undermine any general association between economic deprivation and terrorism. Arana described Spanish migration as 'an invasion by Spanish socialists and atheists', suggesting that if this was colonialism it was that of the poor. Historically, the Basque provinces have been much richer than Spain as a whole, with the exception of Catalonia which has a powerful (non-violent) separatist movement too. Both the Basques and the Catalans were industrious folk who looked down on the backward, sluggish, and snobbish Castilian heartlands from a position of commercial superiority. The Basque country was a wealthy place, with arms firms, banks, iron-ore mines, shipyards and processed steel. In 1969 Guipúzcoa, Vizcaya and Alava ranked first, second and third out of Spain's fifty provinces in terms of per-capita income, with Navarre near by in seventh place. They felt that their productivity was being inequitably taxed so as to support southern idlers and wastrel Castilian aristocrats.[3]

The PNV was a Basque nationalist Christian party that was opposed by both left and right on the eve of the Civil War. The left resented the PNV's creation of a Basque nationalist trades union to compete for the same working-class constituency, while the right thought the Basques were part of a Red–Judaeo-masonic conspiracy to break up Spain. Although the Basques might have gained the sort of autonomy which the Second Republic had granted Catalonia in 1932, the murderous anti-clericalism of the republic's anarchist supporters led to poor relations, and then a sudden lurch to the left when the right came to power in 1934 with the slogan 'Better a Red Spain than a broken Spain'. While the implacably reactionary Carlists supported the 1936 military rebels, the PNV stood by the republic, in the isolation which the rebels succeeded in imposing on Basque provinces cut off from the main areas of Republican support around Madrid. The Basques briefly achieved autonomy at a ceremony held around the ancient oak tree in Guernica, which would shortly be obliterated by the Luftwaffe. On 19 July 1937 general Mola took Bilbao. The Basque nationalist battalions surrendered to Franco's Italian allies in the vain hope of avoiding the vengeance he dealt out to his opponents. The Basque provinces were occupied in ways that earlier Basque nationalist mythology could not have conceived of. US policy towards Franco, who as a Fascist dictator was frozen out, was crucial. The CIA was interested in the PNV, while a US colonel was deployed to train Basque guerrilla fighters gathered at a camp outside Paris. When because of the exigencies of the Cold War the US decided to leave Franco in place, he was able to repress the Basques with impunity.

The Basques were subjected to military rule and their language was outlawed. Priests were banned from using it in services and sermons, while people had to use Spanish in public even in places which were wholly Basque speaking. In a further effort at what some call linguacide – that is, the total eradication of their historic language and identity – Basques were forbidden to give their children identifiably Basque names such as Jon instead of Juan. When Basque-language primary education was eventually conceded, children had to sing the anthem of the authoritarian Falangist movement 'Cara del Sol'.

ETA is the acronym for Euskadi Ta Askatasuna or, in English, Basque Homeland and Freedom. It was founded, as EKIN, the verb for 'to act', in 1952 by youthful supporters of the PNV who belonged to student discussion groups at the university of Deusto in Bilbao. In July 1959 they changed the name to ETA, breaking with the parent party because it appeared too accommodating of Franco. ETA's gestation as an active terrorist organisation was protracted, partly because key leaders were arrested even before the campaign had got under way, but also because the different factions in ETA went in for interminable discussions both at and between their assemblies which supposedly set group policy in the manner of IRA/Sinn Féin's Ard Fheis.

Three fundamental tendencies battled for power within ETA. Traditionalists, of whom José Luis Álvarez Enparanza 'Txillardegi' was the most prominent, stressed ethnological and linguistic factors, arguing that ETA should embrace all those who spoke Basque regardless of class or wealth. By contrast, Paco Iturrioz and others espoused the Marxism of the New Left, wishing to bring about a class struggle in conjunction with Spanish workers, a struggle that would be waged against the Basque oligarchy too. This led them to being dubbed 'españolistas', which was not complimentary in Basque circles. They were also accused of revolutionary *attentisme* – of waiting for the gears of history to grind – and of being Trotskyites by the so-called *tercemundistas* or Third Worldists who were enthused by the guerrilla struggles of Algeria and Vietnam. Their chief spokesman was Federico Krutwig Sagredo, the son of a German industrialist living in Bilbao. This self-styled revolutionary vanguard won the day, expelling the alleged Trotskyists, while the cultural nationalists went their own way.

Despite the heady talk of Che Guevara, ETA's initial activities were on a par with what students do everywhere: daubing slogans or the acronym 'ETA' on walls and surreptitiously flying the red, white and green Basque flag. The more a person demonstrated, the more they were liable to be savagely beaten up by the Guardia Civil, who were not known for their restraint. If you look for trouble, you tend to find it, as a leading ETA member recalled:

> Ten years ago in the festival of Aya, I was wearing a cap with four clusters of ribbons hanging from it. They [the police] grabbed me, they took off the ribbons and they took away my identity card, and they told me to come to Ataun the next day to get it. I went there and they made me return home and come back with the cap that I had on in Aya. I went back with the cap. They slapped me around a little, and yelled at me. And I had to remain quiet. The ribbons were the Basque colours. They gave me a fine of five hundred pesetas and they let me leave.[4]

Participation in strikes and demonstrations was banned across Spain as a whole, and brought a heavy-handed response from the police, who in the Basque provinces were equally brutal towards any manifestation of separate national consciousness. Repression drove Basque militants off the city streets and up into the hills and mountains where they could plausibly claim to be engaged in climbing or hiking. Others joined ETA as their *cuadrilla*, that is the groups of boys who hung around together from childhood, and whose bonds were closer than those of extended Basque families. ETA recruiters identify suitable candidates, and then spend months grooming them, through tasks of escalating risk, until they became fully fledged members of the terrorist organisation. It is a long-drawn-out and considered process, with opportunities for disengagement, rather than a hot-blooded spur-of-the-moment enthusiasm.

On 18 July 1961 ETA attempted to derail a train carrying Nationalist veterans of the Civil War to twenty-fifth-anniversary celebrations held in San Sebastián. The attack failed miserably. In response, 110 ETA members were rounded up and tortured, before being given jail sentences of between fifteen and twenty years. Another hundred or so supporters fled across the border to France, whose three French Basque provinces – Soule, Labourd and Basse-Navarre – became a haven for ETA despite the fact that most French Basques reject ETA's politics. Of course, the highly centralised French state has never conceded its Basques an iota of autonomy.

In exile, the surviving ETA leadership formed an Executive Committee, with four subordinate fronts, for finance, politics, armed struggle and culture. They adopted an eight-year plan, in which propaganda and training would eventuate in an escalating series of terrorist attacks designed to trigger all-out guerrilla war. The Fourth Assembly, held in secret in Spain in 1965, also saw the adoption of the action–repression–action spiral-of-violence theory. Each terrorist attack would provoke a stronger counter-reaction, whose random violence would swell the numbers of ETA supporters. This strategy was much favoured at the time by revolutionaries who seem to have imagined they were directing a play, in control of each actor's action and reaction. In the case of the Monteneros in Argentina and Tupamaros in Uruguay, this proved to be a disastrous calculation, the sort of thing middle-class students envisage in woeful underestimation of the dark forces they stirred up with their ludic Robin Hood ventures. In Uruguay it led to the replacement of Latin

America's sole democracy by a police state, while in Argentina the military obliterated dissidence through torture or disappearances involving suspects being thrown from helicopters.[5]

ETA underwent some organisational changes, not least the creation of an Activism Branch of about thirty men under Javier 'El Cabro' (the Goat) Zumalde, who took to the mountains to wage armed struggle. This was untypical as most ETA terrorists operated within a five- to twenty-kilometre radius of their homes, and did a regular job in between attacks that occurred at half-yearly intervals. Other commandos were created to rob banks, although the first attempt in September 1965 resulted in the arrest of most of the robbers. Armed robberies and shootouts became more frequent in 1965–8, though only one person was killed as opposed to several wounded in what invariably became gunfights. On 7 June 1968 a car carrying ETA militants was stopped at a Guardia Civil roadblock set up in a village called Aduna. One of them shot dead a Guardia Civil called José Pardines before fleeing into another checkpoint where the Guardia Civil dragged Txabi Etxebarrieta from the car and shot him beside the road. His accomplice, Iñaki Saraskueta, escaped, but was captured, tortured and jailed for life. Etxebarrieta's death was the pretext for commemorative masses, demonstrations and riots in the streets of Bilbao, San Sebastián, Eibar and Pamplona. St Txabi became a magnet for future recruits.

ETA decided to capitalise on these disturbances, seeking to provoke the reaction that would convert demonstrations into an uprising. On 2 August 1968 ETA gunmen murdered police commissioner Melitón Manzanas, a man not known for his charitable treatment of suspected terrorists, as he returned home to his house in Irún. Partly because it was raining heavily no one could positively identify the killers. Franco responded by declaring a state of emergency in Guipúzcoa province, which in January 1969 was extended to Spain as a whole. About two thousand people were arrested in the Basque provinces, including Gregorio López Irasuegui and his pregnant wife Arantxa Arruti, a couple suspected of involvement with the murder of Manzanas. Despite her condition, Arruti was tortured by the police, which caused her to miscarry. Her husband, who had been released without charge, was recaptured when he and a colleague tried to break into the prison in Pamplona to liberate her. Ballistics experts established that the Czech machine pistol his accomplice carried matched the weapon used to shoot commissioner Manzanas. This sequence of events led to the arrest of several ETA leaders, including two Catholic priests who belonged to the illegal group. Further raids netted virtually most of the rest, although José María Eskubi managed to flee to France joining Krutwig in exile.

The Franco government used a military tribunal to try the so-called Burgos Sixteen of major ETA figures. Prosecutors asked for six death sentences and aggregate jail sentences of seven hundred years, demands which focused national and international attention on the proceedings. The accused endeavoured to politicise the six-day trial by dismissing their lawyers and reading out calls for Basque self-determination, demands punctuated with revolutionary songs. The military judges flourished their ceremonial sabres. Beyond the courtroom, there were riots in Basque cities that led to ugly clashes with the police, and ETA kidnapped Eugen Beihl, the honorary West German consul in San Sebastián. This was designed to influence the sentencing process after the tribunal had found all of the defendants guilty with the exception of Arruti. A few countries broke off diplomatic relations with Spain, while requests for clemency came from pope Paul VI and Jean-Paul Sartre. The painters Joan Miró and Antoni Tàpies joined three hundred Catalans in locking themselves in Montserrat's monastery by way of protest. Biehl was released four days before the sentences were read out. Six men were sentenced to death, and the rest to 341 years in prison. On 30 December Franco commuted the death sentences to thirty-year jail terms. Demonstrations held in support of his regime uncharacteristically inclined him to clemency over the New Year festive season, because ETA's activities were responsible for a resurgence of the extreme Spanish right within an otherwise senescent Francoism.

That ETA survived was due to the conviction of its military wing (ETA-m) that only sustained violence would stop the loss of members to other groupings on the left that occurred whenever they emphasised political struggle. ETA-m was massively strengthened when in 1970 five hundred members of the PNV youth wing Batasuna went over to ETA, providing the necessary manpower for renewed violence in 1972–5.

The military wing consisted of about fifty to sixty active terrorists organised in five- or six-man commandos, with a ruling directorate of fifteen, at the heart of which was a four-man Executive Committee. They attacked the businesses and homes of known right-wingers in San Sebastián and other towns in the Basque region. In a new development, they kidnapped an industrialist called Lorenzo Zabala Suinaga to influence the outcome of a labour dispute that had led him to dismiss 154 striking workers at his PreciControl factory. ETA demanded their reinstatement, compensation, wage rises and recognition of their union. These conditions were accepted and Zabala was released. Eleven men were arrested in connection with this affair, all aged between twenty-two and thirty-six, with occupations that ranged from butcher, painter and decorator, and truck driver to student. One of them was a Benedictine seminarian called Eustaquio Mendizábal Benito 'Txikia', who led ETA during this phase, organising its bank robberies and kidnappings. He was shot dead by the police when he met a fellow *etarra* at a railway station in April 1973.

In autumn 1972 ETA received a tip that it would be feasible to kidnap admiral Luis Carrero Blanco, Franco's right-hand man and chosen successor as the regime struggled to perpetuate itself. Carrero Blanco attended mass every morning in the same Madrid church, accompanied only by a driver and one bodyguard. The aim of the kidnap was to secure the release of 150 *etarras* in jail. Meanwhile, ETA decided to intervene in another labour dispute, while hoping to also get a ransom for the next kidnap victim. ETA alighted upon the Navarese industrialist Felipe Huarte, scion of a family worth an estimated US$100 million, whose network of factories was plagued by labour troubles. After paying strikers to ensure that a strike at the Torfinasa plant continued beyond its easy resolution, ETA entered Huarte's home on 16 January 1973, locking his three children and four servants in a cellar until Huarte himself and his wife returned. Huarte was spirited away to a cave near Mendizábal's home, and then to a safe house near San Sebastián. A ransom of the peseta equivalent of US$800,000 was paid out to intermediaries in Brussels and Paris. Next, ETA raided a powder magazine in Guipúzcoa, making off with 3,000 kilograms of explosive, some of which was used to kill Carrero Blanco after thoughts of kidnapping were abandoned in favour of assassination.

Four men masquerading as economists had rented an apartment from which they could observe his progress each morning to the Church of San Francisco de Borja, near the US embassy in Madrid. By this time Carrero Blanco had been promoted to head of government; his beefed-up security made kidnapping unfeasible. While other *etarras* were ordered to increase the ambient noise through arson and bomb attacks, four men in a commando named Txikia in honour of the slain Mendizábal moved to carry out Operation Ogro (Ogre). They rented a basement flat at 104 Calle de Claudio Coello, claiming to be sculptors. That explained the noise and dust as they tunnelled under the road, so as to form a tunnel shaped like the letter T. Seventy-five to eighty kilos of Goma 2 explosives were packed in the tunnel, directly below the place where Carrero Blanco would be driven after attending church. A car was double parked to slow his driver down at this deadly spot. On 20 December 1973, ETA commandos disguised as electricians working on cables detonated the bomb as Carrero Blanco's car slowed down. The blast hurled the car over the five-storey-high wall of the church, killing all three occupants instantaneously.

One unanticipated result of this high-profile assassination was that those members of ETA who favoured a more political approach split from ETA-m to join the myriad leftist sects that formed the coalition party Herri Batasuna, which in 1978 would paradoxically emerge as the political wing of the military faction, however much its members deny this fact. Apart from obvious signs that Franco's regime was in its death throes, across Europe these years saw the collapse of Salazar's New State in Portugal and the end of the Greek colonels. A bomb attack on Madrid's Café Rolando, which was favoured by members of the Bureau of Security opposite, which left nine dead and fifty-six wounded, led to the more politically motivated members of ETA seeking to re-establish tighter control over the fighting *etarras*. They wanted greater co-ordination between the military wing and a mass left-wing movement. When ETA-m rejected this strategy, the political–military wing became ETA p-m, which eventually spawned its own political party Basque Left or Euskadiko Ezkerra after Spain had reverted to democracy. Although the ultimate ideological goals of ETA p-m were more revolutionary, the radicality of ETA-m meant that by the early 1980s it had three times as many members, including anyone weary of the slower political–military route to revolution.

Government responses to ETA terrorism included draconian anti-terrorist laws, military tribunals and ubiquitous pairs of Guardia Civil on the lanes and streets. The latter received extra pay in lieu of danger money and generous leave to serve up north. There was also a darker extra-legal response, the first 'dirty war' waged by elements of the police and security services. As the Basques, and many democratic opponents of the regime, celebrated Carrero Blanco's death with the 'Waltz of Carrero', throwing caps, bread and girls in the air while singing 'He flew, he flew, Carrero flew', the latter's admirers struck back in April 1975 when the Mugalde bookshop in Bayonne was bombed by a mysterious group calling itself the Basque Spanish Battalion. A few further attacks followed, many marked by extraordinary incompetence, like the ex-OAS man who blew himself up in Biarritz as he prepared to kill an ETA leader. Following the death of Franco in November 1975, the country moved rapidly to democracy under king Juan Carlos and his moderate conservative prime minister Adolfo Suárez. The rule of law and multiparty democracy were established and the Basques were invited to accept a Statute of Autonomy, which after negotiations that resembled drawing teeth gave them their own regional government and more independence than they had ever enjoyed before. Every single imprisoned member of ETA was amnestied, although this was done on a slow, case-by-case basis, which aggravated the Basques. Instead of responding to this new climate, ETA increased its military operations. This requires explanation, because to outside eyes ETA seemed to have gained most of what it sought.

It is inordinately difficult for anyone who does not use a minority language to understand this mindset, though perhaps one would if one were Welsh or Flemish. The Basque nationalists regarded anything other than total independence as tantamount to linguacide, a view that took little or no account of their fellow Basques' voluntary immersion in a Spanish culture that flourished after the death of Franco, and of the fact that Basque-language literature hardly existed. Some 24 per cent of Basque voters rejected the new constitution in the December 1978 referendum, in contrast to 8 per cent of voters in the rest of Spain. Three months later 10 per cent of Basques voted for Herri Batasuna in elections for a parliament the party refused to recognise. In March 1980, Herri Batasuna's share of the poll rose to 16.5 per cent in the first elections to the autonomous Basque parliament. Support for extreme Basque nationalism has remained at around 12 per cent of the Basque population, with support strongest in Euskera-speaking areas. Forty per cent of ETA terrorists also come from Basque-speaking areas. It is worth stressing that the largest political party in Navarre, the Union of the People of Navarre (UPN) founded in 1977 to oppose Basque nationalism, wins about 37 per cent of the vote in elections, and that the majority of Basques too are opposed to ETA, which has murdered many Basque PNV politicians.[6]

As if to fuel Basque separatist paranoia, in July 1978 mystery gunmen shot up a car driven by former ETA leader Juan José Etxabe in France.

He was badly wounded, but his wife was killed by a hail of bullets that almost cut her in half. Another ETA figure, José Miguel Beñaran Ordeñana, was blown to pieces by a bomb in the sleepy French town of Anglet. Further attacks involved rape, before the female victims were shot, and the killing of two gypsy children when a bomb went off outside a playschool. The tactically driven failure of democratic governments to reform the army, intelligence and police services – which thereby acquiesced in Spain's transition to democracy – meant that parts of the state apparatus were still wedded to the old ways of killing and torture, using Argentine, French and Italian killers to do their dirty work.

In November 1980 about forty people were drinking inside in the Bar Hendayais just across the French border when two men entered and blasted them with a shotgun and bursts from a semi-automatic. Two customers were killed and nine others wounded. The gunmen drove off in a green Renault 18, which sped through the French border post and crashed on the Spanish side. Three men got out with their hands up, and were quickly surrounded by Guardia Civil and armed police. One of those detained proffered a telephone number in Madrid, claiming they were acting under official orders. A policeman then phoned Manuel Ballesteros, head of police intelligence and of the Unified Counter-Terrorist Command, and Spain's leading expert on ETA. He said: 'Let the matter drop. No one has seen or heard anything.' The men disappeared, their identities unknown, never to be seen or heard of again. Across the border, the French police were apoplectic with fury.

The Spanish police intelligence chief was covering for a dirty war waged by an assortment of ultra-right extremists. They included Fuerza Nueva (New Strength) and Guerrilleros de Cristo Rey (Warriors of Christ the King), a version of the Mexican Catholics who had fought the anti-clerical Reds in the 1930s. The personnel included polyglot rightist drifters who washed into Spain on the tide of lost causes: former members of the OAS, the Italian neo-Fascist Ordine Nuovo, the Alianza Anticomunista Argentina or Triple A, and sundry gangsters, fantasists and mercenaries, drawn to what under Franco had been a notorious haven for ex-Nazis and wartime European collaborators. Since this first dirty war has never been extensively investigated, the degree of government involvement remains unclear.

These killings were used as partial justification for ETA's own outrages. Most of their attacks consisted of individual assassinations or killings of small groups of Guardia Civil, who bore the brunt of their violence. In April 1976 one was imaginatively murdered by a booby-trapped Basque flag that electrocuted him. Targeting was extended to the Basque Ertzaintza police when they participated in counter-terrorism campaigns, and to prison officers too, for holding ETA prisoners in remote Spanish jails became a grievance. Erzaintza officers had to wear black balaclavas to disguise their identities. ETA also murdered several mayors and local government figures for alleged collaboration with the Spanish authorities. More senior army officers have died fighting ETA than in any Spanish war. High-value assassinations included several leading figures in the Spanish armed forces, including more than a dozen generals, the aim being to undermine the compromise the armed forces had made with a democratic Spain, a compromise that was rocked sideways in February 1981 when lieutenant-colonel Antonio Tejero and his comrades hijacked the Spanish parliament for a day. The army in particular has regarded itself as the constitutionally decreed defender of Spain's territorial integrity, rattling the sabre whenever concessions to separatist sentiment seemed to get out of hand. Industrialists were a favoured target for kidnappings (and kneecappings), either to raise funds or to curry favour with workers involved in labour disputes. More recently ETA has struck at judges, lawyers and journalists, including any of Basque descent brave enough to criticise these fanatical nationalists. I have had the experience of being interviewed on Spanish CNN, on a subject unconnected with terrorism, by an anchorman whose four police bodyguards waited outside the studio door. At night any decent Madrid restaurant frequented by journalists or politicians has bodyguards loitering along the pavements. Finally, ETA also sought to wreck one of Spain's major industries by leaving bombs at Barajas airport and in such tourist resorts as Benidorm and Marbella. Although ETA prides itself on its precision targeting, and use of prior telephoned warnings, several bomb attacks have resulted in significant innocent casualties. In one incident, a small child was killed after she kicked a bomb that had failed to go off under a passing Guardia Civil jeep. On 19 July 1987 an ETA bomb killed twenty-one people and injured forty-five in Barcelona's Hipercor shopping centre.

ETA also dealt out death in the course of its own faction feuds and against anyone rash enough to seek amnesty through the Spanish government's social reinsertion schemes. In April 1976 ETA p-m kidnapped Ángel Berazadi, another industrialist. He was killed on the orders of Miguel Ángel Apalategui Ayerbe 'Apala', the leader of ETA p-m's

Berezi Commando, who was on the run for killing a Guardia Civil. The murder of Berazadi collided with the strategy of ETA p-m's leader, Eduardo Moreno Bergareche 'Pertur', who at that time was exploring a ceasefire with Madrid in order to take ETA along a political course. On 23 July 1976 Pertur and Apala met in Saint-Jean-de-Luz on the French side of the frontier. Pertur agreed to talk without their respective body-guards and drove off with Apala in a car. He was never seen again. Apala claimed that after their discussion, Pertur had fallen into the hands of Spanish police who had killed him.

In June 1977 Apala was arrested by French police and held in pre-ventative detention in Marseilles as the French refused extradition requests from Spain. A month earlier his Berezi group had abducted the leading industrialist in Bilbao, Javier de Ybarra, demanding the release of twenty-four Basque prisoners, all but two of whom were freed. The arrest of Apala led ETA to up the stakes by demanding a ransom of one billion pesetas, or about US$14 million, a sum even the Ybarra family could not raise. On 20 June his family received a message that he was dead, with a map showing the location of his body, which was eventually found wrapped in a plastic sheet in the highlands of Barazar. To the accompaniment of mass demonstrations in the Basque provinces, French courts endeavoured to decide Apala's fate, a matter rendered emotive by his ongoing hunger strike. In September 1977 his lawyers secured bail for him; he never turned up for his first scheduled appear-ance at Marseilles police headquarters.

Those who decide to renounce ETA violence tend not to live long. María Dolores Katarain was an ETA commander, for, like Herri Batasuna, the organisation espouses several contemporary faiths. A pious Catholic, she had wanted to be a missionary in Latin America, until her fervour was re-routed to a political cause. At seventeen she joined ETA, acquiring the code-name 'Yoyes'. In 1976 she was forced to flee to France where doubts about the organisation she fought for began. She called the life of a terrorist 'this tomb, this living death that was beginning to suffocate me and in which I was physically dying'. In 1980 she moved to Mexico where she studied sociology and had a child called Akaitz. She decided to return to France in order to negotiate her route back to pre-terrorist normality in Spain. The Spanish authorities agreed not to pressure her into renouncing her political views, while ETA assured her she would be safe. In 1985 she returned to Ordizia, where against her will the Spanish government fêted her as a reformed terrorist.

Threatening graffiti appeared on walls. She did not help herself by publicly calling Herri Batasuna 'a puppet of [ETA's] Fascist militarism'. On 10 September 1986 Yoyes walked with her son to see the town fête. An ETA assassin stalked her: 'I went up to Yoyes and said, "Are you Yoyes?" She asked me who I was. I said, "I am from ETA and I have come to execute you." Immediately, I fired two shots from my pistol into her breast. She fell to the ground and I finished her off with another shot to the head.'[7]

In October 1982 ten million Spanish people voted for the Socialist PSOE in a heady dawn that brought many 1960s radicals to power under the charismatic prime minister (or president of the Council of Ministers), the lawyer Felipe González. Among his appointments was José Barrionuevo, who in 1969 had forsaken his Francoist past to join the PSOE. He had been Madrid's deputy mayor, responsible for the city's police. He became Spain's interior minister, retaining many of the intelligence and police officers left over from the Franco years. After ETA had murdered the general commanding the army's elite Brunete Division, the Socialists adumbrated Plan ZEN – the Spanish acronym for 'Special Northern Zone' – which perpetuated the Francoist policy of saturating the Basque country with intrusive policing. This availed them little because ETA could fall back on its cross-border sanctuary in France.

Spanish efforts to get the French to crack down on ETA's organisation failed because the French did not realise that the Socialists were conceding many Basque nationalist demands; the French also clung to a romantic view of political refugees to compensate for their own dubious policies in the 1930s and 1940s. This led senior elements in González's government, which many suspect included the prime minister himself, to launch a second dirty war, which had commenced even before the murder squad GAL was formed when two young ETA members, Joxean Lasa and Joxi Zabala, the latter on the run in France with his friend after a bank raid, vanished in autumn 1983. Although the police did not realise it at the time, their bones turned up on Alicante's coast two years later when they were disturbed by a dog. As it would transpire much later, they had been abducted in Bayonne by Guardia Civil and then held in a disused palace assigned to the civil governor and the Ministry of the Interior. There they had been repeatedly tortured before being shot in the back of the neck. A little after their disappearance, an ETA leader riding a scooter in Hendaye was rammed by a Ford Talbot that loomed into view behind him. Four men put a hood on his head and tried to drag him into the boot of the car. French police stumbled on this attempted abduction and found themselves arresting a police inspector and a captain and two sergeants from Spain's crack anti-terrorism unit. They claimed the incident had been a traffic accident. Later their story shifted to wanting to have a word with their victim. Released on bail, they disappeared back to Spain.

The formation responsible for these nefarious activities was called Grupos Antiterroristas de Liberacíon or GAL, in English Anti-Terrorist Liberation Groups. Its bombers, kidnappers and killers were an idiosyncratic assortment of boxers, publicans, Marseilles gangsters, mercenaries and a lady so short that the recoil from the shotguns and rifles she used to kill nine people with routinely almost knocked her flat. Her nickname was 'the Black Lady', or 'the Blonde Assassin' when she donned a platinum-blonde wig. Unlike the ideological neo-Fascists who ran the first dirty war, these individuals worked like bounty hunters for money. That they had nicknames like 'the Godfather' tells one about the general milieu. Their strategy did not baulk at the occasional collateral French Basque casualty since, as GAL correctly anticipated, in September 1984 this prompted the French to resort to existing national security laws that enabled them to deport ETA terrorists to remote third countries such as Panama or Togo that were paid to receive them. Transcripts of conversations recorded by Spain's intelligence services reveal that, at the time GAL was being mooted, some of the lower-ranking operators had more doubts than their chiefs. A Guardia Civil sergeant Pedro Gómez Nieto said to his chief colonel Enrique Rodríguez Galindo:

> Let's think this through, *mi comandante*: What guarantees do we have that this is really worth doing? That is to say, *mi comandante*, we go there, we take someone out. That is the least of it, you know what we gain from that. You already know that one thing we may achieve is that there will be 10 new members who join ETA as a result of this action. Have you thought about the kind of publicity this will get? What kind of cover-up line are we going to give to the media?

As if to illustrate this objection, on 20 November 1984 two gunmen disguised as gypsies walked into the Bilbao clinic of Santiago Brouard, who was treating a small girl while her parents looked on. In addition to being a much loved paediatrician, 'Uncle Santi' was a leading light of

Herri Batasuna, which he represented in the Basque parliament. The gunmen shot him five times in the head and once in the hand as he tried to defend himself in the only attack GAL conducted on Spanish soil. Apart from the nurse, who recalled bewigged gypsies pushing past her, the parents were the only witnesses, but they failed to appear when the killers were tried. There had been a car accident in which the mother and daughter had been killed; the husband had been blinded. ETA gunmen ambushed a general whose brother had instituted the social reinsertion programme designed to deradicalise ETA supporters. An estimated half a million people turned out for Brouard's funeral. GAL killers had a similar regard for collateral casualties to that of ETA itself. When in February 1985 they attacked the Batxoki bar in Petit Bayonne, girls aged three and five were among those wounded, by gunmen who had expressed their concern about the children's presence, but had been expressly ordered by their chief to disregard it. Exactly a year later GAL assassins who had mounted an ambush on a remote road near Bidarray contrived to kill a sixty-year-old shepherd and a sixteen-year-old Parisian holidaymaker who had been desperate to see some newborn lambs while she stayed in her parents' caravan. The tough interior minister Charles Pasqua in Jacques Chirac's new administration decided to terrorise the terrorists. One ETA leader with refugee status was deported to Algeria, while – making use of a 1945 edict – twenty-six ETA activists were handed directly to Spain.

In addition to making little or no impact on ETA atrocities, which averaged forty deaths a year throughout the 1980s, revelations by investigative journalists and magistrates into the GAL death squads prompted the Socialist government to use every trick in the book to frustrate them in one of the most unedifying and protracted cover-ups in modern European history. The fashionably long-haired idealists of the 1960s had mutated, during what would be fourteen years in power, into a corrupt clique that made policy around a private bar in the Moncloa palace in the company of 'los beautiful', that is their intimate circle of wealthy bankers, while less savoury figures shot at children and shepherds in the Pays Basque.

Dogged magistrates like Baltasar Garzón followed the money trail, discovering 'reserved funds' attached to the Ministry of Interior which were being used to pay for GAL's activities. Individual police officers, like superintendent Amedo, had bank accounts containing exorbitant sums; Amedo's held twenty-seven million pesetas when his net annual salary was just under two million, a disparity that seemed to explain his sybaritic lifestyle. The Socialists used every available method to obstruct investigations into GAL murders – notably withholding evidence and rallying around the accused to prevent them turning state's witness – while smearing journalists, lawyers and the conservative opposition for pursuing this. The belligerently porcine González himself insisted that 'no one will succeed in demonstrating' links between GAL and the state, while simultaneously claiming that 'The rule of law is defended in the courts, and in the salons, but also in the sewers,' a devious way of saying that GAL's actions were justified. Apparently preferring Hobbes to Montesquieu, González would subsequently claim that the judiciary had become over-mighty vis-à-vis the elected executive. Another, disgraceful form of defence was to claim that 'everybody else does it'. González's wife, the noted democrat and feminist Carmen Romero, claimed: 'Why should we lose sleep because of a phenomenon which has happened in Spain like it happened in France, in Germany, in all democratic countries? Phenomena of dirty tricks, settling of accounts, are normal in very many countries.' This was said in the context of José Barrionuevo, her husband's former interior minister, being jailed for ten years for his involvement with GAL, following several very senior police figures into prison.[8]

ETA atrocities ran parallel with these revelations. Brief ceasefires in the late 1980s came to nothing, with ETA complaining about the pace of negotiations. In 1992 it launched its local version of the Palestinian Intifada – the *kale borroka* or street struggle – in which groups of youths and minors vandalised buses, street lamps, ATMs, telephone kiosks and rubbish bins, while beating up anyone carrying a Spanish newspaper. This was designed to increase the flow of recruits who lacked their grandparents' experiences of being beaten up by Guardia Civil. Three years later ETA put forward a 'Democratic Alternative' in which it offered a cessation of violence in return for Madrid recognising the sovereignty of the Basque people over 'their' territory, the right to self-determination, and the release of all ETA prisoners. This was rejected. That year, ETA narrowly failed to kill the opposition leader, José María Aznar, with a car bomb, making an abortive attempt on the life of king Juan Carlos too. In July 1997, by which time Aznar was prime minister, ETA kidnapped a People's Party deputy, Miguel Ángel Blanco, ordering the government to relocate all ETA prisoners within forty-eight hours. He was shot dead when the government did not respond. Six million people demonstrated throughout Spain – including the Basque country – to secure his release, with many more coming on to the streets to scream 'Assassins!' after Blanco had been killed. In 1998 ETA declared a unilateral ceasefire, so as to negotiate with Aznar's government, a ceasefire the terrorists broke in 2000, and which they may only have called so as to regroup and rearm. On 6 November 2001 sixty-five people were hurt by a car bomb in Madrid, with further attacks on football stadiums and tourist resorts. The events of 9/11 led to the banning of Herri Batasuna and the nationalist youth group Jarrai. Spanish police have thwarted several ETA attacks – not least by detecting an enormous truck bomb by a motorway. Another 'permanent' ceasefire declared on 22 March 2006 was called off on 5 June the following year. To herald this development ETA killed two Ecuadorean immigrants in December 2006 as they napped in a car at Barajas airport when ETA collapsed a car park with a bomb. ETA apologised for what it called these 'collateral casualties'.

ETA is engaged in armed struggle to this day. It claims that it has been cheated of the further possibilities allegedly promised when the Basques achieved autonomy. It further claims that many of the things the Basques were granted were never implemented. Relatives of ETA prisoners are aggrieved that they have to make a two-thousand-kilometre round trip on a coach for each forty-minute visit to their fathers or husbands in remote Huelva. People suspected of ETA involvement claim they have been beaten, given electric shocks or threatened with rape with a vibrator, although forensic physicians dispute such claims. What is not in dispute is that ETA has waded sufficiently far out into a river of blood that it cannot psychologically turn back. To do so would dishonour so many of its own glorious dead. Successive Spanish governments have resisted talks with ETA, and eventually banned Herri Batasuna, which meant that a few Basque towns were disfranchised. That in turn meant that supposedly democratic nationalist politicians, beyond Batasuna, emitted ambiguous responses to ETA violence sufficient to justify it. At present, ETA is attempting to extort immense sums of four hundred thousand euros from each of the two thousand Basque businesses it has sent threatening letters to. The situation is so grave and complex that the Northern Irish Redemptorist priest Alex Reid is among those clerics trying to resolve it. There is a wealth of grim experience there too.[9]

II STATES OF SIEGE

The Northern Irish countryside is as lushly green as the Basque country, but the skies tend to be grey and louring rather than blue. The cities are less elegant, consisting at the centre of rows of red-brick terraces of two-up-and-two-down houses, and vast housing estates which feel very grim under the glare of the sodium lights that make so many British cities seem like they have been drowned in a fizzy drink at night. Roman Catholics in Northern Ireland had core political and socio-economic rights, including the vote at general elections, a free press, and levels of state welfare that did not exist in the Irish Republic. This was one of the reasons why the Republic's claims to the North remained largely rhetorical – albeit asserted in its constitution – since picking up the social security tab north of the border would have bankrupted an Eire to which EEC structural subsidies were as yet a dream unfulfilled. Take a few vital statistics.

Although Northern Ireland had half the population of the Republic, in 1964 it had ninety-five thousand children in secondary schools, as opposed to eighty-five thousand in Eire. Northern Ireland's schools were and are some of the best in the United Kingdom. Using contemporary British decimal coin rather than historic shillings, in 1963 the Republic spent 85p per head on university education; the equivalent sum for Northern Ireland was £2.44. In 1969 an unemployed man in Northern Ireland received £4.50 a week while his unemployed opposite number in the South got £3.25; the same disparity existed for a widow's weekly pension in both countries too. Northern Ireland was not South Africa or the US Deep South. Except for a few diehard bigots there were no impediments to social (or sexual) intercourse between Catholics and Protestants in Northern Ireland. Protestant friends of mine from Dungannon say that they often dated Catholic girls, who tended to be more feminine than the butch Unionists. Unlike the US Deep South, they could do this without fear of being lynched. There was another distinction. African-Americans marched for equal rights, not to abolish the Union, which is what many Irish republican civil rights activists wanted.[10]

However, in some parts of Northern Ireland both access to social housing and control of local government were blatantly gerrymandered. In narrowly Protestant-dominated Dungannon, for example, no

Catholics were offered a permanent council house for nearly a quarter of a century. There was also the curious way in which 911,940 registered electors entitled to vote for the provincial parliament at Stormont became 658,778 voters in local government elections. Although Londonderry was 60 per cent Catholic, Unionists had a permanent majority of 12 : 8 on the city council. This was achieved by excluding Catholic lodgers and subtenants from a voting system that favoured resident occupiers, while concentrating ten thousand Catholic voters in one ward so as to guarantee a Unionist majority in the other two.

Protestants were not to blame if it proved impossible to raise the numbers of Catholics in the Royal Ulster Constabulary (RUC) from 11 per cent so as match those from Church of Ireland or Presbyterian backgrounds. After all, if you contest the legitimacy of a state, only an act of monumental hypocrisy would allow you to serve it. Catholics were most likely to be found in unskilled employment, heavily dependent upon catching a foreman's or gang-master's unprejudiced eye, while Protestants had solid skilled trades in engineering and shipbuilding. A father's membership of a lodge belonging to the quasi-masonic Orange Order would help if a boy was seeking an apprenticeship in the shipyards of Harland and Wolff, whose towering yellow cranes dominate the Belfast skyline. Catholics were 31 per cent of the economically active population, but only 6 per cent of mechanical engineers, 8 per cent of university teachers, 9 per cent of senior local government bureaucrats and so on. The one area they were not discriminated against was access to higher education, for by 1971 Catholics were 32 per cent of students at the prestigious Queen's University in Belfast. One of the most memorable aspects of these years was the emergence of a highly articulate generation of Catholic civil rights leaders, such as Bernadette Devlin and John Hume.

But that was a mixed blessing if graduate access to professions was blocked by opaque forces that noted the Christian name Bernadette, Brendan, Finbar, Liam, Malachi or Mary, a Falls Road address, a school called Blessed this or Sacred that, and hair that was black rather than ginger, although one prominent PIRA (Provisional IRA) Belfast leader is inevitably nicknamed 'Ginger' for just this reason.[11] These details marked one out as a 'Croppie', 'Fenian' or 'Taig', this last being the short form for the Gaelic equivalent of Timothy. Even reformist measures seemed always to tilt to one side of the sectarian divide. When a decision was made to establish a new university at Coleraine, this was situated within a predominantly Protestant area, as was a new town provocatively called Craigavon (after James Craig, the Unionist politician ennobled as Lord Craigavon). There was a further fact that is often lost sight of by those inclined always to see one underdog. When new tower blocks went up in predominantly Catholic areas in the 1960s, these seemed luxurious to Protestants living in rat-infested terraced housing where the walls felt damp to the touch. A Protestant recalled what life was like:

> I was from very much a working-class background. We had two small rooms downstairs, two bedrooms upstairs, no hot running water and the old outside toilet. We lived in small, steep streets with terraced houses. You almost felt that if you took the bottom one away, all the rest would collapse like a deck of cards. Not only was I not a first-class citizen, I remember the absolute sense of indignation and outrage whenever I was accused of being one. There was this explicit inference to Catholics being second-class citizens and therefore this inference that I was in some way depriving them of their rights. I can distinctly recall, even as a sixteen-year-old, looking round my humble surroundings at home and saying, 'Well, if this is second-class citizenship, I really wouldn't want to meet the third-class citizens.'[12]

For a very brief moment in the early 1960s it seemed as if change would confound Churchill's famous observation about the grim permanence of this sectarian quarrel. A dash of 1960s optimism characterised the Northern Ireland premiership of Terence O'Neill, acting almost contrary to type. O'Neill had little alternative to modernising the economy since Ulster's linen and shipbuilding industries were in steep decline, creating unemployment rates twice those of the mainland UK. One method was to attract outside investment, luring such firms as Grundig, Goodyear and Michelin, although new manufacturing capacity never matched the closure of the old firms. Another was to end the cold war between Dublin and Belfast, which had ensured that the prime ministers of Northern Ireland and the Irish taoiseach had not met since the 1920s, although there were lesser official contacts on the stands of rugby matches. O'Neill was also the first Unionist premier to visit Catholic schools or to shake hands with nuns. This was revolutionary, since one of his august predecessors had boasted that he had never knowingly employed a Roman Catholic.

In 1965 taoiseach Sean Lemass visited Northern Ireland, with O'Neill making two reverse trips. These developments appalled a thrusting evangelical preacher called Ian Paisley who shouted 'NO MASS, LEMASS!' Paisley was the US-educated moderator of his own Free Presbyterian Church; he became first minister of Northern Ireland in May 2007 at the age of eighty-one . A lumbering charismatic demagogue with a gift for exploiting the bad publicity of an almost entirely hostile media, Paisley articulated a beleaguered brand of Unionist sentiment no longer encompassed by the staid Unionist Party. Working-class Protestants were losing their ingrained deference to the Unionist ruling classes whom Paisley dismissed as 'the fur-coat brigade' living in posh suburbs or country houses.[13]

Paisley spoke for the inner-city Protestant working class and for Protestant farmers in the province's rural sectarian hotspots. These people had a visceral fear of Catholicism, and specifically of the wily ways of the Roman Catholic Church, for after all, through ethnic cleansing and regulations on mixed marriages, Protestantism had been virtually extinguished in the South within living memory. It was obligatory in Eire to have Gaelic to enter state employment, even though few Protestants knew it. Catholic prohibitions on abortion and contraception also made the South seem benighted to those who saw these things as part of modernity. When northern Protestants sang 'Our Fathers knew the Rome of old and evil is thy name', they meant it. Protestants felt besieged, a feeling that came easily to people for whom king James II's siege of Londonderry was part of their historical identity. They lived in Derry City, parading around the fortified walls every August, so as to look down on the majority Catholic population in the extramural slums of the Bogside below. On vast bonfires they burned effigies of the pope; as someone said, Protestants were those who burned wood. Their basic foundation myth was that Ireland had been an undeveloped bog inhabited by feckless idiots until the forces of civilisation arrived in the North.[14]

In 1964 Paisley indirectly provoked the worst rioting in Northern Ireland when he insisted that an RUC that was 89 per cent Protestant enforce the 1954 Flags and Emblems Act by removing an Irish tricolour from republican headquarters in the Catholic Falls Road district of Belfast. Flying that flag, with its faux-ecumenical incorporation of an orange that Catholics insisted was yellow, was an assertion of Catholics 'in' Northern Ireland rather than of Catholics 'of' Northern Ireland.

Catholics did not fear Protestants for reasons of their religion; in their eyes the English Reformation was a theological fix-up to sanction a royal divorce. Rather they feared the prosperity and the political power of Protestants as manifested in the Stormont regime in Ulster, behind whose Unionist MPs lurked the Orange Order, and the raw bigotry that they exclusively attributed to their Protestant neighbours. This was at its most elementally abrasive in the bonfire and marching season of July and August. Youngsters spent weeks collecting wooden pallets and rubber tyres for huge fires, upon which perched effigies of the pope or nationalist MP Gerry Fitt. Orangemen thumped giant Lambeg drums to the jaunty tune of 'The Sash My Father Wore' as their sergeant-majors launched their staffs improbably high in the air, the 'catch-up' marked by a hip-shaking swagger. The piercing pipes gave aggressive menace to songs like 'We are, we are, we are the Billy Boys / We are, we are, we are the Billy Boys / Up to our necks in Fenian blood.' Some commentators find all this quaintly stirring; I find it vaguely nauseating in its abridgement of British values to those of a tribe.[15]

Beyond what was legal, and all this was, darker forces began to stir when in 1966 a small group calling itself the Ulster Volunteer Force or UVF, based in the backstreet bars of the mainly Protestant Shankill Road, decided to attack a quiescent IRA. However, unlike policemen or soldiers, the IRA were not so easy to identify, so the UVF made do with Catholics in general – a policy of brazen casualness. They murdered a seventy-seven-year-old Protestant widow in a firebomb attack on a neighbouring Catholic drink store; a drunken Catholic man wandering up the Falls Road shouting 'Up the Republic, up the rebels!'; and a young Catholic hotel barman who went to a late-night drinking den with his friends and was shot dead when UVF members marked them as supporters of the IRA after mishearing snippets of their conversation.[16]

Inspired by the example of civil rights activists elsewhere, a Northern Ireland Civil Rights Association was formed in January 1967. A highly articulate new generation of Catholic leaders came to the fore. Protestants secretly envied their articulacy, while resenting them as 'uppity' Fenians and Taigs. The movement also included a number of IRA figures, who in search of a pie for their fingers saw it as another route to realising their republican agenda. In no sense were they the decisive or directing hand behind a movement that was too inchoate to control and which was part of a global generational revolt in the 1960s. The extreme-left students who were prominent in the movement consciously sought to provoke what they could characterise as a Fascist reaction from the 'Orange Tories', the necessary prelude to a full-scale revolution. Instead they were engulfed by a sectarian civil war as old monsters surfaced from the sea deeps.[17]

Along with its calls for an end to discrimination by the police or in public housing, the movement crystallised around the slogan 'one man, one vote' in protest against the disqualification of mainly Catholic lodgers, subtenants and young people living at home from voting in local government elections. As the wise Conor Cruise O'Brien once wrote, there was something of Antigone provoking Creon about such civil rights starlets as Bernadette Devlin, known to critics as a three parts innocent abroad. The civil rights movement borrowed the US tactic of marches to the sound of 'We Shall Overcome', in a sectarian context with a very developed sense of 'our' territory. Orange marches were an assertion of dominance; therefore, whatever the civil rights rhetoric, predominantly Catholic marches must be assertions of Roman dominance too. Left-wing activists deliberately selected routes to maximise the likelihood of trouble.

A march that took place despite being prohibited in Londonderry in October 1968 resulted in a police riot which put more than seventy people in hospital. As the young Max Hastings reported at the time, with their revolvers, Sten-guns, armoured water wagons and tear gas, the RUC was not in the mould of Dixon of Dock Green, the avuncular star of a 1960s TV London police drama. There were also the part-time Special Constables or B Specials, that is another eight thousand Protestants armed with guns. Close-up television footage showed a senior RUC officer bludgeoning demonstrators, among them three Labour MPs, one of whom, Gerry Fitt, was soon covered in blood from a head wound.[18] How that situation was engineered for the cameras probably warrants notice. In January 1969 a radical wing of the civil rights movement, called People's Democracy, principally associated with Bernadette Devlin and Eamonn McCann, ignored mainstream advice and marched from Belfast to Londonderry, a route that took them through some heavily Protestant villages. At Burntollet Bridge in rural County Londonderry the marchers were ambushed by loyalists, as the RUC appeared to stand by idly, watching Protestants – including off-duty police officers – smashing up Catholics. The civil rights marchers may have called for civil rights and socialism (while shouting 'Get the Protestants!' despite themselves) but the effect of their actions was to spark deep-seated ethno-nationalist sectarian hatreds.[19]

In the interests of a quiet life, the British had enabled the Unionists to dominate Ulster for fifty years, and the latter had manifestly failed to improve the lives of the minority population. Having alienated them, they were losing working-class Protestant support to self-styled loyalist groupings, that is people whose primary attachment was Ulster itself rather than the United Kingdom. The queen-on-the-wall, red-white-and-blue ultra-Britishness of the Unionists seemed alien to an English majority, beyond a few old biddies in London's East End, for whom demonstrative patriotism is something that Americans and foreigners do. Both major British parties regarded the louder sort of Unionist as embarrassing parodies of their former Victorian selves, although that feeling was stronger among Conservatives than among Labour politicians who had no historic links with Unionism. Labour ministers had no special regard for the upper-class former army officers of the Unionist Party, who insisted on being called 'captain' this or 'major' that more than a decade after the war. Scenes of violence led prime minister Harold Wilson and home secretary James Callaghan to use threats to curtail transferred subsidies to Northern Ireland to force O'Neill to accelerate the pace of reform. The trouble was that 'in a rising market, Unionism always tried, unsuccessfully, to buy reform at last year's prices', offering belated compromises to people whose demands had already moved on. O'Neill was also subjected to a devious campaign of sabotage conducted by the UVF but blamed on the IRA. A homosexual paedophile, William McGrath, and a gay Protestant terrorist, John MacKeague, bombed Belfast's electricity grid and water infrastructure. These attacks were blamed on the IRA so that it would seem that O'Neill's putative liberalism had encouraged them. Although O'Neill had finally accepted 'one man, one vote', in April 1969 he resigned his post in favour of his kinsman, the remarkably similar James Chichester-Clark. In a televised address, O'Neill said: 'For too long we have been torn and divided. Ours is called a Christian country. We could have enriched our politics with our Christianity; but far too often we have debased our Christianity with our politics. We seem to have forgotten that love of neighbour stands beside love of God as a fundamental principle of our religion.'[20]

By August, the height of the local summer marching season, an Apprentice Boys' parade in Londonderry was stoned by Catholic youths after a few coins had flown the other way. The Catholics were attacked by the RUC and Protestant rioters who followed wherever the police opened up a path for them with their batons, tear gas and water cannons. Unhelpfully, the Irish taoiseach, Jack Lynch, set up field hospitals in border areas of the Republic while calling for UN intervention to protect Catholics. Loose talk in Dublin of despatching the Irish army to protect Catholics, at a time when it had a mere 11,500 troops, merely raised Unionist hackles. The rioting spread from Londonderry to Belfast, where the first shots were fired. Near Divis Flats on the Falls Road, rioting youths hurled petrol bombs at the RUC; as night fell, there was the periodic crack and muzzle flash of a sniper as the IRA disinterred ancient guns from attics and floorboards.

The RUC responded by wildly strafing the flats with .30 Browning machine guns mounted on Shorland armoured cars. Patrick Rooney, a nine-year-old Catholic boy, had half of his head blown off when a round flew into his bedroom. Eight people were killed and 750 injured, while some 180 homes were gutted by fire. Eighteen hundred families were forced to flee their homes, like refugees from a war zone. With a total strength of 3,200, the RUC was exhausted and depleted by weeks of dealing with mob violence; this forced Chichester-Clark to ask Wilson to despatch the British army. By the end of August there were six thousand troops on the streets. They came equipped with signs to deter rioters written in Arabic since their last posting had been in Aden. The locals found the accents of Birmingham, East London, Glasgow and Newcastle challenging, just as the soldiers had to get used to 'oul' for 'old' and 'youse' as a plural 'you'. Operation Banner had commenced, with troop numbers rising to over twenty-five thousand by 1972, and enduring until August 2007.

The soldiers were enthusiastically welcomed in the Catholic Bogside, where locals urged them to shoot Protestants throwing petrol bombs, saying 'If you won't use the guns, give them to us who will.'[21] James Callaghan was also popular when he arrived to boss posh Unionist politicians around with the commanding bluntness of a former navy petty officer turned senior cabinet minister. 'Sunny Jim' had a steely interior behind the amiable disposition. But scenes of relieved Catholic housewives inundating British squaddies with tea did not conceal a major error of policy. For, in an act almost guaranteed to confuse the army with the local Unionist agenda, Stormont was perpetuated, as if it was under the protection of British soldiers. British officials conducted separate inquiries into the origins of these disturbances and the conduct of the RUC and B Specials. The latter were abolished and a new, smaller

Ulster Defence Regiment or UDR placed under army control. A senior policeman from London was brought in to reform the RUC. This triggered rioting in the loyalist Shankill Road and the first death of a policeman. A UVF member blew himself up near an electricity pylon in Donegal.

One final aspect of these events was the emergence of the Provisional IRA. The southern-led IRA had been conspicuously slow to fulfil its traditional role of defender of the northern Catholic community in crisis. Contemptuous graffiti reading 'IRA = I ran away' appeared in Catholic ghettos. The southern Marxist leadership was obsessed with the surreal goal of uniting the Catholic and Protestant working classes in the name of socialism. This theoretical gobbledygook led to the breakaway of republican traditionalists in the Provisional IRA and Provisional Sinn Féin on a platform of 'combined defence and retaliation'. Its leader was John Stephenson, or as he preferred Séan MacStiofáin, a forty-year-old with an English father who had been brought up in south London. He was a rabid anti-Communist and a devotee of the Irish language, all reflective of the fanaticism of a convert. His Catholicism was so orthodox that he even refused to import rubber condoms into the Republic for PIRA to test the utility of acid bomb fuses. MacStiofáin was joined by two schoolteachers: the first president of Provisional Sinn Féin, Ruarí O Brádaigh, and Dáithí Ó Conaill (or Dave O'Connell), the first PIRA quartermaster-general. Leo Martin, Joe Cahill and Billy McKee from Belfast also joined the PIRA Army Council, giving the lie to the claim that Gerry Adams and his Young Turk northern friends dramatically wrested control away from southerners in the late 1970s. The Official IRA declared a ceasefire, and were thence known as 'Stickies'.

At the time there were about forty to sixty IRA men in Belfast, a limitation that favoured the rise of an aggressive new generation of local leaders, notably Gerry Adams, who in 1969 became the city's PIRA commander, while his father, mother and siblings (with the exception of a sister) came across too. He married, although he would never allow his wife to engage with the PIRA women's formation. His memoirs rather too vividly conjure up the world of the Falls Road, with its street characters, urchin gangs, wakes, superstitions and belief in fairies.[22] There was, and is, no record that Adams had ever fired a gun or planted a bomb in his life. His talents lay elsewhere. Under the general leadership of Joe Cahill and then Seamus Twomey, Adams was second in command of the Belfast PIRA, with Ivor Bell and Brendan Hughes as his deputies.

The Provisionals gradually established an underground version of martial law within Catholic ghettos from which the police had withdrawn while the army patrolled the perimeters beyond. The Provisional IRA's limited platform, with socialism shorn of Marxism, would appeal to supporters in the USA. The most atavistic republicanism one can encounter is that of Irish-America, not just that of the Boston or New York Ancient Order of Hibernians, but of billionaires rich enough to donate a house in Palm Springs for charity. For the next thirty years there would be plenty of defence and retaliation, and much offence too, for in January 1970 the PIRA Army Council declared an all-out attack on the 'British occupation system'.[23]

In this they were aided and abetted by prominent members of Dublin's Fianna Fáil cabinet which surreptitiously colluded with the Irish intelligence service in supplying the PIRA with combat weaponry, partly so as to diminish the challenge from the Marxist Official IRA in the South by deflecting armed republicanism north. Between 20 August and 2 March 1970, a total of £100,000 of Irish public money was relayed via bank accounts in Dublin and Clones to Belfast, from where some of it went back to other Dublin accounts to be used to purchase arms.

Although key UVF leaders like Gusty Spence were in jail for the murder of Peter Ward, a much larger pool of potential loyalist terrorists was created as Protestants formed local defence associations to protect themselves from IRA or sectarian Catholic attack. Men dressed in camouflage jackets, bush caps and face masks, and armed with baseball bats and clubs, patrolled Protestant areas. One of these groups, the Shankill Defence Association, formed a clandestine elite called the Red Hand Commandos, which was closely linked to the UVF.

In June 1970 republicans killed two Protestants in the Catholic Short Strand enclave of east Belfast, action which led the army to strike against them. Without military intelligence structures in place, the army was fatefully reliant upon the RUC's idiosyncratic identification of republican terrorists, which in turn meant that many innocent people had the experience of soldiers smashing through their front doors, ripping up floorboards or tearing the doors from cupboards, and roughly handling many of those they arrested. In July 1970 troops imposed a curfew on twenty thousand people living in the lower Falls Road, and shot dead three men who breached it, while running over a fourth with an armoured vehicle. The experience of being humiliated by British troops became one of the main recruiting mechanisms for the

PIRA, as did the decision – at the prompting of prime minister Brian Faulkner – on 9 August 1971 to introduce internment for suspected terrorists. This was decided after five engineers had been killed by an IRA bomb while servicing a BBC transmitter, and three off-duty Scottish soldiers – one aged seventeen, his brother a year older – had been lured to a remote spot where while relieving themselves they were shot at close range by PIRA assassins.[24] Ironically, the British general officer commanding Northern Ireland, lieutenant-general Harry Tuzo, was opposed to internment, not least because if it was not simultaneously introduced in the Republic it would be hopelessly ineffective. Thousands of people were picked up under Operation Demetrius. Some of them had not fought for the IRA since the Easter Rising of 1916. It was revealing that, of the 1,590 interned between 9 August and 15 December 1971, only eighteen were eventually charged with criminal offences. It was revealing too that whereas there had been twenty-five deaths in the six months before the introduction of internment, in the following six months the IRA killed 185 people. Some detainees were subjected to rough treatment, or to psychological tortures involving sensory deprivation and white noise. Long-term internees were held at a camp on the disused RAF base at Long Kesh. With its Nissen huts and barbed-wire fences this looked like a Second World War German prison-of-war camp; that was exactly how its terrorist inmates wanted to see it. On the continent, idiot Belgian socialists compared Long Kesh with Dachau in newspaper images one can now see displayed in Belfast's Linen Hall Library of the Troubles.[25] In March 1976 the camp was renamed the Maze prison, and the Nissen huts were replaced by the H-Blocks – reforms which did nothing to lessen the republican propaganda.

Meanwhile, on 15 May 1971 some three hundred members of the Protestant defence associations met in a Belfast school to form an Ulster Defence Association or UDA. Like the PIRA, this had a military structure borrowed from the British army – brigades, battalions, companies, platoons and sections. Eventually some thirty to fifty thousand men joined this legal organisation, which in early 1973 spawned a much more select terrorist group called the Ulster Freedom Fighters or UFF. In July 1972, Gusty Spence was allowed out of Crumlin Road jail for a couple of days to attend his daughter's wedding. He gave his word he would return. Technically Spence honoured this vow by arranging his own kidnapping by the UVF, action that afforded the Orange Pimpernel, as he became known, four months to reorganise the UVF while acquiring arms through raids on police and Territorial Army bases. Many of these men were motivated by a raging desire for revenge after incidents like the 29 September 1971 PIRA bombing of the Shankill Road's Four Step Inn, which led to two deaths and many injured. Fifty thousand people attended the funerals. The PIRA leader, Séan MacStiofáin, had decided to indulge in indiscriminate sectarian murder, although that is not how he would describe it.

Britain had no economic interest in Northern Ireland, and scarcely feared that the severely Catholic South would become another Cuba were it not for the Protestant presence in the North. Nor did the army derive any advantage in terms of training from having its men scuttling along Londonderry back alleys, at a time when the main war it might have to fight was against Soviet tanks on the plains of north Germany. Au fond, Britain was fighting for the territorial integrity of its own domestic empire, for the rule of law against an armed minority, and because ministers believed that 'terrorism, by its very nature, represents a relapse into barbarism and savagery that unites the entire civilised world in determined and unquenchable opposition'.

Policy had to be made against a backdrop of worsening violence. In 1971 a total of 180 people were killed in Northern Ireland, the majority victims of the PIRA. The twenty-nine killed by British troops proved contentious, since some of the victims were teenaged rioters, whom the army routinely claimed had possessed firearms. PIRA attacks against policemen who were invariably Protestant inevitably fuelled a desire for revenge on the other side. The UVF carried out its most deadly attack in December 1971 when a fifty-pound gelignite device demolished McGurk's bar in north Belfast killing fifteen Catholics. They included Mrs Philomena McGurk and the couple's fourteen-year-old daughter Maria, and a thirteen-year-old boy friendly with the McGurks who happened to be visiting them in the flat above the bar. The army endeavoured to lay the blame on the PIRA by claiming that the bomb was being primed inside when it went off. A week later the PIRA struck back, bombing the Balmoral Furnishing Company on the Shankill Road, murdering four shoppers, or rather two adults, two-year-old Tracey Munn and her adopted brother, seventeen-month-old Colin Munn, who were crushed when a wall collapsed on their pram. One wonders what political cause explains that.

Five hundred people died in 1972, the nadir of the Troubles as a whole. The year began inauspiciously with Ireland's Second Blood Sunday. On

30 January thirteen unarmed men were shot dead by soldiers of the Parachute Regiment despatched to contain the violent aftermath of a civil rights rally in Londonderry. The army leadership was exasperated by endless rioting, while mindful that PIRA snipers could be operating within peaceful crowds participating in an illegal demonstration. Claiming they had been fired on, soldiers ran amok, it being questionable why the most battle-hardened regiment in the British army should have been policing an illegal civilian demonstration in the first place. No weapons were found on or near any of those killed. After a contemporary judicial inquiry, widely deemed to have been a whitewash, a further (pointless) inquiry continues to this day, the only beneficiaries being the lawyers who have racked up costs totalling £200 million in a process that many regard as an obscene waste of public money solely designed to placate republicans.

In Dublin an angry mob burned down the British embassy. An Ulster vanguard movement was set up by the Unionist politician William Craig, who told its monster rallies: 'We must build up dossiers on those men and women in this country who are a menace to this country because one of these days, if and when the politicians fail us, it may be our job to liquidate the enemy.' In March 1972 the British government abruptly terminated Stormont and introduced direct rule from the new Northern Ireland Office at Westminster. They had concluded that Stormont was part of the problem rather than the solution; direct rule would provide breathing space for inter-communal and cross-border talks to resolve the problem. That July, four UVF/UDA loyalists, hyped up by the imminent bonfire night on the 12th, broke into the home of a Catholic widow claiming she had IRA hidden weapons in her house. She was robbed and raped. The men took her upstairs where they shot dead her fourteen-year-old retarded son, and then shot her in the hand and thigh. A (Protestant) lodger had a cigarette lighter held under his chin until he could produce the Orange sash that saved his life.

The new Northern Ireland secretary, the koala-like William Whitelaw, introduced Special Category status for prisoners convicted of certain terrorist crimes; this meant they did not have to wear prison uniforms, and effectively gave them political status. Whitelaw also released a few internees, and arranged for various IRA figures, including Gerry Adams and Martin McGuinness, to be flown over for secret talks in the Chelsea home of a fellow minister. This was the first time the government had held direct talks with Irish terrorists. While these men reiterated familiar demands, Whitelaw proposed a power-sharing assembly based on proportional representation to protect minority rights, which would choose an eleven-man executive to restore local rule in the province. The status of Northern Ireland as an integral part of the United Kingdom was repeated like a mantra to assuage Unionists. Brian Faulkner managed to persuade a narrow majority of Unionists to pursue this path, which was vociferously opposed by Ian Paisley. In the autumn of 1971 he had begun forming the Democratic Unionist Party to signal his breach with the landed gentry and urban bigwigs who had dominated the original Unionist Party since its inception.

Subsequent talks held at the Civil Service College at Sunningdale in Berkshire between the British and Irish governments and representatives from Ulster's moderate nationalist and Unionists were designed to set up the bi-national institutions that would ensure the success of local power-sharing, a Council of Ministers and a Council consisting of thirty representatives of the Northern Ireland Assembly and the Irish parliament. This recognised that many nationalists in the North saw themselves as Irish. Clandestine contacts between Michael Oately of MI5 and some of the PIRA leadership may have been intended to draw them eventually into a wider settlement, as was separately indicated by the lifting of bans on both Sinn Féin and the UVF.[26]

Two constituencies rejected the power-sharing settlement: the Protestant majority and the PIRA as a whole. The Irish Republic did not help matters when it publicly reaffirmed its claim to Northern Ireland in clauses 2 and 3 of its constitution, and rejected the extradition of PIRA terrorists from their cross-border bases and sanctuaries. Radical Unionists deposed Faulkner as head of their party, and then went on to win a resounding victory as anti-Sunningdale candidates in elections in February 1973. In a further blow, UK prime minister Edward Heath's Conservatives were replaced by Wilson, whose wish to be shot of Northern Ireland was well known. Unionist workers also underlined their hostility to power-sharing when they launched a general strike in May 1974 which brought the province to a standstill. Hooded masked men from the UDA, armed with wooden clubs, blocked roads and intimidated key workers in power stations into staying at home so as to reduce the electricity generated and transmitted. Since the UDA was not a terrorist threat to the army, the latter left the matter of removing barricades to the RUC, which routinely did nothing to offend people it sympathised with.

Nineteen seventy-four saw the start of something that was discovered by chance three years before. On 30 December 1971 an IRA master bomb maker, Jack McCabe, had been mixing explosives on the floor of his garage when the shovel emitted a spark and he was blown to pieces. Worried that such materials were unstable, the IRA had a ready batch put in a car which was driven into central Belfast and detonated. Two could play at that game. On 17 May 1974 three loyalist car bombs exploded during the rush hour in Dublin killing twenty-two people. A twenty-two-year-old woman, who was nine months pregnant, died as a piece of shrapnel went through her heart, leaving her twenty-two-month-old daughter wandering around alone. Another fatality, twenty-one-year-old Anna Massey, had spent the previous evening writing out invitation cards to her wedding in six weeks' time. She went not to the altar but to the grave. A further five people were murdered in simultaneous car bombings in Monaghan. One hundred and twenty people were injured in attacks whose eventual death toll of thirty-three provided the worst day of the Troubles. The UVF found this attack 'funny', despite the severed arms, legs and heads, and called it 'returning the serve'.

Wilson seriously entertained the Doomsday scenario of British withdrawal from the province so as to extricate England from the mess of Ulster. He went so far as to signal to the PIRA that his government 'wished to devise structures of disengagement from Ireland'; the PIRA responded by proclaiming a ceasefire, which it monitored in republican areas, a first indication of its controlling autonomous green ghettos. Wilson's dark prognostications also had the effect of calling the Republic's bluff, for Irish reality – as distinct from the rhetoric of Irish republicans and the ill-informed fantasies of their US supporters – was that 'we should do everything possible to bring [continued British involvement] about'. That exposed the cold truth that northern republicans were fighting not only to leave a state that did not want them, but to join one that did not want them either. Wilson did not have much time for the loyalists. Venting his fury against the loyalist strikers, he spoke on television of 'people who spend their lives sponging on Westminster and British democracy and then systematically assault democratic methods'. He angrily asked: 'who do they think they are?' In subsequent weeks, loyalists sported small pieces of sponge in their lapels. Within two weeks Faulkner acknowledged the failure of power-sharing and the Executive and Assembly collapsed. One of the most promising peace initiatives prior to the 1998 Good Friday Agreement – described as 'Sunningdale for slow learners' – had failed.

In 1974 the PIRA extended its terror bombing campaign to the UK mainland, both to let militants have their head and to remind the British of the costs of non-negotiation. Deaths in Belfast were so commonplace that only those on the mainland might reignite media interest. In February a bomb exploded on a coach carrying soldiers from Manchester to a barracks in North Yorkshire, killing nine soldiers, a woman and two children. In October two pubs in Guildford, the Horse and Groom and the Seven Stars, frequented by off-duty soldiers as well as the general public, were bombed, killing five people, two of them women. On 7 November 1974 a bomb exploded in the King's Arms near the Royal Artillery Training Centre at Woolwich, murdering a soldier and a civilian. In all of these attacks dozens were injured. On 21 November, bombs went off at the Mulberry and Tavern in the Town pubs in Birmingham, killing nineteen and wounding 182 people. In each case, media and public clamour for a quick result led to unsafe detective and forensic work and the conviction of innocent people who went to jail for very long periods before their convictions were quashed. In December 1975 the four men who were responsible for many of these attacks were cornered in a London flat after they had shot at a restaurant they had bombed a few weeks before. After a five-day siege they surrendered, and in 1977 received forty-seven life sentences and an aggregate two thousand years in jail. An Irish-American citizen who had shot dead a policeman unfortunate enough to alight upon the group's bomb factory was jailed in 1988 for murder after five years of extradition proceedings. Despite these outrages, which led to localised anti-Irish sentiment, especially in Birmingham, the British government developed its contacts with the PIRA. On 10 December 1974 Protestant clergymen from the Irish Council of Churches met PIRA leaders at a hotel in County Clare. A document was prepared which the clergymen took to the home secretary Merlyn Rees, with an offer of a ceasefire from 22 December 1974 to 2 January 1975.

Rees vowed that Britain had no long-term territorial or security interests in Northern Ireland beyond its obligations to a people the majority of whom wanted to remain in the UK. A steady number of republican detainees were released, and prisoners held on the mainland returned to Northern Irish jails. The army was less conspicuous in Catholic neighbourhoods. Managed with the help of clandestine talks between MI5 officers and the IRA, with the only written records stemming from the latter, the ceasefire endured for almost the whole of 1975, although it was punctuated by IRA killings of members of the security forces whenever it deemed its conditions to have been breached. While fewer police and soldiers were killed that year, the ceasefire saw an upsurge in blatant sectarian murders, which a younger generation of IRA figures – including Gerry Adams and Brendan Hughes in Long Kesh and Martin McGuinness in jail in the South – viewed as an indirect consequence of the disastrously naive PIRA leadership's talks with the British who they thought were spinning them along while the loyalists depleted them.

Much innocent blood flowed during the ceasefire. On 13 March 1975, two UVF terrorists planted a gas-cylinder bomb in the entrance to Peter Conway's bar in Belfast; it exploded prematurely, leaving both men badly injured. On 5 April 1975 loyalists left their own gas-cylinder bomb in the doorway to McLaughlin's bar in the Catholic New Lodge area, killing two men watching the Grand National on television. A few hours later, the PIRA shot up Protestants watching the same race-meeting in the Shankill Road's Mountainview tavern, so as to facilitate the throwing of a bomb that murdered five people. Before the night was over, loyalists shot dead a sixty-one-year-old Catholic. On 31 July the Miami Showband were stopped at 1 a.m. as they headed south after a concert in the North by what they took to be UDR soldiers manning a roadblock. They were in fact members of the UVF, although some of them were also part-time soldiers in the UDR. The aim was to plant a bomb in the band's Volkswagen van timed to go off as they went south, the intention being that people would say 'Well, you can't even trust the Miami Showband' not to be PIRA bombers. One of the ten UVF terrorists told the musicians: 'Well, that's great, fellas, thanks for your co-operation, jump in and off you go.' At that moment the bomb exploded prematurely, blowing the head, arms and legs off two of the UVF men. An arm found at some distance had the tattoo UVF on it. The eight remaining gun-men then decided to eliminate any witnesses, putting twenty-two shots into the handsome singer Fran O'Toole's face, before killing Anthony Geraghty and the Protestant trumpeter Brian McCoy. Two of the men convicted of this attack were sergeants in the UDR. On 13 August the PIRA hit back with a bomb and gun attack on the Bayardo bar on the Shankill Road, murdering six Protestants, including one member of the UVF. The leader of the attack was a former seminarian called Brendan

'Bic' McFarlane who would go on to lead PIRA prisoners in the Maze prison in the 1980s.

On 1 September, a PIRA front group murdered five Protestants at the Tullyvallen Guiding Star Orange Lodge in Newtownhamilton. Seventy-year-old farmer William Ronald McKee and his forty-year-old son James died, alongside eighty-year-old retired farmer John Johnston. As the ceasefire ended, loyalist gunmen killed six Catholics living in remote rural areas. On 4 January 1976 masked UVF gunmen burst into a party the O'Dowd family were having around their piano. Three male O'Dowds were shot dead, their bodies collapsing on several children aged under ten. Fifteen minutes later three brothers in the O'Reavey family were killed by the UVF as they watched television. The next day PIRA terrorists stopped a bus carrying ten Protestant workmen home at Kingsmill, South Armagh. They identified one Catholic, the bus driver, and set him aside, before mowing down the remaining nine, their bodies left amid pools of blood and half-eaten sandwiches. The only survivor had been hit by eighteen rounds as he crawled away.

Late 1975 also saw the advent of a UVF unit so ferocious that it was a law unto itself as fellow terrorists were afraid of it. One group to reflect on in what follows are the detectives and forensic scientists who had to cope with the bloody aftermath of what these men did. Thousands of these policemen have never been properly compensated for the traumatising scenes they had to witness – the effects on them including alcoholism, divorce and suicide. The forensic reports were usually so long that it is impossible to quote fully what amount to serial atrocities on the human body.

Hugh 'Lenny' Murphy was a slight man with dark wavy hair and smiling blue eyes. As a child he had extorted money from schoolfellows by threatening them with his elder brothers. Murphy hated Catholics, although with names like Hugh and Murphy (which is why he preferred 'Lenny') he was often teased as a 'Mick' because he was the son of a lapsed Catholic who had married his strenuously Protestant mother – in further illustration that this was not Birmingham, Alabama. The school-boy name-calling did not last long. Central to the successive gangs the adult Murphy formed were Robert 'Basher' Bates, Samuel 'Big Sam' McAllister and William Moore, with such additions as Benjamin 'Pretty Boy' Edwards and James 'Tonto' Watt.

All of these men were members of the UVF, with a visceral hatred of uppity 'Taigs'. Murphy had 'William of Orange, Rem [ember] 1690' and

Ulster's Red Hand tattooed on his upper body, plus a more conventional 'Mum' and 'Dad' on his hands. By the age of twenty, he had developed the strange pastime of frequenting hearings at Belfast Crumlin Road court in his spare time from his job as a shop assistant. He would sit there for hours, in his leather jacket and scarf, listening to the trials of IRA men, and watching their friends and relatives sitting in the public gallery, while learning how to evade a guilty verdict. One of the key things was to deny malicious intent, and to omit key parts of any story, all evident in records of interrogations whenever gang members were arrested.

In 1972 Murphy and his friends abducted a thirty-four-year-old Catholic from a taxi. The man was held in Murphy's 'romper room' in the Lawnbrook Social Club, a loyalist drinking den, until the non-hardcore clientele drifted away. After midnight the man was beaten by those who remained, with Murphy delivering the sickeningly heavy blows that broke bones. Murphy then repeatedly stabbed his victim. At 4 a.m. the victim was shot in the head and his body dumped a mile away. Several more Catholics were selected at random by Murphy and his gang for similar treatment. A forty-eight-year-old mill worker, Thomas Madden, was strung up from a beam in a garage while Murphy went to work on his naked body with a chisel, leaving 147 separate incisions before Madden was choked to death with a pull on the rope. He kept screaming 'Kill me! Kill me!' Forensic reports recorded the distressingly large numbers of wounds Madden had felt.

As a psychopath Murphy was extremely cunning. In September 1972 he set off on a motorbike with Mervyn John Connor, on a UVF contract to shoot a Protestant flautist called Pavis who the UVF thought was selling arms to a friendly Catholic priest acting for PIRA. Murphy shot Pavis in his home. Both Murphy and Connor were arrested in connection with a second shooting, with Connor being persuaded by the police to turn queen's evidence after he had been identified by eyewitnesses. Although Connor was protected in Crumlin Road jail, Murphy resolved to eliminate him. A first attempt, with poisoned custard that would have killed not only Connor but all at his table, failed when the custard went a funny colour. Undeterred, Murphy acquired cyanide from the prison hospital, where he now worked, and a pass to move around, which he used to dodge idle guards so as to enter Connor's cell. There he rammed the cyanide down his friend's throat after Connor had written a letter exonerating him of the Pavis murder.

The only prisoner to witness his crime died shortly after his head was battered into a cell wall.

Returned to his Shankill Road habitat, Murphy set up his gang in the Brown Bear pub, an early recruit being William 'Billy' Moore, a black taxi driver connected to the UVF already – because the UVF 'licensed' the entire Shankill Road fleet, just as PIRA did along the Falls Road. For both organisations this was a lucrative racket, made easier by the fact that many public buses had been burned or otherwise driven from the roads. Moore also had a collection of cleavers and butcher's knives he had stolen before he was sacked from his job in a meat-packing plant. He prided himself on keeping the knives 'as sharp as lances'.

In October 1974 the Murphy gang robbed a Catholic drinks warehouse, shooting dead all four employees after they could not find any cash. When in November 1975 PIRA killed three British soldiers at an observation post at Crossmaglen in South Armagh, Murphy's Butchers went on their next rampage. They set off in Moore's taxi into the Catholic Antrim Road, coming upon a lone walker heading for the city centre. Francis Crossan was clubbed on the head with a wheel brace and dragged into the taxi. Murphy cut into his throat so ferociously that Crossan's head almost came off. When police found his body, the head was at a right angle to it, and shards of glass protruded from his face where it had been rammed with broken beer glasses.

Although Murphy and his men were criminals themselves, the UVF sanctioned them to carry out punishment attacks against petty crooks operating from the rival Windsor bar who had burgled an elderly widow. Usually, punishment involved dropping heavy concrete blocks on legs or heads, followed by a shooting, or a session with an electric drill on the offender's front kneecaps if they did not get the first message. Most frontal kneecappings could be repaired with surgery; Murphy decided a shot to the back of the kneecap would be permanently incapacitating. Three men were kidnapped and taken to a garage; one was shot dead after he tried to flee, while the other two had their kneecaps blown off. Although Murphy was responsible for this murder, he ensured that another gang member was shot dead by the UVF when it exacted retribution for an unauthorised killing.

In early 1976 Murphy and his gang resumed their night hunt for 'Taigs'. The gang would always claim that the idea (and the victim) just popped into their heads whenever they went out for bags of chips. In fact, each killing was hatched as they talked themselves into it during all-day drinking sessions in loyalist bars. They would drag some unfortunate fellow into a black taxi after hitting him on the head with a wheel brace. Inside the victim would be brutally assaulted, while the taxi stopped off to collect butcher's knives or a hatchet for the wet work. Then there would be a long torture session at some dingy loyalist drinking den, which ended when Murphy sawed through the victim's throat and spinal column. Then the corpse would be driven away and dumped – near a republican area if the victim was a fellow Protestant. There was one variation on the theme inspired by the Kingsmill massacre, when Murphy's men launched a gun attack on what they thought was a gang of Catholic workmen on a lorry in the Shankill Road. Two men died and two were wounded. The dead men were both Protestants, information which made Murphy go berserk, vowing to kill twice as many Catholics to make up for the error. He made his first major mistake when he crashed through an army checkpoint after having shot at two young Catholic women in another car. Although in a police station he tried to wash gunshot residue from his hands in the lavatory bowl, he was convicted of attempted murder and sentenced to twelve years in prison.

The resulting six years served did not prevent him from directing an extramural campaign of sectarian murder. In June 1976, after the Times bar was bombed by the PIRA, the Shankill Butchers shot dead three Catholics in the Chlorane bar that same morning. On Friday 29 October they abducted twenty-one-year-old Stephen McCann as he and his girl-friend Frances Tohill returned home from a party late at night. McCann was a dreamy boy who played the guitar and wrote dark adolescent poetry and songs. The gang had spent the day drinking and planning this attack, although, again, they would subsequently claim that the idea of murder came up when they went looking for more chips. McCann was subjected to an horrific assault in the taxi, and then was shot in the head, prior to his head almost being sawn off by William Moore. This was done to distract the police, who suspected that the imprisoned Murphy was the butcher killer. Leadership of the group devolved on Sam McAllister, a bloated tattooed hard man always looking for a scrap. After a drunken brawl with a UDA man was narrowly averted in a loyalist pub, McAllister waited around for his opponent and crushed his head with a breezeblock as he lay on the ground. For this McAllister received two punishment shots to each arm after he had negotiated the penalty up from his precious knees.

In May 1977, after several further murders, the gang's luck expired when, posing as policemen, they abducted twenty-two-year-old Gerard McLaverty late one night. They claimed the idea of 'knocking the bollocks off a Taig' came to them as they cruised Belfast after the bars closed. McLaverty was severely beaten by McAllister with a stick which had two six-inch nails driven through the end, a session so sustained that the gang had to stop for a tea break to catch their second wind. McLaverty was then driven to where they planned to kill him; the fact that they only had a bootlace to strangle him and a small clasp knife to slash his wrists saved his life. The mode of attack not only resulted in the gang's capture, but also the police's realisation that they had those responsible for thirty earlier deaths. McLaverty's testimony and twelve-hour bouts in Castlereagh interrogation centre eventually cracked the gang members' evasions and lies. A broken William Moore at last conceded, 'Murphy done the first three [an underestimate of his lethality] and I done the rest.' He added: 'It was that bastard Murphy led me into all this. My head's away with it.' Eleven men appeared in court charged with nineteen murders. In February 1979 Moore was jailed in perpetuity while most of the others received life sentences, to serve a minimum of eighteen or twenty years. One person was not in the dock.

Lenny Murphy was released from prison on 16 July 1982. There was a party for him that night in the Rumsford Street Loyalist Club. Shortly before midnight a bedraggled vagrant, Alexander Maxwell, drifted in with a view to cadging drinks before hitting his slumbers in a Salvation Army hostel. When Murphy ordered him out, Maxwell made the mistake of giving him too much 'lip'. Murphy took him outside and proceeded to punch and kick him. Maxwell fell unconscious to the ground. Murphy then went inside to fetch some car keys and drove a car back and forth over the vagrant until the man was dead. Within six weeks of his release, Murphy had formed a new gang and was living well from the proceeds of extortion. He drove a smart yellow Rover car. So as to avoid paying the agreed price for this vehicle, he first tried to poison the former owner, and then shot him eight times in a drive-by motorbike shooting. Inevitably, the actions of this maniac eventually caught up with him. He tried to muscle in on a racket related to gambling machines in bars and clubs, while his counter-kidnapping and killing of a Catholic hostage after the PIRA had abducted a UDR soldier aggravated his own side. He seems to have crossed an ex-boxer called Jim Craig, when he tried to get into the same line of work extorting money from construction sites.

Craig was UDA commander in west Belfast. While in the Maze he had explained to a PIRA leader he sat with on the Camp Council his idea of disciplining his own men: 'I've got this big fucking hammer and I've told them that if anybody gives me trouble, I'll break their fucking fingers.' It seems that Craig had also come to an arrangement when in jail with senior members of PIRA as to relative boundaries for their respective extortion rackets, and had quite possibly reached a agreement to murder each other's enemies like the strangers on a train in the Hitchcock movie.

On the evening of 16 November 1982, Lenny Murphy parked his Rover at the rear of his girlfriend's home on a Protestant estate. His wife and children had long ago left him. He had not noticed a blue van in his rear mirrors, nor that it had backed up so as to face his car. The back doors opened as Murphy prepared to get out; he was hit by twenty-six bullets to the head and body, fired by two men in overalls who were spirited away in stolen cars. At Murphy's funeral, six masked UVF gunmen fired a salvo over his coffin which was draped with an orange and purple flag. A piper played 'Abide with Me' as the cortège progressed along the Shankill Road. Murphy had just turned thirty; his mother averred that 'Lenny would not hurt a fly.' His friend 'Basher' Bates, who had got God in prison, was shot dead in 1997, in a UDA revenge killing for Bates's murder twenty years before of dark-complexioned James 'Nigger' Moorehead in the lavatory of a Belfast bar. The vengeful memories were like those in a medieval Icelandic saga. Jim Craig was shot dead by the UFF in a bar in 1988 after his dealings with the PIRA came to their attention.[27]

III DELIVERING CHAOS

If all Irish terrorists were psychopathic criminals like Murphy, there would be no demonstrable ebb and flow to the violence, or shifts in how it was used vis-à-vis other forms of political activity. In fact, many people joined terrorist organisations because they had direct personal experience of injustice or were witnesses to it. Eamon Collins came from a farming family in Crossmaglen, a republican stronghold on the North–South border. His politically pragmatic father raised and traded cattle and bloodstock. His mother was the pious Catholic, responsible for planting in Collins's heart the tear-jerking myths of Irish republican history, and a tension between rebel violence and Christian turning of the other cheek. He had low-level contacts with the IRA, took part in civil rights riots, sold republican papers, and, after odd jobs in the civil service in London, went to Queen's University in Belfast to read law.

On vacation at home, Collins came back to the farm late at night after having drinks with schoolfriends. As he wandered down the lane, British paratroops emerged from the bushes, shouting 'Get your fucking hands up, don't you fucking move. Don't you fucking move.' This was followed with 'Get your arms out. Spread your fucking legs, you cunt.' They then proceeded to beat him with rifle butts, while kicking him with heavy combat boots: 'Get your fucking hands on your head, you Irish cunt.' The soldiers dragged him into the house, pinning him down with the aid of a self-loading rifle shoved into his mouth, which broke some teeth. His guard remarked: 'I'd blow your brains out for tuppence, you rotten Irish cunt.' While his mother screamed hysterically, Collins, his father and brother were arrested, and beaten with rifle butts as they lay on the floor of the Land Rovers that drove them away. Collins was forced to sing 'The Sash' with soldiers marking time by hitting him on the back. After a frightening spell in the army's Bessborough barracks, the three were turned over to the RUC. They were eventually released when forensic scientists determined that the 'explosives' a sniffer dog had detected in the father's car came from spilled creosote used to stain a fence. Collins explained the psychological effects of this mistreatment: 'I would feel a surge of rage whose power unbalanced me: I would sit alone in my room and think with pleasure of blowing off the heads of those para scum.' He became more and more involved in activities designed to support the H-Block prisoners in the Maze. After a lengthy induction period, he joined the PIRA, attending lectures in Dundalk and receiving the organisation's Green Book. This gave the history of the organisation, its military rules and advice on how to resist deep interrogation – the army euphemism for a rough time.

Collins worked as a PIRA intelligence officer under the guise of his day job of Customs and Excise officer in Newry, where he inspected the papers of lorry drivers coming across the border. In his spare time, he was first tenor in the Cloughmore Male Voice Choir. His own colleagues were among the early victims of terrorist attacks he facilitated. He coldly set up major Ivan Toombs of the neighbouring customs house at Warrenpoint, even though Toombs had introduced him to his charming eight-year-old daughter and the two men had got drunk together while inspecting a Russian ship. The forty-seven-year-old Toombs's part-time membership of the UDR was sufficient grounds for him to be shot in his office in January 1981 after Collins had supplied the killer (known as 'Iceman') and his accomplice with details of the building's layout. An obviously intelligent man, although that did not prevent him being beaten to death in 1999 by the PIRA after he had dropped out and narrowly avoided becoming a police supergrass, Collins captured something else about being a terrorist that does not figure as much as it should. This is the desire to bring chaos to the lives of others. After the PIRA had virtually obliterated Newry in a bombing campaign, it looked for a fresher target. It alighted upon Warrenpoint, about ten minutes' drive away. It is worth looking at why Collins made this decision:

> The people there seemed to be cocooned and relatively prosperous. Middle-class Catholics and Protestants lived in harmony, united – as I would have put it from my Marxist perspective – by their class interests in maintaining their high standard of living . . . I loathed the tranquillity of this little seaside town: Warrenpoint was to me a little sugar-plum fairy on the top of a rotten unionist cake . . . Its plump citizens enjoyed a good night-life with pleasant pubs, coffee-houses and restaurants . . . I was going to enjoy bringing Warrenpoint's fairy tale existence to an end.

Shortly afterwards, the Crown hotel in Warrenpoint's main square was demolished when the PIRA deposited keg bombs in which ANFO (a mixture of ammonium nitrate and fuel oil, the so-called fertiliser bomb) was packed into metal milk containers and triggered by gelignite. Chaos had arrived in Warrenpoint.[28]

The so-called 69ers joined the PIRA for uncomplicated reasons. Take Bernard Fox, an apprentice coachbuilder from the Falls Road who joined in 1969, and was rumoured to be a member of the PIRA Army Council. Recalling how he had embarked on a path that would put him in jail for nineteen years, Fox said: 'I was almost shot in a gun attack at Norfolk Street. I came away wanting a gun. It was survival. You wanted to protect your own people . . . my family and myself. When the barricades went up I wanted a gun so I approached this fella who was in the IRA and asked for a gun and he said: could I shoot a British soldier? At that time I hadn't the idea that it was the British government's fault.' Another prominent PIRA figure, rumoured to head the PIRA in west Belfast, joined after his non-political father was shot dead by British soldiers in 1971. The future Brighton bomber Patrick Magee, who almost wiped out Margaret Thatcher's cabinet, claimed that he had been roughly man-handled by soldiers. The young Martin McGuinness was stopped by an army patrol in Londonderry in August 1969 as he left Doherty's butcher shop, where he worked, to fetch some lunch. They told him to remove his shoes and socks before spreadeagling him against a wall: 'Martin was a very shy wee boy, and the soldiers humiliated him in front of all the girls from the shirt factories. They were on their break and stood around staring. Until then, he was a quiet young fellow but after that Martin went down with the rest, throwing stones. He never would have done that,' recalled the brother of a workmate.[29] The injustice of internment was another major contributory factor to volunteers joining IRA ranks, especially since internees developed an elaborate system for smuggling out minutely written accounts of abuse.

One did not actually have to experience brutality or discrimination to feel it, for some leading PIRA terrorists, like Martin Ferris – nowadays a Sinn Féin member of the Irish Dáil – and Sean O'Callaghan, a former head of PIRA Southern Command and member of its GHQ, were from Kerry in Eire's republican deep south. The further away from the North, the more intense the republicanism. Ferris came from a Kerry farming family that augmented income from potatoes, pigs and onions with the haul from oyster beds. His father had spent some time in the US and was a keen amateur fighter. The first song Ferris heard as a child was about an eighteen-year-old hanged by the perfidious British. The best local pub, Mick Lynch's in Spa, doubled as an IRA safe house and a favoured honeymoon venue for people like Gerry Adams's brother Paddy. Ferris was well on the way to being a talented footballer when the first TV sets showed graphic scenes of northern Catholics being 'given the timber' by the baton-wielding RUC and B Specials. After suitable priming by Mick Lynch, on 29 May 1970 Ferris was sworn into the IRA by a local painting contractor and the local vice-chairman of the Gaelic Athletic Association.[30]

O'Callaghan was born in 1954 into a working-class republican family that lived on an estate on the outskirts of Tralee, the largest town in otherwise rural Kerry. Like many PIRA terrorists, he had a happy and uneventful childhood. At the age of nine his paternal grandmother reminded him: 'Never trust a policeman, even a dead one. They should always be dug up and shot again just to be sure.' After seeing the shocking start of the northern Troubles on southern TV, the precocious fifteen-year-old O'Callaghan contacted a man he knew to be a local IRA figure, and was soon being trained in the use of revolvers and high-velocity rifles. By age sixteen he was a proficient instructor in remote PIRA camps where northerners with no experience of weapons came to learn how to use them. He recalled that his trainees had 'a youthful fascination with guns and bombs and a desire to get even with the Prods ... [that] was all the motivation they needed'. In 1972, now aged seventeen, O'Callaghan received a six-month jail sentence after a bomb he was making accidentally detonated and demolished his father's garden shed. That was the start of it.[31]

Another diehard republican area was South Armagh, where Thomas 'Slab' Murphy, a bachelor pig farmer from Ballybinaby with a keen interest in the rough and tumble of Gaelic football, was lord of all he surveyed. The farm complex straddles the North–South border, a location of some use to smugglers who have haunted the area for centuries. There were three brothers, one of whom became mid-Ulster junior heavyweight boxing champion. These were all big men, who took the distinctive soubriquet 'Slab' from their bully of a grandfather. Thomas 'Slab' was at the heart of a major PIRA-organised crime empire that relies on a network of interrelated South Armagh clans and a slow but steady training programme that teaches extreme caution in perpetrating criminal violence. Several members of Murphy's gang, with names like 'the Surgeon' and 'the Undertaker', are or have been key members of the PIRA, although only 'Slab' himself has been its chief of staff. Unlike the more baroquely vicious loyalist terrorists, PIRA's leaders make a virtue of low-key anonymity, which is why there are no lurid biographies of, among others, Brian Keenan, Martin Ferris, Bobby Storey or Padraic Wilson, all at various times members of its Army Council. That is also why they are still alive, in contrast to Dominic 'Mad Dog' McGlinchey, their publicity-seeking rival from the breakway INLA who was shot dead in 1994 by loyalist gunmen.[32]

The decision to embark on a career of politicised violence was invariably construed by PIRA members as something forced upon an individual, in this case by state or sectarian violence against the community that he (or she) was defending, rather than a personal choice that could also reflect a no less keen desire to experience the thrill of clandestine activity in a secret organisation that bestowed status on its members. Status within the PIRA partly derived from belonging to an ultra-republican family already, not least because this brought automatic trust. If the terrorist came from a republican family living in a republican area, like Gerry Adams's home territory on Belfast's Ballymurphy estate, then his adoption of the gun and bomb was both socially sanctioned and morally justified. It was a matter of being true to family tradition. No authority figures were there to argue otherwise, since many Catholic clergy espoused sentimental violent republicanism when they were not vicarious supporters of PIRA violence.[33] To complicate matters, whereas the Irish primate, cardinal Tomás Ó Fiaich, was an advocate of British withdrawal from Northern Ireland, and was hence known to Ian Paisley as 'the IRA's bishop of Crossmaglen', archbishop Cahal Daly of Armagh, which covered the northern counties, was an outspoken critic of armed republicanism and was detested by his parishioner Gerry Adams.[34] Although mothers played a significant role in perpetuating sectarian hatreds across the generations, they were sometimes loath to see their sons (and daughters) involved in political violence. The mother of Declan Arthurs tried to dissuade her son from becoming a Provo:

> What was his future? Life imprisonment? On the run? Or was he going to be killed? I knew his future wasn't going to be any good. I said to him, 'For God's sake, Declan, please think of us because we love you so much.' And he'd just look at me and say, 'I'm sorry, mum, there's nothing else I can do. I have to fight for my country.' I begged him, often I begged him, but to no avail.[35]

Twenty-one-year-old Declan Arthurs was one of eight PIRA members shot dead by the SAS, who ambushed them as they tried to blow up Loughall police station with a bomb in a mechanical excavator on 8 May 1987.

Jail was also not a deterrent in Northern Ireland (or in the South, where many PIRA figures were locked up in atrocious conditions in Portlaoise jail) since paramilitary prisoners invariably dominated their sections in any institution. This is unsurprising in the case of the Maze, where they were gathered in their hundreds, in a geographical context where they could intimidate or murder guards and their families, but was also true of those held in maximum-security prisons on the British mainland. There they would forge alliances with major English criminals who, tantalised by the international scale of PIRA activity, soon realised they were not dealing with a crowd of demented 'Paddies'. Some prisoners reconciled themselves to the long days and nights of nothing;

others regarded every waking hour as a chance to plan a breakout. Jail was an opportunity to practise wartime POW-style feats of derring-do, notably when in 1983 Gerry Kelly led a mass escape by thirty-eight inmates from the Maze, or to improve on the ideological justifications for terrorism. Several imprisoned gunmen of all persuasions have recalled that it was only when they arrived in prison that they were given more elaborate reasons for bombing and shooting people. Veteran loyalist terrorist 'Gusty' Spence always asked incoming prisoners to his section of the Maze at some point, 'Why are you here?' The correct answer was not 'For murdering people.'

In jail terrorists had people to discuss politics with and books to read. Many took the opportunities that distance learning afforded and studied law, history, politics or sociology. This explains why so many former terrorists have a certain autodidactic plausibility, as they convert blood-shed into the anodyne pseudo-sociological jargon of 'identity', 'process', 'situation' and 'tradition'. They sound as if they are almost neutral objective observers of the chaos and mayhem they are largely responsible for creating. Even those who preferred to stick with their psychotic selves at least used time in jail to turn themselves into credible hulks through hours of body-building. Although some twenty-eight Northern Ireland Prison Service officers were murdered during the Troubles, it was not an inert organisation. In the early 1990s it successfully experimented with an early-release scheme, under which carefully identified terrorists in their thirties – with attractive wives, growing children and aged parents – were allowed out on licence, to see the family life they were missing and how far Northern Ireland had improved in their absence. The condition attached to this scheme, which brought early release on licence, was that they would serve their sentences in mixed-community wings of ordinary prisons where they would be away from the corrupting influence of the paramilitary chieftains in the Maze.[36]

Many terrorists in Northern Ireland had few difficulties in reconciling murder with religion. Billy 'King Rat' Wright was forever spouting biblical quotations in the manner of an American Baptist. An uncle of Gerry Adams was both a leading republican and so devout an adherent of the Redemptorists that his workmates dubbed him 'the Bishop'. There were plenty of people in the traditionalist PIRA who were Catholic bigots, motivated by little more than 'wishing to see those Orange bastards wiped out'.[37] IRA membership also granted a status equivalent to that of a Mafia 'made man', able to intimidate by his steely presence, and an object of adoration to women and young boys. Every pretty girl was available, drawn to these ultimate bad boys, whose reality was invariably that they were unemployed or in lowly occupations. For some of the full-time activists the few pounds a week they were paid by the IRA was the only money they had earned in their entire life. The only regular job Sean O'Callaghan has ever had was a year spent on a farm mixing ANFO explosives nicknamed 'blowie', to be used in the North.[38]

There was a certain look that went with being an urban terrorist. Loyalists were often like proletarian thugs in any British city, with their beer bellies, cropped hair and tattoos. They were not sophisticated people; their idea of an exotic meal was to add curry sauce to a bag of chips, while venturing as far as Tenerife for their first overseas holiday. The worst of them, like Johnny 'Mad Dog' Adair, in reality a late developer in the matter of shooting people, overcame his slight stature – he was known as 'the wee man' before he became 'Mad Dog' – building outwards by injecting his arms and thighs with horse steroids and pumping-iron sessions. He used the popular household aerosol furniture polish Mr Sheen to make his shaven head shine.

The urban Provos tended to affect denim jeans and leather jackets, when they were not trying to blend into a covering occupation that required a conventional suit-and-tie appearance. Alex Reid, the Redemptorist priest who played a key role in locking Adams into a peace process, forsook his black robes for a black leather jacket and jeans so as to fit in with his interlocutors. The South Armagh 'Slabs' looked like farmers everywhere in the UK with their checked shirts, gumboots, waxed jackets and flat caps. They also practised a low peasant cunning, calling off operations at the slightest suspicion that something might go awry, which made them harder to detect than the more volatile urban loyalist variety whose loud mouths in pubs were like a neon sign saying 'arrest me'. The PIRA units in South Armagh were notoriously difficult to combat as they had the advantage of knowing every bend in the road, bush or culvert. While many loyalist and republican terrorists acted in a drink-fuelled rage, it is important to recall that former PIRA leader and current deputy first minister Martin McGuinness does not smoke or drink and fly-fishes in his spare time. His colleague, Gerry Kelly, who served a long period in jail for bombing the Old Bailey and Scotland Yard in the 1970s, has the gravely austere manner of a Jesuit priest.[39] The same was true of Billy 'King Rat' Wright, leader of the Loyalist Volunteer Force

(LVF), also a teetotal non-smoker whose pronounced evangelical beliefs meant that unlike many of his loyalist comrades he rarely swore. Many loyalists seem to have felt most at home in Scotland, where they went to support Glasgow Rangers – the Protestant antipode to the city's Catholic Celtic. Indeed, they would like to extend the Anglo-Scottish border westwards. They flirted with English neo-Fascists, but as there were few Blacks in Northern Ireland they found the obsessive racism unfamiliar, although that did not stop them persecuting the local Chinese. Some PIRA terrorists were enthusiastic proponents of Gaelic culture, which they regard as indigenous to their island, its language relying heavily on an archaising Celtic script. A younger generation was just as likely to support English football teams, or to listen to Anglo-Irish–US rock groups like the Eagles, as to avowedly Provo bands such as the Flying Columns (whose name harks back to early IRA formations). In addition to the dirge-like plangent lamentations dedicated to long-dead martyrs like Wolfe Tone or Padraig Pearse, there was also a heavily politicised pop music for those who sought it. As Wolfhound's song 'Little Armalite' has it:

> Sure brave RUC man came up into our street
> Six hundred British soldiers were gathered around his feet
> 'Come out, you cowardly Fenians' said he, 'Come out
>   and fight!'
> But he cried 'I'm only joking' when he heard my Armalite.

Over on the other side, Adair's UFF C Company evolved out of a skinhead 'Oi' band. Having started as admirers of north London's Madness – a 1980s ska band – they graduated to the National Front-supporting Skrewdriver before founding their own combo called Offensive Weapon. Adair played bass guitar. Concerts were an excuse to sniff a lot of glue and to hurl oneself around until a major brawl broke out. The lyrics are instructive:

> I like breaking arms and legs
> Snapping spines and wringing necks
> Now I'll knife you in the back
> Kick your bones until they crack
> [chorus] Evil, evil, evil, evil [× 4]
> Jump up and down upon your head
> Kick you around until you are dead

Fill your body full of lead
See the roads turn red
[chorus]
I don't like trendy cunts who pose
Gonna punch you in the nose
Stick my Marten [boot] in your crotch
Don't like you, you're too much
[chorus][40]

It is revealing that Adair and his associates became terrorists partly to avoid the serious beatings that the UDA periodically delivered to delinquents, drug dealers and petty criminals. Adair himself subsequently set up a satellite group from Tigers Bay, consisting of local low life, or 'Hallions' in local argot, who one policeman remarked 'would have shot their own mothers'. They were now licensed to dole out rough justice themselves. Beyond the bars and republican shebeens (illegal drinking dens) this was also a culture of the mean streets, whose respective kerbstones were painted red, white and blue or orange, white and green. Posters threatened informers or warned against careless talk in pubs that might be with an undercover British agent. In the countryside of South Armagh or Tyrone there were PIRA roadsigns warning 'Sniper at Work', especially after the PIRA acquired a few .50-calibre Barrett sniper rifles which have the same effect on the human body at three-quarters of a mile as a Magnum handgun fired from a few feet. Murals, or as they are known locally 'muriels', were an east Belfast Protestant folk-art form first seen in those areas in 1908. They invariably commemorated King Billy's victory at the Boyne. It was not until the 1980s and the PIRA hunger strikes in the Maze that republicans decided to green the walls of 'their' ghettos aggressively, while the Irish tricolour appeared everywhere. Many of these images celebrated mythical Celtic figures, or intimidated and reassured the population with gigantic masked gunmen brandishing Armalites and AK-47s as old ladies grimly went about their shopping beneath them. The problem here was that the old ladies tended to idolise the murderers among them as nice wee boys who had gone a little off life's rails. Commemorative plaques marked the deaths of volunteers and martyrs. Each side of the sectarian divide cashed in on political violence through souvenir shops selling a wide range of kitsch from commemorative mugs to fridge magnets – 'Proud to be a Prod' – and tea towels as well as tapes (and later CDs) of loyalist or republican music. There are coach tours for anyone too scared to trudge the Falls or Shankill past all those charmers who on a cold February day loiter in T-shirts and lycra shorts with Spiderman tattooed on their bulging calves.

Any terrorist campaign is reliant upon regularly stoking the embers of communal hatred, which in the case of PIRA extends to the huge Irish-American diaspora. The deaths of volunteers – whether killed by the army and RUC or by their own choice as hunger strikers – offered a prime opportunity to mobilise a sense of collective grief and victimhood as well as calls for revenge. Cemeteries like that at Milltown in Belfast's Andersonstown district contained a Provo section with tombstones recalling the careers of dedicated martyrs, while a sentimental shrine has appeared recessed along the Falls Road. The day I visited the cemetery, middle-aged grannies were explaining republican history to toddlers and small children. Crowds of republican sympathisers made up the funeral cortège, with grieving family and friends holding up the coffin draped in the Irish flag. If the dead man or woman was important enough, Gerry Adams – with his bodyguard 'Cleaky' Clark – would be there to say a few words before beetling off in his armoured black taxi. Invariably after the religious rites, masked gunmen would step out from the crowd to fire a salvo over the grave, disappearing so quickly that it was impossible for the watching security services to do more than photograph them through telephoto lenses.

What terrorists mainly do is kill and maim people: 'nutting', 'stiffing' or 'touching out' in a local jargon that uses 'digging' for giving someone a beating with iron bars and baseball bats. The target chosen and the modus operandi are vital since they can bring esteem in the gang and wider community. Anyone so minded can shoot a person randomly on the street from a passing car. Ambushing Gerry Adams as he left Belfast magistrates' court in 1984 brought two decades of kudos for the shooter who hit Adams four times, even though Adams lives, as did firing a rocket-propelled grenade into a police station or loyalist bar. People like Lenny Murphy or 'Mad Dog' Adair did it with relish and wit. Adair would gabble after an expedition, incoherent with excitement, and then would routinely wet the bed when, after partying for days, he joined his common-law wife (also known as 'Mad Bitch', mother of 'Mad Pup') or one of many girlfriends responsive to his rough charms. It is worth giving an account of how one murderous operation started, as it is reminiscent of the psychopathic 'Frank' in David Lynch's movie *Blue Velvet*:

It emerged that the C Company team were present on a Sunday evening in a Shankill Road club with the intention of engaging in a session of drinking. Upon the arrival of the first round of drinks the mood of the party was jovial when one of the assembled dozen or so members shouted 'let's bang a Taig'. Although this comment was intended in jest, Adair picked up on the suggestion and within five minutes had detailed every member of the team to play a specific role in the murder attempt which had now become a reality. Incredibly, fifteen minutes later the operation was underway and it was only then that the team realised that they hadn't actually discussed a target. At this point it was decided to drive into a Catholic area and shoot the first male person they encountered. Approximately twenty-five minutes after the first suggestion, the entire team had returned to the club and resumed their drinking, the celebration of the murder [of forty-four-year-old Sean Rafferty shot dead washing up in front of his screaming children] being led by Adair.[41]

Experience and the performance of elite tasks brought status to people who without terrorism would largely have been unemployed since so many of them had dropped out of school, going on the dole or, like Adams (a barman) or McGuinness (a butcher's boy) or Adair (an apprentice woodturner), into low-skilled jobs. Terrorism invested their lives with significance. Leaders had charisma, evidenced by their Robin Hood acts of kindness to old ladies (breaking the legs of those who stole their purse), or the free chops at the butchers and the rum and cokes 'on me' in the bar. As the case of Adair shows, his charisma did not derive from his being a proficient killer, because unlike his associates he got into that at a relatively late stage, and is thought to have personally killed 'only' once. He routinely missed whenever he tried to shoot someone, and was risibly cackhanded with guns. On stage at a loyalist culture day even the mini-skirted and hooded 'Mad Bitch' got off a salvo while 'Mad Dog' grappled with a flashy automatic pistol on his knees. He also had a big mouth around the detectives who insinuated themselves into his circle, something they could not do with PIRA.

A real killer was like Stevie McKeag, a born-again Christian with two children and a divorce. McKeag was a ginger-haired man in his early twenties with penetrating blue eyes; in addition to his Rottweiler named Butch he kept snakes, an iguana, a parrot, a scorpion and tropical fish in his home. At Christmas he liked to have flashing reindeer on the roof and plastic Santas dotted all over the garden. When he killed first on 28 April 1992, his victim was a Catholic pharmacist called Philomena Hanna. He dismounted from a red Suzuki, walked into the chemist's and shot her six times, bending down over her to put the last bullet into her head at close range. That coolness was his abiding characteristic: 'Everybody, no matter who you were, got sweaty palms. But not Stevie. He just fucking flew through it.' His notoriety increased when he used a bicycle to get away after shooting his first republican victim, the second of dozens of murders he committed. Unlike Adair, who could not keep his mouth shut, McKeag took a professional approach to his work: 'At the end of the day I went out, I pulled the trigger and I came home and I didn't run round shouting and screaming about it.'[42] Less than a decade later, after a couple of severe punishment beatings and bad motorbike crashes, a broken-down McKeag was found dead in his bathroom in his boxer shorts after a cocaine overdose. A crossbow bolt protruding from the inside of a window added to the mystery of his ending. Adair was apparently relieved at the death of a man who had modestly allowed him to thrive in his deadly shadow. Along with notorious hitmen like McKeag, bomb makers or snipers were near the top of the tree, as was anyone involved in internal security units established to root out informing 'touts'. A man like Freddie Scappaticci was a very frightening individual when you were strapped to a chair facing a pair of pliers or immersed in a full bath. This was what the young bucks who joined these organisations wished to be. The lowest level of terrorist was the thug who dealt out punishment beatings. In the eyes of the PIRA these were 'the dregs of the organisation, people who aren't any good at anything else but beating people up'.[43]

In these circles money began to change hands immediately after operations: £10 here, £100 there. All terrorists were aware of police forensics and so would repeatedly shower, using a nailbrush and cotton buds soaked with lemon juice to remove gun residue from nails, noses and ears. Massive amounts of bleach were used if the crime scene was somewhere they habitually used like a club or pub, a trick last used by the PIRA killers of Robert McCartney in a Belfast bar in January 2005 who also removed the CCTV tapes. Since men receiving £40 per week dole money could not afford new clothes, money was handed out to replace those burned after a murder, before many of them took to using cheap workmen's overalls on a job. If they were smart, and many PIRA men were, they would rest up in safe houses – which included Catholic priests' houses – watching their actions recycled on the TV news with some whey-faced priest mawkishly interested in what real men do. If something went wrong with the operation, the PIRA held prolonged debriefing sessions to go over and over the details, to get it right next time, but also on the look-out for informer–saboteurs working for the security services.

Their loyalist analogues seem to have preferred several days and nights partying, although heavy drinking and drug taking do not seem to have cramped their operational efficiency. Emulating PIRA Maze prison commander Brian Keenan, Adair introduced elaborate awards ceremonies for his crew, held in loyalist clubs hosting the annual Loyalist Prisoners' Aid. There was a raffle, with prizes such as bicycles, camcorders and PlayStations before Adair strode on to the stage to a rapturous welcome. To the group's theme song, Tina Turner singing 'Simply the Best' (Ms Turner's record company eventually threatened to sue), Adair presented 'Top Gun UFF' trophies to his men. McKeag had a room full of them, so much so that he had 'Top Gun' tattooed too on his left breast. Massive amounts of alcohol were consumed on these occasions, together with the Ecstasy tablets which Adair's gang were simultaneously trading, for the little acorns of organised crime were growing into sturdy oak trees. In 1991 Adair used £10,000 of UDA money to open Circle Taxis. The police called it 'Murder Cabs' but it was more commonly called 'Dial-a-Drug' as it specialised in door-to-door drug delivery after one had phoned in an order as if for a takeaway Indian meal.

IV SECTARIAN STRATEGIES

We left the narrative of Northern Ireland in the mid-1970s. When on 5 December 1975 the last detainees were released from Long Kesh, internment without trial ended. Prisoners who had been convicted and sentenced remained within the complex, distinguished (thanks to Special Category status) from criminal inmates elsewhere by various privileges such as being allowed to wear their own clothes and not having to work. In September 1976 the former coalminer from Barnsley, Roy Mason, became Northern Ireland secretary, a role he performed with apparent purpose. As he flew in by helicopter to his first day on the job, the PIRA burned seven double-deckers in Belfast central bus station so as to welcome him with the sight of rising smoke.[44] There had already been some changes to British security policy. Diplock courts had been introduced in 1972, replacing juries who could be intimidated with a single senior judge dealing with terrorist cases. A Prevention of Terrorism Act enabled suspects to be held for up to seven days in Castlereagh; allegations of systematic abuse were designed to mitigate the inroads this had by way of PIRA suspects breaking too easily or becoming police informers. A reformed and militarised RUC was put into the frontline of combating PIRA criminality – there was no more talk of war – to be supported by local UDR troops if they needed more firepower. The police were reorganised into Regional Crime Squads roughly shadowing PIRA active service units in each area of operations. Mason was also publicly critical of the British media in their reporting of the conflict, the culture of the left university inclining many television producers and reporters to sympathise with the supposedly left-wing Provos, who spoke their language plausibly, even as they recoiled from the brutal Protestant working class.

Another measure antedated Mason, namely that all prisoners convicted of offences after 1 March 1976 were to be obliged to wear prison uniforms, regardless of whether they claimed to be political offenders. The first test case came in September 1976 when PIRA convict Kieran Nugent refused to don this uniform, and was returned naked to his cell where he cloaked himself in a blanket. Two years later three hundred PIRA prisoners were 'on the blanket', supported by blanket-wearing relatives demonstrating outside. As part of a broader restructuring of the PIRA for what it called the Long War, it was decided by Brendan Hughes, the senior PIRA man in the Maze H-blocks, to escalate the prisoners' protest, as part of a wider effort to build political support for PIRA beyond its diehard republican constituency. In March 1978 the prisoners embarked on the 'no-wash' or 'dirty protest', which meant rejecting the fundamentals of human civilisation by smearing their cells with excrement and allowing food to rot so that it heaved with maggots. Prison officers had to operate in this filth, using high-pressure hoses as a last resort. Further pressure was put on prison officers by having terrorist comrades outside target them for assassination, the fate of six Prison Service members since the abolition of special status. The antics of PIRA prisoners made no impression on Roy Mason, nor on the European Commission of Human Rights which rejected inmate appeals, and were very unlikely to impress Margaret Thatcher either when in May 1979 she became Conservative prime minister.

Two months earlier, the INLA had used a remotely triggered car bomb to murder the Shadow Northern Ireland secretary Airey Neave as he drove out of the House of Commons underground car park. He was a much decorated war hero who had escaped from Colditz Castle and was the architect of Thatcher's Tory leadership bid against Edward Heath. That autumn PIRA reminded the world of its presence with a series of attacks on a single day which made major headlines. A remote-control bomb placed on a boat called *Shadow V* killed the seventy-nine-year-old Lord Mountbatten, his fourteen-year-old grandson, a dowager lady and a young boatman. Later the same day, two trucks containing men from the Parachute Regiment were blown up by a half-ton bomb in milk churns hidden by bales stacked on a hay carrier at Warrenpoint as they rode alongside Carlingford Lough to relieve another unit. The bomb was triggered by the sort of remote-control device used in model aircraft rather than by tell-tale command wires. Six soldiers were killed instantly by the blast, with many others horribly injured.

The survivors ran to the granite gatehouse of a nearby castle and radioed for support as they came under PIRA sniper fire designed to corral them where they had hidden. Twenty minutes after the initial attack, an emergency relief unit was dropped off by helicopter. Just then the gatehouse was demolished by a one-ton bomb that had been placed in anticipation of where the survivors might go to regroup. Twelve men were killed. In the Falls Road graffiti appeared claiming these attacks were revenge for 'Bloody Sunday': 'Thirteen gone and not forgotten – we got eighteen and Mountbatten'.

Inside the Maze the five hundred blanket protesters had made such an investment in this struggle that they decided to go forwards rather than back. Seven prisoners, from 170 who volunteered, resolved to embark on a hunger strike to the death which commenced in late October 1980. In Mrs Thatcher they had picked the wrong opponent. While outwardly she was implacable in her rejection of this sort of blackmail, her secret agents cunningly appeared to concede many of their demands via clerical intermediaries, without having this committed to paper until so late in the day that one of the hunger strikers almost expired. The strike was called off, even though the prison authorities then went on to circumvent what the strikers thought had been agreed.

That resulted in the second hunger strike which began on 1 March 1981 with Bobby Sands, who through chance events shortly became the 'H-Block/Armagh' candidate in a by-election in Fermanagh-South Tyrone after the sitting MP had died. On 9 April Sands heard from an illegal radio that he had been duly elected. Parliament modified the law to disqualify prisoners as candidates. The struggle between the hunger strikers and Mrs Thatcher became personal. She said: 'There is no such thing as political murder, political bombing or political violence. There is only criminal murder, criminal bombing and criminal violence. We will not compromise on this. There will be no political status.' The fact that Special Category status had been conceded in 1972 rather militated against that degree of certainty, as did the wording of the Prevention of Terrorism Act itself, under which these men had been imprisoned, since it spoke of 'the use of violence for political ends'.

After sixty-six days Sands died on 5 May, followed by three other hunger strikers. More men took their place. Two of them were elected in absentia as members of the Dáil Éireann. The death toll rose to six as secret meetings were held between Gerry Adams and representatives of the British government to find a settlement both sides could agree on. Pressure on the PIRA leadership also came from the families of the hunger strikers who were encouraged by the Redemptorist father Dennis Faul to make their views known to those who regarded their sons' and siblings' deaths in purely instrumental ideological terms. Even as four more prisoners starved themselves to death, mothers asserted their right to have their sons force fed, which effectively collapsed the unanimity of the strike. Ten men had died, but hundreds of thousands of angry sympathisers had attended their politicised funerals, and the remaining prisoners had won the right to wear their own clothes and a number of smaller concessions. Meanwhile, Sands and his comrades appeared on several christological murals painted in republican areas so as to boost the idea that they were good holy men. Revealingly, there was more outrage in the US (and in Teheran, where the ayatollahs named a street in Sands's memory) than in the Irish Republic where in Catholic eyes suicide was a sin. Nine years earlier southern republicans had burned the British embassy after Bloody Sunday; a decade of PIRA atrocities had cooled their ardour.

The security forces were not idle during this period. Early efforts to operate covertly included a mobile Four Square Laundry which collected republicans' dirty washing with a view to examining it for traces of explosives while keeping areas under covert surveillance from a hideout in the van. A fake massage parlour was opened, so as to spy on the clients. From 1973 onwards the army deployed a highly secretive unit which became known as Detachment 14 Intelligence Company, many of its members drawn from the Parachute Regiment, and specialised in undercover surveillance in each of the military's three brigade divisions. Its male and female members underwent an incredibly gruelling training course in Templar Barracks in Ashford, Kent and in Wales run by SAS instructors. The least of it was to be woken in the early hours and made to watch a mind-numbing film about the construction of a bamboo hut in South Asia and then be obliged to recall every detail of it. Skilled in such things as breaking and entering, they cleared the way for MI5 and Weapons Intelligence agents to bug homes and businesses or to place tiny transmitters in guns and caches of explosives that made it possible to follow their users' movements. Some explosives were replaced with harmless substances that malfunctioned when ignited; other bombs were prematurely triggered by electronic devices operating on similar wavelengths. RUC Special Branch officers were selected for a unit called E4A to perform such functions. That meant keeping suspects under permanent surveillance even as they moved back and forth across the North–South border, unenviable work done from OP holes in the ground or unmarked Q cars and vans. In the course of the Ulsterisation of the security services, the SAS trained further RUC Special Branch men to become part of Headquarters Mobile Support Units or HMSUs, which killed a number of PIRA and INLA figures. The circumstances were sufficiently dubious to warrant a high-powered police investigation under Manchester's chief constable, John Stalker, which MI5 tried to thwart and whose findings the government suppressed on grounds of national security. Stalker seems to have been so well smeared with allegations of questionable business contacts in his native Manchester that he went on to star in TV double-glazing adverts.

In circumstances where the PIRA was likely to be caught armed and red-handed, SAS troops were deployed, usually with maximum post-operational publicity to satisfy a widespread public desire to see terrorists get their just deserts. Although special forces were obliged to operate within the army's Yellow Card rules of engagement, in practice the nature of their training, and the tense situations in which they were deployed, meant that they were liable to unleash dozens of rounds into the chests and heads of their 'contacts' in circumstances where it was impossible to shout warnings or 'hands up'. When they were not from

Auckland, Cape Town or Fiji, these men were often the products of broken homes with delinquent pasts who had served in places like Oman; when PIRA units encountered them, the probability was that people were going to die. As they had it: 'Big boys' game; big boys' rules'. The Army Legal Service did its best to minimise subsequent appearances by these men – invariably called 'A' or 'B' – before coroners' inquests and courts, although conforming with the rule of law was an important part of the British campaign in Northern Ireland. Successive British ministers adopted the line that they did not dictate security to the security forces while denying that there was a shoot-to-kill policy.[45]

A fairly typical operation occurred on 4 December 1984. Following a tip-off from an informer, an SAS unit staked out a PIRA arms cache at Magheramulkenny. An Armalite rifle had been used in twenty-two attacks on security forces since 1979, including four killings of off-duty policemen in and around Dungannon. Six SAS men, in three groups of two, concealed themselves around the field in which the guns were hidden in a hedge. After two days of lying still and alternating wakefulness and sleep, a Talbot car with three men in it arrived at three o'clock on Sunday afternoon. Twenty-two-year-old Colm McGirr and nineteen-year-old Brian Campbell made for the cache. McGirr pulled out the Armalite and handed it to Campbell who headed for the car. A soldier emerged shouting 'Halt! Security forces!' McGirr turned round holding a shotgun and was hit by a total of thirteen bullets. Campbell turned towards the soldiers, with his Armalite, and was shot twice. The car driver tried to escape, as two soldiers pumped rounds into the car, shattering its windshield. It was found abandoned two miles away with blood inside. A soldier dressed a wound Campbell had in his shoulder, and inserted a breathing tube as he went into shock and died. It is conceivable that the PIRA men could have been photographed carrying the weapons and arrested later by the RUC, but that was not the spirit of those times. If it is true that the British army ensured that the PIRA never achieved its fundamental strategic objective, this was in no small part due to special-forces operations that made it very risky for terrorists to operate. This inculcated the idea that the PIRA faced a military stalemate and hence inclined it to the view that a military solution was a pipedream.

In order to monitor PIRA activities, a vast security net spread over republican areas, whose visible manifestations were watchtowers and observation posts that sprang up in both towns and country. Overhead there were also incessant helicopter flights, some of them carrying heli-teli or cameras recording movements below. RAF surveillance aircraft took aerial photos of country areas looking for signs of ground disturbed by arms dumps or command wires. Electronic eavesdropping devices, hidden cameras and motion sensors all helped intelligence agents to build up a rich picture of their terrorist opponents, as did the replacement of card indexes with ever more sophisticated computers to which foot patrols and roadblocks fed routine fresh intelligence on the movements of suspects. The Provos responded with their own counter-intelligence operations. The number plates of cars owned by respectable middle-class people were cloned, and attached to identical vehicles, which would then raise no suspicions if stopped. They had lookouts watching for undercover agents in unmarked vehicles, or for people whose accents or demeanour did not fit in 'their' territory. Having identified anyone too muscle-bound around neck and shoulders and with too short-cropped hair, the PIRA were soon alert to the scruffy, unshaven, weedy individuals with long hair who replaced them. PIRA technical experts examined weapons that may have been tampered with, and sought out new frequencies for triggering bombs remotely.

By far the sharpest weapon in the security services' campaign against the Provos (and loyalist terrorists) was informers recruited from, or groomed to join, the terrorist organisation, arguably the tactic that would so stimulate PIRA paranoia that the group ultimately lost the armed struggle. In addition to MI5, an army intelligence formation called the Force Research Unit (FRU) was specifically tasked to recruit and handle republican and loyalist agents, a job requiring formidable abilities on the part of those doing it. Most agents and informers were recruited because of familiar human failings. A letter arrived with £50 inside and details of a meeting where more was to be had. A couple of hundred pounds would be handed over. Perhaps the man approached nursed a grudge after squabbling with another Provo. Perhaps he was shown graphic photographs of a local Provo commander sleeping with his wife. Perhaps he just started to talk to the man who deliberately bumped the back of his car so as to provoke a conversation.

For some terrorists the nervous tensions of the job had become unbearable, especially as victory seemed endlessly deferred. A few were appalled by indiscriminate bloodshed in which innocent civilians were killed, a theme underlined whenever relatives of the dead appeared grief-stricken or stunned on television. Apart from those being blackmailed, many probably took up the offer of avoiding a prison sentence when they were caught drunk-driving, dealing drugs or with a gun. A few probably welcomed the £20 a week they were given by their handlers, with the odd £200–300 bonus when they came up trumps with information that led to an arrest. The wife of one agent used to accompany her husband to meetings with his handler, armed with telephone and utility bills, and even the account for the monthly TV rental, knowing that they would be settled by British intelligence. This agent's handlers also enabled him to secure funds from various government employment and community schemes, which boosted his credibility within republican Sinn Féin circles. More senior turncoats had larger sums paid into mainland bank accounts, but they were not allowed to access them lest newfound wealth provoked suspicion. They would ultimately be relocated abroad.

Even a briefcase with £25,000 was scant reward for potentially being abducted, tortured and then shot in the back of the head by the PIRA's dedicated 'nutting squad'. Established in 1980 this was under the sinister command of John Joe Magee, a former member of British army special forces, and Frederick 'Scap' Scappaticci, the son of an ice-cream seller from Belfast's Little Italy. Having failed in his bid to become a professional footballer, Scappaticci had joined the Provos in about 1974. Slight of build but with a ferocious temper, he was quick to take offence when anyone mispronounced his name. By some major irony, he was the British agent code-named 'Stakeknife' or as some prefer 'Steaknife', receiving an estimated £75,000 a year paid into a Gibraltar bank account. He was a so-called walk-in who had contacted British intelligence because he had once been beaten up by the IRA before joining it, and, evidently, because he had an almost pathological detestation of the coldly pious Martin McGuinness, at that time allegedly head of PIRA's Northern Command.[46] On the loyalist side, a former soldier, Brian Nelson, was infiltrated into the UFF, rising to become its senior intelligence officer. He claimed that on behalf of the FRU he redirected UFF violence from indiscriminate slaughter of Catholics to the focused targeting of republican terrorists. Apparently he helped the FRU avert a UFF attempt to assassinate Gerry Adams with a limpet mine attached to the roof of his armoured taxi. But Nelson also set up a number of people as UFF targets, managing to misidentify innocent people, while the FRU itself sometimes deliberately failed to act on his information, thereby enabling the UFF to kill republican targets. He was also involved in the UFF killing of the elderly IRA figure Francisco

Notarantonio, ironically to throw the IRA off the scent of Scappaticci.[47]

Nineteen eighty-one saw the first PIRA supergrass, that is someone who turned prosecution witness in return for soft-pedalling of their own offences. Christopher Black was arrested after participating in a PIRA photo-opportunity dressed in the customary black balaclava. During his interrogation he suddenly said: 'If I help youse, will youse help me?' In return for immunity from prosecution, and a new life in England, Black named thirty-eight people as PIRA members, thirty-five of whom received a total of four thousand years' imprisonment, often on the sole basis of his testimony. Another supergrass, Raymond Gilmour, did for the PIRA in Londonderry, having been recruited by Special Branch as a seventeen-year-old facing bank-robbery charges, before being infiltrated into the PIRA via its rival INLA. As in the cases of Scappaticci, Nelson and others, the security services knowingly allowed Gilmour to take part in a two-year rampage of PIRA criminality so as to extract the maximum information about the organisation. Colluding in criminality was one demerit of using informers; another was their propensity to accuse people they did not like so as to boost their utility to their handlers, the problem that eventually nullified their testimony and led to the overturning of many convictions by Northern Ireland's Appeals Court.[48]

The PIRA bombing campaign in England was designed to exact vengeance on Margaret Thatcher's government and to weaken the resolve of the British public in resisting Irish terrorism. On 18 December 1984 a twenty- to thirty-pound bomb exploded at lunchtime in Hans Crescent outside Harrods department store. A telephoned warning came too late. Six people, including two police officers and an American businessman, were killed and a hundred wounded. On 12 October of that year, a twenty-five-pound bomb hidden in room 629 exploded in the early hours of the morning at the Grand hotel in Brighton, in an attempt to murder Margaret Thatcher and the Conservative cabinet. The blast collapsed the front of the building, killing Sir Anthony Berry, Roberta Wakeham, the wife of the Tory chief whip, and two middle-aged members of local Tory associations. Margaret Tebbit, the wife of senior minister Norman Tebbit, was paralysed from the neck down, while her husband sustained serious injuries and was trapped under rubble for four hours. Despite broken limbs, Tebbit managed to joke with rescuers as they extracted him. PIRA bomber Patrick Magee had left a palmprint and a fingerprint on a hotel registration card when he checked in as 'Roy

Walsh' months before. In 1986 he received eight life sentences, to serve a minimum of thirty-five years. He was released in 1999, becoming a celebrity terrorist with his expressions of qualified regret, most recently on a distasteful radio programme broadcast on the BBC.

On 8 November 1987 PIRA bombers struck at a Remembrance Day ceremony in Enniskillen. A forty-pound gelignite bomb exploded in a community hall near where a small crowd had gathered around a war memorial. PIRA claimed to have been targeting soldiers but the bomb exploded before they arrived. Eleven people were killed – a twelfth man, Ronnie Hill, died in 2000 after being left in a coma for thirteen years – and a further sixty wounded. All of the victims were Protestant civilians, some of them elderly people and five of them women, including a retired WAAF nurse with her war medals and a twenty-year-old nurse called Marie Wilson. Revulsion at this attack swept through southern Ireland, where fifty thousand people signed a book of condolence in Dublin and the country momentarily ground to a halt. Marie Wilson's father became one of the many ordinary people who briefly flitted across public consciousness to remind the wider world that there was a large silent majority of decent people in Northern Ireland.

Bombings like Enniskillen led some within the PIRA leadership to question their sole reliance on a military campaign which could result in such propaganda own-goals. Bobby Sands's 1981 election victory indicated that there might be more mileage in Sinn Féin which many Provos had hitherto regarded as little more than an outlet for their newspapers. Leading republican propagandist Danny Morrison was responsible for the catchy phrase about using the ballot box as well as the Armalite rifle to achieve their goals. In 1982 Adams and McGuinness were elected to a new Northern Ireland assembly, while the following year a Sinn Féin activist won a seat on Omagh district council. On 9 June of that year Adams was elected MP for West Belfast, although he refused to take up the Westminster seat. That November he displaced Ruarí Ó Brádaigh as president of Sinn Féin. Under his leadership, Sinn Féin and PIRA would advance on parallel fronts.

One important effect of the rise of Sinn Féin as an electoral force was that it pushed the governments of Dublin and London closer together in their common desire to stop Sinn Féin from marginalising the constitutional nationalists in the SDLP or from becoming a force in the South's fissiparous coalition politics. On 15 November 1985 Margaret Thatcher and taoiseach Garret Fitzgerald signed the Anglo-Irish Agreement which established institutional mechanisms for the South to have a say in the running of the North as well as enhanced cross-border security co-operation to meet a common threat. The Irish made Northern Ireland a shade greener; Margaret Thatcher could point to a threat to PIRA's southern supply trail and training camps. Although the Agreement stressed that unification would be entirely dependent upon the consent of the northern majority, the Unionists regarded the Agreement as a betrayal and the first step towards a united Ireland. Ian Paisley fulminated: 'We pray this night that thou wouldst deal with the Prime Minister of our country. O God, in wrath take vengeance upon this wicked, treacherous, lying woman. Take vengeance upon here, O Lord, and grant that we shall see a demonstration of thy power.' For the first time the RUC was heavily engaged in battling loyalists mobs, while the UVF attacked the homes of Protestant policemen with firebombs. Although the decision was not related to the Agreement, in the following year Adams and his supporters in Sinn Féin/PIRA abandoned their boycott of the Irish parliament and signalled that Sinn Féin was going to contest southern elections. An abstentionist faction seceded as Republican Sinn Féin, with its own Continuity IRA that is still active today.[49]

While these shifts were happening in the political landscape, a sequence of events occurred that took violence to a new nadir. During the autumn of 1987 British intelligence officers monitored the movements of a Provo active service unit as it moved back and forth between Belfast and Málaga in southern Spain. It gradually became apparent that the PIRA team were bent on driving an enormous car bomb from the Spanish mainland so as to bomb the Royal Anglian Regiment at the Changing of the Guard ceremony in Gibraltar. This was scheduled to take place on 8 March. SAS teams were despatched to join a host of intelligence personnel already present. Their orders specified that they were allowed to fire without warning if a shout might lead to death or injury of a comrade or a bystander. On 4 March 1988 Mairéad Farrell, a thirty-one-year-old former PIRA prisoner, flew in from Brussels, while Sean Savage, aged twenty-three, and Danny McCann, thirty, arrived from Paris. Savage and McCann had assassinated two Special Branch officers in Belfast Docks in August 1987. They hired two Fiesta cars, and used one of them to move 140 pounds of explosives which were then put into the other; this second Fiesta was left in a Marbella car park. They rented a white Renault, and parked it near where the ceremony was to be held, the idea being to replace it with the white Fiesta carrying the bomb so that nobody would notice. Next, Farrell and McCann drove to the border, and then walked over on foot; Savage drove the white Renault. The three wandered around and then walked back along Winston Churchill Avenue to the border. They loitered chatting at a petrol station and then split up to leave. McCann found himself temporarily smiling into a face that did not smile back. Realising his mistake, McCann brought his right arm up suddenly, and was shot by a man in jeans and T-shirt. Farrell went for something in her shoulder bag, and was shot too. Savage was confronted by two SAS men. As he went into combat mode, one soldier fired nine rounds into him; two to the head and seven into his chest as he was trained to do. The soldiers concerned were whisked away from the scene; the British public rejoiced.

Republican supporters turned out in numbers to the funerals of these three in Belfast's Milltown cemetery ten days later. Pandemonium broke out when a UFF gunman, Michael Stone, ran amok hurling grenades and firing at the mourners with a pistol. Before he was rescued by police from a furious mob bent on killing him, Stone had murdered two civilians in their twenties and an older PIRA member called Caoimhin MacBradaigh. His targets had been Adams and McGuinness, in revenge for Enniskillen.

Three days later, republicans gathered to bury Caoimhin Mac-Bradaigh in the same cemetery. A VW Passat suddenly hove into view, leading many of the mourners to think they were under another loyalist attack. As it happened, the two men in the car were off-duty army signals men, one of whom was showing his colleague his first republican funeral. When the car was trapped by an angry mob, one of the soldiers fired a warning shot from his Browning pistol. Any undercover 'Det', FRU or SAS trooper would have shot someone to clear an escape route. The mourners and PIRA stewards dragged the men out of the car. They were assaulted and bundled into a black taxi which drove them to a patch of wasteland. Watched by an army surveillance helicopter, the men were dragged out of the taxi, stabbed and shot. Various mourners were prosecuted under common-cause legislation, but the perpetrators of these two terrible murders were never caught. Prime minister Thatcher joined the soldiers' families when their coffins were flown back to England, where many people, hitherto disinclined to engage in the 'Paddy-whacking' that had become normative in the popular press, regarded their killers as savages.

Against the background of unremitting bleakness, Sinn Féin had come to the bitter conclusion – based on poor poll showings in southern Ireland – that it could only thrive as part of a much broader pan-nationalist front, stretching through John Hume and the SDLP, via Dublin and on to Irish-America and the White House. There Irish issues could be used, for example, to square Democrat Congressmen to support Reagan's war in Nicaragua, with a pay-off in Northern Ireland. The Redemptorist Alex Reid, who had administered the last rites to one of the two soldiers killed at Milltown, was able to arrange a number of meetings between Adams and Hume, talks which were broadened out to include a number of their colleagues and comrades. Hume took full advantage of the recent bloodshed to ask Adams whether Sinn Féin/PIRA thought that 'the methods were more sacred than the cause'. He also said that since the Unionists could only be persuaded into a united Ireland, PIRA should declare a ceasefire and leave the future shape of Ireland to a conference to be convened by the Irish government. Implicitly assuming that the British government was neutral to the outcome, both the SDLP and Sinn Féin built up their support in the US, in the hope that this permutation of cards would trump any noise coming from the Unionists.

On 20 August 1988 PIRA used a two-hundred-pound bomb to kill eight soldiers and grievously injure a further twenty-eight as they travelled on a bus back to their Omagh barracks. Ten days later the SAS killed three PIRA men, including Gerard Harte, the commander of mid-Tyrone PIRA, who were believed to have bombed the bus, in an ambush near Drumnakilly. As the three drove up to kill what they thought was a part-time soldier, they were shot by twelve soldiers concealed in a nearby ditch. In the following years there were further 'contacts' in which PIRA members were wiped out in ambushes in which on each occasion two hundred rounds or more were fired by SAS men. While attacks like these made serious inroads into PIRA's ranks, especially in Tyrone, loyalist paramilitaries switched from indiscriminate sectarian murder to targeting of nationalist sympathisers, who may have been identified for them by renegade members of the security services. The reasoning of Protestant paramilitaries was simple enough. If the British government responded to PIRA pressure by making endless concessions to moderate nationalists at the expense of the Unionists, then loyalist gunmen would deplete the PIRA while warning that if they were sold out they could wage a long war too. For Adair, it was a matter of not letting 'his' community be 'fucking walked on' and of ensuring that those who lived by the sword died by it, which explained his obsessional attempts to kill leading west Belfast PIRA figures. He also went for what he imagined were the brains behind armed republicanism. In February 1989 the UVF broke into the home of a lawyer activist called Pat Finucane who had represented many PIRA clients. Several members of his family were involved in republican organisations; one brother had died in a car crash while on a PIRA active service mission, another was the fiancé of Mairéad Farrell who had been shot on Gibraltar. Finucane was shot four-teen times as he ate his Sunday meal while his wife was shot in the foot. Adair's men nicknamed the victim 'Fork' Finucane; he was still clasping that implement when he died. The killing of Finucane has especially exercised the world's international lawyers, who, incredulous that a lawyer might have terrorist involvements, nonetheless believe PIRA claims that Finucane was set up by elements of the security services colluding with his paramilitary assassins. There was collusion between Adair's gang and individual policemen and soldiers, who passed on montage photos of PIRA terrorists with their addresses, but at no stage has this been found to have been official policy. On 3 March 1991 the UVF planned to hit a senior republican with his wife in Boyle's bar in the republican stronghold of Cappagh, but killed three PIRA volunteers when they drove into the pub car park, as well as a civilian struck by a round in the lavatory. By this time Adair's group had acquired RPG launchers although they were not especially proficient at aiming them.

On the political front the shape of a future settlement was becoming apparent, even though the will to achieve it was manifestly not universal. Moderate Unionists acknowledged that there had to be some form of power-sharing and an Irish dimension of indeterminate proportions, while constitutional nationalists in the SDLP recognised that joint authority was more realistic than a united Ireland. Among the chief reasons why the latter was unrealistic was that southern Ireland was too poor to take up the £6 billion which the UK government was using to subsidise Northern Ireland, funds which paid for its bizarre doppel-ganger infrastructure where there were two of everything from libraries to swimming pools, on each side of the concrete and meshed maze that kept the feuding communities apart.

PIRA continued to commit atrocities on the mainland. This re-emphasis reflected the fact that by then 70 per cent of PIRA operations in Northern Ireland had to be aborted for fear of detection, while of the remaining 30 per cent, 80 per cent were prevented or interdicted by the security forces.[50] On 20 March 1993 two bombs left in a shopping centre in Warrington near Liverpool led to the deaths of a three-year-old boy, Jonathan Ball, and a twelve-year-old, Timothy Parry, who had gone out to buy some football shorts. In response to the December 1993 Downing Street Declaration, PIRA declared a ceasefire on 31 August 1994. The two governments, by now of John Bruton and John Major, issued a Joint Framework Document which promised all-party talks but only when the PIRA had renounced violence. Unionist protests at this deal temporarily lulled republicans into the delusion that they had achieved a sort of victory. A massive explosion on 9 February 1996 in London's Canary Wharf business district was part of a new strategy to damage the British economy at its most lucrative core. Inan Ul-haq Bashir and John 'JJ' Jeffries, who both ran a newsagent's store, were blown to pieces when they took most of the blast. A low-loader with a thousand pounds of ANFO built into it had travelled from County Monaghan via the PIRA Ho Chi Minh Trail in Scotland and then down the motorways to London. Three thumbprints were found, including one on a car magazine left on wasteground where the truck had parked before the bomb-run began, another on an ashtray at a service station covered by motorway CCTV, and a third on a Stena ferry ticket from Belfast. By felicitous coincidence, these belonged to one of several PIRA men caught red-handed when the RUC managed to roll up the South Armagh sniper team, whose final victim had been lance-bombardier Stephen Restorick, the last British soldier to die in the Troubles. The bombers and snipers served a matter of months of very long sentences because of the concurrent impact of the Good Friday Agreement. The Docklands bomb followed on from a one-hundred-pound Semtex bomb a year earlier that caused £1 billion of damage in the older City of London. It killed the fifteen-year-old daughter of a chauffeur returning a car, and injured her eight-year-old sister. A middle-aged doorman and a younger man were also killed. The ambulance driver first on the scene became another casualty. Traumatised by this incident, he shot dead his girlfriend five months later and then repeatedly tried to kill himself in various secure psychiatric hospitals. The Docklands bomb was followed on 15 June 1996 by a 3,500-pound truck bomb which demolished the centre of Manchester, injuring two hundred and causing between £100 million and £300 million worth of damage. Although these operations seemed spectacular, there was something about the execution that also indicated weakness. The bombs originated from South Armagh, indicating the success British security forces had had in rolling up PIRA cells in England. They had learned to watch and wait rather than rounding up the first available group of 'Paddies' at the first opportunity. There was something more. Massive explosions in London undermined Gerry Adams's claim to be able to control PIRA violence, leading Dublin, London and Washington to question the value of dealing with the middle man.

In Ireland that mood spread when on 7 June a PIRA hold-up gang attacked a security van delivering pension money in Limerick, shooting dead Jerry McCabe, a fifty-two-year-old Garda detective in the escort vehicle. The trial of five men for this outrage was hampered by the fact that several eyewitnesses suddenly refused to testify after being intimidated by the PIRA. The police were appalled when a deal was struck allowing four defendants to plead guilty to manslaughter, with Martin McGuinness endeavouring to have them released under the Good Friday Agreement.[51]

Shortly after the election of Tony Blair in May 1997, PIRA restored the ceasefire it had unilaterally broken, in the expectation that a Labour prime minister with a massive majority would be less sympathetic to the Unionists than Major. That was a miscalculation since Blair revealed himself as being strongly pro-Union, believing that the key to the resolution of the conflict lay in a wider policy of devolution within the entire UK. The energetic and youthful Blair brought tremendous energy to the peace process, which he rapidly treated as his domain. He was also a master at the political manipulation of language, having a natural flair for the constructive ambiguity necessary to reconcile implacable antagonists. His first three Northern Ireland secretaries were the former academic Mo Mowlam, the coldly volatile Peter Mandelson and the Glaswegian Catholic John Reid. Unionists intensely disliked Mowlam, although only the really nasty called her 'the pig in a wig' (she had lost her hair through chemotherapy sessions for a brain tumour), because of her foul language and over-familiarity with leading republicans like McGuinness, whom she called 'Martin babe'. Together with the new taoiseach Bertie Ahern, whose role in the peace process was equally important, Blair elaborated what would become the agreed settlement, the Good Friday Agreement reached at Easter 1998.

There would be no change to the Union of Northern Ireland and Great Britain until the majority of the people of Northern Ireland consented to it. Republicans dreamed that demography would do its work in this respect, while they built up political support on both sides of the border, perhaps with an eye to a bid on the Irish presidency, or at least a power-broking role in the Republic's coalition governments. Unionists had to accept power-sharing with the minority and institutionalised cross-border co-operation. If the Provos renounced violence – although establishing that would be a protracted saga in itself – then Sinn Féin would be admitted to the political process without too much talk of murderers. Indeed, the murderers themselves played a role in the peace process. When it threatened to break down after the INLA assassinated Billy 'King Rat' Wright in prison, triggering a further round of tit-for-tat killings, the Northern Ireland secretary Mo Mowlam visited among others Michael Stone and Johnny Adair in the Maze to ensure their continuing commitment to peace.

Although Gerry Adams failed to make much of an imprint on the terms of the Good Friday Agreement, he managed to convey the impression that he had played a major role in it, by virtue of having slipped in matters entirely related to the politics of the gun. These included the early release of paramilitary prisoners, a commission on the fate of the RUC, which after the Patten Report was refashioned as the Police Service of Northern Ireland, and the sanctioning of 'community restorative justice' for those communities which did not trust the regular courts. This effectively handed justice over to paramilitaries who, while in jail, had reconfigured themselves into lawyers and sociologists, except those like Adair who were bent on a life of organised crime and hence concentrated on drugs and weight-lifting. PIRA spent five years prevaricating over the issue of putting its arms dumps beyond use, the face-saving formula adopted for their surrender. For a brief period, the feisty law lecturer turned statesman David Trimble emerged with the Ulster Unionist Party as the strongest grouping in the Northern Ireland Assembly. The dramatic rise in the Sinn Féin vote vis-à-vis that of the moderate SDLP resulted in a corresponding leaching of Unionist voters away from the UUP and Trimble towards the more populist Democratic Unionists of Ian Paisley. To his credit, Blair refused to be deflected from his course, even when, as in August 1998, a huge bomb planted by the breakaway Real IRA demolished the centre of Omagh, killing twenty-nine people and injuring three hundred, in the worst atrocity of the entire Troubles.

While the Provos had been militarily defeated, Sinn Féin was more adroit on the world stage than the loyalists. The latter were hopeless at presenting their case – which should better have resembled the republicans' 'story' – to the wider world. Their most fluent advocates tended to be Tory Roman Catholics and Dean Godson, an Orthodox Jew, writing in the British print media. Sinn Féin–PIRA had a vast propaganda and fund-raising operation in the US. Despite many Irish-Americans being descendants of Ulster Scots, integrated to the point of invisibility, the Unionists had no permanent office in a capital where one can otherwise encounter lobbyists for Burkina Faso and Fiji. It was revealing that when the loyalists got around to stressing their historic role in modernising Ulster through industry, they alighted upon the idea of christening Harland and Wolff shipyard 'Titanic Quarter' after the biggest shipwreck in history. There have also been attempts to rewrite ancient history in order to make the Ulster Scots rival victims to the republicans. The Iron Age inhabitants of Ulster were cruelly expelled by invading Gaels and fled to western Scotland. Their descendants returned, uncorrupted, as Ulster Scots planters in the seventeenth century. Attempts to invent or revive the language are as artificial as the efforts of nineteenth-century Catholic schoolmasters to propagate Gaelic.[52] One missed opportunity was to fail to emphasise Sinn Féin PIRA's unsavoury affiliations with ETA, FARC and the PLO, especially in the wake of 9/11 and the advent of a US climate less indulgent towards terrorists. Where Adams was folksy, slippery and sentimental, with the tone of a sociology lecturer at a provincial university, Trimble was lawyerly and prickly. Although a more articulate loyalist leadership came to the fore, including a number of convicted terrorists who emerged from prison, in September 2001 the world was nauseated by the sight of north Belfast loyalist mobs intimidating infants who, in order to reach the Catholic Holy Cross primary school from the mainly Catholic Ardoyne estate, had to walk four hundred yards through the Protestant Glenbryn estate. This was one of several engineered disputes, designed to attract maximum bad publicity.

Every summer there were also increasingly ugly scenes as the oldest Orange lodge at Portadown asserted its right to march to a Protestant church at Drumcree, via a Catholic district whose residents' association was riddled with republican sympathisers. At these parades cum riots leading Unionist politicians found themselves in the unsavoury company of loyalist paramilitaries bent on using an armoured mechanical digger to attack the RUC.[53] Meanwhile, an Assembly and power-sharing

Executive which had existed for some nineteen months had been suspended after the discovery in 2002 of a Sinn Féin spy-ring at Stormont and the resumption of British direct rule. The following autumn, Tony Blair held fresh elections, partly to confirm the US belief that the conflict could be resolved only when the extremes of Sinn Féin and the DUP were forced to confront the consequences of their own electoral success. David Trimble was offered up as a sacrifice to that goal as his own supporters deserted him. It would take four more years, and the threat to cut off the politicians' salaries, before Ian Paisley became first minister with Martin McGuinness as his deputy.[54]

Repeated Irish and US efforts to achieve this end continually collapsed not just over Sinn Féin–PIRA prevarication over arms decommissioning, but because in 2004 the Provos carried out the largest bank robbery in Northern Ireland's history – whether to buy arms or to provide retired terrorists with pensions is unclear – the most tangible manifestation of the fact that they were operating a Mafia-like crime racket within republican enclaves that has spread to the UK mainland. PIRA did eventually claim to have decommissioned its arsenals, although there is no photographic record of this process, which was conducted under the eyes of a Canadian general. Even the most notorious terrorist prisoners came out through the turnstile of the Maze prison. Johnny Adair was released in September 1999 after serving a quarter of his sentence. Six months earlier, he had taken his wife to a UB40 concert, while out on parole. A republican came up behind him as 'Red Red Wine' played and shot him in the back of the head. The gun may have been tampered with as the bullet merely bounced off the victim's shaven head. Wounded, Adair fled the scene as 'Red Red Wine' resounded.

Loyalist terrorists had one major handicap that almost ineluctably propelled them into criminality. Whereas republicans had an impressive array of welfare organisations that reflected their rejection of the status quo, pro-state loyalist terrorists had no parallel society to fall back on when they could no longer live by the gun. In his new temporary role as a £16,500-a-year prisoners' welfare co-ordinator, a job he failed to hold down like all earlier ones, the peacenik Johnny Adair, all belligerence and testosterone with his pirate earrings and reversed baseball cap, was prominent in organising the decommissioning of loyalist weapons, while reserving the best stuff for himself. These were essential to a major drugs business he operated in Belfast, based on smuggling Ecstasy pills from

England in the detachable hub caps of a Mercedes, while cannabis was dropped off on the coast from Scotland. Since raids by the police routinely unearthed £250,000 worth of drugs at a time, this was a profitable business, with pedlars earning up to £10,000 a week provided they paid their dues and respects to the right terrorist chieftain.

In his bid to be Belfast's Mr Big, Adair endeavoured to merge C Company and the remnants of Wright's LVF, a move that resulted in a lethal feud with the UDA leadership, whose ageing brigadiers were still notionally in charge of loyalist violence. Adair's key allies in both the drugs trade and this feud included the most exotic UDA members, Andre Khaled Shoukri and his brothers, the Coptic Christian sons of an Ulster Protestant mother and an Egyptian father. Demonstrating their customary awareness of the wider world, Adair and his cohorts dubbed them 'the Pakis'. In addition to his involvement in drugs and the feud, Adair simply loved the limelight, forcing his neighbours to keep the streets spotless just in case television crews turned up. An electric road-sweeping cart was forever on his street and he would order his neighbours to move their cars to make way for it. In 2002 he made the criminal big time when he figured in a book called *Hard Bastards* edited by the widow of Ronnie Kray (Ronnie and his twin Reggie had been England's most notorious 1960s gangsters), although the interviewee insisted he was 'a soldier'. He appeared among several gentlemen one would not wish to encounter in a dark alley at night. Adair lost the feud when the massed ranks of the UDA drove his key lieutenants and his wife Gina out of Northern Ireland. Gina had to leave so quickly that the couple's Alsatians Shane and Rebel were left behind. Since fifty or so of these fugitives live in and around Bolton, they are known as the 'Bolton Wanderers' to their erstwhile associates. 'Mad Dog' joined them, but, following the break-up of his marriage, he moved to Scotland where he lives in Ayrshire surrounded by his fellow Glasgow Rangers aficionados. His autobiography claims, 'I will be back,' the cinematic echo being all too deliberate.[55]

It would be misleading to suggest that only loyalists are gangsters. The PIRA runs the largest crime syndicate in Europe, dwarfing the Camorra and Mafia in Italy. Peace has had little or no impact on PIRA-organised criminality, which by the late 1980s was bringing in an estimated £10 million a year. Specialised police units like C13, established by the RUC in 1983, are under-funded and lacking in the confiscatory powers that the Gardaí enjoy in the Republic.

Bank robbery, kidnapping of rich businessmen and the theft of artworks and racehorses have all figured in the PIRA repertory. Since the Good Friday Agreement there have been over four hundred armed robberies in Northern Ireland, including the raid on the Northern Bank that netted £25 million. A senior IRA figure with so many shoes that his friends call him 'Imelda' was repeatedly questioned in the subsequent inquiry into that raid, which in southern Ireland has reached into respectable banking circles. Paramilitary rackets began thirty years ago. By now a lot of the proceeds will have been laundered into outwardly respectable businesses. Money was extorted from firms and shops under the guise of voluntary contributions to prisoner welfare charities that were formalised into a regular Danegeld. When urban bus services were disrupted by hijackers and arsonists the paramilitaries moved into the lucrative licensed taxi trade. Similarly, since many pubs closed at 7 p.m. because of the likelihood of terrorist attacks, all paramilitary groups opened unlicensed drinking dens. As the alcohol sold was usually stolen, these places made an absolute profit, albeit minuscule in relation to the sums later derived from drugs. Unemployed terrorists also gained jobs as bouncers and minders, as the clubs went in for selling stolen goods, food and drink on a large scale. Such men also joined private security services, because firms and shops were charged lower insurance premiums if they employed them. Terrorists colluded with corrupt businessmen in burning down buildings to collect the fire insurance pay-out.[56]

There are the usual scams, including counterfeiting CDs, DVDs, designer goods, perfume and Smirnoff Red Label vodka, this last done by replicating a complex seven-stage distilling process. The fake stuff is sold through pub optics. Irish-Americans provide the latest Hollywood films, which are illegally reproduced on PCs. Then there are gambling machines rigged against the gambler which bars and clubs are encouraged to install, along with the doormen and bouncers who accompany them as part of a package. PIRA has made a big play with being tough on criminals, having shot dead a notorious Dublin racketeer nicknamed 'the General', while shooting the small fry in the legs. Posing as community-spirited vigilantes, PIRA simultaneously licenses approved street dealers, thereby satisfying the moral majority while catering for drug addicts. Those who fail to pay their dues are horrifically beaten and warned to leave the country on pain of death; this has meant the surfacing on the UK mainland of sundry unsavoury characters.

Shockingly, between 1995 and 2003 there were 895 punishment

shootings and 1,512 punishment beatings in Northern Ireland. Although these alarm the police, successive secretaries of state have been loath to use them to suspend political parties linked to the terrorist organisations that carry them out; instead they take rival paramilitary murders as the sole benchmark for proscription. Beatings and shootings are doled out because of some perceived slight to a paramilitary or by virtue of mistaken identity, as well as being inflicted on notorious paedophiles and juvenile delinquents, selected by popular request. As one victim has explained: 'There's one rule for one and another rule for another. See if your da[d]'s in the [I]RA you're sweet, you get away with everything. See if your uncle's in the RA you get away with so much and then they just beat you. See if you've nobody in the RA you're fucked!' What this meant for one child is worth repeating:

> I was about 13 or 14, I got the first beating . . . masked men came round but they only hit us a couple of times in the arms and that was it, and then the next time was about 15. They just beat us again. It was a wee beating, it wasn't hard, and then the last time was March . . . I got black eyes and they beat us all about, beat us about the legs and all. And then it happened . . . again, broke my nose, broke my arm and I was beat with hammers and all, all over my body and I had staples in . . . my head.

It does not take much imagination to see how vigilantism could also be enforced by those seeking to impose local sharia law.[57]

Excise fraud involves the differential duties on diesel and petrol in the Republic and UK, which enables the PIRA to make 15p on each litre smuggled over the border. The PIRA also rinses the dye from low-grade fuel designed for agricultural vehicles, bought at 15–20p a litre, which is then sold at 70–80p as diesel for cars and trucks. Because this fake fuel degrades car engines, a network of motor-repair shops has been established to deal with the inevitable problems. Cigarette smuggling is a lucrative racket as a single forty-foot container brought in from Taiwan houses ten million cigarettes with a street resale value of £1.5 million. A newer racket is the illegal dumping of hazardous waste from the Republic at five sites in Northern Ireland, each of which contains between 5,000 and 25,000 tonnes of rubbish, trucked in for a fee of £5,000 per twenty-tonne load. Livestock are also exported from the Republic, collecting an export subsidy on the way, and are then smuggled back to repeat the same journey later.[58]

In republican areas PIRA experts help people make fraudulent mortgage applications in return for a hefty cut from the loan. Inspectors investigating social security fraud are hampered by intimidation. As the army pulls out of South Armagh, where every second car is a BMW or Mercedes, there will be fewer compensation claims for a herd of cattle that fled over a cliff beneath a thunderous Chinook, only to reappear miraculously at a southern cattle market, or for a £1,000 horse that had drowned in a drain after being frightened by a helicopter which became a chestnut gelding worth £23,500 when the claim went in. Between 1991 and 1997 some £9.5 million was claimed in South Armagh as against £1.9 million for the rest of Northern Ireland; clearly it was not a healthy place for our four-legged friends.[59] As the peace process kicks in, franchising expertise is also a major source of revenue. In an act of wilful stupidity, after 9/11 three senior PIRA technicians were caught training Colombian FARC terrorists, a group the US had proscribed as narco-terrorists, in bomb making, mortar manufacture and sniping; their defence was that they were 'bird-watching'. All three were bailed pending appeal from long sentences. So far neither Jim 'Mortar' Monaghan nor his two associates have returned to Bogotá from the Irish Republic to serve their seventeen-year sentences. It is likely that they were involved in a franchise-type operation with FARC paying the PIRA US$6 million for services which have seen a number of Colombian soldiers killed by sophisticated mortars or snipers using Barrett rifles.[60] Individual PIRA terrorists, and in particular those who live high on the hog in rural South Armagh, are believed to be involved in construction firms in London and Manchester (rebuilding a city centre blown to pieces by a PIRA bomb) and property speculation on the British mainland and in new markets like Bulgaria, Turkey and Libya. A senior PIRA figure is said to have invested indirectly in two hundred properties in Manchester alone. At least one London construction firm is rumoured to be a PIRA front organisation. This turn to Mafia-like activity may be encouraging, although obviously not for people who live in the vice-like grip of these people's 'community leader' friends whose arbitration does not extend to the victims of terrorist violence, as the sisters of the late Robert McCartney discovered when they were driven from their own homes.[61]

The southern Irish 'Celtic Tiger' economy underlined the extent to which war-torn Northern Ireland lagged behind both a booming mainland UK and an Ireland that had been transformed in a generation. It could be that Ulster's energies will henceforth be galvanised, as economic vocations replace careers built on sectarianism and political violence. Former terrorists will eke out modest livelihoods as contemporary witnesses. Anyone with any get up and go moves to more salubrious suburbs, leaving an unemployable, superfluous, proletarian residue to keep the fires of hate burning, along with the disabled, elderly and indigent who cannot move. That people in Northern Ireland talk as much about rising property prices as they do in the Republic or UK is an encouraging sign of returning normality. However much one recoils from the sight of Ian Paisley and Martin McGuinness amiably joshing along over tea and cake, or the convicted bomber Gerry Kelly as Sinn Féin's police and justice spokesman, jaw-jaw is preferable to war-war. One cloud on the horizon is the state-sanctioning of republican areas effectively removed from the control of normal courts and policing. This may set an ominous precedent for other so-called communities on mainland Europe and Britain should they seek to live under sharia law.

Three thousand six hundred and thirty people were killed during the Troubles. One thousand seven hundred and eighty-one of them were murdered by the PIRA, who lost around three hundred personnel, 164 of them slain as a result of PIRA or INLA internecine violence. The army, RUC and loyalist paramilitaries killed 115 PIRA or INLA terrorists. In thirty years, the RUC and UDR lost five hundred men and women, while five hundred British troops were killed. Through some divine injustice, people like 'Mad Dog' Adair and Lenny Murphy live on, on the True Crime shelves of bookstores, while mothers and fathers have grim memories of a knock at the door bringing emptying news of the death of a nineteen- or twenty-year-old soldier son. Police trades union officials, as they sit in homes equipped with armoured doors, reinforced glass and panic alarms, grimly recall attending hundreds of funerals of their colleagues, some blown up when they got into their car. Whether these Troubles will revive in a generation or two is anyone's guess. The ghosts of Padraig Pearse seem quiescent. For at present they have been massively overshadowed by an existential threat to the whole of civilisation, not just in New York or London, but in Jakarta, Sydney and Singapore.[62]

CHAPTER 8

World Rage: Islamist Terrorism

I MOB HYSTERIA

The deeper context of jihadist terrorism involves simultaneous bursts of religious enthusiasm across the Muslim world over thirty years ago. This process was paralleled – without the same violent effects – in other monotheistic faiths from the 1970s onwards. These bursts were sustained by a series of secondary conflagrations, which lent apparent substance to the paranoid jihadist claim that Muslims were the victims of atemporal 'Crusader–Zionist' aggression unchanged since the Middle Ages. This self-serving myth resonated with the more widespread assumption of the moral purity of the oppressed, a source of self-righteous violence from time immemorial within a variety of cultures and traditions, spiritual and secular. Criminals were able to find apologists, supporters and sympathisers from the wider Muslim community by cloaking their activities in an ideology largely derived from a major religious tradition with one and a half billion adherents.[1]

In January 1978 US president Jimmy Carter visited Iran. He lauded his ally, shah Muhammed Reza Pahlavi, and pronounced Iran 'an island of stability', praise he coupled with criticism of the shah's shabby human rights record. The regime's modernising emancipation of women was accompanied by the repression symbolised by Savak, the shah's secret police. Carter's contradictory pronouncements were as helpful to the shah as traffic lights signalling red and green simultaneously are to a motorist. That summer and autumn, Iran was convulsed by demonstrations and strikes, which the shah, already suffering from cancer, answered with limited repression (under a thousand people died in the course of the Revolution) and concessions which his many different opponents brushed aside. The shah left his kingdom, never to return, on 16 January 1978; a year later, an elderly cleric, the ayatollah Ruhollah Khomeini, flew in from his exile in Paris.[2]

Under the influence of the academic ideologue Ali Shariati, who had fused a fashionable Third Worldism with Islam before his untimely death in 1977, Khomeini broke with the political quiescence characteristic of Shia Islam, in which an indeterminate period of occultation would end with the return of a mahdi who had vanished in AD 874. Appealing to the disinherited, in a calculated echo of Frantz Fanon, Khomeini called for the establishment of an Islamic republic, with a dual system of power in which clerics controlled every lever that mattered, notably through a Guardians Council. Liberals and Marxists who had hoped to exploit Khomeini's own manipulation of popular enthusiasms were trumped by the master of this game, who in any case had the unique backing of impressive ranges of Iranian society in what was one of the most popular revolutions in world history. Within a year, the new masters had killed not only the three thousand political prisoners Carter was so exercised about, but more people than Savak had murdered in the previous twenty-five years. One of the ways in which the clerics guaranteed their success was to prolong mass hysteria, which they did through the protracted siege of the US embassy in Teheran, in which 'Death to America' resounded from the erstwhile island of stability, and then through the martyrs who were mobilised for death in the eight years of total war with Saddam Hussein's Iraq. An entire generation of children went to their deaths clutching their plastic keys to paradise. This bloodbath and the regime's domestic repressions alienated even those few silly Western intellectuals, like Michel Foucault, who had celebrated this tantalising eruption against a Western rationalism which bored them. It is striking that, among the subjects that anger so many Muslims today, this obliteration of an entire generation is not among them.

The Islamic Revolution was also for export, notwithstanding the fact that 80 per cent of the world's Muslims were Sunnis. They viewed the Shia as heretics who, in the Persian case, were given to contemptuously racist talk of Arab 'lizard eaters'. But this was counterbalanced by widespread admiration for Khomenei's Islamic regime, its hatred of Israel and its ostentatious defiance of the West, as symbolised by Carter's disastrous attempt to rescue the US embassy hostages. Two immediate manifestations of exporting the Revolution were the creation, by Sunni Palestinian admirers of Khomeini, of a terrorist organisation called

Islamic Jihad, which presaged the transformation of a conflict about rival nationalisms into one involving religion, and the parallel mobilisation of Lebanon's Shi'ites through an Iranian surrogate called Party of Allah or Hizbollah, founded in late 1982, a process the Alawite rulers of Syria aided and abetted to extend their domination over their Westernised Lebanese neighbour. Iran sent an estimated US$50 million to US$100 million per annum to Hizbollah, basing hundreds of training personnel in the Bekaa valley, and using Ali Akbar Mohtashamipour, its ambassador to Damascus, as co-ordinator of Hizbollah's campaign of assassination, bombings and kidnappings.

Islamic Jihad struck first. In what came to be regarded as the first use of suicide truck bombing, on 11 November 1982 sheikh Ahmed Qassir blew up the Israeli headquarters in Tyre, killing or wounding 141 people. Then it was Hizbollah's turn to deal a devastating blow at the US presence in Lebanon. On 18 April 1983 a battered pickup truck, low on its springs due to two thousand pounds of ANFO explosives concealed within, swerved into the exit of the US embassy on Beirut's seafront, and then exploded as it crashed into the main lobby. Sixty-three people, including seventeen Americans, were killed in a blast that momentarily lifted up the entire building before most of it collapsed in a mountain of dust and rubble. The dead included all six members of the CIA's Beirut station, as well as Robert Ames, the CIA's top man on the Middle East and its former liaison with Black September's Ali Hassan Salameh. Ames's hand was found floating a mile away, his wedding ring still visible on a finger.

Six months later two massive suicide truck bombs killed 240 US Marines housed in temporary barracks dubbed the Beirut Hilton, and fifty-eight French soldiers who were also in Lebanon on peace-keeping duties. In the former case, a five-ton Mercedes truck smashed its way through flimsy guard posts at fifty miles an hour early one Sunday morning, enabling the driver to detonate 12,000 pounds of Hexogen high explosives, with tanks of bottled gas tied on to magnify the deadly brisance. The effects of both attacks were like some colossal natural disaster. Over at the French barracks, an uncomprehending lieutenant-colonel stared into a huge crater amid mountains of rubble: 'There are about a hundred soldiers still under there. The bomb lifted up the building. Right up, do you understand? And it put it down again over there.' He indicated a distance of about twenty feet. The Iranian Pasadren and their terrorist helpers in Hizbollah further pressured the

West to vacate Lebanon through a series of kidnappings, including professors at the American University of Beirut, CNN reporters, priests and the local CIA station chief Bill Buckley. Kidnapping of Soviet diplomats was less successful, as the KGB abducted a relative of one of those involved, and began posting pieces of him back to his family to indicate their earnestness. Hizbollah also acted as Iran's long arm by assassinating Iranian or Kurdish dissidents based in Europe on behalf of its paymasters, who were the biggest state sponsors of terrorism in the world. Agents based in Iranian embassies would enable Hizbollah to strike at Jewish and Israeli interests as far away as Argentina.[3]

Although Iran's attempts to export the Islamic Revolution were a striking failure, apart from Hizbollah in the Lebanon, the symbolic example it gave alarmed rulers throughout the Muslim world. Here was an avowedly Islamic state, aggressively challenging the West. In the case of the ultra-conservative Saudis, they already had the mechanisms to try to contain the Iranians, because in 1962 they had established the Muslim World League to counter the national socialism of Nasser's Egypt. Enormous increases in the price of oil after the 1973 Arab–Israeli war enabled the Saudis to propagate their puritanical Wahhabist strain of Islam globally. Named after Mohammed ibn Abd al-Wahhab (1703–92), Wahhabism was the austere version of Islam that underpinned the rule of the Saud dynasty in Arabia through a contract between clerics and rulers.[4] Vast sums were disbursed to build some fifteen hundred mosques around the Sunni world, as well as in western Europe, which were then equipped with books and audio sermons, in the hope that they would speak with the voice of a Saudi moralising conservatism, whose existence was paradoxically underwritten by the kingdom's 'decadent' Western allies. The Saudis further institutionalised their political and financial reach through the Organisation of the Islamic Conference and the Islamic Development Bank, and by donating money to Western and Eastern universities to promote Islamic and Middle Eastern studies.

This petro-Islamic largesse was one of the main contributors to the gradual rise in consciousness of a global Muslim *ummah* or community. This was more viscerally real than the secular nationalism, whether local or pan-Arab, or the socialism that had enthused earlier generations. Saudi influence was also secured through the millions of remittance men drawn to the Gulf states in the 1970s and 1980s from as far afield as Pakistan and the Philippines, not to speak of the two million Muslims who each year made the *hajj* to Mecca, whose infrastructure had been improved by an immigrant Yemeni construction tycoon called bin Laden. For this was the essence of the matter. Whereas the Saudis hoped to keep the words Islam and Revolution separate, the Iranians wanted them to fuse, notably in Saudi Arabia itself, a regime Khomeini hated. Behind that fundamental disagreement lay competition between an ultra-conservative and a reactionary–revolutionary power for dominance within Islam as whole, a struggle that has only increased in recent decades.[5]

The venerable texts which the Saudis were making available on a global basis were amenable to many interpretations, especially when increased literacy enabled people to read them for themselves. Using the frequency of citations from certain authors it is possible to construct a diagram resembling a spider's web of who counts in the mental universe of the jihadis. Modernity is of little account. High on the list would be the writings of Ibn Taymiyya (1268–1323), a contemporary of Dante, who influenced Wahhab himself. His thought was largely conditioned by the depredations various Arab Islamic civilisations experienced at the hands of invading Mongols, depredations made worse by the Mongols' syncretic assimilation of Islam to their existing paganism. Never afraid to make enemies, Taymiyya denounced Muslim clerics whose learned elaborations distracted from the essentials of the faith, as once practised by the *salaf*, the earliest followers of the Prophet. Moreover, rulers who did not accept clerical guidance, by instituting sharia (Islamic religious law), and living lives of conspicuous piety, were apostates whom it was the faithful Muslim's duty to depose. Taymiyya added this duty to the existing offensive and defensive definitions of jihad, which in turn he elevated into a sixth pillar of Islam, along with the declaration of faith, charity, fasting, pilgrimage and prayer. These teachings were subversive in the fourteenth century – Taymiyya was imprisoned five times and died in jail – and they remained so six hundred years later to anyone who dismissed the official clerical *ulema* (including Saudi Arabia's Wahhabi clerical Establishment) as venal apologists for corrupt governments.[6]

At dawn on 20 November 1979 the imam of the Grand Mosque at Mecca prepared to usher in the Muslim New Year with special prayers. He paid no attention to a group of young men with red headbands shouldering coffins – for this was where the dead were often blessed – until they set down their load and produced dozens of weapons. A young man called Juhayman bin Muhammed bin Sayf al-Utaybi who seemed to be in charge declared his own brother-in-law the mahdi, the Islamic messiah, for the date was fourteen hundred years after Mohammed's Hijra from Mecca to Medina, an anniversary already loaded with apocalyptic portents. Attempts to halt this armed manifestation by deploying the monarchy's Bedouin praetorian National Guards proved futile since al-Utaybi was one of their number and he quickly had the entrance gates barred. As the day wore on, he issued damning denunciations of the Saudi ruling dynasty, calling them corrupt apostates who had prospered by allowing their Western allies to plunder the country's oil wealth. Al-Utaybi's well-equipped fighters made mincemeat of regular Saudi soldiers who were despatched to eject them from the mosque, a mission inhibited by the need not to destroy it. Eventually the monarchy called in assistance from France's Groupe d'Intervention de la Gendarmerie Nationale and the Pakistani army. Three hastily converted commandos recommended using mass electrocution by putting a high-voltage cable into the mosque's flooded basements, or nerve gas to flush the Mahdists out. After two weeks of close-quarter combat, al-Utaybi and the other surviving fighters were captured, a task made easier when the construction firm Bin Laden Brothers, which had refurbished the mosque, provided blueprints essential to storming it. Al-Utaybi and sixty comrades were quickly beheaded. At the time this siege seemed like a perplexing incident of cultic violence, as mysterious in meaning, or meaninglessness, as similar events that happened in the Christian world. The fact that during the siege rioting Arab and Pakistani students from Pakistan's Qaid-i-Azam university stormed the US embassy in Islamabad – on the rumour that the Americans and Israelis were behind al-Utaybi's seizure of the Mecca mosque – merely seemed like a bizarre pendant, as did ayatollah Khomenei's warm words to the embassy rioters, which included the observation: 'Borders should not separate hearts.'[7]

II THE BROTHERS AND PHAROAH

Although Egypt is the size of France and Spain combined, 95 per cent of its population of sixty million live on 5 per cent of its land, the lush, lotus-shaped strip that follows the course of the Nile. Beyond lies inhospitable desert, whose only redeeming grace may be that it is unsuited to guerrilla warfare. Mysterious monuments remind Egyptians that they are not really Arabs, but heirs to one of the world's greatest polytheistic civilisations, whose mysterious iconography still shimmers beneath the high art of Christianity. The French left the legacy of Napoleonic law. Egypt became an independent parliamentary monarchy in 1922, although the British remained a powerful, and often resented, commercial and military presence, clinging on to the vestiges of Empire. The flourishing of Western modernity during the 1920s, as manifested in a vibrant press, cinema and literary culture, inevitably triggered an Islamic response, which took the form of the Muslim Brotherhood, established in 1928 by a devout primary school teacher called Hassan al-Banna. Appalled by British military bases, foreign ownership of utilities, Egypt's almost foreign-seeming Turko-Circassian upper class, and a vocal feminist movement, al-Banna incorporated existing charitable and pious associations into a series of cell-like 'families', which were linked by such modern communications as magazines and newspapers as well as sermons. Education and charitable work (or *da'wa*) would lead to social reformation, provided evil Western influences were contained. The Brotherhood patiently built a grassroots base that rapidly reached into every Egyptian province, with a membership of half a million people. One of the main ideological influences upon al-Banna was Rashid Rida, an erstwhile moderniser turned salafist who demanded the replacement of Western-influenced laws by the sharia, and revived the Koranic notion of *jahiliyya* – that is the pre-Islamic state of pagan benightedness – to denounce the regimes of the Arab present. At first viewed sympathetically by a monarch who saw the Brotherhood as less menacing than secular nationalism or socialism, this mood changed when its surface network of charitable and pious foundations was accompanied by an underground military organisation, the Secret Apparatus, that began to infiltrate the armed forces. The Brotherhood was compulsorily disbanded in 1948, prompting it to assassinate the prime minister responsible. By way of revenge, a year later, the forty-three-year-old al-Banna was killed in turn.[8]

Initially, the largely lower-middle-class Brothers welcomed the coup which in 1952 chased out the reforming sybarite king Farouk. They confused their own drive for Islamic unity with the pro-Soviet crypto-totalitarian state being established by Nasser and his junta of young officers. Nasser invited in some twenty thousand Soviet 'advisers', while sending promising young officers, like the air force pilot Hosni Mubarak, to the Frunse Military Academy in Moscow. Relations between Nasser and the Islamists quickly deteriorated to the point where in October 1954 a young Brother called Muhammad Abd al-Latif tried to shoot the president at one of the regime's mass rallies in Alexandria, the shots being broadcast live on radio. Nasser's response was swift and brutal.

As Nasser's supporters burned Brotherhood property, six of its leaders were hanged. Others disappeared into Tura prison in southern Cairo. Their number included the Islamist ideologue Sayyid Qutb, whose thought and travails are essential to the story of modern jihadi-salafist terrorism, perhaps the closest way we can describe this ongoing phenomenon without either indicting Islam and fundamentalism or resorting to terms like Islamofascist or the more appropriate Islamobolshevik. The hyphenated term, which has the virtue of being culturally specific, means armed struggle in the service of the creed of the 'pious forefathers' as reassembled into a politico-religious ideology by men who had no recognised religious authority outside the circles of their supporters. It might be useful to explain how we arrive at this definition.

Simply imagine four circles of diminishing size nestling within one another. The largest circle is the world's one and a half billion Muslims, divided into Sunni, Shia and hundreds of other sects like the Sufi and often as historically accommodating of local non-Islamic beliefs as Christianity is of animism in Africa. Observance can be as casual or fundamental, as grimly austere or colourfully sensuous as religious practice is among Jews, Buddhists, Hindus or Christians, which is why the term fundamentalist does not accurately describe Islamist terrorists. Islamists are the next, smaller circle, that is people who want states to introduce Islamic law, a goal they usually pursue through guns and the ballot box in the tradition of the Muslim Brotherhood. The third smaller circle are salafists, or followers of the wise founders who surrounded Mohammed. They want to establish Islamic states of an extremely puritanical kind. The most influential salafist clerics are Saudis. Most jihadists are salafists, but not all salafists are jihadists, that is people who seek to bring about the violent transformation of societies into Islamic states of which the only known model has been the chaos created by the Taliban in Afghanistan. Some envisage this on a vast scale, a revived caliphate, stretching from Spain through the Balkans, North Africa and the Middle East, and on across the former Soviet 'stans' to South Asia, Indonesia, Malaysia, Pakistan and Thailand and parts of China. Within non-Islamic states, jihadi-salafists take a territorial approach too, with each radicalised mosque being like a separate mini-kingdom, bent on dominance over the immediate neighbourhood. Victory has the smell of derelict bars, pubs and dance halls, and the chill of a draught in a room.

These people would not like being called Qutbists, for to name them after a mere mortal would be blasphemous. The son of a teacher in Upper Egypt, Qutb was a typical beneficiary of Egypt's modernisation, before the schools inspector's politico-religious activities led to his being sent to the US in 1948 on an indefinite fact-finding trip that was intended to get him out of the way. Qutb was repelled by the relatively innocent materialist society he found there, and especially by the succession of women who appeared bent on seducing the middle-aged Arab bachelor in scenes worthy of the actor Peter Sellers. Ironically, many of his responses to the West resembled the strain of cultural pessimism which industrial, urban modernity had evoked among the West's own conservative intelligentsias.[9] He had eccentric observations to make about such subjects as orderly grass lawns and joyless pigeons in anomic city squares. This exposure to the West – in the form of soporifically suburban Colorado – led Qutb to the view that the modern world had reverted to a state of pagan *jahiliyya*, against which the true Muslim had to insulate himself through total submission to Allah. Becoming a slave of God liberated the true believer from the slavery of merely human rulers, and such false creeds as the separation of religion and politics, democracy, human rights, liberalism and so on. In local terms, this meant that wherever Arabs thought they were on the side of the future – democracy, nationalism, socialism and so forth – they were merely rendering obeisance to false idols as worthless, despite their greater sophistication, as the old stone gods of ancient Mecca. They were what Qutb dubbed 'so-called Muslims' and as such they could be killed along with the infidel *kuffar*, in what Qutb envisaged as an endless jihad.[10]

Many have compared Qutb's book with Lenin's *What is to be Done?* Writing with a directness that was unlike the learned disquisitions of the *ulema*, Qutb managed to slip in the very Western, Marxist-Leninist notion of an elite revolutionary vanguard, albeit camouflaged as the belief that only the imprisoned Brothers were true Muslims, the rest being in various states of thrall to false idols. Regimes not solely based on sharia law should be combated with the sword as well as the book. The worst idolaters were the guards in Qutb's prison, who in 1957 responded to the prisoners' refusal to break rocks as part of their sentence of hard labour by entering the cells and killing twenty-one of them. The consumptive Qutb avoided this fate as he was kept in the infirmary.

By the time of his release in May 1964, and by virtue of such writings as *Signposts*, Qutb had become the leading ideologue of the Muslim

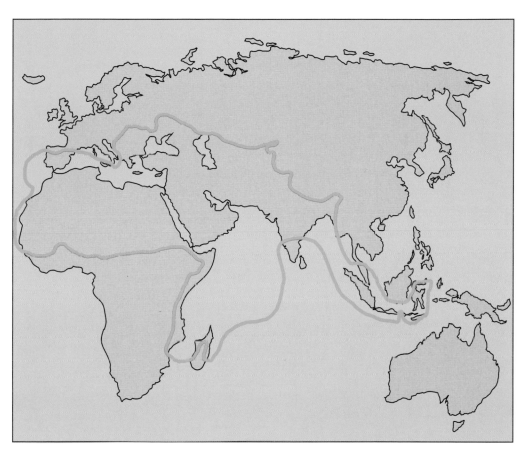

Radical Islamists seek to realise a Caliphate in which political and religious power are fused and whose hypothetical borders are indicated here. One should note that it encompasses the Christian, Confucian, Jewish and Hindu populations of Spain, the Balkans, Greece, central Africa, India and Indonesia.

Abu Sayaf leader Abu Sabaya gives the peace sign in a jungle hideaway in the Philippines. The US missionary Martin Burnham (*centre*) was killed and his wife Gracia Burnham (*right*) badly wounded in a government attempt to release them.

The Egyptian surgeon, Ayman al-Zawahiri, in the dock in 1982 following the assassination by Islamists of president Anwar Sadat the year before. Zawahiri is the strategic intelligence behind Al Qaeda.

The Saudi Wahhabist, al-Khattab or Samir bin Salekh al-Suweilum, who brought especial ferocity to the Chechen terrorist struggle until Russian FSB agents succeeded in poisoning him in 2002.

Sunni terrorists destroyed the Shiite al-Hadi shrine in Samarra in February 2006, bringing further conflict and chaos to Iraq.

The Al Qaeda bomb in Nairobi in 1998 killed hundreds and wounded thousands, many of whom were office workers and shoppers blinded by flying glass.

The perpetrators of the 2002 Bali bombing explicitly sought to kill 'white meat' (that is, Westerners), although they managed to kill many locals, too.

The Solution

رسالة من الشيخ أسامة بن لادن إلى الشعب الأمريكي

All praise is due to Allah, who built the heavens and earth in justice.

As-Sahab

Despite his large ambitions, the Saudi terrorist Osama bin Laden has been restricted to fitful appearances on Al Qaeda's TV station As-Sahab (The Clouds). He is presumed to be hiding in the lawless Tribally Administered zone of Pakistan.

For several years the British authorities allowed the former nightclub bouncer turned preacher, Abu Hamza, to disburse hatred inside and outside a north London mosque that proved to be a nodal point of jihadist terrorism throughout Europe.

Hate-filled faces and murderous slogans at a demonstration in London as part of a delayed action campaign against the notorious Danish newspaper cartoons of the Prophet. The protests claimed the lives of several people in the Middle East.

A girl dressed as a Hamas suicide bomber in the Ain al-Hilweh refugee camp near Sidon, South Lebanon. The backgrounds of such individuals frequently reveal more prosaic motives than a desire for martyrdom.

The blind sheikh, Omar Abdel Rahman, was one of the prime movers behind the 1993 bombing of New York's World Trade Center. This took place more than a decade before the coalition occupation of Iraq, which is often rolled forth in apologetics for this type of activity. Two decades earlier, Islamist fanatics seized the Grand Mosque at Mecca in order to proclaim a returned Mahdi, actions which had nothing to do with western policy, but everything to do with religious issues inside Saudi Arabia.

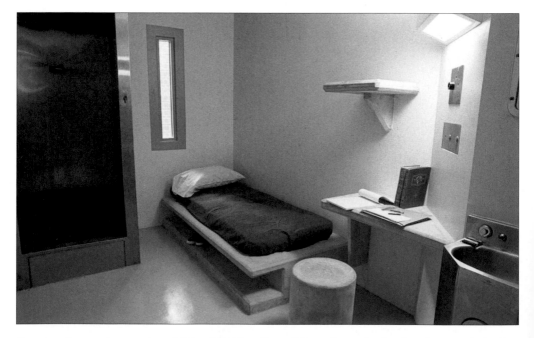

Convicted terrorists, such as Richard Reid or Ramzi Yousef, are destined to live out their days and nights in the Spartan surroundings of the Supermax prison at Florence, Colorado.

Brotherhood as it tentatively sought to regroup. Not every Brother agreed with his violent prescriptions, preferring instead the slow but steady creation of a parallel Muslim society outside the state, a tendency that has periodically enabled Egyptian governments to make peace with the Brotherhood. Qutb was not free for long because in order to boost its credibility vis-à-vis another security agency, the Military Security Services uncovered a wide-ranging conspiracy against Nasser's regime, of which Qutb was alleged to be a leading light. Brutal raids on shanty towns and villages where the Brotherhood was strong, and routine torture of suspects, provided the evidence the regime needed for the existence of a ramified conspiracy that it hoped would galvanise its own supporters. After trial by a military court, Qutb and two colleagues were hanged on 29 August 1966. The decades of abuse he suffered, culminating in such a death, provided a powerful example of martyrdom for the faith that would reverberate around the Muslim world, not least in the form of a lurid biopic that leaves no torture unexplored. One of the places where Qutb's doctrines flourished was in Saudi Arabia. Many exiled Egyptian Brothers were given refuge there as their intellectual skills were locally in short supply. One of them was Mohammed Qutb, Sayyid's brother, who became chief propagator of the martyr's cult, his future disciples including the young Osama bin Laden.[11]

For a decade or so after the Suez Crisis, Nasser basked in the adulation of much of the non-aligned world. Then his vision fell apart, beginning with the failure of the United Arab Republic created by amalgamating Egypt and Syria, although the name lingered on until in 1971 Egypt reverted to being the Arab Republic of Egypt. Widespread disillusionment with Arab nationalism, in the wake of the disastrous 1967 Six-Day War with Israel, and Jordan's Black September, gave a brief boost to socialist alternatives, at least among students who looked to the Paris of 1968 as a model. The fact that the Jordanian Muslim Brothers had supported king Hussein's suppression of the Palestinians inclined many rulers to view Islamism as a useful counterweight. As part of his so-called Corrective Revolution, Egypt's new ruler Anwar Sadat, who came to power in late 1970, first ejected Nasser's phalanx of Soviet advisers, and then released all the Muslim Brothers from prison and allowed exiles to return home.

As elsewhere in the world, Egyptian universities underwent ill-considered expansion in the 1970s, with student numbers rising from two hundred thousand in 1970 to more than five hundred thousand seven years later. Facilities and teaching were atrocious, because any professor of ability had left to earn better money in the Gulf, leaving behind student–teacher ratios of 1:100. Except for a few elite professional faculties, higher education involved learning mimeographed lecture notes by rote, with crash private tuition before exams for qualifications that brought some lowly unsatisfying job in societies where to get ahead one needs some connection to the local Big Man.[12] The state sector could not expand quickly enough to absorb this demi-educated lumpen intelligentsia, whose degrees were the intellectual equivalent of a Western high-school certificate.[13] Overcrowding brought problems peculiar to the Islamic world, since men and women unaccustomed to close physical proximity found themselves pressed up against one another on the campus bus, or jostling three at a time for each available seat in the lecture halls.

The Believing President, as Sadat was known in his own press, encouraged the Jamaat Islamiya student associations to proliferate on campuses, seeing only the virtuous side of multiplying numbers of pious young women wearing veils and bearded men in white robes. Equipped with the funds of the student unions, they were ever fertile in their solutions to the problems of universities, providing sexually segregated housing and transport, free photocopying, and organised camps where religion played a major part. Inevitably, this attempt to realise Islam within the universities had its dark side. Concerts, dances and films were bullied into non-existence by Islamists armed with clubs and iron bars, while intimidation was used to prevent even the most innocent relations between the opposite sexes. In 1980 hundreds of militant students stormed the offices of the dean of the science faculty, to force his compliance with a series of Islamist ultimata. Meanwhile, radical preachers inveighed against nightlife on Cairo's Avenue of the Pyramids, where pious visitors from the Gulf got drunk on bottles of whisky that cost as much as an Egyptian peasant saw in a month, while stuffing banknotes into the bosoms of belly dancers, and against a regime that celebrated the millennia of pre-Islamic Egyptian culture. 'Egypt is Muslim, not pharaonic,' they reminded their own pharaoh when Sadat campaigned to preserve Ramses II's mummy. That Sadat lived increasingly in Farouk's ten palaces further fuelled envy and hostility.[14]

These students included tiny bands of terrorists committed to the violent overthrow of Sadat, especially after his efforts to make peace with Israel in the late 1970s, efforts which meant the Saudis cut off the massive subsidies that mitigated Egypt's chronic economic problems. The first attempted coup by militant Islamist students was suppressed before it started and the ringleaders were hanged. They were succeeded by a group called al-Jamaat al-Muslimin, or the Islamic Group, led by Shuqri Mustafa, an ardent Qutbist agronomist, who pronounced that the whole of Egyptian society was in a state of apostasy, to which the group's initial response was to dwell in desert caves. There their minds took a remarkably prescient turn, forecasting the emergence of an Islamic caliphate that would challenge both the US and the USSR. When a leading Establishment cleric denounced them as heretics, the group kidnapped and killed him. Shuqri was apprehended and put on trial, a theatre he used to denounce the *ulema*, who also got it in the neck from the prosecutors for allowing 'charlatans' like Shuqri to operate within the universities. In that respect they resembled liberal university administrators in the West, with their limitless indulgence towards fanatics' desire for social justice. In 1978 Shuqri and four other members of the Islamic Group were executed. These measures did not halt the proliferation of radical Islamist groups, which found greater grievances than the colossal corruption of the regime. The issues included Sadat's peace deal with Israel, which posted an ambassador to Cairo, resulting in the president becoming a pariah in the wider Arab world; and efforts in 1979, supported by Sadat's wife Jihan, to rebalance marriage and divorce laws to benefit women represented the final straw.[15]

The democratisation of religious opinion as against received authority, and the rage that ensued when mass education did not automatically translate into status, was evident in the group that eventually assassinated Sadat. One cell developed in a Cairo suburb, where a young electrical engineer called Mohammed Abd al-Salam Faraj linked up with two men from the prominent al-Zumr family. Together with Muhammed Zumi, a fugitive from southern Upper Egypt where a further cell developed, they formed Tanzim al-Jihad in 1980. From the start, the group was divided between the northern group which focused on killing Sadat, and southerners more concerned to persecute Coptic Christian goldsmiths and jewellers. The latter's numbers and prosperity had exceeded Islam's threshold of tolerance, while their pope was gaining the ear of Americans concerned about persecution of fellow Christians. Not only were the Copts getting above themselves, but it appeared that their greater assertiveness was being manipulated by their 'Crusader' allies abroad. Minor incidents, perhaps the charge that someone had put the hex on a buffalo, resulted in sectarian violence which the police struggled to contain. It spread to the Cairo slums when in the autumn of 1981 Copts and Muslims attempted to massacre each other.

The conspiracy assumed lethal proportions when it was joined by twenty-four-year-old first-lieutenant Khalid Ahmed Shawqi al-Islambouli, like the al-Zumrs from a prominent family. Frustrated in his desire to become an air force pilot, he had washed up in artillery. The electrician Faraj provided the vision, borrowing bits of Qutb and venerable Taymiyya to justify an attack on the 'near enemy' of apostate Muslim rulers, preparatory to the assault of a consolidated Islam on the 'far enemy' of Israel. Clerical endorsement of this strategy was supplied by a blind lecturer in theology from a southern outpost of Cairo's al-Azhar university, whom Sadat had released from a nine-month prison sentence when he signalled the break with the Nasser era. This forty-something cleric was sheikh Omar Abdel Rahman, thenceforth a pivotal figure in several terrorist atrocities.

Recruitment of others into the developing conspiracy against Sadat occurred in radical mosques, where the more devout were singled out to attend intensive retreats, part of the grooming that draws people into the more select group responsible for acts of terrorism. The next step from these retreats for a select few, whose sense of being the elite within an elite was consolidated, was basic weapons training. The group began by robbing jewellery businesses owned by Coptic Christians in Upper Egypt, robberies which were designed to finance major operations and to make the bumptious Copts – one of whom, Boutros Boutros Ghali, was even foreign minister – feel the Muslim fist. In this climate of sectarian tension, Sadat announced a new line: 'No politics in religion, and no religion in politics'. The regime rounded up about fifteen hundred radicals, including Khalid al-Islambouli's brother Muhammed, leader of Islamic students in the commerce department at Asyut university. This engendered emotions like those that once prevailed in Lenin's family. Their mother recalled: 'When he heard the news, Khalid burst out crying and said to me: "Why have they arrested my brother, who committed no crime?" He cried so much that he had convulsions. When he finally calmed down, he said to me, "Be patient, mother, it is the will of God ... every tyrant has his end." ' On 23 September 1981 Khalid al-Islambouli learned that he was to participate in the parade on 6 October designed to celebrate the moment in 1973 when Egyptian troops had captured a salient over the canal in Sinai. This was the thirty-eighth attempt on Sadat's life; it was horribly successful.

As an army officer al-Islambouli was spared the searches which Sadat's security inflicted on other ranks, who were supposed to surrender their firing pins and live rounds for the day. No checks were made to see that this had been done, although the orders had certainly been given. This laxity enabled al-Islambouli to smuggle ammunition and grenades provided by Faraj into his quarters concealed in a duffle bag. He also pulled rank to bring three assassins dressed as soldiers into his barracks; the following day they took the places of the real soldiers – to whom al-Islambouli gave a day's leave – in his Zil truck as it towed a gun carriage across the parade ground. Only the driver did not know what was going on when al-Islambouli grabbed the handbrake as the truck neared the reviewing stand. He and his accomplices dismounted, removing the safety catches from their weapons.

There, Sadat, his ministers, visiting dignitaries and the 150 men – deployed in concentric groups – supposedly protecting him were distracted by the roaring jets of an air force fly-past. Sadat was dressed in a natty Prussian-style uniform which had arrived from a London tailor the day before. He refused to don a bullet-proof vest, claiming that it would spoil the tunic's line. Besides, as he said when he told his guards to keep their distance: 'Please go away – I am with my sons,' meaning the massed soldiery. When Sadat caught sight of five men running towards him, he stood up, ready with a salute, inadvertently providing them with a clear target. The five hurled grenades, which sent the Egyptian elite reeling, and then, reaching the bottom of the reviewing stand, unleashed about thirty-five seconds of sustained fire from automatic weapons delivered from a range of about fifteen metres. Despite the efforts of the defence minister, who tried to shield his president, bullets tore into Sadat's chest and neck causing massive blood loss. Incredulous at this fate, Sadat's last words were 'Mish Maaqool, Mish Maaqool' or 'impossible, impossible'. Al-Islambouli, whose shots finished off Sadat, repeatedly shouted, 'My name is Khalid Islambouli, I have slain Pharaoh, and I do not fear death!' He did not bother to kill Mubarak too, the self-effacing vice-president. One assassin was killed by security officers, and the rest were wounded and captured.

The plot to take over Cairo, starting with the television centre, unravelled as the captured assassins boasted how these attacks were supposed to unfold, an interpretation probably over-indulgent of the restraint of their interrogators. In the south there was a four-day seizure of parts of downtown Asyut, which ended abruptly when the government sent in paratroopers. Sadat's killers and more than three hundred radical Islamist defendants were tried in a court erected in Cairo's Exhibition Grounds. The surviving terrorists gave reasons for the assassination. They spoke of the 'decadence' represented by alcohol and discotheques, and the dishonouring contempt Sadat had expressed for women dressed in 'tents'. One mentioned the example of the Iranian Revolution and the need to create a Sunni counterweight. There was one exception to the death sentences passed on the main defendants. Lawyers for Abdel Rahman successfully dissociated their client from specific injunctions to harm or kill either Copts or Sadat, while the blind sheikh himself passionately denounced attempts to relativise an immutable Islam so as to conform with modern Western mores. Incredibly, he was acquitted by a court which knew that what he was saying would have been well received by most of the *ulema*, even though one of Mubarak's first acts had been to get the heads of Cairo's prestigious al-Azhar university, the Arab world's Oxford, to condemn the assassins.[16]

Some of the other defendants would achieve even greater promin-ence. Ayman al-Zawahiri was a young surgeon from a distinguished clerical–medical dynasty with a practice in Cairo's Maadi suburb where he had organised a jihadist cell that was on the periphery of the plot to kill Sadat. Although he had learned of the plot only hours before it happened, al-Zawahiri and his friend Aboud al-Zuma were bent on using Sadat's funeral to kill Mubarak and any foreign dignitaries who happened along. On 23 October al-Zawahiri was arrested by the police, the gateway to endless horrors at the hands of Intelligence Unit 75, the government's expert torturers. During the court hearings, he emerged as the defendants' spokesman, using this public forum to give chapter and verse about beatings, electrocution and wild dogs, testimony – all probably true – that provoked chants of 'The army of Mohammed will return, and we will defeat the Jews' from his co-accused. At the end of the three-year trial, al-Zawahiri was sentenced to three years in jail, which he had already largely served on remand. His sentence may have been lightened by intelligence on other terrorists that he gave his tormentors. When he emerged from this ordeal in 1984, al-Zawahiri was no longer the retiring bookish medic with a sideline in militant jihadism. The physical and psychological humiliations of torture, and perhaps the religious ecstasies that extreme pain can generate, had created a suspicious, steely man focused on revenge. The only future question would be, against whom?[17]

III THE RISE OF ISLAMISM IN ALGERIA

The succession of stony-faced army officers who ruled Algeria after it achieved independence in 1962 were confronted by mounting problems that the FLN's brand of single-party national socialism with an Islamic tinge could not solve. Oil and natural-gas revenues were not converted into industrial jobs quickly enough to cope with staggering population growth or the flood of people migrating from the mountains and scrublands to the slums of the major cities. In fact they ended up in Swiss bank accounts of the ruling military elite. Every year 180,000 well-educated youths under twenty-five years of age entered a labour market that grew by only 100,000.[18] Algeria had 8.5 million people in 1954; by 1980 that had become 18.5 million, and 26.6 million thirteen years later. The emigration of about eight hundred thousand workers, largely to France, did not significantly alleviate these demographic pressures, always assuming that people were prepared to put up with the resentment they often faced in the erstwhile colonial metropolis towards the indigent victors of the Algerian War. Moreover, nearly half of the population was aged under fifteen in a society where women had an average of eight children – whose own life expectancy rose because of better medical care.

Many young people had no work; indeed the official unemployment rate reached 28 per cent and that is likely to be an underestimate. Since these boys spent their time slouched against walls, they were referred to as 'hittistes', from *hit*, the Arab word for wall. To these young people, the army and FLN leaderships' constant harping on their allegedly heroic revolutionary role in the 1950s and 1960s meant nothing. They were the corrupt crowd who used the privatisation of state lands in the 1980s to build luxury villas and private factories, and whose security services routinely assaulted and tortured people. Reality for youths in the teeming slums was unemployment, houses so badly built that they sometimes collapsed, and relentless heat made insufferable by chronic water shortages. A distinctive youth culture developed based on gangs, football hooliganism, drugs and *raï* music, which fused North African idioms with rap, reggae and punk. In October 1988 these young males rioted in downtown Algiers, smashing up buses, roadsigns, telephone kiosks, and luxury shops where the local jeunesse dorée, or 'tchi-tchi', were wont to flaunt their wealth. Much sexual frustration was vented against rich young women driving flashy sports cars – dubbed Blonda Hondas by the street youths. Symbolically, they tore down the Algerian flag and raised an empty couscous sack to draw attention to the realities of decades of socialism. When the police counterattacked, killing hundreds of these rioters and torturing detainees, they were called 'Jews', a novel experience for representatives of a state that was pathologically anti-Zionist.

The failure of socialism in Algeria provided militant Islamists with their chance, for it was they who deftly interposed themselves as mediators between the rioters and the government. The regime had fitfully encouraged this trend. In the 1970s president (and colonel) Houari Boumedienne, who had deposed Ahmed Ben Bella in 1965, launched a sustained campaign of Arabisation to expunge every vestige of the hated French. This was despite the fact that French came much more easily to most Algerians than classical literary Arabic as taught by exiled Egyptian Muslim Brothers, and was the surest route to the best professions and jobs, which required expertise in French. Enforced Arabisation did not please the Berbers either, who were proud of their distinctive dialects and cultural identity. In the spring of 1980 the Berber heartland of Kabylia was rocked by demonstrations and strikes which the regime suppressed with its usual violence. The regime also sought to use Islam when socialism palpably failed to create a united Algerian identity. The 1976 National Charter said that 'Islam is the state religion'; the president had to be a Muslim who swore an oath to 'respect and glorify the Muslim religion'. In that year Friday replaced Sunday as a day of enforced rest. Gambling and the sale of alcohol to Muslims were banned. Three years later Muslims were prohibited from raising swine. Partly as a result of Saudi largesse, the number of mosques in the country rose from 2,200 in 1966 to 5,829 in 1980. Many of these were so-called people's mosques which when left half built technically evaded state control. Although the state continued to monopolise the production of audiocassettes, pirate imports brought the radical tidings of Egyptian, Lebanese and Saudi clerics much as printing presses had once universalised the words of Luther and Calvin.[19]

The state's attempt to exploit Islam for purely political ends was resented by many radical Islamists such as Mustafa Bouyali, who declared the regime impious and called for a jihad to overthrow it. After repairing, like the Prophet, to the mountains, Bouyali founded a Mouvement Islamique Armé, with himself as its emir. Until Bouyali was killed in 1987, the FLN–army leaders found themselves playing role reversal with the French who had once battled the FLN in the same bleak countryside. Cooler-headed Islamists decided simply to push the regime towards higher levels of Islamisation. An academic called Abassi Madani called for 'respect for the sharia in government legislation and a purging of elements hostile to our religion'. Among his other demands was segregation of the sexes in education. He was immediately imprisoned, his release being a key future demand of Islamist terrorists. After 1978 the new government of colonel Chadli Benjedid responded to the rise of Islamism by building more mosques, so as to sideline the multiplying number of ad-hoc prayer rooms, and controlling who was allowed to preach in them. An Islamic university was created in the city of Constantine to counter the foreign influences that held sway in the absence of a local Algerian *ulema*. Two distinguished clerics, Muhammad al-Ghazali and Youssef al-Qaradawi, were imported from Egypt, but craftily ignored the regime's efforts to make them its own clerical authorities. Worse, the Islamic faction within the sole ruling party – whom wits called the 'Barbefélènes' because of their beards – began to drift into the orbit of this incipient Islamist movement, mosques being the only legal site of opposition in a one-party state.

Although the October 1988 youth riots petered out, Chadli continued to treat Islamist intellectuals as interlocutors, even though it was not clear at all that they, or anyone else, had much purchase on the young rioters. In a bold move designed to secure his re-election to the presidency, Chadli surprisingly introduced a multi-party system, his intention being to shuffle the parties around so as to give a democratic gloss to a much enhanced presidency. One product of this democratising strategy was the Islamic Salvation Front or FIS, the Islamist party founded in March 1989, which temporarily brought together Algerianists who believed in the creeping, and entirely legitimate, Islamisation of Algerian society, and salafists who were opposed to democracy as a secular foreign imposition, at the same time as they themselves were heavily engaged with fraternal Arab jihadists. The FIS was the first legal Islamic party in the entire Arab world, and the first openly to proclaim the goal of an Islamic republic, while simultaneously promising to restore ethics, justice and warm family kinship. It wanted to revert to the egalitarianism of the early FLN, a distant memory at a time when a corrupt business and military elite was stealing the nation's oil wealth. Unsurprisingly this especially appealed to the first- and second-generation migrants from the conservative countryside huddled in the anomic poor quarters of big cities.

The FIS was both an Islamised political party and a social welfare organisation. The party was governed by a thirty-eight-member Council, called the Madjlis ech-Choura in conscious echo of the Prophet, with day-to-day business in the hands of a twelve-man Executive Bureau. Its local cells were called *ousra* or families, another conscious use of Islamic terminology. Its two main leaders were Ali Benhadji, a charismatic associate of the dead jihadist Bouyali, a demagogue on a motorbike who appealed to young people, and the older Abassi Madani, who was respected by pious traders and shopkeepers. Like the parish structures that had benefited Christian democrat parties in post-war Europe, the mosques provided the FIS with a major organisational advantage over the forty or so rival parties, some of which were led by exiles returned from Europe, whose local appeal was limited. Similar advantages flowed from its charitable activities, which were subsidised by the Saudis, since it provided hospital and funeral funds for the poor, while offering to buy indigent women their veils. In other words, it was like a remoralised version of the early FLN, attracting, beyond the Islamists who made up its hard core, many more protest voters who had had enough of a regime that was neither socialist nor Islamic.

In municipal polls held in 1990 the FIS won 54 per cent of the popular vote, decimating the former governing party. Success led it to overplay its hand. Control of municipal councils resulted immediately in prohibitions on alcohol or on people walking about in shorts and swimming costumes. In Oran, the council banned a *raï* music concert. Another refused to deal with correspondence not written in Arabic. In December 1991 the FIS eventually took part in the first round of legislative elections – after a four-month debate on the propriety of doing so – winning a respectable 47 per cent of a poorly attended poll which suggests that many voters were apathetic about the choices available to them. Four hundred thousand people took part in demonstrations in the capital, chanting 'No police state, no fundamentalist republic!' Correctly fearing that the army had had enough, the FIS made desperate attempts to allay public anxiety about the Islamic society it envisaged for Algeria, even constructing scaled models of a projected Islamic city with cinemas, libraries and sports halls. This did not entirely dispel fears that, if the FIS won the second round of elections, it would abolish democracy, the free press and all other political parties, that being the message from some mosques. On 11 January 1992 the generals mounted a putsch, sacking Chadli and going on to ban the FIS and arrest its leaders. They received lengthy jail sentences, and many of their lesser supporters were despatched to remote Saharan concentration camps. That August a radical Islamist bomb killed ten people at Algiers airport, the beginning of a terror campaign that would eventually be directed at the entire Muslim population.

IV MUSLIM SOUTH ASIA

Of the world's one and a half billion Muslims, only one-fifth live in the Arab world. Arabia bulks large in the Muslim imagination, and Arabic has enormous prestige as the language of Allah recorded in sacred texts, but the demographic strength of Islam lies in the Indian subcontinent and South Asia. Indonesia's 250 million people, consisting of 250 ethnic groups living on the six thousand inhabitable islands in the thirteen-thousand-island archipelago, are nearly 90 per cent Muslim. Since Islam was, as it is said, written over other belief systems, Indonesian Muslims are broadly divided between those who subscribe to this syncretic version and modernisers who sought to make Indonesia conform more tightly to Arab exemplars which exert enormous suasion in the region. Power and wealth in Indonesia sit uncomfortably along ethnic and religious fault lines too. Excepting that part controlled by the ruling dynasts, economic might is largely in the hands of an industrious Buddhist, Christian and Confucian Chinese minority, while bureaucratic, military and political power has been monopolised by a predominantly Christian-educated elite. Although there is a modernised Muslim middle class, the majority of the 49 per cent of Indonesians subsisting on under US$2 a day are Muslims too.

Muslim militias played an important part in fighting the Dutch colonialists, but they broke with the newly established Republic over its refusal to introduce sharia law. A movement called Darul Islam, or the Islamic State of Indonesia, waged a desultory military campaign from its bases in central Java, Aceh and South Sulawesi, until its leaders were captured in 1962. The dictators Sukarno and Suharto propagated a state philosophy called Pancasila, designed to weld this kaleidoscopic nation together. Although Indonesia is a secular state, this creed consists of affirmation of belief in one God, respect for the human individual and social justice, and the unity of the motherland. The pious Muslim minority and the surviving supporters of Darul Islam insisted on adding sharia law, a demand known as the Jakarta Charter. Radical Islam's survival in Indonesia was due to the fact that elements in the security services saw Darul Islam as a useful tool to suppress Communism, as well as due to inflows of Saudi money that financed an Institute for Islamic and Arabic Studies in Jakarta. Another important incubator was the Javanese version of a madrassa or seminary, known locally as a *pesantren*, run by two Arabs, Abdullah Sungkar and Abu Bakar Ba'asyir, at Ngruki in the Solo region. These two were linked to a series of terrorist attacks on bars and cinemas in the 1970s and early 1980s, carried out by a shadowy organisation called Komando Jihad. Though the fact that the attacks always preceded elections may have reflected a government plot to discredit Islamic parties, these two Arabs were tried and jailed for fomenting terrorism. Released on licence, they fled to Malaysia. The restoration of democracy in 1999 saw the mainstream Islamic party achieve fourth place with 11 per cent of the poll. It also saw the development of two terrorist groups. A preacher of Arab descent who was a veteran of the jihad in Afghanistan seems to have been responsible for Laskar-Jihad, a terrorist group formed in West Java to protect Muslims from murderous Christian militias in the Moluccas islands off Sulawesi. Strictly Wahhabist, it also vehemently rejected the presidency of Megawati Setiawati Soekarnoputri (2001–4), largely because of her gender. If Laskar-Jihad has restricted regional ambitions, and would follow Saudi authorities in condemning Osama bin Laden as a sectarian heretic, the front organisation known as Majelis Mujahidin, whose spiritual leader is Abu Bakar Ba'asyir, explicitly wants an Islamic state covering Brunei, Indonesia, Malaysia, Singapore and the Philippines. For convenience sake, regional intelligence agencies refer to this wider South Asian network as Jemaah Islamiyah, and seek to prove its links with Al Qaeda, certain that this will bring US funds for counter-terrorist operations. The links are not imaginary.[20]

The Indian subcontinent is not far behind Indonesia in numbers of adherents of Islam. Already in the nineteenth century, a network of madrassas, whose hub was at Deoband, north of Delhi, propagated a rigorously Wahhabist form of Islam so as to enable Muslims to guard their identity in a hostile Hindu sea. Although secular Muslim intellectuals, and British-trained army officers, had created an independent Pakistan in 1947, for want of anything else with equivalent purchase they had to stress a common Islamic identity to hold its Baluchi, Pashtun, Sindhi and Punjabi tribes together, a problem that became more urgent after 1971 with the secession of the eastern Bengalis into an independent Bangladesh. That loss served to tilt rump Pakistan towards the warm waters of the Gulf states. There was also the longer-standing contest over Kashmir, a princely state under the British Raj, with Sunni Muslims dominant in the Kashmir valley and mixed Hindu, Muslim and Buddhist elsewhere. By force of arms in 1947–9 India succeeded in imposing its will on most of Kashmir, including the Sunni valley, leaving Pakistan in charge of the remaining third, a position it sought to overturn in fighting that recurred in 1965 and 1971. Indian misrule in Kashmir led to vicious attacks by Muslims on Hindus, many of whom fled, and the formation of dozens of militant groups, most of them backed by the army, the intelligence services or Islamist parties in Pakistan, who provide them with arms, money and volunteer manpower. These groups include Hizb-ul-Mujahedin and Lashkar-e-Tayyeba, both of which combine guerrilla warfare with terrorism designed to frighten Hindus or to intimidate moderate Muslims. Pakistani support for these groups makes the country the world's second major state sponsor of terrorism, even if this sponsorship is much more focused in scope than the Iranians'. The general aim is to plague India with a running sore that ties up a quarter of a million Indian troops in the area, while providing a ventilator for radical Islamists in Pakistan itself who might otherwise turn on their own government. That strategy has proved too clever by half, since some Kashmiri and Pakistani militants seek forcibly to Islamise both countries.

For within Pakistan successive governments have sought to instrumentalise Islam with varying degrees of sincerity and success, pandering to a vociferous Muslim lobby that knows how to incite mobs, but whose electoral record – when there have been elections – is modest. A few belated gestures towards Islam in the dying days of the deeply corrupt socialist government of Ali Bhutto did not prevent his overthrow and execution by the military dictator general Zia-ul-Haq in 1977. Zia was a British-trained cavalry officer who while on secondment to Jordan in 1970 had led a group of Jordanian troops he was training into battle against the Palestinians during king Hussein's Black September crackdown. Looking like a slightly oleaginous movie actor with his slickeddown hair and handlebar moustache, Zia admired the Islamist ideologue Mawlana Mawdudi, the journalist who in 1941 had founded a jihadist party called Jamaat-e-Islami, which while harking back to the Prophet's band of followers was also indebted to the vanguardist parties of Europe in the 1930s. Mawdudi was one of the millions of Muslims who went to Pakistan after independence. His party became one element of the broader Pakistani National Alliance with which Zia hoped to stabilise his military regime. Zia brought prominent Islamists into government, briefly including Mawdudi himself, while Islamising education, the law, taxation and so forth. Although he introduced sharia law, the dire penalties for adulterers and thieves were rarely implemented because of scrupulous insistence on the need for many eyewitnesses. Down to his death in 1988, Zia succeeded in dividing the Islamic camp by co-opting the modern Islamist ideologues, while leaving the traditional clerical elite in charge of educating the poor in their burgeoning, Saudi-financed madrassas, the alternative to providing a decent public education system. The number of Deobandi madrassas, which the Wahhabist Saudis favoured, spiralled from 354 in 1972 to seven thousand in 2002. The military regime was also presented with another cause it could pursue with Muslim radicals when the old struggle over Kashmir was joined by the new war in Afghanistan.

V HOLY WAR: THE AFGHAN JIHAD

In the spring of 1978, Afghan Communists killed the country's president Mohammed Daoud, instituting a reign of anti-Islamic terror that has received less notice than their desire to have girls attend schools or encouragement of typists to wear Western skirts and trouser suits. By the end of 1979, some twelve thousand religious and community leaders were in Kabul's jails, where many were quietly liquidated. A revolt broke out in Shia-dominated Herat, in which Islamists hacked to death a dozen Soviet advisers and their families. By way of reprisal, Soviet aircraft bombed Herat, killing about twenty thousand people. The revolt spread to Jalalabad, even as the government's troops began to desert to the mujaheddin. As Soviet leader Leonid Brezhnev and KGB chief Yuri

Andropov wondered how to respond, in Washington national security advisor Zbigniew Brzezinski persuaded president Carter to authorise non-lethal covert support to the Afghan rebels. Medicines and radios with a combined value of half a million US dollars were shipped to Pakistan's Inter Services Intelligence (ISI) for distribution to the Afghan mujaheddin. This was the modest beginning of a major enthusiasm. After murdering the Soviets' first client ruler, Hafizullah Amin clambered to the dizzy pinnacle of power in Kabul, despite KGB suspicions that he was a CIA agent. That rumour sealed his fate when on Christmas Eve Soviet transporters landed paratroops at Kabul, with seven hundred KGB paramilitaries in Afghan uniforms despatched to kill Amin and the current Communist leadership. They were followed by Central Asian Red Army troops – 70 per cent of whom were Muslim – whose armoured vehicles rumbled along the metalled road the Soviets had built in the 1960s. Eventually Soviet forces would peak at about 120,000, although some 650,000 men served in Afghanistan during the eight years of conflict, many of them drug-deranged conscripts blasting away from tanks reverberating with heavy-metal rock music. It is useful to recall that this Soviet invasion led to the formation of the Arab Afghans and ultimately to Al Qaeda.

The Soviet invasion of Afghanistan focused several discrete strategic agendas. The US saw it as a way of bleeding the Russians by using Afghan proxies. Brzezinski wrote to Carter: 'Now we can give the USSR its own Vietnam war.'[21] It cost both blood and treasure. Afghanistan is estimated to have cost the Soviet Union some US$45 billion by the time the Russians retreated, leaving a million Afghan dead at the expense of fifteen thousand Red Army fatalities. Three million Afghans fled to Pakistan, while the same number ended up as refugees in Iran. The US expended much less on its support for the Afghan mujaheddin, perhaps US$5 billion in total, much of it scooped out of the country's fathomless defence budget and re-routed to the CIA to be disbursed via the Pakistanis.

A credulous 'Boy's Own' Western media boosted the mujaheddin as noble savages, nostalgically recalling the massacres these tribesmen had once inflicted on the British, as they contemplated Russian soldiers having their eyes gouged out or genitals cut off if they did not convert to Islam. Responding to widespread Muslim outrage at the invasion of Islamic territory by the legions of the Red godless, the Saudis and other conservative Gulf states saw an opportunity for Sunnis to rival the brightly burning Shia star of ayatollah Khomenei with a cause that would also divert their own militant Islamists to foreign fields. They even introduced discounted fares on the national airline to make it easier to get rid of them to Afghanistan. The Saudis hated the Russians, and through a Safari Club had already co-operated with the US in subverting the spread of Marxist regimes in Africa. In July 1980 the Saudis' intelligence supremo, prince Turki, agreed to match dollar for dollar US support for the mujaheddin. Saudi money was sent to the Washington embassy and then transferred to a Swiss bank account of the CIA, which used these funds to purchase weapons for those Afghans the CIA and the Saudis deemed most worthy of support. This meant that the US$200 million the CIA's Afghan programme received in 1984 became US$400 million courtesy of the Saudis. The problem was that Saudi Arabia's General Intelligence Directorate was not the only game in town, even assuming that it was trustworthy. Also supporting the Islamist cause in Afghanistan were private and semi-official charitable and religious bodies, which funded not only indigenous Afghan Wahhabis, but also the stream of Gulf Arabs heading to Afghanistan to wage jihad. An estimated twenty thousand Arabs went to Afghanistan to fight. The Saudis even paid for the critically wounded to be treated in private Harley Street clinics in London. Lastly, Pakistan's successive regimes, and an Islamised intelligence agency swollen with Saudi and US money, saw a chance to install a friendly neighbouring Islamist regime that would afford Pakistan defence in depth. Moreover, the more far-sighted saw that training camps for Afghan or foreign mujaheddin could become dual purpose, training jihadists to fight India in Kashmir at a time when the US regarded India as a suspiciously pink shape on the Cold War map.[22]

The Afghan–Pakistan border became the site of a bewildering array of camps for some three million people fleeing the Soviets, whose tactics included ruining crops, sowing millions of anti-personnel mines and depopulating villages. Many Afghan boys were subtracted from the desperate environment of all refugee camps, and sent as boarders to the network of Pakistani Deobandi madrassas, where through the medium of ceaselessly chanting the Koran they were refashioned into total Islamic personalities. Many of these boys would return to Afghanistan in early adulthood, after the Russians had left, as the all-conquering Taliban. Meanwhile, foreign intelligence agencies funnelled arms into mujaheddin training camps strung along the Pakistani side of the Afghan border.

As agile as goats, the mujaheddin dominated the high ground, hitting and then running from the Russians, before retiring for long seasonal breaks in the fighting. Second World War-era weapons were replaced by AK-47s, heavy machine guns, mortars and rocket-propelled grenades, together with fleets of trucks to convoy them forwards into Afghanistan. Many of these weapons were purchased from China, allowing the CIA to savour using Chinese Communist arms to kill Soviets. By the mid-1980s the CIA's involvement was deeper, although it baulked at anything like airlifting its own supplies lest it trigger a superpower confrontation. US spy satellites were used to track Soviet positions, which were relayed to the mujaheddin using indecipherable 'burst' communications systems. Next came powerful sniper rifles, plastic explosives and sophisticated detonators, variously intended for sabotage operations and the assassination of Soviet commanders, some of whom were killed by car bombs in Kabul. When the Soviets showed some success by deploying highly trained Speznaz commandos, inserted to ambush the mujaheddin from giant armoured Hind helicopters, the CIA supplied the Afghans with Stinger shoulder-launched guided missiles, whose infra-red sensors invariably found their target. The first successful attack on such helicopters, and the bullets pumped afterwards into the bodies of their crews, was shown on video in the Oval Office. The American budget for the Afghan war climbed to US$470 million in 1986 and US$630 million in 1987, all matched too by the Saudis. The US began paying select mujaheddin commanders a decent salary, partly to offset worrying evidence of another presence, for at no point did the CIA arm or promote foreign Islamist fighters. They moved around in different orbits, with the foreign fighters drawing on different sources of funds and recruits.[23]

The majority of Afghan mujaheddin were suspicious of the Arab volunteers, whom they called Ikhwanis, meaning the Muslim Brothers, or Wahhabis after the puritanical Islamism that rejected more mystical Sufi traditions, saints and shrines. The reason a frontier town like Peshawar was becoming physically Arabised was because that is where the Arabs hung out while not doing any fighting. They would have done the Afghan cause more good by donating the cost of their air tickets. The first Arab presence in Afghanistan consisted of volunteers despatched on humanitarian missions by a wide array of Islamic non-governmental organisations. Since many professionals, such as doctors, were stalwarts of the Muslim Brotherhood, this was how Ayman al-Zawahiri ended up in Peshawar, where he rapidly realised that Afghanistan might be an 'incubator' for the deliverance of his Nilotic homeland from the man he called Pharaoh.

Another Muslim Brother to wash up in Peshawar was a Palestinian called Abdullah Azzam. He had broken with the PLO over Black September, arguing that it should fight Jews rather than Jordanians, which did not spare him from being deported to Saudi Arabia where he taught sharia law at the university of Jeddah. In 1984 he moved to Pakistan, helping to co-ordinate Islamic relief operations from a camp near the Khyber Pass. The Saudis trusted him sufficiently to found a Bureau of Services, designed to monitor the increasing number of Gulf Arabs arriving in Afghanistan to perform, or wage, jihad. Azzam was largely responsible for the romanticised death cult that gained ground among the foreign fighters, since his eulogies to the 'martyrs' were generously filled with perfumed corpses and heavenly virgins. He started a magazine called *Al-Jihad*, and wrote an influential book endorsed by the kingdom's leading cleric, whose generic thrust was that defence of Islamic territory was an individual obligation upon all Muslims rather akin to rescuing a child drowning in the sea. Ominously, the war in Afghanistan was merely the start of it, as Palestine, Burma, Lebanon, Chad, Eritrea, Somalia, the Philippines, South Yemen, Soviet Central Asia and Andalusia, that is two-thirds of modern Spain, were waiting to be delivered too. A wealthy former student, Osama bin Laden, proposed to pay the Bureau's US$2,500 monthly operating costs, while offering expenses of US$300 a month to any Arab that Azzam could lure to Afghanistan in an Islamist cover-version of the International Brigades of the 1930s that had fought Fascism in Spain. Among those whom Azzam inspired (they had met at Mecca in 1987) to follow him was Abu Hamza al-Masri, a hefty Egyptian illegal immigrant to Britain who, having decided Britain was a 'toilet' after working as a bouncer at Soho strip clubs, had got consuming religion. In 1993 Hamza went to Afghanistan where, too bulky to romp easily up and down mountains, he concentrated on bomb making. One such session resulted in the loss of an eye and his hands being blown off, the most plausible reason given for his trademark prosthetic hook.[24]

Afghanistan has always been one of the places that rich Gulf Arabs frequent – to camp and hunt with falcons – on their globalised caravanserai which takes them via the indigent pretty girls of Ethiopia to Annabel's and the tarts of Mayfair and Monaco. Broadly speaking, the

Arabs come to wage jihad were a mixture of fantasists, who simply had themselves photographed with an AK-47 in front of menacing rocks, and the sort of men who would pitch white tents so as to attract the lethal attentions of Soviet aircraft. They actually wanted to die so as to precipitate the sounds and smells of paradise. Bin Laden himself exhibited many of the characteristics of any spoiled rich kid seeking an older mentor and a higher purpose. He found the former in Azzam, but then gradually migrated to al-Zawahiri. In addition to being personally extremely rich, bin Laden had a network of even wealthier supporters.[25]

Gnarled mujaheddin who met the lanky Gulf Arab (his family were originally from Aden in Yemen) thought his hands felt weak while his simpering smile reminded them of a girl's. Actually, the soft exterior, which was slowly reconfigured so that bin Laden seemed like a modest, slow-speaking sage despite his relative youth, concealed a huge ego, a ferocious temper and a cunning organisational mind. Most Arab leaders do not need to be eloquent as repression stands in for the arts of persuasion. By contrast, bin Laden was highly eloquent in his native Arabic. He opened his own training camp – the Lion's Den – at Jaji exclusively designed for Arab jihadists. This was an assertion of independence from Azzam. When the Russians attacked in April 1987, bin Laden and fifty of his supporters allegedly held off two hundred Russian troops for a week. This engagement gave birth to a legend of Arab fighting prowess that served to attract further recruits.

Bin Laden showed an adroit awareness of how to use the media. He had a fifty-minute video made of himself riding horses, firing weapons and lecturing his fighters. These have the indirectness of home videos because bin Laden never addresses the camera. He summoned trusted foreign journalists, notably Robert Fisk, to sit at the feet of this prodigal phenomenon: the millionaire Saudi who had given up the high life to share Afghan caves with scorpions. An easy familiarity enhanced the sensation of celebrity. Visitors noted his simple consumption of water, flat bread, rice and potato and tomato stew.[26] If many Afghan mujaheddin found his renunciation of the good life incomprehensible – most of their own warlords lived rather well in urban villas kitted out with consumer gismos – it played well among his fellow Gulf Arabs. He did not demur when his followers took to calling him 'the sheikh', a dual title that means clan ruler and religious sage. While bin Laden had no theological expertise or spiritual authority whatsoever, any more than the doctors and engineers around him, and was physically hundreds of miles from the traditional sites of Islamic learning, gradually through his mountain-side appearances he assumed all of those roles within the new disorder he was hatching even as US policymakers spoke airily in their big-talking way of the order they were about to impose as the USSR disintegrated. While they described the future architecture of the world in *Foreign Affairs*, *National Interest* and similar journals, thousands of miles away others construed the world through the life and times of the Prophet.[27]

As the Soviet Union under Gorbachev resolved to pull out of its disastrous eight-year campaign in Afghanistan, bin Laden and the other leading Arabs determined to keep the spirit of jihad alive through a secret organisation concealed within a wider guerrilla-training programme which included huge Saudi-financed bases at places like Zhawar Khili and Tora Bora.[28] They may have helped defeat a global superpower, the first major Muslim victory after decades in which Israel had defeated the Arabs and Indian Hindus the Muslim Pakistanis, but the ensuing Afghan civil war showed that they had failed to create an Islamist state in Afghanistan.

Al Qaeda probably came into existence in May 1988, but it was only in August of that year that the leading Arab Afghans discussed it. Originally the word meant 'base' as in military base, so that the US base at Bagram is 'al-Qaeda Bagram'. While the camps would train Arab fighters destined for Islamist mujaheddin factions battling to control Afghanistan after the Soviets had left an isolated client regime behind, Al Qaeda would consist of a more select cadre, of between 10 and 30 per cent of the trainees, destined for open-ended operations. That is the second meaning of Al Qaeda: as a revolutionary vanguard, similar to the Jacobins or Bolsheviks. Recruits came from a variety of social, religious and national backgrounds, which gradually dissolved into a new global jihadi-salafist identity that picked and mixed from secular geopolitics and several extreme Islamic traditions in a thoroughly eclectic post-modern fashion. One can unthread some of the ideological and religious genealogies, but this entirely conventional approach to understanding the jihadists does not really explain the state of mind any more than learned tomes of Teutonic *Geistesgeschichte* which chart the ground from Luther to Lanz von Liebenfels say much about Nazism.

Al Qaeda opened an office in the affluent Peshawar suburb of Hyatabad, where it processed would-be recruits from the thousands of Arabs, and others, who flooded in after the departure of the Soviets to fight fellow Muslims who were squabbling over the ruins of Afghanistan.

There were detailed application forms, terms and conditions of employment, and job specifications for senior positions within the organisation. Suddenly it seemed to the jihadists as if they had got a job with any Western corporation, an impression reinforced by Al Qaeda's use of the language of international business as a code in the network's communications. It even has its own logo, of a white Arabian stallion. On being accepted after extensive vetting, volunteers received a salary of between US$1,000 and US$1,500 depending on marital status, a round-trip airfare to visit home, medical care and a month's vacation. A ruling *shura* or council sat atop various functional sections, which included experts in computers and publicity and the interpretation of dreams. The person chosen to head Al Qaeda's military operations had to be over thirty, with five years' battlefield experience and a degree in a relevant subject.[29]

Quite a lot is known now about Al Qaeda's initial membership. Many of the Arabs, and especially the Egyptians, did not have much choice other than to remain in Afghanistan or Pakistan since they were wanted men in their homeland. Ayman al-Zawahiri would not be availing himself of the free round-trip to Cairo. The psychologist and former CIA analyst Marc Sageman has studied a representative cross-section of Al Qaeda terrorists, including those who were there at its inception. The most important recruits were Egyptians such as al-Zawahiri, Abu Ubaidah al-Banshiri, who drowned prematurely in a Kenyan lake, and Mohammed Atef, its military supremo. Many of these men had already combined terrorism with careers as policemen or soldiers, which explains why Egyptians supplied a disproportionate number of Al Qaeda's ruling group as well as its top military commanders. Like al-Zawahiri himself, many of them had been through Egypt's prison-torture system, emerging as implacable and steely. Egyptians made up over 60 per cent of Al Qaeda's ruling group, and nearly 60 per cent of them had been imprisoned for political reasons before they had volunteered for jihad in Afghanistan. They were dominant within a wider Arab representation from Kuwait, Saudi Arabia, the UAE and Yemen, the latter making up bin Laden's personal bodyguard. Some of these men arrived as little family bands. One Kuwaiti group is instructive, because it shows how a terrorist group relies on existing ties of kinship and friendship. The personal loyalties were semi-forged before Al Qaeda had even emerged.

Approximately half the population of Kuwait are 'bidoon', or foreign migrants servicing the oil industry. Many of these second-class citizens are Baluchis, a people straddling several states including Pakistan. Among these expatriates were Khalid Sheikh Mohammed and his nephew, Abdul Karim, who had been sent by Khalid Sheikh's three elder siblings to study mechanical engineering in the US, where their existing piety had been reinforced in the Muslim circles that Middle Easterners recoiled into upon experiencing the Western world. The three elder brothers went independently to Peshawar. Khalid Sheikh joined them, moving into the orbit of Azzam and bin Laden. He would become the mastermind of the 9/11 attack on the World Trade Center.[30]

Close ties were also cemented by marriage alliances within the emerging group, so that Mohammed Atef's daughter married one of bin Laden's sons, while Al Qaeda's treasurer married bin Laden's niece. That is true of other terrorist groups. Jemaah Islamiyah's Mohammed Noordin Top has two wives, both sisters of fellow jihadists. The next cluster that would become important in Al Qaeda, especially after the false dawning of the Islamic Salvation Front, consisted of Arabs from the North African Maghreb, that is Algeria, Morocco and Tunisia, and a separate group from South Asia, most graduates of two boarding schools run by Jemaah Islamiyah in Indonesia and Malaysia, with the occasional Uighur from China's westerly Xinjiang province.[31] The Maghreb Arabs were the only ones to have prior records for petty criminality such as handbag snatching and credit-card fraud. Those who were not represented in Sageman's sample are no less interesting. There were virtually no Afghans, except for two friends of bin Laden's, and no representatives of the vast Muslim populations of Bangladesh, India, Turkey or Pakistan, although radicalised second- and third-generation Anglo-Pakistani jihadists would make up the deficit. Contrary to expectations, only 17 per cent of these men had received an Islamic education; the majority were products of secular schooling, with over 60 per cent having received some tertiary-level education, and many spoke several languages. Their learning was overwhelmingly in scientific and technical disciplines, such as computer science, engineering and medicine, which in other religious traditions too seem to correlate with fundamentalist religious beliefs born of a desire to extrapolate knowledge from authority. Of course, this could also simply reflect the prestige of utilitarian disciplines in developing societies, although that would not explain why so many engineers and mathematicians are Christian fundamentalists. Unlike other types of terrorist group, some 83 per cent were married men, although only a few – above all bin Laden and al-Zawahiri – insisted on imperilling their wives and children. Marriage for the rest was simply a preliminary to having a child before consigning both wife and offspring to a separate existence.

The Afghan civil war, and the heterogeneous backgrounds of the leaders, led to visceral – and often personal – splits over how Al Qaeda should be deployed. One conspicuous casualty of these was Azzam, who in addition to trying to avoid Arabs fighting Afghans had identified the Lion of the Panjshir, Ahmed Shah Massoud, a minority Tajik, as the most impressive mujaheddin commander, at a time when most Arabs were backing the Pashtun warlord Gulbuddin Hekmatayar. That sealed Azzam's fate, as al-Zawahiri had been spreading lies that he was a CIA agent, and Massoud had been one of the CIA's main clients. On 24 November 1989, Azzam and two of his sons were killed by a roadside bomb as they went to a mosque. Al-Zawahiri spoke sweetly at his funeral.

Having destroyed the Soviets, as he pretentiously viewed it, bin Laden returned to Saudi Arabia as the prodigal become all-conquering hero. The manner began to resemble those self-righteous superannuated rock stars with delusions of grandeur who harangue world leaders about Africa. He tried to interest the Saudi regime in his plans to destroy the Marxist government of the newly minted Republic of Yemen. Yemeni pressure resulted in the confiscation of bin Laden's passport. He warned Riyadh of the threat posed by the secular dictatorship of Iraq's Saddam Hussein, even as the latter was fabricating tensions in order to invade neighbouring Kuwait. When this took place, unleashing a reign of Iraqi terror on the inoffensive little emirate, the desperate Saudis immediately availed themselves of US offers of assistance to prevent Saddam from extending his campaign towards their oilfields. Despite their binge-purchasing of Western armaments, for which the ruling clique were rewarded with bribes and kickbacks, the fact remained that the Saudi army numbered only fifty-eight thousand troops, facing a highly mechanised foe with a standing army of one million. In order to prevent the stationing of defensive US forces in the kingdom, bin Laden offered to raise a force of 'one hundred thousand' from the Arab Afghan mujaheddin and the kingdom's own large numbers of male idle. This offer was rejected as ridiculous. Bin Laden's mood was not improved when the senior clergy issued fatwas to permit the stationing of Christian, Jewish and female US forces in remote parts of the kingdom.

Disgusted by his homeland's craven dependence on infidels and females, bin Laden pulled strings to have his passport returned and flew back to Peshawar. Meanwhile, Saddam began to cloak himself not only in Arab nationalism – thereby securing the support of a PLO that was always the unlucky gambler – but in Islamic rectitude, inveighing against the corrupt rulers of Riyadh and proclaiming 'Allahu Akhbar' upon reaching the Kuwaiti shoreline. Although the multinational coalition expelled Saddam from Kuwait in Operation Desert Storm, unleashing a tempest of high-tech violence that sickened even those responsible for it, in the process Saudi Arabia forfeited its unimpeachable Islamic credentials in the eyes of parts of the Muslim world. The kingdom reaped what it had sown everywhere else. It faced unprecedented domestic discontent, both from Saudis seeking to liberalise the regime through such symbolic acts as allowing women drivers, and, by way of a backlash, from radical Islamists who thought the kingdom needed to restore Islamic funda-mentals. When some of these extremists were expelled, Saudi Arabia's British ally and arms supplier inevitably provided them with a safe haven in London, where they could propagandise amusing tabloid slanders against the Saudi ruling elite entitled 'Prince of the Month'. These were people who would give an aide £1,000 to buy a drink, and then be offended when the aide offered something so mysterious as £990 change. Even bin Laden was allowed to establish offices of a Reform and Advice Committee in the British capital. For 'Londonistan' would soon provide a home from home for more dangerous kinds of Islamist subversive, in one of the most complacent, decadent and irresponsible acts of policy and policing of any Western democracy, all undertaken under the delusion that there was an unwritten 'pact of security' in which the hosts would be safe from attack.[32]

One emerging rival to a discredited Saudi Arabia was the military–Islamist regime of Hassan al-Turabi in the Sudan. The Western-educated al-Turabi advocated the Islamic emancipation of women as well as reconciliation between Sunni and Shia, while waging war on the African animists and Christians of the south. His regime hosted an Arab and Islamic junket to rival the Saudi-dominated Organisation of the Islamic Conference, to some extent seeking to take over the mantle of the dead Khomeini as a beacon of radical Islam. Who contacted whom remains in doubt, but in 1991 bin Laden arrived in Khartoum. He cemented his ties with al-Turabi by taking the latter's niece as his third wife. In a country ruined by war and political turbulence, bin Laden's wealth counted. He deposited US$50 million in the Al-Shamal Islamic Bank, which virtually gave him control.[33] He gave the Sudanese an US$80 million loan to purchase wheat to prevent mass starvation. He helped build an airport and a road from Khartoum to Port Sudan, and invested in a variety of enterprises, including an Islamic bank, a bakery, cattle stations, stud farms, and various import and export businesses. Like many unsuccessful entrepreneurs bin Laden diversified beyond his ken, as when he began importing bicycles from Azerbaijan into a country where nobody rode them. A series of farms doubled as Al Qaeda training camps, for with the aid of Sudanese passports a small multinational army of jihadi-salafists descended upon Sudan. It was one of those curious, lull-like interludes before the storm. Bin Laden spent much time horse-riding, strolling by the Nile and talking bloodstock, with Izzam al-Turabi, his host's son. Family affairs bulked large too as he had all four of his wives, and their children, with him. One wife elected to divorce him; there were concerns about a disabled child. Money flew out at such an alarming rate that bin Laden began calling for retrenchment. This led to rancid recriminations between different ethnic groups among his supporters, and the defection of a Sudanese, ultimately into the hands of the CIA, after he had embezzled a lot of money.

The Sudan period also saw some tentative terrorist operations, especially after the head of Hizbollah's security service, Imad Mugniyah, came to lecture in Khartoum, in the wake of which he set up a suicide-bombing course for Al Qaeda operatives in Lebanon. He had been the prime mover behind the 1983 bombing of US and French peacekeeping troops in Beirut. The first targets were two hotels in Aden where US troops often rested en route to Operation Restore Hope in Somalia. No Americans were hurt in two bomb attacks which killed an Australian tourist and a Yemeni waiter. Ten months later bin Laden's envoys, drawn like mosquitoes to a swamp, watched as khat-crazed Somalia militiamen downed two US helicopters and barbarously killed their crews and US commandos in the middle of Mogadishu. Bin Laden would subsequently claim that it had been Al Qaeda men who shot the Black Hawks down, although in reality his men had run away. Still, behind the retrospective boasting, an idea took shape. His Egyptian mentor was not idle either.

Al-Zawahiri had taken the remnants of al-Jihad to Khartoum because he needed bin Laden's money to pay his men after a month-long fund-raising trip to California had yielded a paltry US$2,000. Although he was effectively on bin Laden's payroll thereafter, al-Zawahiri ran his own operations in his native Egypt. In August 1993 a suicide bomber on a motorbike tried to kill the Egyptian interior minister. Three months later al-Zawahiri tried to murder the prime minister, Atef Sidqi, with a car bomb designed to coincide with the trials of a large number of jihadists. The bomb killed a young girl instead, leading to cries of 'Terrorism is the enemy of God' at her well-attended funeral. Al-Zawahiri would persist in these attacks until they led to Al Qaeda being expelled from Sudan. The next level of violence followed a series of events that remobilised the *ummah* in ways not seen since the response to the Soviet invasion of Afghanistan. In the wake of this, Al Qaeda would emerge as the brightest star in a vaster nebula of violence.

VI ANGER, RAGE AND TV

For much of the 1980s the struggle of the Afghan mujaheddin against the Soviets eclipsed the Palestinian cause as an emotional rallying point for many Muslims. Afghanistan was where the Gulf money flowed, partly because events in the Middle East failed to conform to the simple binary enmities that all myths require. Some neighbouring Arab states like Egypt and Jordan made their cold peace with the Israelis, and the PLO entered into a protracted US-driven process while continuing to practise terrorism. This climate changed with the two Palestinian Intifadas. Together with wars in Bosnia and Chechnya, these provided endless scenes of Muslim victimhood, and sacred causes which legitimised jihadist violence.

The conflict between Israelis and Palestinians has never been the sole conflict in the Middle East, but the formula 'Jews = News' might lead one to imagine that. The world's Muslims see things this way; judging by the indifference of Western Christians to the predicament of their Maronite co-religionists in the Lebanon, a sense of oecumene is much weaker among Christians despite efforts by the Barnabas Trust to raise awareness. A brief recapitulation of Palestinian history is needed to situate the two Intifadas. The PLO had dissipated its energies in the civil wars of the Lebanon, resulting in the ejection of its fighters from Beirut in August 1982 and a Syrian-backed mutiny within the PLO against Arafat. In December 1983, the Saudis brokered a deal with Syria, which was about to crush Arafat's northern redoubt in Tripoli, permitting him and his men to withdraw by sea to Tunis. One minor victory, in the midst of this final débâcle, lay in the 4,500 Palestinian prisoners the Israelis exchanged for six of their own captives as the IDF pulled out of Lebanon. These would play a crucial role in events that put the plight of the Palestinians back in the world's spotlight.

There was always strain between the PLO's foreign-based representatives, with their nice apartments, suits and ties, and their hotel suites in Europe, and the Palestinians in the occupied territories. To them the PLO counselled 'fortitude' or 'steadfastness' while Arafat vainly attempted to defend Fatah's military presence in the Lebanon, whence liberation would come from outside. Arafat may have enjoyed immense personal prestige among the Palestinians as the father of their nation, but his madcap diplomatic gambits had become near irrelevant to the grim experiences of young Palestinians in the occupied territories.[34]

The Gaza Strip is twenty-eight miles long and between three and eight miles wide, and in the 1980s was home to 650,000 Palestinians, including those crammed densely and insalubriously into refugee camps, a burden resented by the indigenous Arab population. There are also powerful clans, which operate somewhere between extended families and Mafia gangs, with memberships of up to five thousand. When it suits them, they adopt titles like Army of Islam to disguise the crime of kidnapping for ransoms. Half the population were under fifteen, the result of an exceptionally high birth rate. Unemployed young men hung around, angry and bored, in the burning summer heat, a problem afflicting the Arab world from the Gulf to the Algerian Maghreb, which teems with superfluous young men, a problem common to many post-industrial Western societies. A skeletal Israeli Civil Administration controlled the Strip with a rigorous inefficiency against which there was little legal redress. The Strip was riddled with undercover officers of the domestic security agency Shin Beth, on the lookout for pliant informers. Although standards of education were good, thanks to external aid, job opportunities were few, with the lucky hundred thousand or so performing manual labour for neighbouring Israelis. Demeaning treatment by Arab or Israeli contractors, squeezing muscles as if they were assessing a mule, was followed by degrading treatment at the exit checkpoints, where bored guards sometimes gave meaning to their dull day by messing Arabs around with that irritating air of nonchalant gun-toting punctiliousness. Every hour in a queue was an hour's lost pay and less for a family to eat. Passive anti-Arab racism was as consequential as the active variety which exists in Israel. The majority of Israelis averted their eyes from the occupied territories and the festering hatreds they were engendering. Their government regarded disturbances as episodic and containable, the handiwork of malign extraneous influences.

The first Palestinian Intifada, or uprising, originated in a sequence of bizarrely random events that crowned months of tension. In May 1987 six members of the terrorist group Islamic Jihad broke out of Gaza Central prison, where they had been confined for such acts as killing Israeli taxi drivers. Sunni admirers of the ayatollah Khomeini, Islamic Jihad's three hundred militants were armed and directed by Islamist elements in Fatah's Western Sector command. Although the fugitives were mostly run to ground, while on the loose they continued their terrorist attacks, thereby acquiring folkloric kudos among young people receptive to their calls for the liberation of Palestine as the prelude to a wider Islamic revival. Even when Shin Beth agents ambushed and killed three of the Islamic Jihad fugitives in October, they lived on in handbills as 'ghosts who will pursue the Jews everywhere and for all time'.

The autumn months of 1987 saw a spate of stabbings of lone Israelis, culminating on 6 December when an Israeli was knifed to death in Gaza's main market. Two days later, the driver of an Israeli truck lost control and hit a car, killing four Palestinian day labourers. A flyer connected the two events as an act of revenge by the Israelis for the earlier stabbing, although the two episodes were wholly unconnected. Thousands of mourners attended the funerals of the four men, shouting 'Jihad! Jihad!' at the fifty-five Israeli reservists holed up in their post in Jebalya, with its sixty thousand inhabitants, the largest of the refugee camps in the Gaza Strip. When patrols sallied forth they came under hails of stones from demonstrators who would not disperse. Further patrols the following day got into difficulties when one unit stopped to pursue a rock-throwing teenager into a house, a move that resulted in their being surrounded by an angry mob. The reservists had no equipment or training to deal with a civilian riot. Warning shots in the air, which had become so frequent during riots that they were ignored, were followed by shots at the demonstrators' legs, and the death of a seventeen-year-old boy. Rioting spread to other sites within the Gaza Strip, each flashpoint marked by acrid smoke from piles of burning rubber tyres. The uprising quickly spread to the West Bank, where similarly only one in eight Palestinian graduates of the seven universities entered a profession, while tensions simmered over such issues as electricity and water. Palestinians needed permits for everything, which were sometimes irrationally denied. In the early 1990s the Israeli authorities rejected a request from Yehiya Abdal-Tif Ayyash, a Palestinian electronics graduate from Rafat, to do a masters degree in Jordan. He had no terrorist hinterland or connections, and, as became abundantly clear, it would have been better had the Israelis let him progress in his chosen career. General Ariel Sharon's provocative purchase of an apartment in east Jerusalem's Muslim Quarter, despite his Negev ranch and his right as a minister to use the capital's luxury hotels, seemed symbolic of a wider, abrasive stance, whether from American or Russian settlers seeking to establish facts on the ground, or a Likud party whose rhetoric tilted rightwards to dark talk, on the part of Israeli right-wing blow-hards, of transferring the Palestinians to Jordan.

The storm-like force of this 'rock revolution' caught both the Israelis and the PLO napping, although the latter's functionaries hastened to take charge. The leadership of the Intifada was elusively mysterious, while its footsoldiers quickly encompassed labourers and devout shop-keepers. As they picked up the first hundred or so putative ringleaders, Israeli interrogators were baffled to discover how apolitical the demon-strators appeared to be. Most were ignorant of even the most elementary PLO platforms. They were young male labourers, rather than students, who had had enough of high-handed treatment by the Israelis. Their tactics mutated too, from a straightforward riot to more sophisticated passive resistance, involving a wholesale disengagement from the Israeli economy. Bits of ground were used to grow vegetables, while chicken coops and rabbit hutches proliferated on roofs.

Nor did the Israelis have a coherent strategy for dealing with riots that involved women and children as well as young men. If it had once sufficed for an Israeli soldier to expose himself to send prudish Palestinian women fleeing, now women appeared to be egging on the demonstrating males. A fifth of the casualties of the first three months' riots were among women, a further outrage to Muslim sensibilities. Soon even grannies were involved, although as they were the bearers of the inter-generational national flame this is perhaps unsurprising.

Historically, revolutions often develop when a regime has many soldiers but few police; the opposite was true of nineteenth-century London, which had plenty of police and no 1848 revolution. The Intifada exposed a fatal blind-spot in Israel's security capability. Soldiers were useless against women and children hurling rocks or firing catapults from within large crowds. Under the massing lenses of the world's photographers and TV, the Israelis blundered into a propaganda disaster, which not only diminished international sympathy, but in its simple-minded misrepresentation of events outraged the wider Muslim world. Although Muslims did not stop to ponder this, Israel is a democracy which allows open access to the media, in marked contrast to conditions prevailing in the entire Arab world. Domestic opponents of the Israeli government gave interviews to the world's press, avenues which do not exist for critics of the governments of, for example, Algeria, Egypt, Morocco or Saudi Arabia, unless they are among well-populated exiled diasporas. Inevitably coverage concentrated on instances of Israeli brutality, without inquiring about the ways in which prolonged exposure of conscripts and reservists to mob violence was responsible for this. Arguably, Israel has never recovered from this public relations disaster, acquiring the reputation of a thuggish bully among mainly left-liberal and Christian circles, already fed up with Jewish moralising about the European Holocaust. Their ranks included an increasing number of liberal Jews in the US too, although for them the Holocaust was alternatively a surrogate religion.[35]

As the Intifada spread to shopkeepers, the Israelis first forced them to keep their shops open, and then welded up their shutters if they refused. This was a small price to pay compared to what the rioters would have done to them. Many of these shopkeepers were devout middle-class Muslims, a matter of import to how the social composition of the uprising mutated from rock-throwing teenagers to more respectable people. A few communities were subjected to collective punishments, involving cutting power supplies and restricting the inflow of food. Although it was infinitely preferable to shooting rioters, the decision to arm soldiers with batons (manufactured by other Palestinians in Gaza) was a public relations disaster, for the world's media focused on outrageous scenes of Israeli troops kicking and bludgeoning Palestinians beyond anything resembling proportionate force, as several cases of people with broken ribs, collarbones or arms that came before Israeli courts confirmed. In the most disgraceful incidents, Israeli high-school students on outings, or drivers ferrying officers about, had been invited to beat up detainees inside army camps. The deployment of rubber rounds was also a mixed blessing as these can be fatal when fired into someone's face. Adverse press coverage, from Israeli and international media, led frustrated IDF soldiers to take out their resentments on journalists and photographers, who met nothing but willingness from the other side, an arrangement that in turn impacted on how the Intifada was reported. The uprising began to leach towards the hitherto quiescent eight hundred thousand Israeli Arabs, who donated blood, medicines and money to the mounting casualties of the uprising.

The PLO leadership succeeded in re-establishing a vestige of remote control over the local Unified National Command which steered the Intifada. This used secretly produced flyers to co-ordinate the myriad grassroots committees that controlled each local epicentre of riot. Local mainstays of both levels of command were students and academics, especially from Bir Zeit university, and the thousands of security prisoners Israel had released in exchange for six soldiers taken hostage, men who had coolly taken the measure of their enemy while in jail.[36] Many of these former detainees joined the strong-arm security squads that proliferated to enforce the Intifada among the Palestinians. Inevitably, the international media did not descend in the same strength on victims of Palestinian violence, notably the Arab 'collaborators', seventy of whom the Intifada's ad-hoc security units killed, or the countless Arabs for whom there was no court to redress the beatings and intimidation they received from Fatah and the Intifada's grassroots supporters, and increasingly from a new actor amid the Days of Rage.

There was a further Israeli own-goal, the result of an idea that both CIA and State Department officials thought 'tried to be too sexy'. As the PLO's bureaucrats and intellectuals clambered aboard the Intifada's bandwagon, a very different type of organisation bid for control. The Civil Administration in the Gaza Strip had encouraged Islamic fundamentalist groups as a way of confounding the left-leaning PLO, especially if they eschewed the terrorism of Islamic Jihad. Defence minister Moshe Arens recalled viewing the rise of radical Islamism 'as a healthy phenomenon'. Right-wingers, by contrast, may have been hoping that the rise of Islamism among the Palestinians would permanently scupper the lengthy talks known as the Oslo peace-process by dividing the enemy.[37]

Funded by the Jordanians, Israelis and Saudis, the number of mosques in Gaza rose from 77 to 160 within two decades, with forty new mosques constructed in the West Bank each year. Despite warnings from moderate Gazan Muslims, the Israelis elected to ignore the rampant anti-Semitism of the Islamic Congress, the local guise of the Muslim

Brotherhood. They regarded its charitable and educational surface activities as preferable, in their steady incremental way, to the bomb and gun attacks of Fatah terrorists. Even better, the Congress's supreme leader, the quadriplegic sheikh Ahmed Ismail Yassin, regularly denounced Arafat and the PLO leadership as 'pork eaters and wine drinkers' who even allowed women into their senior councils. Born in 1938 into a middle-class farming family, Yassin grew up in the al-Shati refugee camp. At twelve he was injured in a wrestling bout; as his condition deteriorated he went from crutches to a wheelchair. After studying at Cairo's Ain Shams university, he returned to Gaza to work as a teacher, and religio-political agitator, until his disabilities forced him to retire in 1984, by which time he had had eleven children. That year the Israelis discovered an arms cache in the mosque Yassin preached in, which flatly contradicted the strategy of encouraging a pacific Islamist rival to Fatah terrorism. Although Yassin received a fifteen-year jail sentence, he was one of those released in exchange for Israeli soldiers captured in Lebanon.[38]

Yassin led a formidable Islamist network, which included al-Azhar university in Gaza, from which Communist and Fatah rivals were expelled by stabbings and acid attacks in an entirely symptomatic striving for totalitarian control. Everywhere the network physically manifested itself: places selling alcohol, displaying female models or playing pop music were smashed up, as was anyone presuming to eat with his or her left hand. The intention was to extrude anything that smacked of a Western hedonism and materialism which, the Islamists thought, was destroying Palestinian resistance by corrupting its austere spirit. Unlike the PLO, the Islamic Congress offered personal redemption as well as national salvation; unlike the PLO it abandoned any attempts to camouflage hatred of Jews. This was a starkly compelling platform for younger people rebelling against both the social hierarchy and the politics of their parents' generation, who could relate to the old sheikh in ways they could not with PLO bosses as they sped from diplomatic junket to junket, or from sell-out to sell-out, in their fleets of Mercedes, in between tripping the light fantastic in villas and luxury hotels. Islamism licensed defiance of the older generation, breaking the narrow bonds of clan or custom in favour of vaster loyalties that at the same time were warmly personal through God.

Yassin was one of the founders in February 1988 of the Islamic Resistance Movement, or Harakat al-Muqawama al-Islamiyya, whose

Arabic acronym was altered from HMS to Hamas, the word for zeal. The others were sheikh Salah Shehada, from the Islamic university in Gaza, an engineer called Issa al-Nasshaar, a doctor, Ibrahim al-Yazuri, Abdul Aziz al-Rantisi, another doctor from Khan Younis, a headmaster and a schoolteacher, all aged between forty and fifty years old.[39] These people did not use the same diplomatic niceties as the PLO. Arriving in Kuwait after being expelled from Gaza, one of its leaders, Halil Koka, baldly announced: 'Allah brought the Jews together in Palestine not to benefit from a homeland but to dig their grave there and save the world from their pollution. Just as the Muslim pilgrim redeems his soul in Mecca by offering up a sacrifice, so the Jews will be slaughtered on the rocks of al-Aqsa.'

In its rivalry with the PLO, Hamas began to dictate the pace of events in the Intifada, by deliberately establishing its own cycle of demonstrations, shop closures and strikes like an alternative calendar to that of the secular nationalists. It issued a charter, which called the destruction of Israel a religious duty. The charter was an odd document, managing as it did to call the Jews Nazis while citing the forged 'Protocols of the Elders of Zion' as proof of a Jewish conspiracy for world domination from the French Revolution onwards. Even the Rotary Club gets a discredit. To call the charter ahistorical would be to understate the ways in which it collapsed time into an eternal struggle between Muslims, Jews and 'Crusaders' from the West.[40] Hamas's public attitude towards terrorism was also changing, although its armed wing, and secret department for killing Arab collaborators, actually predated the founding of the political movement. In July 1988 it lauded a young Gazan who knifed two prison guards while visiting a jailed relative. The organisation had for several years had a small military wing of 'holy fighters of Palestine' who, it now transpired, were planning terrorist attacks on Israel.

That summer, the Israelis struck first at Islamic Jihad by getting the US to force king Hussein to eject the three Fatah chieftains who planned Islamic Jihad's operations. All three were killed by a mystery Mossad car bomb shortly after reaching their sanctuary in Cyprus. Next, Israel detained hundreds of Hamas activists, confining them in Khediot detention camp, where they continued to direct operations by passing and receiving messages through kisses from their families. After initially sparing sheikh Yassin, the Israelis finally detained him too. Despite his disabilities, he and one of his younger sons seem to have been treated in a brutal manner unworthy of a quadriplegic, including being slapped in the face and bashed on the head with a metal tray. Repression only increased the domestic and international appeal of Hamas. Its candidates began to win elections on Palestinian professional bodies, while in 1990 Kuwait alone donated US$60 million to Hamas as opposed to US$27 million to the PLO. The PLO's attempts to neutralise Hamas by co-opting it on to the umbrella Palestinian National Council, as it had done with the PFLP and the Communists, failed when Hamas demanded half the Council seats. The PLO's acceptance of Israel and public renunciation of terrorism through the Oslo Accords deepened the rift between implacable Islamists and Arafat's more diplomatically focused Fatah, however fake Arafat's subscription to non-violence proved.

The human cost of the first Intifada was considerable. By the summer of 1990, over six hundred Palestinians had been killed by the IDF, including seventy-six children under fourteen, with a further twelve thousand people injured. Ten thousand Palestinians were held in detention camps and prisons, a shared experience that served to radicalise even further those affected. On the Israeli side, eighteen people had been killed, including ten civilians, with 3,391 injured, the majority of them soldiers.

During the 1990s Hamas increasingly made the running in terms of devastating terrorist attacks within Israel. In addition to money coming from both Saudi Arabia and Iran, Hamas built a vast charitable money-laundering operation that had important nodal points in the USA, where the Irish republican NORAID was said to have shown how easy it was to raise dollars for foreign terrorism (though NORAID has always denied the allegation that it funded the IRA). Unlike Fatah, or the smaller Marxist Palestinian terrorist groups, Hamas used tight five-man cells to insulate itself against traitors and people who caved in under Shin Beth's notorious interrogation methods. It hit Israel at a very delicate spot when it used killers disguised as Orthodox Jews and cars with yellow Israeli licence plates to abduct and kill IDF soldiers hitchhiking home. Hamas members also ran over and abducted an Israeli border police sergeant, whose body – bearing signs of strangulation and stabbing – turned up in a desert gulley. In response to this, Israel dumped 415 Hamas organisers in the hilly no-man's land on the border with Lebanon. Predictably, the world's left-liberal media descended in sympathy upon these middle-aged accountants, clerics, dentists, doctors and lawyers, shivering in their coats and long-johns around dismal potages of stewed lentils. They did not note that they were fed at night by Hizbollah and Iranian Pasadren agents, who offered money and advanced terrorist training at state facilities in Iran. The men on the hillsides included Abdul Aziz al-Rantisi, Hamas's second in command until Yassin and he were assassinated, and Ismail Haniyah, its bear-like current leader.

A by-product of this expulsion was Hamas's Izzedine al-Qassam Brigade, one of whose first acts was to kill a young Shin Beth agent in a Jerusalem safe house, using axes, knives and hammers to do the job. The flat looked like an abattoir afterwards. They also machine-gunned two traffic policemen dozing in their idling patrol car. The decision to deny Ayyash his chance to study in Jordan to support his wife and son became fateful, as he quickly rose within Hamas as its stellar 'Engineer'. A first attempt to bring the mores of Lebanon to Israel came in April 1993 when a suicide bomber drove a huge bomb hidden in a VW transporter between two buses parked at a crowded service station. Miraculously the blast mainly went upwards, killing a Palestinian who worked in the centre, and the bomber himself.

The murder by Baruch Goldstein, a Brooklyn-born Jewish fanatic, of fifty-five Palestinian worshippers in February 1994 led to the mobilisation of Ayyash's talents in the service of revenge. His chosen instrument was a nineteen-year-old Palestinian, three of whose family had been killed by the Israelis. This youth drove an Opel Ascona in front of a school bus in the town of Afula, detonating five fragmentation grenades nestling within seven propane-gas cylinders, in turn wrapped with thirteen hundred carpenters' nails. Nine young people died and fifty-five were injured. On 13 April a twenty-one-year-old Arab detonated a duffel bag on a bus in Hadera, killing six and injuring thirty. A pipe bomb exploded as the rescuers arrived, in a double tap which indicated some tactical sophistication. As Ayyash moved at each onset of dusk from safe house to safe house, this otherwise modest man assumed the celebrity of a pop star among young Palestinians. His deeds were celebrated by songs recorded on cheap cassettes. Admirers sent wigs and women's clothing to help him with his multiple disguises. In October, Ayyash despatched a suicide bomber on a number 5 bus as it sped through the morning bustle of Tel Aviv's Dizengoff district. The bomber detonated an Egyptian land mine which had been filled with twenty kilograms of TNT. The bomb killed twenty-one Israelis, and the nails and screws it spewed out also seriously wounded fifty people.[41] Ayyash's relentless campaign of suicide bombing began to impact on domestic Israeli politics in that successive prime ministers engaged in peace talks with the Palestinians had to visit the scenes of Ayyash's depredations, increasingly under the gaze of hostile Jewish crowds. Ayyash was also training members of Islamic Jihad in bomb making, including Hani Abed, Islamic Jihad's star terrorist. Abed's sudden death in November 2004 after his Peugeot was destroyed by a booby-trap bomb led to combined operations by Hamas and Islamic Jihad with Ayyash as the mastermind. In January 2005 two men dressed in IDF uniforms blew themselves up sequentially amid soldiers returning from weekend leave. Twenty-one men died and sixty were critically injured in this bombing which occurred at a junction near Ashmoret maximum-security prison – home to sheikh Yassin. As a grim prime minister Rabin surveyed the site of this atrocity, he was lucky that a third bomber had been delayed, making it impossible for him to trigger a bomb hidden in a kitbag by the second suicide bomber. This treble tap might have killed Rabin.

Massive Israeli resources were put into killing Ayyash, who continued with a campaign of suicide bombings that reduced going out to a form of Russian roulette for many urban Israelis. Two senior Izzedine al-Qassam leaders were killed when an apartment blew up in Gaza, and another senior figure was snatched off a Nablus street after he failed to notice two sweaty Sudanese day labourers loitering outside a mosque who were Ethiopian Falasha Shin Beth agents. Islamic Jihad's leader, Fathi Shiqaqi, was assassinated by a Mossad team on Malta. So self-confident was Mossad that, as the killer sped off on a motorbike and caught a boat to Sicily, his colleagues hung around disguised as bystanders to give Maltese police hopelessly inaccurate descriptions. Ayyash's weakness was his family – his wife and son in Gaza, whom he regularly visited, while keeping in touch with his mother and father by mobile phone. Shin Beth stepped up pressure on his mother, with raids on the family home, and prolonged ten-hour bouts of interrogation, designed to infuriate her son. Ayyash was also too comfortable in his routines and grew sloppy.

He accepted the offer of a safe house from a Hamas member in Gaza, unaware that the man's businessman uncle, who owned the building, was on Shin Beth's payroll. Ayyash enjoyed the joke that his apartment was a thousand yards from a major Israeli police checkpoint. Unknown to him this was where his destiny was being settled. He had also discovered mobile phones as an alternative to erratic and easily monitored landlines. He changed them every few weeks, but not before having long calls with his mother and father. On 25 December 1995 Ayyash proudly announced that his wife had borne a second son, rashly telling his father they would speak again on 5 January. In the interim, Shin Beth technicians adapted a mobile phone, inserting fifty grams of RDX high explosive beneath the battery, and a minute detonator that could be remotely triggered. The phone still weighed the same and functioned normally. The phone was passed to his landlord's nephew who said Ayyash could use it any time he liked. The landline in his apartment began to play up. Ayyash told his father that this mobile number, 050–507–497, was his preferred number. Freshly returned home at 4.30 a.m. after a night's mystery activities, Ayyash removed his female clothes and settled down for a few hours' sleep in his purple boxer shorts. The mobile rang at 8.40 a.m.; it was his father. After exchanging a few words, the father found the line disconnected. High in the sky above Gaza, an Israeli agent in a spotter plane had detonated the shaped charge in the phone that took half of Ayyash's head off. A hundred thousand gun-toting Palestinians attended his funeral, straining for a last touch of his coffin. His landlord's uncle was slipped away by Mossad to a new life in the US. An Israeli demolition team erased Ayyash's family home in Riffat. Within four days of Ayyash's death, Hamas suicide bombers killed fifty-seven people in an orgy of attacks that by May 1996 felled the government of Shimon Peres. His tough Likudnik successor, Netanyahu, decided to strike at Khaled Mashaal, the leader of Hamas in otherwise friendly Jordan. In October 1997 two Mossad agents posing as Canadians waylaid Mashaal in his Amman offices, spraying a lethal synthetic opiate into his ear. This was designed to kill him, painfully, forty-eight hours later. Both agents were caught by the Jordanians, who were outraged by this botched violation of their sovereignty. Since king Hussein threatened to hang their agents, the Israelis were forced to hand over an antidote to the poison, and to release fifty Hamas prisoners including sheikh Yassin. When Israeli voters went to the polls they dismissed Netanyahu in favour of Ehud Barak, a war hero we have already encountered in his dealings with Black September in Beirut.

The second, so-called al-Aqsa Intifada erupted in September 2000 and concluded with Israel's unilateral withdrawal from Gaza and northern Samaria and the death of Arafat. Although Arafat had publicly forsworn terrorism, with some parts of his enormous security apparatus erratically co-operating with the Israelis, other elements of this simultaneously doubled as Islamic Jihad or Hamas terrorists. The Israeli navy regularly intercepted big arms shipments from Iran and elsewhere that were destined for Arafat. He also had little control over such hardened veterans of the first Intifada as Marwan Barghouti, leader of an armed Fatah cadre called Tanzim, who were impatient of diplomacy as such. Nor did Arafat control grassroots groups that formed early in the second Intifada, like the Al-Aqsa Martyrs Brigade, created by brothers Nasser and Yasser Badawi and their friend Nasser Awais, in the Balata refugee camp in Nablus about a month into the uprising.

The opposition Likud leader Ariel 'Arik' Sharon chose 28 September 2000 to visit Temple Mount with a large entourage of bodyguards. This was part and parcel of Sharon's marking of territory in east Jerusalem that had begun when he purchased his apartment. Barak sought Arafat's express permission for the visit, insisting that Sharon comport himself with an uncharacteristic dignified quietness. This was akin to telling a bull to wear slippers in his rampage through the china shop. Sharon always exuded an air of bumptious thuggishness, though his admirers say this conceals his more human side.

Predictably, Sharon's visit triggered violent Palestinian riots which spread from Jerusalem to the West Bank and Gaza. Sixty-one Palestinians were killed and 2,657 injured in the first six days. October saw clashes between Arab and Jewish mobs, the latter screaming 'Death to Arabs!' A judicial inquiry under Justice Theodore Or found several faults in the police's handling of these riots, which in any event had escalated into terrorist atrocities. On 12 October 2000, two Israeli reservists in a civilian car got lost in Ramallah, where a funeral was being held for a seventeen-year-old shot by the IDF the day before. They were arrested by Palestinian police and held in a police station. This was attacked by five thousand irate Palestinians chanting 'Kill the Jews!' Although the local Palestinian police chief tried to save the two Israelis, he was overwhelmed by the mob, which beat and stabbed the men to death, throwing one out of the window to be dragged and trampled below. Israelis were horrified by these depredations; their government launched retaliatory air strikes on Palestinian Authority buildings in Ramallah.[42]

Mob violence escalated into all-out armed conflict. Bomb makers trained by Ayyash provided the weapons for new waves of Hamas suicide bombers. These have engendered much incomprehension, despite what we know of medieval Assassins, of Japanese kamikaze pilots, and of airmen and soldiers the world over who undertake missions in which the odds are lethal. Terrorist suicide bombings are far from being an exclusively Muslim thing. The tactic has been most employed by Marxist

Tamil separatists of predominantly Hindu extraction in their war with the Buddhist Sinhalese, as well as by Marxist Kurdish separatists in their conflict with Muslim Turks. In fact, Muslim fundamentalism may paradoxically discourage certain categories of suicide bombers, especially women, who belong in the crib and kitchen. It was the secular Fatah organisation that encouraged women fighters, while men like Hamas's sheikh Yassin were on record as actively opposing this. This may explain why female suicide bombers make up 5 per cent of the total in Palestinian operations, although Hamas has changed its line since.

Hamas adopted the tactic for two reasons. Suicide bombing enabled it to establish a distinctly implacable market share, distinguishing it from Fatah and secular Palestinian terrorist groups. Secondly, its carefully calibrated suicide attacks were designed to scupper the ongoing peace process, while encouraging even the most diehard proponents of Greater Israel to be shot of these unyielding maniacs. The advent of Ariel Sharon as prime minister and his policy of unilateral withdrawal was, in the eyes of Hamas, a development to be welcomed.

Suicide bombing has a comprehensible military logic beneath the superficial insanity of actions from which the genuinely mentally ill are assiduously weeded out by alert handlers. The Palestinians see it as a means of rebalancing the asymmetry due to their lack of aircraft and armour. Whether walk-in volunteers or recruited from among 'sad cases', suicide bombers are expendable extras, rather than highly trained core cadres whose loss might be missed. They do not require much technical training to push a button on their belt or backpack, but they do need a few weeks' or months' careful handling by experienced operators, designed to eliminate doubts and to focus their minds on the mission. The handlers are cold-eyed operators capable of juggling one set of values they apply in their own lives with another that sends others to their deaths. The bombers are shepherded to the point of no return, a moment symbolised by the recording of a video will in which they are surrounded by the martyr's paraphernalia. This helps recruit more suicide killers. Then they are told their target. After that it would be dishonourable to back out, although some do. Handlers routinely escort the bomber on their penultimate journey, making distracting small talk or extolling the delights of the afterlife. Then, briefly, the bomber is on his or her own, smiling sweetly at a representative group of Israelis on their way to work, absorbed in their newspapers, sandwiches or taped music.

Since most terrorists make very careful plans for their escape after an attack, suicide bombing cuts out an entire layer of planning. The tactic enables the bomber to get close to his or her target, giving rise to death tolls that are considerable – in fact four to six times more lethal – compared with gun or grenade attacks below the level of car bombs. Costing an average of US$150 to mount, suicide bombings are cheap.

If we take the Al-Aqsa Intifada, between September 2000 and September 2005 there were 144 successful suicide attacks in Israel among some 36,000 terrorist incidents. Although suicide bombings accounted for a mere 0.5 per cent of all attacks, they caused 50 per cent of deaths and casualties during this period. There is something else worth noting about suicide bombing too. When successful, there is no one to capture – unless the mission fails – while the willingness to die indicates a fanatical belief in a cause. The sheer ordinariness of the bomber indicates that there must be a limitless supply of such people lurking in the hostile population. Denied an obvious object of vengeance, much of the energy of the bewildered opponent goes into working out the motives of why these men and women kill themselves. Such bizarre phenomena as the small child who, in a 2007 Hamas TV advert, swears she is going to follow her deceased mother by becoming a suicide bomber, or the mothers who appear to welcome the deaths of their martyred sons, encourage the view that this is all the fanatical face of a pathological society. In fact, some of the mothers who do not grieve have been bribed, drugged or otherwise intimidated by men, with an interest in ensuring that the martyrs are celebrated.

Israel has around 250 unsuccessful suicide bombers in its prisons, who have been the subjects of extensive investigation by expert psychologists. Some are alive because they lost their nerve, others because their bombs malfunctioned. Their age range begins at fourteen, a boy whom the Israelis captured trying to blow himself up. Many of them were motivated to kill Jews (as they invariably put it) by the loss of family or friends through Israeli military or police action. It is a matter of revenge in a society where blood feuds last generations. This multiplies the carnage. Others saw suicide bombing as a way out of a dysfunctional family, dishonour – especially in the case of women – or sheer boredom. Wafa Idris, a Palestinian woman suicide bomber, had been divorced by her husband after it became apparent she was infertile. Her husband remarried and moved his new wife into a neighbouring house where he threw a party when their first child was born. This sent Wafa Idris over the edge. Several female suicide bombers seem to have disgraced themselves by becoming pregnant with Fatah lovers, or had otherwise acquired a reputation for looseness which *shahid* or martyrdom would expunge.[43] In 2004, Hamas's first woman suicide, a woman with two children, was driven by her husband to the checkpoint where she blew herself up after she confessed to having had an extramarital liaison.

Ironically, some young female would-be suicide bombers saw joining a terrorist group as an opportunity to meet males without supervision. One of them explained: 'We do not live in the West. When I went to training, I told my father that I was going to a girlfriend . . . I had freedom, even though our family is religious. It is natural to go and see girlfriends.' She got cold feet only when the males informed her that the object of these training trysts was for the girls to blow themselves up. One *shahida* explained that when her father refused to allow her to marry a (poor) disabled man with whom she had fallen in love, she got her revenge by becoming a suicide bomber. The vision of life in the Garden of Eden overcame her depression. For women there would not be the seventy-two virgins, but an abundance of food and a doting martyr–warrior. A male failed suicide bomber explained his vision of heavenly delights, much of which was *haram* to Muslims: 'All that is forbidden in this world is permitted in the Garden of Eden. The Garden of Eden has everything – God, freedom, the Prophet Mohammed and my friends, the "shahids" . . . There are seventy-two virgins. There are lots of things I can't even describe . . . I'll find everything in the Garden of Eden, a river of honey, a river of beer and alcohol . . .'[44] Once dead, the suicide bomber joins the rollcall of martyrs, his or her photo ringed with a golden frame at home, and plastered everywhere on posters. Proud parents announce the death in the weddings, rather than obituaries, columns of newspapers. By 2001 Hamas was paying them between US$3,000 and US$5,000 in death benefits. Saddam Hussein raised this to US$25,000, with further perks such as clocks, rugs and TVs. Expectations are so low in places like Gaza and Jenin, that killing oneself can seem like an attractive career option, and a form of social mobility for the entire family or clan. Social endorsement of martyrdom further destroyed residual taboos about suicide, which in any case had been qualified by many Islamist clerics.

Suicide attacks were accompanied by vicious battles between armed elements of the Intifada and the IDF. One of these raged for ten days in a refugee camp at Jenin, home to fifteen thousand people. This was an

Islamist stronghold variously described as 'the capital of martyrs' or 'a nest of cockroaches' depending on one's point of view. Hamas and Islamic Jihad wanted to turn this into an Arab Stalingrad, wiring it with booby-traps and sniping from amid the mounting rubble. As the inhabitants were slow to abandon their homes, they also hoped that any Israeli assault would deliver a propaganda victory, with talk of massacre finding its way from journalists to human rights agencies. In fact, talk of 'hundreds' or even 'thousands' of victims, relayed by Western media outlets, whose presenters could hardly contain their own rage, was misplaced. The final agreed death toll was thirty-two Palestinian armed militants, twenty-two Palestinian civilians, and twenty-three Israeli soldiers. Instead of a non-existent massacre there was steady physical erasure, as helicopters and tanks fired missiles and shells into buildings, while sixty-ton armoured bulldozers nudged down houses and ground down the rubble. If there were human rights violations, these included the Palestinian and IDF decisions to fight a pitched battle in a refugee camp, and Israel's denial of medical and humanitarian relief to civilians caught in the fighting. Scenes like these, repeated endlessly on the world's TV channels, further fuelled the anger of the virtual *ummah*. They were not alone. In 2003 Asif Muhammed Hanif and Omar Khan Sharif, Anglo-Pakistanis in their twenties, who had met studying Islamism under Omar Bakri Mohammed at a college in Derby, volunteered their services to Hamas. They met a Hamas instructor in Syria and then entered Israel via Jordan, mingling with European left-wing activists arriving to insert themselves into the Intifada as part of an Alternative Tourism Group. They seem to have been ferried around various Palestinian towns by a left-wing Italian woman journalist who did not realise they were terrorists, having accepted their cover stories about being interested in Palestinian medical centres. In Gaza they were kitted out with suicide belts and the Italian woman drove them into Israel. Hanif blew himself up outside Mike's Place, a popular Tel Aviv blues bar on the city's waterfront, killing three people. Sharif fled, after a bomb concealed in a book failed to detonate, and his body was washed up on the shore a few weeks later, having drowned in mysterious circumstances.

The mother of a professional Saudi soldier was watching the news with her son one evening in the early 1990s: 'Look what they are doing, they are raping our sisters and killing our brothers. My son, get up, and go, and I don't want to see you again.' Abu Saif, the soldier, and a friend called Abu Hamad al-Otaibi, were soon at the village of Bjala-Bucha in Bosnia. When the Serbs attacked, most of Abu Hamad's head was blown off by a 120 mm shell. Abu Saif was shot dead in the same battle. As they were lowered into one grave, their fellow Arab jihadists said: 'They loved each other in this world and they shall love each other in the next.' Over in east London at the same time, Bangladeshi and Pakistani students at Tower Hamlets College watched a short film, *The Killing Fields of Bosnia*, which made many of them weep. At the London School of Economics, the 'Tottenham Ayatollah', sheikh Omar Bakri, the Syrian-born spiritual head of the extremist Hizb ut-Tahir, had Muslim students jumping to their feet shouting 'Jihad for Bosnia!' after one of his rabble-rousing performances in the main lecture theatre.[45]

Perceptions of Muslims as victims were massively enhanced by the terrible wars that erupted amid the disintegration of Yugoslavia. The Balkans inspired anger, with tales of Serbs using ropes attached to cars to drag the testicles off Muslim males. In March 1992, the predominantly Muslim Bosnia-Herzogovina declared its independence, thereby reminding Muslims elsewhere that they had two million Serbo-Croat-speaking co-religionists indigenous to this part of Europe, South Slavs who had been Islamised under the Ottomans. However, after decades of Communism and secular education, and rates of urban intermarriage of 30 per cent by the 1980s, the Bosnian Muslims were largely Muslim by virtue of culture and tradition rather than fervency. Certain distinct customs and habits marked them out – like drinking coffee from cups with no handles, infant circumcision and distinctive names – but they also drank alcohol and ate pork, and were heavily Europeanised and scarcely hostile to a Western world they regarded as superior to Communism.[46]

Bosnia has an indigenous Islamist tradition, although this was confined to a tiny handful of intellectuals. Alija Izetbegović, the first Bosnian president, was typical of most of these, however, in that he had matured from the Muslim Brotherhood influences of his youth, which had repeatedly landed him in the jails of the Communist dictator Tito, to an endorsement of democracy and an openness towards Western culture. He bent over backwards to accommodate Croat and Serb sensitivities as an independent Bosnia developed. This relatively enlightened position was in marked contrast to the crudity with which former Communists, like Slobodan Milošević, espoused an extreme Serbian

Orthodox Christian national socialism which played upon the still visceral mythology of the Second World War. In Serbian eyes, the Croats were latterday Ustashe – the Catholic Fascist party that Hitler and Mussolini had helped into power – while the two million Bosnian Muslims were Islamist fundamentalists. Ethnically speaking, they were nothing more than Romanised or Islamised Serbs. As had already happened when Croatia and Slovenia declared their independence, Milošević used the combined muscle of the Serb-dominated Yugoslav federal army and sinister ethnic-Serb paramilitaries to fuse the exclaves of territory which he sought to incorporate into a Greater Serbia. This tactic was stymied by the Croats, leaving Milošević to divert this malign energy towards Bosnia, where the psychiatrist turned politician Radovan Karadžić had already declared Serbian Autonomous Regions as a newly independent Bosnia was recognised by the EEC in April 1992.

West European politicians adopted the idiosyncratic strategy of extruding the US from what they protectively claimed was a European problem, while evincing a patrician disdain worthy of Bismarck for the warring savages in the Balkans. They clutched at any historical cliché in their expensively educated imaginations to justify a fateful inertia. By denying the Bosnian Muslims arms, they left them at the mercy of Serb forces with huge stockpiled (and manufacturing) capacity that was immune to an impartial UN arms embargo. British patricians used every slippery evasion to do nothing while butchery, rape and ethnic cleansing took place right under their noses, until the world's media – above all Penny Marshall of ITN – made this impossible by publicising scenes almost worthy of Bergen-Belsen. Western Christians and Jews were as appalled by what they saw as anyone else, in many cases forcing their reluctant governments to do something about it by comparing it with the Holocaust.

At first, the organised Muslim world did not know how to respond to the plight of a Muslim community they knew next to nothing about. In 1992 the subject was discussed at Islamic conferences in Istanbul and Jeddah. The Iranians were the first to offer practical aid, shipping arms and training instructors via Turkey and Croatia to Bosnia, a supply stream that the US tolerated to redress the imbalance between Bosnia and Croatia and Serbia, for many of these weapons fell out of their crates in Zagreb. Egypt and Saudi Arabia donated respectively humanitarian aid and US$150 million, while discouraging a repetition of the Afghan Arab jihad that was already blowing back streams of militants into their countries. Inevitably, since the fall of Kabul in 1992, the free electrons of the jihad were drawn to Bosnia as if by a powerful magnet. Unless they went deeper into Afghanistan, they had nowhere to go, for home was not an option. Pakistan had also blocked the passage of further Arabs into that country. Men connected to Al Qaeda installed the personnel to receive both Arab Afghan mujaheddin and local recruits from among Muslim European immigrants as they made their way to Bosnia via Croatia.

A forty-two-year-old Saudi, sheikh Abu Abdel Aziz 'Barbaros' – the latter word referring to his two-foot-long henna-red beard – was a veteran Arab Afghan also known by the term 'Hown' after the Soviet Hound artillery shell he had used so proficiently. He was one of the first recruits to Al Qaeda. Although he initially thought Bosnia might be situated in the US, Aziz quickly pronounced that the conflict was a legitimate holy war for his fellow jihadi-salafists. Another key participant was a radical cleric, an Egyptian called sheikh Anwar Shaaban, imam of Milan's Islamic Cultural Institute, a mosque installed in a former garage. There are ten mosques in Milan, serving a Muslim population of about one hundred thousand. Most of them are moderate, but the ICI was not, following its London equivalent in Finsbury Park in encouraging worshippers to occupy the pavements in aggressive defiance of motorists and shopkeepers. The mosque was also the hub of an extortion racket which monopolised the supply of halal meat to butchers it terrified into being sole customers.[47] The ICI performed an equivalent role to Abdullah Azzam in Peshawar during the Afghan wars, and both the Jordanian cleric Abu Qatada and Abu Hamza al-Masri in London, in despatching fighters to Bosnia. The hook-handed Hamza went to Bosnia in person, but soon fell out with Algerian Islamists he encountered. Another Italian-based cleric, Mohamed Ben Brahim Saidani, head of a mosque in Bologna, was the direct link between the Bosnian jihad and bin Laden. Beyond these two, a network of Islamist clerics including sheikh Abu Talal al-Qasimy in Cairo and sheikh Omar bin Ahmad in Yemen banged the drum to lure young men to Bosnia. While these clerics provided the theological legitimisation, and many recruits, for this new field of jihad, Algerian and Egyptian veterans of Afghanistan, like Boudella al-Hajj, Moataz Billah and Wahiudeen al-Masri organised the military training at two camps which the jihadists operated from Mehurici and Zenica.

A motley array of volunteers descended on Bosnia. A Bahraini prince and one of the nation's soccer stars, a Qatari handball player and young

British Muslim medical students rubbed shoulders with bulky Arab-Americans from Detroit. The group's official cameraman was a young German Muslim who as a teenager discovered that his German parents had adopted him from a Turkish couple, whom he rejoined. At the age of twenty-one Abu Musa went to Bosnia to fight and film for the mujaheddin, one of his key tasks being to capture the smile on the faces of dying jihadists. A shadowy network of Islamist charities, based in the US, Europe, North Africa and the Middle East, many of which had proven links to Al Qaeda terrorists and which would move its money around too, oiled the assembly and supply of this army. The names, Human Concern International or Third World Relief Agency, belied the evil intent.

The core fighters were wild people, in their Afghan-style flat caps and long quilted jackets, whose cries of 'Allahu Akhbar!' sent a shudder down the spines of UN peacekeepers, who were under orders not to fire at them. They frightened their Bosnian allies, who generally wanted to live, as well as villagers whose pigs they shot. The Arab jihadist presence in Bosnia led to a new apocalyptic rhetoric, in which this complex struggle was portrayed as 'a war between Islam and Christianity . . . a war carried out by the entire West against the Islamic world'. It also led to the introduction of Afghan mores, as when the heads of three captured Serbs were displayed on poles, while others were crudely circumcised with a commando knife. Another Serb prisoner described what happened to him in Arab jihadist captivity: 'As soon as we arrived, the mujaheddins tied us with a hose, into which they let air under pressure, to make it expand and press our legs. This caused terrible pains and Gojko Vujeiae swore [to] God, so one of the mujaheddin took him aside and cut his head off. I did not see what he used to do the cutting, but I know that he brought the head into the room and forced all of us to kiss it. Then the mujaheddin hung the head on a nail in the wall.' Unsurprisingly, captured Serbs, like captured Soviets in Afghanistan, began to accept offers to convert to Islam.

When in 1993 the Arab mujaheddin and their Bosnian allies found themselves fighting the Croats as well as the Serbs, similar atrocities occurred. On one occasion, the jihadists had to be restrained by their Bosnian allies as they attempted to blow up an ancient monastery after they had already scraped images of Jesus and the Virgin Mary from the murals around the altar. Elsewhere they grabbed four young men in a village, cut their throats, and collected the blood so as to tip it back over the victims' heads.[48] Western aid workers became targets too, notoriously when three British men were kidnapped, which resulted in the execution-style killing of Paul Goodhall, and the shooting of two of his friends as they fled the same fate at the hands of the jihadists. Tensions between the Bosnian army and their indispensable foreign friends led to the formation of a separate Battalion of Holy Warriors, whose semi-suicidal propensities were in evidence in several major battles. They were owed a debt of blood by the Bosnian government. This explains why that government ignored warnings that the networks that sustained these foreign fighters were simultaneously engaged in acts of terrorism. In 1995, Algerian jihadists were sent from Bosnia to blast with shotguns an imam of a Paris mosque who had co-founded the Islamic Salvation Front, which by then had fallen foul of the more extreme Armed Islamic Group or GIA. Others connected to the 'charity' Human Concern International were responsible for two bomb attacks on the Paris Métro – the first of which killed ten and injured 116 – as well as a failed attempt to derail a high-speed TGV near Lyons, an early indication that the jihadists were bent on indiscriminate mass casualties.

Warnings from Egypt about this viper's nest in Europe's midst were also ignored by most European governments. After an attempt was foiled to assassinate Hosni Mubarak, the Egyptians decided to strike back. They had the Croatian police arrest Talal al-Qasimy, simultaneously the patron of the Bosnian jihadists and the international spokesman of Al-Gama'at, the terror organisation which had co-operated with Al Qaeda in a bid to murder the Egyptian leader in Addis Ababa. In an early example of CIA-supervised rendition under US president Bill Clinton (for George W. Bush did not patent the policy), al-Qasimy was 'de-territorialised' by being moved to a US warship, and then handed over to the Egyptians. After a spell in the so-called ghost villas maintained by the Egyptian secret service, he was executed in accordance with a death sentence passed in 1992.[49] A decade before major terrorist atrocities in Europe, the Egyptian government issued a clear warning in *Al-Ahram*:

> His [al-Qasimy's] arrest proves what we have always said, which
> is that these terror groups are operating on a worldwide scale,
> using places like Afghanistan and Bosnia to form their fighters
> who come back to the Middle East . . . European countries like
> Denmark, Sweden, Switzerland, England and others, which give

sanctuary to these terrorists, should now understand it will
come back to haunt them where they live.

Virtually every European government, with the honourable exception
of the French, ignored a warning whose chill truth is evident a decade
later.

As sixty thousand NATO peacekeepers descended on Bosnia in
the wake of the Dayton Agreements to halt the carnage, the Bosnian
government enabled many of the Arab jihadists, including those who
had married locally, to become citizens by issuing them with batches
of blank passports. This got around the provision in Dayton that the
jihadists had thirty days to leave the country. The villages where they
settled acquired roadsigns warning 'FEAR ALLAH'. Since the jihadists
regarded the peace deal as a sell-out, and viewed Western NATO troops
as enemies of Islam, any number of ugly incidents occurred when the
two sides met, even as a Canadian suicide bomber attacked a Croatian
police station in revenge for the abduction of al-Qasimy. In December, a
nineteen-year-old British suicide bomber was killed when a car bomb
he was readying for use against Croat forces prematurely exploded. A
spiral of violence ensued, especially after Croat troops ambushed and
assassinated sheikh Anwar Shaaban, the key figure in the entire Bosnian
jihad. As Christmas was celebrated for the first time in four years in
Bosnia, the mujaheddin shot up Croat soldiers returning from mass.

What happened in Bosnia is important for several reasons. The wars
mobilised Muslim opinion across the world, simplifying complex
internecine conflicts into a war between Christianity and Islam – a
view somewhat undermined by the enormous relief efforts made by
Christians in the West who would have recoiled from the nationalist
Orthodox Christianity of the Serbs, whose only firm allies were their
Russian co-religionists. The foreign jihadists acquired further combat
experience and extended the organisational sinews of terrorism into
Europe, under the noses of security services that had yet to learn that
Human Concern International was not quite what the words implied.
Yet there was something else too. The war was resolved by another
Pax Americana and the presence of large numbers of NATO troops,
including many from Muslim countries like Turkey. The jihadists'
attempt to plant Islamist palms in the snows of the Bosnian hills had
failed. The local Muslim population resembled a body that rejects an
organ transplant. Faced with what the jihadists represented, the Bosnian

Muslims opted for their local tradition of confining their religion to the private sphere, laughing off radical calls to ban Father Christmas. That this was all the local Islamist radicals called for was a victory of a notable kind. The trouble was that this evolving reality did not moderate the scenes of jihad that circulated on the internet or via DVDs, for these had joined the timeless fairytale too.[50]

A third conflict enraged the jihadi-salafist imagination by supplying lurid images of Muslim suffering and, one strongly suspects, scenes of retaliatory savagery that often reflected a psychopathic bloodlust. When would-be Anglo-Pakistani jihadists sit down of a night in some dilapidated northern English suburb to watch their spiritual comrades in action, the most gruesome scenes invariably stem from the Chechen wars, whose agonies and complexities have been reduced to a jihadist splatter movie on a DVD costing about US$20.

The implosion of the Soviet Union in December 1991 brought not only the collapse of the Soviet outer empire, but demands for greater autonomy within the newly minted Russian federation, 30 per cent of whose citizens were not ethnic Russians. Only two federal subjects refused to sign the 1992 Federation Treaty, and by 1994 Tatarstan had negotiated a special accord granting it enhanced autonomy. That left Chechnya, the predominantly Muslim part of the former Chechen-Ingush Soviet Republic, a million of whose people Stalin had deported in 1944 to Kazakhstan, from which the remnants returned home in 1957. They found that eight hundred mosques and four hundred religious colleges had been shut down, while the *mazars* or shrines, essential to the Sufi brotherhoods to which many Chechens belonged, had been closed or demolished. Although the Muslim world is entirely unaware of this, it has largely been conservative Western scholars like Robert Conquest and John Dunlop who have spent decades investigating the crimes of the Soviet Union against the Chechen people, studies partly informed by the spirit of the Cold War, but also honouring the struggle of a small nation against a chauvinistic totalitarianism. Others have increased our understanding of Islam's role in Chechen society. The vast majority of Chechens practise a popular Sufi strain of Islam that incorporates local customs, drum and string music, and venerable paganisms; since the 1980s, some 10 per cent have adopted the more bracing beliefs of the Wahhabis.

On 6 September 1991, militant Chechen separatists led by former

Soviet general Dzokhar Dudayev, a Chechen married to a Russian woman, stormed the Chechen-Ingush Supreme Soviet, killing the Communist leader of the capital Grozny and effectively dissolving the government. After having himself elected president by a suspiciously large margin, Dudayev unilaterally declared Chechen independence. When Russia's president Boris Yeltsin declared a state of emergency and flew Interior Ministry troops to Grozny, Soviet president Mikhail Gorbachev declared his action illegal. The Chechens rounded up the Russian troops and bussed them home. Two months later, Shamil Basayev, whose first name evoked the legendary imam Shamil who had fought tsarist invaders in the mid-nineteenth century, hijacked a Russian plane and 178 passengers en route to Ankara in Turkey. He threatened to blow them up unless Yeltsin rescinded the state of emergency. The incident was settled peacefully, but strikingly president Dudayev made Basayev a colonel and gave him a command in his Presidential Guard, a worrying response to an act of terrorism.

In 1992 Dudayev sent Basayev to aid Muslim Azerbaijani national forces fighting Russian-backed Christian Armenians in Nagorno-Karabakh, and then to help Abkhazians fighting for freedom from Georgia. The rumours were ominous. One of the reasons why two hundred thousand ethnic Georgians fled Abkhazia in terror was that, after decapitating a hundred prisoners, Basayev had organised soccer matches for his men playing with the heads of these captives. He returned to Chechnya with a band of brutal 'wolves', although the human variety were a great deal more sinister than the four-legged ones. In 1994 Basayev and twenty of his best men flew to Pakistan where the ISI sent them for advanced training at a mujaheddin camp in Afghanistan. He returned home to Chechnya after being taken ill handling chemical weapons, they and nuclear explosives being a constant in the apocalyptic imprecations he rained down upon Russia.

When a Moscow-backed opposition emerged against President Dudayev's dictatorial rule, Basayev played a leading role in suppressing them, defeating a squadron of Russian tanks operating as freelance mercenaries on the rebel side. Not so covert Russian support for the rebels became an all-out onslaught once the Chechen leader refused an ultimatum from Yeltsin for all sides to disarm and desist. The Russian attack was a shambles, as officers and men refused to participate in actions of dubious legality, while nervous conscripts drafted in from neighbouring regions trembled as they approached formidable Chechen fighters. Encountering resistance in Grozny, most of whose citizens were ethnic Russians, the Russians spent five weeks bombarding the city with heavy artillery and waves of bombers. As the Chechen rebels had fallen back to wage a guerrilla campaign from the mountains, most of the twenty-seven thousand dead in the ruined city were innocent civilians, who unlike the Chechens had no village *teips* or clans to seek sanctuary with.

The Chechen wars were fought with terrible brutality on both sides, even before the Chechens resorted to spectacular terrorist violence. The Chechens used mines and ambushes to disrupt Russian movement, while the Russians, many of whose commanders were routinely drunk, pulverised towns and villages with artillery fire that took no account of a civilian presence. Torture of prisoners was similarly normal on both sides. After the Russians killed eleven members of Basayev's family by dropping two six-ton bombs on his uncle's house, fatalities which included the rebel commander's wife and child, no captured Russian pilot would survive. Basayev made two fateful decisions.

First, he decided to take the war to Russia, or, as he had it, to make the Russians see what blood looks like, the second of many acts of terrorism he committed. These acts played into Russian propaganda that built on the widespread reputation Chechens had among ordinary Russians for Mafia-style activities. In the summer of 1995 he hid 145 of his men in trucks, while others, disguised as Russian policemen, claimed that the vehicles contained the bodies of Russian troops killed in Chechnya. Bribes ensured that the convoy swept through Russian checkpoints until they were stopped in the southerly town of Budennovsk. Escorted to the town police station, Basayev's men leaped from the trucks and killed all the policemen, before initiating a full-scale gun battle with police reinforcements in the town centre. Basayev initially secured the town hospital, situated in a former monastery, so as to treat his wounded, but then decided to use it as a last redoubt. He herded hundreds of civilian hostages into the building, wiring explosives to the entrances and exits. As there were a total of sixteen hundred hostages, this was the biggest incident of its kind in modern history. To show his earnestness, and to settle an old score, he personally shot dead six Russian pilots he unearthed among the patients.

Refusing all offers of compromise, and entreaties from general Aslan Maskhadov downwards, Basayev warned that he would kill everyone in the building if the Russians did not abandon their campaign in

Chechnya. When he was told the Russians were planning to round up and shoot two thousand Chechens, he effectively indicated that they could kill every Chechen in Russia and he 'would not even flinch'. The Russian defence minister decided that four days of this were enough. Russian troops were ordered to storm the building, which resulted in the deaths of over a hundred hostages by the time they had fought their way to the first floor. The following day, prime minister Viktor Chernomirdin decided to negotiate with Basayev, live on TV. As a result of these talks, Basayev and his men (shielded by 139 volunteer hostages) set off back to Chechnya in six trucks, with a refrigerated lorry bringing up the rear with their dead. A peace agreement was signed that July.[51]

Basayev's second stunt was to call upon the services of a Saudi he had fought with in Abkhazia, Samir bin Salekh al-Suweilum, also known as al-Khattab, or as he was variously called 'one-handed Akhmed', 'the Black Arab' or 'the Lion of Chechnya'. Dark, flat-nosed, heavy-set and bearded in an ursine way, al-Khattab's menacing face adorns thousands of DVD covers issued by Hamas and the like (one of his hands had been mangled by a home-made grenade). He had turned down the chance to study in the US in favour of waging jihad in Afghanistan where he fought, for six years, under the aegis of Abdullah Azzam and Osama bin Laden. Perhaps because he claimed that his mother hailed from the Caucasus, or more simply because he saw the fighting there on TV, he went to help the Muslim Azeris, followed by a stint killing Russians in Tajikistan. Having already met Basayev, al-Khattab surfaced in Chechnya in early 1995, bringing eight more Arabs who were contracted as 'consultants' to train Chechen fighters. He brought in more Afghan Arabs, and men he had fought with in Dagestan, to form his own Islamic Regiment. That autumn about forty of these men decimated a hundred Russian troops in an ambush. In their next outing, in April 1996, they attacked a convoy of fifty Russian trucks, killing two hundred Russian soldiers in an action that was videotaped from beginning to end. Al-Khattab is seen brandishing the severed heads of Russian officers, shouting 'Allahu Akhbar!' In August 1996 Basayev and al-Khattab stormed the Russian garrison in Grozny; al-Khattab was given Ichkeria's (Chechnya's) highest decorations and promoted to general. Four months later he murdered six Red Cross relief workers in a hospital, after warning them that he found the ubiquitous crosses offensive. That autumn he also opened the first of four Wahhabist training camps, to which international jihadists flocked for two- to six-month courses in ambushing, hostage taking, armed and unarmed combat, and sabotage. Saudi money paid for the Wahhabist religious infrastructure, which was supposed to presage an Islamic Republic of the Caucasus in embryo, for the plan was to link up Wahhabi enclaves in neighbouring Dagestan after a coup.

General Aslan Maskhadov, a former Red Army artillery officer, was largely responsible for the Chechen separatists getting the upper hand in the First Chechen War. It was he who in December 1996 negotiated a ceasefire at Khasar-Yurt with the Afghanistan war hero general Alexander Lebed. The Russians undertook to withdraw their troops, while agreeing to talks, scheduled for early 2001, to determine Chechnya's future relations with the Russian Federation. Dudayev had been killed in April 1996 by a Russian missile, and Maskhadov succeeded him as president in early 1997. In Russian eyes he was the lesser evil in relation to the other main candidate, Shamil Basayev.

A Second Chechen War erupted in August 1999 as the Russians sought to reverse the de-facto independence that Maskhadov had achieved in the first war against Russia's conscript rabble. From a Russian perspective there were various grounds to restart the war. General lawlessness and kidnappings for huge ransoms were endemic in Chechnya, while the Chechen diaspora in Russia itself was heavily involved in organised crime. Obviously there were many gangsters from other nationalities, but the Chechens enjoyed a reputation for blood feuds and savagery low even by local standards. Worse, if Chechnya gained independence, other regions might make similar bids for freedom, triggering a domino effect that might menace Russia's southern oil and gas supply routes from the Caspian region. There was also a growing Islamic dimension. In order to placate Basayev and the jihadists, Maskhadov introduced sharia law, publicly executing a few offenders at a time when Russia abolished the death penalty, and turned to the Gulf and beyond for external support. He was unable to correct the impression that he was not on top of gangsters and warlords or that the jihadists were out of control. On Basayev's command, al-Khattab and his Arab jihadists attacked Russian troops in neighbouring Dagestan. Suspecting that this was part of a wider effort to Islamise the entire northern Caucasus, the Russian air force was despatched, dropping fuel-air explosive bombs on Chechen villages and killing hundreds of people.

Some people, most of them nowadays dead, view the Second Chechen War as part of a dark conspiracy on the part of the secret police/industrial complex to terminate Russia's passing fling with democracy and free markets. The former KGB lieutenant-colonel Vladimir Putin has been the main beneficiary, and sundry oligarchs the chief losers, as mysterious acts of terror were exploited to reverse the liberalising gains of the Yeltsin era. In September 1999 explosions demolished entire apartment blocks in Moscow and other Russian cities. Hundreds of people were killed. These bombings were attributed to Chechen separatist terrorists, meaning that hapless Chechen emigrants were rounded up and framed by the FSB (the KGB's successor). Discovery of FSB involvement in a bomb that failed to explode in Ryazan was covered up with claims that the whole operation was an 'exercise' involving harmless sugar rather than the explosive hexogen. People who argued otherwise subsequently found that the brakes of their cars failed or, like journalist Anna Politkovskaya, were shot dead or otherwise murdered (former agent Alexander Litvinenko was very publicly poisoned by FSB-connected assassins in the middle of London).

Putin progressed from prime minister to president in a toxic atmosphere of chauvinism, fear and resentment about loss of empire. Using air power and contract professional soldiers rather than hapless conscripts, the Russians attacked Chechen separatists that autumn. They dropped cluster bombs and hit villages with artillery shells and rockets, without any regard for civilian casualties. The Russians dominated the northern Chechen plains and pulverised the ruins of Chechnya's cities. In February 2000 they took Grozny after weeks of fighting that had reduced it to the condition of Dresden in 1945. The deployment of eighty thousand regular troops, and countless security agents, forced the Chechen separatists into fighting a guerrilla war from the mountains and to launch a full-scale terror campaign, whose international ramifications meant that after 9/11 Chechen groups were put on various Western watch lists.

Both sides fought viciously and without rules. As Putin once remarked: 'We'll get them anywhere. If we find terrorists in the shit-house, then we'll waste them in the shithouse. That's all there is to it.' The FSB reached out to 'touch' al-Khattab in 2002 after discovering that his mother in Saudi Arabia regularly sent mail to him via Baku in Azerbaijan which was always picked up by the same courier. In March the courier brought a package containing a Sony video-camera – to record him cutting off heads – a watch and a letter. Al-Khattab retreated to open the letter; he returned deathly pale fifteen minutes later and dropped dead. He had been poisoned with botulism smeared on the letter. His patron Basayev shot dead the courier who he suspected was on the FSB payroll.

As if to signal that al-Khattab's death changed nothing, that summer a massive mine blew up in the midst of a Russian military parade commemorating the end of the Great Patriotic War. On 22 October a large gang of Chechen terrorists – including several women, some in their forties, whose husbands or relatives had died at the hands of the Russians – seized a theatre in Moscow's Dubrovka suburb during the second act of a musical. They took eight hundred people hostage, wiring the auditorium with explosives and strutting about with explosive belts wrapped with nails, nuts and bolts. They started to shoot hostages so as to pressure Russia into withdrawing its forces from Chechnya. At about 3 a.m. on 26 October, Russian commandos released an obscure gas into the theatre, knocking out several hostages and a few terrorists in the front-row seats near an orchestra pit that by this time was the communal lavatory. Two hundred Russian commandos then stormed into the building, killing forty-one terrorists, mostly with a single shot to the forehead. One hundred and thirty hostages also died, since the authorities failed to inform the local hospitals about the type of gas they had used in the assault.

Adopting tactics pioneered by the Israelis, the Russians demolished the family homes of all those terrorists killed in the Dubrovka theatre siege. They dropped fuel-air explosives on the Vedeno Gorge in an attempt to kill Basayev. By this time sporting a wooden leg after stepping on a mine, Basayev was publicly threatening to use Cruise missiles or nuclear bombs, in the 'Whirlwind of Terror' he wished to visit on Russian cities. On 13 February 2004, FSB assassins killed the former acting Chechen president Zelimkhan Yandarbiyev with a car bomb at a villa in Doha, in Qatar, owned by a prominent Saudi arms dealer. The Russians were caught, tried and imprisoned, although their local controller evaded justice by claiming diplomatic immunity. Basayev hit back when a bomb built into the VIP section of the Dynamo Stadium in Grozny killed the pro-Russian Chechen president Akhmad Kadyrov and several members of his government. This killing stopped Putin's policy of Chechenising the conflict through local clients, while triggering a blood feud between Basayev and the dead president's son Ramzan Kadyrov.

Basayev mounted his most dastardly action that autumn, managing to grab the world's attention even though the Russian authorities disbarred and harassed foreign reporters and put psychotropic drugs in the tea of the more venturesome local journalists who flew in to cover it. On 1 September 2004, the Day of Knowledge in the Russian school calendar, thirty-two heavily armed Chechen terrorists took over School Number One at Beslan in Ossetia.

They held twelve hundred schoolchildren, parents and teachers hostage in the gymnasium, immediately killing anyone who spoke Ossetic rather than Russian and fifteen to twenty men whose physique indicated that they might offer resistance. Dehydrated and hungry children were forced to strip off in the terrible heat. While negotiations to resolve the crisis dragged into a third day, explosions inside the school led to an assault by hundreds of men from poorly co-ordinated secret service, military and police formations. While army conscripts fled the scene, local civilians arrived armed to the teeth, causing further chaos and confusion. The roof was set alight with flame throwers while tanks fired anti-personnel shells into the school; the exhausted and confused hostages were too weak to flee. An escaping terrorist was lynched by crazed parents, while the school rapidly burned down in front of one antiquated fire engine with no water. There were no ambulances either to take casualties to hospital. Nearly four hundred hostages died in this chaos, together with eleven Russian commandos and all but one of the thirty-two terrorists. Two of the latter were British Algerians based in London with links to Abu Hamza's Finsbury Park mosque. Before he disappeared into the Russian prison system, the surviving terrorist, Nur-Pashi Kulayev, explained the strategy behind murdering children, namely to trigger a religious war between the Orthodox Christian Ossetians and the Muslim Chechens and Ingush that would engulf the whole Caucasus. On 21 September 2005 Russian special forces tracked down and killed Aslan Maskhadov, by then designated a terrorist fugitive with a US$10 million bounty on his head. A Russian soldier allegedly threw a grenade into his hideout by mistake. On 10 July 2006, FSB agents used an improvised explosive device to kill Shamil Basayev as he drove in a car alongside a truck filled with explosives. The youthful Ramzan Kadyrov still manages to act as Chechen president, with his ménage of pet tigers and hordes of heavily armed men.

Given this poisoned atmosphere, it was inevitable that dark forces would gravitate to Chechnya. In November 2006 Russian police stopped a minivan carrying three men, one of whom identified himself as Abdullah Imam Mohammed Amin, as was confirmed by his Sudanese passport. The photo of a middle-aged man in a suit and tie with neat hair suggested nothing untoward. However, in the van there was US$6,400 in seven currencies, a laptop, a satellite phone, a fax machine and piles of medical textbooks. Closer inspection revealed a visa application for Taiwan, bank statements from a bank in Guandong, China, a receipt for a modem purchased in Dubai, a registration certificate for a company in Malaysia, and details of a bank account in Missouri. The fake Sudanese passport had multiple stamps from Taiwan, Singapore and Yemen. The Russian police called in the FSB, who sent the laptop to Moscow for analysis. Mr 'Amin' was detained for five months, during which time letters flooded in from local Muslim clerics protesting his innocence. At his trial, the judge decided to believe his claims that he was a pious merchant – the accused repeatedly dropped to his knees to pray in the dock – come to scout the prices of leather. He received a six-month sentence for illegal entry, most of which he had already served. In his diary, Ayman al-Zawahiri, for it was he, wrote that 'God blinded them to our identities.' After spending ten days free in Dagestan nursing an ulcer, he left to join bin Laden in Afghanistan.[52]

There was one other conflict in the 1990s whose complexities did not impinge on any Muslim with a crassly polarised view of the world. After the Algerian military had 'interrupted' the January 1992 elections, the Islamic Salvation Front (FIS) was banned and some forty thousand Islamist militants were despatched to camps in the Sahara. The problem with FIS was that although many of its supporters called themselves democrats, others believed in 'one man, one vote, one time'. Armed Islamism predated this coup, since the Algerian Islamic Movement (MIA) was formed in the early 1980s, evolving into the AIS or Islamic Salvation Army a little later, while the rival GIA emerged in 1991. The two organisations fought different types of campaign. Sometimes they briefly merged, more often they attempted to kill each other. Both organisations had a heavy representation of Algerian veterans of Afghanistan, who basked in the glory of successful jihad, members of the FIS who had gone underground, as well as criminals and unemployed street toughs who, combining Levi 501s, the Kalashnikov and the Koran, imposed totalitarian Islamism on their neighbourhoods. Ideologically, the groups encompassed people who still wished to pursue a democratic course from a position of armed might, and jihadi-salafists who regarded democracy as un-Islamic and the entire Algerian population as *kuffar* apostates. This unstable composition led to deadly faction fights within these groups, which were subject to the murderous attentions of the Algerian military and murky intelligence agencies that regard torture as routine. Islamist prisoners arriving at a prison at Blida, where use of a blow torch was normal, were told: 'There is no God or Amnesty International here: you talk or you die.'

In the early 1990s the GIA murdered about ninety Western employees in the oil and gas industry, forcing a mass exodus of six thousand Europeans from Algeria. Twelve Croat technicians were abducted and, their hands bound with wire, had their throats cut in an empty swimming pool. The French interior minister, Charles Pasqua, deported seventeen Islamist clerics to Burkina Faso. The GIA also murdered forty francophone Algerian journalists, writers and doctors, including the Kabylia magazine editor and novelist Taher Djaout, whose *Last Summer of Reason* describes Islamist destruction of the dying remnants of Algeria's cosmopolitan culture. This great left-wing writer was shot dead outside his home in an Algiers suburb. His film-maker friend Merzak Allouache caught the hypocrisy and paranoia of the Islamists in his *Bab el-Oued City*, filmed in an atmosphere so dangerous that he could not return to do second takes in that quarter of the capital. The GIA also abducted and executed an Islamist cleric who refused to issue a fatwa licensing their activities, and in 1998 murdered Lounès Matoub, one of Kabylia's leading *raï* singers. Some six hundred schools were burned down in an effort to eradicate secular education, while sociologists and psychiatrists found themselves token victims of disciplines that the jihadists did not like. Women who did not conform to Islamist notions of decorum were threatened, raped and murdered; people who persisted in accessing 'pornographic' French satellite TV were warned before their severed heads ended up in disconnected dishes.

Late in 1994, four GIA hijackers took over an Air France jet at Boumedienne airport with a view to smashing it into the streets of central Paris. French commandos stormed the plane when it refuelled at Marseilles, freeing 171 passengers and killing the four hijackers. The aim of this attack was to force France to abandon ties with Algeria, thereby weakening the Algerian government to the point of collapse. All it achieved was for the French to stop issuing visas in Algeria, using a central service in Nantes instead, and for Air France to cease flights to Algeria. Although many French people thought that Algeria could 'go hang itself', the French government came under intense US pressure to encourage the military regime to extend its political base. In Algeria itself, the government began arming village patriots to fend off the jihadists who came to commit murder in the dead of night.

The GIA was run by a swift succession of violent emirs, as most met grisly ends. The then emir, Djamel Zitouni, the son of a poultry merchant with a secondary education, alienated many Islamists when he had two leading Islamist ideologues murdered. He exceeded himself when in May 1996 seven French Trappist monks from the desert monastery of Tibhirine were kidnapped and beheaded. That brought to nineteen the number of Christian clergy killed by Algerian Islamists, culminating in the murder of Pierre Claverie, bishop of Oran. The murder of these monks, whose security the GIA had guaranteed, was too much even for Abu Qatada, the GIA mouthpiece in London, who suspended publication of the GIA's *Al-Ansar* bulletin. Zitouni was shot dead, by GIA members fed up with him, a while later. His twenty-six-year-old successor, Antar Zouabri, found a new spiritual guide to replace Qatada in the shape of Londonistan's hook-handed Abu Hamza. They satisfied themselves that the main problem in Algeria was that the majority of the population had become apostates because they were not pursuing their duty of jihad. In the autumn of 1997 several hundred Algerian villagers had their throats cut, including women, who had first been raped, as well as children whose heads were smashed against walls. Attempts to blame this on the Algerian security services, one of whose members claimed that his former colleagues were really behind the GIA, were confounded when Zouabri acknowledged his own authorship of a vulgarly phrased communiqué that called all Algerians '*kuffar*, apostates and hypocrites'. As the US journalist Robert Kaplan reported, relatives of the people massacred by Islamists knew that they rather than the secret police were responsible, although shady army and police units undoubtedly killed many people, sometimes with a view to discrediting the Islamists in the eyes of Western opinion.[53]

In 1998, and with encouragement on a satellite phone from Osama bin Laden, the Salafist Group for Prayer and Combat emerged out of the wreckage of the GIA. The GSPC took several steps back from the GIA's universal war on Algerian society, while simultaneously subscribing to the international jihad. It sought to destroy the Algerian military regime, replacing it with a sharia-based Islamist state, while pursuing the cause of the 'rightly guided caliphate' against Jews and Christians. Even as the

GSPC evolved into one of the world's most deadly terrorist organisations, with a network of supporters throughout Europe, the AIS came
in from the cold, accepting an Algerian government amnesty and
the introduction of the presidential elections that put veteran foreign
minister Abdelaziz Bouteflika in power. It is widely believed that about
two hundred thousand Muslim Algerians were killed in the struggle
between Islamists and the government during the 1990s. The head of the
Algerian secret police, General Smaïn Lamari, was fully prepared to kill
up to three million people in order to wipe Islamism out. No longer
willing to treat Algeria as France's backyard, the US has built up a large
CIA presence in Algiers, spreading its eagle wings over the Bouteflika
regime, which has become an eager partner in the 'war on terror'.[54]

VII TARGETING AMERICA BEFORE 9/11 AND IRAQ

Seeming inevitabilities unravel if one goes back a generation or two.
In 1957, a year after US president Eisenhower brutally brought the
Anglo-French–Israeli invasion of Suez to a halt, he inaugurated a new
building on Washington's Embassy Row. This was a mosque. It was
built after a Palestinian tycoon had attended the funeral of a Turkish
diplomat. He had said to the Egyptian ambassador, 'Isn't it a shame that
the prayer for such a great Muslim is not held in a mosque?' An Italian
architect designed the building, incorporating details recommended
by the court architect in Egypt. Eisenhower dedicated the building:
'America would fight with her whole strength for your right to have
here your own church and worship according to your own conscience.
This concept is indeed a part of America, and without that concept we
would be something else than what we are.' Today, three thousand
people attend the Friday prayers in a building that is the equivalent of
the Episcopalian National Cathedral.

Nineteen fifty-seven is ancient history to most Muslims today, the
majority of whom are so young that they come up to the average
Westerner's waist. The jihadi-salafist imagination deals in racial essences
and ahistorical archetypes, to which history is a necessary corrective.
In their view, the Jews are inherently malevolent, using the USA, the
IMF, the World Bank and the UN for their nefarious purposes. This
explains the bizarre concept of 'Crusader–Zionists'. Anyone with even a

sketchy recollection of medieval history knows that nothing links medieval Christian crusaders, who on occasion massacred Rhenish Jews prefatory to slaughtering Arabs, with a political movement born in the nineteenth century, primarily as an antidote to European anti-Semitism. But facts do not seem to inhibit emotion and prejudice. Even in countries where there are few Jews, like Indonesia, the local jihadi-salafists find them by imagining mercantile 'Chinese–Zionists'. In a sense this proves that anti-Semitism links all jihadists. They are like the man looking at an empty salt cellar who is compelled to talk about Jewish domination of the medieval salt trade or a monopoly 'they' have recently acquired in the Camargue. Although Israel is home to large numbers of conservative Orthodox Jews, it is also an outpost of Western secular modernity. That last part is what Islamists hate, especially when it is combined with the manifest superiority of the high-tech Israeli economy in the region. Instead of allowing this to fructify the neighbourhood commercially, the jihadists are bent on enveloping it in the chaos and violence they create everywhere.

In their view, Israel is the modern incarnation of the Latin Kingdom of Jerusalem, a crusader outpost planted among Muslims by an imperialist West which the Jews control, a claim that passes over the half millennium that separates the crusades from the age of European imperialism, and accords 'the Jews' more power than they could conceivably possess. Intervening events, like the Protestant revolt against the medieval papacy, and the multiplication of hundreds of Protestant denominations, figure not at all in Islamist understanding of the West, which is routinely chastised for not comprehending the division between Sunni and Shia. This is because Islam, at least in Arabia, has overwritten societies where kin or clan are paramount, resulting in indifference or hostility to what lies beyond. In the very few instances where Christians have attacked Muslims (and vice versa), such as Serbia or Indonesia, these attacks have not been endorsed by any Christian religious authorities of any standing. There have been no Christian calls for an anti-Muslim crusade, unlike the many voices demanding warlike jihad.[55]

There is something narcissistic about this assumption that the West is obsessed with Islam and seeks to destroy it. It is not. It is obsessed with itself, followed by China, India and Russia which jostle for Westerners' short attention span. It is drawn, wearily, into so many Middle Eastern crises because this region, with a manufacturing capacity only equal to that of the telecommunications giant Nokia in Finland, is the primary source of instability in the modern world and sits on top of two-thirds of known oil reserves. If huge oil deposits were to be discovered beneath Canada, the West would disengage from the Middle East tomorrow, leaving it to implode amid its multiple conflicts. The West's crusading impulse is allegedly 'in our blood', despatching armed might into the Muslim heartlands to dole out death at the flick of a switch on a console. This massive technological superiority was bitterly resented as it made Arabs seem impotent on any conventional battlefield, reduced to hot spots on the computer screens of electronic weapons systems. Crude conspiracy theories mask entirely local responsibilities. The 'English agent' and 'Jewish criminal' Kemal Atatürk's abolition of the Ottoman caliphate in 1924 destroyed the only institutional basis for resistance, an institution the most extreme jihadists intend to restore.

Some Western secular trends come among traditional societies silently like thieves in the night, notably monogamy and the atomisation of the family, common nowadays among middle-class Iranians. But, notwithstanding the corruption, drugs and vice endemic in many Muslim societies, in their eyes the West is uniquely decadent, hedonistic and secular (despite the US being the most religious society on the planet), spreading its moral pollution, not only through Coca-Cola capitalism, *Baywatch* and MTV, but via the indiscriminate exportation of a vulgar architectural modernism that dwarfed the delicate traditional Islamic architecture of the Middle Ages, not least the minarets of mosques. Globalisation has a way of making mutual hypocrisies visible. Rich Arabs get drunk, gamble, shop and whore in London or Paris. From Dubai to the Maldives, streams of Western tourists descend on traditional societies courtesy of cheap air travel, blissfully unaware of how others might perceive them and wholly ignorant of local mores.[56] If this was one seamy side of globalisation, international jihadist terrorism was another – although this is, emphatically, not to imply any justification or moral equivalence between sunbathing and bombing. As distances shrank and barriers to movement dissolved, terrorists who availed themselves of all the scientific technologies of the contemporary world – much of it manufactured in China and Japan – flailed out in rage against the undermining of their religious identity as they had reconstructed this as an ideology. Religious self-assertion replaced scrutiny of why the Muslim world has made no significant scientific discoveries in the last four hundred years. Although a war would be declared on terrorism – which is a tactic used by a kaleidoscope of groups – a better analogy would have been with the containment of a contagious disease that can never be entirely eliminated, any more than governments can destroy international organised crime.

Farce preceded tragedy when malevolent minds turned to a devastating strike against the West itself. In September 1992, two men arrived at New York's JFK airport in the first-class section of a Pakistani aircraft, for jihadists like to travel in style. (Advised by Khalid Sheikh Mohammed on tradecraft, they seek the deference given to the rich by travelling business or first class and put down a five-star hotel on immigration forms, moving never by taxi but by subway or bus to a cheaper place the following day). This time something went wrong. Immigration officers focused on Ahmad Mohammed Ajaj, a bearded Palestinian, with a Swedish passport whose photograph peeled off in an agent's hand to reveal the image of someone else beneath. Ajaj started shouting that his mother was Swedish, an irrelevance to the fact his face and the passport's real photo did not match. A secondary search revealed British, Jordanian and Saudi passports in his leather case. There were also manuals about forging documents and making bombs, one of which had the words Al Qaeda on the cover. At another immigration desk, Ramzi Yousef, dressed in a colourful confection that included baggy pantaloons, presented an Iraqi passport, with no US visa, and a laminated identity card from an Islamic centre in Arizona, although the names on the two documents did not match. He smiled politely, his face dominated by a bulbous nose and hooded eyes, and requested political asylum. After averring that he was a victim of persecution and giving his correct name, Yousef was told to attend a hearing in three months and released. Apparently the airport detention centre was full that day. Ajaj was sent straight to jail.

Ramzi Yousef was Abdul Basit Mahmud Abdul Karim, the thirty-year-old son of a Palestinian mother and a Pakistani father domiciled in Kuwait. We have encountered him already as the nephew of Khalid Sheikh Mohammed, though the latter was not much older. After studying electrical engineering at the West Glamorgan Institute of Higher Education in Swansea, where high foreign fees talk, and the Muslim Brothers Swansea chapter was active, Yousef had been through an Al Qaeda training camp in Afghanistan. He had the light sensitivity and the burn marks on his hands and feet to prove it, for he was an expert in making bombs. He hated Israel, and the US for supporting it;

US civilians were fair game as they paid taxes which indirectly propped up the Zionist regime. Besides, from firebombing Tokyo, via Hiroshima and Nagasaki, to the use of Agent Orange in Vietnam, the US itself rained death on civilians. Noam Chomsky, John Pilger or Harold Pinter might have written his script. In fact, Yousef was not especially motivated by religious zeal; he was driven more by a sort of criminal fertility that operated under cover of Islam.[57]

Still posing as an Iraqi, Yousef quickly got his bearings in Brooklyn's Arab community, establishing contacts with the Alkifah Refugee Center, a 'charity' established by Abdullah Azzam to funnel money to the jihad in Afghanistan. He frequented mosques in Jersey City, where the blind sheikh Omar Rahman – unconscionably having been given a visa by the US embassy in Sudan – preached. Egyptian requests for his extradition had been refused. Yousef and the sheikh spoke several times on the phone. Yousef recruited a small team of migrant ne'er-do-wells and set about manufacturing sixteen hundred pounds of explosives from commercially purchased chemicals, designed to blow up the World Trade Center. It took three weeks of mixing, spreading and drying, to assemble enough explosives for a gigantic bomb which was kept in rental storage. The detonation system was trickier, so much so that Yousef actually phoned Ajaj in prison to see if he could help. Other comical moments occurred when three of the bombers were almost killed after their car careered out of control late one night, hospitalising Yousef, who nonetheless ordered more chemicals from his hospital bed. The driver, Mohammed Salameh, even though he had failed his test four times, and even though his visa had expired, successfully rented a Ryder van for which he put down a US$400 deposit. In one of his few sentient acts, he even remembered to rent one that would clear the height barriers. Hell bent on collapsing both towers so as to kill a quarter of a million people, Yousef added one last refinement to his ammonium-nitrate and fuel-oil bomb. These were four cylinders of hydrogen gas, intended to propel the initial blast further forwards.

On 26 October 1993, Yousef and a Jordanian, Eyad Ismoil, parked the truck in the basement of the World Trade Center, where it detonated shortly after noon. The blast went through three floors down and two floors up, killing six people, building workers having lunch, and injuring more than a thousand. Yousef flew to Karachi that night while Ismoil took a flight to Jordan. Salameh hung around, brooding about his US$400 deposit. By the time he went to claim it, haggling the sum up from zero to US$200 with an undercover FBI agent, FBI forensic experts had identified the truck used to house the bomb. He was arrested after he left the rental office. Although the attack had killed six and caused half a billion dollars' worth of structural damage, the jihadists around the blind sheikh were not satisfied. Urging them on to greater depravities was the imprisoned Egyptian El-Sayyid Nosair, serving seven years for assassinating the fanatic rabbi Meir Kahane in 1990. Osama bin Laden had paid his legal bills. A motley group, eventually numbering eleven, resolved to blow up the Lincoln and Holland Tunnels into Manhattan. Cars, bomb-making materials and timers were acquired. Justification was sought from sheikh Omar, unaware that one of the key conspirators worked for the FBI and that all of the group were under electronic surveillance. A long series of trials put several of these men, including the sheikh, in jail for the rest of their lives. One of the sheikh's defence lawyers would more recently follow him behind bars for colluding in passing messages from his prison.

These events had no direct connection with bin Laden save that the master bomber had been through his training programme, and he has vowed to wreak havoc if and when the elderly sheikh finally expires from the multiple illnesses he is afflicted by. Refusing medication, the sheikh scoffs immense quantities of fast food from prison canteens so that his diabetes and high blood pressure may expedite this murderous outcome. In 1995 al-Zawahiri's expatriate campaign of terror in Egypt led to the ejection of the entire al-Jihad group from Sudan. Aided by Sudanese intelligence officers, al-Zawahiri conspired to assassinate Hosni Mubarak as he attended an African Unity conference in Addis Ababa. The plan – referred to above in the context of Bosnia – was to kill him as his motorcade drove from the airport into the capital, using teams of shooters equipped with RPGs and automatic rifles. The plot failed, although not before two Egyptian bodyguards had been killed, as Mubarak sped by.

The Egyptian government lashed out at Islamist sympathisers, commissioning five new prisons to house them. Its intelligence agencies decided to strike directly at al-Zawahiri. They kidnapped the young sons of two leading fundamentalists connected to al-Jihad and Al Qaeda, who were drugged and then photographed being sodomised. These compromising photographs were enough to turn them into spies, and to agree to plant a bomb outside al-Zawahiri's Khartoum home. The first bomb was discovered by al-Zawahiri's Sudanese protectors before it went off. Meanwhile one of the boys was being treated for malaria, ironically by al-Zawahiri. The Egyptians tried again, equipping the first boy with a suitcase bomb to kill al-Zawahiri as he attended a meeting. The boy bomber was caught by the Sudanese, who also picked up his ailing companion. Both boys were tried by a sharia court presided over by al-Zawahiri who had them both shot. Their confessions and execution were filmed to discourage others.

This evidence of a state operating within a state angered the Sudanese so much that they ordered al-Zawahiri to leave immediately together with his al-Jihad followers. He fled to Yemen. But he had not finished with the Egyptians. On 19 November 1995, two men fired on the guards outside the Egyptian embassy in Islamabad, scattering them so that two suicide bombers could drive a pick-up truck inside, which exploded killing both drivers and sixteen other people. The Pakistani authorities rounded up two hundred Arab Afghan jihadists; bin Laden appeared offering air tickets to take them to the Sudan. But relations were cooling there too. The Americans had joined the Egyptians and the Saudis in putting pressure on Turabi to expel bin Laden. This was an irresistible combination. Bin Laden might have slept more soundly had he known that White House lawyers, the US military and the CIA were simultaneously frustrating suggestions from counter-terrorism officials that the US simply snatch him in Sudan. Faced with the choice of either staying put, in closely monitored inactivity, or leaving for Afghanistan, bin Laden chose to revisit the scene of his early glories. The crooked Sudanese stripped him of his considerable assets before he flew to Jalalabad. Their claims that they offered up bin Laden to the uninterested Americans are probably lies, even if it is true that at this time the CIA regarded him merely as a 'financier of terrorism'. That year, however, it did set up a special office, code-named 'Alec', the first time it had concentrated such resources on an individual terrorist.[58]

Bin Laden sought refuge among the Taliban, the Pashtu word for students, an Islamist movement supported by Pakistan and Saudi Arabia which built and financed the madrassas from which the Taliban came. In the eyes of Pakistan prime minister Benazir Bhutto, the Taliban would restore order after four years of civil war, a necessary precondition for Pakistan to tranship oil and gas from Turkmenistan to its burgeoning industries. This was the line she sold to the Clinton administration, for whom the Taliban were like some orientalist fable come alive. Bhutto's armed forces also calculated that a Pashtun-dominated Afghanistan would enable Pakistani forces to regroup there if the east of the country ever fell to Indian arms. Saudi Arabia's motives were more straightforward: the Taliban would be a useful Sunni bulwark against Iran. The Saudis dictated the terms of settlement for the wandering prodigal, since they insisted that the Taliban keep bin Laden quiet on the farm he purchased near Jalalabad with a view to going into the production of honey. His men were housed in the expanded facilities of Tora Bora near by. They were not happy, because compared to that oasis of 'progress and civilisation' in Yemen, Afghanistan was a desolate place, 'worse than a tomb' as one Yemeni put it. Nothing worked, with every journey spent perched on an eighth of a car seat, over rutted tracks. The Afghans were child-like, barbaric and venal with an unhealthy interest in boys. There were also clashes of personality, which probably explains why bin Laden initially based himself in Jalalabad rather than Taliban-dominated Kandahar.

Bin Laden's host, mullah Omar, was a tall, forbidding figure with a dark beard, whose sinister air was intensified by his having lost an eye as fragments of Russian shrapnel excavated the upper half of his face. His voice was an almost inaudible whisper. Mullah Omar and his Taliban had their own foundational myth. After experiencing a vision of the Prophet, mullah Omar believed that he had been chosen to deliver Afghanistan from chaos. He gathered together a small group of madrassa students who initially went around like Robin Hoods, rescuing boys and girls from warlord sodomites and rapists. Within a year his band had multiplied into an army of twenty-four thousand that took over most of southern Afghanistan, with Pakistani volunteers arriving at critical moments in the fighting against the Iranian- and Russian-backed Northern Alliance. On 4 April 1996 this obscure village mullah literally wrapped himself in the mantle of the Prophet when he removed a robe from a shrine in Kandahar that was said to be Mohammed's. Ecstatic crowds cheered as he paraded on a roof, clutching this garment, the event that gave rise to the only known photograph of him. From that moment he was unstoppable, going on to take Kabul itself that September. One of the Taliban's first acts was to enter a UN compound from which they dragged out the Communist-era president Najibullah and his brother. Both men were castrated and tortured, shot, dragged behind a car and then hanged from a concrete pillar with cigarettes in the fingers and money spilling from their pockets.

As Pashtun peasant boys who had been through refugee camps and the prayer mills of fanaticism, the Taliban looked with hatred on the sophisticated Dari-speaking inhabitants of Kabul, a city that had had two experiences of cosmopolitan sophistication under the monarchy and the Soviets. Women (who made up 40 per cent of doctors and 70 per cent of teachers) were dismissed from the workplace, the university and schools. Since years of fighting had left many widows, this meant that the streets were littered with black sacks holding their hands out amid their starving children, for all women, including beggars, had to wear the burqa in public, their eyes dimly perceptible behind a sort of mesh. Public buildings fell into desuetude since, to the Taliban, government was an irrelevance; instead senior clerics dictated permissions or pro-hibitions which were jotted down on chits and simply disbursed wads of notes from a treasure chest to reward some needy supplicant. This was 'government' as it had been in Europe in the ninth or tenth centuries, in a country so ruined that, as an American put it, one would have to bomb it up to the Stone Age. The Taliban concentrated on obliterating vice, banning chess, dog and pigeon racing, songbirds and the national pastime of flying kites. Poles were set up from which dangled smashed tape recorders, televisions, computers and VCRs, all enmeshed in unwound audiotapes ripped from people's cars. Even the animals in the zoo were not safe, until a theologian at Kabul's university ruled that the Prophet himself had kept pets. An aged lion called Marjan ripped off the arm of a Talib who had climbed into his den boasting 'I am the lion now,' and then killed him. Marjan was later blinded in one eye by a hand grenade tossed in by the dead man's friends. A deer was shot with an AK-47 after it had bitten a Talib's hand. The sole elephant was killed when a missile strayed off target. Two mangy wolves and a couple of wild boar were safe.

The only licensed entertainment took place each Friday in the Soviet-era stadium where the pop of a Kalashnikov AK-47 and a collapsed burqa indicated the demise of some unfortunate accused of adultery. Since there were no taxes or regulations, commerce thrived, including opium-poppy cultivation which took off in southern Helmand. Despite their insistence on virtue, the Taliban took their cut, estimated at US$20 million a year, of a trade that has resulted in there being four million heroin addicts in Iran alone.[59] Then the Taliban turned on their Iranian- and Russian-backed enemies in the north. In the town of Mazar-e-Sharif they spent two days killing anything that moved, whether human or four-legged, leaving the bodies unburied for an un-Islamic six days to make their point. They rounded up Shia Hazara, a Turko-Mongol mountain people, raping the women and killing the men by shutting them in giant metal containers which were then dumped in the surrounding desert. Taliban clerics gave the surviving Shia three choices: convert to Sunni Islam, leave or die. Between six and eight thousand Shia died. The dead included eleven Iranian consular officials and secret agents, who were taken to a basement and shot.[60]

Bin Laden had various residences in Afghanistan, including a hundred-acre complex at Tarnak Farm outside Kandahar. This consisted of about eighty buildings surrounded by a ten-foot-high mud wall, separating it from the surrounding scrub. Bin Laden also used various villas in Kandahar itself, shifting his location frequently in dim awareness of the US satellites miles above his head. Relations with the Taliban leader were not smooth. The ultra-shy mullah Omar resented bin Laden's obsessions with the modern media, or, as two Al Qaeda men reported it to al-Zawahiri, 'the disease of screens, flashes, fans and applause'. Bin Laden was obliged to acknowledge the supremacy of his host, which may have rankled as he was forever bailing out the feckless Taliban with prodigious amounts of money when they ran through the US$40 million they had received in aid from the Pakistanis. Using one type code systems, Al Qaeda tried to conceal itself within the language of international business. The mullah might have been surprised by coded references to himself and the Taliban as the 'Omar Brothers Company', business partners of the 'Abdullah Contracting Company', meaning bin Laden and comrades, traders (jihadis) in competition with 'foreign competitors', that is the CIA and MI6.[61] Despite these frictions, the Taliban became major state sponsors of terrorism, adopting many aspects of the jihadi-salafist platform. They enabled bin Laden to set up a network of training camps, from which he despatched guerrilla fighters (the majority of those trained) and terrorists to attack in dozens of places, coming and going without visas, while bin Laden himself sped about freely in a heavily armed convoy.

The training camps were multi-purpose, designed to build bodies, minds and skills. They were where the Taliban themselves learned how to calculate artillery ranges, to use high explosives like C-4, and other guerrilla tactics. A special Arab unit called Brigade 005 was deployed to help the Taliban at crucial times in its struggle with the Northern Alliance. The training camps were also useful to the Pakistanis for they were where men destined for Kashmir learned to use M-16s, more suited to Kashmir than the shorter-range AK-47. All Al Qaeda recruits began with a fifteen-day session of physical preparation, involving leaping over gaps or through fiery hoops. Each day began with dawn prayers and ended at about eight at night. This was followed by a forty-five-day period of learning the art of war, from map reading to handling various weapons. A more select band went on to another forty-five-day course in counter-surveillance, counter-interrogation, agent recruitment, forgery, hijacking, assassination and bomb making. Much of this knowledge was codified in a training manual, discovered by British police in Manchester, that eventually reached twelve volumes before being put on a CD-Rom; if one wanted to brew up ricin poisons this was where to look before the internet offered many alternatives. With the help of Pakistani scientists, there were attempts to use such biological and chemical agents as anthrax and cyanide, experiments confined to dogs in glass cages. Indoctrination sessions forged a group mindset, while films starring Arnold Schwarzenegger and other US action movies were shown for relaxation and to pick up useful tips.[62]

It was from amid this charming world that in August 1996 bin Laden issued his 'Declaration of War against the Americans Occupying the Land of the Two Holy Places'. This so-called occupation had gone on for seven years rather than the few months promised by Saudi's rulers. The declaration ingratiated itself with the Saudi in the street by describing the corruption and economic downturn afflicting the kingdom, blaming this on the US military presence in remote desert provinces. In a long literal passage about the joys of martyrdom, bin Laden announced: 'Men of the radiant future of our *ummah* of Mohammed, raise the banner of jihad up high against the Judaeo-American alliance that has occupied the holy places of Islam.' He quoted poetry to describe his type of holy warrior:

> I am willing to sacrifice self and wealth
> for knights who never disappointed me.
> Knights who are never fed up or deterred by death,
> even if the mill wheel of war turns.
> In the heat of battle they do not care,
> and cure the insanity of the enemy by their 'insane' courage.[63]

In an interview that November with Australian Muslim activists, bin Laden praised the bombing of the World Trade Center, and more recent attacks on Americans in Riyadh and at the Khobar Towers apartment complex which killed respectively seven and nineteen people, the majority US servicemen, even though these were Iranian- rather than Al Qaeda-sponsored operations. That operations of an almost fantastic ambition were then entertained was due to a visit by Khalid Sheikh Mohammed, with a story that stretched all the way to Kuala Lumpur and Manila as he searched for a way of hitting the USA.

Khalid Sheikh had come from Karachi where he notionally worked as a public works engineer. He travelled extensively posing as a Saudi businessman. One of his supposed business ventures was in Kuala Lumpur, where his partner was the Indonesian Encep Nurjaman who went by the name of Hambali in honour of an eighth-century Muslim saint. Born in West Java, Hambali had gone to Malaysia in 1985 to deepen his acquaintance with Islam. After a period fighting in Afghanistan, he returned to Malaysia in 1989, settling in Sungai Manngis, a hamlet about sixty kilometres west of Kuala Lumpur, where Abu Bakar Ba'asyir and Abdullah Sungkar, the exiled founders of Jemaah Islamiyah, also lived. This was Terror Central for South Asia. The schemes hatched here were oddly at variance with the ambient squalor. These men hated cosmopolitan and prosperous Singapore, finding local cell members who felt that its materialism and order were spiritually vacuous or who were unnerved by the rational choices a modern society involves. They wanted more certain rules than even this most law-abiding society involved. Perhaps they could stoke enough strife between Chinese and Malays to trigger a war from which the Islamist vanguard would emerge victorious? Hambali lived with his wife in a hut with a zinc roof, one light fitting and a lavatory that was a hole in the ground. He eked out a living selling kebabs and slaughtering poultry. But most of his time was spent preaching and leading discussion groups called *usrah*. These enabled him to identify potential jihadists, whom he sent for military training either with Al Qaeda in Afghanistan or with the Moro Islamic Liberation Front (MILF) which operated in Mindanao in the southern Philippines. The MILF was not the only sympathetic group in the Philippines. The port city of Zamboanga was a hotbed of jihadist militancy. Bin Laden's brother-in-law, Mohammed Jamal Khalifa, had a branch of his International Islamic Relief Organisation there, which had close links with a breakaway MILF faction, of bandits, kidnappers and pirates, called Abu Sayyaf or Bearers of the Sword, named in honour of a giant Afghan jihadist. In March 2000 Abu Sayyaf is said to have received US$25 million from Libya's Colonel Ghaddafi, acting as money man for three European governments, after it released a large number of foreign hostages, money it used to acquire high-powered speedboats.

Hambali became both the operational head of Jemaah Islamiyah, the transnational terror group dedicated to the creation of an Islamic State of South Asia, and the number four in Al Qaeda, the only non-Arab in such a senior position.[64] It is likely that he directed Khalid Sheikh's eyes eastwards. Khalid's terrorist nephew, Ramzi Yousef, lived in Karachi too, where he spent much time with Abdul Murad, a friend who had trained as a pilot, but having failed the exam so many times could not find a job. Their talk turned to killing, for that is what Murad liked to do. 'I enjoy it. You can kill them [Americans] by umm, gas. You can kill them by gun. You can kill them by knife. You can kill them by explosion. There's many kinds,' as he later told Filipino investigators. Murad suggested dive-bombing the CIA headquarters at Langley or the Pentagon with a light aircraft packed with chemicals and explosives, a scheme that caught Yousef's imagination, although he thought spraying the building with deadly chemicals from a crop duster might be more lethal. Osama bin Laden then intervened from afar, suggesting that Yousef assassinate Bill Clinton in November 1994 when he was due to arrive on a five-day tour of Asia. There was talk of using a Stinger missile to down Air Force One as it came in to land. These men were not adolescent fantasists talking large in some Pakistani suburb of Beeston or Leeds, but professional killers with huge rewards on their heads.

Yousef moved into an apartment with Murad where he manufactured bombs. While scraping lead azide from a container – it being a volatile substance used in detonators – it exploded in his face. After a spell in hospital, he flew to Bangkok, not for a rest, but to try to blow up the Israeli embassy. He and Islamist Thai accomplices rented a truck and driver. They strangled the driver and put his corpse in the back, along with a one-tonne bomb wired up to the transmission. Never lucky with his choice of driver, Yousef was appalled when the man he selected crashed the truck into cars and pedal-taxis at an intersection near the embassy. There it remained as the police cars arrived. After a two-month break back in Pakistan, Yousef took up an offer from the Iranian rebel movement, the Mujaheddin-e-Khalq Organisation, to launch a bomb attack on a Shia shrine in Iran. At the height of the Ashura festival, a high-explosive C-4 device made by him demolished a wall at the shrine of Reza, killing twenty-six Muslim pilgrims and injuring two hundred others.

Khalid Sheikh and Yousef plus one Wali Shah arrived in Manila, where the two younger men had already acquired girlfriends in the Philippine capital's many go-go bars. Khalid Sheikh, by now using the name Abdul Majid, and Shah rented apartments there while Yousef took up residence in the Manor hotel. They held meetings in the city's karaoke and go-go bars, plotting holy murder in places filled with mirrors, flashing lights and half-naked dancers. They hired a helicopter to survey the city. Khalid Sheikh took up with a Filipina dentist, sometimes phoning her from the helicopters so she could look up and wave at her paramour. They purchased priests' robes and Bibles, for the reason they were in Manila was to assassinate pope John Paul II, having given up on the heavily protected US president. To that end they rented an apartment along the route his holiness was most likely to take. This was not the only plot under way because, since his discussions with Murad, Yousef had become obsessed with downing large planes. He developed a new bomb, involving nitroglycerine disguised in containers for contact-lens solution, and a timer made from a Casio Databank watch which had the advantage of an alarm that could be set for up to twelve months ahead. The batteries used to power the lightbulbs which (their glass having been deliberately weakened) would set the thing off could be hidden in the heels of shoes, as they did not come within the range of airport X-ray machinery. He tried out a mini-version of this device in a Manila cinema. Then he summoned the pilot Murad. On 8 December, Yousef took a flight from Manila to Tokyo. He assembled his little bomb in the lavatory, and then attached it below his seat, leaving the plane when it refuelled at Cebu. An hour into its second leg, the bomb killed a young Japanese engineer, Haruki Ikegami, who happened to sit where Yousef had placed the device. It ripped the lower half of his body to pieces and almost sent the plane out of control when it burned through the aileron cables controlling the flaps. The pilot managed to force the plane into a turn before landing it on Okinawa, saving the lives of 272 passengers and twenty crew.

Returned to Manila, Yousef moved into the apartment block where the pope would pass by, joining Wali Shah who lived below. Neighbours began to gossip when they noticed the rare spectacle of these Arab men struggling upstairs with boxes and bottles in the torpid heat. They might have found it even odder that on 21 December Yousef threw Manila's only party to celebrate the sixteenth anniversary of the Lockerbie bombing of Pan Am 103. Just after Christmas Khalid Sheikh and Murad arrived, for it was all gloved hands to the pump as two plots got under way, to kill the pope, and something called Boijinka, a made-up word Khalid Sheikh had picked up from Afghanistan or Bosnia. Yousef told Murad to be ready to fly to Singapore on 14 January 1995, one of five men who were going to explode ten Boeing 747 aircraft over the Pacific, by changing planes after the initial legs of their journeys. Yousef reserved for himself the tricky exercise of boarding and leaving three different flights. About three thousand people would have died had this plot been a success.

The 6th of January was intended to be clean-up day in Manila. Yousef was burning off superfluous chemicals on the stove when the flat filled with a cloud of dark smoke too thick to disperse through the windows. It billowed into the hall too, discommoding the neighbours. The fire brigade were called, who arrived with a policeman. Seeing that there was no fire, they accepted Yousef's claim, delivered in the hall where he was frantically dispersing smoke, that he was making fireworks for a belated New Year's party. Firemen and police returned when a fire alarm finally detected the fumes. Police thought they had wandered into the lab of a mad scientist, with nitroglycerine in grape-juice containers, switches, timers, wires, soldering irons, cassocks and maps of the pope's visit. After the two men had fled, Yousef told Murad to retrieve his laptop from the flat. He did. The police arrested him, along with Shah the following day.

While undergoing interrogation by senior superintendent Rodolfo 'Boogie' Mendoza, with the aid of a rubber hose occasionally debouching water into the suspect's lungs, Murad fell for the classic gambit of being told 'You're a shit, a nothing to me' by boasting that he was one of the World Trade Center bombers and an associate of the fabled Ramzi Yousef. Assaults on human vanity usually work for the skilled interrogator. Yousef was holed up in an Islamabad hotel, whose location was betrayed by a potential recruit who had turned him down before deciding to collect the US$2 million reward money. Pakistani and US diplomatic security agents burst in upon him in February 1995, dragging him out blindfolded as he demanded to see the necessary paperwork. On the long flight to New York he bragged about his own atrocities to agents who went to the lavatory to jot down his words. At his trial, in between trying to chat up the pretty blonde court sketch artist, Yousef volunteered that he was a terrorist. On his computer the FBI discovered a business card with 'international terrorist' given as his profession. Yousef is currently imprisoned for life, in solitary confinement and without possibility of parole, in a federal Supermax facility in Colorado.

Khalid Sheikh, who had been staying on the ground floor of the same hotel, used one of his twenty passports to slip away to Doha in Qatar where he had many friends and sympathisers. US pressure on the Qatari government to arrest him, after senior US officials had talked themselves out of a snatch operation, led to Khalid Sheikh's visit to bin Laden, with a portfolio of plans that had been hatched by his ever fertile nephew. Khalid Sheikh mentioned Murad's idea of crashing a plane into Langley or the Pentagon, to which bin Laden responded: 'Why use an axe when you can use a bulldozer?' The plan to crash ten aircraft simultaneously seemed over-ambitious and dependent upon too many changes of planes. Of course, one could combine the two projects, by smashing fewer aircraft into prominent symbolic targets in the US itself, which would be unmistakable from the air. Bin Laden authorised Khalid Sheikh to commence planning such an operation; the Saudi would finance it, and provide the manpower from Al Qaeda training camps. This would not come to fruition until 11 September 2001.

In the course of 1998, the CIA's bin Laden unit studied satellite imagery of the Tarnak Farm. US agents based in Islamabad recruited about thirty Afghan tribesmen for an armed raid to snatch bin Laden. This operation was vetoed at an advanced stage by the CIA itself, because of worries about the legality of assassination, if bin Laden refused to come quietly, and about collateral casualties, because bin Laden and his associates had many women and children around them. Attempts to use newly developed armed Predator drones to kill the Al Qaeda leadership were frustrated by the military's concern that the CIA should pay for them.

Unaware of these deliberations, bin Laden activated an Al Qaeda operation whose feasibility had been established in 1995 when he sent Ali Mohammed to Nairobi. The latter spent four or five days scouting and photographing targets until he had recorded on his Apple PowerBook that the US embassy fronted the street and was lightly protected by Kenyan policemen. No lessons had been learned from the 1983 Beirut bombings about strengthening embassy security, despite a report on this subject by admiral Bobby Inman. A Kenyan Al Qaeda cell had been established in 1994. A Palestinian, Mohamed Sadeek Odeh, opened a fishing business in Mombasa, while Wadi el-Hage opened an NGO called Help Africa People in Nairobi, where he lived with his wife and five children. Other recruits included Fazul Abdullah Mohammed, a native of the Comoros, and Mohamed Rashed Daoud al-Owhali. They rented a single-storey house where an Egyptian bomb maker arrived to assemble a device consisting of 2,000 pounds of TNT concealed in a brown Toyota truck. On 7 August 1998, the eighth anniversary of the arrival of US forces in Saudi Arabia, al-Owhali and a man known only as Azzam drove this truck towards the embassy's small underground garage, after a Kenyan guard had waved them away from the public car park. Al-Owhali dismounted to open the barred gate, dispersing the guards by throwing a grenade, after which he fled.

This bang made many people in surrounding offices rush to the windows. Azzam detonated the truck bomb. The concrete face of the embassy was ripped off, killing twelve Americans, and injuring ambassador Prudence Bushnell, but most of the blast struck a neighbouring secretarial college, while also hitting a bus and passers-by in this busy commercial district. Two hundred and one Africans were killed, with a further 4,500 injured, the majority blinded or cut by shards of flying glass when they had gone to their windows after the grenade had exploded, only to be caught in the second huge blast. Nine minutes later, an Egyptian called Ahmed Abdullah, known as Ahmed the German because of his fair hair, drove a petrol truck laden with gas canisters packed around a similar bomb into the US embassy in Dar-es-Salaam. Luckily, a water tanker absorbed most of the blast, although not enough to save eleven Tanzanian visa applicants who were killed or the eighty-five wounded. The upper half of Ahmed Abdullah hit the embassy roof, still clutching the steering wheel.[65]

In the White House the first priority had been to provide rescue experts while arranging to fly the most serious African casualties to hospitals in Europe. Israel flew in specialist sniffer-dog units which played a major role in rescuing victims buried under tons of rubble. Kenya's emergency services, geared up for a mass catastrophe involving at most sixty people, were overwhelmed. There was no heavy lifting gear, insufficient reserves of blood, and not enough room in the mortuaries. The US offered US$2 billion by way of compensation and reconstruction, although individuals would receive only US$500 for injury and relatives only US$11,000 for a death. The hunt for the perpetrators was relentless, with five hundred FBI agents and hardened CIA counterterrorism operatives like Gary Berntsen descending on Nairobi in C-130s. Odeh was arrested using a false passport when he flew into Pakistan.

At Nairobi airport he was greeted with chilling politeness by Kenyan police: 'Welcome back to Nairobi, Mr Odeh. We have been waiting for you.' He was soon going to talk one way or another. Al-Owahli had been injured in the attack and had visited a hospital. This enabled the Kenyan police and FBI agents to trace him to a hotel outside the city. That his clothes, including his belt and shoes, were pristine despite evidence of cuts on his hands and back was enough to arrest him. His cover story broke when the FBI found bullets and the key to the Toyota on a sill in the hospital. When the CIA produced evidence that Al Qaeda was planning a meeting for 20 August to review the success of these attacks, president Clinton took the decision to launch strikes on Afghanistan and Sudan, where two of the Nairobi bombers had recently surfaced.

Because the Pakistanis could not be trusted, and because they might regard incoming missiles as a sneak Indian attack, a US general was despatched to Islamabad for a dinner with a Pakistani colleague, during which the American would explain that the missiles entering Pakistani airspace were not Indian. Right until the last minute, and despite the concurrent pressures of the Monica Lewinsky affair, Clinton agonised over certain targets in Sudan, but not including the Shifa chemical plant that the CIA had linked to bin Laden because of suspicious trace elements in the compound's soil. Tomahawk Cruise missiles rotated in their tubes on several destroyers in the Arabian Sea as their gyroscopes were orientated. Seventy-five missiles were launched, some circling until the whole flock set off on their contour-hugging two-hour flight into Afghanistan. Each was about twenty feet long, and armed with an assortment of warheads. Some had one-thousand-pound bombs, designed to flatten buildings, if necessary entering via their windows, others were laden with cluster bomblets to kill softer human targets. Each had a payload equal to a Second World War V2 ballistic rocket. During the night these missiles hit six Al Qaeda training camps near Khost, at US$75,000,000 an expensive way of killing a total of six people. Although the National Security Agency (NSA) had been eavesdropping on a satellite phone call made by al-Zawahiri, which might have enabled the US to pinpoint the location of the Al Qaeda leadership, this information was not shared with those who launched Operation Big Reach, which became Big Propaganda Flop. For the Al Qaeda chemical plant in Sudan had been sold on; it was a legitimate business selling repackaged pharmaceuticals locally. Despite this failure, Clinton stationed two nuclear submarines armed with Cruise missiles off the coast of Pakistan, to decrease the response time between actionable intelligence and any attack, while secretly authorising the CIA to use lethal force to deal with bin Laden, thereby breaking with US policy since the Ford era.

These missile attacks led to expressions of anger, easily incited on the streets of Pakistan, while boosting bin Laden's prestige in the Muslim world as his voice announced on radio, 'By the grace of God, I am alive.' Weighing up whether he wanted the US as an enemy, mullah Omar moved closer to bin Laden, who prudently took an oath to Omar as 'the emir of the faithful'. Omar himself vowed in return: 'Even if all the countries of the world unite, we would defend Osama with our blood.'[66] By this time, bin Laden was ensuring his personal primacy over the various separate terrorist 'nations' that had washed up in Afghanistan with a view to waging jihad by making them swear an oath he had devised himself: 'I recall the commitment to God, in order to listen to and obey my superiors, who are accomplishing this task with energy, difficulty and giving of self, and in order that God may protect us so God's words are the highest and his religion victorious.'

One of those to swear this was a young Jordanian, Abu Musab al-Zarqawi, leader of the Bayt al-Imam terrorist group who in 1999 had been freed from a fifteen-year jail sentence as part of a broader amnesty of three thousand prisoners. Al-Zarqawi was a reformed juvenile delinquent from the rough town of Zarqa from which he took his name. Embarrassingly for a jihadist he was covered in tattoos, including a nautical anchor, although he later tried to remove these with hydrochloric acid. People called him 'the green man' because of his body art. He had drifted from crime to radical jihadism, spending time in Afghanistan from 1989. His three years in Jordan's tough Suwaqah prison had been spent body-building and extending his gang of forty Islamist inmates by recruiting imprisoned drug addicts and felons. His prison charisma was cemented by beating people up and washing the bodies of the sick. People obeyed when he blinked his eyes. On returning to Afghanistan, al-Zarqawi and forty of his Jordanian comrades were recruited into Al Qaeda by their high-ranking fellow countryman Abu Zubaydah. Something of a maverick, al-Zarqawi was allowed to establish a training complex near the Iranian border at Herat, whose primary function was to infiltrate Iraqi Kurdistan via a jihadist group called Ansar al-Islam, whose leader mullah Krekar lives in Norway. This would not only help establish an Al Qaeda sanctuary, if they were ever driven from Afghanistan, but also provide a Europe-wide network of Kurdish terrorists who could be co-opted into Al Qaeda. They in turn would be the primary recruiters of European suicide jihadists who went to Iraq to fight Americans after the 2003 invasion.

Al-Zarqawi was also deeply involved in bin Laden's plans for the millennium. One scheme was to blow up the Radisson SAS hotel in Amman, which would be packed with American Christians, and the King Hussein Bridge connecting Jordan to Israel. Fortunately, the Jordanians unmasked the plot and tried twenty-seven terrorists, including the absent al-Zarqawi who received fifteen years in jail.[67] Another plot, to sink the destroyer USS *The Sullivans* off Aden, failed when the boat that was carrying explosives sank a few minutes after being launched as it could not bear the weight. Thousands of miles away, an Algerian named Ahmad Ressam readied himself to cross from Canada to the US, having received US$12,000 expenses from Al Qaeda for his operation. Fortunately, an alert customs officer called Diana Dean was suspicious of the nervous Ressam as he drove off a ferry at Port Angeles, Washington State. She and her colleagues made him open the boot of his car where they found a hundred pounds of urea (to make fertiliser bombs) and quantities of sulphate as well as timing devices. Ressam bolted but was caught within a few blocks trying to steal a car. It dawned on investigators that he was part of a network of US-based sleeper cells that extended from Montreal to Boston and New York. His car contained a map of Los Angeles International Airport, which was his target. All over the US anxious counter-terrorist agents breathed sighs of relief when New Year's Eve passed with nothing louder than fireworks.

There was a further millennium plot under way in the heart of Europe, where the relevant authorities were in a sort of narcoleptic trance. On the night of 20 December 1999, German intelligence officers broke into a Frankfurt apartment being used by an Algerian terrorist cell. They had brought a tracking device as they had learned that a bag of weapons had recently arrived. They found two such bags, and therefore had to choose one in which to insert a trace as they had brought only one device. Early on Christmas Eve, Scotland Yard intercepted a call from a member of this cell to Abu Doha in London in which there was direct talk of an imminent attack. Abu Doha was one of the founders of the Salafist Group for Prayer and Combat, or GSPC. The excesses of the GIA in Algeria during the 1990s had even alienated such spiritual godfathers as

Abu Qatada, the Palestinian Omar Mahmoud Othman, who issued the GIA's newsletter *Al-Ansar* from London. One result of this was the formation of the GSPC, which while refraining from the GIA's mindless violence inside Algeria made up for it by swimming into the wake of Al Qaeda. Abu Doha met bin Laden in Afghanistan and agreed to put his European network at his disposal like a temporary franchising operation. That was how Ahmad Ressam ended up crossing the Canadian–US border to blow up LAX. The call from Frankfurt to London forced the German police to act. They raided the Frankfurt flat, arresting four of the five-man cell. Two of them were failed asylum seekers living in Britain who, despite committing crimes like drug dealing, had not been deported by the British. Another was a convicted GIA terrorist with French citizenship, which did not stop him moving freely between Britain, France and Germany. A fourth was an Algerian who had been refused leave to stay by the Germans when he admitted having procured arms and ammunition for the FIS, but who then disappeared anyway, except when he was repeatedly arrested for theft.

In an apartment used by this cell, German police found thirty kilograms of potassium permanganate, a chemical usually sold in quantities of five to ten grams to treat children with eczema. It is also suitable for making bombs. The men had disguised themselves as respectable doctors embarking on an aid mission to Africa, who visited forty-eight pharmacies near Frankfurt airport claiming they had forgotten they needed prescriptions for the chemical in their haste to reach the paediatric clinics where they intended to do good. This hard-luck story worked on most pharmacists. In another apartment rented by the group, the German police found a twenty-minute videotape recording a journey from Baden-Baden to Strasbourg. In Strasbourg the camera focused on the cathedral façade, and especially on shoppers in the Christmas market. There was a soundtrack in Arabic: 'These are the enemies of God taking a stroll ... These are the enemies of God. You will go to hell. God willing.' The plan seems to have been to put bombs inside pressure cookers, but there is no certainty, for at their trial the defendants maintained silence, only to shriek, 'You are all Jews. I don't need the court. Allah is my defender. Our only judge is Allah,' as they were sentenced. The entire plot had been organised from London, where many members of the cell lived. The British arrested Abu Qatada, and then Abu Doha as he tried to flee from Heathrow. Italian police rolled up a Milan-based cell after their extensive electronic eavesdropping revealed that a Munich-based

Libyan was trying to replay the Strasbourg attack with the aid of a toxic-gas attack.[68]

The continent's lax asylum laws meant that, whereas in 1983 there were eighty thousand asylum seekers, by 1992 the figure was seven hundred thousand, with highly organised smuggling rings bringing in many more illegally, often in deplorable circumstances. This laxity enabled several serious Islamist players to gain a foothold, despite the fact that they routinely told multiple lies to gain the requisite permissions, as when Abu Hamza contracted a bigamous marriage with an Englishwoman in order to gain leave to stay. Even when they broke the terms of their asylum or committed crimes, as in the case of the entire Strasbourg group, it was the exception rather than the rule that any European government would deport those concerned. The Yemeni Ramzi bin al-Shibh claimed to German authorities that he was 'Omar' fleeing persecution in his native Sudan. Even before they rejected his claim, Ramzi bin al-Shibh had acquired the correct registration papers, in his real name, for a German university which he used to obtain a student visa from the embassy in Yemen.[69] There was virtually no co-ordination between courts, interior ministry, immigration authorities, prisons and police, in contrast to the teams of legal activists such men could mobilise if ever they were arrested. At a rarefied level police and intelligence services co-operated, but lower down national jurisdictions ensured no co-ordination of policy in any depth. A conversation recorded by Italian intelligence agents reveals how such men regarded Europe as a soft touch, even without the aid of sympathetic immigration and human rights lawyers, professions that have successfully insulated themselves from all criticism. The named speaker was Mahmoud Abdelkader Es Sayed, a high ranking Egyptian Al Qaeda member, who had anticipated the Italians' curiosity by admitting connections with Islamic Jihad:

> Unknown man: Did you get political asylum?
> Es Sayed: Yes, when I got here I went to Rome. I came to Milan
>   only after obtaining the asylum. Anyway, when I came here,
>   I shaved my beard and I 'shaped up'.
> Man: Yes [laughing] of course they never got to know anything
>   about your extremism . . .
> Es Sayed: I filed my claim in Rome . . . [laughing] naturally
>   I told them I have three brothers in jail . . . I also told them
>   I had been in jail.

Man: Even with the brothers from the Aden Army [he meant
the Yemeni Islamic Army of Aden]?

Es Sayed: This is a thing . . . I left Egypt a long time ago . . . I told
them I was a wanted man . . . I told them I was unjustly
persecuted . . . that my wife had a car accident . . . bad luck
. . . but I told them that the accident had been caused by the
Egyptian secret service.

Man: Very nice!

Es Sayed: All this seemed like persecution and, as a
consequence, they gave me the asylum in the month of
November . . . December.

Italy was in the process of updating its asylum laws, a subject the two
discussed later in this conversation, in a passage which readers might like
to reflect on:

Es Sayed: Now there is a law in Italy which requires that asylum
claims, even those that have already been approved, have to
be reviewed every three months to see if the initial conditions
are still in place . . . this is a very strange thing . . . by doing so
a person can suffer oppression.

Man: This is a form of terrorism.

Es Sayed: Of course it is terrorism . . . Italy is a terrorist country
. . . it is a criminal country . . . all this shows you that in Italy
you cannot obtain a real political asylum . . . the intent of
the government is to take advantage of the Muslims living in
this country.[70]

A further abuse involved European welfare systems, which are
administered by those who have ingested the full multicultural credo.
Abu Qatada received £400 a week in government benefits, broken
down as £322 for housing and £70 a week disability allowances. Abu
Hamza's rent was paid by the taxpayer, to the tune of £2,400 a month,
for a substantial home in a west London suburb. With his large family,
Omar Bakri received a total of £275,000 in welfare payments, which
extended to a £31,000 Ford Galaxy people-carrier to ferry them about.
Europe's traditions of freedom of worship meant that powerful taboos
protected the main sites of Islamist activity. Mosques, together with
the archipelagos of community centres that accompanied them, were
one crucial nodal point in the elaboration of a pan-European jihadist

network. To put this in perspective, French security authorities calculate that of France's 1,685 mosques, which are regularly attended by only 10 per cent of five million French Muslims, eighty or 4.7 per cent gave cause for concern, with 1.1 per cent actually controlled, rather than contested, by radical salafists. Most imams were actually rather meek people, avoiding controversy so as not to offend their congregations or the presbyterian-like mosque committees that controlled the money from collections. The committees often preferred to hire these foreign village preachers because they were cheaper than employing someone with a Western education ranging beyond mastery of the Koran. Control of such committees was one way for radicals to hot up the temperature in the mosque. Radical Islamists were recipients of centralised funding, whether from a local organisation in the host country or from an external source like Wahhabist Saudi Arabia. Unlike some aged peasant cleric preaching in an Urdu that young second-generation Muslims found difficult to comprehend, the radicals frequently operated in the national vernacular, or in authentic Arabic, and were the first to utilise the most modern technologies.[71]

They also knew just which aspects of the local culture to adopt, so that, for example, sheikh Omar Bakri managed to combine the belligerence of his native Syria with a comedic touch worthy of Bernard Manning, an unlamented British racist comedian of a vulgar disposition. Any attempt by moderates to say 'yes, but' could be slammed down with citations from the holy book by 'sheikhs' and 'imams' with no theological grounding whatsoever, but with a feel for life as young Muslims live it. Masters of vituperation, these figures had angry young men eating out of their hands, especially if they bore the physical stigmata of some foreign jihad. Battles for control were fought over moderate mosques, sometimes leading to the bizarre spectacle of a moderate preaching upstairs and a maniac in the basement, or, as in the case of Abu Hamza, out in a London street under the gaze of bored policemen. As in Milan, radicals set up ad-hoc mosques in a former garage or similar premises, or, as in the case of Stepney's East London mosque, gravitated to an alternative venue that they totally controlled. This is what the French call 'Islam des caves', of the basements and cellars in huge public housing projects. Muslim student societies, for this was the generation that enjoyed mass tertiary education, were quickly dominated by bodies like the Young Muslim Organisation, one of the routes into more radically subversive groups such as Hizb ut-Tahir. British academics refused to 'spy' on their students, although they still monitor signs of drug abuse or mental instability. At enormous cost, some European governments, notably the Netherlands, have belatedly commissioned university-based licensing programmes for imams, the goal being to combine Islamic learning with a plural, rationalistic Western education. That 70 per cent of the students are female is not encouraging for the scheme seems doomed to failure in such a male-dominated culture.[72]

The ayatollah Khomeini's parting gift to the world before his death in June 1989 was the issuance of a fatwa calling upon the world's Muslims to murder the novelist Salman Rushdie for insulting the Prophet. This outrage was a bid to reassert Iran's hegemony in the Muslim world – now defined to mean everywhere Muslims lived – after the conclusion of the Saudi-sponsored victory over the Soviets in Afghanistan. It also stymied the efforts of Iranian moderates to reopen doors to the West. After a significant lapse of time, Muslims in India and Pakistan succeeded in whipping up a fury among their co-religionists in Britain. A country that had blithely ignored the religious implications of mass migration, assuming that all immigrants would happily melt into the prevailing secular hedonism, was shocked by scenes of angry people burning books and effigies in northern British cities. This anger has not gone away; it has been regularly re-incited over the last twenty years, to the decreasing amusement of natives who are wearying of the fist-waving and finger-jabbing, the flames and the insatiable anger.

For many European Muslims, their last vision of a functioning multi-cultural society ends when they leave the false dawn of multi-ethnic, multi-faith primary schools for an increasingly segregated secondary school system. There is something deeply tragic about the way this has happened, and it is difficult to see how things can be rectified. These divisions are an inevitable consequence of the formation of de-facto ghettos, the 'dish cities' where the TV satellite receiver is tuned to other shores. Five per cent of British citizens are Muslims, but in some towns they constitute 15 per cent of the population. In a town like Blackburn in Lancashire, people in the Muslim south live separate lives from white people in the north. School children are bussed back and forth, as if visiting a church or mosque in the other part of town was like a trip abroad. According to a recent BBC television programme in May 2007, 'white flight' will result in entirely South Asian or entirely white cities. Politicians express grave concern about such ghettos, but have no idea how to break them up since each fresh initiative seems to fail. In Britain they have to bear in mind that some fifty or so Labour Party MPs are heavily dependent on the Muslim vote, which can be influenced this way or that by telephone calls from a religious or political leader in Pakistan or by fraudulent manipulation of postal voting systems. Politicians of all stripes, except Labour MPs with constituencies containing large numbers of poor whites, ignore polls in which 70 per cent of Britons express their wish to tighten immigration criteria, preferring to side with bien-pensant opinion rather than with what their fellow countrymen – including many Asians and Afro-Caribbeans – actually think. Even to raise these issues was once to be dismissed as a Fascist, a racist or, bizarrely, a eugenicist, a creed that had some purchase on the left too.[73]

One of the major problems is that something for which we already had the neutral term cosmopolitanism, that is all the everyday things about mixed ethnic communities we historically liked, was elided with the activist ideology of multiculturalism, which means far more than buying coffee from a purportedly Algerian store on a gay street in London's Soho run by Italians and Poles, or the fact of (highly ordered) multi-ethnic city states like Hong Kong or Singapore. Some Jews do not like the word cosmopolitan, seeing it as a coded synonym for nineteenth-century Berlin or Vienna, but that is insufficient reason to avoid it.

Multiculturalism means that each diverse group adopted a story of victimhood so as to put itself beyond close scrutiny, enveloping itself in the myth of moral purity that comes with being the historically oppressed. These diverse communities spoke to government through their so-called community leaders, a liberal version of an imperial power dealing through nabobs and tribes with the natives. In fact, the self-appointed leaders of victim minorities can be oppressors too, as anyone familiar with the Bogside, Falls Road or Short Strand will know. There are bullies aplenty in Muslim communities too, in societies like Hizb ut-Tahir that function like gangs. Wild charges of institutionalised or systemic racism shut down discussion of Muslim subordination of women or the hatred they expressed towards gays and Jews, just as some Jews have for decades inhibited criticism of Israel, or of dubious acts involving individual Jews, by automatically insinuating charges of anti-Semitism.[74]

Originating in the Western left university, as a fall-back position after the collapse of Marxism, this creed of multiculturalism was designed to assemble a progressive coalition of minority interests as a counterweight to the nasty nativist majority. It became the prevailing orthodoxy in the Churches, local government, the left-liberal media and wherever cultural self-repudiation has become dominant. In Britain an entire television station, Channel 4, was progressively devoted to propagating it with programmes that are nowadays difficult to parody within the degraded tacky rubbish which it commissions. Like the urgently reactive concern with a merely symbolic Britishness or Dutchness, multiculturalism is similarly negligent of the shared moral values that make civilised living possible, especially when these involve notions of honour or shame and the need for social taboos rather than self-regarding talk of decency or tolerance which are just as traditional in Portugal or Sweden.

There are other insidious aspects of multiculturalism. Behaviour becomes a mere expression of difference rather than of right or wrong, better or worse, civilised or backward, attitudes which have led the police and social services to turn a deaf ear, even towards children being tortured to eject evil spirits, or women facing murder for defying arranged relationships. This policy was most comprehensively pursued by centre-left governments in Britain and the Netherlands, with the passive acquiescence of centre-right opponents terrified of being accused of racism. Centre-left governments have long since walked quietly away from it, but multiculturalism is the bridge between reactionary Islamists and the anti-Semitic and anti-US far left.[75] Only France, with its republican insistence on equality, integration and secularism, was conspicuously opposed to this divisive philosophy. Instead of giving immigrants the training to pursue an economic vocation, this creed actively encouraged a soft form of apartheid, whether by providing translations of official documents, making it unnecessary to learn the dominant language, or actively encouraging welfare entitlement among populations with low levels of educational attainment. Whereas many earlier immigrants, like the Jews, Indians, Greeks and Chinese, regarded welfare payments, assuming they existed, as demeaning handouts, they have now become part of a culture of rights, responsible for such extraordinary facts as Denmark's 5 per cent Muslim minority receiving 40 per cent of its welfare budget. A phenomenon called Islamophobia invented in 1998 – which perhaps should be called 'terrorophobia', or the fear of being killed by Islamist bombers – spares anyone the need to examine what has gone so radically wrong within these communities. BBC news services reflexively help by never connecting terrorists with the constituency they operate in, even when the bombers are last heard crying 'Allah, Allah,' while nervously monitoring its anxieties about a purely hypothetical nativist backlash.[76]

Adolescence and young adulthood bring unique tests for those from a traditional family background who have to make their way in modern, liberal, Western society. Chinese, Indians and Turks seem to have negotiated this very well. Being suspended between Britain and Pakistan, Germany and Turkey, or France, Italy, Spain and North Africa is the common lot of many second- and third-generation Muslims in Europe. Cultural rather than economic issues become hugely significant, for there are no major obstacles to social mobility among South Asians. Do you retreat into the close village your parents have replicated in a suburb of Leeds, Lille or Limburg or do you immerse yourself in a majority society whose mores you find bewildering, decadent and tempting? There seems to be a gender problem too. Whereas Muslim girls toe the line at home, study hard and then rise through work or marriage, Muslim males, cosseted as the 'little prince', seem frequently to go off the rails, with violence as an outlet for pervasive sexual repression in their communities. No wonder they are hell-bent on blowing up scantily dressed 'slags' in British nightclubs, by which they mean young British clerks, nurses and teachers having a night out in clubs and discotheques. Partly by way of generational revolt, many second- or third-generation Muslims turned to Islamism, where they found brotherhood, identity and respect, thereby solving their own existential crises while imbibing a worldview with a clear definition of good and evil. Paradoxically, as Shiv Malik has shown, the ultra-reactionary could be strangely liberating. In addition to rejecting the innocuous piety of their parents, they could also slip free of such traditional practices as arranged marriages with faraway cousins, claiming that this was a Hindu custom falsely adopted by Pakistanis, turning their attentions to the large pool of pious females who donned the hijab, in itself allegedly a form of liberation from the predatory eyes of men. But the veil is also simultaneously totalitarian in the sense that women who do not wear it are routinely intimidated into doing so.[77] Others found their way to radical Islam by way of atonement for a life of crime. Between 50 and 70 per cent of those in French jails are Muslims, while in Spain Muslims are one in ten of prison inmates. British authorities predict that by 2012 a thousand Islamists will be in the prison system, where they already seek to subvert institutional order. Such numbers mean that many jails already have Islamist inmate gangs, who provide security and solidarity to new prisoners and a co-ordinated response, up to riot and mutiny, when one of them is confronted by a prison officer. Many of them are bitter and disillusioned, prey for Islamist recruiters operating either among fellow inmates or as social workers and chaplains. Poorly educated, these men are like empty vessels for jihadist recruiters who can peddle them any version of Islam they wish provided it is implacable enough and promises personal redemption through focusing their aggression on the host society. As Irfan Chishti, an imam who leads prayers at Buckley Hall Prison in Rochdale, has commented: 'You've got someone preaching to an empty shell, someone who has been told Islam is the answer to all their problems, the void can be filled.' With their instrumental view of human beings, Islamist recruiters are infinitely understanding rather than condemnatory, focusing a delinquent's violence on a higher cause. The objects include men like Domenico Quaranta or Ruddy Terranova, street toughs respectively from Sicily and Marseilles, who both converted to Islam while in jail. They even acquired a newfound humility and serenity to conceal the violence raging beneath. Both of these men became active jihadist terrorists.[78]

Richard Reid, the hulking son of a Jamaican father and a white English mother, was typical. His father was so frequently in jail that his wife divorced him. Their son Richard rapidly went astray, as an easily led add-on to south-east London's juvenile gangland. He was the one who was always caught. A stint in a young offenders' institution led to a three-year jail sentence after he was convicted of fifty burglaries. During this time the nominal Christian Reid discovered Islam, pursuing this interest on his release in 1996 at Brixton's Mosque and Islamic Cultural Centre. From there he gravitated into the much more charged scene around Abu Hamza, as externally manifest in his acquired habit of wearing a camouflage combat jacket over flowing white Arab robes. He found a new idol to worship in the bulky form of Zacarias Moussaoui, a French Moroccan who had washed up in Brixton in 1986. As a graduate of business studies at South Bank University, Moussaoui was better educated and more intelligent than the gormless Reid, although he was considerably more volatile. In 1998 Reid moved into the Finsbury Park mosque, where he was talent-spotted by an Al Qaeda recruiter, the Algerian Djamel Beghal. A period of training in Afghanistan followed. Back in Britain by the summer of 2001, Reid went to Brussels where his first act was to put his passport through a washing machine. That got him a new one, without the visa stamps he had acquired en route to Afghanistan. Equipped with a blank passport, he flew to Israel, noting the security levels on the El Al flight, and carried out reconnaissance of various targets in Tel Aviv, Haifa and Jerusalem. His tradecraft was good, including taking empty alcohol bottles back to his hotel to leave around the room, in case Shin Beth poked around. He went via Egypt and Turkey to Pakistan, before returning to Britain to undertake the ill-fated operation involving his shoes that would land him in the Colorado Supermax for life.

Of course, it is wrong to imagine that all jihadi-salafists come from deprived or troubled backgrounds. Ahmed Omar Saeed Sheikh, who is currently on death row in Islamabad for his involvement in hacking the head off *Wall Street Journal* correspondent Daniel Pearl, was not one of life's dispossessed, but a spoiled child. His father ran a successful clothing business, which enabled him to send Ahmed Omar to a minor Essex public school, where he drank too much and vandalised cars. He had his first flirtations with radical Islam when his parents took him back to Pakistan to straighten him out in Lahore. Back at Forest School by the time he was sixteen, he had evolved into a bullying fantasist, touring local pubs as an arm wrestler. He got decent enough A Level grades to get into the London School of Economics to read maths and statistics, but didn't leave much of an impression amid the Eurotrash and Americans doing 'Let's See Europe'. In 1993 he joined an Islamist Convoy of Mercy to Bosnia, but turned back ill at Croatia. After weapons training at an Al Qaeda camp in Afghanistan, he was despatched to India to lure Western backpackers into the hands of Kashmiri terrorists. During such an episode, he terrified hostages by alternately talking cricket and showing how he would cut their throat. He was eventually shot by Indian police and given five years in prison. When Kashmiri terrorists hijacked an Indian jet, Ahmed Omar was one of those released in exchange for the passengers. He went via Afghanistan to Pakistan, while the British government – whose citizens he had recently kidnapped – forswore opportunities to prosecute him. The latest twist is instructive. Al Qaeda puts a premium on well-educated middle-class professional operatives because they live otherwise model lives, and can move around with relative impunity under the cover of doing good, especially if they are doctors employed with minimal vetting by the British NHS.[79]

While German police thwarted the Frankfurt cell, they could not criminalise or investigate every single grouping of dedicated Islamists. During 1998 a tight circle of Islamist friends had congregated in a flat they rented in Hamburg. The group eventually included the dozen men who passed through in the course of the next two years. As far as one can see, they had no grouses against Germany, which had bent over backwards to accommodate them. The key members were the Yemeni Ramzi bin al-Shibh, an Egyptian urban-planning student, Mohamed Mohamed el-Amir Awad el-Sayed Atta, a Lebanese applied-sciences student, Ziad Jarrah, and Marwan al-Shehi, an Emirates soldier taking time out to study marine engineering once he had mastered German. With the exception of Marwan, whose father was a village muezzin, all of these men came from relatively prosperous backgrounds, from which they had been sent to Europe to do well in their designated careers. They spoke European languages, in Atta's case English and German, and they knew how to act and dress Europeanised. Of the group, Atta was the most grimly resolute, while Shibh had the organisational talent.

This group had come to the peripheral attention of German police when they commenced surveillance on Mohammed Haydar Zamar, a loud-mouthed unemployed auto mechanic, and a Syrian businessman, after they had been contacted by an Iraqi jihadist the US had identified as a senior Al Qaeda agent. One reason given for not taking a closer look at the younger men, apart from limitations of police manpower, was that their espousal of an intense Islam was so open; they successfully petitioned Hamburg's Technical university, where Atta was writing a thesis about the architecture of medieval Aleppo, for a prayer room. Much of the group's time was spent praying, listening to taped sermons by Abu Qatada, or watching horror documentaries from Bosnia and Chechnya. The 9/11 Commission Report says that a series of chance encounters, including one with a stranger on a train, led them to wage jihad in Afghanistan rather than Chechnya. A few gaps in our knowledge of Atta's earlier movements make this seem improbable. In late 1999 four of the cell members flew to Pakistan, for the long bus journey to a Taliban office at Quetta, the final staging post en route to bin Laden's Afghan training camps. There they met his operational chief, Mohammed Atef, while Atta, the designated group leader, spent time alone with the sheikh himself.[80]

In January and February 2000 they returned to Germany, equipping themselves with new passports along the way, so as to lose the Pakistani visas. They needed US visas for the flight-training programmes they planned to join as ordered by bin Laden and Atef. Atta, Jarrah and Shehi got theirs without a hitch; as a Yemeni putative economic migrant, Shibh was turned down. Their US$120,000 expenses were wired regularly from the United Arab Emirates by Ali Abdul Aziz Ali, a nephew of Khalid Sheikh Mohammed, with Shibh making up any shortfall from the men's own German bank accounts over which he had powers of attorney. After flying to the US, the three enrolled at two Florida flight schools. Assiduous students, they mastered light aircraft and rented time on simulators for large commercial jets. Across the country in San Diego, two Saudi men, who could scarcely speak English, attempted to enrol at other flight schools. Although both men had been known as terrorist suspects by the CIA, which had monitored their movements in Malaysia, the preferred route to the States, this information had never been passed on to the consular authorities who granted them visas. After frantic attempts to get a visa, Shibh gave up, but not before visiting London where he recruited Zacarias Moussaoui, who, already enrolled at a flight school in Norman, Oklahoma, went first to be appraised by Khalid Sheikh Mohammed, the mastermind of this operation. By the time he reached Pakistan, Khalid Sheikh had identified Hani Hanjour, a Saudi living in the US, who already had a commercial pilot's licence. Shibh's role thenceforth would be as the key fixer, an old friend of the Hamburg cell members now in the US, and, as a Yemeni, someone bin Laden would trust, as he urged Khalid Sheikh to set the plot in motion. Another key element was the thirteen men, all but one a Saudi, who arrived in the US in the spring of 2001. These were the muscle-men who would commandeer aircraft to enable the suicide hijackers briefly to fly them. They left videotaped statements in Afghanistan:

> I am writing this with my full conscience and I am writing this in expectation of the end, which is near. An end that is really a beginning. We will get you. We will humiliate you. We will never stop following you ... May God reward all those who trained me on this path and was behind this noble act and a special mention should be made of the Mujahid leader sheikh Osama bin Laden, may God protect him. May God accept our deeds.

While the muscle-men waited in motels, making extensive use of local gyms, the suicide pilots embarked on non-stop transcontinental travel to explore airport security systems and the routines on commercial jets. They usually travelled first class so as to take a close look at cockpit security, noticing that the door was often open during the ten minutes after takeoff. Many of them acquired Virginia driving licences, which were easy to acquire and would make identifying themselves easier than having to use foreign passports. In July Atta flew alone to Madrid where he spent a week with Shibh, settling the final details of their enterprise. Shibh had obtained two satellite phones, one of which he used to keep in touch with his masters in Afghanistan. On 13 August the suspicious behaviour of Moussaoui at his Oklahoma flight school led to his arrest on immigration-violation charges by the FBI. Although an agent noted down that he was crazy enough to fly a plane into the World Trade Center, no one thought to get permission to search the hard drive of his laptop. In mid-August Atta used an internet chatroom to send Shibh a message: 'The first semester commences in three weeks. There are no changes. All is well.' The internet facilitated Al Qaeda communications, while enabling them to operate various websites such as As Saba, or 'The Clouds'. Messages could be exchanged through chatrooms, or buried within sites dedicated to such things as pornography, the last place anyone might look. Stanographic software programs enabled them to leave messages concealed within innocuous images. By sharing a common password, it was also possible to access messages left in the draft box of a computer, which technically, therefore, were read but never sent, thereby preventing the NSA from intercepting them. Intelligence of Atta's readiness was relayed by Shibh to Khalid Sheikh Mohammed. The attack was coming on 11 September 2001. Atta, Khalid Sheikh and bin Laden had determined on four targets: the twin towers of the World Trade Center, the Pentagon and the US Capitol, ruling out the White House on the grounds of difficulty and the potential absence of its occupant. At Congress it would be full house.

The hijackers' last night alive was well prepared so as to pre-empt doubt, nerves and fear. A fifteen-point list contained military-style instructions about knowing the plan backwards, marshalling the necessary kit and inspecting weapons. They were to don tight-fitting socks and to tie their shoelaces tight, little tasks that concentrated the mind. The shaving of all body hair and dousing with perfume was more ritualistic. They were enjoined to be oblivious to the world: 'For the time for playing has passed, and the time has arrived for the rendezvous with the eternal Truth.' The moment of death would take seconds, before they embarked on the 'gladness' of their wedding and their eternal life with the martyrs and prophets. For this was truly a group death cult. The hijackers were enjoined to recite the words of God: 'You were wishing for death before you encountered it, then you saw it, and are looking for it. And you wanted it.' In Afghanistan, Osama bin Laden and his comrades experienced vivid dreams, bin Laden's consisting of an America reduced to ashes. That he slept at all was partly due to the fact that on 9 September two of his men, posing as Arab television journalists, had assassinated Ahmed Shah Massoud, the leader of the Afghan Northern Alliance, and the first person the US would turn to when George W. Bush sought just vengeance, as he undoubtedly would, for what was forty-eight hours away. The assassination also pacified mullah Omar, who in animated discussions had been keener to direct major operations against the Jews than against the USA.

The twin towers of the World Trade Center were built to sway, like tall poplars in a heavy wind. This is what they initially did, as Atta, murmuring prayers, slammed American Airlines Flight 11 into the north tower, destroying floors 93–99, while Shehi directed United Airlines Flight 175 into the south tower. They were not built to withstand the temperatures of 1,300 degrees Centigrade that erupted when ten thousand gallons of aviation fuel from each plane's heavily laden tanks exploded. The fires collapsed floors and burned through ceilings, melting all that the flames found, while giving out dense black smoke. Trapped inside on the higher floors were, among others, traders from Cantor Fitzgerald and caterers from the Windows on the World restaurant, all starting another day at work on a clear sunny morning. With emergency exists and elevators blocked or incapacitated, terrified people had the non-choice of either burning and choking to death or throwing themselves from broken windows. Fifty to two hundred people made that latter decision, a sight that is so connected to our subconscious terrors that photographic images were quickly taken out of circulation, replaced by epic vistas of the towers burning. Then the towers collapsed, concertinaing hundreds of floors into a seven-storey hill of wreckage as dense clouds of dust billowed down Manhattan streets. Firemen, policemen and priests were among those who died in heroic rescue attempts. A total of 2,792 people perished in a terrorist strike, which included the Pentagon as well as United Airlines Flight 93 which ploughed into a field in Pennsylvania, so major that it resembled an act of war. It had lasted 102 minutes from initial impact to the towers' collapse. George W. Bush was given news of the attacks as he listened to children reading at a Florida primary school, before he was whisked away by the Secret Service to a secure base in Nebraska. The attack spelled the end of his campaign promise to restrict the liberal humanitarian interventionism of his predecessor in favour of a more modest foreign policy. In the White House Presidential Emergency Operation Center, vice-president Dick Cheney watched CNN as the south tower collapsed, his fingers locked under his chin. The room groaned. Cheney closed his eyes after watching the crucial moment, his mind turning to the bureaucratic mechanisms that would wreak destruction on whomever was responsible for this.[81]

VIII AFTERMATHS IN AN AGE OF ANXIETY

While for leading advocates of globalisation, the world out there had become a terrifying other, in their remote Afghan bases the perpetrators paradoxically took a more global view of what they had done. In Afghanistan, bin Laden and his comrades heard news of these attacks over the BBC's Arabic Service. Bin Laden counted off the falling targets on his fingers. Immediately after the attacks he recorded a discussion involving himself, al-Zawahiri and the visiting Saudi militant Khaled al-Harbi, whose mother reported that she had been taking congratulatory calls all day. This tape was released to the press in December. Bin Laden said:

> The sermons they [the 9/11 hijackers] gave in New York and Washington, made the whole world hear – the Arabs, the non-Arabs, the Indians, the Chinese – and are worth much more than millions of books and cassettes and pamphlets [promoting Islam]. Maybe you have heard, but I heard it myself on the radio, that at one of the Islamic centres in Holland, the number of those who have converted to Islam after the strikes, in the first few days after the attacks, is greater than all those who converted in the last eleven years.

'Glory be to God,' added his colleagues exultantly. Bin Laden claimed that he and his planners had expected only the passengers in the planes and people immediately where they crashed to die. But he added, 'I was the most optimistic. Due to the nature of my profession and work in construction, I figured the fuel in the plane would raise the temperature of the steel to the point that it becomes red and almost loses its properties. So if the plane hits the building here [gestures with his hands], the portion of the building above will collapse. That was the most we expected; that the floors above the point of entry would fall.'[82] In his Karachi hidey-hole Khalid Sheikh Mohammed had set up multiple VCRs to tape his handiwork. He was a little disappointed until the towers collapsed. As the US authorities began to estimate the damage, insurance and reconstruction costs, and loss of airline revenue caused by 9/11, in the billions, bin Laden repeatedly emphasised that the entire operation had cost Al Qaeda US$500,000. He may have spoken of the collapsed towers in terms of the smashing of the ancient Meccan moon idol Hudal, but this did not preclude thinking about it in very material modern terms. By 29 September, when an interview found its way into a Pakistani newspaper, bin Laden was cheekily suggesting that the US should look for the culprits among dissidents in 'the US system' or among other systems: 'They can be anyone, from Russia to Israel, and from India to Serbia.' Following the logic of Oliver Stone and The X-Files, he suggested the CIA might have criminalised 'Osama and the Taliban' to secure their funding stream after the end of the Cold War. There was a secret government within a government within the US which knew the truth of the attacks.

Material damage, increased conversion and CIA plots joined the anticipatory assassination of Massoud in bin Laden's estimation of the effects of 9/11. However, he was only one player in the battle that emerged, operating in an environment that his many enemies would shape thereafter. After a remarkably restrained lull, which surprised even close allies, the US government response was to secure the necessary powers to wage what was rapidly, and unsatisfactorily, described as 'the war on terror'. This was meaningless as one cannot declare war on a tactic. The Red Army declared war not on Blitzkrieg but on Hitler's Germany. Had the word been used in the sense of a war on drugs or organised crime – that is, so as to mobilise all resources to minimise these anti-social activities – then that would have been fine. But it was not used like that at all. The word war was used because the mood called for exemplary displays of military might, even though the best way to fight terrorists is through intelligence, undercover operations, informers, propaganda initiatives and so forth, which do not yield instant victories and which are fought beyond the omnipresent eyes and voracious appetites of a media hungry to consume big events.[83] Congress and the Senate authorised Bush 'to use all necessary and appropriate force against those nations, organisations, or persons he determines planned, authorized, committed, or aided the terrorist attacks that occurred on September 11 2001, or harboured such organisations or persons, in order to prevent any future acts of international terrorism against the United States by such nations, organisations or persons'. A request to include the United States itself within this sweeping mandate was removed before the motion passed, 98 to 0 in the Senate and 420 to 1 in the House of Representatives. At the time, Washington took no cognisance of the fact that its European NATO allies regarded terrorism as a crime, rather than an act of war amenable to military solutions. Use of the word war inadvertently lifted groups of criminals on to another moral plane where civilised societies also have rules.[84]

Policy was decided in an atmosphere in which 'flies walking on eye-balls' guys like CIA head of counter-terrorism Cofer Black spoke darkly of sticking terrorists' heads on poles or bringing them back in refriger-ator boxes. When a skull thought to be that of Ayman al-Zawahiri was offered to US military intelligence by Afghans hoping to claim the huge reward, the CIA sought to identify it through a DNA match on a brother in custody in Cairo. Egyptian intelligence offered to 'cut off his arm and send it over'. The CIA settled for a blood sample.

Mainstream CIA spooks were unsettled by this, and by the wholesale recourse to freelance paramilitary contractors, many of whom might otherwise have been robbing banks had it not been for 9/11.[85] The mores of a Wild West movie prevailed as charts appeared with photos and matching biographies of the major culprits who could be crossed out when they were caught or killed. The Texan president talked like a little sheriff about bringing in 'evildoers' dead or alive, terms which sat ill with the military operations he was undertaking. Such talk excited the media, which ignored the duller stuff of orientating vast rival bureaucracies for the war on terror. The CIA and NSA were belatedly forced into reorientating their main activities from a non-existent Soviet threat, so as to focus on myriad shadowy groups capable of mounting international terrorist operations. The CIA's many critics warned that the burgeoning intelligence services attached to the Defense Department might do its job for it, or that the whole field might be contracted out to the private sector. The FBI, with its woeful lack of Arabic speakers – about eight at the time – was told to sharpen up its act and to co-operate with the CIA, a shotgun marriage eventually arranged by the appointment of a coordinator of national intelligence reporting directly to the president.

Having located the source of the attacks, the plan was to step up the

CIA field presence in Afghanistan, in order to combine armed opponents of the Taliban with incoming special-forces soldiers, who would smash the regime (and Al Qaeda) with the aid of US airpower coming in from Diego Garcia or direct from Missouri. CIA agents hurried around Afghanistan with aluminium suitcases and holdalls crammed with millions of dollars to bribe Afghan warlords to fight the Taliban. All this conformed with Donald Rumsfeld's doctrine of using US ground forces lightly, chiefly to guide in precision airpower.

Within weeks of 9/11 Bush became the first US president to acknowledge the desirability of a two-state solution in Israel–Palestine, in an attempt to cauterise the issue that so antagonises the Muslim world. He then spent six years doing nothing about it. But there was another opportunity that was taken. Despite weak evidence that Al Qaeda had any connection with Saddam Hussein, a belligerently abrasive clique, including former Trotskyites turned 'neo-conservatives', who are wearying to listen to, were bent on fusing their long-standing campaign to rid the world of his presence, preparatory to redesigning the entire Middle East around a democratised Iraq. That chimed with grudges lurking within the Bush family, involving the unfinished business of the first Gulf War and Saddam's attempt to kill Bush's father, and a desire, partly born of 9/11, to downgrade the untrustworthy Saudis. The Afghan plan was implemented with extraordinary success, with Al Qaeda's military supremo, Mohammed Atef, an early casualty of an armed Predator drone which killed him on 16 November in a Gardez hotel. His effects included evidence of a Jemaah Islamiyah reconnaissance operation on US interests, and the city subway system, in Singapore.

By that time, US and Afghan forces had killed or captured about 250 Al Qaeda fighters, while its top leadership and eight hundred fighters had fled into the inhospitable terrain of Tora Bora. The US launched a ferocious air assault on this fifteen-square-mile area, including fuel-air bombs so large that they had to be heaved off the back of a transport plane, before devastating an area six hundred yards square in a combustible mist of ammonium nitrate and aluminium whose shockwaves liquefied the internal organs of men hiding in caves. A massive device called Blu-82 was the size of a car and consisted of fifteen thousand pounds of explosives. That was dropped too, before three B-52s cruised overhead, unleashing forty five-hundred-pound bombs on the same target. Northern Alliance fighters watched in awe as their bearded, horse-riding US shadows with names like Dave or Chuck pointed laser beams at Taliban and Al Qaeda positions which were triangulated with smart bombs and missiles. The last direct communications from bin Laden were the orders he barked into the group's short-wave radios, some of which were lifted from Al Qaeda corpses by an Arab-American agent; those who survived the bombing slipped out through a back door that was supposed to have been closed by the Afghans and a force of Army Rangers who were never despatched. Bin Laden is presumably holed up with teams of fanatical bodyguards in one of two ungovernable tribal territories in Pakistan. The hunt for him was fatally disabled when the expert trackers of Task Force 121 were taken off the case and relocated to Iraq to find Saddam and his offspring.[86]

Domestically, the US applied the tactics used in the 1930s to imprison Al Capone, who on learning that he was being prosecuted for tax evasion, blurted out: 'The government can't collect legal taxes from illegal money.' Terrorists of various stripes rely for money not just on Islamist pseudo-charities but on organised crime. A chemical called pseudoephedrine that is used to make anti-allergy or cold medicines is purchased in Canada, shipped to California, and then sold to Mexican drug gangs since it is one of the key ingredients of illicit metamphetamines. As the PIRA discovered, cigarette smuggling can also yield profits of US$2 million a truckload. Cigarettes are purchased in states like Virginia where the tax is 2.5 cents per pack and then resold in New York City for less than the legal price plus the local tax of US$1.50 per pack. A carton of ten packs bought for US$20 doubles in value through this process. Another major means of raising revenue is intellectual property theft, through knockout handbags, T-shirts, trainers, Prozac and Viagra. Viagra is always in demand and pills can be moved around in quantity with low risk attached. In addition to these crimes, which carry heavy penalties, US law enforcement agencies have been active since 9/11 in prosecuting instances of immigration fraud and visa violations, notably those practised by so-called students. This has been in marked contrast to Britain where cash-strapped universities solicit fee-paying customers without making much of an effort to establish their bona fides, and where deportation of bogus and failed asylum seekers is non-existent.[87]

The Al Qaeda and Taliban prisoners represented another problem that the US would contrive to turn into a PR disaster, aided and abetted by fervent human rights lawyers who, while prepared to believe the detainees innocent of every charge of abuse, reflexively believe the worst of the US military and CIA. The phenomenon of activist lawyers aiding and abetting terrorist clients is also not unknown, as we repeatedly saw in the cases of the Red Brigades and RAF in Europe. In Britain, certain legal firms simply migrated from defending IRA Provos to representing Islamist jihadists in their grim determination to thwart the police, knowing that the country's liberal elites – the national characters who appear on BBC *Question Time* or *Any Questions* decade in, decade out – would never dare challenge their usurpation of the civil-liberties high ground. Apart from the dizzying legal aid monies these firms rack up, there is also the under-explored historical fact of lawyers colluding with terrorist clients.

US policy towards terrorist detainees has led to unease among European allies who have likewise zealously occupied the moral high ground, partly because their domestic legal systems had more experience of dealing with terrorists, including – in Roman law systems – far wider powers of search and of investigative and preventative detention, and less restrictive rules of evidence. In these areas the Europeans were not 'surrender-monkeys'. The French police do not need judicial warrants to search someone's home, and the Italians seem to be able to put electronic devices where they like. The French and Italians can detain a suspect for years before he comes to trial as magistrates assemble their case. The Germans can detain prisoners after they have served their allotted sentence, on grounds of public safety. Common law systems, like those of Britain and the US, invariably bend over backwards to guarantee the rights of suspects, ruling out of court great swathes of evidence that in Roman law systems are part of detailed dossiers compiled by investigative magistrates. Rather than fundamentally rewriting the US legal system to make it conform with relatively illiberal arrangements in Europe, both the Clinton and Bush administrations relied on the laws of war. Treating international jihadists as criminals, to be arrested and brought before courts, was not much of an option, given the sanctuary such people enjoyed from the Sudan or the Taliban, who would have to be charged with aiding and abetting terrorists too. Sending in US marshals was a fantasy in these circumstances. The laws of war enabled the US to kill such people, as Clinton tried to do in 1998.[88]

Efforts to keep detainees out of the hands of lawyers who would, doubtless, have become celebrities during any civilian trial led to a PR disaster. Instead of following secretary of state Colin Powell's advice to be seen to follow the rules of the Geneva Convention governing prisoners of war, so as gradually to winnow out un-uniformed enemy combatants, Cheney and his legal advisers resolved to treat them as 'unlawful combatants' without rights under the Convention. This rightlessness could be best guaranteed by keeping these men offshore, at a US base at Guantánamo Bay on Cuba, or in a network of CIA-run centres that was set to expand, with the connivance of the governments of Britain (Diego Garcia), Poland and Romania. Not a new gulag, as the international left preposterously claimed, in its typical ignorance of socialism's grim record, but little pools of extra-legal darkness nonetheless. Then there was the matter of interrogation methods. The high-value target Ibn al-Sheikh al-Libi, for example, was delivered into the hands of the Egyptians. On the Bagram tarmac, a CIA case officer charmingly explained: 'You're going to Cairo, you know. Before you get there, I'm going to find your mother and fuck her.' Renditions to Morocco are said to include encounters between penises and razor blades. The CIA was also pondering what to do with those captives it planned to interrogate itself. They needed precise definition of what was legal. This was not so much a matter of bloodlust as a concern not to fall foul of the US's own legalistic culture, where writs come back to haunt people and modest pensions can be devoured by legal fees.

Cheney's legal team endeavoured to unpick the Geneva Convention's elision of torture with cruel, inhuman and degrading methods of interrogation. While agonising tortures like electric shocks or pulling out fingernails were ruled out of bounds, those that rely on extreme physical or psychological discomfort – shackling, darkness, noise and so on – or, like simulated drowning, that trigger extreme panic, were ruled in. None of the latter leaves any physical trace either. Also legalised were threats to hand the suspect over to countries like Egypt or Morocco where torture is something of a fine art. In fairness, these efforts to 'come off Geneva' were vigorously contested by the Justice and State Departments, while the CIA and the military were extremely anxious to ensure that what they did had precise legal cover. The US Supreme Court is still contesting vital aspects of extraterritorial military jurisdiction in actions brought by the detainees' own military counsel. Ironically, accounts by US military interrogators (mostly civilian reservists) make it abundantly clear that psychological methods of interrogation are more effective than torture is ever likely to be, and never involve the ticking-time-bomb scenario envisioned by torture's academic apologists. The chief advocate, from within the government, where he was deputy assistant attorney-general, was John Woo of Berkeley, while Alan Dershowitz of Harvard, perhaps best known for the acquittal of Claus von Bulow, was keen on judges issuing 'torture warrants'.[89]

The US coalition defeat of the Taliban, whose leader mullah Omar was last seen speeding off on a motorbike, was accompanied by a stealthier war against minor terrorist groups whose absurd gangster names – such as Commander Robot – would not have inclined the US to take them seriously six months earlier. Kidnappings and money from media interviews were the terrorists' main sources of income; after they had got as much as US$10,000 per interview, they logically decided to kidnap the reporters for larger ransoms. In May 2001 Abu Sayyaf terrorists based on the Philippines island of Basilan used high-powered speedboats to raid the island of Palawan (three hundred miles away) so as to kidnap Western tourist divers. This would bring big ransom money and destroy the tourist trade. Instead, they captured three Americans, a middle-aged man living with a Filipina girl, and Martin and Gracia Burnham, a pair of Christian missionaries. The kidnappers also took the Filipino chefs and servants. The group's leader, Aldam Tilao, was built like a brown pit-bull, with a black hip-hop dorag on his head and wraparound sunglasses. He fancied himself as a bit of a DJ whenever he managed to commandeer a local radio station. A long bolo knife and an earring completed the piratical image, although this pirate sang Beatles songs as he sped away with his captives. These men were rapists and murderers who adopted Islamism as an ancillary pose. On their trek into the jungle interior, they grabbed more hostages from a coconut farm, hacking the heads off two men who annoyed them, a fateful decision as it turned out, because one of the victims was the uncle of a tennis coach who boasted that he was Tilao's oldest friend. The US sex tourist also got on their nerves, partly because he stood in the way of the terrorists and his pretty Filipina girlfriend. He was soon led into the dense foliage where his head was cut off too. Along the route to their hideout, a further ten people were decapitated, their heads left every few yards. The survivors included children of ten, six and three, although the three-year-old turned four in the course of this ordeal.

What before 9/11 might have elicited nothing more than diplomatic expressions of concern now attracted the full attention of the CIA when president Gloria Arroyo asked George W. Bush for help in freeing the hostages. The FBI tried paying US$300,000 ransom, but this was absorbed by the Filipino police. Rather than sending in the Marines, the

CIA quietly set up shop in a container parked on a naval base, bringing in tracking devices and spotter aircraft made available from Afghanistan. The tactics adopted minimised a heavy US presence. They would work through the local Marines, including colonel Juancho Sabban and captain Gieram Aragones, a Muslim convert whose hatred of the jihadists' perversion of his religion made him vow not to shave or cut his hair until Tilao was dead. They and the CIA realised that the kidnappers' weak point was when they used couriers to pick up supplies in towns and villages. They recruited Tilao's oldest friend, while playing on the hip-hopper terrorist's vanity. As a test of his friend's reliability, he was instructed to take a local TV reporter, who had interviewed the terrorists before, on a two-day trip into the jungle, which would also establish the group's rough whereabouts. Having tested the connection, the CIA's Kent Clizbee complied with Tilao's request, via his friend, for a satellite phone. This would enable them to track his whereabouts every time he used it. They also made the friend the sole source of supply, by arranging disabling accidents, like a couple of broken legs, for other known couriers. One item handed over was a backpack with a hidden tracking device.

As the Marines kept the group under surveillance, the CIA prepared to deploy a Navy SEAL team to rescue the hostages. That was pre-empted after the Filipino army decided to blunder in, when on 7 June 2002 they stormed Tilao's camp, killing Martin Burnham and a Filipina nurse the group had also abducted. They freed Burnham's wife Gracia, although she was shot in the leg too. With incredible stupidity, Tilao resolved to flee the island on the same high-powered boat he had used to reach it. The Marines turned the two-man crew and hid tracking devices aboard it. When Tilao and his men cautiously left the jungle for the darkened beach, they had no idea that two CIA spotter planes were circling overhead, while four Marine and SEAL teams cruised offshore. The CIA watched black and white images on computer consoles in their container. When the terrorists' boat was far enough out for no one to swim back alive in shark-infested waters, it was suddenly crushed by a heavier Marine craft, hurling the terrorists over the side. Shooting while treading water is not smart since muzzle flashes reveal positions. Tilao did that and was ripped in half by a Rumpelstiltskin-like Aragones who emptied the magazine of an assault rifle into him. Aragones called Clizbee: 'We just killed the motherfucker.' Abu Sayyaf ceased to be anything more than a local nuisance in the southern Philippines.[90]

The first priority for Al Qaeda's leaders was their physical survival and the speedy resumption of operations through networks they had cultivated already. They did obvious things like ceasing to use satellite phones, and constructing camouflaged hides with multiple exits to avoid being crushed and buried alive by bombing. One major setback, in March 2002, was a joint Pakistani–US raid on an apartment building in Faisalabad which netted twelve Al Qaeda suspects, including Abu Zubaydah, the successor of Mohammed Atef. Zubaydah had planned innumerable terrorist attacks and was rebuilding Al Qaeda from the hundreds of men he had recruited. Information gleaned from him, with the use of extreme measures, led to the arrests of Ramzi bin al-Shibh in Karachi and Khalid Sheikh Mohammed in Rawalpindi in September 2002 and March 2003. The US had the key players behind 9/11, although this is often overlooked because of the escape of bin Laden. The arrest of Zubaydah seems to have prompted Abd al-Halim Adl to write to 'Brother Muktar', believed to be Khalid Sheikh Mohammed, complaining that bin Laden was not listening to sound advice, and rushing into ill-considered operations that were making Al Qaeda 'a laughing stock' of the world's intelligence agencies.[91]

All terrorist groups have to adapt to their environment if they are to survive; if they do not they will have the limited life-cycle of nineteenth-century anarchists or nihilists. On the run, Al Qaeda proper decided to use Al Qaeda Plus – that is, the couple of dozen affiliated groups which Al Qaeda armed, financed, trained or influenced through its leaders.[92] Al Qaeda proper would thenceforth be a form of incitement, as well as an example, method or rule that others followed without being directly part of the organisation. Widely perceived as a clever evolutionary move, it in fact reflected a concern with security that overrode the drawbacks of such a strategy.[93]

This networked terrorism is not new, any more than Osama bin Laden is unique as a financial sponsor of international terrorism, a role once performed in Europe by millionaire publisher Giangiacomo Feltrinelli. The PLO was an umbrella organisation for dozens of armed groups. The German RAF had no military-style hierarchy befitting an 'army', and it had extensive contacts with the Red Brigades, ETA, IRA and the Palestinians. Loosely affiliated networks, especially if they consist of ad-hoc amateur groups devoted to a similar objective as the parent firm, have several strengths. Lacking a hierarchy, or state sponsorship, they cannot be decapitated or stopped by regime change. If communication with Al Qaeda merely consists of subscribing to its ideology, and allowing it to claim responsibility for one of the networked groups' atrocities, then they are not regular or sustained enough to represent a weak point that intelligence agencies can exploit.[94] The drawbacks of networked terrorism are multiple, paradoxically jeopardising the very security they are supposed to ensure by the abandonment of hierarchy. It provides opportunities to disaggregate the groups through their own internal dynamics since it is notoriously difficult to plant agents inside.

From Al Qaeda's perspective, there are no means of controlling the operational choices or levels of violence used by remote groups not subject to the discipline of a hierarchical organisation. Indeed, they may be far more violent than the franchising group, whether in terms of launching indiscriminate attacks or killing anyone sent to restrain them. UVF terrorists in Northern Ireland complained that an admiral in the Royal Navy does not have to fear being shot by a renegade rating if the latter decides to sell drugs. Technical information on bomb making has to come from sources like the internet, which leaves plenty of scope for security agencies to fake sites filled with misinformation. This forces groups to contact the parent franchise more frequently, increasing the likelihood that these contacts will be monitored. If it is the case that, for reasons of paranoia, terrorists recruit from kin groups, then pressure on the wider kin will create the perception that this source of recruits is insecure too, and it will be if commitment to terrorism clashes with wider social obligations.

Finance is a further vulnerability. In the absence of centralised funding, and the sort of regular accounting Al Qaeda is known to practise, money has to be raised through crime. This presents opportunities for embezzlement, or the temptation to become full-time drug traffickers, extortionists and armed robbers, presenting many opportunities to be caught. Money derived from crime also has to be laundered, which routinely diminishes the proceeds to a considerable extent as each person in the laundering chain takes a cut. Even the legal *hawala* system, for moving money without wire transfers, intermediary correspondents or cash, usually involves deliberate under-invoicing or the disregarding of reporting requirements, which is a criminal offence in most jurisdictions. For these reasons, it may be advantageous for governments not to advertise attacks on terrorist funding, so as to spread suspicions of fraud throughout the ranks. The people who are engaged in relatively low-risk terrorist financing are widely disliked by those who take the major risks of active operations, especially if there seems to be some ethnic dimension to who does what within an organisation like Al Qaeda. The huge differences in the sentences passed by courts for the two types of activity are beneficial since they help fracture terrorist organisations through different degrees of perceived risk. That is also why Guantánamo Bay is misconceived, on pragmatic rather than moral grounds, since an indeterminate limbo land does not provide the calibrated incentives needed to turn terrorists into betraying their former comrades, in marked contrast to what the Indonesian and Saudi Arabian authorities have achieved by confounding the widespread expectation that arrested terrorists will be routinely tortured.[95]

When Al Qaeda struck back, it was through surrogates who quite independently had sometimes already extended their local operations to attacks on generic Western targets in conformity with global jihadist objectives. This was the case in Indonesia. Between 1999 and 2001 parts of Indonesia had been afflicted by savage violence that began (on Java) with the killing of 160 alleged sorcerers and witches, and spread into vicious sectarian pogroms in which Protestant Christians were just as liable to be the aggressors as Muslims, who were often the victims. The immediate trigger for these attacks, which involved youth gangs sporting white or red headbands to indicate whether they were Muslim or Protestant, which in turn were backed by adult criminals and elements of the security forces, was the country's first free elections held in 1999. Beginning with axes, hammers, iron bars and knives, the weaponry used escalated to firearms. In certain areas the elections threatened to upset the delicate equilibrium with which an authoritarian state had distributed power and patronage between clients from each faith. Worse, the Muslim leaders who came to power (moderate Islamist parties having lost the election to the ecumenical and secularist party of Megawati Soekarnoputri by a margin of 34 to 20 per cent) bent over backwards to accommodate moderate Muslims and non-Muslims by eschewing an Islamic agenda. Democracy spelled defeat for the Islamists. Some of them did not like it.

Although the government got a purchase on this mindless sectarian violence, to the satisfaction of Christian rioters, on the Muslim side the pogroms provided the nationwide recruits for jihadist groups who were formed from the remnants of sectarian gangs and paramilitaries. From 2000 onwards they embarked on a campaign of bombing Christian churches. On Christmas Eve 2000 some forty churches were bombed, leaving nineteen dead and a hundred wounded. The perpetrators were from Laskar-Jihad, the locally focused terrorist group whose leader Ja'far Umar Thalib condemned 9/11 and bin Laden, and from Jemaah Islamiyah, whose leader Abu Bakar Ba'asyir had more expansive aims, and whose group included Filipinos, Malaysians and Thais. Although both groups included men who had fought in Afghanistan, only Jemaah Islamiyah had significant contact with Al Qaeda. As the former US ambassador to Jakarta, deputy defense secretary Paul Wolfowitz, was urging the Indonesian government to crush domestic terrorists, it was unsurprising that the latter readily took up Ayman al-Zawahiri's request to Jemaah Islamiyah to attack a soft Western target in South Asia.

In 1999 the Jemaah Islamiyah cell in Singapore had reconnoitred several targets, taking the family out for the day to camouflage the five films an engineer called Hashim bin Abbas and a printer called Mohammed Khalim bin Jaffar recorded. These had soundtracks: 'This is the bicycle bay as viewed from the footpath that leads to the MRT station [where a shuttle bus dropped off US troops]. You will notice that some of the boxes are placed on the motorcycles – these are the same type of boxes that we intend to use.'

An edited master disc was sent by Hambali to Mohammed Atef in Afghanistan who greenlighted the project. It was found intact in the debris of Atef's house, along with targeting notes that he had taken as Khalim spoke with him. The Singaporean cell had about sixty to eighty members, including women and several people with well-paid jobs. They paid an extra income tax that went to Al Qaeda and to cross-subsidising Jemaah Islamiyah in Malaysia as a whole. While Atef licensed one line of attack, Jemaah Islamiyah's leaders in Malaysia authorised the Singapore cell to attack water pipes on which the city depended and to crash a Russian airliner into Changi airport by way of avenging the Chechens. They also wanted to attack a US warship with a suicide boat at a point where a narrow channel would restrict its evasive manoeuvres. Al Qaeda had this second set of projects shelved while it pushed ahead for a spectacular.

As he put the final touches to 9/11, Khalid Sheikh Mohammed's mind turned to this new venture. The idea was to rig seven trucks with ammonium nitrate and fuel-oil bombs each weighing three tons. Khalid Sheikh Mohammed despatched Farthur Roman al-Ghozi, or 'Mike the Bomb Maker', and an Arab code-named 'Sammy', the former being the master bomber behind the Christmas campaign in Indonesia. The targets were the US and Israeli embassies, the Australian and British High Commissions, a US naval base and other American commercial interests. They used codes like 'market' (Malaysia), 'soup' (Singapore), 'book' (passport) and 'white meat' for Westerners. The targets were filmed and recorded on a video CD entitled 'Visiting Singapore Sightseeing'. As the group had four tons of ammonium nitrate in store, they only had to get a further seventeen. A friend of a friend knew a despatch clerk at a firm of chemical importers. When the friend came to buy the bomb ingredients, he was arrested. His interrogation led to the arrest of twenty-three Jemaah Islamiyah members in Singapore. The Singaporean government insisted that the dominant ethnic Chinese should not blame the Malay-Muslim minority, while explaining to the latter that they would be subject to specific security checks, on the grounds that if you are looking for a stolen Jaguar you do not stop all Mercedes. They did not bother with vacuities about hearts and minds. Lee Kuan Yew, the ever vigilant father of the nation, demanded that Singapore's neighbours co-operate in the fight against terrorism, while simultaneously criticising distortions in Western foreign policy.[96]

Thwarted in their desire to cause simultaneous havoc with seven suicide truck bombs, Al Qaeda fell back on Plan B, soft Western targets in South Asia. Meetings were held in Thailand at which Noordin Top was appointed head of logistics. Dr Azahari Husin of the Technological university of Malaysia was the bomb master, and Mukhlas, a founder of Jemaah Islamiyah, was in charge of the attack. Behind all of them was Hambali, and behind him Khalid Sheikh Mohammed who contributed US$30,000 for the attacks. An engineer and computer expert, imam Samudra, was the field commander. He had named his son Osama. Mukhlas's brother-in-law, Amrozi bin Haji Nurhasyim, bought the necessary chemicals and a car with Balinese plates, for a target had been decided on this predominantly Hindu island.[97]

The specific target was selected after it proved too difficult to hit the Dumai fuelling station or ExxonMobil storage tanks. Sheer racial hatred was the motivating force behind the attack, on the part of a group whose members had travelled from the larger groups with shared prejudice via a more exclusive persecutory bigotry to the obsessional killing rage that characterises many terrorists. This was about killing 'whitey' and nothing else, although that aspect of jihadism rarely receives much consideration. Imam Samudra recruited five young Indonesian men as suicide bombers. For three weeks he and this separate cell kept two bars on Bali's Kuta Beach under surveillance. As Samudra recalled: 'We sat in the car in front of the Sari Club. I saw lots of whiteys dancing, and lots of whiteys drinking there, that place – Kuta and especially Paddy's Bar and the Sari Club – was a meeting place for US terrorists and their allies, who the whole world knows to be monsters.' When it was subsequently pointed out that most of their victims were Australians rather than Americans, Amrozi quipped: 'Australians, Americans, whatever – they're all white people.'

They rented a white L-300 Mitsubishi van. After removing the seats they loaded it with twelve small filing cabinets, each filled with a mix of potassium chlorate, sulphur and aluminium powder. They wired this up to ninety-four detonators made from three grams of RDX plastic explosive and a booster of TNT. Not trusting in fate, there were four separate detonation systems: a mobile phone, a trigger operated by Arnasan, one of the suicide drivers, a timer in case he could not pull this switch, and a booby-trap trigger inside one of the filing cabinets which would go off if opened. At the last minute they discovered that Arnasan could not change gears or turn a car. Ali Imron, a brother of Mukhlas, had to take his place, with Arnasan and 'Jimi', a suicide bomber, alongside. Imron parked the van and left.[98]

At five past eleven at night on 12 October 2002, Jimi walked into a crowded Paddy's Pub on Legian Street. It was a popular haunt of young Australian and American tourists, some breaking their long journeys with an exotic holiday involving cheap booze and easy sex.[99] As Jimi exploded, many patrons rushed outside, where they were incinerated in a double-tap attack by a one-ton device detonated by Arnasan in the white Mitsubishi van. The effects on the 'white meat' were catastrophic, although many Balinese trinket and food sellers died too as the blast set their straw-roofed shacks alight. Two hundred and two people perished, eighty-eight of them Australians, a huge loss for a relatively under-populated country. Many victims received horrific burn injuries and had to be immersed in hotel pools. Others were flown to hospitals in Darwin and Perth. A third smaller device in a package Imron had earlier carefully dropped from a motorbike was detonated outside the US consulate in Denpasar by a mobile phone call, the detonation system representing a new level of sophistication.

Swift police work meant the arrest of the operation's immediate commander, Amrozi, who announced, 'Gosh, you guys are very clever, how did you find me?' His home had the usual bombers' paraphernalia of receipts for chemicals, training manuals and copies of speeches by Abu Bakar Ba'asyir and bin Laden. A mobile phone had the stored numbers of several of his associates, who were arrested too. Ali Imron was also arrested. At a bizarre news conference, he boasted: 'The capability of our group as one of the Indonesian nation [sic] should make people proud.' Attempts to connect Abu Bakar Ba'asyir with the bombing failed, although he was subsequently given a two-year sentence for inciting it and other terrorist outrages. He saw himself as like the salesman of sharp knives who is not responsible for how his customers use them, a peculiar view of the role of religious preacher.[100]

Hambali used US$15,000 to support the families of the imprisoned terrorists. Although he did not need this pretext, from then on Australia's prime minister John Howard, the most successful conservative leader in the world, would be a loyal ally in the 'war on terror', bringing his fellow countrymen's characteristic lack of circumlocution and tough-mindedness to the issues.[101] Azahari was killed during a siege by Indonesia's elite Detachment 88 counter-terrorism unit. He threw bombs from a house, urging the police to enter so as to join him in paradise. Colonel Petrus Reingard Golose of Detachment 88 remarked: 'he said he didn't want to die alone, but I made it clear I didn't want to join him'. Azahari was shot dead by police snipers. Noordin Top fled to fight another day. The most wanted man in South Asia continues to issue bloodcurdling threats against Australia. Imam Samudra set up a website devoted to justifying the Bali atrocity.[102]

Another soft target identified by Al Qaeda for its comeback was Europe. With Afghanistan out of bounds, predominantly Algerian European-based terrorists were despatched via Georgia to camps in Chechnya's Pankisi Gorge for their training. Much of their training involved the use of chemical weapons, the instructor being a one-legged Palestinian jihadist called Abu Atiya. About twenty of these men returned to Europe in the autumn of 2002, entering through Spain. The French DST and two smart magistrates, Ricard and Brugière, encouraged by interior minister Nicolas Sarkozy, were on the case, organising raids on several suburban Parisian apartments, which yielded high-grade arrests and a haul of cyanide, methylene blue (an antidote to cyanide), laboratory equipment and protective suits. Their likely target was the Russian embassy in Paris, as an act of revenge for Russia's assassination of Ibn al-Khuttab, the Arab leader in Chechnya, with a poisoned letter. They were also interested in hitting the Eiffel Tower, a department store and the Métro system.

Inevitably, the sinews of this Paris-based group led to 'Beirut-on-Thames' or 'Londonistan' as the French intelligence services cynically called the British capital. One key player was 'K', who had been deported from Georgia back to London after he tried to enter using a false French passport. 'K' had been denied asylum by the British in 1998 and 2001, being granted temporary admission instead. He disappeared until use of false documents landed him in Yarl's Wood Detention Centre, from which he fled when the detainees burned it down. Together with Abu Doha's replacement Rabah Kadre, 'K' built an Algerian cell in Wood Green's 'little Algiers'. In January 2003 MI5 and the police raided a flat there after the Algerian authorities had warned that the Algerians were about to go active. Six men were arrested, somehow inhabiting a council flat occupied by an Algerian and an Ethiopian who were on benefits. Together with Rabah Kadre, they were charged with attempting to produce toxic substances, which detectives speculated may have included the über-poison ricin, which was to be spread on the handrails of Underground escalators.

On 14 January police and MI5 struck at a house in Manchester in search of a man whose name was connected to the Wood Green cell. Twenty-four unarmed policemen entered the house, where they found three men, including their suspect. A Special Branch detective thought he recognised one of the two extras in the flat. Scotland Yard radioed in the intelligence that this was Kamel Bourgass. What to the three men had seemed like a routine raid on false asylum seekers turned critical once Bourgass was asked to don a forensic suit that would reveal if he had handled toxic substances. Since none of the three was handcuffed, Bourgass lurched at a knife and attacked four officers, killing detective constable Stephen Oake. All three Algerians were failed asylum seekers who had not been deported, through the predictable combination of laxness and incompetence that was now lethal in its effects. Oake's killer had entered the UK illegally in 2000, having already destroyed his identity papers. His requests for asylum were rejected three times, which did not stop him from committing petty crimes, or from murdering detective constable Oake.

Public outrage triggered Operation Mermant, a huge armed raid on Finsbury Park mosque, where police arrested seven men, including an

Algerian described as a major player in the Algerian terrorist group. Bourgass received a life sentence for killing Oake, and another seventeen years for the ricin plot, which was probably focused on the Heathrow Express connecting London to the airport. The mosque had been a home from home, not just to Richard Reid and Zacarias Moussaoui, but to many of the Algerian terrorists in London and Paris. In April 2004, the British finally charged Abu Hamza, notwithstanding the fact that as early as 1998 his son and stepson had kidnapped Western tourists in Yemen, calling 'Dad' in London to report their success. The British refused Yemen's requests to extradite him because of the existence in that country of the death penalty, one of those issues where elite opinion is massively at variance with that of the general public who understand that terrorism is not a risk-free activity. It would take a further outrage to prompt the British government to introduce tougher measures and to adopt a new tone. At the time of writing, the imprisoned Hamza is facing extradition to the US on further terrorism charges.

Medieval Islamic Spain figured prominently in the jihadi-salafist imagination long before the Spanish conservative leader José María Aznar committed thirteen hundred troops to Iraq. It was 'Andalus' or 'the land of Tarek Ben Ziyad', who had conquered southern Spain in the eighth century. Muslims liked to point out that the sprinkling fountains and cool courts of the Alhambra existed when most Europeans were living in rat-infested huts; they don't mention medieval Europe's cathedrals and palaces or that most Iberian Moors lived in rat-infested hovels too, nor the antecedent achievements of Visigothic Spain before the Moors arrived. Apart from this Islamist fantasy, which makes Spanish people laugh, contemporary democratic Spain was also a threat. It is a liberal, modern, prosperous society of enormous vitality, which has lured five hundred thousand legal, and five hundred thousand illegal, North Africans over the short gap separating it from the Maghreb. That is why Spanish governments now seek Catholic Latin American or eastern European migrants. Spain also wants to help transform Morocco's absolutist state into a constitutional monarchy. Grounds for attack aplenty there.

Spanish intelligence agents believe that, from 2001 onwards, jihadist terrorists in Spain were conspiring to attack the nation's train system, in other words long before Spain despatched troops to Iraq. Terrorists struck on the morning of 11 March 2004 when a series of bombs, triggered by mobile-phone detonators, exploded on commuter services at local stations or on trains entering Madrid from the capital's eastern suburbs. Thirteen devices hidden in backpacks exploded on two trains entering Atocha station. They killed a hundred people, including three Moroccan Muslim immigrants, who had gone to Spain to make a new life. Had the trains been in the station, it would have collapsed, crushing thousands of commuters. On one of the trains, two young Romanian girls had flirted with a good-looking Syrian, named Basel Ghalyoun. When he rushed off the train, they shouted that he had forgotten his backpack. When it exploded, it killed one of the girls. Shortly afterwards, two more bombs went off in two suburban stations. All together, within five minutes 191 people were killed and 1,847 injured.

Islamist attacks in Spain had become a racing certainty once Aznar committed troops to the 'coalition of the willing'. The Islamists called the Spanish prime minister Bush's 'tail'. A lucid communiqué, issued by a cyberspace Islamist think-tank, entitled 'Jihadi Iraq: Hopes and Dangers' claimed that Spain was the alliance's weakest link. Al Qaeda was thinking strategically. Britain and Poland could not be bombed out of Iraq, but Spain was another matter. Sixty-seven per cent of Spanish people were opposed to the war, and the country had been devastated when seven of its intelligence agents were massacred outside Baghdad, leaving Iraqi children kicking their corpses. If Spain was forced out of Iraq, then a domino effect might lever Britain and Poland out too.

Not without reason – for three months earlier police had arrested two ETA terrorists planting bombs on trains – Aznar leaped to the conclusion that ETA was responsible for the Atocha outrages, a hard line on Basque separatism being one of the distinguishing marks in the imminent election he was predicted to win. He persisted with that line, which may have been conditioned by earlier efforts by ETA to assassinate him, even as the investigation questioned it. Telephone intercepts revealed that ETA was as surprised by the bombings as anyone else. A van was found at the station from which the bombed trains originated. Inside were detonators and a cassette of Koranic verse. This intelligence was passed to José Luis Rodríguez Zapatero's opposition Socialists, some commentators suspect, because elements of the security services appointed under Felipe González were keen on a Socialist victory. A group claiming to speak for Al Qaeda released a communiqué which said: 'The squadron of death has managed to penetrate the heart of Crusader Europe, striking one of the pillars of the Crusaders and their allies, Spain, with a painful blow. This is part of the old game with Crusader Spain, ally of America in its war against Islam.' Scepticism greeted this since the same group had also claimed responsibility for a major US power outage that was not a terrorist strike at all. Meanwhile some eleven million Spanish people filled the streets in angry vigil.

On 12 March a policeman sifting through personal effects at El Pozo station found a bag with a bomb connected to a mobile phone. The police traced the phone to a shop owned by two Indians in a Madrid neighbourhood. The owners said they had sold a batch of thirty SIM cards to a Moroccan who owned a shop in Lavapiés, a Chinese and North African quarter of the city. Some of these cards had been used to trigger the bombs, but fifteen were unaccounted for. They arrested Jamal Zougam, the shop's owner, and two men, Mohammed Bekkali Boutaliha and Mohammed Chaoui. That night a TV station was directed to a tape in which Abu Dujan al-Afgani identified himself as Al Qaeda's chief military spokesman in Europe. He claimed responsibility for the attacks, notoriously adding, 'You love life and we love death,' a remark that has encouraged the view that Al Qaeda is nothing but a nihilistic death cult. It is, but it also thinks strategically. This communication decided the outcome of the Spanish elections, which the Socialists won. The troops were pulled out of Iraq, although some were quietly redeployed to Afghanistan. No wonder Jamal Zougam's first thought as he appeared in court after five days of isolation was 'Who won the election?'

French and Moroccan authorities had alerted the Spanish police to Zougam months before. Apparently well integrated in Spain, he was connected to Imad Eddin Barakat Yarkas, who had steered Spanish North African migrants to training camps in Afghanistan and Chechnya, while associating with the ominous Abu Qatada in London and mullah Krekar in Oslo. He had also facilitated the meeting between Mohammed Atta and Shibh in Madrid prior to 9/11. The Moroccans had him down as an associate of Abdelaziz Beniyach who in May 2003 had orchestrated suicide bombings in Casablanca, and of Mohammed Fazazi, who had preached to the 9/11 murderers in Hamburg. The Spanish authorities took virtually no action to follow up this huge weight of incrimination against Zougam, partly because the police did not dispose of a single Arabic speaker, except for eight over-worked civilian interpreters and translators, a problem they share with the FBI and MI5.

After Atocha they arrested about seventy people, including two of the men who had planted bombs on the trains. One of them was a professional drug dealer. The investigation gained added urgency when a bag containing twelve kilograms of the same commercial high explosive was found attached to a command wire next to the high-speed railway line from Madrid to Seville – evidence that, even though Spain had retreated from Iraq, this was not going to pre-empt further attacks. Signals from the missing SIM cards drew police to an apartment in Leganés, a lively suburb of Madrid to which commuters return at night. They surrounded a five-storey apartment block on Calle de Martin Gaite, alerting the inhabitants of a flat. Cries of 'Allahu Akhbar!' prefaced bursts of machine-gun fire from the occupants. There were seven men inside, the planners of the Atocha attacks. Warning the police 'We will die killing,' they drank holy water from Mecca and chanted verses of the Koran. They made phone calls. 'Mom. I'm going to paradise. I am ready' was one, and they tried to reach Abu Qatada in Belmarsh maximum security jail. In mid-evening the Spanish police assaulted the apartment, blowing off the lock and firing tear gas inside, shortly before it erupted as the men detonated twenty kilograms of explosives. A Spanish anti-terrorism officer, Francisco Javier Torronteras, was killed in the blast. The body of one of the terrorists flew out into a neighbouring swimming pool.

This was Jamal Ahmidan, a fugitive from Tetuan, where in 1993 he had murdered his accomplice in an armed robbery. Tetuan is the epicentre of Morocco's US$12.5 billion hashish business, with local drug barons joining Lebanese dealers in West African conflict diamonds as an alternative source of terrorist funding after movements of money became harder after 9/11. He and his brother ran a small business in Lavapiés, combining this with dope dealing through his cousin Hamid. Drugs were the medium of exchange when Hamid bartered explosives from a Spanish miner who was a drug addict in return for thirty kilograms of hashish. Deported in 1993, Ahmidan had served a two-and-a-half-year sentence in Morocco where incarceration led to his vehement espousal of Islam. Back in Spain, he had a blousy girlfriend and continued to deal drugs, but he no longer consumed them himself. This was a matter of *takfir*, the art of deluding the infidels. You can drink, smoke, womanise, so long as you have hatred in your heart. He gathered around himself four friends from Tetuan as well as Zougam whose shop was near a barber shop and the Alhambra restaurant where the group hung around. In 2001 Zougam stabbed a stranger who presumed to bring a dog into the restaurant, a bad thing to do when Moroccan Islamists were around. This was when Yarkas, the Al Qaeda cell leader in Madrid, took an interest in this group of dealers and toughs, converting their cultural Islamism into the jihadist variety, through media that would engage their limited attention spans.

A middle-class Tunisian student provided more intellectual sobriety than the drug dealers disposed of, while Rabei Osman Sayed Ahmed, also known as 'Mohammed the Egyptian', was brought in as leader after Yarkas had been arrested. Ahmed was an electronics graduate who had served for five years in the explosives branch of the Egyptian army before going to jail for Islamist activity. By posing as a Palestinian, a common ploy to elicit automatic European sympathy, he had conned his way into Germany, using a special substance to modify his fingerprints whenever the Germans took them and compared them with their databanks. He knew how to 'work' Germany. One just had to rise early, eager for a day's work, which in his case meant being the Lebach asylum centre's resident demagogue arguing 'rights' with German social workers. After simply walking out of this unguarded facility, Ahmed headed for Spain. He rented the country house where the group assembled their eleven bombs, but was careful to leave Spain before the bombings. A lucky break enabled the Spanish police to track him to Milan, where the Italian secret service reported that he was working as a decorator. They bugged a flat he shared with other Egyptians. This is probably the single most important source available for insights into how a jihadist recruiter operates, insights we owe to Italian intelligence.

On 26 May they recorded his efforts to recruit a fellow Egyptian as a 'martyr'. He had audiotapes, a two-thousand-page manual on jihad, and three hundred video-cassettes, for a morbid fascination with heads being sawn off or bomb blasts is very much part of the mindset. So too is a mastery of modern technology. The internet is what bin Laden once described as the electric current connecting the global *ummah*. It makes this 'real' and 'warm' at least in virtual reality, where complete strangers exchange intimate thoughts in Al Qaeda chatrooms such as 'The Fortress', 'The Fields' and 'Reform', none of which can be accessed without the original Arabic titles. How intimate they are can be gauged from the fact that Anthony Garcia, one of the British jihadists jailed after Operation Crevice, 'met', and became engaged to, Zenab Armend Pisheh, a student in Minnesota, in an internet chatroom. Associates of Garcia, whom she never physically met either, soon asked her to wire US$5,000 to support a trip they were planning to an Al Qaeda camp in Pakistan.[103]

The internet also provides a combination of nationhood and morality. The tens of thousands of Islamist sites represent the electronic birth of a nation, because they provide the Islamist equivalent of anthems, flags, patriotic poetry, heroes, martyrs and bloodcurdling injunctions. These sites also increasingly supply the fatwas which license homicidal and suicidal violence, giving the jihadists their peculiar code of ethics which turns homicidal suicides into martyrs. As Mohammed al-Massari, a Saudi dissident based in London, explains on his jihadist internet forum Tajdeed.net, 'No jihadi will do any action until he is certain this action is morally acceptable.' The acceptable includes killing innocent civilian bystanders, who will simply go to heaven or hell as they were meant to anyway. Killing children is not an issue either, as they are not accountable for sin before the onset of puberty. Gone straight to heaven, they will instantly mature to twenty and enjoy the same virgins that the martyrs get. Taxpayers and voters are all liable to be killed since they support enemies of Islam. As Khalid Kelly, a convert of Irish extraction, puts it: 'We have a voting system here in Britain, so anyone who is voting for Tony Blair is not a civilian and therefore would be a legitimate target.'[104]

Wits speak of the net as 'Sheikh Google'. These websites and blogs are simultaneously authoritative and demotic, part of a world where Everyman's thoughts, be they banal or crazed, assume the respectability conferred on the written word. The technology enables a reversion to a pre-Gutenberg world, where anyone can chop and change a key text, rather as medieval scribes inserted their own thoughts between the lines or in the margins of manuscripts. They can be blocked, or filled with porn, by intelligence agencies and freelance counter-terrorist cybernauts, but as the jihadists have commandeered even the servers of the Arkansas Department of Highways and Transportation to bury their trail, this can seem like a losing battle. Incredibly, Al Qaeda's own television outfit, As-Sahab or 'The Cloud', managed to relay itself for a few months via a Centcom satellite conveying orders to US forces in Iraq.[105] The 'television service' consists of a webcam and a mini-editing suite installed in the back of a van, with more fancy technology available in Lahore. Trusted Arab or Afghan cameramen are also brought in to record major statements by Ayman al-Zawahiri or the latest front-man, Azzam the American. The films are copied on to CDs and then passed on through several hands to the television station Al-Jazeera.[106]

In Milan Ahmed and his target watched the internet for hours, taking special delight in al-Zarqawi's beheading of Nicholas Berg, a twenty-six-year-old American businessman. 'Watch closely. This is the policy of the sword. Slaughter him! Cut his head off! God is great!' cried Ahmed. Judging by his actions, al-Zarqawi was addicted to the coppery smell of blood. There was a special audiotape, the one that 'enters inside your veins', which Ahmed repeatedly played to the Madrid jihadists until they had it memorised by heart. Ahmed was especially proud of Oxygen Phone Manager 2 software which enables a computer to command remotely all the functions of a Nokia mobile phone, as it presumably did with the detonators used at Atocha station. In the course of this long conversation, Ahmed lowered his voice and said:

> There is one thing I am not going to hide from you, the attack in Madrid was my project and those who died martyrs' deaths are my very dear friends . . . I wanted to plan it in order that it was something unforgettable, including me, because I wanted to blow up too, but they stopped me and we obey the will of God. I wanted a big load but I couldn't find the means. The plan cost me a lot of study and patience, it took me two and a half years . . . beware . . . beware! Don't you ever mention anything and never talk to Jalil, in any way, not even on the phone . . . You have to know that I met other brothers, that little by little I created with just a few things, before they were drug dealers, criminals, I introduced them to faith and now they are the first ones to ask me when it's the moment for jihad.

Although seventy people were detained in connection with the Madrid attacks, and at the time of writing many have been sentenced, this does not mean that the jihadists have abandoned Spain, even as Zapatero essays inter civilisational dialogue with the Maghreb and Iran courtesy of a Spanish-Iranian oil tycoon. Having attended one of these sessions in Madrid hosted by a foundation that has now been wound up, I can report that they consist of the usual obfuscatory cloud of ecumenical goodwill, in which Anglican female clerics trade homely platitudes with stony-faced imams and muftis in a conference centre ringed by hundreds of armed policemen. A ten-man cell of Pakistanis was broken up as they prepared attacks on high-rise buildings in Barcelona. They were also drug dealers, as 180 grams of heroin were found in their flat. In October 2004 police arrested forty people who were planning to drive five hundred kilograms of explosives into the criminal court where all terrorist cases are held. They may also have been planning suicide attacks on home supporters of Real Madrid. This group, called Martyrs of Morocco under Mohammed Achraf, an Algerian, had been formed among Muslim inmates in a Salamanca jail. They were the usual mix of drug dealers and credit-card fraudsters, contaminated while inside with hardened GIA terrorists. Astonishingly, while serving time in a Zurich jail, Achraf kept in email and mobile contact with his Spanish recruits, receiving correspondence too from Mohammed Salameh, one of the 1993 World Trade Center bombers, buried deep inside a US federal Supermax.

As fine studies carried out by the Police Service of Northern Ireland of IRA prisoners, not grouped in their hundreds in Northern Ireland's Maze, but as half a dozen inmates of Parkhurst on the Isle of Wight, have revealed, they can rapidly achieve positions of organised dominance within the prison, without the IRA threat of murdering the guards' relatives so commonplace in Ulster that many prison officers committed suicide. They do this by teaming up with the roughest London gangsters, who admire the terrorists' dedicated hardness and access to arms and money. Connections with criminals are then used to forge and steal documents, launder money, trade drugs and purchase arms, one of the reasons why Al Qaeda is now currently exploring the lawless 'tri-state' zone of northern Latin America.[107] Spain is discovering the need to treat terrorism holistically, from initial radicalisation, recruitment and training to what happens after sentencing. Terrorism also ventures beyond the grave in more senses than one. The body of Francisco Javier Torronteras, the officer killed in the raid on the terrorists' Madrid flat, was dug up one night. It was dragged away, mutilated, doused with petrol and set on fire.

The invasion of Iraq in early 2003 provided the latest of a series of inflammatory causes which further incensed many Muslims, and millions of non-Muslims too, although only the former seem to respond hysterically to Theo van Gogh's film *Submission*, Danish cartoons mocking the Prophet, or, for the second time, the honouring of writer Salman Rushdie. It is interesting how this rage takes time to be fomented. This is not the place to rehearse the reasons given for war, but it would be simple-minded to pretend that the invasion and occupation of Iraq have not served to re-incite Islamist anger and grievance, which is rather different from accepting the monotone in which such people engage with the world. Despite the evidence of their eyes, most Muslims do not seem to grasp the fact that the vast majority of killings in Iraq are carried out by fellow Shia and Sunni Muslims and not by coalition soldiers, and that it is the strategy of Al Qaeda in and beyond Iraq to trigger a wider sectarian religious war.

The initial demonstration of coalition airpower seemed another instance of Goliath stamping on David, notwithstanding the fact that much of this assault involved precision weaponry devised with a view to minimising civilian casualties in a world where warfare is under twenty-four-hour media scrutiny, with legal repercussions whenever anyone screws up. The US has developed artillery systems which calculate possible collateral damage, so that at a certain point the guns cannot be automatically fired. Apparently a new generation of robot weapons with built-in moral systems to factor out such human emotions as anger and vengeance are only a couple of years from deployment. The massive investment such systems require makes no sense if the intention is to kill Muslims indiscriminately. The technology is designed to do the opposite.

It became apparent that intelligence materials had been deliberately contaminated by political concerns, specifically to support the claim that Saddam Hussein had weapons of mass destruction whose deployment was imminent. The fact that he had used such weapons in the past, notoriously with devastating effect against the Kurds, was elided with flimsy evidence that he was planning to use them against coalition armies, and even flimsier proof that he had been consorting with Al Qaeda terrorists. This double deceit has caused long-term damage to some of the intelligence agencies involved, which may find it hard to make a plausible public case in the event of future conflicts. Promoting one of the key figures involved in putting together that intelligence to the post of director of MI6 seemed dubious to many observers. At least the US largely stuck to the line that its primary goal was to remove a dictator who had flouted any number of UN resolutions.

One consequence of an invasion whose occupying aftermath was culpably mismanaged with the passive connivance of the entire Blair government, including all hold-overs to the Brown administration, was the activation of Europe's Al Qaeda/Ansar al-Islam networks, with the result that some hundreds of Belgian, British, German, French and Italian jihadists were recruited and sent via Kurdistan or Syria to fight coalition troops inside Iraq. The latter were perplexed to discover that one suicide bomber who attacked them was a thirty-eight-year-old blonde, white, Catholic Belgian woman called Muriel Degauque, a convert to Islam who killed herself in Iraq. They became part of a conflict that involves 'former regime elements', Sunnis disgruntled at losing power after ruling Iraq for the Ottomans, the British and Saddam, and some thousands of foreign jihadists of whom the monster al-Zarqawi was the first prominent commander. Although Al Qaeda's Ayman al-Zawahiri had some difficulties with that monster's indiscriminate slaughtering of workmen – especially if they were Muslims – in December 2004 bin Laden eagerly acknowledged al-Zarqawi as 'the emir of the Al Qaeda organisation in the land of the two rivers'. Apart from the running sore of Chechnya, Iraq is likely to be the prime source of highly trained, and battle-hardened, jihadists who may make their terrorist mark in Europe. No European state has seen fit to make it a criminal offence to go abroad to fight its own, or allied, nationals, or to incite others to do the same. Although they have a good idea of who is going where to do what, intelligence and police cannot prosecute any of these fighters. High-level co-operation among European intelligence agencies is good – they have contacts going back decades and are hardwired into each other – but it is revealing that Europol, which holds data on twelve thousand terrorists, complains that national police and immigration services do not access this with apparent regularity.

After the 7/7 London bombing, the then home secretary Clarke claimed that the attack had 'come out of the blue', as the work of so-called 'clean skins'. This turned out not to be accurate. In 2004 Mohammed Siddique Khan and Shehzad Tanweer showed up on the margins of an MI5 surveillance of Islamist meetings. Both men were photographed – although not identified – and Siddique Khan's telephone number was known from his contacts with a suspect who had been monitored since 2003. On one occasion, MI5 had trailed Khan as he drove 150 miles home to Dewsbury in West Yorkshire. The two were deemed a low priority at a time when surveillance resources were stretched to the limit. No attempts were made to identify them, to get clearer pictures, or to show the existing photographs to a detainee held by a foreign intelligence agency who, in early 2004, had testified that Anglo-Pakistanis had visited Pakistan seeking meetings with Al Qaeda. Although Richard Reid had tried to blow himself up on a plane, and two Anglo-Pakistani suicide bombers had attacked Tel Aviv, the security services seem to have been reluctant to believe that British citizens would launch suicide attacks on British soil.

Incredibly, they asserted that there was not a sufficiently developed climate for long-term indoctrination. The first part of that claim, evidently accepted without demur by a House of Commons intelligence committee which reports to the prime minister, was surprising, since for decades the UK had been home to several Islamist fanatics, while anyone seriously familiar with suicide bombers would know that it does not take long to recruit or activate them.

Naturally, the security services work with finite resources, and have to establish priorities, points which conflict with government claims that they receive all the funding they ask for. As the MI5 director Jonathan Evans, appointed in 2007, has underlined, a successful bomb attack is a particularly bitter pill for his agency, whose overriding priority is the safety of the British public. Partly because of the lack of a regional MI5 presence – unlike Germany's security services or the FBI it was centred in the capital – there was little or no in depth familiarity with Islamist culture as it had formed in various central and northern cities. The British knew a lot about Belfast, and much about Arabs and North Africans in London, but their own northern provincial cities were a mystery. Instead of pseudo-academic discussions about how to define terrorism or what to call Islamist fanatics, more effort should have been put into getting a rich picture of the milieu in which jihadists are formed, radicalised and operate. The historic separation of MI5 and the foreign intelligence agency MI6 was anachronistic too in a globalised world where cheap air travel and migration linked Beeston and Bradford with Peshawar in a single continuum of malign activity. Regionally based police Special Branch sections were routinely under-funded, in the interests of high-speed traffic vehicles, helicopters and campaigns against burglars. Key appointments in the Metropolitan Police Counter-Terrorism Branch, notably of its head Peter Clarke in early 2002, have led to much smoother co-operation since.[108]

'7 July began unsettled, with heavy showers in places. The early morning rush in London started as normal.' Only the British could begin a report on a mass atrocity with the weather. The day before, Britain had won the competition to host the 2012 Olympics, and the G8 summit was in full swing in Scotland. Around 4 a.m. a car sped down the M1, containing Mohammed Siddique Khan, Shehzad Tanweer and Hasib Hussain. At 6.49 they met Jermaine Lindsay, parked in a Luton car park. All four donned rucksacks, as if they were going camping. Each rucksack contained two to five kilograms of high explosives. The bombs had been manufactured in a flat they sublet from an Egyptian chemistry student. Prolonged exposure to bleach had started to turn their hair white, something they attributed to the swimming baths they used. The foursome took a train into King's Cross. At the entrance to the Underground, they hugged and split up, two on to the District and Circle line – taking trains going in opposite directions – and two destined for the Piccadilly line. At 8.50 Shehzad Tanweer blew himself up, killing eight people and wounding 171. So did Mohammed Siddique Khan in the second carriage of another train, killing seven and injuring 163. On the Piccadilly line, Jermaine Lindsay blew himself up as the train sped through its deep tunnels, killing twenty-seven people and injuring 340. Meanwhile, Habib Hussain meandered around King's Cross and then took a bus to Euston station. There he switched to a number 30 bus, where, sitting at the back on the upper level, he detonated a bomb which killed fourteen people and wounded 110 near the green oasis of Tavistock Square.

A grim-faced Tony Blair raced back to London to put his characteristic imprint on the occasion. A brilliantly conducted police investigation traced evidence gathered at the crime scenes back through CCTV footage to the cars still parked at Luton and from there up the M1 to a bomb-making factory in Leeds. The men's anxious wives and families had by then declared that they were missing. In September, Al-Jazeera TV would broadcast the six-minute suicide video will of Mohammed Siddique Khan, defiantly jabbing his finger from beyond the grave: 'Until we feel security, you will be our targets. And until you stop the bombing, gassing, imprisonment and torture of my people we will not stop this fight. We are at war and I am a soldier. Now you too will taste the reality of the situation.'[109]

Khan, Hussain and Tanweer were from Beeston, a run-down Pakistani suburb of Leeds, although none of them was deprived himself. Aged thirty when he died, 'Sid' Khan had done a business-studies degree, working voluntarily in a primary school where he helped pupils with special needs, behavioural and language difficulties. He was married, to a woman of his choice, and had a child. Tanweer was the son of a fish-and-chip shop owner. A proficient athlete and cricketer, he had taken a qualification in sports science, but had no job apart from helping his father. Hussain was not very bright either, intermittently attending a business-studies programme. He was the most outwardly religious of the group, going on the *hajj* in 2002, and ostentatiously advertising his support for Al Qaeda after 9/11. This was a tight little world, centred around three mosques, an Islamic bookshop, a community centre and a gym. Evidence for some malign clerical mentor is slight; more probably this was a case of auto-radicalisation in which the group talked itself into violence. The older and more dominant Khan began to give the other two lectures that could also be seen as sermons. They went on group camping, paint-balling and white-water-rafting trips with others, expeditions designed for male bonding and quasi-military training. Some time in 2004 Khan encountered Jermaine Lindsay on the Yorkshire Islamist scene. Of Jamaican origin Lindsay had followed his mother into Islam, taking the name Jamal and adopting an extreme jihadist version of his new faith. After his mother moved to the US in 2002, Lindsay lived on welfare benefits before becoming a carpet fitter. He married a white British convert to Islam and had a child. Between 19 November 2004 and 8 February 2005, Khan and Tanweer visited Pakistan, and probably had contact with Islamist terrorists. After the broadcast of Khan's suicide video, Ayman al-Zawahiri issued a second tape in which he claimed that Al Qaeda had 'launched' the attacks in Britain.

The couple of years it takes to bring terrorists to trial, and rules governing sub-judice reporting, mean that the British justice system almost conspires to minimise the gravity of simultaneous and inter-related terrorist plots. After two-and-a-half years, people can no longer remember why half a dozen people were arrested one night in Leeds or Luton or what connection they had to some other group.[110] On 21 July 2005 a further team of terrorist bombers, with obscure connections to the earlier group, including overlapping periods in Pakistan, launched a second wave of attacks on the London transport system. Four Eritrean, Somali and Ethiopian refugees, Muktar Said Ibrahim, Ramzi Mohammed, Yasin Hassan Omar and Hussein Osman, tried to explode devices on underground trains and a bus in central London, bringing chaos to the capital once again. The number 26 bus stopped directly below my wife's offices. By virtue of the combination of chapatti flour and hydrogen peroxide to make the bombs, and the unseasonal heat, the bombs failed to explode after the detonators went off, although re-creations of their probable effects showed that they would have been devastating. Each plastic bin used to house the bombs was wrapped in tape holding on bolts and screws that would have caused horrendous injuries.

Once again, extraordinary detective work resulted in speedy arrests. Omar was arrested in Birmingham on 27 July, bizarrely standing in a shower wearing a backpack, before he was felled with a taser stun-gun and a rifle butt. Said Ibrahim and Ramzi Mohammed were captured in a west London flat, emerging in their underwear, with their hands up and knowing their human rights. After fleeing to Italy disguised in a burqa and carrying a handbag, Hussein Osman was smoothly repatriated by the Italian authorities, in marked contrast to the prevarications Britain had practised with France, the US and dozens of other governments. A Ghanaian whose name may be Manfo Kwaku Asiedu was arrested in connection with these bombings after he abandoned his device. The hysterical climate these men knowingly engendered was indirectly responsible for the shooting, on 22 July, by Metropolitan Police officers of a Brazilian electrician at Stockwell Underground station whom they misidentified as a suspect and after police radios appeared not to function underground.

In the course of their five-and-a-half months in court, the accused attempted to turn their trial for murder into a trial of British foreign policy, while impertinently proffering their advice to newly anointed prime minister Gordon Brown. To advise on foreign policy one needs more experience and knowledge than that of the son of a northern chip shop owner. They claimed that their explosive devices were of symbolic import, rather than a deliberate attempt to murder their fellow citizens. This suggested a boundless conceit and an unawareness of how democracies function. One of the accused also offered to work for inter-faith reconciliation in the event of an acquittal. As he sentenced them to forty-year jail terms, the judge underlined that this was an Al Qaeda plot to murder at least fifty people, since the men were fully aware of the carnage similarly built bombs had caused on 7/7. The trial itself revealed that Ibrahim had served prison sentences for indecent assault and mugging a seventy-seven-year-old woman. He and his colleagues had also been allowed to travel to Pakistan, despite having camouflage kit, £2,500 cash and a manual on treatment of ballistic wounds in their luggage. At the time there was a warrant out for Ibrahim's arrest for extremist activity, which was not acted on when he left and returned to Britain. Hussein Osman, who claimed to be Somali, was in fact an Ethiopian called Hamdi Isaac, whose lies should have disqualified him from asylum. Assuming they are ever released from prison, their asylum status or citizenship should be revoked and they should be deported, with any appeal having to be launched from outside British jurisdiction. Asiedu was later jailed for thirty-three years.[111]

More recent trials have revealed the extent to which Britain is in the firing line for Islamist terrorists. Operation Rhyme netted an Indian Muslim convert, Dhiran Barot, an Al Qaeda planner almost as malignly fertile as Khalid Sheikh Mohammed. As Barot had had no job or visible sources of income after 1995, it can be assumed he was a high-level Al Qaeda professional terrorist in close contact with Khalid Sheikh Mohammed. He had high tradecraft skills, knowing how to circle a roundabout or to effect sudden changes of lane to throw off surveillance officers. Barot and his gang planned to blow up major financial centres in New York and New Jersey. In Britain they wished to convert stretch limousines into bombs laden with propane gas tanks, or to puncture one of the tube tunnels that run under the Thames in London.

A further group, brought to justice by Operation Crevice, targeted so-called 'slags' having a night out at London's Ministry of Sound nightclub, a generic target also selected by the more recent West End bombers who wished to hit the Tiger White discotheque on ladies' night. In other words, female behaviour, rather than British foreign policy, is legitimate incitement to mass murder by people whom many British people may privately regard as amoral, deracinated scum that has fetched up from various Third World hellholes. Three and a half thousand hours of bugged conversations also revealed that the Bluewater shopping centre in Kent was another major target in a conspiracy that planned to use a thirteen-hundred-pound fertiliser bomb. Members of the group included a would-be male model, an aspiring England cricketer, a gas employee (who stole from Transco the blueprints of Bluewater) and a student who had been radicalised by sheikh Omar Bakri Mohammed at Langley Green mosque in Crawley.[112]

It seems probable, to most informed commentators, that the 'war on terror' is becoming what the generals call 'the long war' which may last for fifteen, thirty or fifty years. This may be the era of long small wars, in which experiences like Northern Ireland (thirty-seven years), Bosnia (fourteen) and Kosovo (seven) become normative, although one hopes that the elementary learning cycle is shorter than the decade this took in Northern Ireland. The purpose of such wars will have to be carefully and intelligently reiterated to domestic publics with short attention spans and a desire for a quick fix urged on them by the media. Attempts to impose artificial timelines and criteria of success or failure have to be resisted in favour of long-term goals – many of them cultural, economic or political – that are vulnerable to the West's own relatively short electoral cycles and its investment in various foreign strongmen.[113]

Without wishing to be prescriptive, some problems raised in this book have prompted a few practical thoughts. Soldiers are only one element of a struggle that has something of the wearying futility of the game 'whack a mole'as they try to suppress Al Qaeda, mainly by killing or capturing its leaders. Denying Al Qaeda operating and training space in Afghanistan, Iraq or Somalia is crucial to the interdiction of major terrorist attacks in the West. Unfortunately, reporting from exotic and violent locations does not make that domestic connection clear enough, so that the armed forces become detached from the societies that despatched them there. The British Ministry of Defence compounded the insult by refusing to award a special campaign medal for those involved in the battle of Helmand Province until a newspaper took up the cause. This is part of a wider failure to educate Western public opinion about what is at stake. In a sense, public diplomacy seems to have failed since 9/11, when there was briefly global unanimity regarding the barbarous nature of this atrocity. One can visit any number of radical Islamist bookshops in Britain to acquire visual materials which make clear at a glance the physical scope of the jihadists' desired caliphate. Far harder is to connect up the sites of jihadist bloodshed into a picture of the sort of nihilistic chaos that sane people the world over seek to avoid, and to educate people about, say, the plurality of conflicts in the Middle East, to counteract a simple presumption of a single Arab–Israeli dispute. What the West needs to avoid at all costs is exclusive identification with authoritarian and repressive regimes, whether in the Middle East, North Africa or Central or South Asia, based on their eagerness to wage the 'war on terror'. Mistakes made in Chechnya are being repeated in South Asia where local groups are being falsely assimilated to Al Qaeda. In the long run that will only result in oppositions coalescing around the jihadists, who will gain mass support they do not deserve.

Regarding the potential jihadists we have, it may be instructive to see what is done elsewhere. Take Riyadh, a place we normally do not look to for lessons. In 2003–4 Saudi Arabia experienced twenty-four terrorist attacks that killed ninety people, many of them Westerners employed in the kingdom. These attacks virtually stopped in 2004–6, and only partly because of large-scale raids to round up militants. The Saudi government introduced an imaginative scheme to wean those on the lower rungs of jihadism off extremism and back to normality. So far the scheme has been applied only to those who have been convicted not of violent offences, but of having jihadist literature and DVDs or low-level involvement in terrorism. A typical example would be twenty-two-year-old 'Ali', a Wahhabist student who started posting on an Al Qaeda website called Sawt al-Jihad. Then the police arrived. In prison 'Ali' was put through a programme based on how people are retrieved from sinister cults.[114] Since 2004, two thousand prisoners have been through it, with seven hundred renouncing their earlier views and being released. The Interior Ministry has established a series of advisory committees, consisting of experts on Islam and psychologists, almost all of them drawn from the universities and mosques. Initially, the experts simply ask why the person is in jail, which leads to a discussion of their beliefs. The clerics concentrate on explaining to prisoners, who invariably have little or no grasp of the religion, that their understanding of it is false, based on corrupt and heretical understandings of Islam. This point is underlined by former jihadist prisoners who, having renounced their views, have become members of these advisory committees.

Those prisoners who respond to short two-hour conversation sessions are put into six-week courses, whose results are examined at the end. Those who pass go on to the next stage of the process, which eventuates in early release. A social and psychological committee assesses the prisoners' wider needs, ensuring from the start that their families' education, health and welfare are immediately taken care of in their absence. This is designed to limit radicalisation to the individual already in prison. Those who are released are helped with cars, jobs and housing, with single males encouraged to marry and start families. They are monitored by the secret police and its informers. Since one of the objects of cults is to detach people from their friends and families, the programme strives to re-establish such connections. The wider clan is encouraged to take responsibility for the individual released. According to the Saudis, the programme has an 80–90 per cent success rate, with only nine or ten prisoners having been rearrested for security offences. Saudi sceptics argue that a few more public beheadings of such people would achieve the same results. What this programme does show, however, is that Al Qaeda is ideologically vulnerable and not like an unstoppable machine hurtling towards its malign objectives. Its momentum can be checked.

Guantánamo-style arrangements, where all inmates are lumped together as 'evildoers', impede similar outcomes. Efforts, by their lawyers, to concentrate the increasing number of jihadist inmates in single wings of prisons should be resisted, not least because they will be followed with cries of abuse from Mudassar Arani, Gareth Peirce, Clive Stafford Smith and their ilk within about ten minutes.[115]

Although police and military activity is obviously vital, there are broader cultural issues at stake in what many claim is a latterday Cold War. During the Cold War, the West went to great lengths to advertise the superiority of its freedoms over totalitarian Marxist-Leninism, and this included covert CIA support for the work of Jackson Pollock. The Australian lawyer Peter Coleman wrote an outstanding book on these operations. Not much of this talk seems to translate into concrete policy suggestions as to how cultural warfare might actually be waged. Would it be primarily designed to subvert the jihadists' ideology, or to solidify the West's own morale? The old Atlanticist model does not seem particularly relevant if the victims of terrorism are also in Bali or Kenya while US conservatives heap scorn on 'Euroids'. There are additional problems in reviving this tactic since we live in a less serious age, and one which has progressively marginalised high intellectual endeavour. Within my lifetime, academics studied such subjects as the comparative history of parliaments or war finance; they are now more likely to be experts on gay and lesbian body art, serial killers or the persecution of witches, rivalling television in their popu-list pursuit of the lurid or trivial. A glance through any catalogue of academic books – that is, those written in incomprehensible jargon and with pages of footnotes to prove earnestness – shows how unserious academics have become as a group. How can politicians defend Western values if their conception of them is to demonstrate familiarity with the Arctic Monkeys, while being almost embarrassed about going to the opera? All societies should do more to educate all their citizens in the history of the individuals and institutions that make living in them a relative privilege. This should include discussion of the historic separation of Church and state in the West, with religion confined to matters of public and private morality, and the advantages that accrue from local permutations of that broad arrangement. This has never prevented the religious from playing to their advantages in dealing with the depressed, elderly, suicidal and so forth.[116]

Ultimately the battle with jihadism will only be won by Muslims themselves, albeit with our discreet encouragement and involvement, because despatching huge armed forces is manifestly unsatisfactory, whether in creating more jihadists or exposing the West's internal divisions and indisposition to suffer extensive casualties in what is, for the time being, still the age of pre-robotised warfare. It is salutary to recall that more British soldiers were killed in Northern Ireland in a single year than have so far perished in the entire campaign in Afghanistan. Since the suffering of the vast virtual *ummah* – which is not the suffering of Africa or Tibet – seems to be at the heart of contemporary problems with jihadism, anything that contributes to a sense of nation or statehood may reverse that tendency, as will anything that encourages the considerable number of reasonable people in Muslim countries who are historically averse to being ruled by overmighty clerics and their mob-like followers. Here the West might take a much greater interest in the high culture of these societies, since very often novelists and the like are on the front line, assuming they have not been killed. In one or two places, successful pop singers have bravely propagated anti-jihadist sentiments. They speak for large constituencies whom we need on our side, and we remain indifferent to them at our peril.

All of which is to say that the Muslim and non-Muslim worlds need to exercise more curiosity about each other. We should avoid the colonial cum multicultural approach of viewing highly variegated groups of individuals through the false prism of so-called community leaders, who invariably speak for a purposive coterie. That applies to both government and the mass media. One reason we have the problem of jihadism is that various Western institutions and professions are not treated with sufficient scepticism. Their massive political bias is simply accepted as in the nature of things, as if homogeneity of opinion had not been deliberately brought about over decades through clientelism and recruitment of the liberally likeminded, something ruefully acknowledged by the BBC.

Universities are allowed to use free-speech arguments to defend sinister Islamist organisations active on campuses, rather than challenged about their greed for high overseas fees. What are already highly politicised universities are allowed to receive dubious foreign funding for regional-studies or Islamic-studies programmes which are biased against Western interests, at a time when they routinely reject Western government funding if it emanates from the military.

Since Islamist terrorism is a deviant outgrowth of a religion, much attention needs to be paid to the terms on which that religion is permitted to function in non-Muslim societies. For a start, it should be directly related to how Muslim societies treat adherents of other faiths, or people who espouse none. The British government should flatly prohibit current plans to build a vast mosque in east London, until such time as Churches are allowed to operate in all Muslim countries without fear of persecution. Proselytism should also be based on a similar absolute quid pro quo. Allowing Wahhabism to grow in our societies just because of lucrative aircraft contracts is an outrage. Given the potential danger they constitute, Muslim clerics require careful supervision and training. The Dutch authorities have introduced an imam-licensing programme, based at such universities as Leiden, whose object is to create a responsible clergy who realise that integration is no barrier to practising their religion.[117] The French have shown how close surveillance of what is preached in mosques can drastically lessen the likelihood of attack. The French, of course, are just as much signatories of the European Convention on Human Rights as any other member of the EU. The French internal security service, the Renseignements Généraux or RG, have had a section called Violent Fundamentalist Environment which not only watches mosques, but gets its hands on copies of each Friday's prayers, which are collated and analysed. Using such indicators as encouragement to jihad, the RG asks the criminal police to summon the imam concerned, who (provided he is not a French national) can be threatened with expulsion under laws passed in the mid-1990s. The local city council will also warn the imam that all local funding for the mosque will cease. In 2005, eleven out of the thirty imams who received these warnings were expelled, with the remainder heeding this ultimate sanction. It might help, too, if mosques and imams ceased to be the primary Muslim role models, by encouraging alternatives drawn from business, charity, the arts and sports.[118]

In the wider world, Muslim governments should be held responsible for what is said by clerics on the state's payroll, for it is obvious that they can control these clerics when it suits their domestic interests, and can turn them on or off like a pressure valve. Commercial contracts and aid should be contingent on unconditional co-operation with Western security interests. Western private and public pension funds have enormous power to discourage companies which use our money regardless of its wider political or strategic impact. Ethical investment is not confined to airlines, cigarettes or sweat shops, as the comptroller of New York City's pension fund showed when he persuaded several giant corporations from Conoco to Halliburton to disinvest in Iran.[119] Western advocacy of democratisation should follow, rather than precede, support for a secular civil society developed enough to challenge the Islamists who have often usurped that function in one-party dictatorships. If democracy merely leads to the election of parties which believe in 'one man, one vote, one time', then it is perhaps not worth encouraging at all. That also means investment in liberal, secular alternatives to the infrastructures Islamists have established – notably the madrassas, but also clinics and hospitals – starting with primary education, where the cartoon characters will no longer blow up Jews, and going on to Arabic translations for university students of the classical texts of Western freedom, from Burke to Orwell and Solzhenitsyn. We need a samizdat culture in reverse. The advent of an Arabic Booker Prize is encouraging. That might remind Muslims that the West consists of more than MTV or chatlines where one can ring pouting Pauline. The thrust of educational campaigns should be especially directed towards younger children, for they are as yet unradicalised, despite the best efforts of Hamas and the like to do so by having Mickey Mouse kill Jews.[120]

On a much larger scale, non-Arab Muslim states should be encouraged to contest the imperialist dominance, within the faith, of Arabic and Arab authorities, while the Arab states themselves should be enjoined to spread oil and gas wealth more fairly within their societies, so that young men have some meaningful careers other than that of full-time jihadist. The West has a direct interest in the creation of affluent and aspirant middle classes with a cosmopolitan outlook. Even in a predominantly Muslim society like Indonesia, where about twenty local districts and municipalities are currently trying to impose sharia law, there are plenty of people to protest against this. Women do not like having the lengths of their skirts dictated, and young couples do not like being arrested for kissing on a park bench or going dancing under so-called anti-pornography laws. In the industrial city of Tangerang, west of Jakarta, authorities made it illegal for a woman to go out after 7 p.m. unaccompanied by a man, despite there being numerous textile and Korean-owned shoe factories which rely on women working night shifts. A local mother of two out at night was convicted of prostitution because police found lipstick in her bag. The governor of Bali has threatened to secede if these laws are applied to Western tourist resorts, so catastrophic is the predicted effect on Bali's economy.[121]

The West should also encourage moderate forms of Muslim orthodoxy, which stress the mystical and personal, as well as the 'next-worldly', both in the real and the virtual electronic realms. It should also grasp that Muslim fundamentalism is no more inherently menacing than its Christian, Jewish or secularist equivalents. Western priests and rabbis should understand that any ecumenical dialogues must automatically involve clear and unambiguous denunciation of terrorism by all of those involved and as a precondition for participation. It was dismaying to learn in August 2007 of the advice issued by Tiny Muskens, bishop of Breda, that Dutch Catholics should call God 'Allah', in the interests of easing tensions between Muslims and Christians. The abandonment of clerical appeasement and equivocation might also realign clerics with what most of their Christian parishioners think (92 per cent of more than four thousand people polled disapproved of bishop Muskens's lame proposal). Since the jihadists exploit the internet so thoroughly, and since we apparently cannot emulate the Chinese or Singaporeans by controlling it, efforts need to be made to disrupt sites or to sow disinformation, about bomb making for example. Since most servers are US based, they should avail themselves of a new, free, electronic translation service so that they can comprehend what they are funnelling on to the internet, the precondition for the servers refusing to host such sites.

Above all, perhaps, all those opposed to terrorism should be highlighting the chaos and criminality that accompany jihadi-salafist activity and which would characterise their rule, judging from the only known instance of it under the Taliban. Islamist supremacism is as unattractive as any other, and equally relies on coercion and intimidation. The chaos and bloodshed we witness each day in Iraq are the element in which these people operate. The most reliable assessments of future Al Qaeda strategy suggest that they want to provoke an all-out Sunni–Shiite war, which will be a cataclysmic disaster for the Middle East. The jihadi-salafists have no positive vision, except the desire to visit chaos and bloodshed elsewhere. If that is clearly understood by enough people, particularly in the Muslim world, we may have a rather shorter long war. Looking back over the history of terrorism, we can see any number of ideological causes which once fed violent passions but which have passed into oblivion. These things take time. The Cold War lasted from 1947 to 1989. On that calendar, we are in the equivalent of 1953 in the struggle with the jihadi-salafis.[122]

AFTERTHOUGHTS

Some historians argue that their academic colleagues should be drawn into policy-making in the manner of lawyers, economists, or food and drug experts. This strikes me as dubious, partly because only 'professional' historians, meaning other academics, are eligible. Historians would be no less susceptible to emotive group-think than anyone else who has to make crucial decisions in real time as part of a team. That does not mean that historians have no role in suggesting what History counsels or counsels against, for they may just be more than a subsidiary branch of the entertainment industries, alongside cooking, gardening or home-makeover programmes. They can continue to do that through the tried and trusted medium of helping to shape a historically aware population, from which politicians will continue to be drawn.

History crops up fitfully in our present conflicts; we reflexively use the past to make sense of what is happening in the present. Soldiers, for example, have scoured the history of the 1948–57 Malayan Emergency – a classic case of learning on the job – for examples of how to combat insurgents in contemporary Iraq. Even the term 'emergency' itself has been recommended as an alternative to 'war on terror', partly because it suggested only a temporary suspension of legal norms in the pertinent theatre rather than a wholesale rewriting of legal norms through such devices as the US Patriot Act or European counter-terrorism legislation. The British army of that period gradually learned to refer to the Malayan Races Liberation Army as the 'Communist Terrorist Organisation'. These semantic questions have become important in contemporary conflicts.[1]

After 9/11 the US proclaimed a 'war on terror', or 'WOT' or 'GWOT' if one adds the prefix global. Some deemed this to be as descriptively meaningless as a war on Blitzkrieg and as futile as a war on drugs, or felt that the word war unnecessarily elevated criminals. Most European allies of the US prefer to regard the struggle against terrorism as a law-enforcement issue, an approach which in some countries has duly led to lawyers and judges frustrating the impact of intelligence and police work. Among the alternatives to the WOT are the 'long war', a term used by the Provos to describe thirty years of violence in Northern Ireland; 'the first global terrorist war'; or, more plausibly, Australian strategist David Kilcullen's 'war on the global jihadist insurgency'. None of these has the descriptive precision of, say, the Cold War, a concept that also recurs in discussions about winning Muslim hearts and minds and/or about how the West represents itself. What to call the enemy is also being revised in a fashion which some find Orwellian. An example of how the British government thinks was revealed when it enjoined the bureau-cracy to talk of 'anti-Islamic extremism', not only eschewing the 'T' word altogether, but evading the source of the problem. Similar semantic recommendations, or 'Words that Work and Words that Don't', were handed down in the US by the National Counterterrorism Center (NCTC) in March 2008. 'Extremism' is favoured over an abruptly pro-scribed 'jihadism'. Retired law-enforcement agents with long memories recall that in the 1970s the Carter administration similarly told Immi-gration and Nationalisation Service inspectors to refer to illegal aliens as 'undocumented workers' while avoiding announcing themselves as 'criminal inspectors'.[2]

Although this conflict, which US officials think will be an inter-generational struggle, has scarcely begun, there is already debate about what will constitute victory. President George W. Bush's premature declaration about the ending of major combat operations in Iraq from the flight deck of a warship did not anticipate the asymmetric war of attrition that was barely under way, an insurgency that partly reflected the wholesale dismissal of the Iraqi police and army, which have had to be painstakingly reconstructed from scratch. Since then over four thousand US troops have lost their lives, while many more have been blinded or left limbless, mainly because of sophisticated improvised roadside explosives. Expectations have been scaled down considerably, although advocates of the war in Iraq also periodically redefine the nature of victory.[3] Inadvertently echoing Tory Northern Ireland secretary Reginald Maudling's talk in the 1970s of 'acceptable levels of violence', in 2004 Kilcullen observed:

Different societies exhibit different normal, chronic levels of armed violence. Victory does not demand that we reduce violence to zero, or establish peace and prosperity in absolute terms. It only requires that we return the system to what is normal – for that society, in that region, in this period of history – so that society can re-establish normal pre-insurgency patterns of interaction.

Perhaps that realistic view is all we can hope for given that more ambitious strategies seem to have failed, and, in any case, go against powerful foundational traditions in US foreign-policy thinking which disdain seeking out monsters to slay.[4]

History is also pressed into service to give the enemy a familiar face through a semantic shorthand. This has recurred several times in my lifetime, with Nasser, Galtieri, Saddam or Mugabe described as another Hitler who should never be appeased under any circumstances. Commentators and politicians have often metaphorically substituted steel helmets for the chequered keffiyahs and turbans. We have heard much about 'Islamofascism', especially from the liberal left, and also about 'Islamobolshevism', depending on whether the emphasis is on the anti-Semitic and homophobic or on the vanguardist aspects of jihadism.[5] Both terms risk boxing our thinking into the past even as they give needless offence to about 1.6 billion Muslims by insinuating that they are latterday Nazis. Hence the NCTC recommendations seek to proscribe 'Islamofascism' too.

Top US officials think they can learn from the advertising industry. Michael Doran, a Middle East expert responsible for counter-terrorism strategy at the Pentagon, is more interested in what the advertising industry has to say about the success and failure of global brands in their quest to delegitimise Al Qaeda within the Muslim world than in looking for past European precedents that cut no ice in such circles. Doran wants Al Qaeda to go the way of Ford's failed Edsel – a preposterous car with elongated tail fins that became a loss-maker of epic proportions – rather than imitate Audi, BMW, Coca-Cola or Nike. The aim is to discredit Al Qaeda and cognate organisations by stressing that 'they create nothing, they only destroy'. They are what the British lieutenant-general Graeme Lamb crisply describes as 'architects of chaos'.[6] Ironically, as Steve Coll shows, it was largely the bin Laden clan that was responsible for the vulgar architectural modernisation of Saudi Arabia, including apartment blocks and shopping malls adjacent to Mecca, as well as the huge advance bases needed for Operation Desert Storm, which Osama bin Laden so deplores, even though he financially benefited from shares of the corporate profits.[7]

Many Europeans think that because of their experiences with the Provos or ETA they know about terrorism. This delusion is especially evident in Britain where defence secretary Des Browne has suggested we talk to the Taliban, as well as Hamas and Hizbollah with whom we are not at war. He ruled out talking to Al Qaeda. No such restraint was evident when in March 2008 Tony Blair's former chief of staff Jonathan Powell said, in the course of promoting a book about the Northern Ireland peace process, that we should be negotiating with Al Qaeda on the basis of his covert and overt dealings with Martin McGuinness and Gerry Adams (whom he allowed to skateboard with his children in an intermission during negotiations). Apparently the same indulgence should be shown to a 'repentant' Osama bin Laden; what American readers make of that suggestion is not hard to imagine. Leaving aside the post-imperial hubris lurking behind these attempts to export conflict-resolution studies – on the idiosyncratic basis of Northern Ireland – I am reminded of a story related to me by a senior Mossad officer who had many dealings with Irish Special Branch in the shape of a giant rugby player with big ears and a collapsed nose. The Mossad man was told that the Irish police already knew about terrorism. He pointed out that the first concern for any Provo terrorist planning an operation was how to get away, a minor concern for jihadis who are seeking martyrdom and paradise. After due reflection on such suicide tactics, the Irish detective conceded: 'S——, you know what, we'll keep the Provos and you can have Hamas and Hizbollah.'[8]

That this is also a war of competing ideas means that the Cold War is often referred to. British prime minister Gordon Brown is said to be impressed by a history of the Congress of Cultural Freedom by Frances Stonor Saunders, a left-wing journalist whose book is a polemic against the politicisation of culture by various donor front organisations covertly funded by the CIA.[9] The book may have influenced the prevention part of Britain's CONTEST counter-terrorism strategy, a feeble replica of the multi-layered and polyvalent strategies the US has adopted to combat global terrorism. It seeks to instrumentalise Islamic Studies in higher education – with the aid of £1 million of hypothecated funding – as a means of deradicalising young British Muslims, many of whom, like Ed

Husain, author of *The Islamist*, were indoctrinated in further-education colleges through the presence of Hizb ut-Tahrir.[10] This also means blithely ignoring the intent behind the £200 million-plus donated to British universities from the Arab Middle East, as well as disregarding the ostentatious refusal by British academics to acknowledge that they have any public responsibilities in terms of notifying the authorities about Islamist extremism among their students. An Islamist underworld exists within these universities in prayer rooms and societies, all passively tolerated by vice-chancellors. British dons take Saudi money – £8 million was given to Cambridge in 2008 – while their trades union seeks to exclude military recruiters or to boycott Israel, which they view as an apartheid state like South Africa. Oxford's notorious St Antony's College employs the sinuous Tariq Ramadan despite his being banned from France and the US as an undesirable influence.[11]

During the Cold War the CIA despatched the Boston Symphony Orchestra into the cultural lists and covertly funded both abstract expressionism and serial music as alternatives to social realism. It is debatable whether the West needs to do this nowadays, although it is surely right to suggest that the sums it expends on public diplomacy are derisory. Does the US really need to burnish Brand America when the world's enterprising classes line up for entry, or when the functioning of democracy was so manifest in the 2008 presidential primaries, notwithstanding Abu Ghraib or Guantánamo Bay? Where else elects district attorneys, judges and sheriffs? Where else so subtly separates Church and state, without prejudicing the rights of the religious, or differentiates between sin and crime – a failure to effect such a separation being one of the main conceptual failings of the Muslim world? Surely, if the problems are primarily in the Muslim world, then the West should be supporting the shoots of pluralism that already exist, through such enterprises as the Arabic Booker Prize and other manifestations of a liberal artistic, journalistic and visual culture. Are there no liberals and socialists in the entire Middle East? Do Muslims really savour dictation by mullahs? They would be extraordinarily unlike most Christians if they did. There are many Muslims around the world who no more wish to live in theocracies than Westerners do, being all too aware of the ignorance and megalomania of clerics.

Several unsavoury regimes based on corruption and violence have used the war on terror to suppress voices that have nothing to do with radical Islamism. Pakistani president Pervez Musharraf's arrests of lawyers and judges provide one conspicuous example of this process, acts which automatically subtracted forces hunting down murderous Islamists who assassinated prime ministerial candidate Benazir Bhutto in late December 2007. This problem is also evident in the Middle East and North Africa. Some 300,000 people demonstrated in Algiers in 1992 on the eve of elections that the Islamic Salvation Front won, marching under the slogan 'neither a police state, nor an Islamic state, but a democratic state'. Similar constituencies of the cosmopolitan intellectual or mercantile bourgeoisie exist in Cairo: the West's task is discreetly to help organise them, perhaps along the lines of Freedom House's role in the 'colours' revolutions in Georgia and Ukraine, for they could be one of the building blocks from which a more pluralistic Middle East and North Africa may emerge. After all, democracy is not inherently alien to that region, whatever differences societies based on clans and tribes may impose on its local elaborations. Since 1961 Kuwait has had a parliament, replete with committees that grill ministers. Since 2006 women have had the vote and can stand as candidates. That some Kuwaitis are attracted to the brash modernisation pursued by the alternative sovereign-autocracy model in neighbouring Bahrain, Abu Dhabi or Qatar only suggests that, in this respect, they are not much different from Russians.

Instead of trying to sell a way of life whose attractions are evident from queues of people seeking visas, the West should also simply represent hope by bringing fresh water and school buildings to places without either, or by providing major disaster relief in emergencies such as earthquakes, like those that hit Iran and Pakistan, or the Asian tsunami and the Burmese cyclone.[12] It should also be encouraging voices of Islamic authority beyond the Arab world, for example in Turkey or Indonesia. The Turkish Ministry of Religious Affairs has sought to conform the hadith to life in the twenty-first century. The West should also stand firm for the rights of women, denouncing such abominations as so-called honour killings, prohibitions on educating girls and gender-biased divorce and inheritance laws.

There is no point in elderly conservatives being nostalgic for the Cold War or for a West that in important respects no longer exists for kids who listen to world music or take their pre-university gap years in Africa or South America. Even an oldie like this author has CDs of raï music, the Egyptian chanteuse Uhm Khaltum and more arcane recordings from Mali, mixed in with Bach and Beethoven, while some of the most interesting novels I have read have been by Algerians and Egyptians. The entire world is just a click of a mouse away. During the Cold War, enterprises like the Congress for Cultural Freedom confronted state propagandists in the Eastern bloc, in place of today's Al-Manar, As-Sahab or Al Jazeera, plus six thousand or so websites bouncing back and forth mainly on the West's own servers. In addition to jihadist websites, there are also chat-rooms and social networks, perhaps the real sites of auto-radicalisation among young Muslims, although the technology changes so swiftly it is difficult for someone of my age to tell.[13]

Given the confusions in our own cultures, not least their institutionalised saturation with the dogmas of multiculturalism, and the widespread post-modern rejection of authority, truth and meaning, how exactly do rationalists project a single view of Western society's values? Do states need civic religions? What do we do about the growing number of people who inhabit a virtual world where, as in TV's *X-Files*, everything is a hidden conspiracy and where a three-month inquest has not comprehensively dispelled belief that MI6 murdered Princess Diana? How do rational people counter a pervasive fascination with the irrational or such potent myths as the 'Crusader–Zionist' conspiracy against the global *ummah*? Merely setting out the historical truth of the matter is clearly insufficient, just as it is for dedicated Holocaust-deniers, a category that often overlaps with such circles.[14]

One approach gaining international ground is for high-level Muslim clerics unequivocally to condemn Al Qaeda-inspired terrorism. The Saudi cleric Shaykh Salman bin Fahd wrote an open letter this year to Osama bin Laden saying: 'How much blood has been spent? How many innocent people, children, elderly and women have been killed, dispersed or evicted in the name of al Qaeda?' A similar condemnation came from the grand mufti of the Al-Azhar Mosque in Cairo. While prison-based schemes in Egypt, Indonesia, Saudi Arabia, Singapore and Malaysia have chalked up some success in reorientating people imprisoned for low-level bloodless extremism (an option that does not exist in the West), Britain has seen the launch of the Quilliam Foundation. Led by Maajid Nawaz, a British Islamist imprisoned for five years in Egypt, the Foundation aims to confront young Muslims with the perils of extremism. It bluntly recommends cutting all ties with Saudi religious funding. It further insists that Muslim communities should ignore charges of being collaborators and stooges by co-operating with the intelligence services and police to root out extremists. They should also ignore attempts by a few Islamist activist human rights lawyers, who represent many terrorist suspects, actively to frustrate such co-operation by offering on their websites

494 · BLOOD AND RAGE

advice on how to resist it. The Foundation says that 'the foreign policy of the British government will not be held hostage by any one community', and, in a revolutionary act of self-awareness, suggests that Muslims should 'turn their attention to corruption within mosques, gender inequality at community level, domestic violence, forced marriages, incest, drug abuse, abortion and low rates of educational attainment'.[15]

Naturally, the Islamists do not inhabit a social vacuum, although one might be forgiven for thinking so given their insistent solipsism. How the rest of society reacts to them is no less important, although considerable efforts have been put into concealing this subject by public media obsessed with Islamophobia. The BBC persists in airing dramas about British skinhead-type Fascists attacking reasonable-seeming jihadist sympathisers, even though there are no instances of this happening in reality, an example of how the left needs to oxygenate itself through the myths of anti-Fascism.

No significant section of Western elite opinion is sympathetic to the jihadists, as many were to Marxist-Leninism in the 1930s, but throughout Europe there are left-liberals (and a few pro-Arab 'Camel Corps' right-wingers) whose hatred of the US, and Israel, is so pathologically ingrained that they have become apologists for the most reactionary elements within Islam. Think of the Cambridge classics professor, and ubiquitous *Times Literary Supplement* presence, Mary Beard, who shortly after 9/11 wrote in the taxpayer-subsidised *London Review of Books* that 'the US had it coming to it', a line Americans have also heard from Pastor Jeremiah Wright. Think too of the notice given to activist human rights lawyers who are prepared to believe every crime ascribed to the US or UK governments, without anyone daring to raise the matter of their own collusive involvements with terrorists, relationships for which there are ominous precedents in recent European history. Moreover, don't human rights lawyers rake in colossal fees in return for public moralising?[16]

British judges have also played their part, in ruling that control orders on terrorist suspects they have released from detention are illegal, a courtesy extended to Al Qaeda ideologue Abu Qatada, on the ground that while Qatada might not be tortured in his native Jordan (following agreements between the two governments), *witnesses* used against him might have been subjected to it to secure their testimony. If British lawyers are so casual in the case of Abu Qatada, a truly dangerous man, what hope is there that lesser lights will regard Britain as anything other than a safe haven? The latest judicial refinement, in April 2008, is to stymie efforts to block the sequestration of terrorist finances lest they find it humiliating to account to the UK Treasury for what they spend each week on groceries. Apparently while such sequestration is permissible under UN guidelines, it has never been formally approved by the British parliament. In June senior judges insisted on freeing a man only identified as 'G'. According to British intelligence sources, G had undergone military training at a camp in Kashmir, before being sent back to Britain as an Al Qaeda fund-raiser and recruiter. Those who write books about terrorism are also not immune to rich foreigners successfully exploiting Britain's draconian libel laws to suppress information about the financing of terrorism, even though the authors are not actually British citizens. Only Nick Cohen, writing in the satirical magazine *Private Eye*, has had the guts to report the most egregious examples. This scandal has resulted in US Congressmen attempting to pass laws designed to nullify the effects of such rulings in the US itself.[17]

Even the armed forces and police are not immune to some of these pathologies. The Royal Navy, once the scourge of pirates, refuses to detain Somali pirates on the ground that their rights might be infringed if they handed them over to neighbouring states, or to take them back to Britain because they might contend they required asylum and welfare thanks to the hypothetical persecution applying in the first scenario. The police have also been loath to investigate honour killings in the Muslim community, or the abusive treatment of women, because of cultural 'sensitivities'. The police seem to have turned a blind eye to instances where sharia courts adjudicated in cases that manifestly should have come before criminal courts, such as grievous bodily harm resulting from some unfortunate being hit over the head with an iron bar.[18]

Beyond such examples of elite political correctness and smug irresponsibility, there is a less exclusive penumbra of people who have graduated from the extreme left to supporting parties that are halfway houses to the reactionary Islamists. One thinks especially here of George Galloway's Respect party which has literally absorbed the older Socialist Workers Party. Mrs Cherie Blair's half-sister, the celebrity Palestinian activist and right-wing Sunday-newspaper columnist Lauren Booth, is a leading light of this ultra-left party. The left-wing former mayor of London, Ken Livingstone, was also zealous in extending the hand of friendship to Sheikh Youssef al-Qaradawi, who is banned from even seeking medical treatment in Britain because of his indulgence of Palestinian suicide bombers and his hatred of homosexuals. This was

part of a multiculturalist electoral strategy in which people were supposed to vote according to a given identity, after calculations had been
made whether there were more Muslim than, say, Black or gay voters.
The spectacle of left-liberal sympathy for Islamists, whom many regard
as latterday Fascists, has become too much for a number of decent
prominent British left-wingers, including Anthony Andrew, Nick Cohen
and Rod Liddle who have been traduced by their erstwhile comrades
on the *Guardian*. They shouldn't worry too much since many of their
most angry critics are merely playwrights like David Edgar or, to move
down several notches, Ronan Bennett – who has a noteworthy past in
Northern Ireland. Even the Labour-supporting Ed Husain has been
abused on television by a British-based Hamas activist – in 2004 this
gentleman had told the BBC he would be pleased to be a suicide bomber
– on the grounds that Husain was a 'neo-conservative', the all-purpose
term of abuse in such circles.[19]

Once upon a time, theologians like Reinhold Niebuhr and Paul Tillich
knew how to respond to evil without limp equivocation. That tradition
has been continued by the present pope and his immediate predecessor.
Many Western Protestant Churches are nowadays so suffused with
secular liberal messianisms that they are indistinguishable from common
or garden progressive opinion.[20] A particularly jarring example is an
archbishop of Canterbury who, in some circles, enjoys the reputation of
a profound thinker, despite his self-description as 'a hairy leftie'. Rowan
Williams sought to make common cause with Muslim clerics (against
militant philosophical or scientific secularists and degraded materialism
in general) by contemplating the licensing of enclaves of soft sharia
law, a concession that would wholly undermine the common law of
England, while opening the gates to hard sharia law in the future.
Williams thinks we live in a 'market state', a concept he borrowed from
the constitutional lawyer Philip Bobbitt, although recent NATO caveats
about the war in Afghanistan suggest that the nation state is alive and
well when it wants to be, as is the only licensed European nationalist
sentiment, that of unthinking anti-Americanism. Another line of
justification for thoughts that outraged the British public, despite the
archbishop's sly resort to Greco-German theological 'unclarity', was that
the banking sector has already noiselessly introduced sharia-compliant
finance (and insurance) – even though this does not exist in Egypt.
Evidently what is good enough for folks in Cairo is no longer good
enough for London.[21]

Like it or not, Islam in Europe is a proselytising religion which asserts its presence through such demands as those for amplified muezzin in a predominantly non-Muslim suburb of Oxford or a 35,000-capacity mega-mosque to be situated next to London's 2012 Olympic complex. Both of these projects have occasioned deep public unease. There are also quotidian acts of minority-within-a-minority self-assertion, ranging from schoolgirls insisting on wearing the hijab and jilbab, to imams petitioning NHS hospitals with demands that patients' beds be turned to Mecca five times a day, and female Muslim NHS surgeons refusing to bare their arms for scrubbing up, in defiance of health regulations designed to prevent MRSA. These are not fantasies of right-wing tabloid newspapers, but facts about life today in the UK and in many other parts of western Europe where those strident in their criticism of Islam have to live under constant police guard or go into exile, the fate of Ayaan Hirsi Ali and the Dutch MP Geert Wilders.

Islam is a more territorial religion than Christianity or Judaism, with no tradition either of Christianity's separation of the temporal and spiritual or of accepting the predominance of the host society and its laws as orthodox Jews do everywhere with their Beth Din arbitration courts. Western Europe is witnessing the gradual emergence of Muslim no-go areas, of enclaves based around nodal mosques and community centres, and public housing projects or rows of private terraced housing from which the White indigenous population is decamping. According to a BBC *Panorama* investigation, these Whites are fleeing because they feel alienated in their own country, both because they have become surrounded by people who have not bothered to learn the language and customs of the host society, and because of a more sinister chill emanating from professional Islamists who ensure the collapse of such things as the betting shop and the street-corner pub. The BBC documentary revealed that in justice minister Jack Straw's Blackburn constituency there was almost zero interaction between the White north and the Muslim south of this small Lancashire town. Lax immigration policies, cheap flights and phone calls and satellite TV mean that many immigrants do not make the mental break with home that is normative in the USA.[22] Instead they simply transplant their home village to British cities – most glaringly when a group of Mirpuri families bought sixteen houses in suburban Slough, knocking down the garden walls so that they could replicate the village environment they had known in Kashmir. Their excuse for resisting integration (as opposed to assimilation) is that they despise what they are being asked to join, namely the popular culture of binge-drinking and television dominated by *Big Brother* – an especially pernicious reality show produced by the descendant of the eminent Bazalgette who, ironically, built Victorian London's ring sewers. Much the same state of affairs exists in what Ian Buruma has dubbed the 'dish cities' of the Netherlands or in the peripheral *banlieues* around some French cities.[23]

So far governments, notably in Britain and the Netherlands, have responded with state programmes to intensify the inculcation of local values through formal citizenship tests and public ceremonies even as they sneer at America's ubiquitous flags on the lawn. Many new citizens find such ceremonies moving. In these two countries in particular, there has been a rapid theoretical abandonment of the divisive doctrine of multiculturalism, although no commensurate attempt to uproot its massive bureaucratic footprint in education, the media and local government. Indeed, the solution to radicalisation seems to be to create more bureaucrats, presumably to counter the influence of those we already have. It has taken about four years for the British government to realise that the old imperial habit of ruling so-called communities, which are as complex as any other, through self-nominated chiefs – in this case the Muslim Council of Britain – was self-defeating because these people often reflected a highly conservative Deobandist Islam, akin to Wahhabism, which was part of the problem rather than the solution. The former MCB leader Sir Iqbal Sacranie has never retracted his comment that 'death would be too easy for Salman Rushdie', while the current leader, Dr Abdul Bari, has a history of involvement with the Jamaat-e-Islami movement. The French Muslim umbrella organisation has similar problems. Because of lucrative arms contracts, no efforts have gone into stemming the flow of Gulf money into propagating Wahhabism, whether through mosques or the venal universities and their Islamic Studies programmes. In other words, government policy lags behind what reformed radicals themselves have been proposing.

II 'THE END OF THE BEGINNING?':
EPISODES FROM THE JIHAD 2007–2008

As the principal target for global jihadist terrorism, the US has sophisticated and various ways of dealing with it. The key difference between the
US and Europe is that the former is fighting something 'out there', largely
by front-loading military power, while Europeans already have 'it' in
their midst in the shape of North African, Bangladeshi and Pakistani
second- or third-generation citizens, as well as those to whom they have
sometimes been foolish enough to grant asylum. In reality things are not
so straightforward. For Europe is likely to be the main source of clean-
skin terrorist attacks within the US, a process FBI director Robert Muller
has graciously decided not to stymie by rescinding the visa-waiver
programme for short-term visitors. The US has multi-layered defences
which begin with investment in securing nuclear materials in faraway
Georgia and Kazakhstan, the screening of containers in ports, and the
close monitoring of foreign visitors that commences when they purchase
their air ticket. The INS and other agencies are keepers of the gates when
they disembark, carrying out their task firmly but with courtesy and
sensitivity.

The US also plans for nightmare scenarios, including terrorist access
to micro-bacteriological labs or nuclear weapons. In April 2008, for
example, the Senate Committee on Homeland Security heard authoritative evidence about the effects of a nuclear strike on the US capital. The
chairman, senator Joe Lieberman, said: 'The scenarios we discuss today
are very hard for us to contemplate, and so emotionally traumatic
and unsettling that it is tempting to push them aside.' His Committee
heard that a ten-kiloton bomb left in a truck near the White House would
erase a two-mile radius of downtown federal buildings, killing about
100,000 people, the majority African-Americans in clerical positions.
More people would die of burns, for at present the national capacity to
treat such cases is restricted to fifteen hundred people. A radioactive
plume would drift, with the winds, from the west to the south-east, affecting predominantly African-American neighbourhoods where there is a
single major hospital. As Lieberman said: 'Now is the time to have this
difficult conversation, to ask the tough questions, and then to get answers
as best we can.' That this is not some alarmist fantasy on the part of
hysterical Americans can be gauged from the fact that in July 2007 the

Canada Border Services Agency rescinded a visa granted to a recently arrived Anglo-Pakistani man by the High Commission in London on the grounds that 'he is a suspected terrorist implicated in Al Qaeda's mass destruction weapons program'. After a night in a Toronto jail he was deported to Manchester, although his current whereabouts are unknown.[24]

Al Qaeda has mutated since 9/11, exchanging a military-style hierarchy for a loose franchised network, although it is currently rebuilding both the hierarchy and the training camps in the Federally Administered Tribal Areas and North-West Frontier Provinces of Pakistan. This reflects the success of a NATO coalition and the reconstituted Afghan National army in restoring some modicum of stability to twenty-nine of the country's thirty-four provinces. Al Qaeda's restoration of a base in Pakistan was facilitated by Pervez Musharraf's August 2006 Waziristan Accords, which the current government of Pakistan is bent on perpetuating. In return for non-interference by the Pakistani army and Frontier Corps, the tribal leaders agreed to keep a lid on jihadism within their areas. The result was a rapid extension of extremist activity into the peaceful Swat Valley, which is peaceful no more. Informed commentators like Steve Coll think bin Laden himself is ensconced in or around Miram Shah, a Taliban stronghold in North Waziristan. Whether the political culture of the FATA approves of Al Qaeda simply recreating the conditions it enjoyed under the Afghan Taliban is a moot point. Al Qaeda may have to invest so much effort in squaring its endemically fractious hosts, notably the Haqqani clan, that it has little energy left to conduct international terrorism. Moreover, ethnic Chechens, Tajiks and Uzbeks captured by coalition forces have revealed the disdain in which they are held by Al Qaeda's Arab core, within which individual risks are not fairly run by Egyptians, Libyans, Lebanese, Moroccans, Algerians and Yemenis.[25]

Stemming the flow of fresh recruits is equally important. Approximately two thousand entry-level jihadists have passed through the Saudi Arabian prison re-education scheme. As a psychologist involved in the programme has said: 'we have to deal with the minds and the emotional passions of the extremists. Fixing minds is like fixing a building with sixty floors. It's not easy.' According to researchers from Princeton University, of the 700 people released from the scheme, only nine have gone on to reoffend, although whether or not the hard-drives of their minds have been cleansed remains known only to them.[26]

As Olivier Roy has cogently argued, although Al Qaeda cannot realise its caliphate – for that would give the US a concrete object to destroy – it can expand the lawless grey areas in which it thrives. It has sought to exaggerate its global reach through regional affiliates: hence Al Qaeda in the Land of the Two Rivers, Al Qaeda in the Islamic Maghreb and, if it is to be believed, Al Qaeda in Britain. In the first two cases it is seeking to subsume local conflicts, presumably to reorientate these fighters against US and other Western targets by emphasising the ultimate source of their local ills. It wishes to transform itself from being a bright star into a glistening galaxy or nebula. Again this is not as straightforward as it seems. The strategy is vulnerable to the extirpation of the key figures who link the centre with the area concerned. That was why the January 2008 killing in Pakistan of Abu Laith al-Libi, the driving force behind bringing the Libyan Islamic Fighting Group into Al Qaeda's orbit, was so crucial. The second, successful Cruise missile strike on Adan Hashi Ayro on 1 May 2008 in Somalian Dhusamareb may similarly disable the Al-Shabaab movement in that country.[27]

Creating vast regional umbrella organisations, such as Al Qaeda in the Islamic Maghreb, papers over real tensions between, say, Algerian and Libyan militants derived from the fact that in the 1990s the Algerian GSPC killed many Libyan volunteers as apostates. Algerian Islamism itself is riven with strategic differences about whether to focus on toppling the Bouteflika regime or to hit Western targets. Having alighted upon the Berber Kabylia as terrain suitable for waging terrorism, Al Qaeda in the Islamic Maghreb has alienated many Berbers with the reign of terror it has established in towns like Tizi Ouzo.

Because of the multiple pressures Al Qaeda has experienced in Algeria, Egypt, Morocco and Saudi Arabia, it has sought to extend operations to Mauritania and other states of the Sahel, that is the belt of countries running from Mali to Somalia. Mauritania has seen the murder of European tourists and has become so unstable that the annual Paris–Dakar rally, which passes through, was cancelled. The regime in Yemen has also reversed its earlier co-operation in the war on terror, by releasing jihadist prisoners, including those responsible for killing seventeen US sailors on the USS *Cole*, who have gone on to attack US interests and foreign adventure tourists, just as some of the released Guantánamo detainees have become suicide bombers.[28] Since the US-sponsored Ethiopian invasion of Somalia in December 2006 to depose the Islamic Courts regime, conditions there have gone from bad to worse, with 1.5 million refugees and another 1.5 million dependent on UN food aid. The

Ethiopian presence also enables the jihadists to masquerade as defenders of Somali nationalism and sovereignty, a pose adopted by some of the coastal pirates – fishermen who claim, in the absence of central government, that they are warding off Spanish trawlers infringing a notional 200-mile fishing limit. Somalia and Yemen should therefore be regarded as areas where Al Qaeda may set up a future territorial base should the Afghan–Pakistan borderlands prove inhospitable.

While the picture in these countries is dispiriting, elsewhere there are signs of hope. There has been a marked lull in jihadist activity in South Asia, where, as in Indonesia and Malaysia, aggressive counter-terrorism tactics by special forces has been accompanied by softer programmes designed to disengage the minds of imprisoned extremists. Perhaps the head of Indonesia's counter-terrorism police was taking things too far when he invited some of the imprisoned Bali bombings conspirators to a party in his home in September 2007. 'We make them our brothers, not our enemy,' explained General Surya Dharma. There has been no major jihadist terrorist incident in Indonesia since 2005 – surely a consequence of more than two hundred arrests. In Turkey, two roundups in January and April 2008 netted some fifty Al Qaeda extremists, while revealing the parallel world they had established, including a school system that even issued regular report cards.[29]

One issue has clearly exacerbated jihadist terrorism: Iraq. Because this has also telescoped the already short-term memories of so many commentators (for according to professor Akbar Ahmed one can find jihadists under Nor Mohammed seeking to take over Waziristan in the mid-1970s) I decided to give it marginal attention in the book. In case anyone has forgotten, Algerian Islamists attempted to crash a passenger aircraft into the Eiffel Tower in the mid-1990s.[30] Whether the US should have invaded or occupied Iraq is not a subject that belongs in a history of terrorism, and nor does the question of whether Iraq will ultimately remain a unitary state, which can be left to futurologists. It may break up; it may become a Middle Eastern version of post-war Finland. I also instinctively recoil from those who so eagerly believe that the US administration acted in bad faith, that it is a captive of Israel – or an American-Jewish lobby – or that it has established a regime of terror akin to the gulag or Nazi Germany. Much of this is not even worthy of comment. As a conservative realist, sceptical of the zealous neo-cons, I hold no brief for former assistant defense secretary Douglas Feith, but to compare him with the Nazis is tastelessly wrong – and not only because nine members of his family perished in the Holocaust.[31]

After four years of floundering around in Iraq, effective counter-insurgency strategies seem to have been adopted by the US. In part this reflects mistakes made by their opponents. Al Qaeda's leadership lost control over one major franchisee, Abu Musab al-Zarqawi, who discredited the brand through his penchant for videoing the beheadings of hostages. Even Ayman al-Zawahari was moved to protest at the time. Commencing in 2006, a US-inspired Sunni Awakening movement has thrown off the regime of terror which mainly foreign jihadists erected in some central provinces, reasserting the rule of conservative tribal elders into the bargain. To overcome their own distaste for relying on former insurgent opponents to crush the jihadis, the US military recorded data on these new forces and their weapons that make it possible to track them quickly should they turn against the Americans in future.

Deploying five fresh combat brigades, generals David Petraeus and Raymond Odierno launched operations to destroy the insurgency through combined military, political, economic and diplomatic methods. The essence of this was to deny Al Qaeda the outlying and suburban strongholds from which they had launched the urban roadside bombs and suicide missions that were killing six thousand Iraqis a month. It was a variant of the counter-insurgency tactics used by General Sir Gerald Templer in Malaya, although US forces have been used aggressively and without any equivalent to the British colonial police. Large-scale follow-up operations like Phantom Strike hit the jihadis as they fled towards Mosul. At the same time Petraeus took many unemployed young men off the streets by instituting essential public works programmes designed to fix things that should have been fixed on day one.

Judging from the discontent revealed in Al Qaeda in Iraq's internal correspondence, these surge operations have stemmed the flow of foreign volunteer martyrs coming from Libya and Saudi Arabia. They arrive, hang around, grow disillusioned and leave because the major urban attacks have been interdicted. They want the big money-shot (for the structure of jihadist suicide videos resembles that of porn movies) and not some minor attack that kills a couple of American civilian contractors. Insofar as most Iraqis are keen to retain democratic elections while their elected government is urging the US to maintain a military presence, these operations can be said to have been a political success, even if the main geopolitical consequence of the war has been to extend Iran's influence westwards, thereby triggering improbably improved relations between Saudi Arabia, Syria and Israel. Al Qaeda in Iraq has also conspicuously failed in its twin objectives of creating an Islamic state and plunging the country into a sectarian civil war. However, one worries about how many men may have experienced training and combat in Iraq, and how many of them are Europeans who may try to commit acts of terrorism on their return home. In that sense, Iraq may play a similar role to the Afghan–Soviet war of the 1980s. In 2005 French counter-terrorism officials rounded up the so-called 19th arrondissement cell. This was the handiwork of a twenty-six-year-old Franco-Algerian called Farid Benyettou, an ex-janitor turned imam, who had recruited suicide bombers to go to Iraq.

In Europe, intelligence and police work has frustrated several conspiracies to murder. As a result of the concentration of powers of investigation, detention and punishment in the *juges d'instruction* such as Jean-Louis Bruguière and Jean-François Ricard, the French have been the most aggressive in combating terrorism and religious subversion, holding suspects for periods of time that would embarrass the US itself. French skill in this area is indirectly reflected in the fact that the main CIA station for counter-terrorism is in Paris, while the Spanish intelligence services have agreed joint operations that take no notice of the Pyrenees as a border. This co-operation has paid off. Thanks to a tip-off from a French agent inserted into a Pakistani network, on 19 January 2008 Spanish police arrested eleven Indian and Pakistani males who were allegedly conspiring to blow up Barcelona on 11 March so as to force the tiny Spanish contingent out of Afghanistan. It is striking that although France has been largely spared major terrorist incidents since the 1990s, while its government ostentatiously refused to get involved in Iraq, it nevertheless sees itself as an integral part of Western civilisation under jihadist attack. The hardline domestic approach to terrorism does not prevent a highly nuanced French diplomacy towards the Arab world. In April 2008 the US homeland security secretary Michael Chertoff and the German interior minister Wolfgang Schäuble concluded controversial intelligence-sharing arrangements based on data-mining to counteract the possibility that German jihadists may attack US interests. Italian counter-terrorism magistrates such as Armando Spartaro have also been assiduous in closing down jihadist cells based in Italy, although co-operation with the US was damaged when in 2003 thirteen CIA agents kidnapped Abu Omar in broad daylight from a Milan street, spiriting him to Cairo where he was tortured.[32]

Britain has much experience in the field of terrorism, although not in the sense that the British themselves like to advertise. Although other countries have problems with murderous jihadis (notably Denmark and the Netherlands) Britain, according to a recent Europol report, is actually the epicentre of European jihadism. This news was buried in brief two-hundred-word accounts in the newspapers that bothered to notice it. In 2007 some 203 people were arrested in Britain on suspicion of terror offences; the figure for the whole of the rest of Europe was 201.[33] A large number of terrorist cases, under investigation for several years, have also passed through British courts. They have included Dhiran Barot, the Hindu convert and Al Qaeda mastermind who conspired to blow up US targets. Several men were convicted in the wake of Operation Crevice for planning to kill shoppers at the Bluewater complex in Kent and 'dancing slags' in South London nightclubs. Also convicted was the cyber-jihadist Younis Tsouli, codenamed 'Irhabi 007', who graduated from assisting the late Abu Musab al-Zarqawi, by using the home movies of US soldiers to help Al Qaeda pinpoint attacks, to becoming Al Qaeda's pre-eminent internet expert. Another was Pervez Khan, who with his accomplices sought to abduct a British Muslim soldier on leave in Birmingham, with a view to filming his decapitation in a garage so as to 'give Young Tony [Blair] something to think about'. Further trials concern the supporting cast in the 7/7 and 21/7 bombings (after the failed bombers of 21/7 had been given long jail sentences), and last but not least, the eight men accused of plotting to blow up multiple trans-Atlantic flights with the aid of liquid explosives concealed in bottles of Lucozade. Pre-recorded suicide videos, and a lot of forensic evidence, will not help their case. Several prominent rabble-rousers, notably Abu 'The Claw' Hamza and Trevor 'Abu Izzadeen' Brooks, have also received jail sentences, with Hamza facing extradition to the US after he has completed his seven-year sentence. Among those yet to come to court is the Iraqi who survived the failed alleged attack on Glasgow airport using gas-cylinder bombs and Andrew Ibrahim, an alleged 'lone wolf bomber'. These cases have confirmed that 70 per cent of conspiracies in Britain have links to Pakistan. The plotters invariably went to Pakistan with a view to waging armed jihad, only to be subtly redirected, because of their uselessness on a battlefield, to carrying out atrocities on home ground in operations that were subsequently green-lit from abroad.

There have been other revelations regarding the mentality of British jihadists. One case has revealed a video pre-recorded by 7/7 lead bomber Mohammed Siddique Khan in which he bade farewell to his infant daughter before leaving to fight in Afghanistan. This touching scene, which moved the more credulous or relativist sort of British columnist, was counterbalanced by evidence in the trial of Pervez Khan regarding his conversion of the living room in his Birmingham house into a replica mujaheddin encampment. MI5 recorded his attempts to indoctrinate his son. As a young man, Khan had shown no interest in religion. He drank, smoked, went clubbing and supported a local amateur soccer team. All changed when he visited Pakistan, after which he began shipping night-vision glasses and camouflage gear to jihadist fighters. Perhaps the most instructive aspects of the conversations MI5 bugged in his home (their code-name for Khan was 'Motorway Madness') were his efforts to beat his worldview into his five-year-old son Abrar, who like all the Khan children was sleeping on groundsheets at home. Abrar: 'I love Sheikh OBL.' Khan: 'Allah and?' Abrar: 'Sheikh Abu Hamza.' Khan: 'And who else do you kill?' Abrar: 'Bush I kill.' Khan: 'And who else?' Abrar: 'Blair I kill.' Khan: 'And?' Abrar: 'Both, I kill.' Khan: 'I speak, my son. Who else you kill? *Kuffar* [infidels].' Abrar: 'Yeah, *kuffar*.' Khan: 'What do you do with these people?' Abrar: 'Shoot them.' Khan: 'How do you kill them? Cut their neck. Show me. Good.'[34]

While not denying that trained theologians issue fatwas licensing violence, most European jihadis come from technical educational backgrounds (rather than the arts), while the leaders of the global jihad include an engineer and a surgeon, both remote from such centres of Islamic learning as Cairo's Al-Azhar university.[35] Indeed the backgrounds of some prominent inciters of jihad in Europe are instructive because they suggest that some sort of compensatory born-again mechanism for a life of dissolution is at work. Abu Hamza worked as a bouncer (doorman) at a London strip joint. Over in Paris, the Algerian Omar Saiki:

> went to bars and frequented prostitutes more often than he attended the mosque or went to listen to Abu Qatada's sermons . . . Saiki was typical of those who have landed up in the Islamist movement by 'accident' and whose zeal redoubles when they find themselves in terrorist cells which provide them with a remedy for the frustrations felt by a whole group of North African men. Having learned to repeat some half-baked theolog-

ical ideas, Saiki styled himself Professor of Theology and began to contaminate other young people similarly.[36]

In Europe, many terrorists are products of a greatly expanded tertiary-education sector – engineering and IT particularly – who are then disappointed when their low-level attainments at institutions whose qualifications employers regard with some scepticism do not translate into rewarding careers, let alone the capacity to dictate foreign policy. Major delusions and pretensions are at work in such circles, perhaps compounded by the 'little prince' syndrome operative in many Asian households. There are also fashionista jihadis like twenty-three-year-old Samina Malik, a shop assistant working airside at London's Heathrow Airport, who described herself as a 'lyrical terrorist' because of her penchant for writing poems praising martyrs on the back of till receipts.

The footsoldiers are also recruited from the expanding underclass with its subculture of absent fathers and prolific mothers. A remarkable number of European prison inmates are Muslims compared with their percentage of the general population. In Belgium 15 per cent of prisoners are Muslims, but only 2 per cent of Belgians in general. In the Netherlands they are 20 per cent of prison inmates, and less than 6 per cent of the Dutch population. In France, 60–70 per cent of prisoners are Muslim, in a country where Muslims are 5–10 per cent of the population. Finally in Britain they are 11 per cent of the prison population and only 3 per cent of the total population. Many prisoners convert to Islam, for two main reasons: either because their lives are self-evidently such a mess that Islam brings order and meaning, or because of the 'don't mess with the Muslims' syndrome. Jailed Muslims form powerful gangs within prisons, affording the new recruit a significant degree of protection – in US terms rather like joining the Aryan Nation, Hell's Angels, the Bloods or the Crips. The career of Richard Reid, the Afro-Caribbean shoe bomber currently residing in Florence, Colorado, is symptomatic of the type: he converted to Islam while serving one of many sentences for petty offences. The Brotherhood – in his case around north London's radical Finsbury Park Mosque – provided the warmth and purpose his life had not known, the entry stage for a trajectory that finished when he was prevented from exploding the bomb concealed in his shoes. (In the latest twist, as reported by Channel 4, jihadist preachers are licensing south London Muslim gang members to rob the *kuffar* provided they give a cut of the proceeds to the extremists' cause.)

Given that some 1,600 Muslim extremists are likely to be imprisoned in Britain by the end of the decade, how to stop them radicalising very vulnerable fellow inmates should be a matter of urgent concern, for in future jihadism may commence, rather than culminate, in life behind bars. Should the authorities allow them to be consolidated in one place (as they and their lawyers insist) or should they be dispersed throughout the general maximum-security jail population – with the risk of their recruiting others or being subject to serious assault? The US has a similar problem because some 30,000–40,000 prisoners in American jails convert to Islam each year.[37]

III SOME EUROPEAN PERSPECTIVES

The current condition of Europe has triggered much alarmism, with talk of a neutralised 'Eurabia' on the one hand and a future Muslim Holocaust on the other, depending on whether, like Bat Ye'or or Bruce Bawer, one views Europeans as 'wimps' or, like the maverick Colonel Ralph Peters, as mass murderers. The latter is a popular view in a society that consumes so much material on the Holocaust. A book on the 'Old Continent' by veteran terrorism expert Walter Laqueur published in 2007 included the words 'Last Days' and 'Epitaph' in its title.[38]

In recent years the trans-Atlantic rhetoric has overheated, a fact that can only give the West's jihadist enemies cause for hope given that Al Qaeda's strategy includes offers of truces designed to divide and rule. Europeans don't much like being called cowardly 'Venusians' slipping into abject dhimmitude in an Islamised 'Eurabia'. One has also heard enough for one lifetime from abrasive neo-cons such as Kenneth Adelman and John Bolton who can't quite play against typecasting on BBC television discussion shows. Presumably vanity plays its depressing role as it is easy to decline a *Newsnight* request for an interview just by saying no. It is similarly galling for a sophisticated people like the Americans to be defamed by ignorant Europeans (of whom there are many) as gun-toting cowboys, all the more so because for the last sixty years US commitment to Europe's security has enabled it to divert huge resources from defence into social welfare and health programmes. Beyond this public chatter, much of it emanating from public intellectuals, US and European intelligence and police forces are quietly

hardwired into one another, although the higher British judiciary sometimes actively frustrate their co-operation in the erroneous belief that
that they are living in Hendrik Verwoerd's South Africa.

There are problems in Europe, but they are not solely the crude demographic ones that pessimists routinely point to when prognosticating
about 'Eurabia'. After all, second- or third-generation Muslims will be
as exposed to ambient secularising pressures as anyone else. Like other
Europeans (and middle-class Iranians for that matter) they will also
realise that two children are cheaper than six or seven. Religion is almost
absent from public discourse about identity. This arises from a fear of
offending Muslims, and from the dogmatically secular nature of some
European countries. Compared to the noise generated by aggressive
atheism and secularism, European Christianity is relatively timorous,
although Benedict XVI occasionally surprises, with his Regensburg
Address of September 2006 or his baptism eighteen months later of an
Egyptian-Italian Milanese newspaper editor. A number of distinguished
European intellectuals such as Regis Debray or Umberto Eco have also
recently argued in favour of reclaiming and reasserting the West's
Christian heritage. On a popular level, despite spasmodic resurgences of
'cultural Christianity' which repeated Islamist provocations have elicited,
the Churches themselves are so suffused with secular liberalism that
they are indistinguishable from it. Western Christendom is an embarrassment from the deep past, although not quite yet something the
Churches feel obliged to apologise for except in relation to the Crusades
or slavery – even though, as the historically aware will know, Europe
itself experienced both. Indeed on some moral issues one can find a
variable geometry of religious opinion, as when in February 2007 the
Catholic archbishop of Lyons, a rabbi and an imam conjointly issued a
declaration against gay marriage.[39]

There is little prospect either of a confident political identity at the
European federal level as long as voters in major states regard the undemocratic nature of such a project with deserved scepticism, while
national leaders are divided as to whether to extend the project eastwards
or southwards. Intra-European political wrangling largely instigated
by Germany has seen off Nicolas Sarkozy's imaginative plan to offer
North Africa and Israel associate status. Nor are countries which are
themselves mostly federal, composite mini-empires going to have success in re-establishing core national identities, especially since the entire
thrust of fashionable academic opinion is that the nation state is a mere

ideological 'construct' that is in any case being superseded by Bobbitt's wretched 'market state'. When the British government essayed identity-building, the Scots and Welsh immediately protested their separate identities. Much the same has happened, or might do so, in Belgium, Italy or Spain should anyone push the matter, all of them states facing powerful separatisms. Likewise – and Britain may or may not be a uniquely vulgarised place – one does not notice contemporary politicians speaking up for the culture of Bach and Rubens rather than the Arctic Monkeys or the Killers, whom they believe they must favour if they are to pursue the talismanic 'yoof' vote.[40]

Judging by the amount of restiveness indigenous peoples (and one includes Chinese, African, Afro-Caribbean, Hindu and Sikh immigrants in that description) are expressing in the face of the incremental demands of assertive Islamists, it will be a rash politician who fails to accommodate such sentiments in making policy before some cataclysmic terrorist event forces a more knee-jerk reaction.[41] The Prodi government's failure to tackle the twin issues of crime and immigration has already led to the re-election of Italy's Silvio Berlusconi, and a cabinet heavy with Northern League separatists and post-Fascists. We are likely to sound more Australian in future; in other words, politicians of all party persuasions will seem to present a united front in making it clear that there are lines in the sand, regarding the liberal democratic nature of our societies, which are not going to be crossed.[42] Liberal Protestant clerics seem to provoke the loudest popular responses. It was made abundantly clear to the Dutch bishop Tiny Muskens when he suggested renaming God 'Allah' and to Rowan Williams with his donnish enthusiasm for licensing sharia law in Britain that these were steps too far. There are further straws in the wind.

Across Europe, conservative parties have found an anodyne way of talking about immigration as 'population movements' in order to neuter charges of racism. But such charges no longer have the debate-silencing effect they had even a decade ago, especially since it is older immigrants who often lead the way in calling for restrictions against uncouth newcomers. The fact that many recent migrants have been white Catholic Poles and other east Europeans has also helped defuse the issue of colour-obsessed racism. The people disproportionately responsible, it is alleged, for crime in Italy are Albanians or Romanians; the 800,000 children whose non-existent or poor English strains the British school system are largely east European. Borders will be policed by dedicated policemen – whose charms Yankees will shortly encounter when they debouch at Fiumicino, Schiphol or, heaven help them, Gatwick or Heathrow. There will also be more efforts to insist that immigrants have a mastery of the relevant local language, just as there will be a more graduated, extended process of achieving citizenship after fulfilling various reciprocal requirements. In other words citizenship is going to be conditional or probationary. Tougher measures will be taken against employers who cynically rely on illegal immigrant labour. Some would like to go further in restricting access to state benefits – it being notable that so many of those plotting to kill people in Britain do not refuse substantial welfare entitlements. Indeed they regard this not only as an entitlement, but as evidence of the decadence they see at the heart of the western European way of life. There should also be a few deft alterations to local law. People deported for terrorist-related offences should be allowed to mount appeals (at their own expense) only after they have been removed from the country. A local Bill of Rights in the UK should override European human rights law, while making it impossible for foreigners to exploit libel laws to quash legitimate inquiry into terrorist finance.

One purpose of these afterthoughts has been to update our current predicament in the global jihadist insurgency. Events in Pakistan or Somalia really do re-impact on Europe or the US, just as events in Europe do on the States and those in the States on Europe. To recall Michael Doran's concern with advertising branding, I suspect that the bin Laden brand is not what it was in 2001. Perhaps Doran is right to talk too in Churchillian tones of 'the end of the beginning'. I have left one matter to the end. On 7 July 2005 four Islamist suicide bombers murdered fifty-two people travelling on London's transport system. The survivors of that mass atrocity are writing accounts of their experiences, which should be part of any history of the most recent terrorist activities, although it sometimes seems that this is an exclusive two-way dialogue between the authorities and Muslim minorities. Actually it is not. Among the best accounts of 7/7 are Canadian journalist Peter Zimonjic's account of that morning when he embarked on another trip to purgatory on the overcrowded London tube. Within a few minutes, three men blew themselves up on trains packed to capacity which, depending on the line, were between fifteen and seventy feet underground. For those unfamiliar with such journeys, that means about a thousand people jammed noses to armpits in a metal cylinder in tunnels that are so tight it is impossible to walk between the train and the walls. That is bad enough, without some maniac trying to kill you.

The victims on 7/7 included Danny Biddle. He had gone to work reluctantly rather than take the day off because of a bad migraine. He was a couple of seats away from Mohammed Siddique Khan when the latter calmly reached into his rucksack and detonated a powerful bomb. Danny was hurled out of the train into the tunnel. After a few seconds he realised he was in flames, and was thinking 'Fuck, I'm on fire. Fuck, fuck, fuck.' His metal watch was burning into his wrist. After some minutes it dawned on him that the leg he was contemplating some way off was his own. It had been blown off at the hip. His right leg had also disintegrated into the shreds of his trousers. His head was both swollen and cut across the entire forehead. An eye was missing. It took forty-five minutes for paramedics to reach him, during which time two strangers managed to stop massive blood loss with primitive tourniquets made from torn-up shirts. There are many academic definitions of terrorism. Try this one:

> Danny was certain he was going to die in that tunnel. He looked at Adrian and Lee, shadows fidgeting in the darkness around him, and he thought that these two men, two strangers, were the last people he would ever see. It broke his heart. He was going to die in the dark, with no one who loved him by his side, with no one who knew him even aware of what was happening. The thought terrified him. 'I don't want to die. I don't want to die,' he thought. 'I am twenty-six. I don't want to die this way. Not like this. I have a lot of things left to do. Not like this, please.' With the panic came guilt. He was going to leave his fiancée behind, alone without him. For the rest of her life she would have to live with the thought that he had died in the dark, afraid, staring up at the dirty ceiling of some filthy tunnel with no one to tell him they loved him.[43]

ACKNOWLEDGEMENTS

I must thank Victoria Barnsley of HarperCollins for the brilliant idea of including a lengthy Afterthoughts chapter both to update the book and to offer some general conclusions. Since the book was first published in the UK I have been heartened by the highly enthusiastic responses of several people who are informed counter-terrorism practitioners, rather than academic theoreticians of terrorism. What I describe without superfluous editorialising commentary is what they have encountered. In no particular order I would like to warmly thank General the Lord Guthrie, Britain's former Chief of the Defense Staff; Lieutenant-General Graeme Lamb, the head of the UK Fighting Army; the former Spanish president, José María Aznar, who kindly came to the Policy Exchange in London to interview me about the book; and Assistant Commissioner Peter Clarke, the former head of the Metropolitan Police Anti-Terrorism Branch, who moved the vote of thanks on that occasion. I was very glad to hear that Peter has recommended it for a new MA in Counter-Terrorism at my alma mater. David Cameron, the Conservative Party leader, most generously referred to the book in a major speech in March 2008 on terrorism. I am also grateful to Eric Edelman and Michael Doran of the US Defense Department for the opportunity to learn how these issues are viewed by our US friends and allies. Harvey Sicherman and James Kurth organized a memorable discussion at the Foreign Policy Research Institute in Philadelphia.

Michael Burleigh
June 2008

NOTES

Chapter 1: Green: The Fenian Dynamiters

1 Alvin Jackson, *Ireland 1798–1998* (Oxford 1999) pp. 177–8
2 For these preliminary remarks see especially Paul Bew, *Ireland. The Politics of Enmity* (Oxford 2007) pp. 240ff. and Jackson, *Ireland 1798–1998*
3 The best recent book on Irish nationalism is Richard English, *Irish Freedom. The History of Nationalism in Ireland* (London 2006) pp. 179ff.
4 Patrick Quinlivan and Paul Rose, *The Fenians in England 1865–1872* (London 1982) p. 5
5 R. V. Comerford, *The Fenians in Context. Irish Politics and Society 1848–82* (Dublin 1985)
6 Alan O'Day, *Irish Home Rule* (Manchester 1998) p. 8
7 *The Times* 14 December 1867 has detailed reports on the atrocity in Clerkenwell
8 See the comprehensive study by Seán McConville, *Irish Political Prisoners, 1848–1922. Theatres of War* (London 2003)
9 See especially Lindsay Clutterbuck, 'The Progenitors of Terrorism: Russian Revolutionaries or Extreme Irish Republicans?' *Terrorism and Political Violence* (2004) 16, pp. 154–81
10 G. I. Brown, *The Big Bang. A History of Explosives* (Thrupp 2005) pp. 92ff.
11 See especially K. R. M. Short, *The Dynamite War. Irish-American Bombers in Victorian Britain* (Dublin 1979) pp. 218–19
12 Henri le Caron, *Twenty-Five Years in the Secret Service. The Recollections of a Spy* (London 1893)
13 On Sullivan see Terry Golway, *Irish Rebel. John Devoy and America's Fight for Ireland's Freedom* (New York 1998) pp. 155ff.
14 *The Times* 21 May 1883
15 Roland Quinault, 'Underground Attacks' *History Today* September 2005 pp. 18–19 has some charming illustrations
16 Richard English, *Armed Struggle. The History of the IRA* (London 2003) pp. 3–13
17 Bew, *Ireland* p. 375; for Pearse and Republican Catholic nationalism see Conor Cruise O'Brien, *Ancestral Voices. Religion and Nationalism in Ireland* (Dublin 1994) pp. 103–17
18 English, *Armed Struggle* p. 18
19 Peter Hart, *The IRA at War 1916–1923* (Oxford 2003) pp. 141ff.
20 See the excellent account in Jackson, *Ireland 1798–1998* pp. 257ff.
21 Christopher Murray, *Seán O'Casey. Writer at Work* (Dublin 2004) pp. 163ff.
22 Jackson, *Ireland 1798–1998* pp. 345–6

Chapter 2: Russian Nihilists and Revolutionaries

1 Edvard Radzinsky, *Alexander II. The Last Great Tsar* (New York 2005)
2 For the general issues see John Horgan 'The Search for the Terrorist Personality' in Andrew Silke (ed.), *Terrorists, Victims, and Society.*

Psychological Perspectives on Terrorism and its Consequences (Chichester 2003) pp. 3–27

3 All details from Vera Figner, *Memoirs of a Revolutionist* (DeKalb, Illinois 1991)

4 Jay Berman, *Vera Zasulich. A Biography* (Stanford 1983) p. 4

5 On Populism see Franco Venturi, *Roots of Revolution. A History of the Populist and Socialist Movements in 19th Century Russia* (London 2001)

6 Gary Saul Morson, 'What is the Intelligentsia? Once More, an Old Russian Question' *Academic Questions* (1993) 6, pp. 20–38; see also Martin Malia 'What is the Intelligentsia?' in Richard Pipes (ed.), *The Russian Intelligentsia* (New York 1961)

7 Ronald Hingley, *Nihilists. Russian Radicals and Revolutionaries in the Reign of Alexander II (1855–81)* (London 1967)

8 Nikolai Chernyshevsky, *What is to be Done? Tales of the New People* (Moscow 1983); William F. Woehrlin, *Chernyshevskii. The Man and the Journalist* (Cambridge, Massachusetts 1971); Irina Paperno, *Chernyshevsky and the Age of Realism. A Study in the Semiotics of Behavior* (Stanford, California 1988). There is much insight on these issues and personalities too in Joseph Frank, *Dostoevsky* (Princeton 1976–2002) five volumes

9 Richard Pipes, *Russia under the Old Regime* (London 1974) pp. 271–2

10 Adam B. Ulam, *Prophets and Conspirators in Pre-Revolutionary Russia* (New Brunswick 1998) pp. 1–3

11 See Roger Scruton, 'The Nature of Evil' in his *A Political Philosophy. Arguments for Conservatism* (London 2006) pp. 176ff.

12 References from Berman, *Vera Zasulich*

13 Richard Pipes, *The Degaev Affair. Terror and Treason in Tsarist Russia* (New Haven 2003) tells the story with great skill

14 These debates are carefully charted by Norman Naimark, *Terrorists and Social Democrats. The Russian Revolutionary Movement under Alexander III* (Cambridge, Massachusetts 1983)

15 Anna Geifman, *Thou Shalt Not Kill. Revolutionary Terrorism in Russia, 1894–1917* (Princeton 1993) p. 16

16 On this see now Simon Sebag Montefiore's gripping *Young Stalin* (London 2007)

17 Boris Souvarine, *Stalin. A Critical Survey of Bolshevism* (New York 1939) pp. 94ff. is still the best account

Chapter 3: Black: Anarchists and Terrorism

1 See James Billington, *Fire in the Minds of Men. Origins of the Revolutionary Faith* (New York 1980) pp. 72–92 and François Furet and Mona Ozouf (eds), *Critical Dictionary of the French Revolution* (Cambridge, Massachusetts 1989) pp. 179–85. The quotation from Kropotkin is from Peter Marshall, *Demanding the Impossible. A History of Anarchism* (London 1992) p. 316. For an excellent collection of key texts on the influences that comprised modern terrorism see Walter Laqueur (ed.), *Voices of Terror* (New York 2004)

2 Carl Wittke, *Against the Current. The Life of Karl Heinzen* (Chicago, Illinois 1945) is reliable but overly sympathetic; as a corrective see Benjamin Grob-Fitzgibbon, 'From the Dagger to the Bomb: Karl Heinzen and the Evolution of Political Terror' *Terrorism and Political Violence* (2004) 16, pp. 97ff.

3 Frederic Trautmann, *The Voice of Terror. A Biography of Johann Most* (Westport, Connecticut 1980) for these details of Most's life

4 See 'Assassination' *Alarm* 18 April 1885; 'Dynamite' *Alarm* 27 June 1885; 'Explosives' *Alarm* 18 April 1885; 'Dynamite' *Alarm* 21 February 1885

5 James Green, *Death in the Haymarket* (New York 2006)

6 Arthur Holitscher, *Ravachol und die pariser Anarchisten* (Berlin 1925) is sympathetic to Ravachol and his successors

7 See the reports in *The Times* dated 16 and 21 February 1894 and David Mulry, 'Popular Accounts of the Greenwich Bombing in Conrad's *The Secret Agent*'

Rocky Mountain Review of Language and Literature (2000) 54, pp. 43–64

8 Conrad to Edward Garnett 4 October 1907 in Frederick R. Karl and Laurence Davies (eds), *The Collected Letters of Joseph Conrad* (Cambridge 1988) vol. 3, p. 488

9 John Batchelor, *The Life of Joseph Conrad. A Critical Biography* (Oxford 1994) pp. 156–7 and Ian Watt, *Essays on Conrad* (Cambridge 2000) pp. 112ff.

10 Joseph Conrad, *The Secret Agent* (London 1963) quotations from pp. 74, 93, 101–3, 265. See also Ben MacIntyre, 'Insignificant, Shabby, Miserable – The Banal Stamp of a Terrorist' *The Times* 13 May 2006 p. 21 for some astute reflections on literature and Britain's 7/7 bombers

Chapter 4: Death in the Sun: Terror and Decolonisation

1 Stefan Wild, 'Zum Selbstverständnis palästinensisch-arabischer Nationalität' in Helmut Mejcher (ed.), *Die Palästina-Frage 1917–1948* (Paderborn 1993) p. 79

2 Anton La Guardia, *War without End. Israelis, Palestinians and the Struggle for a Promised Land* (New York 2003) p. 77. This is an extraordinarily fair-minded account by a distinguished British journalist of a conflict where rival passions mean that an agreed version is impossible

3 Yehoshuah Porath, *The Palestinian Arab National Movement* vol. 1: *The Emergence of the Palestinian Arab National Movement 1918–29* (London 1974) pp. 31ff.

4 See A. J. Sherman, *Mandate Days. British Lives in Palestine 1918–1948* (London 1997)

5 For this outline see Martin Gilbert's fair-minded *Israel. A History* (London 1998) which sympathetically portrays the British view

6 See the discussion in Ilan Pappé, *A History of Modern Palestine. One Land, Two Peoples* (Cambridge 2004) especially pp. 109–16

7 Uri M. Kupferschmidt, *The Supreme Muslim Council of Islam under the British Mandate for Palestine* (Leiden 1987) p. 250

8 Martin Gilbert, *Churchill and the Jews* (London 2007)

9 Amos Perlmutter, *The Life and Times of Menachem Begin* (New York 1987) p. 33 is an outstanding guide to the politics of Revisionist Zionism

10 The best account of Hassan Salameh is in Michael Bar-Zohar and Eitan Haber, *The Quest for the Red Prince* (Guilford, Connecticut 1983) pp. 17–44

11 Naomi Shepherd, *Ploughing Sand. British Rule in Palestine* (London 1999) is a well-documented account

12 Porath, *The Palestinian Arab National Movement* pp. 178ff.

13 Joseph Heller, *The Stern Gang. Ideology, Politics, and Terror 1940–1949* (London 1995) pp. 78–91

14 Gerald Cromer, '"In the Mirror of the Past": The Use of History in the Justification of Terrorism' *Terrorism and Political Violence* (1991) 3, p. 171

15 Michael Bar-Zohar, *Ben-Gurion* (London 1978) p. 123

16 As recalled by my late friend Amos Perlmutter

17 *The Times* 23 July 1946 p. 4 for the details of the bombing

18 Sherman, *Mandate Days* p. 205

19 Ibid., pp. 207–8

20 Christopher Sykes, *Crossroads to Israel* (London 1965) pp. 380–84. I am deeply grateful to the late Frank Johnson for recommending this fascinating book by a former diplomat and SAS officer during a memorable lunch hosted by Antony Beevor and Artemis Cooper a few weeks before Frank died

21 Bruce Hoffman, *Inside Terrorism* (New York 2006) p. 53

22 See Ilan Pappé, *The Making of the Arab–Israeli Conflict 1947–1951* (London 2001) pp. 87ff.

23 Abu Iyad, *My Home, My Land: A Narrative of the Palestinian Struggle* (New York 1981) pp. 4 and 12

24 Pappé, *History of Modern Palestine* p. 177

25 La Guardia, *War without End* p. 190

26 John Ruedy, *Modern Algeria. The*

Origins and Development of a Nation
(Bloomington, Indiana 2005) pp. 150–52

27 Alistair Horne, *A Savage War of Peace.
Algeria 1954–1962* (New York 2006)
p. 17. This is not only the best single
book on Algeria, but one of the finest
examples of modern historical writing
known to me

28 Paul Aussaresses, *The Battle of the
Casbah. Counter-Terrorism and Torture*
(New York 2005) pp. 33ff.

29 Entry dated 9 March 1956 in Mouloud
Feraoun, *Journal 1955–1962. Reflections
on the French–Algerian War* trans.
Mary Ellen Wolf and Claude Fouillade
(Lincoln, Nebraska 2000) pp. 84–5

30 Christopher Bayly and Tim Harper,
*Forgotten Wars. The End of Britain's
Asian Empire* (London 2007) p. 489

31 Horne, *Savage War of Peace* pp. 262–3

32 Martha Crenshaw Hutchinson,
*Revolutionary Terrorism. The FLN in
Algeria 1954–1965* (Stanford 1978)
pp. 121–2

33 Benjamin Stora, *Algeria 1830–2000*
(Ithaca 2001) pp. 51–2

34 Alf Andrew Heggoy, *Insurgency and
Counterinsurgency in Algeria*
(Bloomington, Indiana 1972) p. 236

35 Aussaresses, *Battle of the Casbah* p. 77

36 Hoffman, *Inside Terrorism* p. 58

37 Horne, *Savage War of Peace* p. 186

38 Alexander Zervoudakis, 'A Case of
Successful Pacification: The 584th
Bataillon du Train at Bordj de l'Agha
(1956–57)' in Martin Alexander and
J. F. V. Krieger (eds), *France and the
Algerian War 1954–62. Strategy,
Operations and Diplomacy* (London
2002) pp. 54–64

39 Tony Walker and Andrew Gowers,
Arafat. The Biography (London 2003)
pp. 20–32

40 On Habash see John K. Cooley, *Green
March, Black September. The Story of
the Palestinian Arabs* (London 1973)
pp. 133ff.

41 Nelson Mandela, *Long Walk to Freedom*
vol. 1: *1918–1962* (London 2002) p. 135

42 T. Dunbar Moodie, *The Rise of
Afrikanerdom. Power, Apartheid and the
Afrikaner Civil Religion* (Berkeley 1975)

43 The best recent history of South Africa

is R. W. Johnson, *South Africa. The First
Man, the Last Nation* (London 2004)
especially pp. 139ff.

44 David Harrison, *The White Tribe of
Africa* (Berkeley 1981) p. 129

45 Ibid., pp. 301–400 for Mandela's
account of these debates

46 Oliver Tambo, *Beyond the Engeli
Mountains* (Durban 2004) pp. 318ff.

47 For these details see Stephen M. Davis,
*Apartheid's Rebels. Inside South Africa's
Hidden War* (New Haven 1987)
pp. 36ff.

48 Adrian Guelke, *Terrorism and Global
Disorder* (London 2006) p. 224

49 Steven Mufson, *Fighting Years. Black
Resistance and the Struggle for a New
South Africa* (Boston 1990) pp. 199–200

50 For examples see Francis Meli, *South
Africa Belongs to Us. A History of the
ANC* (London 1989) pp. 195–8

51 See the website 'Afriforum' for these
issues

Chapter 5: Attention-Seeking: Black
September and International Terrorism

1 On the early history of hijacking see
Timothy Naftali, *Blind Spot. The Secret
History of American Counterterrorism*
(New York 2005) pp. 19ff.

2 Patrick Seale, *Abu Nidal. A Gun for
Hire* (London 1992) pp. 77–8

3 Tony Walker and Andrew Gowers,
Arafat. The Biography (London 2003)
p. 139

4 Simon Reeves, *One Day in September*
(London 2000) p. 41

5 On the leadership see Christopher
Dobson, *Black September* (London
1974) pp. 51ff.

6 For these biographical details see
Michael Bar-Zohar and Eitan Haber,
The Quest for the Red Prince (Guilford,
Connecticut 1983) pp. 92ff.

7 For these quotations see William R.
Farrell, *Blood and Rage. The Story of
the Japanese Red Army* (Lexington,
Massachusetts 1990) pp. 130–44

8 See especially Aaron J. Klein, *Striking
Back. The 1972 Munich Olympics
Massacre and Israel's Deadly Response*
(New York 2005)

9 Barry Rubin and Judith Colp Rubin, *Yasir Arafat. A Political Biography* (London 2003) pp. 63–5

10 Dobson, *Black September* p. 129

11 Bruce Hoffman 'All You Need is Love: How the Terrorists Stopped Terrorism' *Atlantic Monthly* December 2001. Since Hoffman is one of the world's leading authorities on terrorism, there seems little reason to doubt this story, even if his Palestinian interlocutors obviously seek to exonerate PLO terrorism

12 On this see Yossi Melman, *The Master Terrorist. The True Story behind Abu Nidal* (New York 1986) pp. 108ff.

13 Christopher Dobson and Ronald Payne, *The Carlos Complex. A Pattern of Violence* (London 1977) pp. 103ff.

Chapter 6: Guilty White Kids: The Red Brigades and the Red Army Faction

1 Leonard Weinberg, 'Violent Life: Left-wing and Right-wing Terrorism in Italy' in Peter Merkl (ed.), *Political Violence and Terror. Motifs and Motivations* (Berkeley 1986) pp. 147–8

2 Paul Ginsburg, *A History of Contemporary Italy 1943–1980* (London 1990) pp. 354ff.

3 Alison Jamieson, *The Heart Attacked. Terrorism and Conflict in the Italian State* (London 1989) pp. 19–21 for these statistics. These obviously exclude casualties from later terrorist attacks, which have continued sporadically into the early 2000s

4 Alberto Ronchey, 'Guns and Grey Matter: Terrorism in Italy' *Foreign Affairs* (1979) 57, p. 930

5 Stefan Wisniewski, *Wir waren so unheimlich konsequent . . . Ein Gespräch zur Geschichte der RAF* (Berlin 2003) p. 17

6 Raimondo Catanzaro, 'Subjective Experience and Objective Reality: An Account of Violence in the Words of its Protagonists' in Catanzaro (ed.), *The Red Brigades and Left-wing Terrorism in Italy* (London 1991) p. 184

7 Richard Drake, *The Revolutionary Mystique and Terrorism in*

Contemporary Italy (Bloomington, Indiana 1989) p. 96

8 Salvatore Veca, 'Sixty-eight: Ideas, Politics, Culture' in Omar Calabrese (ed.), *Modern Italy. Images and History of a National Identity* (Milan 1985) vol. 4 p. 81

9 Mario Moretti, *Brigate Rosse. Eine italienische Geschichte* (Berlin 2006) pp. 24–34

10 Mara Cagol, *Una donna nelle prime Brigate Rosse* (Venice 1980) pp. 119–20

11 Ibid., p. 64

12 Alberto Franceschini, *Mara, Renato e io. Storia dei fondatori delle BR* (Milan 1988) p. 204

13 Moretti, *Brigate Rosse* p. 49

14 Adriana Faranda interviewed in Jamieson, *The Heart Attacked* p. 271

15 Catanzaro, 'Subjective Experience and Objective Reality: An Account of Violence in the Words of its Protagonists' p. 184

16 Moretti, *Brigate Rosse* pp. 111–13

17 Jamieson, *The Heart Attacked* p. 157

18 Patrizio Peci, *Io l'infame* (Milan 1983) pp. 81–106

19 Ibid., p. 63

20 Ibid., pp. 14–15

21 Ibid., p. 195

22 Rino Genova, *Missione antiterrorismo* (Milan 1985) p. 150

23 Richard Drake, *The Aldo Moro Murder Case* (Cambridge, Massachusetts 1995) is admirably tough-minded in refuting all the conspiracy charges that have enveloped the facts of the Moro case

24 Dennis Bark and David Gress, *A History of West Germany. Democracy and its Discontents 1963–1988* (Oxford 1989) vol. 2 pp. 120–21

25 Butz Peters, *Tödlicher Irrtum. Die Geschichte der RAF* (Frankfurt am Main 2006) pp. 81–4

26 Wolfgang Kraushaar, 'Antizionismus als trojanisches Pferd. Zur antisemitischen Dimension in den Kooperation von Tupermaros West-Berlin, RAF und RZ mit den Palästinensern' in Kraushaar (ed.), *Die RAF und der linke Terrorismus* (Hamburg 2006) vol. 1 pp. 676ff. This line is still fashionable among such

former salon Marxists as New York University's self-regarding Tony Judt and his attempts to construe himself as a martyr to the likes of Abraham Foxman, the head of the Anti-Defamation League

27 Bommi Baumann, *Wie alles anfing* (Munich 1979)

28 See especially Klaus Stern and Jörg Herrmann, *Andreas Baader. Das Leben eines Staatsfeindes* (Munich 2007)

29 Wolfgang Kraushaar, 'Rudi Dutschke und der bewaffnete Kampf' in Kraushaar (ed.), *Die RAF* vol. 1 pp. 222–5; and Kraushaar, Karen Wieland and Jan Philipp Reemsta, *Rudi Dutschke, Andreas Baader und die RAF* (Hamburg 2005)

30 Herfried Münkler, 'Sehnsucht nach dem Ausnahmezustand. Die Faszination des Untergrunds und ihre Demontage durch die Strategie des Terrors' in Kraushaar (ed.), *Die RAF* vol. 2 pp. 1220–21

31 Susanne Bressen and Martin Jander, 'Gudrun Ensslin' in Kraushaar (ed.), *Die RAF* vol. 1 p. 428

32 Martin Jander, 'Horst Mahler' in Kraushaar (ed.), *Die RAF* vol. 1 p. 381

33 The best biography of her is Alois Prinz, *Lieber wütend als traurig. Die Lebensgeschichte der Ulrike Meinhof* (Weinheim 2003)

34 Stefan Aust, *Der Baader–Meinhof Komplex* (Hamburg 1998) p. 107

35 Ibid., pp. 155–6

36 Wisniewski, *Wir waren so unheimlich konsequent* p. 38

37 Hans Josef Horchem, 'The Decline of the Red Army Faction' *Terrorism and Political Violence* (1991) 3, pp. 67ff.

38 Jander, 'Horst Mahler' pp. 390–97

39 Rolf Sachsse, 'Prada Meinhof. Die RAF als Marke. Ein Versuch in politischer Ikonologie' in Kraushaar (ed.), *Die RAF* vol. 2 p. 1260

Chapter 7: Small-Nation Terror

1 An analogy made by a Basque nationalist who appears in Julio Medem's polyphonic 2004 documentary *Basque Ball* (available on DVD from Tartan DVDs). The Spanish Partido Popular and ETA had difficulties in participating in the film so in a sense it is incomplete

2 'Starkoch gibt Restaurantkomplex auf' *Der Spiegel* 19 February 2007

3 Robert P. Clark, *The Basque Insurgents. ETA, 1952–1980* (Madison, Wisconsin 1984) p. 15

4 Robert P. Clark, 'Patterns in the Lives of ETA Members' in Peter Merkl (ed.), *Political Violence and Terror. Motifs and Motivation* (Berkeley 1986) p. 296

5 See the discussion in Matthew Carr, *Unknown Soldiers. How Terrorism Transformed the Modern World* (London 2006) pp. 109ff.

6 Barbara Loyer, 'Basque Nationalism Undermined by ETA' *Le Monde Diplomatique* (February 1998) pp. 1–7

7 Ibid., pp. 181–3

8 See the detailed account by Paddy Woodworth, *Dirty War, Clean Hands. ETA, the GAL and Spanish Democracy* (New Haven 2001) from which all quotations are taken

9 'Pay Up or Else, ETA Terrorists Tell 2,000 Spanish Businesses' *Daily Telegraph* 7 August 2007 p. 15

10 See F. S. L. Lyons, *Ireland since the Famine* (London 1971) pp. 741–2 for these statistics

11 Glenn Patterson's novel *Burning your Own* (London 1988) is a vivid depiction of life on a predominantly Protestant housing estate in 1969 which sheds light on these subtle cultural matters. The book's hero, a ten-year-old boy, is the son of mixed-religious parents, who christened him 'Malachy' but always shorten this to the less Catholic 'Mal'. ' "Read the birth certificate," her husband said. "You'll find no Malachy there." "Because you cheated me," she shouted. "Cheated me when I was too sick from having him to fight you." "Look!" Mr Martin thumped the table. "We compromised, remember? Mal we would christen him and Mal we would always call him. Right?" . . . "Ignoramus!" Mrs Martin burst out. Her laughter was feverish. "Terrified people will think he's a Catholic when if

they had an ounce of education they'd know the name's Hebrew." "I don't care if it's flaming Zulu, it sounds Catholic" ' (p. 69).

12 Roy Foster, *Modern Ireland 1600–1972* (Oxford 1988) pp. 582–5; Peter Taylor, *Loyalists* (London 1999) p. 50

13 The best study of Paisley is still Steve Bruce, *God Save Ulster! The Religion and Politics of Paisleyism* (Oxford 1986)

14 One of the most brilliantly evocative histories of Ulster is A. T. Q. Stewart, *The Narrow Ground. Aspects of Ulster 1609–1969* (Belfast 1977). For a study of the group mindset see Susan McKay, *Northern Protestants. An Unsettled People* (Belfast 2000) and Sarah Nelson's earlier *Ulster's Uncertain Defenders. Loyalists and the Northern Ireland Conflict* (Belfast 1984)

15 Conor Cruise O'Brien, *States of Ireland* (New York 1972) pp. 168–9

16 David McKittrick and David McVea, *Making Sense of the Troubles* (London 2001) pp. 26ff.

17 Simon Prince, 'The Global Revolt of 1968 and Northern Ireland' *Historical Journal* (2006) 49, pp. 851–75

18 Max Hastings, *Ulster 1969. The Fight for Civil Rights in Northern Ireland* (London 1970) pp. 28–30. I am grateful to Max for interesting discussions about this period

19 See especially Paul Bew, *Ireland. The Politics of Enmity* (Oxford 2007) especially pp. 492ff. I am grateful to my friend Lord Bew for his help with everything related to Northern Ireland terrorism

20 Hastings, *Ulster 1969* p. 114

21 Ibid., p. 149

22 Gerry Adams, *Falls Memories* (Dingle, Co. Kerry 1993)

23 Ed Moloney, *A Secret History of the IRA* (London 2003) pp. 74ff.

24 See David McKittrick, Seamus Kelters, Brian Feeney, Chris Thornton and David McVea, *Lost Lives* (Edinburgh 2004) pp. 70–73. This outstanding book is the most sombre memorial to the Troubles

25 Peter R. Neumann, *Britain's Long War. British Strategy in the Northern Ireland*

Conflict, 1969–98 (London 2003) p. 57

26 Peter Taylor, *Provos. The IRA & Sinn Fein* (London 1997) pp. 163ff.

27 Martin Dillon, *The Shankill Butchers. A Case Study in Mass Murder* (London 1989) is gruesomely definitive

28 Eamon Collins, *Killing Rage* (London 1997) pp. 98ff.

29 Liam Clarke and Kathryn Johnston, *Martin McGuinness. From Guns to Government* (London 2003) p. 41

30 J. J. Barrett, *Martin Ferris. Man of Kerry* (Dingle, Co. Kerry 2006) pp. 44–5

31 Sean O'Callaghan, *The Informer* (London 1998) p. 55. I am grateful to Sean O'Callaghan for many memorable conversations about terrorism

32 Toby Harnden, *'Bandit Country'. The IRA & South Armagh* (London 1999) pp. 36ff.

33 For examples see Martin Dillon, *God and the Gun. The Church and Irish Terrorism* (London 1997)

34 See the insightful discussion of Church politics in Moloney, *A Secret History of the IRA* pp. 228ff.

35 Taylor, *Provos* p. 267

36 See Bruce Hoffman 'All You Need is Love: How the Terrorists Stopped Terrorism' *Atlantic Monthly* December 2001 pp. 1–4

37 Richard English, *Armed Struggle. The History of the IRA* (London 2003) p. 123

38 Maxwell Taylor and Ethel Quayle, *Terrorist Lives* (London 1994) pp. 28–34

39 See the important book by Kevin Toolis, *Rebel Hearts. Journeys within the IRA's Soul* (London 1995) p. 288

40 David Lister and Hugh Jordan, *Mad Dog. The Rise and Fall of Johnny Adair and 'C Company'* (Edinburgh 2007) p. 37

41 Ibid., pp. 100–101

42 Ibid., p. 140

43 Andrew Silke, 'Rebel's Dilemma: The Changing Relationship between the IRA, Sinn Fein, and Paramilitary Vigilantism in Northern Ireland' *Terrorism and Political Violence* (1999) 11, p. 62

44 Roy Mason, *Paying the Price* (London 1999) p. 163

45 Mark Urban, *Big Boys' Rules. The Secret*

Struggle against the IRA (London 1992) pp. 69–78 for an insightful discussion of the army and the law

46 Martin Ingram and Greg Harkin, *Stakeknife. Britain's Secret Agents in Ireland* (Dublin 2004) pp. 6off. for Scappaticci's background and character by one of his former handlers

47 Peter Taylor, *Brits. The War against the IRA* (London 2001) pp. 288–96

48 Taylor, *Provos* pp. 259–65

49 Bew, *Ireland* p. 532

50 Neumann, *Britain's Long War* p. 157

51 McKittrick et al., *Lost Lives* pp. 1393–5

52 Brian Graham, 'The Past in the Present: The Shaping of Identity in Loyalist Ulster' *Terrorism and Political Violence* (2004) 16, pp. 12–14

53 For the grim details see Chris Ryder and Vincent Kearney, *Drumcree. The Orange Order's Last Stand* (London 2002)

54 For this see Dean Godson's excellent *Himself Alone. David Trimble and the Ordeal of Unionism* (London 2006)

55 Kate Kray, *Hard Bastards* (London 2002) pp. 35–48 and Johnny Adair, *Mad Dog* (London 2007) p. 250

56 See Keith Maguire, 'Fraud, Extortion and Racketeering: The Black Economy in Northern Ireland' *Crime, Law and Social Change* (1993) 20, pp. 273–92

57 Rachel Monaghan, ' "An Imperfect Peace": Paramilitary "Punishments" in Northern Ireland' *Terrorism and Political Violence* (2004) 16, p. 444

58 'IRA plc Turns Terror into the Biggest Crime Gang in Europe' *The Times* 25 February 2005. Obviously since these people are skilful, there may be further activities not mentioned here, some of which – involving front businesses on the UK mainland – are not given in great detail for legal reasons

59 Harnden, *'Bandit Country'* pp. 451ff.

60 Edna Leahy, 'Farc Rebel "Admits IRA Trained Him" ' *The Times* 15 May 2005

61 Michael Burleigh, 'Sinister Mutations' *Spectator* 18 February 2006 is based on interviews with serving PSNI officers regarding paramilitary criminality

62 For these statistics see the appendix in McKittrick et al., *Lost Lives* pp. 1525ff.

Chapter 8: World Rage: Islamist Terrorism

1 Gilles Kepel, *The Revenge of God. The Resurgence of Islam, Christianity and Judaism in the Modern World* (University Park, Pennsylvania 1994) is an excellent comparative study of the resurgence of the three Abrahamic faiths from the mid-1970s

2 Patrick Clawson and Michael Rubin, *Eternal Iran. Continuity and Chaos* (London 2005) pp. 87–93

3 Mike Davis, *Buda's Wagon. A Brief History of the Car Bomb* (London 2007) pp. 78–86 and Robert Baer, *See No Evil* (London 2002) pp. 97ff.

4 See especially Charles Allen, *God's Terrorists. The Wahhabi Cult and the Hidden Roots of Modern Jihad* (London 2006) pp. 42ff.

5 Gilles Kepel, *Jihad. The Trail of Political Islam* (London 2002) pp. 69–75

6 Jarret Brachman (ed.), *Militant Ideology Atlas* (West Point 2006) Appendix 1 p. 12

7 Steve Coll, *Ghost Wars. The Secret History of the CIA, Afghanistan and Bin Laden, from the Soviet Invasion to September 10, 2001* (London 2005) pp. 24–37; Yaroslav Trofimov, *The Siege of Mecca* (London 2007)

8 Brynjar Lia, *The Society of the Muslim Brothers in Egypt. The Rise of an Islamic Mass Movement* (Reading 1998)

9 As discussed by Ian Buruma and Avishai Margalit, *Occidentalism. A Short History of Anti-Westernism* (London 2004)

10 For a good explication of his views see Mary Habeck, *Knowing the Enemy. Jihadist Ideology and the War on Terror* (New Haven 2006) pp. 35–7

11 For an informed discussion see Gilles Kepel, *The Roots of Radical Islam* (London 2005) pp. 36ff.

12 As starkly depicted in Alaa Al Aswany's *The Yacoubian Building* (London 2007)

13 Carrie Rosefsky Wickham, *Mobilizing Islam. Religion, Activism, and Political Change in Egypt* (New York 2002) pp. 36ff.

14 Ibid., pp. 145–55

15 For a brilliant memoir of contemporary

Egypt see Mary Anne Weaver, *A Portrait of Egypt. A Journey through the World of Militant Islam* (New York 1999) which is especially good on the Sadat years

16   See Youssef H. Aboul-Enein, 'Islamic Militant Cells and Sadat's Assassination' *Military Review* (2004) pp. 1–8; and Daniel Benjamin and Steven Simon, *The Age of Sacred Terror* (New York 2002) pp. 81–5

17   Lawrence Wright, *The Looming Tower. Al-Qaeda's Road to 9/11* (London 2006) pp. 49–59

18   Martin Stone, *The Agony of Algeria* (London 1997) p. 97

19   Benjamin Stora, *Algeria 1830–2000. A Short History* (Ithaca 2001) pp. 171ff.

20   See the very useful paper by Martin van Bruinessen, 'Genealogies of Islamic Radicalism in Post-Suharto Indonesia' at http://www.let.uu.nl/~Martin.van. Bruinessen/personal/publications/genealogies_islamic-r

21   Wright, *Looming Tower* p. 99

22   Coll, *Ghost Wars* pp. 81–2

23   Marc Sageman, *Understanding Terror Networks* (Philadelphia 2004) p. 57

24   Sean O'Neill and Daniel McGrory, *The Suicide Factory. Abu Hamza and the Finsbury Park Mosque* (London 2006) pp. 23–9 for the two versions of this story. In the other, the engineer Hamza was tracing the outlines of structures on the ground with a stick and triggered a land mine

25   J. Millard Burr and Robert O. Collins, *Alms for Jihad. Charity and Terrorism in the Islamic World* (Cambridge 2006) pp. 51–2. *Alms for Jihad* has been the subject of legal action in London. Citing it does not imply that I endorse all its assertions

26   See the astute interview in Abdel Bari Atwan, *The Secret History of Al-Qaeda* (London 2006) pp. 19–30

27   See Faisal Devji, *Landscapes of Jihad. Militancy, Morality, Modernity* (London 2005)

28   Jason Burke, *Al-Qaeda. The True Story of the Radical Islam* (London 2003) pp. 77–8

29   For extensive documentation on Al Qaeda see West Point Counter-Terrorism Center's Harmony Project. Employment Contract AFGP-2002–600045 and Organisational arrangements AFGP-2002–00078 and AFGP-2002–000080

30   Terry McDermott, *Perfect Soldiers. The 9/11 Hijackers* (New York 2005) pp. 107–19

31   Peter Brookes, *A Devil's Triangle. Terrorism, Weapons of Mass Destruction, and Rogue States* (Lanham, Maryland 2005) p. 102

32   Melanie Phillips, *Londonistan. How Britain is Creating a Terror State Within* (London 2006) tells it as it really is

33   Burr and Collins, *Alms for Jihad* p. 94

34   For the above see mainly Tony Walker and Andrew Gowers, *Arafat. The Biography* (London 2003) pp. 208ff.

35   Bernard Lewis, 'The Other Middle East Problems' in his collection *From Babel to Dragomans. Interpreting the Middle East* (London 2004) pp. 332–42

36   Ze'ev Schiff and Ehud Ya'Ari, *Intifada. The Palestinian Uprising and Israel's Third Front* (New York 1989) p. 154

37   David Pratt, *Intifada. The Long Day of Rage* (Glasgow 2006) p. 51

38   As well as numerous obituaries of the sheikh, see Matthew Levitt, *Hamas. Politics, Charity, and Terrorism in the Service of Jihad* (New Haven 2006) pp. 34–7

39   Zaki Chehab, *Inside Hamas. The Untold Story of Militants, Martyrs and Spies* (London 2007) p. 23 and Shaul Mishal and Avraham Sela, *The Palestinian Hamas. Vision, Violence, and Coexistence* (New York 2006)

40   'Hamas Covenant 1988' in the Avalon Project edition available at www.yale.edu/lawweb/avalon/mideast/hamas.htm pp. 1–25 and as an appendix in Mishal and Sela, *The Palestinian Hamas* pp. 175–99

41   Samuel M. Katz, *The Hunt for the Engineer. How Israeli Agents Tracked the Master Bomber* (Guilford, Connecticut 2002) is a brilliant account of Ayyash's career

42   Pratt, *Intifada* pp. 108ff is vivid

43 See especially Ami Pedahzur, *Suicide Terrorism* (Cambridge 2005) pp. 134ff. and the less interesting Robert A. Pape, *Dying to Win. Why Suicide Terrorists Do It* (London 2006) and Diego Gambetta (ed.), *Making Sense of Suicide Missions* (Oxford 2005)

44 Anat Berko and Edna Erez, ' "Ordinary People" and "Death Work": Palestinian Suicide Bombers as Victimizers and Victims' *Violence and Victims* (2006) 20, pp. 603–23

45 Ed Husain, *The Islamist* (London 2007) pp. 74–81

46 Noel Malcolm, *Bosnia. A Short History* (London 1994) pp. 220–22 is characteristically humane and intelligent

47 Lorenzo Vidonio, *Al Qaeda in Europe. The New Battleground of International Jihad* (Amherst, New York 2006) pp. 215–31

48 Evan Kohlmann, *Al-Qaeda's Jihad in Europe. The Afghan–Bosnian Network* (Oxford 2004) pp. 85–6

49 'The 1995 and 1998 Renditions' Human Rights Watch at http://dR//hrw.org/reports/2005/egypt0505h5.htm

50 Kepel, *Jihad* pp. 251–3

51 Paul Murphy, *The Wolves of Islam. Russia and the Faces of Chechen Terror* (Washington DC 2006) pp. 20–24

52 Andrew Higgins and Alan Cullison, 'Saga of Dr Zawahiri Sheds Light on the Roots of Al Qaeda Terror' *Wall Street Journal* 3 July 2002

53 Evan Kohlmann, 'Two Decades of Jihad in Algeria: The GIA, the GSPC, and Al-Qaida' www.nefafoundation.org (2007) pp. 1–28. Mohammed Samraoui, *Chronique des années de sang* (Paris 2003) should be used with caution as it has been the object of libel actions in French courts. See especially Martin Evans and John Phillips, *Algeria. Anger of the Dispossessed* (New Haven 2007) pp. 235ff.

54 Stora, *Algeria 1830–2000* pp. 213ff. is good on politics in the 1990s

55 For the first point see Mark Allen, *Arabs* (London 2006) p. 30

56 Habeck, *Knowing the Enemy* pp. 83ff.

57 Simon Reeve, *The New Jackals. Ramzi Yousef, Osama bin Laden and the Future of Terrorism* (London 1999) pp. 125–32 is a persuasive account of Yousef's mind

58 Richard A. Clarke, *Against All Enemies. Inside America's War on Terror* (New York 2004) pp. 140–47

59 Burke, *Al-Qaeda* p. 127

60 See mainly Ahmed Rashid, *Taliban. The Story of the Afghan Warlords* (London 2001) pp. 72–5

61 See Alan Cullison, 'Inside Al-Qaeda's Hard Drive' *Atlantic Monthly* (September 2004) pp. 1–16. Cullison's brilliant reporting from Afghanistan for the *Wall Street Journal* includes details from abandoned Al Qaeda computers he purchased in Kabul

62 Daniel Byman, *Deadly Connections. States that Sponsor Terrorism* (Cambridge 2005) pp. 205–9

63 McDermott, *Perfect Soldiers* Appendix C p. 264 for most of this text

64 Baradan Kuppusamy, 'Hambali: The Driven Man' *Asia Times* 19 August 2003

65 Lucien Vandenbroucke, 'Eyewitness to Terror: Nairobi's Day of Infamy' and Patience Bushnell, 'After Nairobi: Recovering from Terror' *American Foreign Service Bulletin* (2000) June, July issues

66 Michael Griffin, *Reaping the Whirlwind. Afghanistan, Al Qaeda and the Holy War* (Sterling, Virginia 2003) p. 174

67 Jean-Charles Brisard and Damien Martinez, *Zarqawi. The New Face of Al-Qaeda* (Cambridge 2005) is essential on Zarqawi as it is based on extensive Jordanian documentation

68 Vidino, *Al Qaeda in Europe* pp. 147ff.

69 McDermott, *Perfect Soldiers* pp. 37–46

70 DIGOS (Italian secret service) report 'Al Muhajroun 3' dated 21 November 2001

71 Shiv Malik, 'My Brother the Bomber' *Prospect* (June 2007) p. 34

72 Gerald Robbins, 'Dutch Treat: The Netherlands Tries to Assimilate its Muslim Immigrants' *Weekly Standard* 13 July 2007 pp. 1–2

73 George Walden, *Time to Emigrate?* (London 2006)

74 Paul M. Sniderman and Louk

Hagendoorn, *When Ways of Life Collide* (Princeton 2007) pp. 27ff.

75 See especially Nick Cohen's honest and informed *What's Left? How the Liberals Lost their Way* (London 2006)

76 Walter Laqueur, *The Last Days of Europe. Epitaph for an Old Continent* (New York 2007) p. 85; and for the final discussion see the clear-minded piece by Rod Liddle, 'The Public Know How These Attacks Happen – Unlike the Politicians' *Spectator* 7 July 2007 pp. 14–15

77 This important point is made by Ed Husain, *The Islamist* pp. 69–70

78 Jamie Doward, 'Extremists Train Young Convicts for Terror Plots' *Observer* 15 July 2007

79 Jason Burke, *Evening Standard* 8 August 2007

80 Thomas H. Kean and others, *The 9/11 Commission Report* (New York 2002) p. 166

81 Barton Gellman and Jo Becker, 'Angler: The Cheney Vice Presidency' Part ii, *Washington Post* 24 June 2007 p. 5

82 Fawaz A. Gerges, *Journey of the Jihadist. Inside Muslim Militancy* (Orlando 2006) pp. 207–9

83 See the useful discussion by Michael Howard, 'War against Terrorism' Royal United Services Institute Address 30 October 2001 pp. 1–5

84 Ron Suskind, *The One Per Cent Doctrine. Deep Inside America's Pursuit of its Enemies since 9/11* (London 2006) p. 17

85 See the interesting memoir by Tyler Drumheller, *On the Brink* (New York 2006) p. 48. Drumheller was the head of CIA clandestine operations in Europe

86 Christina Lamb, 'The Invisible Man' *Sunday Times* magazine 18 March 2007 pp. 48–57 is an informed account of the search effort

87 David Gartenstein-Ross and Kyle Dabruzzi, 'The Convergence of Crime and Terror: Law Enforcement Opportunities and Perils' Center for Policing Terrorism 26 March 2007 pp. 1–24

88 For the above see David Rivkin and Lee A. Casey, 'Family Feud: The Law in

War and Peace' *National Interest* (2007) 89, pp. 66–75 and John Yoo, *War by Other Means. An Insider's Account of the War on Terror* (New York 2006)

89 See the thoughtful review by Alasdair Palmer, 'American "Oppressors" Have a Right to a Fair Trial Too' *Sunday Telegraph* 3 June 2007 reviewing Clive Stafford Smith's new book on Guantánamo Bay

90 Mark Bowden, 'Jihadists in Paradise' *Atlantic Monthly* March 2007 pp. 54–75

91 West Point Counter-Terrorism Center Harmony Project Adl to Muktar dated 13 June 2002

92 See Rohan Gunaratna, 'Terrorism in Southeast Asia: Threat and Response' *Hudson Institute* (New York 2006) pp. 1–12

93 Jason Burke, 'Al Qaeda after Madrid' *Prospect* (June 2004)

94 See the discussion by David Tucker, 'What's New about the New Terrorism and How Dangerous is It?' *Terrorism and Political Violence* (2001) 13, pp. 1–14

95 See the important paper by Stanford University's Jacob Shapiro, 'The Terrorist's Challenge: Security, Efficiency, Control' Center for International Security and Cooperation 26 April 2007 pp. 1–36

96 For recent examples see Lee Kuan Yew, 'Winning the War on Terrorism' *Foreign Affairs* January/February (2007) 86, pp. 2–7

97 Simon Elegant, 'The Terrorist Talks' *Time*/CNN 5 October 2003 p. 2 which quotes from CIA briefings

98 The most detailed account is by Maria Ressa, *Seeds of Terror. An Eyewitness Account of Al-Qaeda's Newest Center of Operations in Southeast Asia* (New York 2003) pp. 143ff.

99 Arabinda Acharya, 'The Bali Bombings: Impact on Indonesia and Southeast Asia' *Hudson Institute* (New York 2006) pp. 1–5

100 Kumar Ramakrishna, 'The Making of the Jemaah Islamiyah Terrorist' in James J. F. Forest (ed.), *Teaching*

Terror: Strategic and Tactical Learning in the Terrorist World (Oxford 2006) pp. 223ff.

101 For a splendid account of contemporary Indonesia see Tracy Dahlby, *Allah's Torch. A Report from behind the Scenes in Asia's War on Terror* (New York 2005) as well as the equally informative John T. Sidel, *Riots, Pogroms, Jihad. Religious Violence in Indonesia* (Ithaca 2006) especially pp. 196ff.

102 Zachary Abuza, 'JI's Moneyman and Top Recruiter: A Profile of Noordin Mohammed Top' *Terrorism Focus* (25 July 2006) 3, pp. 1–2 and Jay Solomon and James Hookway, 'In Indonesia, War on Terror Shows Both Gains and Worrisome Trends' *Wall Street Journal* 8 September 2006

103 'Terrorists Proving Harder to Profile' *Washington Post* 11 March 2007

104 Michael Moss and Souad Mekhennet, 'The Guidebook for Taking a Life' *New York Times* 10 June 2007 pp. 1–4

105 See Lawrence Wright, 'The Terror Web' *New Yorker* 2 August 2004

106 Kathy Gannon, 'Cameraman Sheds Light on al-Qaida Tactics' Associated Press 26 June 2006

107 Douglas Farah, *Blood from Stones. The Secret Financial Network of Terror* (New York 2004) is the authoritative account by the *Washington Post* West African bureau chief

108 House of Commons Intelligence and Security Committee (Chairman Paul Murphy MP) *Report into the London Terrorist Attacks on 7 July 2005* (London 2006) for these remarks on the Committee's findings. That the Committee is heavy with MPs with intelligence and military connections tends to render it the elected version of what it is supposed to monitor rather than a forum that asks original questions. The need for secrecy (pervasive in Britain) counts for more than the ability to pose questions from beyond the security community's conceptual horizons. An important corrective is Crispin Black, *7/7. The London Bombs. What Went Wrong?* (London 2005)

109 *Report of the Official Account of the Bombings in London on 7th July 2005,* HM Stationery Office (London 2006) for these details

110 Sean O'Neill, 'Silence in (and out) of Court' *The Times* 12 May 2006 p. 24. This point was made by Peter Clarke in *Learning from Experience. Counter-Terrorism in the UK since 9/11* Colin Cramphorn Memorial Lecture at Policy Exchange (London 2007) pp. 34–5

111 Sean O'Neill, 'Refugees Who Tried to Wage War on London' *The Times* 10 July 2007 front page and pp. 6–7

112 'How 7/7 killers Slipped MI5 Net' and related stories in *Daily Mail* 1 May 2007

113 Anon., 'An Army on Operations'. I am grateful to Antony Beevor for a copy of this Kermit Roosevelt address by a senior British general to a US audience

114 Terence Henry, 'Get Out of Jihad Free' *Atlantic Monthly* June 2007 pp. 39–40

115 Christopher Boucek, 'Extremist Reeducation and Rehabilitation in Saudi Arabia' *Terrorism Monitor* (2007) 5, pp. 1–4; a similar Egyptian scheme has been hampered by lack of funds, see Manal El-Jesri, 'Given the Chance' *Egypt Today* October 2007

116 Peter Coleman, *A Liberal Conspiracy* (New York 1989)

117 Gerald Robbins, 'Dutch Treat. The Netherlands Tries to Assimilate its Muslim Immigrants' *Weekly Standard* 13 July 2007

118 Pascale Combelles Sigel, 'An Inside Look at France's Mosque Surveillance Program' *Terrorism Monitor* (2007) 5, pp. 1–3 is an excellent analysis of French domestic security measures

119 See Frank Gaffney and others, *War Footing* (Annapolis, Maryland 2006) pp. 68–70

120 See Mitchell D. Silber and Arvin Bhatt, *Radicalization in the West: The*

NOTES · 527

Homegrown Threat New York City Police Department Intelligence Division (New York 2007)
121 Solomon and Hookway, 'In Indonesia'
122 Peter Grier, 'Where Does Al Qaeda Stand Now?' *Christian Science Monitor* 5 March 2007; for an up-to-date assessment of where Al Qaeda is now see Fred Burton and Scott Stewart, 'Gunning for Al Qaeda Prime' *Stratfor Terrorism Intelligence Report* 27 June 2007 pp. 1–4

Afterthoughts

1 See John A. Nagl, *Learning to Eat Soup with a Knife. Counterinsurgency Lessons from Malaya and Vietnam* (Chicago 2005) pp. 59ff.
2 Jeffrey Imm 'Who is America Fighting – Jihadists or Extremists?' *Counter-terrorism Blog* 25 April 2008 pp. 1–6
3 For example Frederick W. Kagan, 'How We'll Know We've Won: A Definition of Success in Iraq' *Weekly Standard* 5 May 2008 pp. 1–6
4 Lieutenant Colonel (Dr) David Kilcullen, 'Countering Global Insurgency', paper delivered on 30 November 2004, p. 39
5 The term Islamofascism is used by Martin Amis, Christopher Hitchens and countless commentators. Islamobolshevism is less frequently employed by among others Niall Ferguson
6 See Michael Doran, 'Statement on CIST Strategy', which argues that Muslim self-perception is more important than how the US is perceived by others. I am grateful for the opportunity to have discussed these issues with Mr Doran
7 See Steve Coll's marvellous *The Bin Ladens* (London 2008)
8 Jonathan Powell, *Great Hatred; Little Room. Making Peace in Northern Ireland* (Oxford 2008); briefing session with Under-Secretary Eric Edelman at the Carlton Club, London, 14 March 2008. The Irish anecdote comes from a source who prefers to remain anonymous

9 Frances Stonor Saunders, *Who Paid the Piper? The CIA and the Cultural Cold War* (London 1999). There is a much better book by Peter Coleman, the former editor of *Quadrant*, called *The Liberal Conspiracy. The Congress for Cultural Freedom and the Struggle for the Mind of Postwar Europe* (London 1989)
10 Ed Husain, *The Islamist* (London 2007) is an important account of Trotskyite-style entryism by Islamists into Britain's low-grade higher- and further-education colleges
11 See the forthcoming Centre for Social Cohesion report by Anthony Glees, *Islam in Britain. The Government's Security-driven Plans to Reform the Teaching of Islam in English Universities* (London 2008)
12 Martin Evans and John Phillips, *Algeria. Anger of the Dispossessed* (New Haven 2007) p. 170
13 For a good discussion of the internet and terrorism see Marc Sageman, *Leaderless Jihad. Terror Networks in the Twenty-First Century* (Philadelphia 2008) pp. 109–23. The Dutch intelligence services have also produced a number of high-grade reports on this issue. Of course, one should not neglect the radicalising impact of satellite TV, especially in the 'dish cities' of the Netherlands, or of mainstream satellite and terrestrial news broadcasters who recycle scenes of atrocity at half-hourly intervals. See also Fred Burton, 'The Web of Jihad: Strategic Utility and Tactical Weakness' *Stratfor* 13 June 2006 pp. 1–4
14 Damian Thompson, *Counterknowledge. How We Surrendered to Conspiracy Theories, Quack Medicine, Bogus Science and Fake History* (London 2008) is one of many recent titles dealing with these broader cultural issues
15 See the director Maajid Nawaz's *In and Out of Islamism* (London 2008) and Quilliam Foundation (ed.), *Pulling Together to Defeat Terrorism. Recommendations for Uprooting Islamist Extremism* (London 2008)
16 See Michael Burleigh, 'Lawyers Sap our

Will to Combat Terrorism' *The Times* 27 July 2007 p. 17

17 Floyd Abrahams, 'Foreign Law and the First Amendment' *Wall Street Journal* 30 April 2008. Unfortunately, the laws of libel prevent my being any more specific, but interested readers can consult the magazine *Private Eye* for some relevant examples of the problem

18 Sean O'Neill, 'Terror Suspect Who Won Court Battle Identified as "Senior Al-Qaeda Agent"' *The Times* 26 April 2008

19 Relevant books include Nick Cohen, *What's Left?* (London 2007) and Andrew Anthony, *The Fallout* (London 2007)

20 For an interesting discussion on the Churches and 9/11 see Jean Bethke Elshtain, *Just War against Terror. The Burden of American Power in a Violent World* (New York 2003)

21 Among the many commentaries on Williams' remarks see Melanie Phillips, 'Seven Deadly Reasons Why the Archbishop Should Not be Allowed to Get Away with It' *Daily Mail* 13 February 2008 p. 14. The archbishop was essentially responding to aggressive Islamist self-assertion by saying that Britain should become a bit more Muslim. He was also unmindful of a worldwide flock that in some countries (including areas of the UK as well as Nigeria, Pakistan, Somalia and Sudan) is under siege by Muslim extremists

22 Philip Jenkins, *God's Continent. Christianity, Islam and Europe's Religious Crisis* (Oxford 2007) pp. 52–3

23 See the important article by John Cornwell, 'Are Muslim Enclaves No-go Areas, Forcing Other People Out?' *Sunday Times* 16 March 2008 pp. 1–7, and Ian Buruma, *Murder in Amsterdam* (London 2006)

24 'Terror Suspect Obtained Visa' *Star* 25 April 2008; recent books on nuclear proliferation include William Langewiesche, *The Atomic Bazaar. The Rise of the Nuclear Poor* (London 2007)

25 Center for Combating Terrorism (West Point) (ed.), *Cracks in the Foundations. Leadership Schisms in al-Qa'ida*

1989–2006 (West Point, NY 2007) is a well-documented study of these divisions

26 Josh Lefkowitz, 'Terrorists behind Bars' *NEFA Foundation Report* 5 May 2008 pp. 31–6. This also deals with Singapore's Religious Rehabilitation Group

27 Olivier Roy, *The Politics of Chaos in the Middle East* (London 2007) pp. 141ff.

28 Olivier Guitta, 'Africa is the Next Stage of the War' *Examiner* 6–7 October 2007; Jane Novak, 'Yemen's Truce with Al Qaeda' *Weekly Standard* 31 October 2007 pp. 1–2; Andrew McGregor, 'Military Rebellion and Islamism in Mauritania' *Terrorism Monitor* (2005) 3, pp. 1–3; J. Peter Pham, 'Violence, Islamism, and Terror in the Sahel' *World Defence Review* 22 February 2007 pp. 1–3

29 Thomas Renard, 'Police Raids Uncover Al-Qaeda's Parallel World in Turkey' *Terrorism Focus* (2008) 5, pp. 5–7

30 Akbar Ahmed, *Resistance and Control in Pakistan* (London 1991), a book informed by the author's role as a frontier officer in Waziristan as well as by his anthropological training

31 Notably by British human rights lawyer Philippe Sands, *Torture Team* (London 2008)

32 Marc Reuel Gerecht and Gary Schmitt, 'What France Does Best' *American* March/April 2008 pp. 1–4, and Craig Whitlock, 'French Push Limits in Fight against Terrorism' *Washington Post* 2 November 2004

33 'Britain is Europe's Top Terror Centre, Arrests Show' *Sunday Telegraph* 27 April 2008

34 Andy Dolan, 'Fanatic Tried to Brainwash Son' *Daily Mail* 19 February 2008 pp. 20–1

35 Shmuel Bar, *Warrant for Terror. The Fatwas of Radical Islam and the Duty of Jihad* (Stanford 2006)

36 Mohamed Sifaoui, *Inside Al Qaeda* (London 2003) p. 65

37 Lefkowitz, 'Terrorists behind Bars' pp. 9–13 for the European and US prison statistics

38 Bat Ye'or, *Eurabia: The Euro-Arab Axis*

(Madison 2005) and Ralph Peters, 'The "Eurabia" Myth' in his *Wars of Blood and Faith. The Conflicts that will Shape the Twenty-First Century* (Mechanicsburg, PA 2007) pp. 332–4. See also Walter Laqueur, *The Last Days of Europe. Epitaph for an Old Continent* (New York 2007)

39 Roy, *Politics of Chaos* p. 66

40 I am referring to Michael Burleigh, *Earthly Powers. Politics and Religion from the French Revolution to the Great War* (London/New York 2005) and *Sacred Causes. Politics and Religion from the European Dictators to Al-Qaeda* (London/New York 2006)

41 For a pre-emptive reordering of our legal universe see Phillip Bobbitt's *Terror and Consent* (London 2008)

42 Gerard Henderson, *Islam in Australia. Democratic Bi-partisanship in Action* (London 2007). I am grateful to Gerard for the opportunity to discuss these questions at the Sydney Institute

43 Peter Zimonjic, *Into the Darkness. An Account of 7/7* (London 2008) pp. 196ff.

PICTURE CREDITS

I

Ricard O'Sullivan Burke, leader of the Irish Republican brotherhood in England, 1887. Courtesy of Mrs T. Lynch of Coachford.
John Holland in the turret of his 'Fenian Ram'. © Bettman/CORBIS
Assassination of Tsar Alexander II.
Bomb explosion in the Liceo Theatre, Barcelona, 1893. Art Media/Heritage Images.
Film still from Gillo Pontecorvo's *The Battle of Algiers*: Colonel Matthieu. Ronald Grant Archive.
Film still from *The Battle of Algiers*: Saadi Yacef. The Kobal Collection.
1972 'wanted' poster for members of the Baader–Meinhof gang. akg-images.
Mario Moretti stands trial. © Gianni Giansanti/Sygma/Corbis.
Andreas Baader, 1977. akg-images/Ullsteinbild.
Unexploded bomb found in Little Wormwood Scrubs Park, 21 July 2005. Rex Features.
Lead globe bomb used in the Chicago Haymarket Bombing, 1886. Chicago Historical Society.
BATF Explosives Standards chart. The Bureau of Alcohol, Tobacco, Firearms and Explosives.
Lenny Murphy, 1999. Pacemaker, Belfast.
Johnny Adair with colleagues outside the Maze prison, 1999. Pacemaker, Belfast.
'Sniper at Work' road sign. © Photo: Allan Leonard.
Brian Gillen, 1995. Pacemaker, Belfast.
IRA prisoners, including Padraic Wilson, in the IRA wing of the Maze prison, 1998. Stephen Davidson/Pacemaker Belfast.
Brian Keenan at a Republican funeral. Pacemaker, Belfast.
Martin Ferris and Gerry Adams, 1997. Pacemaker, Belfast.

II

Map of Osama bin Laden's speculative Caliphate.
Abu Sabaya with the couple he kidnapped, Martin and Gracia Burnham.
    © Reuters/CORBIS.
Ayman al-Zawahiri, 1982. Getty Images/Stringer.
Al-Khattab aka Samir bin Salekh al-Suweilum. © Reuters/STR New/Getty
    Images.
Iraqis step over the rubble of the al-Hadi shrine, Samarra, 2006.
    © epa/CORBIS.
Civilians and firemen work to remove bodies following the Al Qaeda
    bombing of the US Embassy in Nairobi, Kenya, 1998. AFP/Getty Images.
Indonesian rescue workers remove a body after the bomb blast in Bali, 2002.
    © Reuters/Stringer Indonesia/CORBIS.
Osama bin Laden, 2007. Still photo taken from footage released by Al Qaeda's
    media wing, As-Sahab, and provided by the SITE Intelligence Group.
    AFP/Getty Images.
Abu Hamza, Finsbury Park mosque. PA Photos.
Muslim protesters chant slogans as they march toward the Danish Embassy
    in London, 2006. Lefteris Pit Arakis/AP/PA Photos.
A young girl dressed as a Hamas suicide bomber in the Ain al-Hilweh refugee
    camp, South Lebanon. © Reuters/CORBIS.
Sheikh Omar Abdel Rahman, giving an interview to *Time* from his jail cell,
    1995. Time & Life Pictures/Getty Images.
A Supermax prison cell, Florence, Colorado. © Lizzie Himmel/Sygma/
    CORBIS.

While every effort has been made to trace the owners of copyright material reproduced herein, the publishers would like to apologise for any omissions and would be pleased to incorporate missing acknowledgements in any future editions.

SELECT BIBLIOGRAPHY

The internet is indispensable for information on the constant mutations of contemporary terrorism. The Washington DC-based website Counter-terrorism.org brings expert perspectives to bear on global terrorist issues, especially the contributions of Douglas Farah, Evan Kohlmann and Walid Phares. It monitors trials as well as police and military counter-measures. Jamestown.org, the Site Institute website and West Point's Counter-Terrorism Center are all of equal merit, especially since the CTC website has useful documents captured from Al Qaeda in a section entitled the Harmony Project. A commercial site called Stratfor.com also has much information, primarily designed for corporations. Among US media, the *Atlantic Monthly*, *Foreign Affairs*, the *New Yorker*, *Time* and especially the *Wall Street Journal* have exemplary commentary and reporting on many of the areas discussed in the last half of this book, as do the *Daily Telegraph*, the *Daily Mail*, the *Observer*, *The Times* and the *Sunday Times* in the UK. Since a new book on terrorism is published every nine hours, the following list will necessarily be even more incomplete by the time readers get up in the morning than it was before they went to bed the night before.

Abu Iyad *My Home, My Land. A Narrative of the Palestinian Struggle* (New York 1981)

Abuza, Zachary 'JI's Moneyman and Top Recruiter: A Profile of Noordin Mohammed Top' *Terrorism Focus* (25 July 2006) 3, pp. 1–2

Acharya, Arabinda 'The Bali Bombings: Impact on Indonesia and Southeast Asia' *Hudson Institute* (New York 2006) pp. 1–5

Adair, Johnny *Mad Dog* (London 2007)

Adams, Gerry *Falls Memories* (Dingle, Co. Kerry 1993)

—— *An Irish Journal* (Dingle, Co. Kerry 2001)

Alexander, Martin and Keiger, J. F. V. (eds) *France and the Algerian War 1954–62. Strategy, Operations, Diplomacy* (London 2002)

Algemene Inlichtingen en Veiligheidsdienst (AIVD) *Violent Jihad in The Netherlands* (The Hague 2006)

Allen, Charles *God's Terrorists. The Wahhabi Cult and the Hidden Roots of Modern Jihad* (London 2006)

Allen, Mark *Arabs* (London 2006)

Anderson, R. *Sidelights on the Home Rule Movement* (London 1906)

Andrews, Anthony 'The Price of Peace' *Observer* 6 March 2005

Atwan, Abdel Bari *The Secret History of Al-Qaeda* (London 2006)

Aussaresses, Paul *The Battle of the Casbah. Counter-Terrorism and Torture* (New York 2005)

Aust, Stefan *Der Baader–Meinhof Komplex* (Hamburg 1998)

Baer, Robert *See No Evil* (London 2002)

Balestrini, Nanni *The Unseen* (London 1989)

Bar, Shmuel *Warrant for Terror. The Fatwas of Radical Islam and the Duty of Jihad* (Stanford 2006)

—— 'The Conflict between Radical Islam and the West: Origins, Prognosis and Perspectives' (unpublished paper Tel Aviv 2006)

Bar-Zohar, Michael *Ben-Gurion* (London 1978)

—— and Haber, Eitan *The Quest for the Red Prince* (Guilford, Connecticut 1983)

Bark, Dennis and Gress, David *A History of West Germany. Democracy and its Discontents 1963–1988* (Oxford 1989) 2 volumes

Barrett, J. J. *Martin Ferris. Man of Kerry* (Dingle, Co. Kerry 2006)

Bawer, Bruce *While Europe Slept. How Radical Islam is Destroying the West from Within* (New York 2006)

Bayly, Christopher and Harper, Tim *Forgotten Wars. The End of Britain's Asian Empire* (London 2007)

Bell, J. Bowyer 'The Inherent Inefficiency of the Underground' *Terrorism and Political Violence* (1990) 2, pp. 193–211

Benjamin, Daniel and Simon, Steven *The Age of Sacred Terror* (New York 2002)

—— *The Next Attack. The Globalization of Jihad* (London 2005)

Berko, Anat and Erez, Edna ' "Ordinary People" and "Death Work": Palestinian Suicide Bombers as Victimizers and Victims' *Violence and Victims* (2006) 20, pp. 603–23

——, Wolf, Yval and Addad, Moshe 'The Moral Infrastructure of Chief Perpetrators of Palestinian Suicide Terrorism' (typescript) pp. 10–47

Berman, Paul *Terror and Liberalism* (New York 2003)

Berntsen, Gary with Pezzullo, Ralph *Jawbreaker. The Attack on Bin Laden and Al Qaeda* (New York 2005)

Bew, Paul *Ireland. The Politics of Enmity* (Oxford 2007)

Black, Crispin *7–7. The London Bombs. What Went Wrong?* (London 2005)

Blair, Tony 'A Battle for Global Values' *Foreign Affairs* (2007) 86, pp. 79–90
—— 'What I've Learned' *Economist* (2007) 283, pp. 29–31
Blanford, Nicholas *Killing Mr Lebanon. The Assassination of Rafik Hariri and its Impact on the Middle East* (London 2006)
Boucek, Christopher 'Extremist Reeducation and Rehabilitation in Saudi Arabia' *Terrorism Monitor* (2007) 5, pp. 1–4
Bowden, Mark *Killing Pablo* (London 2001)
—— *Guests of the Ayatollah* (New York 2006)
—— 'Jihadists in Paradise' *Atlantic Monthly* March 2007 pp. 54–75
Brachman, Jarret (ed.) *Militant Ideology Atlas* (West Point 2006)
Brisard, Jean-Charles and Martinez, Damien *Zarqawi. The New Face of al-Qaeda* (Cambridge 2005)
Brookes, Peter *A Devil's Triangle. Terrorism, Weapons of Mass Destruction, and Rogue States* (Lanham, Maryland 2005)
Brown, G. I., *The Big Bang. A History of Explosives* (Thrupp 2005)
Bruce, Steve *God Save Ulster! The Religion and Politics of Paisleyism* (Oxford 1986)
—— 'Turf War and Peace: Loyalist Paramilitaries since 1994' *Terrorism and Political Violence* (2004) 16, pp. 501–21
Burke, Jason *Al-Qaeda. The True Story of Radical Islam* (London 2003)
—— *On the Road to Kandahar. Travels through Conflict in the Islamic World* (London 2006)
—— ' "Islamism" Has No Place in Terror's Lexicon' *Observer* 26 August 2007
Burleigh, Michael *Sacred Causes. Politics and Religion in Europe from the European Dictators to Al Qaeda* (London 2006)
—— 'Sinister Mutations' *Spectator* 18 February 2006
—— 'Winning Muslim Hearts and Minds' *Daily Telegraph* 30 November 2006
—— 'Victors' Justice is Bloody, But in the End Someone had to Pay' *Sunday Times* 31 December 2006
—— 'The Iranian Who Wants an Apocalypse' *Daily Telegraph* 5 January 2007
—— 'Lawyers Sap our Will to Combat Terrorism' *The Times* 27 July 2007
Burr, J. Millard and Collins, Robert O. *Alms for Jihad. Charity and Terrorism in the Islamic World* (Cambridge 2006)
Buruma, Ian *Murder in Amsterdam. The Death of Theo van Gogh and the Limits of Tolerance* (London 2006)
Bushnell, Patience 'After Nairobi: Recovering from Terror' *American Foreign Service Association* (Washington 2000)
Byman, Daniel *Deadly Connections. States that Sponsor Terrorism* (Cambridge 2005)
—— 'Do Targeted Killings Work?' *Foreign Affairs* (2006) 85, pp. 95–111

Cagol, Mara *Una donna nelle prime Brigate Rosse* (Venice 1980)

Carr, Caleb *The Lessons of Terror. A History of Warfare against Civilians* (New York 2002)

Carr, Matthew, *Unknown Soldiers. How Terrorism Transformed the Modern World* (London 2006)

Catanzaro, Raimondo (ed.) *The Red Brigades and Left-wing Terrorism in Italy* (London 1991)

Center for Defense Information (Washington) 'In the Spotlight: Abu Sayyaf' www.cdi.org/terrorism/sayyof.cfm 5 March 2002

Chandler, Michael and Gunaratha, Rohan *Countering Terrorism. Can We Meet the Threat of Global Violence?* (London 2007)

Chehab, Zaki *Inside Hamas. The Untold Story of Militants, Martyrs and Spies* (London 2007)

Clarke, Peter *Learning from Experience. Counter Terrorism in the UK since 9/11* (London 2007)

Clawson, Patrick and Rubin, Michael *Eternal Iran. Continuity and Chaos* (London 2005)

Cohen, Nick *What's Left? How the Liberals Lost their Way* (London 2007)

Coll, Steve *Ghost Wars. The Secret History of the CIA, Afghanistan and Bin Laden from the Soviet Invasion to September 10, 2001* (London 2005)

Collins, Eamon *Killing Rage* (London 1997)

Cook, David 'Paradigmatic Jihadi Movements' *The Combating Terrorism Center* (West Point 2006) pp. 1–32

Corera, Gordon *Shopping for Bombs. Nuclear Proliferation, Global Insecurity and the Rise and Fall of the A. Q. Khan Network* (London 2006)

Cotton, James 'Southeast Asia after 11 September' *Terrorism and Political Violence* (2003) 15, pp. 148–170

Coulter-Smith, Graham and Owen, Maurice (eds) *Art in the Age of Terrorism* (London 2005)

Cruise O'Brien, Conor *States of Ireland* (New York 1972)

—— *Ancestral Voices. Religion and Nationalism in Ireland* (Dublin 1994)

Cullison, Alan 'Inside Al-Qaeda's Hard Drive' *Atlantic Monthly* September 2004 pp. 1–16

D'Ancona, Matthew *Confessions of a Hawkish Hack. The Media and the War on Terror* (London 2006)

Dahlby, Tracy *Allah's Torch. A Report from behind the Scenes in Asia's War on Terror* (New York 2005)

Davis, Mike *Buda's Wagon. A Brief History of the Car Bomb* (London 2007)

Devji, Faisal *Landscapes of the Jihad. Militancy, Morality, Modernity* (London 2005)

Dillon, Martin *The Shankill Butchers. A Case Study in Mass Murder* (London 1989)

Dobson, Christopher *Black September* (London 1974)

—— and Payne, Ronald *The Carlos Complex. A Pattern of Violence* (London 1977)

Drake, Richard *The Revolutionary Mystique and Terrorism in Contemporary Italy* (Bloomington, Indiana 1989)

—— *Apostles and Agitators. Italy's Marxist Revolutionary Tradition* (Cambridge, Massachusetts 2003)

Eagleton, Terry *Holy Terror* (Oxford 2005)

English, Richard *Armed Struggle. The History of the IRA* (London 2003)

—— *Irish Freedom. The History of Nationalism in Ireland* (London 2006)

Ensslin, Christiane and Ensslin, Gottfried (eds) *Gudrun Ensslin: 'Zieht den Trennungsstrich jede Minute'. Briefe an ihre Schwester Christiane und ihren Bruder Gottfried aus dem Gefängnis 1972–1973* (Hamburg 2005)

Enzenberger, Hans Magnus 'The Radical Loser' *Spiegel Online* 20 December 2006 pp. 1–9

Ernesto, Cyrus 'From Revolutionary Dreams to Organizational Fragmentation: Disputes over Violence within ETA and Sendero Luminoso' *Terrorism and Political Violence* (2002) 14, pp. 66–92

Evans, Martin and Phillips, John *Algeria. Anger of the Dispossessed* (New Haven 2007)

Fallows, James 'Declaring Victory' *Atlantic Monthly* September 2006 pp. 60–73

Farah, Douglas *Blood from Stones. The Secret Financial Network of Terror* (New York 2004)

Farrell, William R. *Blood and Rage. The Story of the Japanese Red Army* (Lexington, Massachusetts 1990)

Feraoun, Mouloud *Journal 1955–1962. Reflections on the French–Algerian War* trans. Mary Ellen Wolf and Claude Fouillade (Lincoln, Nebraska 2000)

Fishman, Brian *Al-Qaida's Spymaster Analyzes the US Intelligence Community* (US Marine Academy 6 November 2006)

Forest, James J. F. (ed.) *The Making of a Terrorist. Recruitment, Training and Root Cause* (Westport, Connecticut 2006) volumes 1–3

—— (ed.) *Teaching Terror. Strategic and Tactical Learning in the Terrorist World* (Oxford 2006)

Foster, Roy *Modern Ireland 1600–1972* (Oxford 1988)

Friedman, George *America's Secret War. Inside the Worldwide Struggle between the United States and its Enemies* (London 2004)

Gal-Or, Noemi (ed.) *Tolerating Terrorism in the West. An International Survey* (London 1991)

Gambetta, Diego (ed.) *Making Sense of Suicide Missions* (Oxford 2005)

—— and Hertog, Steffen 'Engineers of Jihad' CSCW-PRIO workshop Oslo 17–18 August 2006

Garvin, Tom *Nationalist Revolutionaries in Ireland 1858–1928* (Oxford 1987)

Gebrauer, Matthias and Musharbash, Yassin 'Islamist Terrorists Planned Massive Attacks in Germany' *Spiegel Online* 5 September 2007 pp. 1–4

Geifman, Anna *Thou Shalt Not Kill. Revolutionary Terrorism in Russia, 1894–1917* (Princeton 1993)

Gerges, Fawaz A. *The Far Enemy. Why Jihad Went Global* (Cambridge 2005)

—— *Journey of the Jihadist. Inside Muslim Militancy* (Orlando 2006)

Gilbert, Martin *Israel. A History* (London 1998)

Glucksmann, Andre *Dostoievski en Manhattan* (Madrid 2002)

Golway, Terry *Irish Rebel. John Devoy and America's Fight for Ireland's Freedom* (New York 1998)

Gove, Michael *Celsius 7/7* (London 2006)

Gray, John, *Al-Qaeda and What it Means to be Modern* (London 2005)

Green, James *Death in the Haymarket* (New York 2006)

Grier, Peter 'The New Al Qaeda: Local Franchises' *Christian Science Monitor* 11 July 2005

—— 'Where Does Al Qaeda Stand Now?' *Christian Science Monitor* 5 March 2007

Gunaratna, Rohan 'Terrorism in Southeast Asia: Threat and Response' *Hudson Institute* (New York 2006) pp. 1–11

Habeck, Mary *Knowing the Enemy. Jihadist Ideology and the War on Terror* (New Haven 2006)

Halevy, Efraim *Man in the Shadows* (London 2006)

Halliday, Fred *Islam and the Myth of Confrontation* (London 2003)

Harnden, Toby *'Bandit Country'. The IRA & South Armagh* (London 1999)

Hart, Peter *The IRA at War 1916–1923* (Oxford 2003)

—— *Mick. The Real Michael Collins* (London 2005)

Hashim, Ahmed S. *Insurgency and Counter-Insurgency in Iraq* (London 2006)

Hastings, Max *Ulster 1969. The Fight for Civil Rights in Northern Ireland* (London 1970)

Heggoy, Alf Andrew *Insurgency and Counterinsurgency in Algeria* (Bloomington, Indiana 1972)

Heller, Joseph *The Stern Gang. Ideology, Politics and Terror 1940–1949* (London 1995)

Hingley, Ronald *Nihilists. Russian Radicals and Revolutionaries in the Reign of Alexander II (1855–81)* (London 1967)

Hoffer, Eric *The True Believer* (New York 1951)

Hoffman, Bruce 'All You Need is Love. How the Terrorists Stopped Terrorism' *Atlantic Monthly* December 2001

—— *Inside Terrorism* (New York 2006)

Horchem, Hans-Josef 'The Decline of the Red Army Faction' *Terrorism and Political Violence* (1991) 3, pp. 61–74

Horgan, John (ed.) *The Psychology of Terrorism* (London 2005)

—— and Taylor, Max 'The Provisional Irish Republican Army: Command and Functional Structure' *Terrorism and Political Violence* (1997) 9, pp. 1–32

Horne, Alistair *A Savage War of Peace. Algeria 1954–1962* (New York 2006)

House of Commons Intelligence and Security Committee (Chairman Paul Murphy MP) *Report into the London Terrorist Attacks on 7 July 2005* (London 2006)

House of Representatives Permanent Select Committee on Intelligence *Al Qaeda: The Many Faces of the Islamist Extremist Threat* (Washington DC June 2006)

Hroub, Khaled *Hamas. A Beginner's Guide* (London 2006)

Hsu, Spencer and Pincus, Walter 'US Warns of Stronger Al-Qaeda' *Washington Post* 12 July 2007

Husain, Ed *The Islamist* (London 2007)

Hutchinson, Martha Crenshaw *Revolutionary Terrorism. The FLN in Algeria 1954–1962* (Stanford 1978)

Ignatieff, Michael *The Lesser Evil. Political Ethics in the Age of Terror* (Edinburgh 2005)

Ingram, Martin and Harkin, Greg *Stakeknife. Britain's Secret Agents in Ireland* (Dublin 2004)

Jamieson, Alison *The Heart Attacked. Terrorism and Conflict in the Italian State* (London 1989)

Jaulmes, Adrien 'Ben Laden: six ans d'une traque vaine' *Le Figaro* 10 September 2007

Jesri, Manal El-, 'Given the Chance' *Egypt Today* October 2007

Johnson, R. W. *South Africa. The First Man, the Last Nation* (London 2004)

Jurgensmeyer, Mark (ed.) *Violence and the Sacred in the Modern World* (London 1991)

—— *Terror in the Mind of God. The Global Rise of Religious Violence* (Berkeley 2000)

Kepel, Gilles *The Revenge of God. The Resurgence of Islam, Christianity and Judaism in the Modern World* (University Park, Pennsylvania 1995)

—— *The War for Muslim Minds. Islam and the West* (Cambridge, Massachusetts 2004)

—— *The Roots of Radical Islam* (London 2005) a reissue of *The Prophet & Pharaoh. Muslim Extremism in Egypt* (London 1985)

—— *Jihad. The Trail of Political Islam* (London 2002)

Khalili, Laleh *Heroes and Martyrs of Palestine. The Politics of National Commemoration* (Cambridge 2007)

Klausen, Jytte *The Islamic Challenge. Politics and Religion in Western Europe* (Oxford 2005)

Klein, Aaron J. *Striking Back. The 1972 Munich Olympics Massacre and Israel's Deadly Response* (New York 2005)

Kohlmann, Evan *Al-Qaeda's Jihad in Europe. The Afghan–Bosnian Network* (Oxford 2004)

—— 'Two Decades of Jihad in Algeria: The GIA, the GSPC, and Al-Qaida' www.nefafoundation.org (2007) pp. 1–28

Kraushaar, Wolfgang (ed.) *Die RAF und der linke Terrorismus* (Hamburg 2006) 2 volumes

—— , Wieland, Karen and Reemtsma, Jan Philipp *Rudi Dutschke, Andreas Baader und die RAF* (Hamburg 2005)

Kray, Kate, *Hard Bastards* (London 2002)

Kumar, Nishant *Hijacking. A War by Other Means* (Delhi 2000)

Lamb, Christina 'The Hunt for Osama bin Laden' *Sunday Times* colour magazine 18 March 2007 pp. 46–59

Langewiesche, William *The Atomic Bazaar* (London 2007)

Laqueur, Walter *A History of Terrorism* (New Brunswick, New Jersey 2001)

—— *No End to War. Terrorism in the Twenty-First Century* (London 2004)

—— (ed.) *Voices of Terror* (New York 2004)

Lawrence, Bruce (ed.) *Messages to the World. The Statements of Osama bin Laden* (London 2005)

Leahy, Edna 'Farc Rebel "Admits IRA Trained Him" ' *The Times* 15 May 2005

Levitt, Matthew *Hamas. Politics, Charity, and Terrorism in the Service of Jihad* (New Haven 2006)

Lewis, Bernard *From Babel to Dragomans. Interpreting the Middle East* (London 2004)

Linen Hall Library (ed.) *Troubled Images* (CD-Rom Belfast 2006)

Lister, David and Jordan, Hugh *Mad Dog. The Rise and Fall of Johnny Adair and 'C Company'* (Edinburgh 2007)

Litvinenko, Alexander and Felshtinsky, Yuri *Blowing Up Russia. The Secret Plot to Bring Back the KGB* (London 2007)

Loyola, Mario 'Operation Phantom Strike: How the US Military are Demolishing al Qaeda in Iraq' *Weekly Standard* 3 September 2007

Lyons, F. S. L. *Ireland since the Famine* (London 1971)

McDermott, Terry *Perfect Soldiers. The 9/11 Hijackers* (New York 2005)

McGinty, Stephen 'The English Islamic Terrorist' *Scotsman* 16 July 2002

McKay, Susan *Northern Protestants. An Unsettled People* (Belfast 2000)

Mackey, Chris and Miller, Greg *The Interrogator's War. Inside the Secret War against Al Qaeda* (London 2004)

Magee, John *Northern Ireland. Crisis and Conflict* (London 1974)

Maguire, Keith 'Fraud, Extortion and Racketeering: The Black Economy in Northern Ireland' *Crime, Law and Social Change* (1993) 20, pp. 273–92

Malik, Shiv 'My Brother the Bomber' *Prospect* (June 2007) pp. 30–41

Mason, Roy *Paying the Price* (London 1999)

Melman, Yossi *The Master Terrorist. The True Story behind Abu Nidal* (New York 1986)

Merkl, Peter (ed.) *Political Violence and Terror. Motifs and Motivations* (Berkeley 1986)

MI5 (anonymous) 'The Radicalisation of Muslims: Speaking Notes' (London 2006) typescript pp. 1–16

Miles, Hugh *Al-Jazeera. How Arab TV News Challenged the World* (London 2005)

Mishal, Shaul and Sela, Avraham *The Palestinian Hamas. Vision, Violence, and Coexistence* (New York 2006)

Monaghan, Rachel ' "An Imperfect Peace": Paramilitary "Punishments" in Northern Ireland' *Terrorism and Political Violence* (2004) 16, pp. 439–61

Montefiore, Simon Sebag *Young Stalin* (London 2007)

Moretti, Mario (with Rossana Rossanda and Carla Mosca) *Brigate Rosse. Eine italienische Geschichte* (Berlin 2006)

Morris, Richard *John P. Holland* (Annapolis, Maryland 1966)

Morrison, Danny *All the Dead Voices* (Cork 2002)

Morson, Gary Saul 'What is the Intelligentsia? Once More, an Old Russian Question' *Academic Questions* (1993) 6, pp. 20–38

Moss, David *The Politics of Left-wing Violence in Italy, 1969–85* (London 1989)

Mueller, John *Overblown. How Politicians and the Terrorism Industry Inflate National Security Threats and Why We Believe Them* (New York 2006)

Mufson, Steven *Fighting Years. Black Resistance and the Struggle for a New South Africa* (Boston 1999)

Musharbash, Yassin 'What al-Qaida Really Wants' *Spiegel Online* 12 August 2007 pp. 1–4

Naylor, Sean *Not a Good Day to Die. The Untold Story of Operation Anaconda* (London 2005)
Nelson, Sarah *Ulster's Uncertain Defenders. Loyalists and the Northern Ireland Conflict* (Belfast 1984)
Neumann, Peter R. *Britain's Long War. British Strategy in the Northern Ireland Conflict, 1969–98* (London 2003)
Noonan, Peggy 'Hatred Begins at Home' *Wall Street Journal* 17 August 2007
Norton, Augustus Richard *Hezbollah. A Short History* (Princeton, New Jersey 2007)

O'Callaghan, Sean *The Informer* (London 1998)
O'Connor, Frank *Classic Irish Short Stories* (Oxford 1985)
O'Doherty, Malachi *The Trouble with Guns. Republican Strategy and the Provisional IRA* (Belfast 1998)
O'Neill, Sean and McGrory, Daniel *The Suicide Factory. Abu Hamza and the Finsbury Park Mosque* (London 2006)

Packer, George *The Assassins' Gate. America in Iraq* (New York 2005)
Pape, Robert A. *Dying to Win. Why Suicide Terrorists Do It* (London 2006)
Pappé, Ilan *The Making of the Arab–Israeli Conflict 1947–1951* (London 2001)
Patterson, Glenn *Burning your Own* (London 1988)
Pearl, Mariane *A Mighty Heart. The Brave Life and Death of my Husband Daniel Pearl* (London 2003)
Peci, Patrizio *Io l'infame* (Milan 1983)
Pedahzur, Ami *Suicide Terrorism* (Cambridge 2005)
Perlmutter, Amos *The Life and Times of Menachem Begin* (New York 1987)
Peters, Butz *Tödlicher Irrtum. Die Geschichte der RAF* (Frankfurt am Main 2006)
Phares, Walid *Future Jihad. Terrorist Strategies against America* (New York 2005)
Phillips, Melanie *Londonistan. How Britain is Creating a Terror State Within* (London 2006)
Pipes, Richard *The Degaev Affair. Terror and Treason in Tsarist Russia* (New Haven 2003)
Politkovskaya, Anna *A Dirty War. A Russian Reporter in Chechnya* (London 2001)
Porath, Yehoshuah *The Palestinian Arab National Movement 1918–1939* (London 1974–7) 2 volumes

Posner, Richard A. *Preventing Surprise Attacks. Intelligence Reform in the Wake of 9/11* (Stanford 2005)

Prince, Simon 'The Global Revolt of 1968 and Northern Ireland' *Historical Journal* (2006) 49, pp. 851–75

Quinlivan, Patrick and Rose, Paul *The Fenians in England 1865–1872* (London 1982)

Rashid, Ahmed *Taliban. The Story of the Afghan Warlords* (London 2001)

Reeve, Simon *The New Jackals. Ramzi Yousef, Osama bin Laden and the Future of Terrorism* (London 1999)

—— *One Day in September* (London 2000)

Reich, Walter (ed.) *Origins of Terrorism. Psychologies, Ideologies, Theologies, States of Mind* (Washington DC 1998)

Ressa, Maria *Seeds of Terror. An Eyewitness Account of Al-Qaeda's Newest Center of Operations in Southeast Asia* (New York 2003)

Richardson, John *Paradise Poisoned* (Kandy, Sri Lanka 2005)

Richardson, Louise *What Terrorists Want. Understanding the Terrorist Threat* (London 2006)

—— (ed.) *The Roots of Terrorism* (New York 2006)

Riedel, Bruce 'Al Qaeda Strikes Back' *Foreign Affairs* (2007) 86, pp. 24–40

Rivkin, David and Casey, Lee A. 'Family Feud: The Law in War and Peace' *National Interest* (2007) 89, pp. 66–75

Robbins, Gerald 'Dutch Treat: The Netherlands Tries to Assimilate its Muslim Immigrants' *Weekly Standard* 13 July 2007 pp. 1–2

Roy, Olivier *Globalized Islam. The Search for a New Ummah* (New York 2004)

Rubin, Barry and Rubin, Judith Colp *Yasir Arafat. A Political Biography* (New York 2003)

Ruedy, John *Modern Algeria. The Origins and Development of a Nation* (Bloomington, Indiana 2005)

Sageman, Marc *Understanding Terror Networks* (Philadelphia 2004)

Schiff, Ze'ev and Ya'Ari, Ehud *Intifada. The Palestinian Uprising and Israel's Third Front* (New York 1989)

Scruton, Roger *The West and the Rest. Globalization and the Terrorist Threat* (London 2002)

—— 'I Resent your Success. I Hate You and your Kind. So I Bomb You' *The Times* 9 July 2005

—— 'Islamofascism' *Wall Street Journal* 17 August 2006

Seale, Patrick *Abu Nidal. A Gun for Hire* (London 1992)

Shapiro, James 'The Terrorist's Challenge: Security, Efficiency, Control' Center for International Security and Cooperation Stanford University 26 April 2007

—— and Siegel, David 'Underfunding in Terrorist Organisations' *International Studies Quarterly* (2007) 51, pp. 405–29

Shepherd, Naomi *Ploughing Sand. British Rule in Palestine* (London 1999)

Sherman, A. J. *Mandate Days. British Lives in Palestine 1918–1948* (London 1997)

Short, K. R. M. *The Dynamite War. Irish-American Bombers in Victorian Britain* (Dublin 1979)

Sidel, John T. *Riots, Pogroms, Jihad. Religious Violence in Indonesia* (Ithaca 2006)

Siegel, Pascale Combelles 'An Inside Look at France's Mosque Surveillance Program' *Terrorism Monitor* (2007) 5, pp. 1–3

Silber, Mitchell D. and Bhatt, Arvin *Radicalization in the West. The Homegrown Threat* New York City Police Department Intelligence Division (New York 2007)

Silke, Andrew 'In Defence of the Realm: Financing Loyalist Terrorism in Northern Ireland' and 'Drink, Drugs, and Rock n' Roll: Financing Loyalist Terrorism in Northern Ireland' *Studies in Conflict and Terrorism* (1998 and 2000) 21, pp. 331–61 and 23, pp. 107–27

Smith, Michael *Killer Elite. The Inside Story of America's Most Secret Special Operations Team* (London 2006)

Solomon, Jay and Hookway, James 'In Indonesia, War on Terror Shows Both Gains and Worrisome Trends' *Wall Street Journal* 8 September 2006

Stern, Jessica *Terror in the Name of God* (New York 2004)

Stern, Klaus and Herrmann, Jörg *Andreas Baader. Das Leben eines Staatsfeindes* (Munich 2007)

Stewart, A. T. Q. *The Narrow Ground. Aspects of Ulster 1609–1969* (Belfast 1977)

Stone, Martin *The Agony of Algeria* (London 1997)

Stora, Benjamin *Algeria 1830–2000. A Short History* (Ithaca 2001)

Tamimi, Azzam *Hamas. Unwritten Chapters* (London 2007)

Taylor, Maxwell *The Terrorist* (London 1988)

—— and Quayle, Ethel *Terrorist Lives* (London 1994)

Taylor, Peter *Provos. The IRA & Sinn Fein* (London 1997)

—— *Loyalists* (London 1999)

—— *Brits. The War against the IRA* (London 2001)

Tong, Goh 'Beyond Madrid: Winning against Terrorism' Council of Foreign Relations transcript (Washington DC 6 May 2004) pp. 1–9

Toolis, Kevin *Rebel Hearts. Journeys within the IRA's Soul* (London 1995)
Townshend, Charles *Terrorism. A Very Short Introduction* (Oxford 2002)
Trofimov, Yaroslav *The Siege of Mecca* (London 2007)
Tucker, David 'What's New about the New Terrorism and How Dangerous is It?' *Terrorism and Political Violence* (2001) 13, pp. 1–14

Urban, Mark *Big Boys' Rules. The Secret Struggle against the IRA* (London 1992)

Vandenbroucke, Lucien 'Eyewitness to Terror: Nairobi's Day of Infamy' *American Foreign Service Bulletin* (2000)
Venturi, Franco *Roots of Revolution. A History of the Populist and Socialist Movements in 19th Century Russia* (London 2001)
Vidino, Lorenzo *Al Qaeda in Europe. The New Battleground of International Jihad* (Amherst, New York 2006)

Walden, George *Time to Emigrate?* (London 2006)
Walker, Tony and Gowers, Andrew *Arafat. The Biography* (London 2003)
Weinberg, Leonard *A Beginner's Guide to Global Terrorism* (Oxford 2005)
—— and Eubank, William Lee *The Rise and Fall of Italian Terrorism* (Boulder, Colorado 1987)
—— and Pedahzur, Ami (eds) *Religious Fundamentalism and Political Extremism* (London 2004)
Weiner, Tim *Legacy of Ashes. The History of the CIA* (London 2007)
West, Bing *No True Glory. A Frontline Account of the Battle for Fallujah* (New York 2005)
Windschuttle, Keith 'The Nation and the Intellectual Left' *New Criterion* 27 January 2007 pp. 1–11
Wisniewski, Stefan *Wir waren so unheimlich konsequent . . . Ein Gespräch zur Geschichte der RAF* (Berlin 2003)
Wittke, Carl *Against the Current. The Life of Karl Heinzen* (Chicago, Illinois 1945)
Woodward, Bob *Bush at War* (New York 2002)
Woodworth, Paddy *Dirty War, Clean Hands. ETA, the GAL and Spanish Democracy* (New Haven 2001)
Wright, Lawrence 'The Terror Web' *New Yorker* 2 August 2004
—— *The Looming Tower. Al-Qaeda's Road to 9/11* (London 2006)

Yoo, John *War by Other Means. An Insider's Account of the War on Terror* (New York 2006)

Zuleika, Joseba *Basque Violence* (Reno, Nevada 1988)

INDEX